Sweet Anticipation

Sweet Anticipation

Music and the Psychology of Expectation

David Huron

A Bradford Book
The MIT Press
Cambridge, Massachusetts
London, England

First MIT Press paperback edition, 2007

This book was set in Stone Sans and Stone Serif by SNP Best-set Typesetter Ltd., Hong Kong, and was printed and bound in the United States of America.

Library of Congress Cataloging-in-Publication Data

Huron, David.
Sweet anticipation : music and the psychology of expectation / David Huron.
    p.   cm.
"A Bradford book."
Includes bibliographical references (p.   ) and index.
ISBN 978-0-262-08345-4 (hc : alk. paper)—978-0-262-58278-0 (pb : alk. paper)
1. Music—Psychological aspects. 2. Expectation (Psychology). I. Title.

ML3838.H87   2006   781'.11—dc22   2005054013

10 9 8 7

Sweet Anticipation

Music and the Psychology of Expectation

David Huron

A Bradford Book
The MIT Press
Cambridge, Massachusetts
London, England

First MIT Press paperback edition, 2007

© 2006 Massachusetts Institute of Technology

This book was set in Stone Sans and Stone Serif by SNP Best-set Typesetter Ltd., Hong Kong, and was printed and bound in the United States of America.

Library of Congress Cataloging-in-Publication Data

Huron, David.
Sweet anticipation : music and the psychology of expectation / David Huron.
   p.   cm.
"A Bradford book."
Includes bibliographical references (p.   ) and index.
ISBN 978-0-262-08345-4 (hc : alk. paper)—978-0-262-58278-0 (pb : alk. paper)
1. Music—Psychological aspects. 2. Expectation (Psychology). I. Title.

ML3838.H87   2006   781'.11—dc22   2005054013

10 9 8 7

Contents

Preface

This book describes a psychological theory of expectation. I call it the *ITPRA theory*—a name that will be explained in the first chapter. When I began this research, my interests were limited to music. I was aiming to better understand how listeners form music-related expectations, and how these expectations might account for various emotional responses. As the work progressed, the ITPRA theory evolved into a general theory of expectation and so expanded beyond my parochial concerns about music. Although my principal motivations remain musical, this book should prove informative to a more general audience of readers interested in cognitive science and evolutionary psychology.

For musicians and music scholars, this book offers psychologically based insights into such venerable topics as meter, syncopation, cadence, tonality, atonality, and form. Detailed accounts of musical tension, deception, and surprise are given, and I suggest how music is able to evoke emotions such as spine-tingling chills and musically induced laughter. I provide moment-by-moment analyses of the psychological effects of common musical devices such as the appoggiatura, suspension, and anticipation, and discuss the role of expectation in crafting effective performance interpretations. In addition, I suggest how the organization of the brain might account for the taken-for-granted aesthetic distinctions of *work*, *genre*, and *rendition*. The book offers psychological interpretations of various historical events in Western music, notably the advent of musical modernism as exemplified in the works of Wagner, Stravinsky, and Schoenberg. Finally, I speculate about how the psychology of expectation might be exploited to create entirely novel musics. In general, the book attempts to show how both biology and culture contribute to the subjective phenomenal experiences that make listening to music such a source of pleasure.

For psychologists and cognitive scientists, this book offers a general theory of expectation. I suggest how the phenomenon of surprise can lead to fear, laughter, frisson, or awe. I endeavor to reconcile competing theories of emotion, most notably cognitive appraisal theories with physiologically inspired theories such as the James–Lange theory. Along the way, I propose a new interpretation of the Mere Exposure effect and suggest that misattribution is an artifact of the biological world's response to the problem of induction. An important part of the book deals with the origin of auditory expectations. In general, the experimental evidence reported here supports the emerging consensus for statistical learning. Finally, I address the problem of how expectations are mentally represented. I note that the apparently chaotic patterns found in the research on musical development are consistent with neural Darwinist theories. I further note that the differences between innate and learned representations (such as those observed in auditory localization) can be explained by the Baldwin effect. In general, I attempt to tell an uninterrupted story, from the patterns of the objective world, through imperfectly learned heuristics used for predicting that world, to the phenomenal *qualia* we experience as we apprehend the world.

In retrospect, music provided me with a serendipitous starting place for theorizing more generally about the psychology of expectation, I think for three reasons: First, most everyday experiences are too complicated to provide fruitful cases for analysis. For example, one of the most important expectation-related experiences is *surprise*. Unfortunately, many of the surprises that people experience involve complex social contexts that are often difficult to interpret. Even the simple "peek-a-boo" surprise between parent and infant involves a social dynamic that makes it hard to study. Although music is not simple, there are often fewer confounding factors to consider. A second advantage is that many musicians actively seek to provoke emotional responses in their listeners. Although different musicians pursue different goals, manipulating expectations has been a common technique used to create an emotional effect. In general, without manipulation, causality is difficult to infer; so this aspect of music often provides helpful clues about the cascade of causal events. Finally, music typically provides detailed records (in the form of notated scores) that chronicle the precipitating events as they unfold in time. Musical scores provide a convenient database for testing specific hypotheses about expectation. In short, music offers a number of advantages as a case study of the psychology of expectation. My hope is that psychologists will find the theory engaging, even if they have no interest in music.

While my main audience is intended to be musicians, I have tried to make the underlying theory of expectation accessible to nonmusician readers. Where possible, I have bracketed the technical musical descriptions as independent chapters. In chapters 1 and 2 the theory itself is described in general terms with little reference to music. Chapter 3 describes the experimental methods used to study the phenomenon of expectation. Chapters 4, 5, and 6 identify five general patterns of expectation exhibited by listeners familiar with Western music. Chapters 7, 8, 11, and 12 expand on the basic theory. While the theory itself is described in general terms, the illustrations in these chapters are drawn almost entirely from the field of music. Parallel examples in visual perception, linguistics, social behavior, and ethology will readily come to mind for those readers who are knowledgeable in such areas. Nonmusicians may wish to skip the applied discussion of music, especially chapters 9, 10, and 13 to 16. The concluding chapter (17) provides an analytic summary of the basic theory.

For readers who don't read music, the notational examples may feel irksome or irrelevant. Let me assure readers that the musical examples are genuinely illustrative. The examples have been "field tested," and for most listeners they evoke fairly reliable phenomenal experiences. To help readers grasp them more fully, recorded versions of all of the notated examples are available on the World Wide Web.[1] Professional musicians themselves may want to refer to the recorded examples since they often include performance nuances that enhance the effect.

The purpose of this book is to describe a set of psychological mechanisms and illustrate how these mechanisms work in the case of music. Some of these mechanisms are able to evoke particular emotional responses. However, this book does not provide a comprehensive theory of music and emotion; there are many other factors that contribute to musically evoked emotion that do not arise from expectation. In discussing emotional responses to music, much of the book will concentrate on how expectations are able to generate *pleasurable* experiences for listeners. The discussion will focus on general principles and will not deal directly with individual differences, such as why a person might dislike a particular tune. The emphasis on pleasure may seem controversial to some readers. Although pleasure is recognized as an important psychological motivator, it is a factor that has sometimes been overlooked or denigrated by arts scholars as merely hedonistic. It should be noted that pleasure does not trump all other values: the best music is not necessarily music that fills its listeners with pleasure. But without a significant dose of pleasure, no one would bother about music.

Pleasure does not preclude effort. Minds need to *reach*, not simply *grasp*. Brains need to be *challenged*, not simply *pampered*. If the arts are to achieve all that can be achieved, it would be wrongheaded to focus on the limitations of human minds. But neither is it the case that anything is possible. Humans are biological beings living in a social and physical world. In pursuing some artistic goal, there are often constraints that must be taken into account if the goal is to be attained.[2] To ignore these constraining phenomena is to exist in a naive delusional world. One must not mistake ignorance for imagination. Nor should wishful thinking masquerade as artistic insight.

It is essential that musicians understand that I am attempting to describe psychological processes, not aesthetic goals. My musical aim in this book is to provide musicians with a better understanding of some of the tools they use, not to tell musicians what goals they should pursue. If we want to expand artistic horizons and foster creativity there is no better approach than improving our understanding of how minds work.

Many artists have assumed that such knowledge is unnecessary: it is *intuition* rather than *knowledge* that provides the foundation for artistic creation. I agree that intuition is essential for artistic production: in the absence of knowledge, our only recourse is to follow our intuitions. But intuition is not the foundation for artistic freedom or creative innovation. Quite the contrary. The more we rely on our intuitions, the more our behaviors may be dictated by unacknowledged social norms or biological predispositions. Intuition is, and has been, indispensable in the arts. But intuition needs to be supplemented by knowledge (or luck) if artists are to break through "counterintuitive" barriers into new realms of artistic expression.

Accordingly, the best I can aim for in writing a book like this is to provide artists with some conceptual tools that might lead to something new. In the concluding chapter I highlight some of the opportunities afforded to both musicians and music scholars by taking the cognitive sciences to heart.

Acknowledgments

Research is never done in a vacuum and the research reported in this book is no exception. Much of this work was inspired by research carried out in my Ohio State University laboratory by postdoctoral fellow Paul von Hippel and doctoral student Bret Aarden. Paul von Hippel took my intuition about the possible influence of regression to the mean in melodic organization and wove a marvelous story about how listeners hear melodies. In particular, von Hippel's experiments made clear the discrepancy between what people hear and what they expect. Bret Aarden took my interest in reaction-time measures in judging melodic intervals and turned the paradigm into a truly useful tool for investigating musical expectation. His work has transformed the way we understand previous work on tonality. I am indebted to both Paul and Bret for being such tolerant listeners and for mentoring me as much as I mentored them.

Although I have always preferred so-called structural theories of tonality to functional theories, I have benefited enormously by having David Butler (the principal advocate of functional tonality) as a departmental colleague. Professor Butler's knowledgeable criticisms of structural theories led me to a better understanding of the importance of parallel mental representations. My discussion of rhythmic expectation builds on the research of another colleague, Dr. Mari Riess Jones. Along with her collaborator, Dr. Ed Large, she assembled a theory of rhythmic attending that provides the core for understanding the "when" of expectation.

Throughout the book I report a variety of statistical measures based on several databases of encoded musical scores. I am indebted to the late Helmut Schaffrath for making available his Essen Folksong Collection. I am also indebted to the Center for Computer Assisted Research in the Humanities at Stanford University for providing access to the MuseData electronic scores. Particular thanks go to Walter Hewlett, Eleanor Selfridge-Field, and Craig Sapp. In addition, my thanks go to Tom Recchia for encoding the database of pop chord progressions.

Without wishing to minimize my debt to my colleagues and collaborators, I must acknowledge that the most important people in any research program are one's critics.

Over the years, I have come to greatly value the preventive medicine provided by the peer review process. The sad truth about writing a book is that it is immensely difficult to cajole knowledgeable people into providing critical feedback. The distinguished hearing scientist, Georg von Békésy, once lamented that his successful career had resulted in the loss of his best critics. For von Békésy, former critics were ultimately transformed into friends, and with that, he felt that the quality of his research had suffered. One way to compensate for the paucity of critics is to encourage friends to put aside their affections and pull out their scalpels. I am grateful to those of my associates who recognize the value of mixing encouragement with pointed criticism. My thanks to Bob Snyder, Ian Quinn, Elizabeth Margulis, David Temperley, Fred Lerdahl, Zohar Eitan, Marc Perlman, Dirk-Jan Povel, Peter Desain, Ryan Jordan, Donald Gibson, William Conable, Peter Culicover, Kristin Precoda, Simon Durrant, James Wright, Jonathan Berger, Joy Ollen, Randolph Johnson, Joshua Veltman, Judy Feldmann, Marion Harrison, Freya Bailes, and Bruno Repp.

1 Introduction

The world provides an endless stream of unfolding events that can surprise, delight, frighten, or bore. Such emotions provide the intimate experiences that define our personal lives. Sometimes emotions are overwhelming—as when we experience great pleasure or great agony. More often, emotions add subtle nuances that color our perceptions of the world. Emotions add depth to existence; they give meaning and value to life.

How do emotions arise? What purposes do they serve? What accounts for the distinctive feelings we experience? These questions have stimulated philosophers for centuries. More recently, these questions have inspired the curiosity of psychologists and cognitive scientists. But they are also questions that attract the attention of the "practitioners" of emotion. Playwrights, novelists, poets, film directors, musicians, choreographers, comedians, and theatrical magicians all have a professional interest in what distinguishes delight from boredom. Therapists, game designers, carnival operators, and traffic engineers have good reasons to try to understand what causes people to be surprised or fearful. Even advertisers and politicians have practical motivations for understanding how the flux of events shape human emotional experiences.

It is no coincidence that the performing arts have figured prominently in attempts to understand the dynamics of emotion. Over hundreds of years, poets, actors, comedians, and musicians have developed a sort of folk psychology about how certain emotions can be generated. Of the many arts, music has perhaps faced the most onerous challenges. Where the poet or playwright can evoke sadness by narrating a recognizably sad story, musicians must create sadness through abstract nonrepresentational sounds. Where a comedian might evoke laughter through parody, wordplay, or absurd tales, musicians must find more abstract forms of parody and absurdity. Where magicians evoke awe by appearing to transgress the laws of physics, no comparable recipe exists for creating musical awe. Despite the difficulties, musicians have amply demonstrated an exquisite skill in evoking the profoundly sad, the twistedly absurd, and the deeply awe-inspiring.

In each of the arts, codes of practice, heuristic rules of thumb, and speculative theories have been passed from teacher to student across the generations. These folk psychologies are based on a combination of intuition and tried-and-true techniques. In music, composers absorb a number of clichés—useful devices that are most easily observed in film scores. Trained musicians will readily recognize some commonplace examples: *tragedy* can be evoked by using predominantly minor chords played with rich sonorities in the bass register. *Suspense* can be evoked using a diminished seventh chord with rapid tremolo. *Surprise* can be evoked by introducing a loud chromatic chord on a weak beat.

For many thoughtful musicians, such clichés raise the question, "Why do these techniques work?" To this question, an ethnomusicologist might add a second: "Why do they often *fail* to work for listeners not familiar with Western music?" And an experienced film composer might insist on adding a third: "Why do they sometimes fail to work, even for those who are familiar with Western music?" In addressing these questions, intuition and folk psychology provide important starting points. But if we want to probe these questions in depth, we must ultimately embrace a more systematic approach. In theorizing about music and emotion, it is inevitable that we must move beyond folk psychology to psychology proper.

Many of the arts achieve specific emotional effects through a sort of stylized depiction or representation of common emotional displays. The mime exaggerates human body language and facial expressions. The cartoonist distills these same expressions into a few suggestive pen strokes. Even when a dancer aims for a strictly formal performance, her body movements will still tend to imply natural gestures or socially defined expressions. Music too involves mimicry of some natural emotional expressions. But aesthetic philosophers and music commentators have long noted that music is not a "representational" art in the way that painting or sculpture can be. How is music so successful in evoking emotions when its capabilities for representing the natural world seem so constrained?

In the 1950s, the renowned musicologist Leonard Meyer drew attention to the importance of *expectation* in the listener's experience of music. Meyer's seminal book, *Emotion and Meaning in Music,* argued that the principal emotional content of music arises through the composer's choreographing of expectation. Meyer noted that composers sometimes thwart our expectations, sometimes delay an expected outcome, and sometimes simply give us what we expect. Meyer suggested that, although music does contain representational elements, the principal source for music's emotive power lies in the realm of expectation.[1]

As a work of music theory, Meyer's approach was pioneering in its frequent appeals to psychological explanations. Despite Meyer's interest in psychology, however, *Emotion and Meaning in Music* was written at a time when there was little pertinent psychological research to draw on. In the intervening decades, a considerable volume of experimental and theoretical knowledge has accumulated.[2] This research provides an opportunity to revisit Meyer's topic and to recast the discussion in light of contemporary findings. The principal purpose of this book is to fill in the details and to describe a comprehensive theory of expectation—a theory I have dubbed the "ITPRA" theory.

Of course, expectations are not the province of music alone; expectation is a constant part of mental life. A cook expects a broth to taste a certain way. A pedestrian expects traffic to move when the light turns green. A poker player expects an opponent to bluff. A pregnant woman expects to give birth. Even as you read this book, you have many unconscious expectations of how a written text should unfold. If my text were abruptly to change topics, or if the prose suddenly switched to a foreign language, you would probably be dismayed. Nor do the changes need to be dramatic in order to have an effect. Some element of surprise would occur if a sentence simply ended. Prematurely.

Any theory of musical expectation necessarily presupposes a general theory of expectation. The ITPRA theory is intended to provide such a general theory. The theory is ambitious in scope and aims to account for all of the main psychological phenomena related to expectation. In particular, the ITPRA theory endeavors to account for the many emotion-related elements of expectation. The theory attempts to explain how expectations evoke various feeling states, and why these evoked feelings might be biologically useful.

The story of expectation is intertwined with both biology and culture. Expectation is a biological adaptation with specialized physiological structures and a long evolutionary pedigree. At the same time, culture provides the preeminent environment in which many expectations are acquired and applied. This is especially true in the case of music, where the context for predicting future sounds is dominated by cultural norms. In attempting to understand expectation, it is essential to take both biology and culture seriously. Accordingly, my text will freely meander through such topics as physiological and evolutionary psychology, learning, enculturation, style, and music history.

From an evolutionary perspective, the capacity to form accurate expectations about future events confers significant biological advantages. Those who can predict the future are better prepared to take advantage of opportunities and sidestep dangers. Over the past 500 million years or so, natural selection has favored the development of perceptual and cognitive systems that help organisms to anticipate future events. Like other animals, humans come equipped with a variety of mental capacities that help us form expectations about what is likely to happen. Accurate expectations are adaptive mental functions that allow organisms to prepare for appropriate action and perception.

But what about the emotional "feelings" that are often conjured up as a result of expectations? What gives *anticipation* or *surprise* their distinctive phenomenological characters? The story of emotion is intertwined with the psychology of behavioral motivation. Emotions are motivational amplifiers.[3] Emotions encourage organisms to pursue behaviors that are normally adaptive, and to avoid behaviors that are normally maladaptive. In this regard, the emotions evoked by expectation do not differ in function from other emotions. As we will see, the emotions accompanying expectations are intended to reinforce accurate prediction, promote appropriate event-readiness, and increase the likelihood of future positive outcomes. We will discover that music-making taps into these primordial functions to produce a wealth of compelling emotional experiences. In this way, musicians are able to create a number of pleasurable emotional experiences, including surprise, awe, "chills," comfort, and even laughter.

The biological purpose of expectation is to prepare an organism for the future. A useful place to begin is to consider, in general, what it means to be prepared.

Preparation

When you switch on a light, electrical energy streams down a convoluted path of wires from a distant power station. The speed with which this happens is impressive. The electricity flows at nearly the speed of light, which means that the power you consume was generated less than one one-thousandth of a second earlier. There is no time at the power station to "gear up" for your demand. The turbine generators must already be producing the electricity that the power company thinks you (and other customers) might need. Any energy generated that is not used by current customers is simply wasted: fuel is burned for no good reason. Clearly, power companies have a strong incentive to anticipate precisely how much power should be produced at any given moment in time.

All biological organisms consume power—power to maintain metabolisms, to move muscles, and to spark nervous systems. This power is expensive. It must be generated from the food the animal consumes, and gathering food is difficult, time-consuming, and very often dangerous. As with the electrical grid, the amount of power required by an organism changes from moment to moment, so it is important for the animal to avoid waste by matching the amount of energy generated with the amount the animal needs.

Commercial power producers employ teams of statisticians whose sole job is to try to predict power demands. They estimate what time people will get up on Saturday morning, how many people are likely to watch the big game on TV, and whether the outside temperature will entice customers to turn on their air conditioners. The predictive models used by utility companies are elaborate and impressive feats of human ingenuity. But like so many other human creations, the complexity and efficiency of these predictive models pale when compared with the achievements of nature.

Organisms are constantly trying to conserve energy. Bodies (including brains) drift toward low states of arousal when no action or thought is needed. In a static unchallenging environment, minds grow bored and bodies grow limp. We respond to these environments by invoking nature's all-purpose energy-conservation strategy—*sleep*. Of course, sometimes the events of the world do require some appropriate action, and so the body and mind must be roused in preparation. Like a machine that has been turned off, a certain amount of time is needed for us to "power up."

When you unexpectedly hear the sound of a barking dog, your heart will quicken and the volume of blood flowing to your muscles will increase. At the same time, an important hormone, norepinephrine, will be released in your brain making you more alert and attentive. In truly dangerous situations, this response, quick as it is, may prove to be too slow. Like a power "brown out," the demands of the body might momentarily exceed the supply of resources. Many animals have become another animal's dinner in the split second required to respond to danger. If only one could have known in advance to increase the power output and pay closer attention. If one could have anticipated the danger, a more effective response might have been rallied.

Over the eons, brains have evolved a number of mechanisms for predicting the future. The biological purpose of these mechanisms is to prepare the body and mind for future events while simultaneously minimizing the consumption of metabolic resources. From a physiological perspective, there are two interrelated systems that influence metabolic consumption: *arousal* and *attention*. The arousal system controls heart rate, respiration, perspiration, and many other functions associated with movement. The attention system is more subtle. Attention spurs the brain to be more engaged with the world. Instead of looking at nothing in particular, our gaze becomes focused. Instead of tuning out a conversation, we pay close attention to what is being said. Instead of daydreaming, we become grounded in the here and now. All of this takes energy.

Arousal and attention levels fluctuate according to both the actual and the anticipated demands of the environment. When we think of arousal and attention reacting to the environment, there is a tendency to think foremost of them as *increasing*. However, the arousal and attention systems can also *reduce* or *inhibit* responsiveness. The experiences of boredom and sleepiness are no less manifestations of metabolic fine-tuning than are the experiences of excitement and exhilaration.

We may also tend to think of arousal and attention as systems that deal necessarily with the uncertainties of life. But even if we knew with exact precision and certainty all of the future events in our lives, we would still need anticipatory mental and corporeal changes to fine-tune our minds and bodies to the upcoming events. Suppose, for example, that I know that at 9:18 A.M. I will encounter an obstacle on the path requiring me to steer my bicycle around it. This godlike foreknowledge does not absolve me from having to attend to the object and make the appropriate motor movements at the appointed time. Nor can I execute any of the needed mental or corporeal maneuvers before they are required. So perfect knowledge of the future would not change the fact that attention and arousal levels must fluctuate according to the moment.

Of course, such perfect knowledge of the future doesn't exist; we do live in a world in which the future is uncertain, and this uncertainty does make it more difficult to produce the optimum arousal and attention. How do we prepare for a future that has untold possibilities? Sometimes this uncertainty doesn't matter. There are some situations where the precise outcome is highly uncertain, but where all of the potential outcomes would require the same type of mental and physical preparation. In a casino, a roulette croupier has no idea which number will appear on the wheel, but the croupier's ensuing actions are highly practiced: collect the chips from the losing bets and reward any successful bets. While the croupier's actions are obviously guided by the result on the roulette wheel, the croupier's response depends very little on the specific outcome—unlike the responses of the gamblers!

These sorts of situations are not commonplace, however. More commonly, different outcomes will require different optimum responses. The body typically faces a quandary: which of several possible outcomes does one prepare for? In preparing the body and mind for these outcomes, our instincts are depressingly pessimistic. Like a grumbling naysayer, nature tends to assume the worst. Consider, for example, the slamming of a door. Even though we may see that the door is about to slam shut, it is difficult to suppress the impending startle or defense reflex. We know the door poses no danger to us, but the sound of the slamming door provokes a powerful bodily response anyway. Despite our annoyance, nature knows best: it is better to respond to a thousand false alarms than to miss a single genuinely dangerous situation.

As we will see later, nature's tendency to overreact provides a golden opportunity for musicians. Composers can fashion passages that manage to provoke remarkably strong emotions using the most innocuous stimuli imaginable. As every music-lover knows, simple sequences of sounds hold an enormous potential to shape feelings. As we will see, it is nature's knee-jerk pessimism that provides the engine for much of music's emotional power—including feelings of joy and elation.

The object of expectation is an event in time. Uncertainty accompanies not only *what* will happen but also *when* it will happen. Sometimes the *when* is certain but not the *what*. Sometimes the *what* is known, but not the *when*. Later, we will see how music manipulates both kinds of uncertainty, and how the different what/when combinations produce different emotional responses.

Along with *what* and *when*, brains also predict *where* and *why*—but these are more specialized operations. For sound stimuli, the *where* expectations are associated with physiologically ancient structures for sound localization. Musicians have sometimes manipulated the locations of sounds (as in the antiphonal works of Giovanni Gabrieli or the electroacoustic works of Karlheinz Stockhausen), but they have less often manipulated listener *expectations* of location. The *why* expectations are associated with physiologically recent structures associated with conscious thought. In contrast to the *what* and *when* of prediction, the *where* and *why* components of auditory expectation have played little role in musical organization and experience. But they represent opportunities for future enterprising composers.

Emotional Consequences of Expectations

As I have noted, the ability to anticipate future events is important for survival. Minds are "wired" for expectation. Neuroscientists have identified several brain structures that appear to be essential for prediction and anticipation. These include the substantia nigra, the ventral tegmental area, the anterior cingulate cortex, and the lateral prefrontal cortical areas.[4] Most people will regard such biological facts as uninteresting details. For most of us, the more compelling details pertain to the subjective experience. From a phenomenological perspective, the most interesting property of expectation is the feeling that can be evoked. What happens in the future matters to us, so it should not be surprising that how the future unfolds has a direct effect on how we feel.

Why precisely do expectations evoke various feeling states? I propose that the emotions evoked by expectation involve five functionally distinct physiological systems: imagination, tension, prediction, reaction, and appraisal. Each of these systems can evoke responses independently. The responses involve both physiological and psychological changes. Some of these changes are autonomic and might entail changes of attention, arousal, and motor movement. Others involve noticeable psychological changes such as rumination and conscious evaluation.

Outcomes matter, so the evoked emotions segregate into positive and negative kinds. That is, the feeling states are *valenced*. Positive feelings reward states deemed to be adaptive, and negative feelings punish us for states deemed to be maladaptive. The word "deemed" here is important. Positive feelings are evoked not by results that are objectively adaptive, but by results that the brain, shaped by natural selection, presumes to be adaptive. From time to time the evoked emotions are wrongheaded. For example, a family pet may experience acute distress when being taken to the veterinarian—despite the fact that the medical attention objectively increases the animal's well-being. Like the family pet, we can feel that our world is falling apart even while good things are happening to us. Each of the five response systems makes different assumptions about what is good or bad. So different emotions can be evoked by each of the five systems.

The five response systems can be grouped into two periods or epochs: *pre-outcome* responses (feelings that occur prior to an expected/unexpected event) and *post-outcome* responses (feelings that occur after an expected/unexpected event). Our discussion begins with two types of pre-outcome responses: those of the imagination and the tension systems.

1 Imagination Response

Some outcomes are both uncertain and beyond our control. The weather provides a good example. It may or may not rain, but you are helpless to influence either outcome. Other outcomes, however, may lie within our control. If it rains, you might get wet; but if you carry an umbrella you can reduce the probability of that outcome. In short, people have no control over "rain," but we sometimes have control over "getting wet."

At some point in animal evolution, the ability to predict aspects of the future led to the emergence of other mental mechanisms that attempted to ensure that particular future outcomes were more likely to occur than others. Once an animal is able to predict that some events are likely, there is a lot to be gained if one behaves in a fashion that increases the likelihood of a favorable outcome.

Imagining an outcome allows us to feel some vicarious pleasure (or displeasure)—as though that outcome has already happened. You might choose to work overtime because you can imagine the embarrassment of having to tell your boss that a project remains incomplete. You might decide to undertake a difficult journey by imagining the pleasure of being reunited with a loved one. This *imagination response* is one of the principal mechanisms in behavioral motivation. Through the simple act of day-dreaming, it is possible to make future outcomes emotionally palpable. In turn, these feelings motivate changes in behavior that can increase the likelihood of a future favorable result.[5]

Neurological evidence for such an imagination response is reported by Antonio Damasio, who has described a clinical condition in which patients fail to anticipate the feelings associated with possible future outcomes.[6] In one celebrated case, Damasio described a patient ("Elliot") who was capable of feeling negative or positive emotions after an outcome had occurred, but was unable to "preview" the feelings that would arise if a negative outcome was imminent. Although Elliot was intellectually aware that a negative outcome was likely, he failed to take steps to avoid the negative outcome because, prior to the outcome, the future negative feelings were not palpable and did not seem to matter. Damasio's clinical observations have established that it is not the case that we simply think about future outcomes; when imagining these outcomes, we typically are also capable of feeling a muted version of the pertinent emotion. We don't simply *think* about future possibilities; we *feel* future possibilities.

The imagination response provides the biological foundation for deferred gratification. Feelings that arise through imagination help individuals to forgo immediate pleasures in order to achieve a greater pleasure later. Without this imaginative emotional capacity, our lives would be dominated entirely by petty excitements. From time to time, pop psychologists and self-appointed spiritual advisors have advocated that people focus on living in the here and now and let go of their concerns for the future. Damasio's patients have achieved exactly such a state. For these individuals, the future is a gray abstraction that is irrelevant to the business of living. As a consequence, they lose their friends, go bankrupt, and live lives in which present-tense joys become increasingly hard to achieve because they are unable to plan ahead. It is important to pause and smell the roses—to relish the pleasures of the moment. But it is also crucial to take the imaginative step of planting and nurturing those roses.

If we think of positive and negative feelings as hills and valleys in a complex landscape, the imagination response helps us avoid getting stranded at the top of the nearest hill. Imaginative *thought* allows us to see the higher peaks that might be experienced if only we are willing to first descend into one or more valleys. But it is imaginative *emotions* that motivate us to undertake the difficult journey to reach those higher peaks.

2 Tension Response

A second form of pre-outcome emotional response originates in the mental and corporeal preparation for an anticipated event. At a party, a friend approaches you with a balloon in one hand, and a sharp pin poised for action in the other hand. The grin on your friend's face suggests that the balloon is not likely to remain inflated for long. You squint your eyes, put your fingers in your ears, and turn your face away.

Preparing for an expected event typically involves both motor preparation (arousal) and perceptual preparation (attention). The goal is to match arousal and attention to the expected outcome and to synchronize the appropriate arousal and attention levels so that they are reached just in time for the onset of the event. Usually, events require some increase in arousal. Heart rate and blood pressure will typically increase, breathing will become deeper and more rapid, perspiration will increase, and muscles will respond faster. In addition, pupils may dilate, eyes may focus, the head may orient toward (or away from) the anticipated stimulus, and distracting thoughts will be purged. These (and other) changes help us to react more quickly and to perceive more accurately.

If we want to conserve the maximum amount of energy, then we ought to wait until the last possible moment before increasing attention or arousal. If it only takes a second or two to reach an optimum arousal, then we shouldn't begin increasing arousal until a second or two prior to the outcome. This simple ideal is confounded, however, by uncertainty—uncertainty about *what* will happen, and uncertainty about *when* it will happen. When we are uncertain of the timing of the outcome, we must raise arousal or attention levels in advance of the earliest anticipated moment when the event might happen. If the actual event is delayed, then we might have to sustain this heightened arousal or attention for some time while we continue to wait for the event.

I once saw a couple moving from their second-storey apartment. Having tired of running up and down the stairs, they had resorted to dropping bundles of clothing from their apartment balcony. She would toss bags over the railing while her partner would try to catch them before they hit the ground causing the plastic bags to split. Unfortunately, the physical arrangement prevented the two of them from making eye contact. As a consequence, her partner stood on the ground with his arms perpetually outstretched, unsure of when the next bag would drop out of the sky. I recall this incident because the man looked so silly—like something out of a Laurel and Hardy film. At one point, I could see that the woman had gone back into the apartment to fetch some more bags, but the man was still staring intently upward, arms out-stretched, rocking back and forth in anticipation. He was wasting a great deal of energy because the timing of expected events was so uncertain.

Apart from uncertainty regarding *timing*, we may have difficulty tailoring the *level* of arousal or attention. When the exact nature of the outcome is uncertain, it can be difficult to match precisely the arousal and attention levels to the ultimate outcome. The safest strategy is to prepare for whatever outcome requires the highest arousal and/or attention level. In a baseball game, a fielder can clearly see the pitcher's windup and whether or not the batter swings. There is little doubt about the timing of out-comes. The uncertainty resides principally with the *what*: Will the batter hit the ball? And if so, will the ball be hit into the fielder's area of play? The actual probability of a batter hitting any given pitch into the vicinity of the fielder is comparatively low. Nevertheless, the fielder's best preparation is to assume the worst—namely, a hit into the fielder's area. Unfortunately, this vigilance comes at a cost. With each pitch, arousal and attention peak and then subside (presuming no action is needed). Maintaining high levels of arousal and attention will cause the player to expend a lot of energy. In an important championship game, a fielder is apt to be exhausted by the end of the game, even if the player never had to field a ball.

In the case of the man catching bags of clothing, the uncertainty relates mostly to the *when*, not the *what*: a bag of clothing would surely drop out of the sky, but the timing was uncertain. In the case of the baseball fielder, the uncertainty pertains mostly to the *what*, not the *when*: the ball can only be hit after the pitcher throws the ball. But the outcome of each pitch is uncertain.

The most uncertain situations are those where both the *when* and the *what* are unknown. A soldier on guard duty, for example, might have reason to fear a possible attack. Although the shift may pass uneventfully, the heightened attention and arousal engendered by the expectation of a possible attack is likely to produce acute mental and physical exhaustion.

As it turns out, the physiological changes characteristic of high arousal are also those associated with stress. Not all high arousal is stressful: positively valenced emotions such as joy and exuberance will evoke high arousal with little stress. But anticipating negative events is sure to be stressful. In dangerous situations, organisms respond with one of three classic behaviors: *fighting*, *fleeing*, or *freezing*. The greatest stress tends to occur when high arousal coincides with low movement. Consequently, it is the *freeze* response that engenders the most stress. Fighting and fleeing are active responses, while the freeze response is often symptomatic of helplessness. This is thought to be the reason why the worst health effects of stress are to be found in those people who are unable to do anything to alleviate their stressful conditions.

When anticipating some future event, our physiological state is often akin to that of the freeze response. We may experience elevated heart rate and perspiration without any motor movement. The word "dread" captures the stressful feeling that accompanies anticipating a bad future outcome. By contrast, anticipating something positive evokes a feeling something like being "heartened." But even anticipating something positive has some accompanying stress. In the pre-outcome period, nothing is certain, and so our heartened state is likely to be mixed with a nagging fear that an anticipated positive result may not actually come to pass.

Since stress commonly accompanies the rise of anticipatory arousal, I have chosen the word "tension" to characterize these sorts of pre-outcome responses. Both the baseball fielder and the man catching bags of clothing were experiencing distinct physiological states in anticipation of future outcomes.

Unlike the imagination response, the tension response is linked to the period immediately prior to the anticipated moment of outcome. As the arousal and attention levels move toward an optimum level in anticipation of the outcome, the physiological changes themselves evoke characteristic feeling states. The feelings that accompany the tension response are artifacts. The evoked feeling states have no particular function by themselves, but are simply consequences of the physiological changes that accompany preparation for an anticipated outcome.

The "artifact" status of certain emotions was famously proposed by William James and Carl Lange roughly a century ago.[7] In an often quoted passage, James argued that fear was evoked by the act of trembling, sorrow was evoked by the act of crying, and so on.[8] This "James–Lange" theory of emotion has a checkered history. Some important research supports the theory.[9] One example is found in a simple experiment carried out by Fritz Strack and his colleagues where participants were asked to hold a pencil in their mouth.[10] In one condition, participants held the pencil using their teeth without allowing their lips to touch the pencil. In a contrasting condition, participants held the pencil with their lips only. Strack showed that the manner by which participants hold the pencil has a direct effect on how they feel. Grasping a pencil between your teeth causes you to feel happier than grasping it with your lips. The difference can be traced to the flexing of the zygomatic muscles: holding a pencil between your teeth produces something very similar to smiling. It is not just that you smile when happy—you can feel happy *because* you smile.[11]

The research by Strack and others notwithstanding, there is also research that is wholly inconsistent with the James–Lange theory.[12] It is probably the case that the sort of physiologically induced emotions described by James and Lange are limited to a handful of particular circumstances. I propose that the tension response is one of the circumstances in which the James–Lange theory holds. Simply flexing muscles in anticipation of catching a ball will change a person's feeling state. The evoked feelings will depend on which muscles are flexed. Flexing abdominal muscles will tend to evoke a different affect than squinting eyes, smiling, or clutching a steering wheel.

There are several factors that influence the character and magnitude of the tension response. These include the degree of uncertainty, the importance of the possible outcomes, the difference in magnitudes between the best and worst plausible outcomes, and the estimated amount of time before the outcome is realized. Sometimes outcomes are utterly certain and have little consequence. These situations evoke little tension. In other cases, we may have little idea about what will happen. If one or more of the possible outcomes involves a high stake (something very good or very bad), then we will tend to be more alert and aroused as the moment approaches when the outcome will be made known.

In general, organisms should try to avoid situations of high uncertainty. High uncertainty requires arousal and vigilance, both of which incur an energy cost. Consequently, it would be adaptive for an organism to experience high tension responses as unpleasant. That is, even if only positive outcomes are possible, high uncertainty will lead to a certain amount of unpleasant stress.[13]

3   Prediction Response

Once some event occurs, there ensues a convoluted sequence of physiological and psychological changes. It is useful to distinguish three post-outcome responses.

As you might suppose, organisms respond better to expected events than unexpected events. Accurate predictions help an organism to prepare to exploit opportunities and circumvent dangers. When a stimulus is expected, appropriate motor responses are initiated more rapidly and more accurately. In addition, a stimulus is more accurately perceived when it is predictable.

Since accurate predictions are of real benefit to an organism, it would be reasonable for psychological *rewards and punishments to arise in response solely to the accuracy of the expectation*. Following a snow storm, for example, I might predict that I will slip and fall on the sidewalk. In the event that I actually fall, the outcome will feel unpleasant, but the experience will be mixed with a certain satisfaction at having correctly anticipated this dismal outcome. This expectation-related emotion might be dubbed the *prediction response.* When the stimulus is expected, the emotional response is postively valenced; when the stimulus is unexpected, the emotional response is negatively valenced.

Psychological evidence in support of a prediction response is found in the classic work of George Mandler.[14] An abundance of subsequent experimental research has affirmed the importance of this response. In fact, this response is considered so important in the extant literature on expectation that it is commonly referred to as the *primary affect.*[15] Confirmation of expected outcomes generally induces a positive emotional response even when the expected outcome is bad. It is as though brains know not to shoot the messenger: accurate expectations are to be valued (and rewarded) even when the news is not good. We will devote an extended discussion to this important response in chapter 8.

4   Reaction Response

The most obvious emotions in the post-outcome epoch are those that pertain to the pleasantness or unpleasantness of the outcome itself. Once an outcome is known, our emotions reflect some sort of assessment of the new state. For example, we might experience fear when encountering a snake, sadness when receiving a poor grade, or joy when meeting an old friend. These emotional responses occur only after the outcome is known.

Extensive research has established that there are two types of responses to the advent of events. One type of response is very fast. The other type of response is more leisurely. The fast response represents a "quick-and-dirty" assessment of the situation followed by an immediate somatic (bodily) response. The second response represents a more "thoughtful" assessment of the situation—a response that takes into account complex social and environmental factors. I propose to call the fast response a *reaction response,* and the more complex slower response an *appraisal response.*

Reaction responses exhibit three characteristic features: (1) The response has a fast onset. Typically, the onset of the response begins less than 150 milliseconds following the onset of the outcome. Although the onset of the response is fast, the somatic changes arising from the response might continue for several seconds afterward. (2) The response is not mediated by consciousness. No conscious thought or rumination is involved. Some reaction responses can even occur when we are asleep. (3) The response is defensive or protective in function. The reaction assumes a worst-case scenario, and responds accordingly.

An example of a reaction response is a *reflex.* Suppose that you accidentally touch a hot oven. A well-documented reflex will cause your hand to be abruptly withdrawn from the hot surface. Surprisingly, this reflex is so fast that it happens in less time than it takes for a neural signal to travel from the hand up to the brain and then back down from the brain to the muscles of the arm. Physiologists have determined that the reflex originates in the spine rather than in the brain. So-called *reflex arcs* in the spine connect the sensory neurons in the hand to the motor neurons of the arm. You have withdrawn your hand before your brain even registers the sensation of the hot surface. The reflex has a fast onset, is not mediated by consciousness, and has a defensive function.

Reflexes are examples of reaction responses, but not all reaction responses are technically reflexes. As we will see later, reaction responses can also be *learned*—which is not the case with reflexes. More specifically, we will see that learned *schemas* are used in reaction responses. These learned reaction responses are easiest to observe in situations of surprise. By way of example, consider wrong with speak. Violations of grammar—such as in the preceding sentence—evoke a mild but rapid surprise. Of course English grammar is entirely learned, so the reaction can't be considered a reflex—despite its speed and automaticity. The surprise here arises from a discrepancy between an actual outcome and a highly practiced schema.

Learned schemas span a huge range of behaviors. Schemas can relate to practiced motor skills (such as brushing your teeth) or perceptual norms (such as watching traffic flows). Schemas can involve social norms (such as polite greeting rituals) or cultural norms (such as framing an object so that it is recognized as "art"). As long as the schema is well entrenched in a mind, it becomes possible to provoke reaction responses by violating the schematic expectation. In chapter 2 we will consider such reactive surprises in greater detail, and focus specifically on the feeling states that can be evoked.

5   Appraisal Response

Suppose you answer the phone and are pleasantly surprised to hear the voice of a close friend. Within a second, your pleasure turns to acute embarrassment as you realize that you have forgotten your friend's recent birthday. Or, imagine an experienced biologist is walking in a forest and is startled when a large spider drops onto the sleeve of her jacket. Her negative feelings immediately turn to joy as she realizes that she may have discovered a new species of spider.

Our initial reactions to events are susceptible to revision or augmentation. What we find initially exciting or startling may be completely transformed by further thought. The *reaction response* is quick and unconscious. Once conscious thought is engaged, the assessment of a situation is the province of the *appraisal response*. The above examples are illustrations of when the appraisal response and the reaction response evoke contrasting emotions. But the two responses may also reinforce one another. A near accident in an automobile might quickly evoke a feeling of fear. The subsequent recognition that you were not wearing a seat belt and that any accident would have likely proved fatal might provoke an even stronger sense of fear. Moreover, further conscious thought might lead you to realize that you are behind in your life insurance payments, and that had you died, your children would not have been adequately provided for—hence evoking even greater fear.

As you continue to ruminate about a situation, several successive appraisal responses might ensue. The important point is that appraisal responses can involve conscious thought that often draws on complex social and contextual factors. By contrast, the reaction response involves no conscious thought.

The reaction response and the appraisal response are independent and need not be consistent with each other. As we have seen, a single outcome can produce a negatively valenced reaction response and a positively valenced appraisal response (or vice versa). We will see many examples of such paradoxical feeling states in later chapters. In addition, different people may experience similar reaction responses, but contrasting appraisals. Consider, for example, two office workers who are both startled by the unexpected ringing of their telephones. After the initial start, the worker in the sales department may become excited because the call represents the possibility of making a sale (with an accompanying commission). But the worker in the customer service department might react more negatively, since the call likely represents a customer with a complaint.

In general, positive and negative emotions act as behavioral reinforcements. The pain caused by biting your tongue teaches you to chew carefully and avoid tissue damage. Bad tastes and bad smells reinforce the aversion to ingesting unhealthy foods. The pleasure caused by engaging in sex encourages procreation. The enjoyment of playing with our children encourages parental investment and nurturing. Positive emotions encourage us to seek out states that increase our adaptive fitness. Negative emotions encourage us to avoid maladaptive states.

The ITPRA Theory of Expectation

To summarize: I have distinguished five expectation-related emotion response systems. Each response system serves a different biological function. The purpose of the *imagination response* is to motivate an organism to behave in ways that increase the likelihood of future beneficial outcomes. The purpose of the *tension response* is to prepare an organism for an impending event by tailoring arousal and attention to match the level of uncertainty and importance of an impending outcome. The purpose of the *prediction response* is to provide positive and negative inducements that encourage the formation of accurate expectations. The purpose of the *reaction response* is to address a possible worst-case situation by generating an immediate protective response. The purpose of the *appraisal response* is to provide positive and negative reinforcements related to the biological value of different final states. All of these goals are biologically adaptive. Table 1.1 summarizes these five response systems and presents them in their approximate order in time.

Table 1.1

Response system	Epoch	Biological function
(I) *imagination response*	pre-outcome	future-oriented behavioral motivation; enables deferred gratification
(T) *tension response*	pre-outcome	optimum arousal and attention in preparation for anticipated events
(P) *prediction response*	post-outcome	negative/positive reinforcement to encourage the formation of accurate expectations
(R) *reaction response*	post-outcome	neurologically fast responses that assume a worst-case assessment of the outcome
(A) *appraisal response*	post-outcome	neurologically complex assessment of the final outcome that results in negative/positive reinforcements

Informally, we might characterize the "feeling" components to these responses by posing five questions:

1. What do you think might happen, and how do you feel about that prospect?
2. Are you ready for what's about to happen? How do the preparations make you feel?
3. Did you "place a good bet"—did you predict the outcome accurately? Are you pleased or disappointed by the accuracy of your wager?
4. Assuming the worst, how have you reacted? How does this reaction make you feel?
5. Upon reflection, how do you feel about how things have turned out?

Once again, these five response systems are evoked at different times in the expectation cycle. The imaginative function may begin years prior to an expected event. A person might imagine the sense of achievement associated with graduating from college or paying off a mortgage. As an anticipated event approaches, the emotions evoked by the imagination become dwarfed by the feelings evoked by the mental and corporeal preparations for the actual event—especially if the outcome is uncertain. These preparatory responses relate predominantly to a sense of stress or tension. Once the outcome is known, three response systems are set in motion. One component simply responds to the accuracy of the prediction. In tandem with this prediction response are the emotional states evoked by the reaction and appraisal responses. A short-lived reaction response is typically replaced by the more nuanced appraisal response. Like the imagination phase, the appraisal emotions have the potential to last for years. One may still feel good about some long-ago success, or feel regret about some long-ago failure. The time course of these different emotional responses is illustrated in figure 1.1. It is this time-course that leads to the acronym ITPRA: Imagination–Tension–Prediction–Reaction–Appraisal. Since the prediction and reaction responses

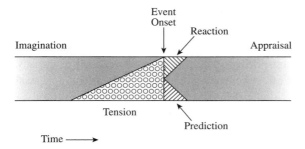

Figure 1.1
Schematic diagram of the time-course of the "ITPRA" theory of expectation. Feeling states are first activated by imagining different outcomes (**I**). As an anticipated event approaches, physiological arousal typically increases, often leading to a feeling of increasing tension (**T**). Once the event has happened, some feelings are immediately evoked related to whether one's predictions were borne out (**P**). In addition, a fast reaction response is activated based on a very cursory and conservative assessment of the situation (**R**). Finally, feeling states are evoked that represent a less hasty appraisal of the outcome (**A**).

occur in tandem, one might equally call it ITRPA (reversing the R and P), but I prefer the more pronounceable ITPRA.

As I have noted, I propose that these five response systems arise from five functionally distinct neurophysiological systems. Each response system solves an important problem in tailoring behavior so that it is optimally adapted to a given environment. Since each response system addresses a different biological problem it is possible that each system represents a distinct evolved adaptation. One might even propose a plausible order of evolution for these systems. The oldest response system is probably the (unconscious) reaction response. Clearly, an organism must take appropriate actions in response to what actually happens in the world; outcomes (and our responses to them) are what matter most. An organism that always assumes the worst outcome has a better chance of surviving those occasional situations that are truly dangerous. Since these hasty reaction responses are commonly exaggerated, some basic elements of the appraisal response probably evolved next. This would have begun as an (unconscious) inhibitory function, suppressing those reaction responses that are excessively conservative. The tension response was likely next to evolve. Simple classical conditioning might allow an organism to anticipate what happens next, and there are clear advantages to tailoring the arousal and attention to the expected event. Since the prediction response provides a way to evaluate the predictions implicit in the tension response, the prediction response must have appeared after the advent of the tension response. Finally, the imagination response is probably the most recent evolutionary addition. Once one achieves some modicum of success in predicting the future, there is obvious value in trying to change the future through our own actions.

Each of these five proposed systems is able to evoke various feeling states—although some systems are more constrained than others. The tension and reaction responses, for example, have a limited range of affective expressions. By contrast, the appraisal response is able to evoke a huge range of feeling states, from jealousy, contempt, or loneliness, to compassion, pride, or humor.[16] For any given situation, these five proposed systems combine to create a distinctive limbic cocktail. Actually, "cocktail" isn't quite the right word, because it is a dynamic phenomenon rather than a simple static mixture. Expectation-related emotions can begin long before an event occurs and can linger long afterward. Within this time span, a dynamically evolving sequence of feelings can arise.

As we will see later, these systems combine to produce a wealth of different feeling experiences in different circumstances. Of all the "practitioners" of emotion, musicians, I believe, have proved the most adept at manipulating the conditions for these different dynamic responses. Although I have used nonmusical examples in this chapter, the principal focus of this book will be on using the ITPRA theory to explain many aspects of musical organization. In chapters 13 to 15 we will see how musicians make use of these psychological systems, and in chapter 16 we will see how the psychology of expectation has shaped a major event in Western music history. But before we apply the ITPRA theory to specific musical circumstances, there are a number of supporting topics that need to be addressed. How does a listener know *what* to expect? How are expectations acquired? Are all expectations learned, or are some innate? How are expectations mentally represented? How are expectations tailored to a particular context? How do the different response systems interact? These and other questions will occupy the next several chapters.

2 Surprise

When I was in sixth grade, we held a surprise party for our teacher, Ms. Bradley. One of my classmate's parents had invited Ms. Bradley to dinner. Hiding in the basement was my entire sixth-grade class. Under the pretense that dinner wasn't yet ready, Ms. Bradley was led down into the darkened room. When the lights came on we all shouted "SURPRISE!" at the top of our lungs. The effect couldn't have been more satisfying to a child's mind: Ms. Bradley nearly jumped out of her skin. There was an expression of sheer terror on her face: her chin had dropped, leaving her mouth wide open, and the whites of her eyes were visible all the way around her pupils. But the expression of terror quickly dissolved into laughter as she regained her composure.

When a surprising event occurs, two brain processes are initiated: a rapid reaction response and a slower appraisal response. Research by Joseph LeDoux and his colleagues at New York University has helped to trace the corresponding pathways through the brain.[1] Figure 2.1 provides a schematic diagram of the reaction and appraisal tracks. Whether the stimulus is visual or auditory in origin, information is first relayed to the thalamus, where some basic processing occurs. At this point the fast and slow tracks are known to diverge. The fast track proceeds directly to the amygdala, which plays an important role in the assignment of affective significance to sensory stimuli. If fear is evoked, activity can be seen in the midbrain periaqueductal gray—which coordinates a number of defense responses. In addition, the paragigantocellularis lateralis will be activated. This is a region of the brain that initiates changes to the viscera that contribute to the sensation of fear. When an event makes you feel something in the pit of your stomach, it is the paragigantocellularis lateralis that is responsible.

The slow track amounts to a long detour between the thalamus and the amygdala. The detour here is via the cerebral cortex—the massive outer layer of the brain, which, among other things, is responsible for conscious thought. Here the stimulus causes activation throughout large areas of the cortex, especially in the frontal lobe region—areas associated with cognitive rumination and evaluation. All sorts of complex social,

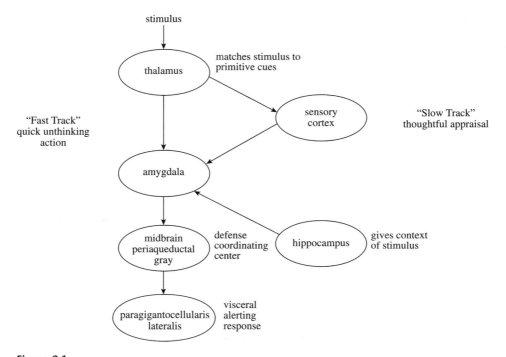

Figure 2.1
Schematic diagram of the brain mechanisms involved in the fear response. Concurrent fast and slow pathways are activated. The fast track involves a direct connection between the thalamus and the amygdala. The slow track leads through the sensory cortex—the large mass located on the exterior surface of the brain.

environmental, and behavioral considerations are brought to bear in appraising the situation. All of this neural activity makes this track the more complicated pathway.

The fast and slow pathways converge in the lateral nucleus of the amygdala. In fact, the two pathways converge onto single neurons in the amygdala.[2] If the slow track leads to the assessment that fear is unwarranted, then the cortex will generate an inhibitory signal that effectively turns off the amygdala and arrests the fear response. Compared with reaction responses, such cognitive processes result in a more accurate, nuanced, and realistic appraisal of dangers, risks, or opportunities afforded by some situation. Unfortunately, this appraisal process is comparatively slow.

For both the fast and slow pathways, the context of the stimulus is known to influence the fear response. Several studies have shown that the context for fear associations depends on the hippocampus. That is, the hippocampus helps us interpret the fear-evoking stimulus.[3]

As noted, the rapid reaction response to surprise assumes the worst. The body responds quickly—under the presumption that the outcome is bad and that the body must belatedly rally resources to deal with an unanticipated situation. When it comes to the unexpected, our physiological reflexes reveal that biology is deeply suspicious and pessimistic: bodies don't like surprises.

One consequence of this rapid reaction response to surprise is activation of the sympathetic nervous system: heart rate increases, and there is increased perspiration, increased glucose uptake, and an increase in the rate and volume of respiration. The purpose of the respiratory response is to bathe the body's tissues in oxygen (and purge carbon dioxide) in preparation for a possibly major energy expenditure. In addition to this increase in arousal, another consequence of surprise is an increase in attention. Sensory systems become more acute. Irrelevant thoughts are purged and attentional resources are focused on the immediate events.

The heightened arousal and attention associated with surprise can be observed directly in the characteristic facial expression for surprise. Recall that Ms. Bradley's chin dropped so that her mouth was wide open, and her eyelids were fully retracted producing a "wide-eyed" look. The open mouth facilitates respiration, which is a component of raising arousal. The open eyes facilitate visual perception, which is a component of increased attentiveness.

Contrastive Valence

Surprising people for fun appears to be a cross-cultural universal.[4] Ronald Simons has documented many instances of "recreational" surprise in various cultures. Most cultures have an equivalent of the "peek-a-boo" interaction between parents and infants, and in nearly all cultures children take delight in sneaking up on each other.

It is not simply the case that surprises are fun for those doing the surprising. In some circumstances (such as Ms. Bradley's surprise party) surprises can also be fun for the person being surprised. But the observation that at least some surprises can be pleasurable raises a biological puzzle. Recall that the purpose of expectation is to enhance readiness. The phenomenon of "surprise" represents a failure of expectation. From a biological perspective, surprise is *always* a bad thing. Even when the surprising outcome turns out to be good, failing to anticipate the outcome means that the brain has failed to provide useful information about possible futures. Predictive failures are therefore cause for biological alarm. If an animal is to be prepared for the future, the best surprise is no surprise.

So if surprise is biologically bad, how is it possible for some surprises to activate the physiological machinery for pleasure? How can people possibly enjoy being surprised? It turns out that an answer to this question can be found on any basketball court. Consider the following experiment carried out by psychologist Peter McGraw.[5] McGraw asked amateur basketball players to take shots from different locations around the court. Before each shot, the player was asked to estimate the likelihood of scoring a basket. Following each shot, the player rated how good he or she felt. As you would expect, players are happiest when they successfully make a shot and are unhappy when they miss a shot. Emotions are positively valenced for positively appraised outcomes and negatively valenced for negatively appraised outcomes. However, the degree of satisfaction or dissatisfaction is also related to the player's expectation. McGraw found that basketball players experienced the greatest unhappiness when they missed shots judged easy, and were happiest when they scored baskets judged to be difficult. The magnitude of the emotional response is amplified when there is a large contrast between predicted and actual outcome. In general, *unexpected* fortune or misfortune causes the biggest emotional responses.[6] That is, low expectation amplifies the emotional response to the outcome.

When we are surprised, a limbic contrast will sometimes arise between the reaction response and the ensuing appraisal response. The fast biological response to surprise is perpetually negative. But the slower appraisal response might be neutral or even positive. At Ms. Bradley's surprise party, the momentary terror she experienced was quickly displaced by a highly positive appraisal response. Her amygdala was switched on and then abruptly switched off. As with McGraw's basketball players, it was the limbic contrast that rendered the experience so powerful. In less than a second, Ms. Bradley's brain went from experiencing profound terror to happy celebration.

In the case of McGraw's basketball players, the limbic contrast was between the prediction response and the appraisal response. In the case of Ms. Bradley's surprise party, there was similarly a contrast between the prediction and appraisal responses, but the main limbic contrast was between the (very negative) reaction response and the (very positive) appraisal response.

Limbic contrasts between the fast and slow pathways are not limited to the extreme circumstances of a surprise party. In our daily lives we experience hundreds of small moments of surprise: a telephone rings, a pen runs out of ink, the car ahead changes lanes, a petal falls from a cut flower. Many of these episodes fail to reach conscious awareness. Most are ultimately appraised as innocuous.

The interaction of the fast and slow pathways has repercussions for how listeners experience sound. If a nominally unpleasant sound is not expected by a listener, then the sound will be perceived as even more unpleasant or annoying. Conversely, if a nominally pleasant sound is not expected by a listener, it will tend to be perceived as more pleasant. A lengthy dissonant passage is likely to lead listeners to expect further dissonant sonorities. If the music shifts toward a more consonant texture, then the resulting contrast will tend to evoke a pleasing effect that can be greater than experiencing only the consonant passage.

More interestingly, even neutrally appraised sounds have the capactiy to generate limbic contrast. Whether or not a sound is regarded as inherently pleasant or unpleasant, if it is unexpected, it is capable of evoking a negatively valenced prediction response—which may contrast with an ensuing neutral appraisal.

An apparent problem for the contrastive valence theory is accounting for why an unexpected good outcome would be experienced as more positively valenced than an expected good outcome. In the case of an expected good outcome, a person should feel good about the outcome and should also feel good about the predictive accuracy. In the case of an unexpected good outcome, a person should feel good about the outcome but also feel bad about the poor predictive accuracy. Why then does an unexpected good outcome sometimes evoke a more positive emotion than an expected good outcome? It is possible that the contrast between the positive appraisal and negative reaction is the more powerful effect. But if so, it would be maladaptive to consistently experience a positive emotion whenever one's predictions prove wrong. Perhaps the only important lessons for an organism to learn occur when a wrong prediction accompanies a negative appraisal of the outcome.

A better understanding of the phenomenon comes from looking at some of the physiological research. When we experience stress, it is typically accompanied by the release of endogenous opiates such as endorphins. These natural opiates produce an analgesic effect that reduces the experience of pain. You've probably experienced a panic situation, such as where you've had to run to catch a bus. Only after you are settled in the bus do you realize that you inadvertently cut yourself in your frantic rush. Oddly, the pain is much more subdued than if the same injury had been inflicted while at rest. That is, the energetic panic had somehow attenuated the experience of pain. Working at Stanford University, Albert Bandura, Delia Cioffi, Barr Taylor, and Mary Brouillard carried out an experiment where individuals were artificially induced to fail at some task. Half of these individuals were administered a saline solution while the other half received naloxone—an opiate receptor antagonist that blocks the effect of any endorphins present. The participants were then given a test that measured their tolerance for pain. Those individuals who had received naloxone were significantly less pain tolerant, indicating that the stress caused by failing at the task had resulted in a release of endogenous opiates.[7]

The body appears to release opiates whenever we experience a negatively valenced emotion such as pain or fear. Suppose that a wild bear appeared and injured you. Immediately, analgesic opiates are released by the body to counteract the pain and allow you to continue to function. Now, suppose that it turned out that you weren't actually injured, but the opiates were released anyway. The net result is simply the opiate release—and the ensuing pleasant feelings. The physiological origin of contrastive valence might follow a path akin to this sequence of events.

The potential for increased pleasure provided by contrastive valence might explain a number of seemingly peculiar conscious strategies people use when mentally preparing for future outcomes. Recall that the imagination response occurs in the pre-outcome epoch—prior to the outcome event. Normally, the imagination response serves a motivational function. By imagining different outcomes (and experiencing a foretaste of the feelings associated with these outcomes) we are encouraged to take actions that will reduce future negative outcomes and increase the likelihood of future positive outcomes. Even for the most certain positive outcomes, if time permits, we will have an opportunity to consider the possibility that the positive outcome will not happen. The imagination response for such scenarios is sobering. We realize that even at the cost of reducing the predictive accuracy, it is better to lower the subjective probability of a positive outcome in order to mute the bad emotions that might ensue from an unexpected negative outcome.

Support for this view comes from a common mental strategy. When a good outcome seems highly probable, a person will sometimes mentally deny or minimize the likelihood of the positive result. ("Everyone seems certain that Caroline will agree to marry me, but I think there is a real chance that she will say no.") This conscious mental strategy has the effect of reducing the magnitude of the negative feelings should a negative outcome ensue, while simultaneously increasing the pleasure evoked by a positive outcome. Similarly, people will occasionally exaggerate negative predictions. ("My coat is ruined; I bet that stain will *never* come out.")

This view is reinforced by the reverse scenarios—found in the experience of *Schadenfreude*—pleasure in others' misfortune. When a rival seems poised for failure, we may minimize the likelihood of their negative outcome ("Aaron is certain to escape punishment for what he did"). This conscious mental strategy will minimize the disappointment if our rival escapes the negative outcome, and increase the pleasurable *Schadenfreude* should the negative outcome be realized. Conversely, when a rival seems poised for success, we may amplify the likelihood of their success ("Barbara is certain to inherit the house"). This will maximize the *Schadenfreude* if the rival in fact does not succeed, and increase the positively valenced prediction response if the outcome for our rival is positive ("I absolutely *knew* that Barbara was going to get the house").

Notice that these strategies are necessarily conscious. They supplant the underlying unconscious intuitions about the likelihood of various events and intentionally bias the subjective probabilities in order to maximize positively valenced emotional states. Since these strategies require conscious rumination, a certain amount of time is needed in order for a person to formulate the strategy. When events unfold quickly, there is insufficient time to arrange these strategies. By way of example, consider once again the case of the basketball players predicting the success of sinking baskets. The theory of contrastive valence can be used to make the following prediction. After a basketball player has predicted the likelihood of making a shot, suppose we stop the player from shooting. We then ask the player to pause and reflect again on the shot: "With a moment's thought here, would you like to consider revising your estimate of the likelihood of making this shot?" My prediction is that the players will tend to reduce the probability of making the shot. That is, in general, the longer the time interval for contemplation, the lower the assessed probability of a positive outcome. Moreover, if a large (monetary) reward is offered for completing a shot, I predict that the effect will be magnified: the larger the monetary reward, the greater the likelihood that the assessed probability will drop below the objective empirical likelihood of making the shot. That is, people will tend to adopt an overtly pessimistic attitude in order to minimize possible disappointment and maximize future pleasure.

All of this presumes a "contrastive valence" theory of the magnitude of positive and negative emotions. How we ultimately feel about an event is not simply tied to an appraisal of some absolute benefit or penalty associated with that event. Our feelings also seem to depend on limbic contrast.[8] This is not a new insight. In his *Essay on Human Understanding*, John Locke spoke of the pleasure arising from the removal or attenuation of pain. Edmund Burke explicitly argued that the aesthetic experience of the "sublime" depends on an initial sensation of fear that is ultimately appraised as inconsequential. Nor do these ideas originate with these eighteenth-century European philosophers. Throughout history, sages have recognized that pleasure is enhanced by contrast: happiness is not so much a state of being as it is a state of becoming. People who fast periodically probably benefit from contrastive valence. As the Spartans understood, hunger is the best spice.

Three Flavors of Surprise

Listening to music can give rise to an enormous range of emotions.[9] Music can engender a joyous exuberance or transport us into a deep sadness. It can evoke a calm serenity or generate spine-tingling chills. It can lead to a sense of ominous darkness or convey a mysterious sense of awe and wonder. Music can even cause listeners to laugh out loud.

Apart from these strong "whiz-bang" emotions, music is also able to generate a wealth of "microemotions"—more subdued or muted feelings that are not easy to describe but occur more frequently while listening to music. These more nuanced feelings will be considered in later chapters. For the remainder of this chapter I would like to focus on three strong emotions that are closely linked to surprise: *laughter*, *awe*, and *frisson*. *Laughter* is a state of jocular amusement that is characterized by a distinctive "ha-ha-ha" vocalization. *Awe* is a state of astonishment or wonder that may cause a person to gasp. *Frisson* is the feeling you have when "chills" run up and down your spine and the hair stands up on the back of your neck. (All of these responses will be described more carefully later.)

These strong emotions are not common while listening to music, but when they occur they are memorable. Such emotions are typically sparked by particular musical moments or passages. Of course, not all listeners will respond to these passages in the same way, and even a single individual listener may not have the same emotional experience each time the passage is encountered. When they are evoked, however, these emotions are distinctly pleasurable and so listeners often seek out these experiences. Although *laughter*, *awe*, and *frisson* appear to be very different from one another, I will suggest that they share a deep biological kinship. We will see that each of these emotions is related to a violation of expectation. All three are specialized varieties of surprise.

Extreme surprises lead to the characteristic "surprise" facial expression. Interestingly, the "surprise" expression is the same as the one for horror.[10] The common element is simple fear. When in a fearful state, an animal has recourse to one of three behaviors. One response is to stand one's ground and attempt to defeat, disarm, or neutralize the danger; the goal here is to prevail over the fear-inducing situation. Another response is to run away as quickly as possible; the goal here is to escape the fear-inducing situation. A third response is to hide by remaining perfectly immobile and quiet; the goal here is to escape notice while the fear-inducing situation passes. These three primordial behaviors of fight, flight, and freeze can be observed throughout the animal kingdom. Even insects respond to danger by generating one of these three behaviors.

In everyday life, these responses are rarely manifested as full-blown behaviors. Instead, they are occasionally glimpsed as momentary or fleeting states. In the case of the surprise party, the person being surprised will often exhibit the characteristic "surprise" face with the gaping mouth and wide-open eyes. The "surprised" facial expression can pass in the blink of an eye. It is sometimes so quick, that it is apparent only later when viewed on video. The surprised expression is soon replaced by smiles and laughter as the celebrated individual realizes the true meaning of the unanticipated event. But in that first brief moment of fear lies much that is important.

Laughter—A Pleasurable Panting

In chapter 14 we will see examples of musical passages that cause listeners to laugh out loud. People don't often laugh while listening to music, but musically induced laughter does occur from time to time. Occasionally, composers explicitly set out to create works that provoke laughter—such as Mozart's *Ein musikalischer Spass* ("A Musical Joke"), Haydn's string quartet opus 33, no. 2 ("The Joke"), or Peter Schickele's wacky *Pervertimento for Bagpipes, Bicycle and Balloons*. In chapter 14 we will see evidence that whenever music causes listeners to laugh, the response can be traced to a massive violation of expectation. But for now, let's simply accept my claim that musically induced laughter is one of the responses a listener can experience when surprised.

What is it about some violations of expectation that will cause listeners to laugh? A tempting answer is to say that the violations are "humorous." But this begs the question. Consider a more literal version of our question: Why do people sometimes make a "ha-ha-ha" sound in response to violated expectations? Why don't listeners make a "hissing" sound, grit their teeth, or tug on their earlobes? What is it about violated expectations that can evoke the distinctive "ha-ha-ha" vocalization we call laughter?

Scientific studies on laughter can help answer this question—but the story is a little circuitous.[11] Perhaps the single most important lesson from research on laughing is that laughter is predominantly a *social* response. Robert Provine estimates that people are thirty times more likely to laugh in the presence of another person than when they are alone.[12] Field studies have established that most laughter is not in response to humor. Social inferiors laugh more in the presence of their social superiors. Social inferiors are also more likely to laugh at the instigation of social superiors than vice versa. For those of us who love to laugh, the scientific research on laughter seems depressing: the principal function of laughter seems to be to dissipate social fears. Laughter is a common response to humor, but humor is not necessary for laughter. For example, people frequently laugh at the misfortunes of their enemies, or laugh nervously in the face of danger.

Although laughter is predominantly a social phenomenon, the laughter response itself is innate rather than learned. All over the world, people laugh with a characteristic "ha-ha-ha . . ."[13] Even congenitally deaf people who have never heard anyone laugh make the same sound. Of course there are many variations on a theme. Some people make little sound—simply allowing their chest to jiggle in paroxysms of laughter ("chuckling"). Other people squeal, bellow, or roar. Yet others exhibit all manner of giggling, yukking, snickering, and snorting. Despite these variations, the basic laughter pattern remains.

Provine describes laughter as a "punctuated exhaling." The onset-to-onset time between "ha's" occurs at regular intervals of about 210 milliseconds. If the vocalization is high pitched and quiet, the sound is regarded as "giggling." If the mouth remains closed during laughing, the sound is better described as "snickering." If the mouth opens and closes in synchrony with the "ha's" then the sound becomes one of "yukking." If the mouth is rounded and remains open, then the sound is modified to a distinctly Santa-like "ho-ho-ho." Each laugh-phrase is followed by a deep inhalation. If the inhalation relies on the nose alone, then sometimes a snorelike vibration of the soft palate will cause a distinctive "snorting" sound (often to the embarrassment of the person laughing). Sometimes the laughter is preceded by a high-pitched squeal.

In general, however, the basic laughter pattern consists of a punctuated exhaling that occurs at a rate of roughly five times per second.[14]

Humans are not the only animals that laugh. Recognizably laughlike responses are also observed in chimpanzees, bonobos, orangutans, and gorillas. For example, tickling a young chimpanzee will typically cause the chimp to produce a rapid "oo-oo-oo-oo" sound. Similar sounds are produced during rough-and-tumble play such as when an animal is being chased by a playmate. Interestingly, the rate of such punctuated breathing is comparable to the rate found in human laughter. However, the laughter of chimpanzees, bonobos, orangutans, and gorillas differs in one important respect from that of humans. Humans laugh by exhaling only. The "oo-oo-oo-oo" sound of nonhuman primates involves a rapid alternation of inhaling and exhaling that doubles the tempo of the vocalizations to about ten per second.[15]

Robert Provine has argued that the human exhale-only version of laughter is a recent evolutionary development since the inhale–exhale version is shared by the other primates. Says Provine, "The human variant with its looser respiratory-vocal coupling evolved sometime after we branched from chimpanzees about six million years ago. Evidence of the primacy of the chimp form comes from the identification of chimplike laughter in orangutans and gorillas, apes that split off from the chimpanzee/human line several million years before chimpanzees and humans diverged."[16]

The inhale–exhale laughter of chimpanzees, bonobos, orangutans, and gorillas is essentially a form of *panting*. In fact, when Provine played ape recordings to university students and asked them to identify the sounds, the most common response was to describe the sounds as "panting." Going beyond Provine's research, we might observe that panting is a common component of physiological arousal: panting prepares an animal for physical exertion by drawing in large quantitites of oxygen and expelling carbon dioxide. When an animal fails to anticipate an event, this failure represents a potential danger. Like increased heart rate and increased perspiration, panting is a wholly appropriate response to surprise.

There are different types of laughter. *Nervous laughter* tends to occur when we are aware of an impending threat or danger. There is *slapstick laughter* where we laugh at physically awkward or calamitous body movements of others (or sometimes ourselves). *Sadistic laughter* occurs when we laugh at the misfortunes of our enemies. If our enemy is present, we may direct the response *at* the person as *mocking laughter*. *Surprise laughter* tends to occur when an event (such as a bursting balloon) is completely unexpected. *Social laughter* is the sort of polite or gregarious laughter that signals our participation or desired membership in a particular social group. In social laughter, we may be aware that nothing is particularly funny, but we may still laugh as a way of reducing any social tension. Finally, *humor laughter* is an overt form of pleasurable entertainment, usually relying on some form of joke-telling. Humor does not require laughter (we can find things amusing without laughing). Nor does laughter necessarily indicate humor.

These different forms of laughter would seem to defy any single explanation. What is it that all of these situations share? Why do nervousness, surprise, sadism, slapstick, humor, and social politeness all tend to lead to a characteristic "ha-ha-ha" respiratory reflex? I think that Aristotle already had the answer 2,500 years ago. In his *Poetics*, Aristotle described laughter as "a species of the base or ugly . . . some blunder or ugliness that does not cause pain or disaster."[17]

Aristotle's view was reiterated by the eighteenth-century German philosopher Immanuel Kant when he characterized laughter as arising from "the sudden transformation of a strained expectation into nothing." The key here is the contrast between the fast *reaction response* and the slower *appraisal response*.

The different forms of laughter all share two features: (1) Each situation is tinged with risk or fear, although this fear may arise simply because of a failure to anticipate the future (i.e., surprise). Remember that the reaction response always assumes the worst in surprising situations. (2) However, cognitive reflection either eliminates or inhibits the assessment of fear or risk. In the case of slapstick, the fast reaction response arises from *empathy*—the brain's disposition to "mirror" the psychological experiences of others. For example, research by Tania Singer and her colleagues at University College, London, has shown that similar brain regions are activated when we see someone else experience pain as when we ourselves experience pain.[18] The fast reaction response responds to the physical danger (whether to ourselves or others), but the ensuing cognitive appraisal recasts the apparent danger as inconsequential. The same pattern characterizes *Schadenfreude* when we laugh sadistically at the misfortunes of those we exclude from our social in-group: these are the misfortunes of *others*—not ourselves. Once again, there is a rapid recognition of the existence of harm, followed by an appraisal that we ourselves are not endangered—we might even benefit from the situation. In the case of nervous and social laughter, these rely on a cognitive appraisal that a social superior will not mistreat us, for example.

Consider the simple game of "peek-a-boo." The game is surprisingly resilient. Pediatrician Dr. Robert Marion describes how his sympathy for a distressed infant led to a long game of peek-a-boo: "I covered my face with a hospital towel and pulled that towel away for nearly three hours, to the delighted squeals of this one-year-old."[19] How is it that the sudden appearance of a face can cause such delight? Once again, it is the combination of "innocent surprise." The surprise causes a fast biological alarm, followed by the appraisal that no harm will happen. But how is it possible to sustain such a response for nearly three hours?[20]

There are excellent reasons why the fast-track brain should not lower its guard. The sole purpose of these reaction responses is to defend against those rare circumstances that are truly dangerous. The whole fast-track system is designed to tolerate large numbers of false alarms. Unlike the townsfolk in Aesop's fable, the fast-track pathway tends to respond to the cry "wolf" no matter how many times it occurs. The fast-track system maintains its vigilance. It never grows tired of assuming the worst. If the fast-track system did adapt or habituate to all the false alarms, then the reaction responses would not be available for those rare occasions when they are really needed.

Musical surprises fall almost exclusively into the category of innocuous risks.[21] In generating musical humor, composers are taking advantage of the biology of pessimism. As we have noted, surprise is always a sign of adaptive failure, and so the initial limbic response is necessarily negative. However, the slower appraisal mechanism intercedes and the ensuing contrastive valence results in a broadly pleasant experience.

Laughter's Origin

If laughter is an innate reflex, then laughter must originate as an evolutionary adaptation with its own unique biological history of development. The idea that laughter originated as a type of fear response does not seem to square well with our human experience of humor. Laughing is fun. How is it possible that a species of fear became transmuted into something pleasant? If I might be permitted some evolutionary speculation, I would like to suggest that the development of human laughter might have evolved along the following path:

1. Unvocalized panting occurs in response to surprise. This panting is part of a generalized increase in physiological arousal. Like the gaping mouth of the "surprised" face, panting prepares the animal for action.
2. For highly social animals (like humans and great apes) the biggest dangers come from other members of our species (conspecifics).
3. Threats from other conspecifics also evoke unvocalized panting. The threatening animal recognizes the panting as a successful provoking of a momentary state of fear in the threatened animal. The evoked fear means that the threatened animal has been successfully cowed. Panting becomes a signal of social deference. As an aside here, we might note that dogs exhibit "social panting"—where submissive animals begin panting when a dominant animal (sometimes a human owner) appears.[22]
4. Being able to evoke panting in another animal reassures the dominant animal of its dominant status. Similarly, panting in the presence of another animal serves to communicate one's submissiveness. For both animals, this communication is valuable because it establishes the social hierarchy.

5. In order to enhance the communication of deference, panting becomes *vocalized*—that is, the vocal cords are activated. Vocalized panting becomes a specific signal of deference or submissiveness.

6. Vocalized panting generalizes to most surprising circumstances.

7. In some primates, "panting-laughter" is reserved specifically for surprise linked to nondangerous outcomes. In highly socialized animals, most dangers are social in origin, so panting-laughter is commonly associated with social interaction.

8. In hominids, panting-laughter becomes explicitly social. Mutual panting-laughter within a group becomes an important signal of reciprocal alliance, social cohesion, and peaceful social relations.

9. The contrast between negative reaction feelings and neutral/positive appraisal feelings evokes an especially pleasant state. Human culture expands on these agreeable feelings through the advent of "humor" as an intentional activity meant simply to evoke laughter.[23]

10. Laughter becomes commonplace in hominid social interaction. In order to reduce the energy cost of laughter, the inhaling–exhaling form is replaced by the more efficient vocalized exhaling (i.e., modern human laughter).

Evolutionary storytelling is fraught with dangers, so the above story should be viewed pretty skeptically. My story is offered only as an illustration of how the innate behavior we call laughter might have evolved from surprise-induced fear. Biology is a complicated business, and most physiological functions develop in strikingly convoluted ways. The actual origin of human laughter is probably much more complicated. But as a universal human reflex, there is no doubt that laughter has an evolutionary history.

Awe—Takes Your Breath Away

Laughter is not the only response that can be evoked by surprise. Imagine that you are making your way through a dense jungle where tangled branches render your progress fitful. The thick vegetation obscures your vision so you can only see a foot or two ahead. Suddenly, you break through a mass of vegetation and find yourself standing immediately on the edge of a high cliff. A few more steps and you would plunge over the precipice. While laughter might be a possible response to this situation, a more likely response is to gasp. A *gasp* is an abrupt inhaling followed by a momentary holding of one's breath.

This imaginary scenario differs from the usual fight-or-flight response. There is no need for an impending expenditure of energy. Instead, the danger is more suited to the often-overlooked *freeze* response. Standing at the cliff's edge, *panting* would serve no useful purpose. But freezing *is* an appropriate response. A single rapid inhale provides a reservoir of oxygen that allows us to hold our breath.

Other situations that might evoke a freeze response are easy to imagine. You might encounter a snake, or a sparking electrical cable, or someone pointing a gun. In Brazil, I once encountered a spider's web the size of my outstretched arms and legs—it stopped me dead in my tracks, and I distinctly recall holding my breath. The enormous web was beautiful—brilliantly illuminated in the sunshine. But it was simultaneously a fearsome sight.

Holding one's breath has several benefits. It reduces movement and sound, which makes it more difficult for a possible predator to see or hear us. Reducing movement and sound also makes it easier for us to listen intently, and to see more clearly. Marksmen are better able to hit the bull's-eye when they stop breathing and shoot between heartbeats. A cricket will merrily chirp away until approached. Then it will become silent until it assumes you have moved away.

The freeze response is most probable when the danger remains fixed. The danger associated with the cliff remains as long as we are near the edge. The danger associated with encountering a snake remains as long as the snake is nearby. Laughter, by contrast, is more likely to occur when an apparent or actual danger rapidly dissolves. The bursting of a balloon represents a momentary rather than sustained danger. I might slip on a staircase, but immediately recover my footing without falling—an event that then results in my laughing. A parent says "boo" to a child, who subsequently erupts in laughter.

In short, laughter is a response to an apparent or momentary danger, whereas the gasp is a response to a sustained danger. Following the gasp, subsequent appraisal of the situation will determine whether the danger is real or "manageable." If the danger is real, then the gasp will be a prelude to sustained fear. If the danger is manageable, then the gasp will be a prelude to *awe*. Wobbling on the edge of a cliff we may experience fear. Standing securely on the edge of a cliff we may experience awe. Being in close proximity to a venomous snake we may experience fear. If the snake is being held by an experienced snake handler then we may experience awe.

Like laughter, the gasp can be vocalized or unvocalized. The unvocalized rapid inhale is the quiet, clandestine form. Silence is an appropriate response to sustained danger. The vocalized "ah!" when we gasp is more unusual, because it is rare for humans to vocalize while inhaling. Vocalizing also makes it more difficult to remain unobserved. But the vocalized form of the gasp is more audible to others and so may have some communicative function. In short, the unvocalized gasp is a self-serving defense response, whereas the vocalized gasp is a more altruistic response that can alert others to potential danger.[24]

As in the case of laughter, the gasp can be evoked by stimuli that at first appear dangerous, but on reflection are recognized as not actually dangerous. That is, the reaction response is acutely negative, but the appraisal response is either neutral or positive. It is this contrast that transforms the experience into something pleasurable.

Accordingly, we might characterize awe as a form of pleasurable surprise, one that mixes a sense of apparent sustained danger with an appraisal that the situation is okay or good. This characterization of awe is reinforced by the word's etymology. In English, the word "awe" traces a circuitous historical path that nicely echoes the combination of positive and negative emotions. My Webster's dictionary reports the archaic meaning of the word "awe" as "the power to inspire dread." The word originates in the Greek *achos*, which means pain. Webster's defines the more modern meaning of "awe" as follows:

emotion in which dread, veneration, and wonder are variously mingled: as 1: fearful reverence inspired by deity or by something sacred or mysterious 2: submissive and admiring fear inspired by authority or power (he stood in ~ of the king) 3: wondering reverence tinged with fear inspired by the sublime

Standing on the edge of the Grand Canyon is both dangerous and a wonderful opportunity to get a good look around. The sight is surely awesome—it takes your breath away. If God is to be both loved and feared, then meeting God would be a good reason for a person to feel awe.

Frisson—Thrills from Chills

Fear can provoke many different types of physiological reaction. When threatened by another animal, we might prepare to *fight* rather than flee or freeze. In the fight response, the first order of business is to produce an aggressive display. By signaling one's readiness to fight, it is possible that the threatening individual might back down, and so an actual fight can be avoided. Aggressive displays can include the displaying of teeth, making eye contact with the other animal, and generating low-pitched vocalizations. In addition, there are a series of behaviors that are all intended to make the individual appear bigger—and so more intimidating. This includes rearing up (to appear taller) and the bristling of hair (to appear more massive). Cats, by way of example, will arch their backs and make their hair stand on end.

All of these responses are also evident in humans. For example, human aggression can be signaled in the wrinkling of the upper lip, which, if the mouth is open, makes the upper cuspids (or canine teeth) more visible. Although humans are comparatively hairless as mammals go, fear can still cause the hair on the back of your neck to stand on end—a reflex technically known as *piloerection*.

Piloerection also occurs when a person is cold. Shivering causes the skin to tighten and hair follicles to pucker—causing the characteristic "goose flesh" texture. When it is cold, piloerection helps capture a layer of insulating air—a warming technique that works a lot better for animals with more hair than us humans. Even when piloerection occurs in response to fear (rather than cold), we still have a feeling which is often described as "chills." I think that this feeling is another example of the comparatively rare emotions that conform to the James–Lange theory. Recall from chapter 1 that James and Lange argued that the physiological response itself can precede and lead to a characteristic feeling. In chapter 1 we saw an example of such feelings in the Strack pencil task—where making people flex their cheeks (in a smile-like manner) causes them to feel happier. Here "chills" are evoked by piloerection. Fear doesn't make us "cold." Instead, fear causes piloerection, and this response evokes the phenomenal feeling of coldness—a feeling that would be a normal sensation when piloerection is evoked by cold temperatures.

This raises the question of why the linkage is not the other way around. Why is it that when we experience fear, we feel chills, but when we are cold, we don't feel fear? I suspect that the reason for this asymmetry harkens back to the very distant evolutionary past. Piloerection almost certainly arose first as a method of thermoregulation. For animals with lots of hair, making one's hair stand on end is a good response to a cold environment. Later, natural selection "discovered" that piloerection is a welcome addition for creating a convincing aggressive display (a physiological borrowing that biologists call a "preadaptation" or "exaptation"). Once the neural wiring was added so that aggression generated piloerection, the phenomenal sensation of chills simply came along as an artifact.

The phenomenon of "chills running up and down your spine" is technically referred to as *frisson*—a useful loan-word from French. The phenomenon has been variously described, including "thrills," "shivers," "chills," and "goose flesh." Psychophysiologists Gunther Bernatzky and Jaak Panksepp have proposed the memorable term "skin orgasm"—but their term has failed to gain currency.[25] A handful of studies regarding musically evoked frisson have been carried out, including work by Jaak Panksepp, Robert Zatorre, Anne Blood, Richard Gray, Avram Goldstein, and John Sloboda.[26] In chapter 14 we will examine a number of examples of musical passages that evoke frisson. We will see that the frisson response is correlated with two conditions: (1) loud passages, and (2) passages that contain some violation of expectation—such as an abrupt modulation.

Loudness is known to increase physiological arousal. There are good reasons for this connection: loudness is indicative of events in the environment that entail a large expenditure of physical energy. Whether physical energy is embodied in animate agents (such as a herd of elephants) or in inanimate objects (like boulders rolling down a slope), high levels of physical energy are more likely to pose a danger than low levels of energy. There are good reasons for organisms to be highly aroused by loud sounds.

In my own listening experience, I have found that I can reliably manipulate the magnitude of a frisson episode by adjusting the playback volume on my stereo. Louder reproduction enhances the frisson evoked by a musical passage, while quieter reproduction reduces the frisson. Incidentally, I've also observed that frisson is influenced by temperature: I am less likely to experience frisson when I am warm or hot. Cinemas and concert halls with lots of air conditioning might well enhance the emotional experiences of patrons.

Along with loudness, frisson is more likely to occur when there is an unexpected modulation, or an abrupt chromatic mediant chord, or an unexpected onset. In Beethoven's "Ode to Joy," many listeners have pointed to the pleasure evoked by a memorable moment when one of the phrases abruptly begins half a beat early.

As we have already noted, surprise is biologically bad. Both loudness and surprise evoke negatively valenced *reaction* responses. The loudness is symptomatic of high energy with a concomitant potential for physical injury. Surprise is symptomatic of an unpredictable environment. Together, these factors represent the potential for significant biological danger.

As in the case of laughter and awe, the frisson response originates in a reaction response shaped by fear. The fast-track brain responds to the combination of loudness and surprise with its usual pessimistic presumption. At the same time, the slower appraising mind concludes that the musical sounds are entirely safe. Once again, the negatively valenced piloerection response is in stark contrast with the neutral or positively valenced appraisal response. Once again, the magnitude of this contrast amplifies an overall sense of pleasure.

Fight, Flight, and Freeze: The Aesthetics of Pessimism

As noted earlier, physiologists have identified three classic responses to danger: the *fight*, *flight*, and *freeze* responses. The fight response begins with aggressive posturing and threat displays. The flight response is characterized by a quick increase in arousal, including rapid preparatory respiration. The freeze response is characterized by sudden motor immobility, including breath-holding.

My idea should by now be obvious. There is a striking similarity between the fight, flight, and freeze responses, and the experiences of frisson, laughter, and awe. The piloerection characteristic of frisson suggests a kinship with the fight response. The modified panting of laughter suggests a kinship with the flight response.[27] And the rapid inspiration and breath-holding of awe suggest a kinship with the freeze response.

When musicians create sounds that evoke laughter, awe, or frisson, they are, I believe, exploiting the biology of pessimism. The fast-track brain always interprets surprise as bad. The uncertainty attending surprise is sufficient cause to be fearful (at least until the more thorough appraisal process can properly evaluate the situation). Depending on the specific circumstances, that fear is expressed as one of the three primordial behaviors of fight, flight, or freeze.[28]

Because the fast-track brain never lowers its guard, musicians can rely on sounds to evoke pretty much the same response each time the music is heard. If the fast-track brain weren't so pig-headed in its pessimistic interpretation of surprise, then familiar musical works would rapidly lose their power to evoke the emotions of frisson, laughter, or awe. Of course, listening does change with exposure. But the fast-track brain responds primarily based on schematic expectations, and these schemas change only with extensive exposure. (I'll have more to say about this in later chapters.)

It might seem odd that the experiences of frisson, laughter, and awe rely on the evocation of fear. But this fear appears and disappears with great rapidity and does not involve conscious awareness. The appraisal response follows quickly on the heels of these reaction responses, and the neutral or positive appraisal quickly extinguishes the initial negative reaction. As listeners, we are left with the contrast in valence between the reaction/prediction and appraisal responses—a favorable contrast that leaves us with the sort of warm glow that contributes significantly to the attractiveness of music. In effect, when music evokes one of these strong emotions, the brain is simply realizing that the situation is very much better than first impressions might suggest. In this regard, music is similar to other forms of pleasurable risk-taking, such as hang gliding, skydiving, riding roller coasters, or eating chili peppers.[29]

The truly remarkable thing is that these powerful emotional responses can be evoked through the innocent medium of mere sounds. Of course, not just any sounds will do. Listeners must be enculturated into specific auditory environments where some events or patterns are more predictable than others. As we will see in the ensuing chapters, it is the learned schemas that provide the templates that enable the fast-track brain to make predictions, and in some cases, to be surprised.

If a musician wishes to evoke the experience of laughter, awe, or frisson, then the musician must be intimately familiar with the normative expectations of ordinary listeners. This is not a novel observation. Music scholars have long noted the importance of *convention* as a basis for generating various emotional responses. For example, in her book, *Haydn's Ingenious Jesting with Art*, musicologist Gretchen Wheelock describes many of the devices and elements in Haydn's music that relate to humor. Wheelock quite rightly emphasizes the necessity of convention to humor. Humor requires surprise; surprise requires an expected outcome; and an expected outcome requires an internalized norm. Composers must activate either normative schemas (such as styles) or commonplace clichés in their listeners if their violations of expectation are to have the desired effect. Leonard Meyer recognized this half a century ago.[30]

In each of laughter, awe, and frisson, an initially negative reactive response has been followed by a neutral or positive appraisal. What about the possible situation where an initially negative reaction response is followed by a *negative* appraisal? That is, what would happen (musically), if fight, flight, or freeze were allowed to be expressed unimpeded? Negative appraisals can arise for all sorts of reasons. A listener might find the style distasteful, regard the work as overvalued, dislike the musicians, or have unhappy past associations. A listener might be disappointed by the content of the lyrics, be embarrassed by the amateurism, be offended by an apparent plagiarism, or be disgusted by crass commercialism. But the sounds themselves will inevitably lead to the conclusion that the stimulus is "just music." Unlike the growling of a bear, the sounds do not represent an imminent danger. There is no need to run, flee, or hide from these sounds.

Of course it is possible to imagine fantastic scenarios where "just music" might be truly terrifying. For example, suppose you had just watched a horror film at the cinema with your friends, and then returned home alone. As you step into your darkened house, music from the horror film comes blaring at you from your stereo. (Perhaps you have inventive friends whose notion of "fun" suggests some need for psychological counseling.) In such a circumstance, most people would genuinely flee. But the ensuing flight would not really be evoked by the music. It would be evoked by the appraisal that either an intruder must be in your home, or that there really are evil spirits out to get you. These are both good reasons to feel genuine fear.

The "just music" assessment might explain why, of laughter, awe, and frisson, it is frisson that is the more common experience for listeners. An organism is most in command of a fearful situation when it chooses to fight, rather than flee or hide. That is, if the fear-inducing situation proves to be manageable, then one would expect an aggression display, rather than gasping or panting. The least fearful reaction response would generate frisson rather than laughter or awe.[31]

When surprised, how does a brain decide whether to initiate a fight, flight, or freeze response? Even though no conscious thought is entailed, some assessment must be involved—however crude the judgment. In general, if the danger is assessed to be relatively mild or manageable, then a fight response should be more likely. If the danger is assessed to be sustained, then the freeze response should be more likely. If the danger is assessed as an intermediate threat, then fleeing might be more likely. Almost certainly, context will play a role. When gathering with friends, for example, surprises are probably more likely to evoke laughter than awe or frisson. When alone in a dark alley, by comparison, the same surprise is not likely to result in laughter.

Interestingly, these same experiences of laughter, frisson, and awe can be evoked by purely intellectual pursuits—as when attempting to solve a problem. For example, consider the intellectual charge or pleasure that we feel when coming to understand, grasp, or solve some problem—an experience that is commonly dubbed the "insight" or "aha" phenomenon. The experience of solving a problem can also evoke laughter, frisson, or awe. But these different responses appear to be linked to distinctive characteristics of the problem-solving experience. For example, laughter is more likely to arise when the solution to a problem is suddenly recognized to be trivial. Frisson is more likely to arise when we make a connection that simplifies a problem. Awe is more likely to arise when we realize that the solution to a problem turns out to be massively complex. That is, frisson accompanies the experience of "gaining command" over a problem. Awe accompanies the experience of "losing command" over a problem. Laughter accompanies the experience of transforming a problem into something trivial.

A task as commonplace as solving a crossword puzzle can be the occasion to experience all three such emotions. We might have individual moments of insight. A chuckle may attend one solution, for example. As we finish the puzzle, we may have a frisson-like experience as we realize a previously unrecognized thematic unity that links the puzzle words together. Turning the page, we might have an awe-like response when we see that the next crossword puzzle is much larger (and harder).

In this chapter I have argued that laughter, frisson, and awe are three flavors of surprise. Since surprise represents a biological failure to anticipate the future, all surprises are initially assessed as threatening or dangerous. The body responds by initiating one of three primordial responses to threat: fight, flight, or freeze. The physiological basis for these responses can be seen in some characteristic behaviors: hair standing up on the back of your neck, shivers running up and down your spine, laughter, gasping, and breath-holding. In most real-world situations, evoking fight, flight, or freezing behaviors will prove to be excessive—an overreaction to innocuous situations. A slower cognitive process ultimately makes this assessment and begins to inhibit or modify the fast reaction response. Although the situation begins with a negatively valenced limbic response, it is replaced by a neutral or even positively valenced limbic response. The contrast between these successive assessments generates a subjective experience akin to relief. What begins as a brief moment of fear is transformed into a strikingly positive phenomenal experience.

In this chapter I have also argued that reaction responses are necessarily conservative or "pessimistic." To maintain their effectiveness, especially in environments that may generate lots of false alarms, reaction responses must be resistant to habituation or extinction. That is, reaction responses should be difficult to "unlearn." Notice, however, that this situation does not preclude learning. That is, there is no theoretical impediment to learning *new* ways of being surprised. In fact, there are significant biological benefits to be gained if an organism is able to learn new ways to become fearful. When it comes to fear, learning should be easy, but unlearning should be difficult.

At the beginning of this chapter I identified a number of types of emotions that can be evoked by music. But the discussion here has considered only three of these emotions: laughter, awe, and frisson. What about some of the other strong emotions that can be evoked by music, such as joy, exuberance, serenity, angst, sadness? Here I need to remind readers that the purpose of this book is to address the phenomenon of expectation (and the emotions that arise from expectation). While expectation probably plays a role in these other emotions, I suspect that the phenomenon of expectation is less relevant in evoking emotions such as sadness or exuberance.

Reprise

In this chapter, I have introduced the phenomenon of surprise. Expectations that prove to be correct represent successful mental functioning. The experience of surprise means that an organism has failed to accurately anticipate possible future events. From a biological perspective, surprise is always bad—at least initially. I have noted that there are different expressions of surprise and that these expressions echo the primordial behaviors of *fight*, *flight*, and *freeze*. Musical surprises are capable of initiating these responses, but the responses themselves are short-lived because an ensuing appraisal ultimately judges the stimuli as nonthreatening. The appraisal response inhibits the full expression of fight, flight, or freeze and also prevents the individual from becoming consciously aware of their brief brush with fear. Instead, the listener is left with a corresponding response of frisson, laughter, or awe. Evidence in support of this account can be found in the various physiological responses associated with fight, flight, and freeze that can also be observed among music listeners: piloerection, chills, changes of heart rate, laughter, gasping, and breath-holding.

I have suggested that the pleasure associated with these responses arises from limbic contrast—a phenomenon I've called *contrastive valence*. Pleasure is increased when a positive response follows a negative response. While surprise is biologically bad, surprise nevertheless plays a pivotal role in human emotional experience. Surprise acts as an emotional amplifier, and we sometimes intentionally use this amplifier to boost positive emotions. Suppose you had the opportunity to know in advance all of the future times and places when your most cherished goals or ambitions would be fulfilled. I doubt that many people would want such knowledge. Part of the joy of life is the surprise that accompanies achieving certain wishes. When all of the uncertainty is removed, the capacity for pleasure also seems to be diminished.

There is a tired old joke that begins by asking "Why do you keep beating your head against the wall?" Neuroscience gives some credence to the answer: "Because it feels so good when I stop." Of course there are more effective forms of head-banging. Music is one of them.

3 Measuring Musical Expectation

Without some way of gathering information about what individuals expect, all theories of expectation would remain purely speculative. If we want to hold our views accountable, we must be able to compare theories with evidence about how real minds anticipate the future. How then, do we go about determining what someone is expecting?

This question raises a host of related questions. What does it mean to have an expectation? How precise are expectations? Do we expect specific events, or do we expect "classes" or types of events? Can a person truly anticipate more than one possibility at a single time—that is, is it possible to have "plural" expectations? How do expectations manifest themselves as psychological or physiological states? How would one go about measuring what a person expects?

One definition of expectation might classify it as a form of mental or corporeal "belief" that some event or class of events is likely to happen in the future.[1] Such "beliefs" are evident in a person's "action-readiness"—that is, changes of posture, metabolism, or conscious thought that prepare the individual for certain possible outcomes but not for others. Such expectations can differ in strength of conviction or certainty.

Over the past four decades, researchers have devised a number of methods for gauging or estimating what people expect. The purpose of this chapter is to describe some of the experimental methods used to characterize listener expectations. Many of the same techniques are used to characterize nonauditory expectations, such as visual expectations. In addition, we will introduce some useful concepts from probability and information theory. These concepts will provide a convenient quantitative method for characterizing the range of expected possibilities, and for expressing the relative strength of conviction or certainty for various expectations.

Experimental Methods in Expectation

At least eight different experimental methods have been used to characterize a listener's expectations. Each method has strengths and weaknesses. Some methods are laborious whereas others are easy; some give fine-grained detail about the relative strengths of various possibilities, where others merely indicate that some outcome is possible for one listener. Some methods require the listener to reflect and introspect; others require no conscious thought at all. Some require the listener to be musically skilled; other methods require no special skills. Some methods are suitable only for adult listeners who can communicate verbally; other methods can be used with pre-verbal infants and nonhuman animals. Some methods require that the sound experience be periodically halted; other methods can be used without interrupting the listening experience. Each method is able to provide some useful information, but no method is a panacea. Becoming familiar with the different methods will help us better interpret the various experimental results, and also help us understand why different methods sometimes produce diverging—sometimes even conflicting—results.

It is important to understand that none of the following methods measures "expectation" in any direct sense. "Expectation" is a theoretical construct whose meaning and definition is open to debate. In experimental research, theoretical entities are rarely directly observable. Instead, researchers must operationally define some measureable quantity that is assumed to correlate with the theoretical construct. In reading the descriptions of the following experimental methods, it will become obvious that each measurement method is open to the legitimate charge "that's not what expectation really is." But in interpreting the experimental results we need to maintain some perspective. No method will capture the entire essence of expectation, but on occasion, some methods will allow clearer glimpses of how "expectation" operates.

1 Method of Tone Detection

Perhaps the earliest method for measuring auditory expectation was devised by Gordon Greenberg and Willard Larkin in the 1960s.[2] Working at the University of Illinois, Greenberg and Larkin had participants listen to tones in the presence of continuous loud noise. The listeners' task was simply to indicate whether or not they heard the tone.

Greenberg and Larkin discovered that listeners were better able to detect a tone if they expected a tone of a specific pitch to occur at a particular moment. They found that expectation allows listeners to direct their attention in both frequency and time: this directed attention has the effect of lowering the threshold of sensation for the sound. Greenberg and Larkin showed that there was a band of frequencies that was facilitated when listeners were expecting a particular frequency. If a listener expected a tone of 500 Hz, she was still able to detect a partially masked 550 Hz tone, but not a tone of 800 Hz. In effect, Greenberg and Larkin showed that listeners can direct their attention at particular frequency regions and time spans, and they used the method of detection to determine the shape and width of these "attentional bands."

Working at the Catholic University in Washington, Jim Howard, Alice O'Toole, Raja Parasuraman, and Kevin Bennett extended this method so that listeners were asked to detect a tone in some patterned context.[3] Listeners heard a twelve-note sequence presented along with a concurrent sustained noise. Two presentations of the sequence were given. One presentation was complete; the other presentation was missing one of the tones. Listeners were asked to indicate which of the two presentations was complete. The researchers established that the preceding sequence of tones facilitated the detection of some tones but not others. That is, they showed that the *melodic context* influences where listeners direct their attention.

The method of tone detection is rarely used today in experiments related to auditory expectation. But the work of Greenberg and Larkin remains important because it demonstrates two general principles concerning expectation. First, *accurate expectation facilitates perception.* When the events of the world conform to our expectations, we are better able to detect, perceive, and process these events. Over the past half century, this facilitating effect has been observed many times.[4] It is a principle that holds for both visual as well as auditory events. A second lesson from Greenberg and Larkin is that low-level sensory processes (like the hearing threshold for detecting a tone) are influenced by higher-level mental processes (like expectation). It is as though higher mental functions are able to reach down into the sensory apparatus and do some fine-tuning. Sensory systems don't just present information to the higher mental functions; in addition, higher mental functions can reconfigure a sensory system to focus on particular aspects of the sensorial world.

2   Method of Production

At the University of Washington in Seattle, James Carlsen, Pierre Divenyi, and Jack Taylor pioneered the simple technique of having listeners sing a continuation to some interrupted musical phrase.[5] Carlsen and his colleagues simply played a sequence of tones and asked listeners to sing what they thought would be an appropriate continuation. Carlsen used this method to compare the melodic continuations of American, German, and Hungarian listeners.[6] In analyzing the sung continuations, Carlsen found significant differences between the three groups, suggesting that one's cultural background influences listener expectations of what might happen next.

This method has a number of disadvantages. Notably it requires that participants have some singing ability (and be willing to sing while being recorded).[7] The method also relies on the participants' facility and comfort with improvising. Sung continuations can be confounded by vocal constraints. For example, if the antecedent context is low in pitch compared with the singer's vocal range, then there will be a natural tendency for the singer to produce a continuation that rises in pitch. Conversely, if the antecedent context is high in pitch compared with the singer's vocal range, then there will be a tendency for the singer to produce a continuation that falls in pitch.

Thus the melodic contour will reflect the participant's vocal range, rather than general melodic trends. (This problem can be controlled to some extent by determining the singer's vocal range prior to the experiment, and then tailoring the stimuli so they are positioned near the center of the participant's range.) When the antecedent context is short (such as a two-note interval), it may be impossible to infer the key that a participant might be using. In experiments by William Lake, this problem is eliminated by playing a tonic-establishing cadence before the start of the stimulus.[8] Another problem relates to deciphering what a singer sang. When singers are not well trained, the pitch and timing is often quite ambiguous. This introduces onerous technical challenges for the experimenter when transcribing what pitches and durations a singer produced or was intending to produce.

A variant of the method of production has been used by Mark Schmuckler. Instead of having participants sing, Schmuckler asked pianists to perform a continuation on a keyboard. Compared with sung continuations, the use of a keyboard circumvents the problems of pitch transcription, but it introduces a potential problem with skill. In order to reduce the need for keyboard skills, participants are given opportunities to try several different continuations, and rehearse their preferred continuation until they are satisfied with their response. This variation of the method of production has been popular with those researchers, such as Dirk-Jan Povel, who want to reduce the uncertainties introduced by pitch transcription.[9]

Yet another variant of this technique has been developed by Steve Larson at the University of Oregon. Larson contrived a task involving musical notation and expert music theorists.[10] He simply provided a notated antecedent context and asked music theorists to compose a suitable melodic continuation. In some ways, music theorists are ideal participants since they can draw on a lot of experience and know how to respond precisely. But music theorists often pride themselves on being musically clever, so a potential danger with this approach is that participants will be tempted to compose technical flights of creative fancy rather than commonplace or more intuitive melodic continuations. Larson explicitly instructed his participants to compose what they thought would be the most common or obvious continuation. As an inducement to this end, he offered a prize whose winner would be selected from the group of theorists who wrote the same (most frequent) continuation. That is, he gathered all of the responses, identified the most commonly occurring response, and then awarded a prize to one of the theorists (drawn at random) who had composed the most common continuation. One advantage of this approach over Carlsen's method is that it is possible to use complex harmonic or polyphonic stimuli (and responses) that would not be suitable for a sung response. However, there are a number of disadvantages to this method. The principal disadvantage is that notationally literate musicians often hold their own theories about melodic organization, and so the responses hold the potential to be confounded by theoretical preconceptions. Like

Schmuckler's keyboard task, the notation task lacks the spontaneity of improvised singing. That is, it encourages conscious, contrived, and reflective responses.

As we have seen, the principal drawback to the method of production is that participants in the experiment must have considerable musical competence—as vocalists, keyboardists, or by having facility with musical notation. This tends to limit the technique to participants who are relatively musical. Further, in requiring participants to "perform," the method of production also assumes that expectation facilitates not perception but *motor production*. Finally, Mark Schmuckler has pointed out that the method of production also requires a certain degree of conscious attention, whereas under normal listening conditions expectations may be largely unconscious and effortless.[11]

Compared with other methods, a unique benefit of the method of production is that it doesn't artificially limit a participant to producing a single tone following the given musical context. That is, whereas many other experimental methods assume that the preeminent expectation will pertain to the immediately succeeding tone, the method of production readily allows a participant to suggest several continuation notes as a coherent group. Later, we will see evidence indicating that a listener's strongest expectation may relate to an event that does not occur until after several intervening tones. The method of production provides better opportunities for an experimenter to study such possible long-term expectations, rather than focusing exclusively on note-to-note relationships.

3   Probe-Tone Method

Without question, the best-known experimental method for testing musical expectations is the probe-tone method pioneered by Roger Shepard and Carol Krumhansl.[12] Krumhansl and her colleagues at Cornell University have carried out numerous experiments using this technique. In simple terms, a musical context is presented—such as several chords or the initial notes of a melody. Following this context, a single tone or chord is played, and the listener is asked to judge this target (or "probe") sound according to some criterion. Often, the listener is asked to judge how well the tone or chord "fits" with the preceding musical context. The original contextual passage is then repeated and a different probe tone or chord is played. Following each presentation, the listener is asked to judge how well the new tone or chord fits with the preceding context.

In probe-tone experiments, a dozen or more repetitions of the same contextual passage may be presented—each presentation followed by a different probe. For example, several dozen possible continuations (probes) might be presented on successive trials. In this way, numerical ratings can be gathered for a large number of possible continuations. Thus, a significant advantage of the probe-tone method is that a detailed picture can be assembled where the listener provides information concerning several possible continuations, rather than only a single continuation. For example, with the probe-tone method a given participant might judge two or three continuations equally good. In the method of production, by contrast, participants must choose just one continuation, so it is problematic for the experimenter to infer that several different continuations would be equally acceptable for the participant. In addition, the probe-tone method can also establish which continuations sound "bad." That is, the method can be used to identify implausible as well as plausible continuations.

An obvious difficulty with the probe-tone method is that it is tedious. Each possible continuation must be tested separately. In practice, the total range of possibilities is reduced by the experimenter. For example, there are 88 tones available on a piano, but most of these tones are unlikely candidates to follow some melodic passage. Most tones will be implausibly high or low. Typically, the experimenter will reduce the candidate pitches to those within a two-octave range (one octave above or below) of the current pitch.

Yet another way to limit the number of possible continuations is to use so-called Shepard tones as probes. Shepard tones are specially constructed complex tones consisting of octave-spaced partials spanning the entire hearing range.[13] This encourages the listener to judge "goodness of fit" according to pitch-class rather than according to a single pitch. In Western music, there are only twelve pitch-classes, so using Shepard tones reduces all possible pitch continuations to just twelve. Using Shepard tones, however, means that the experimenter cannot directly infer the pitch direction (or contour) expected by the listener, given that each pitch class represents several possible pitches.

Apart from the tediousness of the probe-tone method, another difficulty is that it stops the music. When a listener judges "goodness of fit" one might imagine the response to arise from a combination of two sorts of judgments: (1) how well does this tone follow the previous note? and (2) how well does this tone terminate the tone sequence? Theoretically, it is possible that a tone follows well from the previous tone, but it might be judged as a poor fit because it evokes little sense of perceptual closure or completion. Conversely, a tone might follow poorly from the previous tone, yet evoke a strong sense of tonal closure, and so be rated highly by listeners. We will have more to say about these divergent interpretations in chapter 9.

Progressive probe-tone method   In some cases, exhaustive experiments have been carried out to trace the changes in the listener's experience as the music progresses. For example, the first three notes of a melody may be played, followed by a probe tone. This procedure is repeated until a large number of continuation tones have been probed. Then the first *four* notes of the melody are played, again followed by one of several probe tones. This procedure continues for the first five notes, six notes, and so on. The progressive probe-tone method has been used to trace in detail such phenomena as how a modulating chord progression begins to evoke a different tonal center.[14]

Continuous probe method   An obvious difficulty with the progressive probe-tone method is the tediousness of repeating the stimulus for each probe tone. If twelve probes are used following each note, a simple eight-note sequence will require 96 repetitions of the simulus in order to map the changing expectations over the course of the passage. In 2002, Carol Krumhansl and her colleagues introduced a variation of the probe-tone method in which a single probe tone (or chord) is sustained throughout the passage and the listener provides continuous responses as to the appropriateness of the probe at each moment in time.[15]

A problem with the continuous probe method is that it is hard to regard the responses as relating to expectations. Suppose, for example, that a tonic pitch is sounding continuously throughout a passage. As a cadence approaches, the dominant chord might sound. However, the harmonic clash between the dominant chord and the tonic pitch is not likely to result in a high rating for the tonic. Yet, one might presume that following a dominant chord, a high rating would be expected for the tonic. By comparison, if the penultimate chord is a subdominant chord, the probe-tone tonic is likely to receive a very high rating (because it is consonant with the sounding chord). Yet the dominant chord may well have evoked a greater expectation for an ensuing tonic than is the case for the subdominant chord. Said another way, one would expect the responses to continuous probe tones to be confounded by the resulting harmonic congruence: harmonic congruence is apt to play a much stronger role than expectation for subsequent events in determining a listener's response.

4   Betting Paradigm

Although the various probe tone methods do provide some information about the magnitude of various expectations, it would be useful to gather more precise measures of the subjective probabilities of different outcomes. In the *betting paradigm*, participants are given a "grub stake" of poker chips and asked to place bets on a set of possible continuations. Participants hear an antecedent passage and are invited to bet on what pitch they think will occur next.

I and my collaborators, Paul von Hippel and ethnomusicologist David Harnish, used this approach to compare the expectations for two cultural groups—Balinese musicians and American musicians. The experiment works as follows. Bets are placed on the keys of a mock-up of an instrument (in our experiment, a Balinese *peng ugal*). Bets need not all be placed on a single outcome. Instead, participants are free to distribute the poker chips across several possible continuations—varying the number of chips wagered according to the degree of certainty or uncertainty. Bets placed on the correct pitch are rewarded tenfold. Bets placed on incorrect pitches are lost. Participants are instructed to try to maximize their winnings.

As in the progressive probe-tone method, responses (wagers) can be collected following each note of a melody. The experiment begins with the participant hearing the first note of the melody while the pitch is indicated on a computer monitor. The participant is then invited to bet on what she or he thinks will be the second note. Once bets are placed, the actual second note is revealed, the winnings tabulated, and a sound recording of the melody is played, stopping before the third note. The participant is then invited to bet on what she or he thinks will be the third note. This process is repeated until a complete melody has been revealed.

In our experiment both American and Balinese musicians were tested on a traditional Balinese melody.[16] Throughout the experiment, participants could see the notation up to the current point in the melody, and could try out different continuations using a digital keyboard sampler that emulated the sound of the *peng ugal*. The betting context helped participants consider other possibilities apart from the first one that came to mind.

The principal benefit of the betting paradigm is that it allows the experimenter to calculate the subjective probabilities for different continuations. Assuming that the participant is behaving rationally, bets should be placed in proportion to the subjective likelihood of subsequent events. For example, if a participant thinks that a certain pitch is twice as likely as another pitch, then the participant ought to place twice as large a bet on the more probable pitch. Later in this chapter we will discuss how information theory provides a useful way to quantify such subjective probabilities.

A related advantage of the betting paradigm is that it allows the experimenter to measure confidence independent of relative probabilities. Suppose, for example, that the Balinese and American participants had roughly the same expectations ("A" is more likely than "B" which is more likely than "C"), but differed significantly in their confidence. A lack of confidence would be evident by participants' spreading their bets out more evenly. Once again, this can be calculated using information theory.

There are also several problems with the betting paradigm. For one thing, the procedure is even more tedious than the progressive probe-tone method. On average, we have found that it takes roughly three minutes for participants to complete their wagers for each note in the melody. A thirty-five-note melody thus can take as long as two hours to complete. Fortunately, the majority of our participants report that the task is fun, and that the gambling aspect of the task is highly motivating.

Like the notated version of the method of production, the betting paradigm encourages a conscious-reflective response rather than a spontaneous response. Unlike the method of production, the participant knows that there is a real melody involved, and is motivated to correctly anticipate the next note. Even more so than the method of production, the betting paradigm requires a degree of musical skill. In this regard, the probe-tone method is notably superior, not requiring any musical expertise.

A further problem with the betting paradigm is that the data may be confounded by a learning effect. Since the participants receive constant feedback about the accuracy of their wagers, they are likely to become progressively better at placing their bets as the experiment continues. Typically, experiments last more than an hour, so there is plenty of opportunity to improve and refine one's betting skills. Any apparent decrease in uncertainty as the melody progresses may therefore be an artifact of becoming a more savvy gambler.[17]

5   Head-Turning Paradigm

When we hear an unexpected sound, we will often turn our head in the direction of the sound. This basic reflex is referred to as the *orienting response*, and it is evident in all vertebrates, including young infants and adults. If a stimulus is repeated, after a while an individual will *habituate* to the stimulus and fail to orient to it. Further repetitions are unlikely to provoke a response. If a change is then made to the stimulus, and if the change is sufficiently novel, then a listener might reorient to the sound. This reorienting to a modified stimulus is called *dishabituation*. If an infant reorients to a modified sound, then one might interpret this as evidence that the infant didn't expect the sound.

Experiments employing a dishabituation paradigm typically repeat a stimulus until the participant becomes habituated to it. When habituation is complete then a new stimulus is introduced. If the new stimulus is perceived as the same (or similar) to the preceding stimuli then the participant will typically show no dishabituation. Conversely, if the new stimulus is perceived to differ from the preceding or expected stimuli then the participant is likely to show evidence of dishabituation by orienting to the stimulus.

The dishabituation paradigm is typically used when studying preverbal infants or nonhuman animals. The paradigm is used less commonly among adults since adults can verbally report perceived similarity or difference.

In research with infants, the head-turning paradigm has proved quite popular. There are a number of variants of this experimental method. In some cases, the experimenter merely tabulates whether or not a participant reorients to a modified stimulus. Another variant of the method measures the duration of orienting. This assumes that the greater the discrepancy between the expected and actual stimulus, the longer an infant will look in the direction of the stimulus. Yet another method will compare how quickly an individual habituates to two related events.[18]

Most of the experimental methods described in this chapter are not suitable for use with young children or infants. The principal advantage of the head-turning paradigm is that it can be used with infants and nonhuman animals. Also, unlike the bradycardic method (see below), it requires no special instrumentation apart from a video camera. One problem with the head-turning paradigm is that it requires that the participant first become habituated to the stimulus before some change is made. This makes the procedure extremely time-consuming. Newborn infants have difficulty controlling their head movements, so typically, the head-turning paradigm cannot be used until the infant is at least two or three months old.

An example of an experiment using the head-turning paradigm is one carried out by Michael Weiss, Philip Zelazo, and Irina Swain.[19] Weiss and his colleagues had infants listen to a nonsense word repeated until they habituated to it. The infants then heard either the original sound or one of four variants in which the pitch had been altered. Specifically, the frequency was modified by either 7, 14, 21, or 28 percent. They found that infants were most likely to reorient to the stimulus when the frequency of the nonsense word had been altered by 14 percent or more.

6   Bradycardic Response Method

Another version of the dishabituation paradigm examines changes of heart rate rather than head movements. When a stimulus deviates from an expected stimulus or attracts the attention of an individual, a measureable reduction of heart rate is often observed. Typically, such stimuli will result in a reduction of heart rate of about two to four beats per minute, followed by a recovery back to the normal rate. This response is referred to as *bradycardia*. Bradycardic changes of heart rate are associated with *interest* and *attending* to a stimulus.

Like the head-turning paradigm, the bradycardic response method is useful for studying the expectations of nonhuman animals, and especially for studying preverbal infants. Unfortunately, the method is tedious and the equipment can be cumbersome. Unlike the probe-tone method and the betting paradigm, each trial gives comparatively little information, and building a picture of infant expectation may require hundreds of trials from dozens of participants.

7   Reaction Time Method

Recall that Greenberg and Larkin showed that accurate expectation facilitates perception. When you hear an expected sound, you will typically be able to process it more quickly and respond to it faster (if a motor response is required). A quick reaction time is therefore correlated with high expectation. While reaction-time measures have long been used in experiments related to visual expectation, the method has gained favor only recently in research on auditory or musical expectation. Bret Aarden has shown that the method shows great promise for the study of melodic expectation.[20]

Aarden concocted a task where listeners were required to process and respond to sounds as quickly as possible. While they listened to an ongoing melody, Aarden asked his listeners simply to indicate whether the pitch contour of the melody had ascended, descended, or remained the same. In this task, there are three alternatives, and the listener must press one of three keys as quickly as possible after each note in the sequence. The responses are collected, including the elapsed time between the onset of the heard tone and the key press. The method is based on the assumption that if the pitch contour of a note moves as expected, then this will have a facilitating effect and so produce faster reaction times. Conversely, if a tone moves to an unexpected tone, this will increase the processing time and so result in a slower reaction time.[21]

The reaction time method has two notable advantages over other methods we have seen. First, it can be used in a continuous listening task where data are collected after every tone (except the first). The task is fairly difficult, so stimulus melodies are typically played using a tempo that is about 60 percent of the normal speed.[22] However, apart from the reduced tempo, there are no musical interruptions or pauses. As we will see later, compared with other methods, this method reduces the closure confound—where long pauses encourage listeners to respond to how well the tone provides a good ending point. A related advantage is that data collection is much faster than other methods. Rather than spending an entire experimental session on a single melody, a single session can collect data for dozens of melodies or tone sequences representing many different contexts. Another advantage is that the task happens so quickly that it is difficult for participants to engage in conscious reflection.

The reaction time method also has a number of drawbacks. First, unlike the betting paradigm or the probe-tone method, the reaction time method does not collect data for all of the different possibilities at each moment. Instead, we have a record of the processing time for specific contours within the heard sequence. When a listener makes a slow response, we have no idea of why this occurs—except that the heard tone evoked a more time-consuming mental process. There is no explicit information to tell us which alternative stimulus might have been processed more quickly. Finally, we must note that the reaction time method is fully premised on the idea that accurate expectations facilitate response times. At the moment, not enough is known about this relationship to know what sorts of confounds might be lurking.[23]

Despite these problems and caveats, the reaction time method shows excellent promise. As we will see in chapter 9, the results of the reaction time method and the probe-tone method sometimes diverge dramatically. We will see that these differences illuminate some important aspects of auditory expectation.

8   Evoked Response Potential (ERP)

The activity of neurons results in tiny electrical currents. When large numbers of neurons are active at the same time, the aggregate electrical current can often be detected through the scalp using suitably sensitive electrodes. The complicated hills and valleys of electroencephalographs have been studied for decades. Most of the activity remains an enigma; however, a consensus has slowly emerged about the interpretation of several specific features.

The most pertinent research related to expectation involves those electrical patterns that arise in response to a particular stimulus, like a tone. Since the recorded brain activity is in response to a stimulus, the ensuing electrical behavior is referred to as an *evoked response potential* or ERP.

Researchers still have difficulty interpreting individual ERP recordings. Typically, researchers average together many trials in which the same stimulus condition exists. It is the averaged data set—sometimes averaged across many subjects—that is able to tell a story. After the onset of the stimulus, a characteristic sequence of peaks and troughs can be observed in the ERP data. For convenience, successive peaks are designated P1, P2, P3, and so on, while successive troughs are designated N1, N2, and so on.

Suppose that a repeated sequence of identical sounds is interrupted occasionally by a deviant sound. Typically, this change is reflected in the listeners' response as an increased amplitude of the N2 waveform, which usually peaks around 100 to 250 milliseconds following the occurrence of the deviant sound. Because the electrical potential is negative and because it occurs in response to stimuli that fail to match the expected sound, the event is referred to as a *mismatch negativity* or MMN. MMNs can occur in response to changes of pitch, changes of loudness, and changes of timbre, among other things. MMNs also occur if any expected tone is replaced by a silent rest. Interestingly, MMNs occur if the listener *expects* to hear a change in the sound even if the sound remains unchanged.[24]

MMNs have been observed in listeners who are asleep and even in anesthetized rats, so the mismatch negativity can be evoked without conscious awareness of changes in sound. The magnitude of the effect is influenced, however, by attentiveness. For example, distracting tasks will attenuate the MMN.

The location in the brain of the evoked MMN is known to change depending on the type of stimulus change. For example, a change in frequency will evoke the largest MMN response along the sides of the head (temporal cortex). However, suppose an auditory pattern A–B–A–B–A–B is interrupted by the repetition of either A–A or B–B. In this case the site of maximum MMN response shifts toward the top of the head.[25]

ERP methods have a number of advantages and disadvantages. Like the head-turning paradigm and the bradycardic response method, ERP can be useful for studying the expectations of nonhuman animals, and especially for studying preverbal infants. No verbal responses are necessary, and no conscious awareness or thought is required. Unfortunately, many trials must be averaged together in order to infer anything.

Subjective Probability and Uncertainty

Having described the major experimental techniques for characterizing a listener's expectation, let us now turn to a second question: How do we express the strength of conviction or certainty of an expectation?

Suppose you are a participant in a betting paradigm experiment. There might be ten possible notes, and your task is to place your bets according to how likely you think each outcome is. There are lots of possible circumstances. If you are completely clueless, the best strategy would be to simply spread your poker chips evenly across all ten possibilities. Conversely, if you are completely certain of the outcome, the best strategy would be to place all of your chips on the expected note. In the first case, the bets reflect that you are completely uncertain of the outcome, whereas in the second case the bets indicate you are absolutely certain. Of course, there are many intermediate situations. You might be pretty sure that a certain outcome will happen, but you are less than 100 percent certain. In this case, you might place a small bet on all ten outcomes, but place most of your chips on the one outcome you think is most likely. Alternatively, you might be absolutely certain that one of the ten outcomes will *not* happen. In this case, you might spread your bets evenly across the remaining nine possibilities—placing no chips on the outcome you are certain won't occur. A more complicated situation might arise if you are moderately certain that only three outcomes are likely. Here you might split the majority of the poker chips between the three most likely outcomes, while placing small bets on the remaining possibilities.

From a research perspective, it would be convenient if we could distill any complex arrangement of bets into a single number representing the overall degree of certainty or uncertainty. Such a summary measure is provided by information theory. Using the so-called Shannon–Weaver equation, any arrangement of probabilities can be summarized by a single value that represents the aggregate uncertainty—measured in *bits*. When the number of bits is high, it means that the bets (probabilities) represent a high degree of overall uncertainty. Conversely, a low number of bits is indicative of high certainty.[26]

We won't bother to explain the equation here. However, the flavor of using bits to characterize uncertainty can be conveyed by some examples. Suppose we want to characterize the uncertainty of tossing a fair coin. With two possibilities (heads or tails) the amount of uncertainty is precisely 1 bit. Think of a bit as equivalent to one "yes-or-no" question: Did the coin come up heads? A single yes-or-no answer to that question is all we need to know to resolve the uncertainty. Similarly, if there are four equally likely outcomes, the number of bits is 2. If we have to choose from 8 equally likely pitches, then the uncertainty is 3 bits ($2 \times 2 \times 2$).

In the case of the von Hippel, Huron, and Harnish experiment described earlier, the *peng ugal* instrument provided ten possible tones. If all ten tones were equally

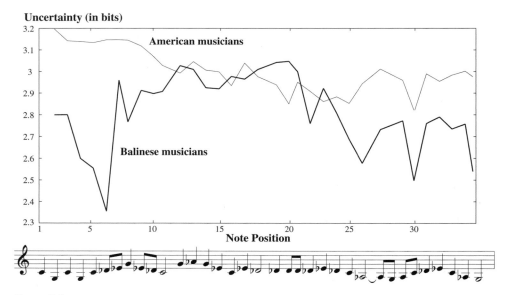

Figure 3.1
Average moment-to-moment uncertainty for Balinese and American musicians listening to an unfamiliar traditional Balinese melody. Uncertainty is plotted as entropy, measured in bits. In general, Balinese listeners show less average uncertainty. Note positions correspond with underlying notational rendering. The pitch levels shown in the notation are only approximate.

probable, then the uncertainty would represent 3.32 bits. A completely clueless listener (acting rationally) would place equal bets on all ten notes, and the Shannon–Weaver equation applied to this arrangement of bets would result in 3.32 bits of uncertainty.

Figure 3.1 plots the average uncertainty (expressed in bits) for the Balinese and American listeners in our experiment. Notice that after the first note, the average uncertainty for the American musicians was 3.2 bits. Since maximum uncertainty for ten outcomes is 3.32 bits, this means that after hearing the first note, the American musicians were almost perfectly clueless about what might happen next. After hearing the first note, the average uncertainty for the Balinese listeners was 2.8 bits, which corresponds almost precisely with seven equally probable states. This advantage is equivalent to being able to eliminate three of the ten notes as possible successors. By the fifth note of the melody, the average uncertainty for the Balinese musicians was roughly 2.35 bits. This is equivalent to being able to exclude five of the ten notes as possible successors.

Notice that by about ten notes into the melody, the American musicians are now comparable in confidence to the Balinese musicians in placing their bets. However, the Balinese musicians continue to exhibit less uncertainty—especially as the end of the melody approaches.

It is important to understand that figure 3.1 portrays average *uncertainty*—not predictive *success*. One can be confidently wrong as well as confidently right. In this case the Balinese musicians were not only less uncertain than the American musicians; they were also more accurate in their bets. A simple summary measure of predictive success is to compare "winnings." We started our participants with a nominal grubstake of $1.50 (not real money—for reasons that will soon become apparent). We rewarded accurate bets tenfold, while inaccurate bets were lost. If a player simply distributed the bets equally across all ten notes on the *peng ugal*, and left them there throughout the melody, then the final winnings would be the same as the initial $1.50 grubstake.

With regard to predictive accuracy, the differences between the American and Balinese musicians were striking. By the end of the melody, the most successful Balinese musician had amassed a fortune of several million dollars. The most successful American musician failed to do as well as the least successful Balinese musician. Moreover, several American musicians went bankrupt during the game and had to be advanced a new grubstake in order to continue.

Not surprisingly, Balinese musicians do better than American musicians in forming accurate expectations related to a Balinese melody. Although the specific melody was unfamiliar to both the Balinese and American listeners, the Balinese were able to take advantage of their cultural familiarity in forming suitable melodic expectations. Familiarity with a musical genre leads to both more accurate expectations and less uncertainty. However, it would be wrong to conclude that the American musicians were utterly clueless when listening to Balinese music. On average, the American listeners performed much better than chance. Either the American musicians were able to adapt quickly to the unfamiliar music, or they were able to successfully apply intuitions formed by their extensive experience with Western music—or both.

Conditional Probabilities—The Role of Context

In casino gambling, there is no link between a previous outcome and a future outcome. Each time we roll a pair of dice, the number that is rolled is independent of numbers previously rolled (this is true even for loaded dice). But in many real-world phenomena, subsequent probabilities do depend on preceding states. The probability of the occurrence of the letter "u" in text increases considerably when the preceding letter is "q." Likewise, in tonal music, the probability of occurrence of the tonic degree increases when preceded by the leading tone (the seventh degree of the scale). When the probability of an event is dependent on some preexisting state, it is referred to as a *conditional probability*.

In describing conditional probabilities, two concerns are the *contextual distance* and *contextual size*. Some states are influenced only by their immediate neighbors (i.e., small contextual distance). Other states are influenced only by states that are far away in space or time (i.e., large contextual distance). At the same time, states might be influenced by just a few other states or by a large number of other states. The size of the context of probabilitistic influence is sometimes also called the *probability order*. When the probability of occurrence for elements is totally independent of preceding elements (as with fairly thrown dice) the probability order is called the *zeroth order*; context sizes that take into account a single preceding element are called *first order*; *second order* denotes the probability order in which two preceding elements are taken into account, and so on.

It is important to note that the contextual size or probability order is independent of the contextual distance. Some event or state might be constrained only by its immediate neighbor (near context, small order). If an event is constrained by many neighbors, it will have a near context and large order. If an event is constrained by the presence of a single distant event, then it will have a distant context and small order.

By way of illustration, consider the following four contrasting examples:

1. Far context, small order   A worker who receives a bonus might decide some weeks later to go shopping for a new jacket. Here, the likelihood of a future event (purchasing a jacket) is constrained by a single, somewhat distant earlier event.
2. Near context, small order   Hearing her child cry, a mother might pick up the child. Here the future event (picking up the child) is evoked principally by a single immediately preceding state.
3. Near context, large order   At a bingo parlor, a winner shouts out "bingo!" This event is provoked only by many preceding events, each of which caused another number on the card to be marked or covered.
4. Far context, large order   A talented scientist might carry out a number of experiments leading to a major discovery that many years later results in her receiving a Nobel prize. The prize arose from many activities that were carried out decades earlier.

As we will see in later chapters, music exhibits a complete range of such dependencies. Most of the time, the principal constraints are of low probability order and involve a near context (e.g., one note influences the next note). But music also exhibits distinctive patterns of organization where distant contexts are more influential than near contexts and the probability order is quite large.

Reprise

In this chapter we have covered some basic background that will help us in discussing some of the experimental research pertaining to expectation. In the first instance we have described eight experimental paradigms used to characterize listeners' expectations. None of the methods is without difficulties. Each method makes different assumptions and provides subtly different information.

In addition, we have shown how information theory provides useful tools for measuring the strength or uncertainty of an expectation. We have also provided some conceptual language that will help us describe how the occurrence of a particular event might be shaped by other neighboring or distant events.

4   Auditory Learning

Where do expectations come from? Are they learned or are they innate? If they are learned, how are they acquired? If they are innate, what purpose do they serve and how did they evolve? Using the various experimental methods discussed in the previous chapter, most researchers have been led to the conclusion that the majority of auditory expectations are learned through exposure to some auditory environment. In this chapter, we consider some of the evidence in support of this view. But first, we begin with some general remarks about learning.

The Problem of Induction

Philosophers distinguish two grand methods for acquiring knowledge about the world: *induction* and *deduction*. Deductive knowledge is generated by deriving statements (called propositions) from a set of assumptions (called axioms). If the axioms are true, then properly derived propositions must also be true. For example, if one accepts the premises that *all humans are mortal* and that *Socrates is human*, then it necessarily follows that *Socrates is mortal*. Such deductive methods provide the foundation for propositional logic and all mathematics.

By contrast, *induction* is the process by which some general principle is inferred from a finite set of observations or experiences. Having seen many blue jays fly to my bird feeder, I infer the general proposition that "blue jays are capable of flight." Learning from experience is regarded by philosophers as the premiere example of inductive reasoning.

The eighteenth-century Scottish philosopher David Hume drew attention to a fundamental problem with induction. Hume noted that no amount of observation could ever decisively establish the truth of some general statement. For example, no matter how many white swans one observes, an observer would never be justified in concluding that *all swans are white*. Modern philosophers agree with Hume. In contrast to deductive reasoning, inductive reasoning is inherently *fallible*. From a purely logical point of view, it is not possible to infer solely from experience the true principles underlying the world.

Suppose I eat an apple for lunch and later become sick. What conclusion (if any) can I draw from this experience? Perhaps I should wash food more thoroughly before eating it. Or perhaps I have a food allergy. Perhaps I should avoid purchasing apples at the farmer's market. Or perhaps eating apples in general is bad. Alternatively, the culprit might be eating food at midday. Or perhaps holding a round red object while sitting in a particular location will make one feel sick. Perhaps I shouldn't eat lunch on Thursdays if the sun is shining. Or perhaps I simply forgot to offer proper thanks to the pagan Apple God. The problem is that the observational data (eat apple, get sick) are consistent with thousands of possible interpretations or theories. In fact, it can be formally demonstrated that any observation is consistent with an infinite number of theories (though not with all theories).

Since science attempts to discover general truths about the world via observation, the problem of induction plagues all of the sciences. Not surprisingly, the problem of induction has exercised the brightest minds in the philosophy of knowledge. It remains an intractable problem—one that philosophers believe can never be solved. This dismal prospect notwithstanding, there are practical solutions that help to minimize the sorts of errors that commonly accompany induction.[1] In all of these solutions, statistical reasoning plays a central role.

At first, the problem of induction would seem to make knowledge about the world impossible. But clearly, organisms do indeed learn and benefit from experience. The problem of induction merely places restrictions on this knowledge. Inductive knowledge is necessarily contingent and fallible. Inductive knowledge is vague and adaptive, rather than precise and certain.

How, we might ask, has biology addressed the problem of induction? On what basis do organisms infer general principles from the patterns exhibited by the world? How do animals learn from experience? Like modern empirical science, biology has not "solved" the problem of induction. Instead, organisms have assembled a bunch of ad hoc mechanisms that are fallible but useful. Interestingly, it appears that biology approaches the problem of induction in a manner quite similar to the methods of modern science. As we will see, experiential learning also appears to rely on statistical inference. One of the most important discoveries in auditory learning has been that listeners are sensitive to the probabilities of different sound events and patterns, and that these probabilities are used to form expectations about the future.

The Baldwin Effect

People will often engage in heated debates about whether a particular behavior is innate or learned. We seem preoccupied with the origins of different behaviors. Nature has no such preoccupation. Whether innate or learned, the acid test for all behavior is whether it promotes the adaptive fitness of an organism in its environment. Both instincts and learning are the products of biological evolution.

From a biological perspective, there is a clear criterion for when it is best for a behavior to be instinctive and when it is best for a behavior to be learned. The critical determining factor is *the stability of the environment.* When an environment changes little over the eons, then conditions favor the evolution of an instinctive or innate behavior. Instincts allow an organism to act quickly and efficiently. Conversely, when an environment changes relatively rapidly it becomes difficult for an adaptive instinct to evolve. In such circumstances it is better for behavior to be learned. Examples of this phenomenon abound. For example, the most flavorful insect eaten by a species of salamander keeps changing color markings every decade or so. Rather than evolving an instinct to eat insects with a fixed coloration, the salamander has evolved the capacity to learn which color markings are indicative of a tasty food source. With a little trial and error, the salamander learns to recognize the appropriate color markings.

When we observe some behavior, it is typically hard to figure out whether the behavior has been learned or is instinctive. Instinctive behaviors are most apparent when the environment changes in some dramatic fashion. Consider, for example, the eating behavior of the Pacific bullfrog. During the Second World War, American soldiers stationed on Pacific islands discovered an unusual frog behavior. Soldiers discovered that if they rolled lead pellets from a shotgun shell toward a bullfrog, the frog would immediately thrust its tongue forward and eat the pellet. Curiously, the frog would do this repeatedly, never learning to avoid consuming the lead shot.

This is not a nice thing to do to a frog. But the story highlights an important fact about frog behavior. Since the frogs never learned to avoid eating the lead shot, it is reasonable to infer that the behavior is instinctive. It would appear that the pattern "small-black-moving" automatically causes the frog to catch-and-eat. Usually, this instinctive behavior is beneficial for the frog. But unfortunately in the environment of bored soldiers with shotgun shells, the frog's behavior is utterly inept. For the Pacific bullfrog, this behavior is instinctive, so the frog is incapable of learning a more nuanced behavior. While there are important advantages to instinctive behaviors, the case of the Pacific bullfrog vividly demonstrates why learned behaviors can sometimes be superior to prewired instincts.

The difference between an instinctive prewired behavior and a learned behavior is not that the instinctive behavior is "genetic" and that the learned behavior is "environmental." Learning occurs by changing the physical structure of a brain—a brain that is genetically predisposed to change its structure. The capacity for learning almost certainly involves the participation of more genes than any instinctive behavior.

Moreover, the evolution of an instinctive behavior happens only through sustained interaction with an environment over eons. Instincts are more strongly shaped by environment than are learned behaviors. Let me say that again. Contrary to intuition, learning involves the operation of more genetic machinery than does a behavioral instinct, and instincts reflect a longer and more profound interaction with the environment than does learning. The principal issue separating learning from instinct revolves around the stability (or predictability) of the environment. In order for a behavior to be learned, it is necessary only that learning proves more adaptive in the long run than other potential alternatives.[2]

The process of learning is just as much a product of evolution by natural selection as any prewired instinct. This idea that evolution can account for the capacity to learn without invoking a Lamarckian notion of inherited learning was postulated in 1896 by James Baldwin. An *evolved capacity to learn* is consequently referred to as the Baldwin effect.[3]

Conceptually, we might suppose that auditory expectations include both innate and learned components. A number of aspects of human audition appear to be innate. For example, a loud abrupt sound will reliably evoke a *startle response* in virtually all animals that have a sense of hearing. Similarly, the *orienting response* is another innate reflex that causes listeners to direct their auditory gaze at unexpected sounds. However, apart from a handful of such reflexes, the existing research strongly implicates learning as the main factor influencing our auditory experience. This reliance on learning, in turn, implies that the auditory environment in which humans evolved was characterized by a high degree of "semiotic variability." Like the salamander eyeing the color markings of an insect, humans could not be assured that a given sound would maintain a reliable or invariant "meaning" across the eons. In the environments experienced by prehistoric humans, the meanings of different sounds were too variable to allow the development of instinctive responses. In some circumstances, a particular sound or sound property would be associated with "threat," whereas in other circumstances the same sound or sound property would be associated with "opportunity." In such inconsistent environments, learning is the appropriate biological strategy.

Incidentally, this evolutionary background holds important repercussions for music—especially for music's creative future. If learning plays the preeminent role in forming auditory meanings, then this suggests that musicians have considerable latitude in creating a wide range of musics for which listeners may form appropriate responses. In the long pleistocene period of human evolution, if the auditory environments had not been so variable, then our current capacity to shape musical meanings would have been much more constrained. The great variety of music we see around the world owes its origin, at least in part, to the Baldwin effect.

The Hick–Hyman Law of Learning

Over the past few decades, it has become an article of faith for many music scholars that "it's all learned." Our responses to music, our likes and dislikes, are all a matter of learning, not instinct. This assertion masks three problems. The first is simply that not all aspects of human audition are learned. The second problem is the tendency to forget that learning is a biological process: learning is not some disembodied social phenomenon, but an evolved neurological process in which aspects of the environment are invited to influence the microstructure of the brain. The third problem is the failure to go beyond the slogan and consider how learning actually takes place.

So how does auditory learning occur? Over the past half century, experimental research has shown that both humans and animals are attuned to *how often* various stimuli occur in their environments. This sensitivity to the frequency of occurrence of patterns is evident in auditory, visual, and tactile stimuli, and has been observed in many species.[4]

In the 1950s, W. E. Hick (at Cambridge University) and Ray Hyman (at Johns Hopkins University) independently discovered a general relationship between the frequency of occurrence of some stimulus and the speed with which that stimulus is mentally processed.[5] Suppose, for example, that you are shown a series of photographs of faces and asked to identify as quickly as possible whether the face is that of a man or a woman. In the sequence of photographs, we might vary the familiarity of the faces. For example, we might include photographs of members of your family, well-known politicians, and movie stars. In addition, we might include people you are unlikely to have ever seen, including faces of people from unfamiliar nationalities or cultures. As you might expect, you will be faster in identifying the sex of people you know well, less fast for people with less familiar faces, and slowest for people from an unfamiliar culture. What Hick and Hyman showed was that the reaction-time responses follow an orderly "law" related to exposure. The familiarity of a face can be characterized using information theory, and the amount of information in each face measured in bits. Highly familiar faces have a low information content, whereas unfamiliar faces have a high information content. When reaction-time is plotted against information in bits, there is a linear relationship: the greater the information content, the slower the reaction time.

The Hick–Hyman law has been observed using all kinds of stimuli, including abstract visual patterns as well as sounds. With increased exposure to a particular stimulus, mental processing becomes faster. Said another way, *processing of familiar stimuli is faster than processing of unfamiliar stimuli.* You might notice that this is very similar to the findings of Greenberg and Larkin discussed in chapter 3. Recall that they showed that *accurate expectation facilitates perception.* Notice that if we assume that people expect the most familiar stimuli, then the work of Greenberg and Larkin is simply a restatement of the Hick–Hyman law: perception is more efficient for expected stimuli than for unexpected stimuli.

A music-related example of this principle can be seen in the phenomenon of *absolute pitch* (AP)—or what most musicians call "perfect pitch." A person who possesses absolute pitch can name or identify the pitch of a tone without any external reference. Wake up an AP possessor in the middle of the night, play an isolated tone, and the AP musician will accurately identify the pitch. Fewer than one person in a thousand has this seemingly magical skill, so it is not surprising that it has been a compelling topic of research in music perception.[6] Obviously, absolute pitch must involve learning, since the pitch categories and pitch names are culture-specific. But the evidence for learning runs much deeper. Japanese researcher Ken'ichi Miyazaki has shown that people who have absolute pitch are faster at identifying some pitches than others. For example, the pitches C and G are more quickly identified than E and B; similarly, the pitches C# and F# are more quickly identified than D# and G#.[7] In general, identifying black notes takes longer than white notes. Why?

My student, Jasba Simpson, and I carried out a study that simply tallied how often each pitch occurs in a large sample of music. As you might expect, white notes are more common than black notes, and pitches like C# and F# occur more frequently than pitches like D# and G#. Simpson and I went on to show that the relationship between speed of identification and frequency of occurrence is consistent with the Hick–Hyman law.[8] This finding implies that AP is learned through simple exposure, and that AP possessors learn best those sounds that occur most frequently in the sound environment.

This tidy story of learning by exposure is not complete, however. There remains at least one problem with the idea that absolute pitch is learned by exposure. The most important thing to say about absolute pitch is that not everyone has it. If pitch identity is learned by exposure, why doesn't everyone who is exposed to Western music have absolute pitch? In chapter 7 we'll return to this interesting question. But for now, let's press ahead and consider a pitch-related perceptual phenomenon that is much more widespread.

First Impressions

Most listeners experience pitch as a *relative* rather than *absolute* phenomenon. Two forms of relative pitch are commonly distinguished by music theorists: *interval* and *scale degree*. In the case of intervals, it is assumed that listeners experience successive pitches by coding the distance separating them. In the case of scale degree, it is thought that listeners experience pitches by coding their position in some established scale, such as the Western major or minor scales.

Let's consider the simplest case of hearing a single tone. A single isolated pitch can theoretically be heard as any possible scale degree. For example, if you sing a pitch, this might be the first pitch in "My Bonnie Lies Over the Ocean," in which case it is the dominant or fifth scale degree. But if that same pitch is conceived as the first pitch in "Three Blind Mice," then it would be the mediant or third scale degree. If it is conceived as the beginning of "Somewhere Over the Rainbow," then the pitch would be the tonic or first scale degree.

If we hear just the first pitch of some melody, how do we know which scale degree to hear it as? One possibility is that listeners suspend all scale-degree perceptions until they have heard enough of the melody to infer the key. Another possibility is that listeners begin with some scale-degree assumptions and then revise these assumptions as more information becomes available. For example, a listener might begin by supposing that the first tone heard is the most commonly occurring scale tone. Since the dominant pitch is the most common pitch in Western music (see chapter 9), listeners might simply assume that the first pitch will be the dominant. Other scale degrees might also be possible, but there would be some uncommon scale tones that would be discounted as highly unlikely.

We can test whether listeners make such assumptions by measuring how quickly people process different scale degrees in isolation. I asked a dozen university-level music students to imagine an isolated tone as some particular scale degree.[9] For example, the pitch G# might be played and the listener instructed to imagine the tone as the mediant pitch. Once they were able to hear the pitch as the specified scale degree, they responded by pressing a key. To ensure that my musicians were responding honestly, a harmonic cadence was played immediately following the key-press, and they were asked to indicate whether the cadence corresponded to the correct key or not. Figure 4.1 shows the average response times for only those responses where the listener correctly recognized that the cadence passage was in/out of the correct key.

As can be seen, the fastest average response time is for the tonic pitch (do), followed by the dominant (so). That is, listeners were most easily able to imagine an isolated tone as the tonic or dominant. Some scale tones, like the second scale degree (re) and fourth scale degree (fa), are much slower. The pitch "fa" proved to be the slowest of all the scale tones. This result might strike musicians as odd since "fa" is not a notably rare pitch. If the speed of perceptual processing is supposed to relate to exposure, then this graph doesn't seem to reflect very well the actual frequency of occurrence of the various scale degrees.

The results make better sense if we consider the pitches as *initial notes* of melodies. For major-key melodies, it turns out that "fa" is the least likely scale tone to begin a work.[10] The pitches of the tonic triad (do, mi, so) are the most likely starting pitches, with re, ti and la much less common. Western melodies tend not to begin with "fa,"

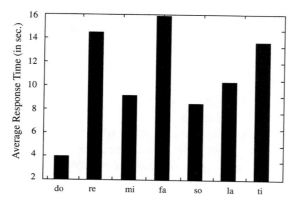

Figure 4.1
Average response times for musician listeners to hear an isolated tone as a specified scale degree. Data are shown only for responses where the listener correctly recognized that an ensuing cadence passage was in/out of the correct key.

and this fact seems to be reflected in the difficulty musician listeners have in conceiving an isolated tone as "fa."

None of this proves that listeners *expect* certain notes to begin a melody. Rather, it simply shows that listeners are able to process more quickly those pitches that are most likely to occur as the first notes in a melody. If the purpose of expectation is to facilitate action and perception, then the results are certainly consistent with the idea that listeners expect an isolated tone to be (say) "do" rather than "fa."

In a subsequent follow-up experiment, I asked musicians to *imagine* a variety of different sounds. In one case, I simply asked them to imagine any tone (without singing or producing a sound). After the participant had formed a stable mental image of some tone, a series of probe tones were played until we zeroed in on the pitch of the tone they were imagining.[11] The average pitch height for my participants was near F4—the F just above middle C. This is just two semitones away from the average pitch height in real music, which lies near E♭4.[12] In other words, when asked to imagine some tone, listeners tend to imagine a sound of average pitch.

In this same experiment, I asked musicians to imagine some sounding chord. I then asked a series of questions designed to determine what chord my musicians were imagining. As it turned out, 94 percent of my participants imagined a major chord. Sometimes the chord was imagined as a three-note triad, sometimes as a four-note chord. Most reported hearing the chord as an "up-and-down" arpeggio, while a few heard it as a block chord. But all of the participants imagined a chord in root position. It will come as no surprise that the most common chord in Western music is the major chord, and that root position chords are two to three times more common than chords in another inversion.[13] In other words, when asked to imagine some chord, listeners tend to imagine the most commonplace or typical chord.

At this point, I don't expect readers to be convinced that these tendencies represent listener "expectations." Nevertheless, there are some general observations that can be noted here. First, people with absolute pitch process some isolated pitches more quickly than others (e.g., C and G versus D# and G#). Second, musician listeners process some isolated scale degrees more quickly than others (e.g., do and so versus fa and la). In both cases, the speed of processing is proportional to the frequency of occurrence of these sounds in the environment we call "Western musical culture." When asked to imagine some unsounded tone, listeners tend to imagine a sound of average pitch height. When asked to imagine some unsounded chord, listeners imagine the most commonplace chord in its most common position. All of these results are consistent with the idea that listeners are sensitive to the frequency of occurrence of different stimuli in the environment. If the biological purpose of expectation is to enhance mental and corporeal readiness, then we shouldn't be surprised that listeners are better prepared to perceive those sounds that have occurred most frequently in their past auditory experience.

Even before the first note in a musical work is sounded, listeners appear disposed to process commonplace sounds more quickly than rare sounds. When the first tone appears, listeners process the tone faster if it conforms to a common way of beginning the music. Listeners seem to jump to conclusions about what they are hearing, even when the amount of available information is miniscule.[14]

Contingent Frequencies

The above results pertain only to isolated sounds, and so one might argue that they have limited pertinence to music. A more interesting case involves sequences of tones. As we learned in the previous chapter, future events can be influenced by context. For example, the probability of hearing the tonic pitch is increased if we are currently hearing the leading tone. What if we could demonstrate that patterns involving several successive sounds were learned by a purely statistical process?

Jenny Saffran, Richard Aslin, and their collaborators at the University of Rochester carried out a set of seminal experiments that demonstrate the statistical manner by which tone sequences are learned by listeners.[15] In one of their experiments they constructed small musical "vocabularies" consisting of three-note "figures." An example of a vocabulary containing six basic melodic figures is notated in figure 4.2. Using these figures, Saffran and her colleagues constructed a long (seven-minute) tone sequence that consisted of a random selection of the six figures. Figure 4.3 shows a sample excerpt from the sequence; it begins with figure 2, followed by figure 4, followed by figure 6, followed by figure 5, and so on. The random sequences

Figure 4.2
"Vocabulary" of six three-note melodic figures used by Saffran et al. (1999). See also figure 4.3.

Figure 4.3
Excerpt of a sample tone sequence used in the exposure phase of Saffran et al. (1999). Sequences lasted for seven minutes and were constructed by randomly stringing together the three-note figures shown in figure 4.2. Tone sequences were constrained so that no single figure was repeated twice in succession.

Figure 4.4
Sample test stimuli used by Saffran et al. (1999). Listeners heard two three-note sequences and were asked to identify which sequence was more familiar.

were constrained so that no individual three-note figure was repeated twice in succession.

Twenty-four listeners heard the seven-minute sequence three times for a total of twenty-one minutes of exposure. Note that the listeners had no prior knowledge that the tone sequence was conceptually constructed using a vocabulary of three-note figures: listeners were simply exposed to a continuous succession of tones for twenty-one minutes.

In order to determine whether listeners had passively learned to preferentially recognize any of the three-note figures, the twenty-one-minute exposure phase was followed by a test phase. For each of thirty-six trials, listeners heard two three-note stimuli. One stimulus was selected from the six vocabulary items whereas the other three-note stimulus had never occurred in the exposure sequence. A sample test item is illustrated in figure 4.4. The first sequence is a vocabulary item whereas the second sequence is not. Listeners were asked to identify which of the two three-note items was more familiar. The results were clear: listeners correctly identified the three-note sequences they had been exposed to.

A possible objection to Saffran's experiment is that four of the six vocabulary items shown in figure 4.2 end on the pitches of a D-major triad (D, F#, A). The pitches used in this experiment seem to suggest the key of D major, so perhaps Saffran's listeners were merely preferring test items that implied some sense of completion or tonal closure.

Actually, the experiment was a little more sophisticated. The twenty-four listeners were divided into two groups. Only half of the listeners were exposed to the tone sequences described above. The other listeners were exposed to a different sequence constructed from six entirely different vocabulary "figures." Both groups of listeners were tested, however, using precisely the same test materials. The pairs of three-note figures were organized so that what was a vocabulary item for listeners in Group 1 was a nonvocabulary item for listeners in Group 2 and vice versa. What one group of listeners deemed "familiar" was the precise opposite of what the other group deemed familiar.

This experimental control allows us to conclude that what listeners heard as a figure has nothing to do with the structure of the figures themselves, but relates only to their simple probability of occurrence. A simple linguistic analogy might help to clarify the results. Suppose you heard a long sequence of repeated syllables: *abababababa* . . . How would you know whether you were supposed to hear *ab*, *ab*, *ab*, *ab*, *ab* . . . or *ba*, *ba*, *ba*, *ba*, *ba* . . . ? In effect, Saffran trained two groups of listeners, one to hear the sequence as *ab*, *ab*, *ab*, and the other to hear the sequence as *ba*, *ba*, *ba*. (In fact, in an earlier experiment, Saffran, Aslin, and Newport had done exactly this for spoken nonsense syllables.)[16] For each item in the test phase, one group of listeners heard as a figure what the other group heard as a nonfigure and vice versa.

Saffran and her colleagues went on to repeat both the musical and linguistic experiments with eight-month-old infants. Using a head-turning paradigm they were able to show that the unfamiliar figures were perceived as exhibiting greater novelty for the infants. Once again, the infants were divided into two groups and exposed to different random sequences. That is, in the test phase, what was a vocabulary item for one group of infants was a nonvocabulary item for the other group, and vice versa. In short, both infants and adults learned to recognize the most frequently occurring patterns—whether tone sequences or phoneme sequences. Moreover, those patterns that occurred most frequently were the patterns that both adults and infants best recognized.

It is important to note that there were no silent periods, dynamic stresses, or other cues to help listeners parse the figures. From the listener's perspective, the figures might have consisted of two-note groups, three-note groups, or some other group size or mixture of group sizes. Also recall that none of the figures was repeated twice in succession. Since two groups of listeners learned diametrically opposite "motivic vocabularies," the internal structure of the figures had no effect on the perception of grouping. This means that the only possible conclusion is that listeners were cuing on the simple statistical properties of various tone sequences. More precisely, listeners were learning the *contingent frequencies:* given pitch X, the probability of pitch Y is high, but the probability of pitch Z is low, and so on.

The twenty-one-minute period of exposure allowed listeners to form a sense of the likelihood of different pitch successions. Table 4.1 shows the long-term conditional probabilities for sequences using the six figures shown in figure 4.2. The vertical axis indicates the antecedent state (initial note) and the horizontal axis indicates the consequence state (following note). For example, the probability of a C followed by a C# is 0.056. That is, 5.6 percent of all successive pitch pairs involve C followed by C#.

Applying these probabilities to the original exposure sequence, we can identify the likelihood of each pitch-to-pitch transition. Figure 4.5 provides a schematic illustration of the transitional probabilities for the sequence shown in figure 4.3. Thick lines indicate pitch successions that have a strong probability of occurrence. Thin lines are

Figure 4.5
Sample exposure stimuli showing the long-term statistical probabilities of pitch-to-pitch transitions. Thick lines indicate high probability. Thin lines indicate medium probability. Absence of line indicates low probability.

Table 4.1
Transitional probabilities for pitch successions arising from the melodic figures shown in figure 4.2.

	Consequent state										
	c	c#	d	d#	e	f	f#	g	g#	a	b
c	0	0.056	0	0	0	0.056	0.056	0	0	0	0
c#	0	0	0.056	0	0	0	0	0	0	0	0
d	0.011	0	0.022	0.011	0	0.078	0	0.022	0	0.022	0.056
d#	0	0	0	0	0.056	0	0	0	0	0	0
e	0.011	0	0.011	0.011	0	0.011	0	0.011	0	0.011	0
f	0.056	0	0	0	0.056	0	0	0	0	0	0
f#	0.011	0	0.011	0.011	0	0	0	0.011	0	0.011	0
g	0	0	0	0	0	0	0	0	0.056	0	0
g#	0	0	0	0	0	0	0	0	0	0.056	0
a	0.011	0	0.067	0.011	0	0.011	0	0	0	0.011	0
b	0.011	0	0.011	0.011	0	0.011	0	0.011	0	0	0

Antecedent state

less strong. No line indicates a weak likelihood. Notice how the three-note structure of the figures can be inferred simply by recognizing strong conditional probabilities. Saffran's experiments establish precisely this fact: in order for a listener to learn to hear this sequence as constructed from three-note vocabulary "motives," the listener would have to recognize, in some sense, that the boundaries between vocabulary motives have relatively low probabilities.

The work pioneered by Richard Aslin and Jenny Saffran provides just one of many examples showing how people (and animals) learn from exposure. Much of the research in this area pertains to vision, but Saffran and Aslin have shown that the same statistical learning processes occur for adult and infant listeners—both when listening to speech as well as when listening to tone sequences. In effect, both adult and infant listeners build some sort of mental representation of the transitional probabilities between adjacent tones in a tone stream, grouping together tones with high transitional probabilities, and forming group boundaries at locations in the tone stream where transitional probabilities are low. The statistical properties of the sequence are learned as a by-product of simple exposure without any conscious awareness by the listener.

Reprise

In this chapter I have presented some preliminary evidence suggesting that auditory learning is shaped by the frequency of occurrence of individual stimuli and groups of stimuli. We noted that musicians with absolute pitch identify more quickly those pitches that occur most frequently in music. We also noted that musician listeners process more quickly those isolated scale degrees that are more likely to begin a melody. When listeners are asked to imagine some unsounded tone, they are most likely to imagine a sound of roughly average pitch height. When asked to imagine some chord, listeners tend to imagine the most common chord in the most common position. When exposed to a novel uninterrupted sequence of pitches, listeners are likely to perceive groups of pitches where the boundaries between the groups coincide with points of low-probability pitch successions. While these observations do not constitute proof of statistical learning, they are all consistent with statistical learning. That is, these observations are all consistent with the idea that listeners somehow absorb the statistical regularities evident in their sound environment.

Recall that speed of mental processing is one of the hallmarks of expectation: we process most quickly those stimuli we most expect. The above observations suggest not only that auditory learning may be statistical in nature, but that this statistical learning might form the basis for auditory expectation. What we expect might simply reflect what we have experienced most frequently in the past.

As mentioned above, these statistical patterns are absorbed with little or no conscious awareness by listeners. In particular, the experiments with eight-month-old infants indicate that much, most, or all of this learning must occur at a preconscious level. Without the involvement of consciousness, there are not many plausible alternatives to the statistical learning theory. Without the sophisticated mental resources provided by consciousness, one can readily see why brains might rely on simple probability of occurrence: in predicting a future stimulus, our best prediction would be the stimulus that has occurred most frequently in the past. Similarly, given a particular sequence of tones, the most likely next tone is that tone which has most frequently followed after the antecedent context in the past.

At this point I don't expect readers to be convinced that auditory learning is dominated by statistical exposure. (More evidence will be presented in the ensuing chapters.) But with this initial evidence, I hope you will be at least willing to entertain statistical learning as a real possibility. Given this viewpoint, let's see where it takes us.

5 Statistical Properties of Music

As we saw in the previous chapter, listeners appear to be sensitive to the frequencies of occurrence of different auditory events. In Jenny Saffran's experiments, listeners heard tone sequences whose statistical properties were artificially contrived. If we want to understand music-related expectations, then we need to identify the statistical regularities evident in real music.

There are lots of stable probabilitistic relationships that can be observed in music. Some patterns are unique properties of individual musical works. For example, a repeated musical motive or theme may become a statistical feature of a particular composition.[1] Other probabilities appear to reflect properties of particular styles or genres.[2] Yet other probabilities appear to reflect properties of music as a whole. We might begin our musical story by looking for statistical regularities that seem to characterize Western music in general. More narrowly, we might begin by restricting our discussion to melodies.

Mental Representation

Before continuing we might ask what is it that listeners represent when they form mental analogues of probability structures? For example, are tone sequences represented as pitches or as intervals? Are melodies mentally represented as up/down pitch contours? Or coded as pairs of successive scale degrees? Or perhaps music is mentally stored as a combination of two or more such representations? As we will see later, how minds represent music has repercussions for what listeners remember, what listeners judge to be similar, and other musically important functions.

In this chapter, however, we will simply sidestep the issue of mental representation for music—leaving a more thorough discussion for two later chapters. Notice that Saffran's experiments (described in the previous chapter) also sidestepped the issue of how the tone sequences are mentally represented. For example, Saffran's experiments did not directly address whether her listeners learned fixed pitch sequences (such as absolute pitches) or relative pitch sequences (such as intervals or scale-degrees). In principle, these questions can be answered through further experimentation.

As noted, in this chapter we will ignore issues of representation and simply focus on the task of identifying some basic statistical regularities evident in real music. Our sample will be biased primarily toward Western art and folk melodies. But we will draw on music from a number of cultures, including Albanian, American, Bulgarian, Chinese, English, German, Hassidic, Iberian, Irish, Japanese, Macedonian, Norwegian, Ojibway, Pondo, Venda, Xhosa, and Zulu. There are many statistical regularities to be found in music, so we must limit our discussion to a handful. A useful starting point is to identify first those regularities that are the most pervasive or obvious. In this chapter, we identify five such regularities related to melodic organization: *pitch proximity, step declination, step inertia, melodic regression,* and *melodic arch.*

1 Pitch Proximity

One of the best generalizations one can make about melodies is that they typically employ sequences of tones that are close to one another in pitch. This tendency to use small intervals has been observed over the decades by many researchers.[3] Figure 5.1 shows a distribution of interval sizes for samples of music from ten cultures spanning Africa, America, Asia, and Europe.[4] For this sample of cultures, small intervals

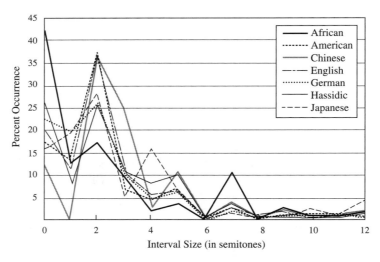

Figure 5.1
Frequency of occurrence of melodic intervals in notated sources for folk and popular melodies from ten cultures. African sample includes Pondo, Venda, Xhosa, and Zulu works. Note that interval sizes only roughly correspond to equally tempered semitones.

tend to predominate. There are exceptions to this general trend—such as Swiss yodeling and Scandinavian "yoiks." But overall, there is a marked tendency to construct melodies consisting mostly of small pitch movements.

If real melodies tend to favor small intervals, what about listeners' expectations? Do listeners *expect* successive melodic intervals to be small? Since accurate expectation promotes event readiness, evidence consistent with an expectation for pitch proximity would show that listeners process small intervals more quickly than large intervals.

In 1978, Diana Deutsch at the University of California, San Diego, showed that listeners are more efficient when processing tones preceded by small intervals than by large intervals. A year later, Paul Boomsliter and Warren Creel at the University of Toronto found that when exposed to extremely brief tones, listeners are faster to form pitch sensations when the stimuli are embedded in sequences where successive pitches are close together.[5] By contrast, listeners take longer to form pitch sensations when the pitch distance separating successive tones is large.

In a musical context, evidence of listeners' expectations for proximate pitch continuations has been assembled from experiments carried out in my Ohio State University laboratory by Bret Aarden.[6] Using a reaction-time method, Aarden asked participants to listen to a number of folksong melodies. As each note in the melody was played, listeners had to indicate whether the pitch was higher, lower, or the same as the previous pitch. Aarden found that listeners respond significantly faster when the successive tones are closer in pitch.

None of the above experiments proves that listeners expect small intervals. It is theoretically possible that these observations have some other explanation. But given the facts that melodies tend to use mostly small intervals and that the auditory system appears to be sensitive to frequently occurring phenomena, it is not unreasonable to suppose that listeners might have learned to expect small intervals. At a minimum, we can conclude that small pitch intervals are a common feature of real music, and that listeners familiar with Western music process small intervals more easily than large intervals.

2 Step Declination

Working at the University of Nijmegen in the Netherlands, Piet Vos and Jim Troost discovered that large melodic intervals are more likely to ascend and that small melodic intervals are more likely to descend.[7] Figure 5.2 shows the frequency of occurrence of ascending intervals for different interval sizes. The dark bars show the results for Western classical music whereas the light bars show the results for mainly Western folk music. Fewer than 50 percent of small intervals ascend. The reverse holds for large intervals.

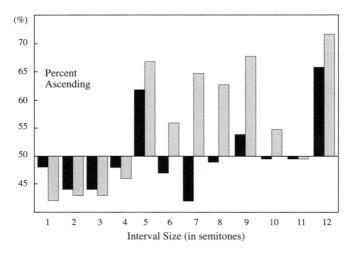

Figure 5.2
Proportion of non-unison melodic intervals that ascend in pitch. Dark bars: sample of thirteen Western composers. Light bars: sample of Albanian, Bulgarian, Iberian, Irish, Macedonian, Norwegian, and African-American folk songs. From Vos and Troost 1989.

In my laboratory we have replicated this asymmetry for many other cultures. The tendency for large intervals to ascend is evident in Australian aboriginal music, Chinese folk songs, traditional Korean music, Ojibway, Pondo, Venda, and Zulu songs. Of the many musical samples we've examined over the years, only a small sample of north Indian classical music failed to display this feature.[8]

There is another way of interpreting this asymmetry between ascending and descending large intervals. Melodies tend to meander around a central pitch range—what goes up must come down (and vice versa). If most large intervals go up, then it necessarily follows that most small intervals will go down. And, as we have already seen, most melodic intervals are small rather than large. So instead of saying that most large intervals ascend, we might simply say that the majority of melodic movements are descending small intervals.

Ethnomusicologist Curt Sachs long ago noted the tendency of certain cultures to produce what he called *tumbling melodies*. Tumbling melodies are dominated by phrases that typically begin with an initial ascending leap and are followed by a series of steplike descending tones. Sachs speculated that the tumbling phrase derives from a sort of impassioned "howl" or "wail." These sorts of descending lines are plainly evident in a number of repertoires—for example, in Russian laments, in Australian aboriginal music, and in Lakota (Sioux) music.[9]

The tumbling strain is very similar to descending pitch patterns that are common-place in speech. Researchers who study the pitch contours of speech ("intonation") have observed that the initial part of an utterance tends to ascend rapidly, and then the pitch of the voice slowly drops as the utterance progresses. There are a few exceptions, such as the "up-speak" apparent in the speech of some American adolescents, as well as in the final syllables of some interrogative forms. But in general, the pitch of the speaking voice tends to descend. In the field of linguistics, this ubiquitous prosodic pattern is known as *declination*.[10] The origin of pitch declination in speech is thought to be the drop in subglottal air pressure as the air supply in the lungs is exhausted.

Since singing requires sustained control of pitch height, it is unlikely that the tumbling melodic phrase pattern originates in the loss of subglottal air pressure. However, given the similarity between the pitch patterns in speech and the prevalence of descending small intervals, we might borrow the linguistic term and dub the musical phenomenon *step declination*.

Having identified this widespread asymmetry of occasional ascending leaps and frequent descending steps, we might ask whether experienced listeners come to expect this pattern. We'll postpone discussing the pertinent experimental evidence until our discussion of melodic regression (see below).

3   Step Inertia

Leonard Meyer suggested that small pitch intervals (1 or 2 semitones) tend to be followed by pitches that continue in the same direction. Paul von Hippel has coined the useful term *step inertia* to refer to this property of melodic organization. Music theorist Eugene Narmour (a former student of Meyer) has suggested that listeners form such "step inertia" expectations, and has even suggested that these expectations might be based on innate dispositions.[11]

The first question to ask is whether melodies themselves are actually organized according to step inertia. Is it the case that most small pitch intervals tend to be followed by pitch contours that continue in the same direction? The answer to this question is a qualified yes. Von Hippel examined a large sample of melodies from a broad range of cultures. His results are shown in table 5.1. Von Hippel found that only descending steps tend to be followed by a continuation in the same direction. Roughly 70 percent of descending steps are followed by another descending interval. However, in the case of ascending steps, no trend is evident. When an ascending step occurs, melodies are as likely to go down as to continue going up.

But what about listeners' expectations? Do listeners expect a step movement to be followed by a pitch movement in the same direction? Two critical experiments were

Table 5.1

Probabilities for step–step movements in a large sample of Western and non-Western musics.

	Followed by ascending step	Followed by descending step
Initial descending step	30%	70%
Initial ascending step	51%	49%

carried out in my laboratory—the first by Paul von Hippel and the second by Bret Aarden.[12] Von Hippel's experiment used randomly contrived pitch sequences whereas Aarden's experiment used actual melodies. Von Hippel's listeners heard a randomly generated twelve-tone row. This was done to minimize the possible confounding influence of tonality-related expectations. After hearing the twelve tones, listeners were asked to indicate whether they expected the next (13th) note in the sequence to be higher or lower than the last pitch heard. Since the sequences were random, there is no "correct" response to this question; von Hippel simply looked at the interval formed by the last two notes in the sequence. If the last two notes formed a descending step, were listeners more likely to say the ensuing note would be lower? If the last two notes of the sequence formed an ascending step, were listeners more likely to expect the ensuing note to be higher? Von Hippel's results showed that listeners do indeed expect descending steps to be followed by another descending interval. Surprisingly, listeners also expect ascending steps to be followed by another ascending interval.

In a subsequent reaction time study by Aarden, listeners were asked to judge whether the pitch in a folksong melody went up, down, or remained the same. Aarden's results fully replicated von Hippel's earlier study. After hearing a step interval, listeners respond more quickly and accurately when the ensuing note moves in the same melodic direction. It doesn't matter whether the pitch sequence is ascending or descending.

These results are a nice vindication of Meyer's and Narmour's intuitions about step inertia. In light of Narmour's suggestion that step inertia might be innate, the results also seem to go against the statistical learning theory of expectation. Real melodies exhibit a tendency for step inertia *only* for descending intervals. If expectations are formed by apprehending statistical regularities in the music, then why do listeners expect step inertia for both ascending and descending contexts?

In response to this problem, Paul von Hippel has suggested that listeners tend to overgeneralize in forming their melodic expectations. Notice that since ascending steps have a fifty–fifty chance of going in either direction, there is no penalty for (wrongly) assuming that ascending steps should typically continue to go up. That is, for ascending contours, the expectation for step inertia is no worse than chance. Since the strategy of expecting step inertia pays off for descending intervals, listeners who always form a step-inertia expectation will still, on average, have more accurate expectations than a listener who has no step-inertia expectation.

Furthermore, if ascending and descending steps were equally prevalent, then a step-inertia expectation would prove correct in just over 60 percent of cases. But ascending steps account for only about 42 percent of all step motions. This further reduces the penalty for wrongly expecting that an ascending step is likely to continue in the same direction. On average, a step-inertia expectation will prove correct in roughly 62 percent of cases. Interestingly, if listeners relied on the "correct" heuristic and expected step inertia only for descending intervals, then the proportion of correct predictions would be the same—62 percent. That is, there is no practical difference between expecting step inertia only in the descending case, and expecting step inertia in both the ascending and descending cases. It would seem that listeners who form expectations based on the step-inertia heuristic are performing near the optimum level, even though they are employing the wrong rule.

Notice, moreover, that the same predictive accuracy would occur if listeners simply assumed that melodies tend to descend. (Rule: Always expect the next pitch to be lower.) So why do listeners form a step-inertia expectation rather than a pitch-descent expectation? One plausible answer goes as follows: Incorrect heuristics are most likely to be revised or discarded when falsifying instances are obvious. Melodic leaps are more perceptually salient or noticeable than steps. Most large intervals ascend in pitch. Therefore, each occurrence of an ascending leap represents a salient observation that contradicts the general inference that pitches tend to descend whether by steps or by leaps.

A possible objection that can be levied against this account is that it is contradicted by another plausible scenario. Most intervals are descending steps. Most large intervals ascend in pitch. On average, this means that most ascending large intervals are preceded by a descending step. Melodic leaps are more perceptually salient. Therefore, each occurrence of an ascending leap preceded by a descending step represents a salient observation that contradicts the inference that descending steps are followed by another descending interval.

Notice, however, that in the first scenario, *all* ascending leaps are falsifying observations, whereas in the second scenario, only the *majority* of ascending leaps are falsifying observations. Although this difference might not seem convincing, it might nevertheless explain why listeners come to favor the step-inertia heuristic over the descending-pitch heuristic.

There is one further finding from von Hippel's experiment that must be mentioned. Von Hippel tested both musician and nonmusician listeners and found step-inertia expectations only for the musician participants. The nonmusicians had no discernible pattern related to step-interval antecedents. This result raises problems for the idea that step-inertia may be innate, since if it were innate, one might expect to see it operating in all listeners. Although other explanations might account for this finding, the greater musical experience of musicians provides a plausible source for this difference—with the implication that learning plays the formative role.

4 Melodic Regression

We have seen that listeners expect melodies to consist mostly of small pitch intervals. Experienced listeners also expect that small intervals tend to be followed by pitches that preserve the melodic direction—although melodies exhibit step inertia only for descending intervals. What about expectations for what follows large intervals?

Since at least the sixteenth century, music theorists have observed that large intervals tend to be followed by a change of direction. Most of the theorists who have commented on this phenomenon have further suggested that large intervals tend to be followed by step motion in the opposite direction. Since most pitch intervals are small, any interval should tend to be followed by step motion. The important part of the claim is the idea that large leaps should be followed by a *change* of direction. Following Paul von Hippel, we can call this purported tendency *post-skip reversal*.[13]

Once again, the first question to ask is whether actual melodies conform to this principle. Do most large leaps tend to be followed by pitches that change direction? In 1924, Henry Watt tested this idea by looking at melodic intervals in musical samples from two different cultures: Lieder by Franz Schubert and Ojibway songs. Watt's results for Schubert are shown in figure 5.3. For intervals consisting of 1 or 2 semitones, roughly 25 to 30 percent of contours change direction. That is, the majority of small intervals continue in the same direction. However, as the interval size increases, the graph tends to rise upward to the right. For octave (12 semitone) intervals, roughly 70 percent of intervals are followed by a change of direction. (There is no data point corresponding to 11 semitones because there were no 11-semitone intervals in Watt's sample.) Watt found similar results for the Ojibway songs.

Paul von Hippel and I carried out further tests of this idea using a broader and more diverse sample of melodies from cultures spanning four continents: traditional European folk songs, Chinese folk songs, South African folk songs, and Native American songs. For each of these repertories we replicated Watt's finding: the majority of large intervals are indeed followed by a change of direction.[14]

Paul and I proposed a rather unexciting reason for the existence of post-skip reversal, namely, *regression to the mean*. Statisticians have shown that whenever a distribution exhibits a central tendency, successive values tend to "regress toward the mean." That is, when an extreme value is encountered, the ensuing value is likely to be closer to the mean or average value. For example, when rolling a pair of dice, the highest pos-

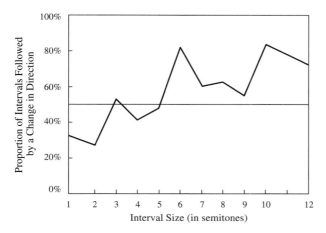

Figure 5.3
Watt's (1924) analysis of intervals in Schubert Lieder. Larger intervals are more likely to be followed by a change of melodic direction than small intervals. Watt obtained similar results for Ojibway songs. No data point corresponds to eleven semitone intervals because of the absence of such intervals in Watt's sample. From von Hippel and Huron 2000.

sible combination is twelve (two sixes) and the lowest combination is two ("snake eyes"). The most common outcome is the number seven. If you roll a pair of dice with an outcome of, say, ten, the likelihood is that the next roll will be lower than ten. Similarly, if you roll an outcome of three, the next roll is likely to be higher. That is, successive values tend to "regress" toward the mean.

A similar phenomenon could conceivably occur with melodies. In general, most large intervals tend to take the melody toward the extremes of the melody's range. For example, a large ascending leap has a good probability of placing the melody in the upper region of the tessitura or range. Having landed near the upper boundary, a melody has little choice but to go down. That is, most of the usable pitches lie below the current pitch. Similarly, most large descending leaps will tend to move the melody near the lower part of the range, so the melody is more likely to ascend than to continue descending.

Another analogy might help to illustrate this point: When you encounter a very tall person, the next person you encounter is likely to be shorter. But the shorter person is not "caused" by the previous encounter with a tall person. It is simply a consequence of the fact that most people are near average height. There is no "force" or "magnet" drawing values toward the mean. Regression to the mean is simply a numerical artifact—a necessary consequence of the fact that most values lie near the center of some distribution.

Figure 5.4
Four hypothetical interval relationships relative to the median (or average) pitch (represented by the bold central line): (1) median-departing leap, (2) median-crossing leap, (3) median-landing leap, and (4) median-approaching leap. See also figure 5.5.

Like human heights, the distribution of pitches in melodies exhibits a central tendency. Melodies do not simply wander around in an unbounded pitch space. Melodies also display a stable range or tessitura. The most frequently occurring pitches in a melody lie near the center of the melody's range. Pitches near the extremes of the range occur less commonly. This makes melodies a candidate for regression to the mean.

If post-skip reversal were merely a consequence of regression to the mean, then we ought to see a difference for leaps depending on where they occur in the range. Consider the ascending intervals shown in figure 5.4. In this schematic illlustration, the mean or median pitch for the melody is represented by the bold center line in the staff. The first ascending leap takes the contour above the median. Both regression to the mean and post-skip reversal would predict a change of direction to follow. In the second case, the ascending leap straddles the median pitch. Once again, both regression to the mean and post-skip reversal predict a change of direction. In the third and fourth cases, the two theories make different predictions. In the third case, the leap lands directly on the median pitch. Post-skip reversal continues to predict a change of direction, whereas regression to the mean predicts that either direction is equally likely. Finally, in the fourth case, the leap lands below the median pitch. Here regression to the mean predicts that the contour should tend to continue in the same direction (toward the mean), whereas post-skip reversal continues to predict a change of direction. So how are real melodies organized? Are they organized according to post-skip reversal? Or according to regression to the mean?

In order to answer this question, we studied several hundred melodies from different cultures and different periods. For each melody we calculated the median pitch and then examined what happens following large leaps. Our results are plotted in figure 5.5 for the case where a "skip" is defined as intervals larger than two semitones. The black bars indicate instances where an interval is followed by a change of direction. The white bars indicate instances where an interval is followed by a continuation of the melody in the same direction.[15]

If post-skip reversal is the important organizing principle of melodies, then we would expect to see taller black bars than white bars in each of the four conditions.

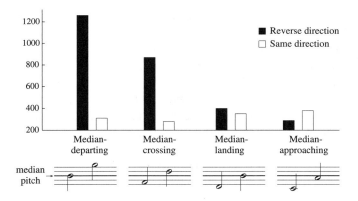

Figure 5.5
Number of instances of various melodic leaps found in a cross-cultural sample of melodies. Most large intervals that approach the median pitch continue in the same melodic direction. Large intervals that land on the median pitch are as likely to continue in the same direction as to reverse direction. Results support the phenomenon of melodic regression and fail to support post-leap reversal. From von Hippel and Huron 2000.

By contrast, consider regression to the mean. This would predict that black bars should be taller than white bars for the median-departing and median-crossing conditions (which is the case). For skips that land on the median pitch, regression to the mean would predict roughly equivalent numbers of continuations and reversals (that is, we would expect the black and white bars to be roughly the same height). Finally, in the case of median-approaching skips, regression to the mean would predict that melodies ought to be more likely to continue in the same direction toward the mean (that is, we would expect the white bar to be taller than the black bar). The results shown in figure 5.5 are clearly more consistent with regression to the mean than with post-skip reversal.

Paul von Hippel carried out further statistical analyses that reinforce the above result. With regard to large intervals, melodies behave according to regression to the mean and are not consistent at all with the idea of post-skip reversal. The further the leap takes the melody away from the mean pitch, the greater the likelihood that the next pitch will be closer to the mean. If a leap takes the melody toward the mean, then the likelihood is that the melody will continue in the same direction. Incidentally, we tried a number of different definitions of "large" leap. The results are the same no matter how a leap is defined in terms of size. We also looked for possible "delayed" resolutions. That is, we looked to see whether the second or third note following a large leap tended to change direction. Once again, the aggregate results always conformed to regression to the mean, and not to post-skip reversal. This was true in

Schubert, in European folk songs, in Chinese folk songs, in sub-Saharan African songs, and in traditional Native American songs.

We also entertained the possibility that melodies might be organized according to some combination of regression to the mean and post-skip reversal. Perhaps regression to the mean accounts for (say) 70 percent of the resolution following large intervals, and post-skip reversal accounts for the remaining 30 percent. To test this possibility we carried out a multiple regression analysis. After the effect of regression to the mean is removed, we found that post-skip reversal accounted for *none* of the residual. Zero. The results were unequivocal.

For musicians, this finding is an attention-getter. For hundreds of years musicians have been taught that it is good to resolve a large leap with a step in the other direction. Surely at least some composers followed this advice? The statistical results from von Hippel and Huron imply that for each passage where a composer had intentionally written according to post-skip reversal, then they must have intentionally *transgressed* this principle in an equivalent number of passages. Otherwise the statistics would not work out. This led von Hippel on a quest to see if any composer's music showed genuine evidence of post-skip reversal. Using our extensive database of scores, he found one: Palestrina. Palestrina's music does exhibit evidence of post-skip reversal above and beyond the effect of regression to the mean. However, the magnitude of the effect is small. Even in Palestrina's music, the overwhelming share of contour change following a large leap is accounted for by regression to the mean. Since Palestrina himself promoted the idea of post-skip reversal, we shouldn't be surprised that he sometimes took his own advice.

Palestrina notwithstanding, these studies simply refute the idea that post-skip reversal is an organizational principle in melody. This is true not just in Western music, but also in music in many (perhaps all) of the world's cultures.

It bears reminding that most large intervals are indeed followed by a change of direction. (For skips of 3 semitones or greater, roughly 70 percent are followed by a reversal of contour.) But this is only because most large intervals tend to take the melody away from, rather than toward, the mean pitch for the melody. When looking at notated music, one finds that the most noticeable leaps are precisely those where the melody moves to an especially high or low pitch. Unless one remains aware of the relationship of the interval to the tessitura, it is easy to see how theorists might have been deceived.

Having investigated the organization of actual melodies, we might now turn to the question of what listeners expect. Even if melodies are not organized according to post-skip reversals, might it not be the case that listeners *expect* large intervals to be followed by a change of direction? Or do listeners expect the next pitch to move in the direction of the average pitch?

Once again consider my earlier analogy to people's heights. When we encounter a tall person, do we (1) expect the next person to be of average height (the "real" phenomenon) or (2) expect the next person to be shorter—an artifact of (1)? This question was answered experimentally by Paul von Hippel in my laboratory.[16] Paul played large intervals in a variety of melodic circumstances, and asked listeners to predict whether the melody would subsequently ascend or descend. The melodic contexts were arranged so that some large intervals approached the mean and other large intervals departed from the mean. If listeners' expectations are shaped by post-skip reversal, then they ought to expect all large intervals to be followed by a change of direction. However, if listeners' expectations are shaped by regression to the mean, then they ought to respond according to the register of the interval: intervals in the low register (whether ascending or descending) should be followed by higher pitches while intervals in the higher register (whether ascending or descending) should be followed by a lower pitch.

The results were clear: the register or tessitura of the interval doesn't matter. Listeners typically expect large intervals to be followed by a change of direction without regard to the location of the median pitch. That is, listeners' expectations follow the post-skip reversal principle, rather than regression to the mean. As before, these results apply only in the case of musician listeners. Von Hippel's nonmusician listeners showed no discernible pattern of responses. Although the difference between musicians and non-musicians might suggest some sort of genetic or innate difference, a more plausible possibility is a difference due to learning, either formal training or through passive exposure.

But why would musicians' expectations follow post-skip reversal over regression to the mean? A quick glance at figure 5.5 reminds us that roughly 70 percent of all large intervals are followed by a change of direction. If listeners adopt the simple post-skip reversal heuristic, their expectations will be correct 70 percent of the time. A regression-to-the-mean heuristic would be more accurate. However, in order to use a regression rule, the listener would need to constantly be inferring the tessitura or distribution of the pitches in the melody, in order to judge whether the current pitch is relatively high or relatively low. Post-skip reversal provides a simple and efficient heuristic that serves well enough to keep the listener's expectations on track.

5   Melodic Arch

To this point we have only been considering the note-to-note organization of music. What about larger structures such as phrases or whole melodies? Does music exhibit stereotypic phrase-related patterns? And if so, do listeners form expectations that reflect such patterns?

Earlier, I mentioned Curt Sachs's notion of a *tumbling* melody where phrases tend to start on a relatively high pitch and then slowly descend via small intervals. Such falling phrases are commonplace in Australian aboriginal songs and in many Native American songs. Another popular phrase-related pattern is the so-called *melodic arch*. For centuries, music scholars have observed a general tendency for phrases to rise upward and then descend in pitch, forming an arch-shaped contour. Examples of such melodic arches include the initial phrases of "Twinkle, Twinkle, Little Star," "On Top of Old Smoky," "Itsy Bitsy Spider," and "We Wish You a Merry Christmas." The phenomenon isn't limited to Western music. In Tuvan throat singing (from central Asia), for example, nearly every phrase rises and then falls in pitch.

In Western music, not all phrases are arch-shaped. For example, both "Joy to the World" and "The Star Spangled Banner" begin with a marked descending-then-ascending contour. Is there any truth in the notion of the melodic arch? In 1996 I published a comprehensive study of phrase contours in a collection of over six thousand European folk songs. Using well-defined criteria, I had a computer classify each phrase into one of nine types: ascending, descending, concave, convex, horizontal (hovering), horizontal-ascending, horizontal-descending, ascending-horizontal, and descending-horizontal. Nearly 40 percent of the roughly ten thousand phrases analyzed were classified as convex (i.e., arch-shaped)—the most common classification. Convex contours were four times more common than concave contours, even though the classification criterion was exactly symmetrical. Ascending and descending phrases were the next most common contour types, accounting for nearly 50 percent of all phrases between them.

Interestingly, further analysis showed that ascending and descending phrases tend to be paired together (thus forming an "arch" over two phrases). Moreover, while ascending phrases tend to be followed by descending phrases, the reverse is not true: descending phrases are not more likely than chance to be followed by an ascending phrase.

The arch tendency within phrases is illustrated graphically in figures 5.6 and 5.7. Figure 5.6 shows what happens when six thousand seven-note phrases are all averaged together. The first value shows the average pitch of all the first notes in the phrases; the second value shows the average pitch of all the second notes, and so on. (Pitch heights are given in semitones above middle C.) The arch shape evident in this graph also occurs for phrases containing different numbers of notes, from five-note phrases to seventeen-note phrases. However, for phrases longer than twelve notes, a central dip tends to appear—what I like to call the "McDonald's effect." This dip might appear because two shorter phrases were inadvertently notated as a single long phrase, or because long phrases exhibit subphrase structures.

Incidentally, I found that if one represents each phrase by the average pitch-height of all the notes within the phrase, then whole melodies also tend to exhibit an arch

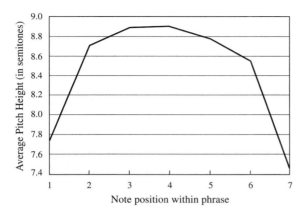

Figure 5.6
Average contour for 6,364 seven-note phrases taken from *The Essen Folksong Collection* (Schaffrath 1995). The graph shows the average pitch height (measured in semitones above middle C) according to serial position in the phrase. This arch shape contour is present for 5-note, 6-note, 7-note, 8-note, 9-note, 10-note, and 11-note phrases. From Huron 1996.

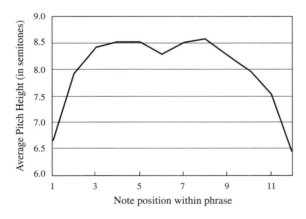

Figure 5.7
Average contour for 1,600 twelve-note phrases taken from *The Essen Folksong Collection*. The graph shows the average pitch height (measured in semitones above middle C) according to serial position in the phrase. The dip in the middle of the arch ("McDonald's effect") is evident in 12-note, 13-note, 14-note, and 15-note phrases and suggests possible subphrase structures. From Huron 1996.

contour. Over 40 percent of all melodies have successive phrases that tend to increase in overall pitch and then descend in overall pitch. However, no hierarchical relationship exists between convex phrases and convex melodies. That is, a melody that is convex overall is not more likely than other melodies to exhibit convex phrases.[17] In subsequent unpublished research I have found the same arch tendency in samples of other Western music. The effect is robust; however, it appears to be slightly less marked in instrumental music than in vocal music. To be sure, not all phrases in Western music exhibit an arch contour. Nevertheless, it is a clearly notable tendency.

Since Western phrases tend to exhibit arch-shaped contours, the next question is whether experienced listeners form appropriate "arch" expectations. Do listeners expect pitches to rise and then fall over the course of a phrase? Using music students at the Ohio State University, Bret Aarden was able to test this hypothesis. In a reaction-time study, listeners heard a number of folksong melodies. After each tone they indicated as quickly as possible whether the tone went up, down, or stayed the same. Aarden divided all of the reaction-time data into two sets: responses that occurred in the first half of phrases and responses that occurred in the second half of phrases. He then looked to see whether listeners are faster at recognizing an ascending interval in the first half of the phrase and whether they are faster at recognizing descending intervals in the second half of phrases. The results showed a clear pattern: musician listeners are no faster at identifying ascending versus descending intervals in the first half of phrases. However, in the second half of phrases, musicians are much faster in responding to descending intervals than to ascending intervals. In short, the results are consistent with the notion that listeners expect descending intervals in the latter half of phrases.

These results are difficult to explain. When a musical phrase begins, the listener is in no doubt that they are listening to the first half of the phrase. Surely, this should make it easy for listeners to expect that successive pitches will tend to rise upward in pitch. In contrast, it is much less clear how a listener determines when she is listening to the second half of a phrase. The number of notes in musical phrases varies considerably; surely, it is more problematic for a listener to infer that she is listening to the latter half of any given phrase. Nevertheless, it is the final descent of the phrase that listeners seem to expect, not the initial pitch ascent. The experimental results seem to contradict intuition.

Reprise

In this chapter I have highlighted five robust melodic tendencies that are evident in (notated) Western music: *pitch proximity, step declination, step inertia, melodic regression,* and *melodic arches.* Many of these organizational patterns can be found in non-Western musics as well. With the exception of yodeling and Scandinavian yoiks, *pitch proximity* is pervasive throughout the world's music. With the possible exception of Hindustani music, *step declination* also appears to be a common musical pattern. *Melodic arches,* by contrast, are clearly limited to certain cultures. *Melodic regression* may well be universal, while the extent of *step inertia* awaits cross-cultural study.

In identifying musical patterns, we have only scratched the surface. In chapter 7 we will discuss some further pitch-related statistical patterns, and in chapter 10 we will look at some patterns related to rhythm and timing. In chapter 11 we will consider patterns that are style- or genre-specific.

Many of the patterns discussed in this chapter have long been known to music theorists. But the precise nature of these patterns has not always been recognized. As we will discover in the next chapter, it can be instructive to review how various music scholars have interpreted these musical patterns.

6 Heuristic Listening

We've seen that when listeners anticipate sounds, they often rely on heuristic knowledge—imperfect rules of thumb about what is likely to happen next. These rules of thumb are helpful in most situations, but they are only approximations of the structure of the melodies as notated. In light of the observations made in the previous chapter, let's pause and consolidate what we understand so far. We can now compare how melodies are notationally structured with how experienced listeners *think* they are structured. Of course, we should bear in mind that our discussion here is limited to Western melodies and Western-enculturated listeners.

Notated Melodic Structure—Expected Melodic Structure

Melodies show the following organizational elements:

1. Pitch proximity   Successive pitches tend to be near to one another. Pitch proximity is not merely an artifact of central tendency. That is, pitch proximity doesn't arise simply because most of the pitches in a melody lie near the center of the distribution. If pitch proximity were the only organizing principle for melodies, then melodies might look something like the pitch sequence shown in figure 6.1. Here we see a randomly generated "melody" in which the only constraint is a bias toward smaller rather than larger intervals. The result is a so-called *random walk*—what engineers call "Brownian noise."

2. Central pitch tendency   If melodies were constrained only by pitch proximity, then long melodies would inevitably wander out of range at some point. However, like the vast majority of other phenomena in the world, the most frequently occurring pitches in melodies tend to lie near the center of some distribution. If this central tendency were melodies' only organizing principle, then melodies might look something like the pitch sequence shown in figure 6.2. Here we see a randomly generated "melody" whose pitches were generated according to a normal distribution centered on middle C.[1] Engineers call this kind of distribution "Johnson noise" or "white noise."

Figure 6.1
"Brownian" or "random walk" melody. Successive pitches are constrained only by the principle of small distances to the preceding pitch.

Figure 6.2
"Johnson" or "white noise" melody. Pitches are randomly selected from a normal distribution centered on middle C. Pitches are less likely to occur as the distance from middle C increases.

Since melodies are organized according to both pitch proximity and central tendency, melodies exhibit a sort of intermediate character between Brownian and Johnson fluctuations. Incidentally, Johnson noise has a so-called power distribution of $1/f^0$ (= 1), whereas Brownian noise has a power distribution of $1/f^2$. When these two principles are combined, the resulting power distribution approaches $1/f$—the so-called *fractal distribution*.[2] In 1975, Richard Voss and John Clarke showed that melodies exhibit a power distribution similar to $1/f$ noise. At the time, this was thought to be an important discovery and it received considerable coverage in the popular press. There are in fact a large number of natural phenomena that exhibit this distribution, and there is nothing particularly magical about this observation. The $1/f$ fractal distribution arises whenever a phenomenon exhibits both central tendency *and* proximity. Said another way, a $1/f$-like power distribution will characterize all phenomena that are both "clumpy" and "stringy." A huge number of phenomena fit the bill, including vegetation, clouds, rock piles, conversations, waterways, traffic flows, human limbs, and melodies—to name but a few.

3. Ascending leap tendency/descending step tendency   In general, melodies tend to exhibit relatively rapid upward movements (ascending leaps) and relatively leisurely downward movements (descending steps). The reason for this asymmetry is not yet known.[3] However, as I noted in the previous chapter, the phenomenon is similar to pitch *declination* in speech. Figure 6.3 shows a randomly generated "melody" that is constrained only by an asymmetrical distribution favoring ascending leaps and

Figure 6.3
Random melody generated using an asymmetrical interval distribution that favors descending steps and ascending leaps.

Figure 6.4
Random melody constructed from phrases exhibiting an arch-shaped contour tendency.

descending steps. The melody behaves as a modified random walk and so, as in figure 6.1, would inevitably drift out of range.

4. Arch phrase tendency In general, Western melodies tend to exhibit arch-shaped pitch contours. The lowest pitches in the phrase tend to occur near the first and last serial positions while the highest pitches tend to occur near the middle of the phrase. Once again, the reason for this pattern is not yet known.

The phrases in figure 6.4 were generated by randomly selecting a phrase length (in notes) from a distribution of actual phrase lengths. A random pitch was selected for one of the notes positioned at or near the center of the phrase. The pitches of the remaining notes were randomly generated so that the pitch height is negatively correlated with the distance of that note from the central position in the phrase.

In an ideal world, these four common musical patterns would lead to the following subjective expectations in experienced listeners:

1. Pitch proximity Listeners would expect an ensuing pitch to be near the current pitch.
2. Regression to the mean As the melody moves farther away from the mean or median pitch, listeners would increasingly expect the next pitch to be closer to the mean.
3. Downward steps Listeners would expect most intervals to be descending steps.
4. Arch phrases Listeners would expect phrases to begin with ascending pitch sequences and to end with descending pitch sequences.

Instead, experienced listeners show the following expectational tendencies:

1. Pitch proximity   Listeners expect an ensuing pitch to be near the current pitch.
2. Post-skip reversal   Listeners expect a large interval to be followed by a change in pitch direction.
3. Step inertia   Listeners expect a small interval to be followed by a subsequent small interval in the same direction.
4. Late-phrase declination   Listeners expect pitches to descend in the latter half of phrases.

Like the Pacific bullfrog, experienced listeners of Western music rely on patterns that are serviceable, but not exactly right.

Narmour's Theory of Melodic Organization

The first three expectations described above conform very well to a theory of melodic organization proposed in 1990 by the University of Pennsylvania music theorist Eugene Narmour.[4] Narmour's theory of melody distinguishes two kinds of melodic situations: those that are *implicative* (that is, evoke a strong sense of what might happen next), and those situations that are *non-implicative* (that is, evoke little sense of what might happen next). Narmour's theory, known as the *implication-realization theory*, attempts to describe what listeners expect when the musical context is strongly implicative.

For implicative melodic contexts, Narmour proposed five predispositions that shape a listener's expectation for melodic continuation.[5] Two of these predispositions are central to Narmour's implication-realization theory. The first is *registral direction* and the second is *intervallic difference*. The principle of registral direction states that small intervals imply continuations in the same direction whereas large intervals imply an ensuing change in direction. The principle of intervallic difference states that small intervals imply a subsequent interval that is similar in size, while large intervals imply a consequent interval that is smaller in size.

Narmour's theory of melodic implication inspired a fruitful legacy of perceptual experimentation. Shortly after his theory was published, a study by Lola Cuddy and Carol Lunney at Queen's University in Kingston, Canada, showed that predictions from the theory conform quite well to listener behavior.[6] However, Cuddy and Lunney also showed that Narmour's original five principles could be simplified without loss of predictive power. Further research conducted by Glenn Schellenberg at the University of Windsor (also in Canada) showed that the theory could be simplified even further.[7] Schellenberg noted that Narmour's theory for implicative contexts could be reduced to just two principles. One is the pitch proximity principle. The second principle, Schellenberg suggested, is a combination of Narmour's registral direction and registral return dispositions.[8] Five years later, a statistical analysis by Paul von Hippel showed that the combination of registral direction and registral return can be simplified even further: they are approximations of post-skip reversal.[9] In short, most of the predictive power that was recognized in Narmour's original theory can be distilled to the twin principles of pitch proximity and post-skip reversal.

A major success in Narmour's theory is his reiteration of Leonard Meyer's intuition that listeners expect small intervals to be followed by another interval in the same direction. Unlike pitch proximity, step inertia is *not* a property of the music as notated in the score or as propagated through the air. In Western music, only descending steps are likely to be followed by another descending interval. Moreover, the ensuing interval is no more likely than chance to be a *step* rather than a *leap*. However, the experimental work carried out by Paul von Hippel showed that listeners' expectations follow the Meyer–Narmour view even though the actual musical organization does not warrant this presumption. Experienced listeners really do expect a small interval to be followed by another interval in the same direction, regardless of whether the intervals are ascending or descending. The expectation for step inertia across the board appears to be an imperfect inductive approximation of an underlying objective tendency for downward steps.

A less successful component of Narmour's theory is the concept of *registral return*. This concept might be regarded as Narmour's version of the principle Leonard Meyer called *gap fill*. According to Meyer, gap fill is the psychological tendency to return to states that have been omitted in some sequence. For example, if a melody ascended along some scale and skipped one of the scale tones, Meyer suggested that there would arise a slight psychological yearning to return at some point and "fill" the gap that had been created. Meyer's notion of gap fill was proposed as a general (Gestalt) principle of which post-skip reversal is but one manifestation. Initially, experimental work by Mark Schmuckler at the University of Toronto appeared to show that listeners' responses are consistent with the notion of gap fill.[10] However, subsequent experimental and statistical work by von Hippel overturned this interpretation. The appearance of gap fill is an approximation of post-skip reversal. The expectation for post-skip reversal is, in turn, attributable to regression to the mean, and regression to the mean is an artifact of central pitch tendency.[11]

Narmour proposed that these expectations are somehow innate. But the experimental evidence does not support this view. At face value, the experimental research suggests that the expectations are learned, and that the predictive heuristics used by listeners are the product of sustained exposure to commonplace musical patterns. Apart from the work of Bret Aarden and Paul von Hippel, independent support for a statistical model has been assembled recently by Marcus Pearce and Geraint Wiggins at the City University, London. Pearce and Wiggins found that a straightforward statistical model provided a better account of existing perceptual data than either

Narmour's Gestalt-inspired heuristics or Schellenberg's simplified model. More than 80 percent of the variance in the observed patterns of expectancy can be accounted for by the induction of statistical regularities found in the music itself.[12]

Theoretically, it is possible that my account here has the cause and effect reversed. It is possible that the organization of music has been shaped by *a priori* expectational tendencies rather than vice versa. That is, it is possible composers *intend* to create music conforming to *post-skip reversal* (say), but then somehow erroneously construct melodies shaped by regression to the mean instead. This view is not very plausible, however. Regression to the mean is a property of all distributions that exhibit a central tendency. The vast majority of distributions in nature show such central tendencies, so regression to the mean is found wherever one cares to look. Moreover, there is a perfectly reasonable explanation for why distributions of musical pitches would display a central tendency. When singing, vocalists find that it is physically easier to perform near the center of their range. Both high and low notes are physiologically more difficult to sing than midrange pitches. Similarly, most instruments are easier to play in some central register. There are good reasons why pitch exhibits a central pitch tendency, and so there are good reasons why pitch successions would exhibit regression to the mean.

In the case of pitch proximity, there are similarly good physical reasons why one might expect successive real-world sounds to be close in pitch. In the physical world, there are a number of ways by which the frequency of a vibrator can be changed. For example, frequency can be increased by shortening the physical dimensions of the vibrator, or decreasing its mass (such as decreasing the volume of a resonant cavity), or by increasing the tension. When moving from one frequency to another, there is commonly a physical continuum in which the physical vibrator must pass through a series of intermediate values. For example, when increasing a vibrator's tension from 5 newtons to 10 newtons, one must momentarily pass through a gradient of intervening tensions: 6, 7, 8, etc. An obvious repercussion is that small changes of frequency are easier to produce than large changes of frequency. In most physical circumstances it is easier to change a frequency by X rather than $2X$ or $3X$. There are exceptions to this principle. For example, in the case of a guitar string, one can abruptly change the vibrating length from 40 centimeters to 20 centimeters by engaging one's finger at a particular fret. In this case, the length of the vibrating string does not pass through the intermediate lengths. Similarly, different modes of vibration can be induced that may cause discontinuous jumps of frequency. However, these circumstances are less common.[13]

Narmour's theoretical intuitions have been remarkably good, especially in drawing attention to step inertia. However, the explanatory framework that Narmour proposed to account for these expectations is not tenable. In light of Paul von Hippel's work, we can see that these listener expectations are better regarded as inductive approximations of underlying objective patterns of musical organization rather than innate Gestalt principles. Moreover, the most likely origin of these inductive heuristics is through the mechanism of statistical learning.

Schenkerian Theory

The tendency to expect descending pitches in the latter half of a phrase is reminiscent of a theory of musical organization devised by the early twentieth-century Austrian theorist, Heinrich Schenker. To put it in overly simplified terms, Schenker proposed that tonal musical works tend to exhibit an overall descending pitch structure. Specifically, Schenker proposed that the musical foreground of a work can be regarded as an elaboration of one of three structural templates or scaffolds. One scaffold consists of three descending pitches—mi, re, do. A second scaffold consists of five descending pitches—so, fa, mi, re, do. A third (more rare) scaffold consists of an eight-pitch descending line—do, ti, la, so, fa, mi, re, do.

Using a sophisticated series of "rewrite" rules, Schenkerian analysts progressively distill a musical foreground to a successively reduced set of structural tones, until finally, an entire work or movement is reduced to a three-, five-, or eight-line scaffold called an *Urlinie*.

Since the middle of the twentieth century, Schenker's theory of tonal music has been without peer. There are few music theorists who have not been inducted into the refinements of Schenkerian analysis. Nevertheless, some scholars have viewed Schenkerian analysis with skepticism. The rewrite rules used for reductions are not fully systematic and so there is considerable latitude for interpretation. No controlled studies have been carried out to determine whether analysts are unduly influenced by confirmation bias. (Knowing that the "right answer" must be one of three descending lines is a recipe for self-deception during analysis.) For most theorists who learn Schenkerian analysis, the method seems stable enough to dispel doubts about confirmation bias. The descending *Urlinie* often seems to jump out as an obvious feature in some musical works.

In Schenkerian analyses, the highest pitch of the *Urlinie* tends to occur relatively early in the work. In nearly all published analyses, the remaining tones of the *Urlinie* tend to appear in the latter half of the work; often the final tones of the *Urlinie* occur quite close to the end of the work.

In both Western and many non-Western melodies, phrases and works have a statistical tendency to fall in pitch toward the end. Even if one were to make a random selection of pitches near the end of a work, these pitches will tend to descend. This implies three contrasting interpretations. One interpretation is that Schenker understood that Western music has an objective tendency to decline in pitch, especially toward the ends of phrases or works. A second interpretation is that Schenker succeeded in identifying a common subjective experience when listening to music—namely, the psychological tendency to expect late-phrase declination. A third, less charitable, interpretation is that the *Urlinie* is an approximation of the more fundamental phenomenon of late-phrase declination.

In some ways, it matters little which interpretation is correct. The important point is that expectations do not always reflect accurately the way musical sounds are actually organized. We have seen that musician listeners are faster to respond to descending pitch sequences in the latter half of phrases. Whether or not this expectation arose through an imperfect apprehension of melodic arches, it is nevertheless a common way of listening, and potentially a significant part of the listening experience.

Imperfect Listeners

The last two chapters provide important lessons regarding music listening and music theorizing. The first lesson is that experienced listeners are far from perfect in learning to form accurate expectations about music. Listeners make systematic errors in comprehending the organizational features of music—including regression to the mean, descending step tendency, and melodic arches. Given these misperceptions, it is theoretically possible to construct a computer program that would do a better job of predicting subsequent musical events than an experienced listener. Real listeners are imperfect listeners.

While music scholars might find this situation surprising, psychologists will recognize a familiar pattern. For over a century, psychologists have documented innumerable ways in which human perceptions, cognitive processes, and methods of decision making are approximate, flawed, or sometimes downright illogical. When we learn from the world, what we learn is selective, simplified, and imperfect: we do not have access to some unvarnished truth. What we learn is constrained by the ever-present problem of induction.

The foregoing studies also highlight an important distinction: the biological goal of expectation differs from the musical goal. The biological goal of expectation is to form adaptively useful predictions about future events. Often, this aim is served by attempting to form *accurate* expectations about the world. When our expectations about future events are based on faulty heuristics, then we are courting potential biological disaster. However, the musical goals of expectation are very different. In most situations, the musical goal will be to evoke a pleasing or compelling emotional dynamic. From a musical point of view, it does not matter if experienced listeners form inaccurate expectations about future events. It is only important that individual listeners form broadly similar expectations under the same musical conditions. Suppose, for example, that individual listeners had their own unique sets of mental heuristics for forming expectations about how music unfolds. The thwarting of one listener's expectation

might be the fulfillment of another's. In such a world, expectation would be an ineffective instrument for music-making. If you don't have a group of listeners who
respond in a broadly similar fashion, then you can't create a musical culture—at least
not one based on the psychology of expectation.[14]

Naive Realists

Another lesson arising from the last two chapters is a sobering one for music theorists.
Philosophers have described an intellectual position known as *naive realism*. Realists
believe that there exists a world external to ourselves. Naive realists believe that our
senses provide unbiased windows through which we directly apprehend this world.[15]
Modern perceptual psychology has amply demonstrated that naive realism is not
tenable. Perceptual research shows that our senses interpret the world in ways that
typically distort our experiences in systematic ways. Some of these distortions occur
because of "imperfections"—such as the eye's blind spot. Other distortions are "useful"
deceptions.[16]

For hundreds of years, music theorists have been looking at notation as naive realists. We have tended to make two assumptions: that the structures we see are ones we
experience, and that the structures we experience can be seen in the notation. For the
most part, these assumptions are serviceable. But as we have seen, these assumptions
are not trustworthy. There are structures in notated or sounded music (like regression
to the mean) that are not experienced by listeners, and there are structures in experience (like post-skip reversal) that do not exist in the notated or sounded music. If the
field of music theory is to develop, we must abandon the habits of naive realism. We
must be more careful to discriminate between various forms of description, and to
methodically test our claims and intuitions—rather than relying solely on informal
analyses or impressions. For hundreds of years, musicians looked at musical notation
and thought they saw a pattern of large skips being followed by a change of direction.
It is only through careful statistical analysis that we can show that this appearance is
a delusion.

It would be wrong, however, to find the situation embarrassing or cause for despair.
On the contrary. As long as our ears and eyes agree with each other, people have little
curiosity about how we experience or construct the world. However, when the anoma-
lies between different perspectives become large, we can no longer be complacent
about what we are seeing or hearing. Far from being a cause for despair, these discrepancies provide wonderful opportunities to better understand the phenomenon of
music. We now have a question with lots of promise: Why are listeners so imperfect
in their musical expectations? To address this question, we must look in more detail
at the nature of mental functioning.

7 Mental Representation of Expectation (I)

When I answer the phone, I expect to hear a human voice reply to my "hello." When I turn on the faucet, I expect to hear the sound of flowing water. When I hear footsteps just outside my door, I expect to hear more footsteps, continuing on their way. If we ask "what do listeners expect?" the natural answer is "sounds of a certain sort"; we expect particular sound events with specific properties at given moments in time.

A problem with this answer is that brains do not store sounds per se. Auditory images are not organized in the brain like phonograph recordings. Instead, brains *interpret*, *distill*, and *represent* sounds. As noted earlier, expectations imply some sort of mental representation. The *what*, *when*, and *where* of expectation exist as mental codes.[1] These mental codes are not disembodied abstractions. They exist as real biological patterns that have taken up residence somewhere inside people's heads.

When a listener correctly anticipates a sound, that *real* sound will appear as two time-variant pressure fluctuations—one for each of the left and right eardrums. A listener ultimately anticipates a pair of signals like those shown in figure 7.1. The core question is: What is it about these signals that was correctly anticipated by the listener?

Suppose for the moment that you know nothing about sound or human audition. Suppose that you are a resourceful Mother Nature, attempting to build a biological organ that can predict two pressure signals such as the ones shown in figure 7.1. Our hypothetical sound-prediction organ (SPO) might anticipate that the fluctuations will begin at a particular moment. Or perhaps the SPO anticipates that the squiggles will exhibit upward spikes (rather than downward ones). Or perhaps it anticipates that the upper squiggle (the left ear) will begin slightly before the lower squiggle (right ear), or that the upper squiggle will be slightly taller. Perhaps our SPO correctly anticipates that the squiggles will grow large, then diminish, grow large again, and then diminish. Or perhaps it anticipates that there will be a repeated pattern of three little humps followed by one big spike.

First, let's dispense with the idea that there is a "right" way to describe such pressure signals. It is a common misconception to suppose that mathematics tells us how best

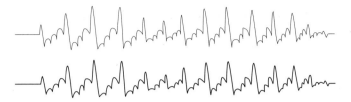

Figure 7.1
Any anticipated sound appears as two time-variant pressure signals, one for each of the left and right ears. What is it about these signals that is correctly anticipated by a listener?

to characterize such waveforms. The French mathematician Jean Baptiste Joseph Fourier famously devised a method for describing a periodic function as the sum of a series of harmonic sinusoids of various amplitudes and phases. The details here are not important. Suffice it to say that Fourier's theorem is a masterly bit of mathematics that is justly celebrated. But we should not be blinded by the formal beauty of Fourier analysis. One can similarly create a method that describes any function as the sum of harmonic *square waves* of various amplitudes and phases. Or one could use triangle waves. Or, for that matter, the facial profile of Napoleon Bonaparte (in whose army Fourier served with distinction). There are infinitely many such methods. Moreover, few sounds are precisely periodic, so any unadulterated Fourier analysis is strictly impossible for most real sounds. Finally, there are entire universes of nonlinear and nonharmonic ways of describing a function. With a moment's thought, it becomes plain that the number of ways of describing a sound function is unbounded. It is true that Fourier analysis holds some special mathematical properties, but that doesn't mean Fourier analysis provides the single "right" way for a biological system to represent a sound.

If the possibilities seem mind-boggling, the existence of functioning auditory systems indicates that real minds aren't completely boggled. The brain does somehow represent these squiggles (or, at least, properties of these squiggles) and is able to use these representations to form expectations about the properties of future squiggles.

Localization

Hearing scientists, psychoacousticians, and auditory neurologists have been able to identify many aspects of sound functions that brains represent. A useful place to begin is with the seemingly lowly phenomenon of sound localization. Location is biologically important. A priority for any auditory system is to establish the location of possible prey and predators. In seeking food and avoiding danger, biology follows the real-estate agent's maxim: *location, location, location*. The biological importance of localization is evident in comparative auditory physiology. The neural structures that decipher sound location are among the oldest in the brain. Localization represents an evolutionarily ancient neurophysiological adaptation. Not all animals experience pitch, but all animals that have a hearing organ can localize sounds.

Several factors are known to influence the perception of auditory location. Two factors figure prominently. One is the relative time difference between pressure fluctuations in the left and right ears. A second is the relative difference in the magnitude or amplitude of these signals. Both of these factors rely on differences between the ears—so-called *interaural* differences. These interaural squiggle-properties provide useful correlates with the physical *location* of a sound source.

When localizing sounds, interaural time and amplitude differences reflect genuinely stable physical relationships between sound sources and pairs of listening devices (like ears). In a homogeneous medium the speed of sound is constant, so even in the most reverberant of environments the onset of a sound will always reach the nearer ear prior to the more distant ear. Similarly, the inverse-square law describes a simple geometric fact whose consequence is that sounds lose energy with increasing distance from the source. Given the width of the head, the magnitude of these interaural differences will be systematically related to the horizontal direction or *azimuth* of a sound. If a sound originates from your left, the pressure disturbance will arrive at your left ear prior to your right ear; it will also be more energetic in your left ear. As noted in chapter 4, when an environment remains stable, then evolution is likely to favor the creation of an innate mechanism.[2] In the case of azimuth, there are some stable physical principles that make it possible for Mother Nature to build such innate mechanisms.

The perception of the horizontal azimuth of sounds contrasts notably with the perception of their vertical position or *elevation*. Whereas two-eared ("binaural") organisms can infer a sound's azimuth, they cannot infer the elevation of a sound from universal geometric facts such as interaural time or amplitude differences. Instead, the perceived elevation of a sound is known to be facilitated by the distinctive shape of the external visible part of the ear known as the *pinna*. The outer ear acts as a complex resonant filter, changing the tone color of sounds depending on their vertical projection onto the surface of the pinna. A sound coming from above will have a slightly different timbre than the same sound coming from straight ahead, or from below.

Notice that the ability to infer the elevation of a sound presupposes that an organism "knows" (in some sense) what the unfiltered timbre should sound like, and is then able to use timbral modifications as cues for elevation. Since the world is full of lots of different sounds of various elevations and timbres, this implies that elevation is probably a *learned* aspect of localization—unlike horizontal azimuth. Current auditory research provides good support for this view. Paul Hofman and John Van Opstal at the University of Nijmegen fitted volunteers with binaural plastic molds that modified the shape of their pinnas. These molds immediately abolished the ability of listeners to judge the elevation of sounds but did not disrupt their azimuth (left–right) judgments. However, after wearing the molds for periods of up to five weeks, all listeners had adapted to the plastic molds and had regained their ability to judge elevation. That is, listeners were able to learn how the novel spectral transformations relate to elevation.[3]

In a contrasting experiment, Hofman and his colleagues outfitted participants with full-spectrum "in-the-ear-canal" hearing aids that were contralaterally wired: the sounds arriving at the left ear were shipped over to the right ear and vice versa. The immediate effect of this manipulation was to swap the horizontal azimuth: listeners judged sounds from the right as originating on the left, and vice versa. With the passage of many weeks, listeners failed to learn to adapt to this new arrangement. Listeners never stopped hearing the sounds as laterally displaced, even though the auditory cues were constantly contradicted by what they were seeing.[4]

In short, *azimuth* perception appears to be innate, whereas *elevation* perception appears to be learned. Notice that these differences are in accord with the Baldwin effect discussed in chapter 4. Recall that the Baldwin effect says that innate mechanisms are more effective when the environment is relatively unchanging, while learned mechanisms are more effective when the environment is more variable. Those aspects of localization that can be linked to stable physical properties in the world (like principles of geometry) appear to lead to innate coding mechanisms. By contrast, those aspects of localization that rely on variable factors (such as the familiarity of different timbres) lead to mental codings that appear to be learned.

Research suggests that there are several *levels* of representation involved in what we call "localization." Neurophysiologists have identified specific regions in the brain where neurons "code" interaural time and amplitude differences. We might say that location is represented using the codes of interaural time and amplitude differences. But auditory processing does not stop with these representations. Other parts of the auditory system translate these (and other) sensory codes into the more useful representations of *azimuth, elevation,* and *distance.* These perceptual codes are much more useful to an organism. When we experience a sound, we have no conscious access to the neural representations of interaural time difference or interaural amplitude difference. Instead, we experience a mental representation that says "over to the left," "up high," or "pretty far away."

Of course, the auditory system doesn't just attempt to resolve the current location of a sound. It also endeavors to predict the location of future sounds. In the realm of expectation, *where next* is probably the first predictive mechanism to have evolved in the primordial auditory system.

The *where-next* function requires yet another set of mental representations. Since the perceiving animal may be in motion, it is useful to translate the relative relationships of azimuth, elevation, and distance to an absolute location—namely, the representation of *place* rather than *bearing*. By creating a mental code for place, we can better predict a sound location that compensates and eliminates the possible effects of our own movements. In addition, a place-based mental representation might integrate information from the visual system to provide a more robust coding. Finally, a mental representation of *speed* and *trajectory* can help us better predict location when the sound source itself is in motion.

By way of summary, there exist several levels of mental representation for localization. The lowest (unconscious) representational level includes interaural time, amplitude differences, and spectral shape. A higher (subconscious) representational level includes azimuth, elevation, and distance. With further processing, conscious representations emerge, such as place, speed, and trajectory.

Having described some functionally useful representations, let's return for a moment to consider the problem of predicting sound functions such as those shown in figure 7.1. In the case of localization, only some of the features evident in these sound functions are pertinent. The most important features are the relative time relationship and the difference in amplitudes.[5] From the perspective of predicting location, it is important to predict that the upper sound function begins slightly before the lower one, and that the upper function also exhibits a slightly higher amplitude. Note that most of the features one could describe about these two sound functions are simply not germane to the task of localizing a sound—or predicting its future location. The mental representation is strongly shaped by the physiological function.

The case of sound localization illustrates an important fact about mental representation. One might think that an ideal mental representation would be one that accurately reflects the organization of the real world. However, the business of biology is survival and procreation, not truth or accuracy. In order to understand the nature of mental representations, we must consider what biological functions they serve and what types of pertinent information are available in the world.

Notice that we have not resolved the question of which *level* of localization-related mental codes might form the basis for expectation. Suppose, for example, that a listener anticipates that the next sound will come from a more central location. How is this expectation represented? Does the listener's brain anticipate the shortening of the *interaural time difference* between the ears? Or does the listener's expectation make use of a higher level representation, such as anticipating that the *azimuth* will shift toward the body's midline? Which mental code or codes are used in anticipating the future? In what "language" are predictions expressed?

The existing auditory research doesn't yet have an answer to this question. It is a difficult question because there are lots of possibilities. For example, a higher-level representation (such as *trajectory*) might be used to "calculate" an expectation, but that expectation might be concretely expressed as, say, an anticipated interaural amplitude difference. Alternatively, a low-level representation such as interaural amplitude difference may play no role in the forming of an expectation, except that interaural amplitude difference is used as an intermediate stage in calculating the higher-level codes that *are* expected. Yet another possibility is that all of the mental representations related to localization are concurrently involved in independent predictions about what will occur next.[6] These are empirical questions that can be answered only through future experimental research.

The problem of predicting auditory location might seem to have little pertinence to music.[7] But our discussion highlights some useful lessons about mental representation in general. First, just because we can identify (mathematically) certain features in a sound does not necessarily mean that these features are germane to brains. Mental representation is shaped by physiological function. Second, there may be several representations pertinent to a particular function—as in the case of interaural time differences and interaural amplitude differences. Third, representations can build on one another. For example, auditory "bearing" probably depends on underlying representations such as interaural time and amplitude codes. Fourth, mental codes rely on features of stimuli that maintain a stable relationship to the environment—either the long-term environment of evolutionary history, or the short-term environment of individual learning. A change in the attended feature should reliably reflect a pertinent change in the real world.

Representing an Expected Pitch

Consider now the more musically pertinent problem of pitch representation. How is the pitch of an expected tone mentally represented? We might begin by pointing to the usual suspects. Theoretically, a listener might expect a particular absolute pitch, such as the pitch B3. Or the listener might expect a particular pitch-class—for example, the set of all Bs including B2, B3, B4, B5, and so on. Or the listener might expect a particular contour; for example, the listener might simply expect the next pitch to be higher than the current pitch. Alternatively, the listener might expect a particular interval, such as the interval of a rising major second. Or the listener might expect a particular scale degree, such as the seventh scale step or leading tone. The listener might expect an ensuing pitch to be a member of some specific chord; for example, any of the pitches of the G major chord G3, B3, or D4. More subtly, rather than expecting particular notes of a particular chord, the listener might expect the pitch to be a member of "the dominant chord." Or the listener might expect the pitch to be a member of any dominant function, such as the tones of a dominant minor-ninth chord or an augmented dominant triad.

There are also lower-level representations that must be considered. For the psycho-acoustician and hearing scientist, *pitch* is already a remarkably high-level representation. At the level of the sensory organ, the cochlea encodes nothing that resembles pitch. At the cochlear level, all sounds appear to be represented in two forms. In the first instance, different frequencies cause different places along the basilar membrane to be excited. Each place is associated with the firing of different sensory neurons. This sound–place mapping is referred to as a *tonotopic* representation, and this tono-topic coding of sound can be observed at many places throughout the auditory system—including on the auditory cortex.

A second representation relates to the rate and pattern of firing of various auditory neurons. Throughout the auditory system, neurons exhibit a tendency to fire in syn-chrony with the frequencies driving the ear drum. Neurons cannot fire faster than about 1,000 times per second. Since humans are able to hear frequencies well above 10,000 Hz, there are limits to this synchronous firing. Nevertheless, the rate of firing is known to play a role in the representation of pitch. The idea that frequency is mentally represented using a combination of tonotopy and neural firing was first proposed in the 1950s by Joseph Licklider. This two-component theory is referred to as the "duplex theory" of pitch.

As in the case of localization, it is possible that an expected sound is represented by a combination of several underlying representations. For example, a listener might expect a tone to be from a particular pitch-class, *and* to activate particular tonotopic points. Or a listener might expect that the pitch will be very close to the current pitch, but will also be a member of the dominant seventh chord. Or a listener might expect that the contour will ascend to either the fourth or sixth scale degrees. In addition, it is possible for combinations to involve non-pitch-related representations. For example, a listener might expect a combination of long duration and particular pitch-class.

So how precisely are musical pitches represented in the brain? What precisely do listeners expect? First, let's consider why a profusion of different representations might be useful for a listening brain.

Neural Darwinism

As I have already emphasized, when a phenomenon is stable over a long period of time it becomes possible to evolve specialized innate representations such as interaural time and amplitude differences. However, when an environment is highly variable, then it is better to evolve the capacity for learning. When learning proves to be the most adaptive strategy, it is appropriate not only for the specific expectations to be learned, but also for the underlying representation itself to be learned rather than innate. A good mental representation would be one that captures or approximates some useful organizational property of an animal's actual environment.

In the case of audition, we know that learning plays a dominant role. If the real world of sound is organized according to scale degrees, for example, then scale degree might be an appropriate mental representation for expressing pitch-related expectations. If the real world is organized according to a combination of (say) pitch contour, metric position, and diatonic interval, then an appropriate mental representation might echo this mixed organization.

But how does a brain know which representation is the best? How can an auditory system learn to discard one representation in favor of another? Here expectation may play a defining and perhaps essential role. Expectation is an omnipresent mental process; brains are constantly anticipating the future. Moreover, we have seen that there is good evidence for a system of rewards and punishments that evaluates the accuracy of our unconscious predictions about the world. A defective mental representation will necessarily lead to failures of prediction. Conversely, a mental representation that facilitates useful predictions is likely to be retained. In effect, our mental representations are being perpetually tested by their ability to usefully predict ensuing events.

This claim carries an important implication. It suggests that the auditory system is spontaneously capable of generating several representations from which the less successful can be eliminated. This in turn suggests that *competing concurrent representations* may be the norm in mental functioning.

Neurophysiologists have posited precisely such competitive concurrent neural structures. The foremost advocate of this view has been the Nobel laureate Gerald Edelman, who has dubbed this theory *neural Darwinism*. Other advocates include William Calvin.[8] Edelman and Calvin have assembled strong neurophysiological evidence supporting this view. According to the neural Darwinism theory, "cortical real estate" is the resource over which different functions and representations compete. "Unsuccessful" functions atrophy and their cortical resources are taken over by the more "successful" functions.[9] (This competition is restricted primarily to the cortex and is less evident in subcortical brain areas.) It has been suggested that this competitive process accounts for much of the flexibility or plasticity that is evident in the brain.

According to Edelman and Calvin, representations compete with each other according to Darwinian principles applied to patterns of neural organization. Those representations that prove most useful in predicting future events are preserved and reinforced, while less useful representations atrophy. Such neural competition is possible only if more than one representation exists in the brain. That is, in forming expectations, the normal brain would maintain multiple concurrent representations. Relying on a single representation would mean either that the brain had achieved near perfection in forming predictions about the world, or that the representation is genetically ordained, or that the brain has become pathologically structured.

Viewed from a functional perspective, something like the prediction response would be a logical necessity in order to provide feedback concerning the relative success of different representations. The whole process involves a sort of feedback loop: representations are used to form expectations, and the accuracy of these expectations is used to select among the various alternative representations.

Notice that this feedback loop would be highly sensitive to the type of auditory environment in which a listener resides. Given different environments, we would expect people to differ in their mental representations for sound. For example, if the prevailing music in some culture were dominated by contour-related regularities, then we would expect contour-related representations to be foremost in the mental functioning of members from that culture. In a different culture, the prevailing musical organization might favor some other pitch-related mental representation among experienced listeners.

As we will see later in this chapter, recent research on absolute pitch will support this interpretation. That is, we will see evidence of multiple concurrent music-related representations, of competition and atrophy, and evidence that the preeminence of one or another representation depends on listener-specific circumstances and environments.

Expectation serves at least three functions: *motivation*, *preparation*, and *representation*. First, by anticipating future events, we may be able to take steps now to avoid negative outcomes or increase the likelihood of positive outcomes. That is, expectations have the capacity to motivate an organism. Second, even if we are unable to influence the course of future events, expectations allow us to prepare in appropriate ways. For example, accurate expectations allow us to adopt a state of arousal that is better suited to what is likely to happen next. Accurate expectations also help us orient in the direction of an anticipated stimulus, and so increase the speed and accuracy of future perceptions. That is, expectation allows us to prepare suitable motor responses and craft suitable perceptual strategies. Finally, expectation provides the test-bed for evaluating various mental representations. That is, expectational success and failure provides the "natural selection" mechanism for the neural competition that may underlie mental representation.

If it is true that mental representations are in competition according to neural Darwinism, then two consequences follow. First, there must be a mechanism for generating new representations. It is possible that this mechanism is only or at least predominantly active early in life and becomes inactive in adulthood. But at some point in a listener's life, there must be a process that generates alternative auditory representations. Second, selection can take place only if all of the competing representations are simultaneously engaged in generating expectations. Selection can take place only if there are competing (and diverging) predictions. This implies that normally more than one mental representation is involved in activating expectations.

These points bear on our earlier question: Do listeners expect a particular pitch, or a particular scale degree, or a particular interval, or a particular contour? If I am correct, for any given auditory stimulus, the listener's brain is generating predictions using several representations. However, the predictions arising from the different representations are by no means treated equally. Each listener will have a distinctive listening history in which some representations have proved more successful than others. A typical listener will hold a combination of differently favored expectations. Informally, we might regard a listener's expectation as some sort of weighted sum, say, 70 percent scale degree, 15 percent harmonic function, and 10 percent pitch contour.

Acquiring a Representation—The Case of Absolute Pitch

In chapter 4 we briefly discussed the phenomenon of absolute pitch (AP)—the ability to identify the pitch of tones without the use of any external reference. Absolute pitch is one of the most studied phenomena in music perception. Experimental research concerning AP has been carried out for more than a century. The intense curiosity about absolute pitch arises from its relative rarity. If everyone had AP we wouldn't give it a moment's thought. What makes it a compelling topic is the fact that only a few people develop this skill. Why?[10]

Some correlational evidence suggests that the capacity to develop AP may involve a genetic predisposition.[11] But even if genetics plays a role, the existing research suggests that a critical learning period is involved. One of the best generalizations one can make about "perfect pitch" is that its possessors typically begin musical instruction or involvement at a comparatively early age—often before the age of six or seven years.[12]

Many musicians would like to acquire perfect pitch and so there is a ready market for "methods" that purport to help adults develop it. Occasionally, an adult does succeed in developing AP, but the methods produce inconsistent results. One of my former students, Peter Sellmer, spent a year attempting to develop AP. He worked at it daily and regularly tested his progress. At one point he was even convinced that he was improving. But systematic pre- and post-tests established that his year-long effort had been fruitless. It turns out that those individuals who succeed in acquiring absolute pitch as adults typically began their music involvement at an early age. Adults who began musical involvement as teenagers almost never acquire perfect pitch.[13]

An often overlooked precondition for the development of absolute pitch is that the pitch environment remain stable. A person cannot learn to name pitches if the pitch of nominally identical tones keeps changing. Some musical instruments, such as the guitar and the violin, must be frequently retuned. If there is no stable external pitch reference for tuning such instruments, then it will be impossible for a person to develop absolute pitch. In many cultures, there is no fixed tuning standard. For example, the instruments of a traditional gamelan are typically tuned to one another, but the overall tuning will change from ensemble to ensemble. Since most gamelan instruments are metallophones, they retain a fairly constant pitch. This means that a musician may develop absolute pitch related to an individual instrument, or to a specific group of instruments. But this skill may not transfer to the gamelan in a neighboring village.

The human voice is perhaps the most obvious example of an "instrument" without fixed tuning. Unless a culture maintains instruments with stable tuning, a predominantly vocal culture is anathema to the development of absolute pitch.

The phenomenon of pitch instability or variable tuning might explain why not all people acquire absolute pitch. In 1901, Otto Abraham proposed a theory that has come to be known as the "pitch unlearning" theory. A century ago this theory was largely regarded as an implausible curiosity, but today the theory is regarded much more favorably.[14] Abraham pointed out that in many music-making environments, there is no fixed tuning standard. Consider, for example, the sort of musical activity commonly found in a nursery school or kindergarten. Most such environments don't have a piano; the music-making is often voice-only. Today, the children might sing "Happy Birthday" for Jill in the key of E major; tomorrow, the children might sing "Happy Birthday" for Ken in the key of G major. As long as individual musical works are sung in different keys, there is no possibility of "coding" the tune as a sequence of absolute pitches. In such an environment, there is simply no advantage for a brain to represent events in terms of absolute pitch. Said another way, in a pitch-variable environment, an absolute pitch encoding provides no predictive advantage whatsoever.

Abraham suggested that people might have a natural tendency to acquire absolute pitch. However, when exposed to an auditory environment characterized by high pitch variability, any latent perfect pitch capacity is likely to atrophy. It is not quite correct to say that people "unlearn" perfect pitch. But it is an appropriately colorful name for Abraham's theory.

Yet there is an even more compelling reason why brains should be indifferent to perfect pitch: there are better possible mental representations. If one of the purposes of a mental representation is to facilitate prediction, then a *relative pitch* representation will prove much more useful for music-related pitch. In the singing of "Happy Birthday," a relative pitch representation will prove consistently more accurate in predicting ensuing tones.

Given the greater value of relative pitch representations, one might ask why *anyone* would retain an absolute pitch ability. What possible advantage does absolute pitch confer? Musicians will note that absolute pitch is useful for tuning without a reference pitch, that it helps performers maintain accurate intonation, that it facilitates recall of musical works from memory, and that it aids in transcribing music by ear. But however much these skills might be useful for professional musicians, they hold only negligible value from the perspective of mental functioning. Indeed, researchers have shown that there are significant *disabilities* that attend perfect pitch (see below). Later we will see why a brain might develop this skill, despite its limited utility.

Recall that in chapter 4 we reviewed some of the evidence in support of absolute pitch as a learned phenomenon. One of the strongest pieces of evidence is to be found in reaction-time studies for pitch identification. Recall that people with absolute pitch are faster when identifying the most commonly occurring pitches, and that the reaction-time measures are consistent with the Hick-Hyman law.[15] As we noted in chapter 4, this finding implies that AP is learned through simple exposure.

In the past decade, researchers have become more aware of how absolute pitch interferes with certain musical tasks. A seminal study was carried out by Ken'ichi Miyazaki at Niigata University.[16] Miyazaki demonstrated that in certain circumstances, absolute pitch possessors perform worse than non-AP possessors. Consider, for example, the rising major sixth interval from C4 to A4. Both AP and non-AP possessors could readily identify this interval—although AP possessors responded slightly faster than non-AP musicians. Now consider the rising major sixth interval from C#4 to A#4. Here non-AP possessors identified this interval just as quickly as the interval C4 to A4. However, the AP possessors responded significantly slower. Miyazaki's study demonstrates that many AP possessors "calculate" the interval from the pitch names. That is, many AP possessors hear the pitches C4 and A4, and then determine that the interval must be a major sixth. However, when the pitches are C#4 and A#4, the interval calculation becomes more complicated—especially since many AP possessors tend to identify the A sharp as a B flat instead. Because of the enharmonic change, musicians are slower to identify the interval between C sharp and B flat.

In effect, Miyazaki showed that for many AP-possessors, the ability to identify pitches impedes their ability to learn intervals by ear. Rather than identifying intervals from the relative distance separating the tones, AP-possessors often rely on deriving intervals from pitch names. Miyazaki's work suggests that many possessors of AP have no native mental representation for intervals.

For music teachers this situation would seem highly problematic. Identifying intervals by ear is considered a basic musicianship skill. But we shouldn't be too quick to judge. First, why do musicians attempt to learn to identify pitch intervals? The answer is to be able to reproduce heard or imagined sounds. That is, we learn to recognize intervals so that we can notate pitch sequences, or reproduce them when playing on an instrument. Notice, however, that both of these tasks could be carried out perfectly well if we could always recognize the pitch of a sound. What incentive is there for a person with absolute pitch to ever use interval-recognition when notating music? For the relative pitch user, once the key is established, intervals are translated back into pitches anyway. Why not just represent the pitches directly?

Music teachers have a ready answer for this. It is often useful to be able to transpose music into a different key. For example, singers have different vocal ranges and it is important to be able to perform the music at a different absolute pitch height. If the singer has absolute pitch, this is hard to do. If the notation reads "F#," it is hard for the AP-possessor not to imagine and sing F#.

It may well be that developing brains begin by assuming a simple representation (such as absolute pitch). If the world is not organized in a manner consistent with absolute pitch (as in the persistent singing of "Happy Birthday" in different keys), then some other representation (such as interval or scale degree) will become more appropriate. However, any latent absolute pitch representation will be preserved to the extent that it retains some value in predicting the future.

Let's review, then, the basic facts about absolute pitch as they are currently understood.

1. Not everyone develops absolute pitch.
2. If absolute pitch emerges, the basis for it tends to be laid in early life.
3. Reaction time data shows that AP is acquired by exposure to the environment—faster reaction times happen for those pitches that are encountered most often.
4. Possession of AP doesn't mean that the person can *only* code pitches this way.
5. Nevertheless, possession of absolute pitch can retard the development of relative or intervalic pitch coding.
6. Absolute pitch proves useless in situations where there is no standard tuning.
7. Absolute pitch never develops in sound environments where it is not useful.

Notice that all of these facts are consistent with the principles of neural Darwinism: all of these facts are consistent with the notion that representations that prove the most useful in predicting future events are preserved and reinforced. Representations that fail to provide accurate predictions about the world are less likely to develop. In short, the case of absolute pitch is consistent with three theoretical claims:

1. There are competing mental representations for sound.
2. Representations are shaped by exposure to the environment.
3. Representations are differentially favored depending on their predictive success.

The evidence in support of this view is not extensive; further research is needed. Nevertheless, the phenomenon of absolute pitch is consistent with my earlier suggestion that one of the functions of the prediction response is as an engine of selection for mental representation.

Correlated Representations

Over the years, perceptual research in music has shown that listeners are sensitive to many different experimental manipulations. Reading this research literature, one might conclude that there exists a multitude of concurrent representations that are involved in music listening. The research implies that at least some listeners are able to code sounds as absolute pitches, pitch chromas (or pitch classes), scale degrees, intervals, scale-degree dyads (successive scale degrees), contours, durations, relative durations, metric positions, harmonic functions, chord qualities, and spectral centroids—to name a few. Some mental representations are apparent only in certain tasks. Other representations (like absolute pitch) are available only to a minority of listeners. Some research explicitly suggests that musical coding involves more than one concurrent representation.[17] There is, however, a problem that should make us wary of accepting the research at face value. The problem becomes evident only when we directly compare several different possible representations.

Figure 7.2 plots the flow of information for the tune "Pop Goes the Weasel." Information is plotted (in bits) for five different representations. The uppermost plot shows information according to the probabilities of different scale degrees. Less common scale degrees (such as $\hat{6}$—pitch E) convey more information compared with frequently occurring scale degrees (such as $\hat{1}$ and $\hat{5}$—pitches G and D). The second plot shows information according to scale-degree successions or scale-degree dyad. Here high probabilities (low information) events include the succession $\hat{1}$ followed by $\hat{1}$ and $\hat{4}$ followed by $\hat{3}$. Low probability (high information) events include $\hat{1}$ followed by $\hat{6}$ and $\hat{6}$ followed by $\hat{2}$. The third graph plots metric position for 6/8 meter. High probability events include notes whose onsets coincide with the downbeat of each measure. For 6/8, a low probability (high information) event occurs for notes whose onsets coincide with the second eighth of the measure. The fourth graph plots interval. Common intervals include the unison repetition and the rising major second. Uncommon intervals include the rising major sixth and the descending perfect fifth. Finally, the fifth graph plots interval dyad (pairs of successive intervals). High probability events include a unison followed by an ascending major second and an ascending major second followed by a unison. Low probability events include the rising major sixth followed by the descending perfect fifth, and the falling perfect fifth followed by the ascending minor third. The probabilities used in figure 7.2 were derived from an analysis of some six thousand European folk songs.

Notice that the information for both scale-degree and melodic interval representations peak at the word "pop." For scale degree dyad and interval dyad the word "pop" coincides with the second highest information value—with the maximum value following immediately after the word "pop." There appears to be an element of musical "surprise" at this point that is echoed in the lyrics. As a children's action

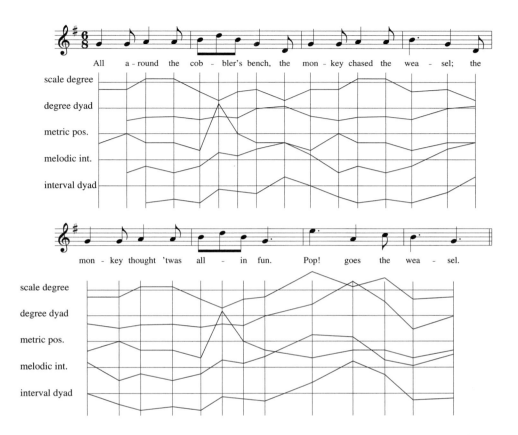

Figure 7.2
Information theoretic analysis of "Pop Goes the Weasel" showing changes of information (in bits) as the piece unfolds. Graphically, high points represent less probable events; low points indicate highly probable events. Note that the word "Pop!" tends to exhibit high information, characteristic of surprise. Plotted information includes scale degree, successive pairs of scale degrees (degree dyad), metric position, melodic interval, and successive pairs of melodic intervals (interval dyad).

Table 7.1
Correlation matrix showing similarities in information fluctuation for five representations used to analyze "Pop Goes the Weasel." Pitch-related representations are highly correlated.

	degree	degree dyad	metric position	interval	interval dyad
degree	+1.00				
degree dyad	+0.45	+1.00			
metric position	−0.31	−0.05	+1.00		
interval	+0.17	+0.74	−0.00	+1.00	
interval dyad	+0.30	+0.90	+0.02	+0.77	+1.00

song, this point is usually accompanied by some abrupt action, also suggestive of surprise.

Note, however, that there is no comparable peak in information for metric position. That is, the interval/pitch/scale-degree may be relatively surprising, but the *moment* of its occurrence is not surprising. This highlights the independence of the *what* and *when* of surprise. Here, the *what* is relatively surprising but not the *when*. In other musical situations, the *what* is expected, whereas the *when* may be relatively unexpected. (More musical examples will be considered later in chapter 14.)

With the exception of the metric position information, all of the pitch-related information values are broadly similar. That is, they are positively correlated. Table 7.1 shows a correlation matrix for the information content (measured in bits) for the various representations used in the above analysis of "Pop Goes the Weasel." Three representations are closely intertwined: interval, interval dyad, and scale-degree dyad. The average correlation between these three representations is a remarkable +0.80 (of a theoretical maximum of +1.0). These positive correlations are not limited to Western music. I have carried out analyses of some 200 melodies from American, Chinese, Dutch, Pawnee, and Xhosa sources and found that these large positive correlations are typical.

The fact that different musical representations are positively correlated is both good and bad news. An advantage of this correlation is that it suggests that probabilistic analyses of music are fairly insensitive to the choice of pitch-related representation. For some analytic tasks, knowledge of the precise nature of the mental representation may not be important. The disadvantage of this high correlation is that it invites onerous mistakes of interpretation. When an experimenter manipulates some pitch in a stimulus passage, it is not just pitch that changes. Typically, a change of pitch will also cause a change of scale degree, a change of chroma, a change of interval, and a change of scale-degree succession, among other changes. A change of pitch might also lead to a change of melodic contour. Suppose that the experimenter finds that this change is noticed by a listener. Can we conclude that the listener has heard a change of pitch? No. Unless the experimenter takes care to ensure that no change in contour, interval, scale degree, interval dyad, and so on took place, it is impossible to interpret the listener's discrimination. In research methodology, this problem is referred to as "the third variable problem."[18] If a listener distinguishes stimuli that differ according to property *A* it does not follow that the listener is "sensitive" to or "encoding" property *A*. By changing *A*, an experimenter might inadvertently be changing property *B*—and it may be property *B* that listeners are able to code or distinguish.

Nearly all of the experiments that purport to manipulate some pitch-related property (like interval) also end up transforming other properties as well. This means that taking an experiment to suggest that people are sensitive to, say, pitch contour may be entirely wrong. The high correlation between the various pitch-related representations means that we must be very careful in interpreting experimental results. Music psychologists have largely failed to be sufficiently discerning when manipulating different pitch-related parameters. As a result, much of the existing research related to the mental representation of music needs to be redone. Incidentally, the high correlation between various pitch-related representations does not mean that it is impossible to ever resolve which representations are coded mentally. It is possible to organize experiments so that these confounds are controlled, minimized, or circumvented. However, implementing such experiments requires careful planning.

The Enigma of Melodic Interval

A few years ago I began to doubt whether I hear melodic intervals. Don't get me wrong: I'm as capable of generating and recognizing intervals as the next music teacher. If you ask me to sing an ascending major sixth, I'll readily oblige—but I know that I'm cheating. I'll really be singing the first two pitches of the song "My Bonnie Lies Over the Ocean." I might sing the syllables "la la"—but really, my mind is thinking "so–mi."

I'm also aware that when I hear a major sixth interval, I find it much easier to recognize if the tonal context for the interval is "so–mi" rather than, say, "re–ti" or "fa–re." If the interval occurs in an uncommon context, I sometimes check my intuition by mentally transposing the key so that I can hear the interval as "so–mi." Then I really *know* it's a major sixth.

All of this raises the interesting hypothesis that I have no native mental code for melodic interval. Instead, I may have a scale-degree code, and perhaps a scale-degree dyad code. I tend to hear the rising perfect fourth as "so–do" or sometimes "mi–la"— but almost never as "re–so" or "ti–mi." Rising minor thirds I hear as either "mi–so" or "do–may." Major and minor seconds are an exception: I seem to hear these intervals in a more automatic fashion without being tied to scale relationships.

In many ways, my identification of melodic intervals resembles some of the AP musicians observed by Ken'ichi Miyazaki. I seem to identify the notes and then mentally infer the interval. Since I don't have absolute pitch, I'm not able to identify the pitches per se. Instead, I'm experiencing the tones as scale degrees and then "calculating" the interval. While I can consciously recognize that "so–do" and "la–re" are the same interval, they don't sound at all the same to me. I seem to have no native representation for the concept "perfect fourth" apart from a willfully imposed classification that groups together a bunch of obviously different things.

When I've spoken with other musicians about this, about a third report having similar experiences. If nothing else, it is at least reassuring to learn that I'm not alone. But do some listeners really experience intervals this way or are my introspective descriptions flawed?

With my collaborator, Bret Aarden, I carried out an exploratory experiment to try to determine whether other musicians fail to "hear" pitch intervals. In our experiment we had musicians identify various melodic intervals while we measured their reaction times. Rather than simply playing the intervals to our participants, we preceded each interval by a key-defining context. Specifically, we played a I–IV–V–I harmonic cadence before each trial. Between trials we played a random atonal pitch sequence to try to erase any lingering key that might interfere with the next trial.[19] We predicted that if listeners encode intervals as scale-degree dyads, then certain key-congruent presentations should be more quickly identified than other presentations. Figure 7.3 illustrates two sample trials from our experiment. If a listener tends to experience a major sixth interval as "so–mi" then trial (a) should result in faster interval identification than the "fa–re" presentation of trial (b).

Of course, even with the key-defining context, it is possible that some of our listeners would rapidly change the mental key in order to more quickly identify the presented interval. To control for this possibility, we followed the interval-identification task by a second task. After the participant had identified the interval, we immediately played a ii^6–V–I harmonic cadence and asked our listeners if this cadence was in the same key as the original key-defining cadence that began the trial. This second cadence had a 50 percent chance of being in the same key. We used this latter judgment to gauge whether the listener had maintained the original key or had inadvertently drifted to a different key while making the interval judgment.

Trial (b) in figure 7.3, for example, shows a key-incongruent test cadence. The trial begins in the key of C major and presents a major sixth interval as "fa–re." If a listener tended to hear the interval as "so–mi" then they would have had to reconceive of the pitches in the key of B-flat major. If they did this, it would increase the probability that they would falsely claim that the ensuing test cadence was the same as the initial key-defining cadence.

Figure 7.3
Two sample trials used in Huron and Aarden's (unpublished) study of the effect of key context on interval identification. Listeners first heard a key-defining context (I–IV–V–I cadence) followed by an ascending melodic interval. In (a) the interval is an ascending major sixth between scale degrees $\hat{5}$ and $\hat{3}$. In (b) the same interval is played between scale degrees $\hat{4}$ and $\hat{2}$. Musician participants then identified the interval. We predicted that responses to (a) would be faster than to (b). After the participant identified the interval a test cadence is heard (a ii⁶–V–I cadence). In (a) this cadence is consistent with the original key-defining context. In (b) the test cadence is consistent with the different key of B-flat major. Participants had to identify whether the key of the test cadence corresponded with the initial cadence. If participants tended to code ascending major sixths as $\hat{5}$ to $\hat{3}$ then we would predict that in stimulus (b), participants would be more likely to incorrectly claim that the test cadence was consistent with the original key.

Our results were somewhat mixed. Some intervals for some musicians appear to be facilitated for certain key contexts. But apparently, not all musicians experience melodic intervals the way I do. With further research, we may be better able to resolve the issue of pitch-interval representation. But there is more work to be done.

Even if we assume that all listeners develop no native code for successive pitch intervals, it does not follow that it is useless to train musicians to consciously identify intervals. Intervals are useful objects in music, and there are lots of circumstances where it is helpful to identify intervals—and to identify them without regard to key context.[20] But we should be careful to distinguish native mental representations from consciously derived labels. At least in my case, it is doubtful that I hear melodies as successions of intervals. My subjective intuition is that I experience melodies primarily as successions of scale degrees. However, this type of introspection is fraught with dangers. Consider, by way of example, the hypothetical mental organization shown in figure 7.4.

Here we see an auditory system that begins with a pitch representation from which an interval representation is generated. In this hypothetical organization, both of

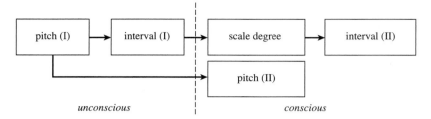

Figure 7.4
A hypothetical mental network for pitch-related representation. In this hypothetical scheme, pitch is a low-level sensory representation from which interval is derived. This interval representation is not experienced consciously, but it is used to derive a mental representation for scale degree. Both pitch and scale degree are then experienced "natively" as a *conscious* perceptual experience. Musical training allows this individual to mentally determine or "calculate" interval based on scale degree.

these mental representations are *unconscious*—codes that are not accessible to consciousness. From the interval representation, a scale-degree representation is created. Also, the pitch representation is duplicated and refined (Pitch II). Both of these latter representations are available to consciousness. Through musical training, this individual has learned to identify intervals (Interval II). This is a conscious task that makes use of the scale-degree code that is accessible to consciousness. Ironically, in this hypothetical scheme, conscious interval recognition would be a reconstruction from a scale-degree representation that itself is constructed from an earlier interval representation that is not accessible to consciousness.

My point is that although my introspective intuition suggests that my preeminent pitch-related representation is scale degree, this does not necessarily mean that interval is perceptually unimportant to my mental representation. In some ways it is difficult to imagine how a scale-degree representation can arise without some sort of intervalic information. Of course, if there is some unconscious interval coding, it will not employ the verbal labels musicians use (major second, minor sixth, etc.).

If such convoluted mental organizations seem far-fetched, there is a precedent for such odd arrangements in the phenomenon of localization. Recall that the auditory system makes use of interaural time and amplitude differences in determining the left–right azimuth for sounds. However, interaural time difference is not accessible to consciousness or introspection. We hear that a sound is "located off to the left," not that the pressure variation in the right ear lags behind the left ear. That is, the representation accessible to introspection differs from the lower-level mental code used to derive it.[21] Biology does not follow the principle of parsimony. Mental representation is not necessarily straightforward.

Other Possible Pitch Representations

Inspired by the twelve-tone music of Arnold Schoenberg, music theorists in the latter part of the twentieth century proposed a number of new music-related representations. The representations suggested by theorists pertained mostly to pitch—or more commonly, pitch-class. Among the more popular representations, theorists would include interval vectors, Z-relations, and Tn and TnI relations.[22] All of these representations pertain to *relative* pitch-class structures, so they are better described as "interval-class" representations. Nevertheless, the designation "pitch-class" (PC) has stuck and remains the common name within music theory circles for these types of representations.

Right from the beginning, these representations spawned skepticism in certain quarters. While many theorists embraced the representations and applied them in their music analyses, other music scholars felt that the constructions were artificial and had little to do with the experience of listening. Much of the disagreement arose from a lack of clarity about the epistemological status of analytic representations in general.[23] A representation does not have to have a perceptual basis in order for it to be useful. For example, a useful representation may pertain solely to the means of musical composition. As I have argued elsewhere, there are plenty of structures in music that have nothing to do with human perception, and that does not make these structures somehow vacuous, wrong-headed, or unworthy of investigation.[24]

The problem arises when an analytic representation is presumed to serve some perceptual or cognitive function. The music analysis literature is full of intimations that a particular set structure has some sort of psychological effect or is important in the aesthetic apprehension of the work by a knowledgeable listener. These presumptions can be tested experimentally, and, over the past half-century, many have been. Pertinent experiments have been carried out by Francès (1958), Thrall (1962), Largent (1972), Lannoy (1972), Millar (1984), Bruner (1984), Gibson (1986, 1988, 1993), Samplaski (2000, 2004), and others. Each of these experiments called into question the ability of listeners to hear the pitch-set relationships posited by some theorists. Don Gibson's 1988 work is especially noteworthy since he studied thirty-two professional music theorists. Gibson showed that even professional theorists perform near chance levels in discriminating pairs of chords according to pitch-class identity.[25]

To be fair, one can't fault theorists for wanting to describe possible new ways of experiencing music. There is little glamour in describing the ordinary—the commonplace musical experiences. The good news from research in music cognition is that, if it is true that mental representations emerge from patterned exposure, then there ought to be many opportunities for artists to shape new and different ways of experiencing sounds. However, the mere proposing of a music representation does not mean that listeners are capable of experiencing music this way. In particular, brains may have a hard time experiencing already familiar music according to novel mental representations. Moreover, the opportunities to learn new musical representations may be limited to critical periods during childhood.

The theoretical controversy aside, these studies on the perceptibility of pitch-set relations provide important clues concerning mental representation for music. They imply that certain forms of pitch-related representations may be difficult or impossible to form in the adult human auditory system, in the same way that it is difficult or impossible for most adults to acquire AP. Certain music-related representations seem to be preferred. Oddly, these representations may be preferred even though they are just approximations of a theoretical representation that would prove much better at predicting the world. What accounts for our representational preferences?

Representational Preferences

Why do brains appear to favor some types of mental representation over others? Here I'd like to propose four general principles that may influence the preferred mental representations for pitch. All four principles manifest a preference for simplicity over complexity in mental representation. In brief, the preferences are for (1) lower-order relationships, (2) neighboring over distant relationships, (3) lower-derivative states, and (4) event-related binding.

Recall from chapter 3 that a "lower-order relationship" is a relationship between a small number of elements. If the occurrence of state X is influenced by the presence of states Y and Z, it is said to have a higher-order relationship than if X were influenced by Y alone. The lowest order relationship is a "zeroth-order" relationship; this exists when the presence of some state is independent of any other states. For example, in English text, the most common letter is "e." That is, without considering any context, the highest zeroth-order probability is for the letter "e."

Notice that when we speak of "order relationships," we do not necessarily mean that these relationships are between adjacent or neighboring elements. An event might depend on only a single other event, but that event might be quite remote in time or space. When I push the elevator button in a high-rise building, it might be some time before the elevator appears. But despite the passage of time, the probability that the elevator will appear in response to my pushing the button is almost certain.

Mental representations also appear to favor *neighboring* over *distant* relationships. In the sequence of successive states $A, B, C, D \ldots$ it is easier to recognize a relationship between neighboring states (e.g., A and B) than more distant states (e.g., A and D). One way to think of the preference for neighboring rather than distant relationships is to suppose that it is preferrable for brains to minimize the size of temporal memory. Holding two successive events in short-term memory is easier than holding four events.

Figure 7.5
Four objects illustrating the failure to code spatial interval. Most observers fail to spontaneously notice that the distance between the salt shaker and the cup is the same as the distance between the pepper shaker and the candle.

Consider now the representation of derivative states. When characterizing relationships between two or more states, we can measure the amount of change, or the change in the amount of change, or the change in the change of the amount of change, and so on. For example, pitch successions might be represented by the amount of change (e.g., interval), or by the amount of change in the interval, and so on. In the language of calculus, we are identifying the derivatives: first derivative, second derivative, third derivative, and so on. Mental representation appears to favor lower derivatives. For example, in vision, the representation for *position* appears to take primacy over *velocity*, while *velocity* takes primacy over representations for *acceleration*, which in turn exhibits primacy over representations for *jerk*.

Finally, mental coding appears to favor representations that bind to auditory events. Consider the nonauditory analogy shown in figure 7.5. When I asked some colleagues to describe this illustration, all of them began by noting that there are four objects: what appear to be a salt and pepper shaker, a cup, and a candle. There is a special relationship between these objects. Can you see it?

The relationship is that the distance between the salt shaker and the cup is the same as the distance between the pepper shaker and the candle. Obvious, right? Of course, this relationship is not at all obvious to viewers. In parsing a visual field, we focus foremost on objects and their positions rather than distance relationships. This is not to say that minds don't apprehend distance relationships, only that our first disposition is to apprehend objects. In the case of sound, we focus foremost on sound events. In fact, observations of electroencephalographic behavior establishes that the brain responds most energetically to events, not to, say, the distance separating events. Brains are especially sensitive to the onsets of events.

In the field of perception, an important mental function is so-called *binding*. When we perceive an object, many different parts of the brain participate in calculating various features of the object. For example, in the case of vision, color is processed separately from shape, while object recognition occurs in yet another part of the brain. But when we see an apple, the phenomenal experience is unified: the shape, color, name, and other properties all adhere together as a single object.

A similar phenomenon occurs in audition. When we hear a sound, the pitch and timbre are not experienced as separate entities. We hear a "cute sound" or a "harsh sound." We don't hear "a sound" accompanied by an independent feeling of "cuteness" or "harshness." The various sound properties—loudness, pitch, location, timbre—all adhere together as a single event-object. Of course, if we are motivated to do so, we can introspect and focus on just the pitch, or just the location, for example. But the brain's disposition is to assemble an integrated "package." The object is experienced as a unified entity rather than a smorgasbord of disparate properties.

When we hear a melodic interval, the experience of interval doesn't somehow replace the two tones. We don't experience the interval as occupying the space between the two tones. Instead, the interval is manifested by the onset of the second tone—the interval feels as though it is a quality or property of the second tone. Although we tend to think of an interval as a certain kind of relationship between two tones, a melodic interval may be better described as a distinctive way of approaching a single tone. Although interval is obviously a distance relationship between two sound events, it is not some disembodied quality. The quality we call "melodic interval" is a property that binds to the ensuing tone.

A demonstration of this disposition is evident at phrase boundaries. Ask a musician friend to indicate whenever they hear a melodic leap while you sing "Happy Birthday." There is a strong likelihood that your friend will miss one or more of the leaps that occur *between* phrases. I think that event-related binding explains why the interval between the last note of one phrase and the first note of an ensuing phrase is often not salient.

My argument here is not that minds don't represent relationships. Rather, my argument is that minds favor event- or object-bound representations. It is easier to process, code, or manipulate representations when they are mentally attached to events or objects.

Preferred Representations

With these four principles of preferred mental representation in mind, let's apply these principles to some concrete examples in mental coding for music. Consider first the phenomenon of post-skip reversal. Why might listeners expect post-skip reversal rather than regression to the mean? In order to infer regression to the mean, a listener would need to retain a cumulative distribution of all the pitches heard up to a given moment and use this distribution to infer the average pitch. That is, a regression-to-the-mean expectation would require a mental representation based on high-order relationships. All of the preceding pitches would participate in the calculation of an expected pitch. At the same time, a regression-to-the-mean expectation would also require that the representation encode long relational distances. By contrast, with post-skip reversal, a listener need retain only the previous two pitches—inferring the size and direction of pitch motion. Post-skip reversal would require calculating the first derivative—and so would involve a more complicated representation (interval or direction) compared with pitch alone. But the cost of this more complicated representation would be offset by the significant computational savings incurred by not having to maintain a complete past history of pitch heights.

What about the case of absolute pitch? Absolute pitch is the ultimate zeroth-order pitch representation. According to our four principles, it is the simplest possible pitch-related representation. So why doesn't everyone have absolute pitch? In the modern world, stable tuning systems mean that absolute pitch is useful in predicting ensuing tones. If you hear Chopin's Nocturne opus 62, no. 2, a person with AP will know that the initial B3 is followed by G#4. What could be simpler?

As I have already noted, the predictive utility of absolute pitch is limited. Nor is this limited utility merely a product of the variable tuning of voice and instruments for music-making. Consider the research suggesting that there may be a genetic component to AP.[26] If there are genes that facilitate the development of AP, then we are talking about the wrong environment if we focus on modern music-making. The vast majority of human evolution occurred during the long Pleistocene period when hominids slowly took on all of the characteristics of modern *Homo sapiens*.[27] If it is true that there is a genetic disposition that favors absolute pitch, then the sound environment under which it evolved was the Pleistocene savannah, not the salons of eighteenth-century Europe. In the Pleistocene environment, it is hard to imagine any stable absolute pitches. Early humans probably recognized the higher and lower voices of their various friends, but the pitch variability would have been large compared with the better than semitone resolution of modern AP possessors. For millions of years in human evolution, absolute pitch would have had little or no utility.

Moreover, once *Homo sapiens* began to sing, the more pertinent auditory skill would not have been absolute pitch, but a refined form of relative pitch. The triumph of relative pitch in human music-making might even have been the precipitating event for the decline of any existing absolute pitch abilities. If absolute pitch requires one or more enabling genes, then the advent of human music-making may have been the selective agent that has *reduced* the prevalence of these hypothetical genes in the human genome. Ironically, the advent of human music-making may be the reason why so few people have absolute pitch.

The existing research, however, does not favor a genetic account for explaining the variability in AP possession. The capacity for absolute pitch appears to be built into the hearing organ itself with its absolute mapping of frequency to place on the basilar membrane and its faithful phase-lock coding of the temporal fine-structure of sounds. Instead, the existing research suggests that it is the pitch stability of the childhood environment that is the principal determining factor in AP development. Most children fail to encounter an environment where AP significantly enhances accurate expectation, and so the latent capacity either withers or fails to compete with more successful codes such as relative pitch.

Our four principles also provide a plausible reason why pitch interval appears to be problematic. Interval entails calculating the first derivative. At the same time, the interval calculation requires some coding of the two pitches involved. However, if the brain simply encodes pitch-dyad instead of interval, then no derivative need be calculated. Pitch-dyad is a simpler representation than pitch interval.

These four principles of mental representation are admittedly speculative. Additional research may well establish that these suggested principles are incorrect. What they share in common is computational simplicity. Each principle either minimizes the amount of memory needed, or minimizes the number of operations required to code a state.

I think these principles are plausible for several reasons. First, neural networks are easily configured to calculate changes. One neuron can be connected to respond to the difference in potential between two other neurons. This process can be repeated so that a neuron is responding to the difference between two differences and so on. Calculating derivatives is neurologically plausible. Note, however, that each derivative recruits an additional layer of neurons. If, as the research suggests, there is competition for neural real estate, then the brain ought to favor lower-level derivatives over higher-level derivatives.

For similar reasons, the brain ought to favor calculations involving fewer states—hence favoring lower-order relationships. Higher-order relationships would require the recruitment of many more interconnected neurons. Similarly, there are plausible reasons to favor neighboring relationships over distant relationships. Distant relationships can be recognized only when a large number of states can be held in memory, and only when a large number of comparisons between states can be made.

Finally, I suspect that in the evolution of nervous systems, it was inevitable that the "divide-and-conquer" strategy would emerge in analyzing sensations. Brains can apply several different concurrent analyses to a sensation, in some cases using specialized neural tissues for different analytic functions. However, such a strategy incurs a cost: each perceptual property is free-floating and so the experience of the world is fragmented. I suspect that brains have somehow evolved to compensate for this problem by ensuring that perceptual properties are assembled into a unitary percept. In the case of the auditory system, the profusion of perceptual properties is handled by assembling them into "a sound"—whose phenomenal existence is linked to the onset of an acoustic signal.

A Theory of Auditory Representation

The above discussion, in effect, offers a theory of auditory representation. It is appropriate to take a moment and explicitly summarize the main points of this view.

The theory proposes that the auditory system allows a number of competing neural networks to blossom—each network processing the sensory information in its own way. All of these networks ultimately start with the information provided by the auditory nerve: tonotopic position and firing-rate codings.

Expectations are neural circuits whose activation depends on the pattern of sensory inputs. In practice, these energized circuits facilitate certain motor behaviors and/or cause attention to be directed in particular ways. Motor behaviors may be facilitated directly or may be facilitated indirectly by evoking feeling states that act as motivators. Those neural circuits that predict well the ensuing events evoke a positive prediction response—a positively valenced limbic reward. Different neural representations compete with one another, and it is the prediction response that judges each performance and hands out the prizes. Networks that fail to predict ensuing states atrophy, while those that have some predictive success are retained and strengthened. In evaluating predictive neural networks, the brain follows an ancient biblical adage: the way to identify false prophets is by their false prophecies.

In the development of the auditory system, the initial representations are simple, relying on the codes passed along from the auditory nerve. These representations are low-order and make use of little or no contextual information. However, as auditory development proceeds, networks can connect with and draw information from other networks that have proved successful in predicting ensuing events. As a consequence, subsequent auditory development permits higher-order relationships and more distant contextual information to play a role in the representations that are spontaneously being generated.

In the case of pitch, for example, one might imagine that the brain begins with a simple absolute pitch representation. If a person lives in an environment where absolute pitch provides useful predictive information, then the mental coding for absolute pitch flourishes. Conversely, if the individual lives in an environment where absolute pitches provide little information of value in predicting future events, or where absolute pitch has difficulty competing with the emerging juggernauts of relative pitch prediction, then the capacity for absolute pitch withers.

Notice that the success of a representation is determined largely by the structure of the stimuli encountered by the auditory system. If the auditory environment is organized in a particular way, then mental representations that approximate that external structure will be favored.

Most of the competitive development of auditory representations occurs early in development—probably in infancy and childhood. New representational networks may continue to be spawned later in life, but they have difficulty competing with existing extensive networks that have long proved their worth.

In spawning new representations, simplicity is preferred over complexity. The brain is more likely to form mental representations that code (1) lower-order relationships, (2) neighboring over distant relationships, (3) lower-derivative states, and that (4) can be coordinated or "bound" with sensory events.

Since the auditory system must find its own way in assembling useful representations, there is plenty of scope for individual variation. However, this variation may be masked because different representations are often correlated with one another. Differences may also be masked because brains will normally rely on multiple concurrent representations. Although different listeners may respond to sounds in similar ways, they may be using very different mental codes to perform the same task.

It bears emphasizing that music-related representations exist as real biological patterns in individual brains. They aren't just formal abstractions. With advances in brain imagining, neuroscientists are beginning to show how brain organization reflects the organization of the auditory world. A landmark in music-related neural imaging is the work by Peter Janata, Jeffrey Birk, John Van Horn, Marc Leman, Barbara Tillmann, and Jamshed Bharucha. In Western tonal music, music theorists have long noted a complex web of relationships between major and minor keys. Neighboring keys are related by the "circle of fifths" while major and minor keys are related by a sequence of minor thirds. Music theorists have shown that these relationships can be graphically represented as a three-dimensional torus (donut) shape.[28] By using specially composed music that visited all of the major and minor keys through a series of modulations, Janata and his colleagues were able to observe the activation of torus-like topographies in individual listeners using magnetic resonance brain imaging. The tonal structure of the music was thus evident as a dynamic topography in a part of the rostromedial prefrontal cortex. Note that the torus tonal structure is unique to Western music. Only Western tonal music employs a system of "relative" and "parallel" major and minor keys and dominant/subdominant key-relatedness. The toroidal structures observed by Janata and his colleagues provide direct evidence of neurological adaptations to a particular musical environment.[29]

One final observation is worth highlighting from the work of Peter Janata and his colleagues. The observed toroidal structures were unique to each listener. Each listener's brain exhibited a toroidal pitch-class structure, but the precise organization differed from cortex to cortex. It was like looking at floor plans for houses. Each house might have a kitchen, living room, bathroom, and master bedroom, but the floor plans differed from house to house. These differences imply a unique learning path for each listener—consistent with the theory of neural Darwinism.

In this chapter I have introduced the subject of mental representation—principally by discussing pitch-related representations. Much of my discussion has centered on absolute pitch and interval. From time to time I have also alluded to the role of scale-degree representation, but without much in the way of detail. In chapter 9 we turn our attention exclusively to the phenomenon of scale degree. Scale degree is almost certainly the most musically important mental representation related to pitch for Western-enculturated listeners. But first, let's return to the subject of emotion.

A century ago, the German psychologist Max Meyer carried out a simple musical experiment. Meyer composed a set of short piano works that he described as "oriental-like" in style. He asked people to listen to these works and tell him how well they liked them. He then repeated each piece—each time asking his listeners to judge how well they liked what they heard. Meyer continued to repeat the works until his listeners had heard twelve performances of each composed piece. He found that listeners liked his pieces more, the more times he played them.[1]

The idea that people prefer the familiar is a long-standing piece of folk psychology. More than two thousand years before Max Meyer's experiment, Aristotle had already observed that familiar music sounds better than unfamiliar music, and wondered why this was so. Meyer's 1903 experiment is not alone. At least a dozen other experiments have also shown that the more listeners hear a piece of music, the more they like it.[2]

Most of us have an instinctive negative reaction against the idea that familiarity leads to increased liking. Surely if Max Meyer had continued to repeat his little compositions, there would be a point where his listeners became bored, irritated, or downright annoyed. Surely there is a point where "familiarity breeds contempt."

Before we get ahead of ourselves, it is helpful to trace the research legacy that followed from Max Meyer's observations. Over the past century, the experimental evidence in support of the general principle that "familiarity breeds liking" has become nothing short of monumental. Central to modern experimental efforts has been the American psychologist, Robert Zajonc. Zajonc (pronounced ZAH-yonts) carried out several experiments in the 1960s and 1970s that inspired many other researchers. Over two hundred experiments have been published concerning a phenomenon that Zajonc dubbed the *mere exposure effect*—often simplified to the *exposure effect*.[3]

Exposure Effect

People prefer familiar foods to unfamiliar foods, familiar smells to unfamiliar smells, familiar faces over unfamiliar faces, familiar words, familiar photographs, familiar objects, drawings, paintings, sounds, nonsense words—even familiar polygons and familiar Chinese characters over their unfamiliar counterparts. When people are shown photographs of themselves, they prefer the mirror images to the actual photo. That is, we prefer the version of ourselves that we regularly see in the mirror.[4] People also show a preference for the "average" face—suggesting that liking-the-familiar might generalize to classes of stimuli rather than being limited to particular tokens. A preference for the familiar is not limited to humans: ethologists have shown that all kinds of animals prefer familiar over less familiar stimuli.[5]

Some of these preferences might be explained by other plausible causes. For example, food normally evokes a positive limbic response, so a preference for familiar food might simply be explained by classical conditioning. Past experience conditions us to anticipate that eating a familiar food will be enjoyable. Novel foods are unable to evoke such positive associations. However, although classical conditioning might seem like a reasonable explanation for preferring the familiar, it accounts for only a small part of the effect. A preference for the familiar has been amply demonstrated, even when the possibility of conditioning has been eliminated through experimental control.

Despite this general tendency to prefer the familiar, there are some occasional discrepancies from this pattern in the research literature. For example, several studies seem to indicate that complex stimuli are rated as more pleasing than simple stimuli. And in some circumstances repeated stimuli have been rated by participants as less pleasing. However, these discrepancies disappear under a very telling condition.

The Role of Consciousness

An important discovery has been that the exposure effect is independent of stimulus recognition. Participants do not need to be consciously aware of which stimuli they have encountered before in order to show a preference for the most familiar.

Two techniques have been used to prevent participants from becoming consciously aware that some stimuli are more familiar than other stimuli. One technique involves subliminal presentation where visual stimuli are presented too quickly to register in consciousness. The second technique involves distracted presentation, where the stimuli are presented while the participant is attending to some other task.

Jennifer Monahan, Sheila Murphy, and Robert Zajonc, for example, exposed viewers to individual Chinese characters for just 5 milliseconds. Such presentations appear as a brief flash. When participants were asked to identify which images they had seen before in the experiment, their performance was at chance level—indicating that they were unable to identify whether or not they had seen the characters before. Nevertheless, when asked to judge which Chinese characters they preferred, participants showed a marked preference for those characters they had been exposed to most frequently. They preferred certain Chinese characters without knowing why.

In his comprehensive review of the research literature, Gettysburg College psychologist Robert Bornstein identified sixteen experiments involving subliminal or unattended presentation of the stimuli. All sixteen experiments showed that the exposure effect is independent of stimulus recognition.[6] In fact, studies using subliminal or unattended stimuli produce more robust exposure effects than studies that don't use these techniques. In Bornstein's meta-analysis of the studies on the exposure effect, he found a correlation of 0.34 for experiments where participants were able to recognize the stimuli, but a larger correlation of 0.53 for experiments where participants were unable to recognize the most frequent stimuli because they were presented subliminally. In other words, conscious recognition of the stimulus actually *inhibits* the exposure effect.[7]

John Kihlstrom has suggested that when participants are consciously aware of the stimuli, they are able to suppress or stifle their natural inclination to prefer the familiar. Bornstein has suggested a number of further "countercontrol" mechanisms and strategies that may account for the reduced impact of the exposure effect when participants are conscious of the manipulation of familiarity. It is as though we are offended by the thought that we will automatically prefer whatever the experimenter has most exposed us to.[8]

Two implications arise from this result. One is that conscious awareness of which stimuli occur most frequently may somehow encourage experimental participants to think about the stimuli, and therefore to use more complex cognitive and aesthetic strategies when forming their like/dislike responses. The possible interference from conscious thought is confirmed in a study by Thomas Burgess and Stephen Sales, who found that participants who reported negative feelings about the experiment in general showed no exposure effect.[9] This suggests that some participants consciously counteract the tendency to prefer familiar stimuli in their responses. Said another way, it is only when participants are consciously aware of the fact that some stimuli occur more often than others that they will respond in a manner that suggests they prefer novelty over familiarity.

A second (related) implication is that the exposure effect originates in the "fast" brain rather than the "slow" brain. That is, the tendency to prefer frequently occurring stimuli is primarily a function of fast, unconscious, reflex-like processing. The exposure effect is most apparent when the slower (cortical) brain is taken out of the loop—that is, when conscious mental processing is disrupted or distracted.

Further evidence in support of this automatic aspect of the exposure effect is found in studies where a time delay is introduced between the stimulus exposure period and the testing of stimulus preferences. Following a delay of several days or weeks, the exposure effect becomes *stronger*. Interestingly, this strengthening can also be observed in the small number of participants who, for experiments involving nonsubliminal presentation, report a preference for the more novel stimuli: if a delay of days or weeks is introduced, these same participants will exhibit a preference for those stimuli that occurred most frequently during the exposure phase. As Bornstein properly notes, the effect of delay in strengthening the exposure effect implicates the role of long-term memory and supports the idea that the exposure effect arises from automatic unconscious learning.[10]

Auditory Exposure Effect

While most of the experiments related to the exposure effect have used visual stimuli, several experiments have shown that the same phenomenon can be observed with purely auditory stimuli.[11] In one of the Moreland and Zajonc early experiments, tones of different pitches were used. As in the case of the visual stimuli, listeners were unable to distinguish which pitches they had been exposed to previously. Nevertheless, they showed a distinct preference for the most frequently occurring pitches.

For music theorists, the finding that the most frequently occurring pitch is preferred by listeners does not seem especially impressive. Music theory provides a seemingly more congenial explanation. Listeners will tend to assume that the most frequently heard pitch is the tonic. Listeners "like" these tones because they hear them as tonics, not because they like more familiar pitches. Many music theorists are likely to regard the exposure effect as too simplistic, whereas *tonality* provides a richer and more satisfying explanation for these preferences. We will pick up this debate again in chapter 9.

As in the case of visual stimuli, research using auditory stimuli has also confirmed the inhibiting role of conscious awareness on the exposure effect. Unlike visual images, it is difficult to present sounds as "subliminal" stimuli. Nevertheless, William Wilson was able to devise an experimental method that allowed him to reduce the possibility of conscious attending. Specifically, Wilson employed a distractor task to draw listeners' attention away from the pitch sequences. Wilson employed a so-called *dichotic* listening task where the left and right ears heard different sounds. Tone sequences were presented to one ear and spoken language was simultaneously presented to the other ear. Participants received a transcript of a spoken story, which they read aloud in unison with the recorded speaker. However, the text and speaker often diverged, and participants were required to identify all of the errors in the printed text as the task continued. As you might imagine, this task proved to be very effective in forcing participants to ignore the melodies heard in the other ear. When later asked to identify which melodies they had heard during the exposure phase, participants performed at a chance level.

Despite the distractor task, Wilson's listeners exhibited a clear preference for those melodies they had heard during the exposure phase. That is, entire melodies were preferred in a manner analogous to individual tones.[12] In the next chapter we will consider in greater detail the relationship between the exposure effect and music. In particular, we will ask whether the exposure effect or tonality provides a better account of the observations. At this point, we might note that one of the advantages of the exposure effect over tonality is that the exposure effect also explains why groups of pitches and whole melodies are preferred by listeners—not just isolated tones.

You might expect that with continued exposure, at some point, the exposure effect would disappear or reverse itself. However, the experimental research doesn't support these intuitions. The exposure effect continues to strengthen with each stimulus presentation. A single exposure has the greatest impact on whether participants will prefer that stimulus over other stimuli. Each additional repetition tends to increase the preference, but the amount of increase gets progressively smaller. After about thirty repetitions, the increase in preference can become very small. Nevertheless, continuing to present the stimulus still results in an increased liking.[13]

Origin of the Exposure Effect

Where does the exposure effect come from? What possible benefit is conferred by experiencing familiar stimuli as pleasant? Why is there a general tendency to prefer commonplace sounds and images?

Two theories concerning the exposure effect have been proposed. Robert Zajonc's own explanation for the exposure effect is that familiar stimuli reduce the likelihood of orienting responses, and that this reduces an organism's arousal level. The result is a more relaxed state—which is experienced as more pleasant.[14] In effect, familiarity gives us the luxury of paying less attention to the world. Familiar stimuli allow us to lower our guard. According to Zajonc's theory, familiarity is the path to contentment.

A second theory has been offered by Robert Bornstein and Paul D'Agostino, who argue that when we perceive a familiar stimulus, we misinterpret the ease of processing as a good stimulus. This is known as the "perceptual fluency/attributional" theory.[15] My own theory can be viewed as a direct offshoot of the Bornstein and D'Agostino theory. But before I present my account, it is helpful to discuss another well-known psychological phenomenon, *misattribution*.

Misattribution

In the early 1970s, Donald Dutton and Arthur Aron from the University of British Columbia carried out a famous experiment on two foot-bridges at the beautiful

Capilano canyon north of Vancouver. In this study, male university students were brought to the canyon. Each participant was shown a photograph and asked to tell a story related to the picture. As explained to the participants, the ostensible purpose of the research was to study the effect of the natural environment on creativity. The experimenter was an attractive female graduate student.

The Dutton and Aron experiment entailed two conditions. In one condition, the participant crossed the Capilano foot-bridge—a wood and cable suspension foot-bridge that wobbles and sways wildly. I have walked across this bridge and can vouch for the fact that the great height and constant swaying make for a memorable experience—not everyone would willingly walk across this bridge. In the control condition, the location of the experiment was changed so that participants crossed a nearby solid concrete bridge. At the end of the experiment, the female experimenter offered the male participants her home telephone number and said they were welcome to call her if they had any questions about the experiment.

The dependent measure for this experiment will come as a surprise to most readers: Dutton and Aron wanted to know how many of the participating men would telephone the female experimenter in order to ask her out for a date! Those participants who had walked across the suspension bridge were significantly more likely to contact the experimenter and ask her for a date than those participants who had walked across the nearby concrete bridge.

The most popular interpretation of this experiment is that the men crossing the foot-bridge experienced increased physiological arousal due to the vertigo. This limbic response was then consciously or unconsciously misconstrued by the participants. Looking at a beautiful woman, the men were more likely to interpret their state as one of infatuation rather than one of vertigo. That is, the cause of the physiological arousal was *misattributed*. Although this particular experimental design was challenged by other researchers, a subsequent flurry of research has established that misattribution is commonplace. Activation of the limbic system can often lead to incorrect attributions of the cause—resulting in indiscriminant or arbitrary associations.

In general, research has shown that whenever we experience a strong emotion, the brain has a tendency to associate the emotional state with whatever salient stimuli exist in the environment. The net is cast quite widely.[16]

Expectation, Misattribution, and the Exposure Effect

Why does misattribution occur? Linking an emotion to the wrong cause is an obvious recipe for disaster. What possible benefit is there in misattributing vertigo to love? How has misattribution survived the sharp scalpel of natural selection? Why does Nature tolerate such blatant misconstruals of the world?

Positive and negative emotions are important motivators that help organisms learn. Suppose I am robbed in a dark alley. I experience highly negative emotions whose purpose is to encourage me to avoid similar situations in the future. But what, precisely, is the lesson I should learn? Should I learn to avoid dark alleys? Should I avoid encounters with other people? Should I avoid walking on concrete sidewalks? Should I avoid eating a sandwich for lunch? Should I avoid people wearing balaclavas? Once again, we are faced with the problem of induction: what general principle can one infer from a finite number of observations? Moreover, since such highly emotionally charged events tend to be rare, what can one reasonably learn from just *one* observational event?

Whenever we make an inference from observation, we can make two kinds of errors. One error is that we falsely conclude that X is the cause of Y (when in fact, X is not the cause of Y). Methodologists call this a Type I error, or *false positive error*. Alternatively, we might falsely conclude that X is not the cause of Y (when in fact, X is indeed the cause of Y). This is a Type II error, or *false negative error*.

Most scientists would tell us that no conclusion is possible from a single observation. They would recommend that we try to collect further data. They would eschew any conclusion because there would be a high probability of making a false positive error. But ordinary living does not allow the luxury of waiting for more observations. We might simply throw up our hands and conclude that "no conclusion is possible." But this means we would learn nothing from isolated incidents.

In real life, Nature is willing to pay the price of possible Type I errors by nevertheless jumping to a conclusion. In fact, in order to try to learn some useful lesson, Nature jumps to *many* conclusions. Nature addresses the problem of learning by casting a very wide net. When we experience strong emotions, we tend to remember many details about the experience. A person trapped in a crashed automobile will tend to retain vivid memories of the crash site, the face of the ambulance attendant, and the music playing on the car radio. Research on misattribution has established that we tend to associate strong emotional experiences with all salient perceptual cues (time of day, facial features, manner of speaking, location, colors, etc.). Since the experience is highly charged, it is better to draw excessively broad conclusions (which have a better chance of catching a true cue) than to draw narrow lessons (which have a high chance of failing to capture a pertinent cue).

In other words, misattribution is a predictable consequence of the problem of induction. In trying to ensure that we learn a useful lesson, our minds tolerate learning all sorts of wrong lessons as well. Misattribution is the price we pay for trying to draw conclusions from small amounts of information.

Since learning is most likely to occur when we experience emotions, misattribution is emotion's constant companion. Whenever emotions are evoked, the potential for misattribution arises. In chapter 1, I introduced the five emotional components of the ITPRA theory. Recall that the five response types are the *imagination* response (where a foretaste of possible future emotions occurs), the *tension* response (where arousal and attention are tailored to anticipated outcomes), the *prediction* response (where predictive accuracy is rewarded), the *reaction* response (where a quick defensive response is initiated), and the *appraisal* response (where a leisurely assessment of the final state leads to encouraging or discouraging reinforcement).

In musical melodies, the most common event is a pitched tone. As individual tones, one tone is pretty much the same as another. There is nothing inherently more pleasant about the pitch G4 versus F4. Consequently, the *appraisal* of these states will be virtually identical. What can differentiate G4 from F4 in a melody is their predictability. One tone might be highly expected, while the other tone is highly unexpected. For individual tones, the strongest emotional responses will relate to the *prediction response*.

Whenever emotions are activated, misattribution is not far away. I contend that this is the situation with the prediction response. When a listener accurately predicts some stimulus, misattribution is ready to pin the positive emotion onto any convenient bystander. Similarly, when a listener fails to predict some stimulus, misattribution is ready to spread the blame.

So who are these innocent bystanders? The answer is the stimulus itself. There is nothing inherently pleasant about the pitch G4. But if a listener predicted the occurrence of G4, then the tone itself is likely to be experienced as pleasant. In effect, the prediction response says "congratulations for predicting the pitch G4." The real prize ought to go exclusively to the mental circuit that succeeded in making the correct prediction. But misattribution also tacks the warm positive feelings onto the stimulus itself. The result is that G4 "sounds nice." Conversely, if we unexpectedly hear the pitch F4, the prediction response is negatively valenced. We ought simply to feel some element of discomfort for failing to predict this stimulus. But instead, misattribution spreads the blame to include the most salient stimulus in the environment—the tone itself. As a result, the unpredicted F4 "sounds bad."

In response to the question of why listeners are sensitive to the frequency of occurrence of different events, I have offered a straightforward answer: because it increases the listener's ability to predict the future. If we ask what is the most likely future event? Our best prediction is: the most frequently occurring past event. The combination of the *prediction response* and *misattribution* now allows us to offer a plausible explanation as to why commonly occurring stimuli would evoke a positively valenced emotional response.

If my account is correct, then it is not frequency of occurrence per se that accounts for the experience of pleasure, but sure and accurate prediction. That is, the pleasure of the exposure effect is not a phenomenon of "mere exposure" or "familiarity." It is accurate prediction that is rewarded—and then misattributed to the stimulus. If the view I have offered here is right, then "exposure effect" is a poor label for this phenomenon. A more appropriate label would be the "prediction effect."

My proposal that the relationship between exposure and affect is a consequence of prediction rather than exposure can easily be tested experimentally. Imagine a sequence of stimuli where the stimulus *A* is more common than other stimuli. However, the appearance of stimulus *A* is random, and so not predictable using any contextual cues. Now suppose that we add two less common stimuli: *B* and *C*. The appearance of stimulus *B* is always followed immediately by stimulus *C*. My prediction is that participants will tend to judge stimulus *C* more positively than stimulus *A*—even though stimulus *A* occurs more frequently than *C*. A "prediction effect" would imply that the more predictable stimulus *C* would be preferred; a "mere exposure effect" would imply that the more familiar stimulus *A* should be judged more positively.

As we will see in the next chapter, a natural form of this experiment has already been carried out on a massive scale. In Western tonality, the dominant pitch is the most frequently occurring scale degree; however, the tonic pitch—when it occurs in a predictable cadential context—is judged by listeners as evoking the greater pleasure.

Repetition Effect

Further support for the prediction effect as the underlying cause of the exposure effect can be found by comparing results from experiments using repeated visual stimuli with the results from experiments using repeated auditory stimuli. In Western melodies, unisons are less common than changes of pitch. That is to say, it is more common for a tone to be followed by a subsequent tone that differs in pitch. Given this pattern, one might predict that experienced listeners would generally expect a change of pitch rather than a repetition. In his reaction-time experiments, Bret Aarden found this to be the case: listeners are slower to respond to unisons than to other intervals.[17]

This result appears to conflict with research in vision. In reaction-time studies using visual stimuli, researchers have reported a facilitating effect for immediate repetition. That is, viewers are faster to respond to successive repeated visual images.[18] This has been reported as a hypothetical "repetition effect." If such an effect exists, then why don't we observe a "repetition effect" when listening to tones in melodies? Two points are pertinent here. First, in everyday vision, most images are followed by nearly identical images (think of the successive frames of a motion picture film). At any given moment in time, the image you see is very similar to the image you saw a second ago. When our brains parse a visual scene, that resulting information helps us parse the visual scene at the next moment in time. By contrast, the essence of both speech and music is dynamic change. Without this moment-to-moment fluctuation, speech and music would fail to be very communicative. It may be that the real-world contrast between relatively static visual signals and relatively dynamic auditory signals accounts for the observed differences in the so-called repetition effect.

Second, in visual experiments, typically the arrangement of successive images is random or nearly random. Such random sequences are alien to most viewers' experience. Viewers of these image sequences have no pertinent dynamic-visual schemas to draw upon when predicting the next image. This is quite contrary to the case of listening to melodies where listeners have extensive pertinent schematic experience to draw on. Bret Aarden has proposed that the "repetition effect" is mislabeled in the visual tasks. He has proposed that it is more parsimonious to regard the observations as arising from enhanced prediction.[19] In melodies, pitch repetitions are less likely than pitch changes, so we observe faster reaction times when pitches are *not* repeated. In random sequences of visual images, viewers have no useful expectations—except zeroth-order probabilities of the preceding images. In these contexts, the best prediction is the preceding image—hence we observe facilitation due to repetition.

Predictable Music

The foregoing discussion would seem to raise an unsettling problem. If predictable stimuli lead to positively valenced responses, then wouldn't the most enjoyable music be entirely predictable—utterly banal? Wouldn't the most pleasurable music avoid all novelty? The idea that good music should exhibit extreme predictability seems implausible—even offensive. Surely boredom would set in.

First, remember that we are not defining "good" music. We are simply discussing *one* mechanism by which pleasure may be evoked. Second, proposing that predictability evokes pleasure does not preclude the existence of other psychological phenomena that tend to limit the effect of repetition. For example, independent or interrelated brain mechanisms might exist that reward novelty, or reward novelty-seeking behaviors, or punish boredom, or reward boredom-avoiding behaviors. Physiologists have long known, for example, that simply repeating a stimulus leads to *habituation:* a desensitization that reduces the magnitude of the response.

Finally, the prediction response is only one component of the ITPRA theory. Recall that the ITPRA theory proposes that post-outcome responses can be divided into three types: *prediction, reaction,* and *appraisal.* What I have called the "prediction effect" pertains only to the prediction response. When music is highly predictable, I propose that the prediction responses are indeed dominated by positively valenced limbic responses. The prediction response serves the biologically essential function of rewarding and reinforcing those neural circuits that have successfully anticipated the ensuing events. However, the reaction and appraisal responses need not be so sanguine when encountering such banal music.

Music that is highly predictable can be "unpleasant" in a number of ways. A loud dissonant sound may evoke a negatively valenced reactive response, even though its occurrence is entirely expected. At the same time, a saccharine-sweet musical passage might lead to a negative cognitive appraisal—especially if we feel that we are being treated as musical children. The fact that the prediction response is positively valenced doesn't mean that the reaction and appraisal responses must also be positive.

The overall emotional effect can also depend on the interaction between different responses. Many of the most exciting and memorable moments in music arise from surprise. In chapter 2, I described three flavors of surprise—leading to laughter, frisson, and awe. I argued that the pleasures associated with such surprises originate in a contrastive limbic valence. Later, in chapter 14, we will see concrete musical examples of these forms of surprise. Without predictable norms, it would be impossible to arrange the sort of deviant phenomena that make such pleasant surprises possible.

These caveats notwithstanding, it is important to understand that, all other things being equal, predictability, by itself, will be experienced as pleasant. The easiest path to predictability is through repetition. In this regard, music amply fits the bill. In chapter 13, we will review studies that measure the amount of repetition in music. For music scholars who have learned to focus on novelty, the results will be shocking. We will see that there is probably no other stimulus in common human experience that matches the extreme repetitiveness of music.

Reprise

In this chapter, I have reviewed some of the literature related to the "mere exposure effect." In general, people (and animals) prefer familiar over unfamiliar stimuli. This tendency to prefer the familiar is most clearly observed when people are not consciously aware of the relative novelty or familiarity of different stimuli. Conscious thought tends to obscure the effect, which suggests that the exposure effect originates in an unconscious, reflex-like process.

I have suggested that "exposure effect" is a misnomer, and that a more parsimonious account lies in prediction: fast minds prefer stimuli that are predictable. If accurate prediction is rewarded, and if emotions are susceptible to misattribution, then it is easy to see how a limbic reward for accurate prediction might spill over so that the stimulus itself is experienced in a positive (or negative) manner.

In the following two chapters, I will focus on two classes of schematic structures whose predictability create opportunities for both the pleasure arising from accurate prediction and the contrastive valence arising from innocuous surprises. These two classes of auditory schema are commonly known as *tonality* and *meter*.

9 Tonality

The word "tonality" has been used by musicians in a wide variety of senses. One simple definition of tonality is a system for interpreting pitches or chords through their relationship to a reference pitch, dubbed the *tonic*. Once the tonic is established, the relationship of this pitch to other pitches can be designated using scale-degree names or numbers.[1] Each scale degree evokes a different psychological quality or character. As we saw earlier, by an act of will, musicians can imagine a single tone as either the leading-tone, the submediant, the dominant, and so on. The ability of listeners to imagine a single tone as serving different tonal functions indicates that scale degrees are *cognitive* rather than *perceptual* phenomena. That is, "scale degree" is how minds interpret physically sounding tones, not how tones are in the world.

The phenomenon of tonality is one of the most venerable topics in the field of music theory. Many Western theorists would consider tonality to be *the* principal theoretical foundation in Western music. It is a subject that has attracted sustained and detailed scholarly attention, especially over the past century.[2] Some theorists restrict the idea of tonality to the specifics of the Western major/minor scale system. Other theorists view tonality as a more embracing concept that can be observed equally in the scale systems of non-Western cultures. For most theorists, tonality evokes thoughts of cadences, modulations, thematic key areas, and long-term key closure. For many Western theorists, tonality represents a deep organizational principle that shapes a vast array of musical details. At the same time, a number of composers have endeavored to either challenge, expand, overthrow, or ignore the concept of tonality (e.g., Claude Debussy, Arnold Schoenberg, Edgar Varèse, Henry Cowell, Harry Partch). Within art-music circles, tonality has been variously viewed as an essential musical foundation or as an oppressive monopoly that has restricted the creative enterprise of music.

In parallel with the work of music scholars, tonality has also been the subject of considerable interest among psychologists. Dozens of experimental studies related to tonality have been carried out, especially in the past three decades.[3] Much of the psychologically inspired research has focused on how listeners infer the key of some passage or sequence of tones.

The subject of tonality has such rich connotations for music theorists that my discussion here is necessarily partial. Although I have entitled this chapter "Tonality," my ambition here is rather narrow. My principal goal is to account for the various feelings evoked by different scale degrees. Philosophers use the word *quale* to refer to the subjective feelings that accompany sensory experiences.[4] When I touch a glass object, for example, I experience a distinctive sensation of smoothness and coolness mixed with pleasure. No words can communicate the actual feeling—the feelings are ineffable and private. But you can draw on your own experiences and so imagine how it feels to touch a glass object. *Qualia* accompany all consciously experienced sensations, including the sensation of sounds. When I hear an isolated leading-tone, I experience a strong sense of precariousness or instability mixed with some urgency and accompanied by feelings of yearning or aspiring upward. That is, the leading-tone evokes a striking and distinctive *quale*. In this chapter, I propose to explain how scale tones might acquire their unique psychological characteristics.

Scale Degree *Qualia*

For listeners experienced with Western music, each scale tone appears to evoke a different psychological flavor or feeling. A simple *qualia* survey illustrates the point. I asked ten experienced Western-enculturated musicians to describe the different scale degrees for the major key. Each musician received the following instruction:

For each of the following scale degrees describe as best you can the distinctive quality or character of that tone. Describe how the tone makes you feel in as much detail as possible. Imagine the tones for the major key only. Please think of pitches rather than chords.

Asking musicians to perform a task like this makes a lot of assumptions. The task assumes that isolated tones are able to evoke *qualia* independent of some musical context. It assumes that musicians can introspect about such matters without actually hearing the sounds. The task assumes that language can be used to express the ineffable qualities people experience. The survey is also limited to the major scale with no consideration of the various minor scales.

A summary of my survey results is given in table 9.1. The first column identifies the scale degree—tonic, supertonic, and so on. The second column identifies the most frequent words and themes given in the participants' descriptions. Some sample responses from the participants are provided in the third column.

In reading the various descriptions offered by my survey particants, one is immediately struck by the richness of the descriptions. Many of the descriptions are

Table 9.1

Scale tone	Common descriptors	Sample responses
tonic	stable, pleasure, home, contentment	stable, extremely satisfying, centered, foundational, solid, resolved, strong
raised tonic	strong, upward, bold	edgy, unstable, uncertain, upwardly mobile, mildly precarious
lowered supertonic	surprise, abruptness, pause	somewhat dark, a sense of almost inevitable further descent, murky, unexpected richness, mild surprise
supertonic	solid, movement, resolve	hanging, dangling, transitory, moderate expectancy of more to come, part of a flow
raised supertonic	longing, unstable	needling, moderately harsh, jarring, unstable, off-balance
mediant	bright, love, warmth, beauty	light, lifted, bright, point of many possible departures, yet also strongly restful, peaceful and calm
subdominant	descending	awkward, tentative, strong sense of being unfinished, "Now what?" no clear expectation of future, hanging feeling, would be happy to fall by half step
raised subdominant	intentional, motivated	moderately anxious, interrupted flow to dominant, somewhat curious about possibilities, fluidity, transitory
dominant	strong, muscular, balance, possibility, pleasant	strong, towering, height, sense of looking down from a tall building and being comfortable, but knowing you'll eventually take the elevator back to the street level
raised dominant	leading, aspiring	leading to something, sense of implication, unfinished, leaning, mildly uncomfortable
submediant	balance, open, lightness	airy and open, temporary suspendedness, neutral, evokes mild curiosity in regard to direction
subtonic	falling, lightness drifting downward, shifting	heavy, like walking with a limp, unexpected, open new possibilities, sheds a new light on things
leading tone	unstable, pointing, restless	sense of inevitability, highly unstable, uncomfortable, squirmy, itching, restless

delightfully poetic. In responding to the survey, my participants did not simply offer abstract formal characterizations or bald statements of fact. Instead, the descriptive language of their responses is imbued with a sensitivity and nuance that suggests that musicians think something important is being addressed—something musical.

Another striking result is the remarkable level of agreement evident in many characterizations. For example, seven of the ten participants used the word "unstable" in describing the leading-tone. Six of the ten participants used the word "bright" in describing the mediant pitch. All of the participants associated the tonic with pleasure, satisfaction, or contentment.

To be sure, there were several discrepancies evident. For example, one participant described the subtonic (lowered leading-tone) as "light" whereas a second participant described this same pitch as "heavy." The dominant pitch was described as both "stable" and "unstable." However, overall, such discrepancies were the exception: the descriptions showed a relatively high level of agreement.

So where do these *qualia* come from? What accounts for the different feelings described by my survey participants? Since the participants were all trained musicians, it is possible that the reported *qualia* simply reflect what musicians learn through formal training. That is, it is possible that these descriptions merely echo textbook descriptions rather than genuine subjective feelings. While this account is possible, I don't think it is likely. Apart from Deryck Cook's 1959 book, *The Language of Music*, I don't know of any books that include material akin to the information in table 9.1.[5] In order to reassure myself that these descriptions aren't merely the delusions of musicians, I recruited two nonmusician friends for an informal experiment. I played a key-defining context on the piano and then played a particular scale tone. They were given descriptions of three different scale tones, one of which was the tone in question. I repeated this with eleven of the thirteen tones described in table 9.1. With only a few errors, my nonmusician friends were quite accurate in selecting which *qualia* description went with which tone.

So what accounts for these shared *qualia*? A helpful starting point is to examine the descriptions in detail and see if we can decipher some patterns. Working from a complete list of words used in the musicians' descriptions, I clustered together similar terms, including synonyms and antonyms. My respondents used a large number of metaphors to describe their feelings, including lightness/darkness, open/closed, rising/falling, irritation/comfort, and so on. However, seven semantic categories seem to account for most of the descriptions. My seven categories include (1) certainty/uncertainty, (2) tendency, (3) completion, (4) mobility, (5) stability, (6) power, and (7) emotion. Let's take a moment to illustrate each of these categories.

My first proposed category pertains to *certainty/uncertainty*. In my sample of scale-degree descriptions, obvious *certainty/uncertainty* words included "inevitable," "unexpected," "surprise," "abrupt," "many possible departures," and "now what?"

The second semantic category has to do with sequential *tendency*. For example, most of the participants described the raised tonic as "upward tending." Sample descriptive terms included "tending," "leading," "leaning," "pointing," "upward," and "downward." Other words that might be included in this category are "longing," "motivated," "falling," and "intentional."

The third category might be dubbed *completion*. Sample words included "unfinished," "hanging," "dangling," and "transitory," as well as "resolved," "home," "finished," and "complete."

The fourth category appears to relate to *mobility*. Sample words included "movement," "repose," "flow," "fluidity," and "drifting."

The fifth category relates to *stability*. For example, eight of the ten participants described the tonic pitch as "stable." Other stability/instability words included "balance," "precarious," "solid," "foundational," "squirmy," "restless," "transitory," and "unstable."

The sixth category relates to *power*. Power words included "muscular," "heavy," "towering," "energized," "bold," "light," and "delicate."

The final category appears to relate to emotional valence—that is, words indicating positive or negative feelings. *Emotion*-related words included "pleasure," "love," "calm," "satisfying," "contentment," and "beauty." Negative assessments are evident in words such as "edgy," "anxious," "harsh," "jarring," "itching," and "uncomfortable."

Later in this chapter we will return to these *qualia* descriptions and attempt to identify some possible origins. At this juncture, we might simply note that scale degrees are wonderfully evocative. Given a particular key context, a simple pitched tone seems to be capable of evoking a cornucopia of psychological impressions or feelings. Moreover, these feelings are not merely idiosyncratic to different listeners: Western-enculturated listeners appear to experience broadly similar *qualia*.

Statistics of Scale Degrees

In the preceding chapters I have presented evidence implicating statistical learning for pitch-related sequences. For at least some phenomena, listeners are sensitive to the frequency of occurrence of sounds. Can simple statistical learning somehow account for the *qualia* evoked by different scale degrees? Can we account for the feelings listeners experience by understanding the statistical patterns evident in the music itself?

At first, this question seems not just simple-minded, but utterly moronic. How can the poetic qualities evoked by different scale degrees arise from the prosaic world of mere numbers? Here readers will have to bear with me. Whatever misgivings we may have about this approach, we can at least be reassured that no statistical fact or argument can change how we, as listeners, experience different scale degrees. When

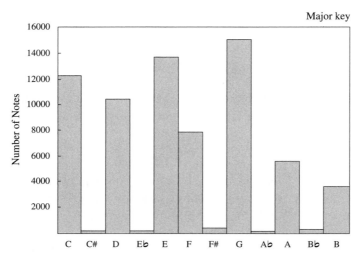

Figure 9.1

Distribution of scale tones for a large sample of melodies in major keys (>65,000 notes). All works were transposed so the tonic pitch is C; all pitches are enharmonic. Modulating passages were excluded. From Aarden 2003.

biologists tell us that *love* is nature's way of promoting pair-bonding and procreation, this does not render the experience of love any less beautiful, profound, or passionate. If we are ever able to understand how music works, music will not suddenly cease to be beautiful because of this knowledge.

An obvious place to begin is to consider the simple *event frequencies* for scale degrees. Like pitches, not all scale degrees occur with the same frequency. My collaborator, Bret Aarden, has tabulated scale-degree distributions based on a large sample of musical melodies. Figures 9.1 and 9.2 show the frequency of occurrence of scale tones for works in major keys (first graph) and for minor keys (second graph). For convenience, both graphs are normalized by transposing all works so the tonic pitch is C.[6]

For both major and minor keys, the most common pitch is the fifth scale degree (dominant). In the major key, the second and third most common pitches are scale degrees three (mediant) and one (tonic). In the minor key, the order of the tonic and mediant is reversed with the tonic occurring more frequently than the mediant. In both major and minor keys, scale degrees four and two are next most common, followed by scale degrees six and seven. The nonscale or chromatic tones occur least frequently.

The major and minor distributions shown in figures 9.1 and 9.2 are not merely artifacts from averaging a large number of musical works. Most individual (Western) musical works exhibit very similar distributions to those shown here. In fact, the

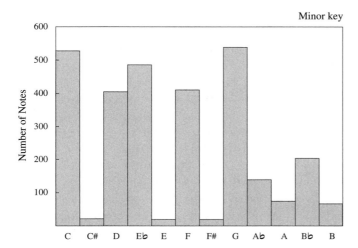

Figure 9.2
Distribution of scale tones for a large sample of melodies in minor keys (>25,000 notes). All works were transposed so the tonic pitch is C; all pitches are enharmonic. Modulating passages were excluded. From Aarden 2003.

scale-degree distributions are sufficiently stable that one can use them to predict the key of individual musical works.

Working at Cornell University, psychologists Carol Krumhansl and Mark Schmuckler devised a useful key-determination method based on distributions similar to those shown here. The Krumhansl–Schmuckler method simply tabulates the number of occurrences (or alternatively, the total duration) of the different pitch-classes evident in a musical work or passage. This distribution of pitch-classes is then correlated with the major and minor distributions for all possible keys; the highest correlation is used as an estimate of the tonic and mode (e.g., G minor). For example, when applied to the 48 fugues from J. S. Bach's *The Well-Tempered Clavier* the method successfully identifies the conventional key designations for 46 of the 48 works.[7] The average correlation between the works and the distributions given in figures 9.1 and 9.2 is an impressive +0.92.[8]

Such high correlations turn out to be typical.[9] In fact, the values for the fugues in *The Well-Tempered Clavier* are understated because these works include passages that modulate to other keys. For musical passages that do not modulate, the correlations are even higher.

Evidently, the distributions shown in figures 9.1 and 9.2 capture some stable and ubiquitous pattern in ordinary Western tonal music. If the biological goal of expectation is to make accurate predictions about the future, then one might suppose that good listeners would internalize these distributions and use them to make predictions about future pitches. If a listener is asked to guess what scale degree she is about to hear, in the absence of any other information, the best guess would be the *dominant.*

As we saw in chapter 6, it is important to test whether listeners really do take advantage of a particular feature of musical organization. So do listeners use distributions like those in the above figures to form expectations? In an ingenious set of experiments, Bret Aarden showed that listeners' expectations conform to the distributions shown in figures 9.1 and 9.2.[10] Aarden established this in a reaction-time study where listeners were asked to judge the up/down/same pitch-movement in various unfamiliar melodies. As we have already noted, when listeners correctly anticipate an ensuing note, this is reflected in a faster reaction time. When the data were collapsed according to scale degree, Aarden found that average reaction times are inversely proportional to the frequency of occurrence. That is, listeners are faster when responding to scale degrees that occur more frequently in Western music.

It is important to understand that these results are independent of the local melodic context in which the notes appear. Whether the contour goes up or down or remains level, listeners are generally faster at responding to the dominant pitch (for example) than the mediant pitch. Similarly, listeners are slower (on average) to respond to the sixth and seventh scale degrees no matter what the melodic context. The slowest reaction times are those that involve the nonscale tones.

In chapter 6 we saw that the expectations listeners form are often imperfect approximations of the actual musical structures. But in the case of the scale-degree distributions, Aarden found that listeners' expectations are pretty well on the mark. As in the case of pitch proximity expectations, listeners have the right idea when it comes to scale degree.

Bret Aarden's work provides excellent empirical support for a theory first proposed by Carol Krumhansl. Krumhansl suggested that tonal schemas are learned through exposure to music from a given culture or genre. Specifically, Krumhansl suggested that one of the primary factors influencing tonality perception is the simple frequency of occurrence of different tones.[11]

Key Profiles

Readers already familiar with the existing music cognition research will have found the above description unorthodox. I have essentially restated the theoretical position advocated by Carol Krumhansl, but without using any of her experimental results. Why?

In the early 1980s, Carol Krumhansl and Ed Kessler exposed listeners to a key-defining context, such as an ascending scale followed by a cadential harmonic progres-

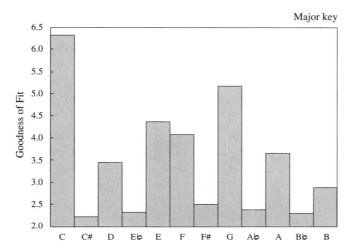

Figure 9.3

Krumhansl–Kessler "key profile" for major context. From Krumhansl and Kessler 1982.

sion. They then played an isolated probe tone, and asked listeners to rate how well the tone fit with the preceding context. They repeated this task using all twelve pitch-classes and applied this procedure for both the major and minor key contexts. Their results are shown in figures 9.3 and 9.4.[12]

For a number of years, it was recognized that the Krumhansl–Kessler key profiles are similar—but not identical—to the frequency of occurrence for scale degrees in the actual music. In her landmark 1990 book, Krumhansl argued that this similarity impli-cates learning-from-exposure. The psychological schemas for the major and minor key profiles are cognitive reflections of an objective statistical regularity in Western musical practice. Unfortunately, the evidence seemed imperfect. As we have seen, the domi-nant is the most frequently occurring pitch in both the major and minor modes, yet the Krumhansl and Kessler profiles consistently rate the tonic higher than the domi-nant. In addition, the second and fourth scale degrees (supertonic and subdominant) are rated significantly less highly than the actual presence of these tones would suggest. Why do the Krumhansl–Kessler "key profile" distributions differ from the pitch-class distributions of the music itself?

The problem was resolved in my laboratory by Bret Aarden.[13] As we noted in chapter 3, the probe-tone method used by Krumhansl and Kessler requires that the musical passage stop. When the listener judges "goodness of fit" there is the danger that the judgment will be confounded by perceptual *closure*. Instead of judging how well the tone fits with the preceding tones, the listener's judgment might be influenced by whether the tone represents a good place to stop.

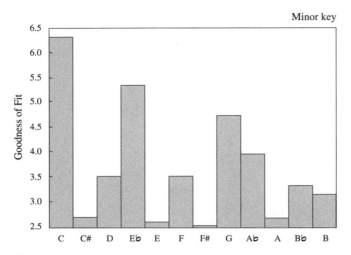

Figure 9.4
Krumhansl–Kessler "key profile" for minor context. From Krumhansl and Kessler 1982.

Aarden resolved this issue as follows. First, he collected a large sample of musical works and determined the distribution of scale degrees that *end* musical phrases. As you might expect, many phrase endings tend to involve tones from the tonic triad. In major keys, the most common phrase-terminating pitch is the tonic, followed by the dominant, followed by the mediant. In minor keys the mediant occurs more frequently than the dominant, but the tonic remains foremost. What if listeners form an independent "closure schema"? That is, what if listeners internalize a scale-degree schema that is explicitly linked to points of musical closure?

To test this idea, Aarden carried out another reaction-time experiment in which he collected data only for the last note in a melodic phrase. Listeners heard eighty phrases from unfamiliar folk melodies and watched a numerical counter count down the number of notes remaining before the end of the phrase. The purpose of the counter was to abolish any uncertainty of when the phrase ended. When the phrase-terminating note appeared (count zero), listeners made a single response to the pitch contour (up/down/same) as quickly as possible. Aarden found a very high correlation between the average reaction times and the frequency of occurrence of *phrase-final tones*. Listeners were faster when responding to scale degrees that occur most frequently as the terminal pitches in a phrase. Aarden's listeners were fastest when the phrase ended on the tonic. In major key contexts, they were next fastest when responding to the dominant pitch, and so forth. At the same time, Aarden found that average reaction times correlated much more weakly with the general frequency of occurrence of various scale degrees. That is, the phrase-final reaction times correlated weakly with the pitch distributions shown in figures 9.1 and 9.2.

Aarden's results suggest that listeners experienced with Western music maintain at least *four* different expectational schemas for scale degrees. Two schemas are associated with the simple frequency of occurrence for scale degrees in major and minor key contexts. Two further schemas are associated with the simple frequency of occurrence for scale degrees as phrase-final tones—one for the major key context and another for the minor key context. To these four schemas we might add a fifth: the schema used by listeners to predict what scale degree initiates a melody, as discussed in chapter 4. (In this latter case, no distinction is made between major and minor, since the mode is ambiguous for the first pitch in an unknown melody.)

If it is truly the case that the probe-tone method is confounded by closure, then we might predict that the discrepancies between the Krumhansl–Kessler key profiles and the actual distribution of scale degrees in music will be accounted for by the "closure distributions" assembled by Aarden. Aarden showed that the Krumhansl–Kessler key profiles are very close approximations of the actual distribution of phrase-terminating pitches. Using a multiple regression analysis, Aarden further showed that the residual difference between the Krumhansl–Kessler key profiles and the phrase-terminating pitches is accounted for by the general scale-degree distribution. The results indicate that, in a probe-tone task, listeners are responding primarily to musical closure rather than according to a sense of continuation.

Aarden's studies vindicate and reinforce Krumhansl's theoretical intuition that scale-degree schemas are learned from simple exposure. Once a distinction is made between *phrase-final* contexts and *mid-melody* contexts, the evidence for statistical learning of scale degrees is even stronger than formerly supposed. Moreover, these results reinforce the research we examined in earlier chapters. Recall that the relationship between speed of identifying absolute pitch and the distribution of pitches in music strongly implicates statistical learning. The findings by Jenny Saffran and her colleagues for arbitrary pitch patterns also implicates statistical learning. As we will see in the next chapter, work by Peter Desain and Henkjan Honing will show that rhythmic patterns are also perceived in a manner that is consistent with statistical learning. In the world of audition, statistical learning appears to be pervasive.

Closure

An important discovery in Aarden's work is that listeners are sensitive to the scale-degree distribution at points of interruption or closure. Clearly, listeners make a distinction between events that happen mid-melody and events that happen at points of melodic termination or repose. For music theorists, the cadence is the quintessential gesture for defining a tonal framework. The great nineteenth-century theorist Hugo Riemann regarded the tonic–subdominant–dominant–tonic progression as the prototypical tonality-defining structure. It was this I–IV–V–I mixed cadence that Krumhansl and Kessler played when collecting their original probe-tone data.

The word "cadence" comes from the Italian word *cadenza*—meaning to fall or decline. The label is apt since, as in speech, the final pitch in music is very often approached in a descending contour. In many cultures, tumbling phrases epitomize this phrase-final fall. As we saw in chapter 5, there is a tendency in Western music for phrases to exhibit arch-shaped contours, and musician listeners form expectations that the notes in the latter half of a phrase are likely to descend in pitch. In music, cadences are not restricted to the final moments of a work, but also occur at the ends of individual phrases. Cadences can differ in their degree of closure. Like different punctuation marks (commas, semicolons, periods) some cadences sound more final than others.

Music theorists have long observed that cadences tend to be organized in a stereotypic fashion. It is not simply the final note of the cadence that is predictable; the final note is often approached in a characteristic or formulaic manner. If cadences are truly stereotypic, then this fact should be reflected in measures of predictability.

As we saw in chapter 3, information theory provides some useful tools for characterizing uncertainty. Using the Shannon–Weaver equation, we can measure information content (in bits) for pairs of successive scale degrees. For tonal melodies, one of the highest probability events is the dominant pitch followed by a repetition of the dominant. I have measured this transition as 4.1 bits. By contrast, a low probability (high information) sequence consists of the lowered seventh followed by the raised seventh (13.4 bits). Using a sample of three hundred folk songs, the average information content for scale-degree successions is 5.5 bits. However, the information content for the final two notes of each phrase is 5.0 bits.[14] Without even considering meter, rhythm, melodic contour, or other factors, phrase endings exhibit scale-degree patterns that have a comparatively high probability of occurrence.

When harmony is considered, the difference in probability is even more pronounced. I have measured the average information content for two-chord successions in J. S. Bach's chorale harmonizations to be 8.6 bits. However, the information content for the final two chords of each phrase averages 4.8 bits. Cadences are both melodically and harmonically more predictable than other segments of the music.[15]

Such stereotypic cadential patterns are ubiquitous throughout music—both Western and non-Western. The stereotypes of musical closure can be readily observed and have been described in detail by music theorists. Figure 9.5 illustrates a handful of the innumerable cadential formulae found in Western music. Figure 9.5a shows a "Landini cadence"—a common pre-Renaissance way of terminating phrases (named after the fourteenth-century Italian composer, Francesco Landini, who used it consistently). Figure 9.5b shows a typical cadence associated with gypsy (Romani) music—what

Figure 9.5
Four examples of cadences in Western music: (a) Landini cadence, (b) gypsy or Magyar cadence, (c) authentic cadence employing a German sixth and cadential 6–4, and (d) common jazz cadence ending on a tonic chord with added major seventh and ninth.

composer Franz Liszt dubbed the "Magyar cadence."[16] Figure 9.5c shows a German sixth chord resolving to an authentic cadence via a cadential 6–4 chord—a common cadential progression using an augmented sixth chord. The last example shows a common twentieth-century jazz cadence ending on the tonic chord with an added major seventh and ninth. The tonic chord is approached here by a "tritone-substitution" chord—a chord based on the Neapolitan seventh rather than a dominant seventh.

There are many other examples of stereotypic cadences in both Western and non-Western musics.[17] Cadence-related increases in predictability can be observed in such disparate repertoires as Gregorian chant and Korean *p'iri* music.[18] Figure 9.6 shows some typical cadences for Chinese, Moroccan, and Pawnee musics.[19] In Chinese *bawoo* (bamboo flute) it is common to terminate works or phrases with sustained trills. In Moroccan *Jajouka* music and Pawnee songs it is common to terminate works or phrases

Figure 9.6

Three examples of cadences in non-Western music: (a) final cadence in a Chinese bamboo flute melody, (b) Moroccan Jajouka cadence, and (c) the ending of a Pawnee song. (Notated pitches are rough approximations of the actual sounded pitches.)

with a series of repeated pitches. Not all music is organized into phrases; nor does all music end with final closing gestures. But for music that does exhibit cadences, these points of closure are among the most clichéd aspects of the music.

As we might expect, the increase in predictability observed in the notated or transcribed music is echoed in a decreased uncertainty for listener expectations. Consider again the Balinese melody discussed in chapter 3, where a marked decrease in listener uncertainty is evident as the end of the melody is approached (see figure 3.1). Incidentally, the high degree of predictability when approaching a phrase boundary is also evident in speech. Speech researchers have shown that people are very good at predicting the end point for a spoken utterance, even when they have no knowledge of the speaker's language.[20]

A high degree of predictability in approaching a point of closure is not the only characteristic feature of closure. Another feature is the increase in uncertainty that commonly follows *after* the closure point. Consider once again the information content in folksong melodies. The average information for scale-degree successions is 5.5 bits. However, the information context between the last note of one phrase and the first note of the next phrase is 6.2 bits. A similar pattern can be observed in Bach's chorale harmonizations. Whereas the average information content for the final two chords in a cadence is 4.8 bits, the information content between the last chord of one phrase and the first chord of the following phrase is much higher. Phrase boundaries exhibit both an increase in predictability as the cadence is approached, and an increase in uncertainty about what will follow after the cadence.

Musicians have long regarded the cadence as a sort of "reset" point. When learning to write melodies, for example, musicians are commonly advised that they can begin a new phrase with almost any scale tone they want. Further evidence in support of this view can be seen in measures of pitch proximity. In folksong melodies, for example, the average within-phrase interval size is 2.0 semitones. The average interval between the end of one phrase and the beginning of the next is significantly larger at 2.9 semitones.[21]

The effect of closure on expectation has been one of the recurring themes in Eugene Narmour's theory of melodic expectancy. We saw some of Narmour's principles of melodic expectancy in chapter 6. But Narmour takes pains to bracket his expectancy principles—claiming that they only apply in "implicative" contexts. In some situations, pitch successions may evoke little sense of what might happen next. For Narmour, the preeminent example of such a nonimplicative context is found at the end of a cadence. Narmour's conception of closure is rather convoluted. But Northwestern University theorist Elizabeth Margulis has provided an admirably succinct characterization of closure in Narmour's theory. The simplest way to think of Narmour's notion of closure, says Margulis, is as an event that suppresses expectancy.[22]

The statistical measures of notated music support this interpretation of Narmour's view. The strengths of melodic expectations fluctuate over the course of the composition. Some events provoke clear premonitions of ensuing events, whereas other events leave little sense of what might happen next. It should not be surprising that the strength of expectation is related to perceptual grouping. It is entirely reasonable that brains would group together stimuli that exhibit a strong statistical association. (This statistically defined grouping tendency was precisely what was demonstrated in the experiment by Jenny Saffran and her colleagues, discussed in chapter 4.) When there cease to be expectations about what may happen next, it makes sense for brains to experience a sense of the loss of forward continuation—a loss of momentum, of will, determination or goal. In short, it makes sense for brains to experience a sense of repose or quiescence whenever the implications cease. The relative absence of expectation defines the boundaries of perceptual chunks: segmentation is primarily statistical. At the same time, the absence of expectation evokes a sense of closure.[23]

Of course statistical segmentation may not be the whole story. Western music theorists have proposed a number of explanations of the phenomenon of musical closure. In general, these theories have attracted little experimental attention. A notable exception can be found in the work of musicologists Roland Eberlein and Jobst Fricke working at the University of Cologne.[24] Eberlein and Fricke carried out a series of nine experiments in which Western-enculturated listeners judged the degree of closure for a great variety of stimuli inspired by cadences from different historical periods. Eberlein and Fricke tested a number of popular theories of closure in Western harmony. For example, they tested whether rising semitones, root movement by a descending fifth, and simple frequency ratio relationships contribute to a sense of closure. Their

Table 9.2

First-order scale-degree probabilities (diatonic continuations)

		Consequent state							
		$\hat{1}$	$\hat{2}$	$\hat{3}$	$\hat{4}$	$\hat{5}$	$\hat{6}$	$\hat{7}$	rest
Antecedent state	$\hat{1}$	0.03416	0.02806	0.01974	0.00210	0.01321	0.00839	0.02321	0.03678
	#$\hat{1}$	0	0.00042	0.00004	0	0	0.00003	0.00002	0.00002
	$\flat\hat{2}$	0.00004	0	0.00001	0	0	0	0	0
	$\hat{2}$	0.04190	0.02632	0.03282	0.00678	0.00825	0.00201	0.00586	0.01521
	#$\hat{2}$	0	0.00000	0.00018	0	0	0	0	0.00000
	$\flat\hat{3}$	0.00030	0.00108	0.00001	0.00071	0.00010	0	0	0.00017
	$\hat{3}$	0.01555	0.04865	0.03142	0.02644	0.02365	0.00281	0.00029	0.02357
	#$\hat{3}$	0	0	0.00000	0	0	0	0	0
	$\hat{4}$	0.00054	0.01260	0.04127	0.01506	0.01712	0.00441	0.00125	0.00537
	#$\hat{4}$	0.00003	0.00016	0.00037	0.00010	0.00257	0.00040	0.00003	0.00013
	$\hat{5}$	0.02557	0.00530	0.02854	0.03653	0.04835	0.02076	0.00369	0.02284
	#$\hat{5}$	0	0	0.00001	0.00001	0.00000	0.00027	0.00003	0.00002
	$\flat\hat{6}$	0.00001	0.00000	0.00001	0.00003	0.00021	0	0	0.00002
	$\hat{6}$	0.00238	0.00168	0.00065	0.00342	0.03642	0.01261	0.00854	0.00410
	$\flat\hat{7}$	0.00062	0.00003	0.00001	0.00003	0.00043	0.00119	0.00000	0.00025
	$\hat{7}$	0.02025	0.00510	0.00035	0.00029	0.00323	0.01327	0.00448	0.00275
	rest	0.01974	0.01096	0.01644	0.00706	0.03082	0.00487	0.00241	—

principal finding was that *familiarity* with cadential formulae from different historical periods contributes most to the listener's experience of closure: "The only way completely to explain the results is by invoking the subjects' degree of musical experience" (p. 258). Eberlein and Fricke's results are complicated—so one cannot claim that familiarity alone accounts for the psychological experience of closure. However, their results are consistent with a prominent role for statistical learning.

Tendency

As we have seen, some successions of scale degrees are more likely than others. Tables 9.2 and 9.3 show the results of a detailed analysis of scale-degree successions in a sample of several thousand Germanic folk songs in major keys. Each table shows the probabilities for various transitions between antecedent scale degree (rows) and consequent scale degrees (columns). The frequency data presented in these tables are based on an analysis of more than a quarter of a million tone pairs. Table 9.2 shows the transitions where the consequent tones are diatonic scale members. Table 9.3 shows

Table 9.3
First-order scale-degree probabilities (chromatic continuations)

Antecedent state	Consequent state								
	$\#\hat{1}$	$\flat\hat{2}$	$\#\hat{2}$	$\flat\hat{3}$	$\#\hat{3}$	$\#\hat{4}$	$\#\hat{5}$	$\flat\hat{6}$	$\flat\hat{7}$
$\hat{1}$	0.00006	0.00002	0.00001	0.00021	0	0.00013	0.00000	0.00003	0.00099
$\#\hat{1}$	0.00004	0	0.00001	0	0	0	0	0	0
$\flat\hat{2}$	0	0.00000	0	0.00000	0	0	0	0	0.00000
$\hat{2}$	0.00033	0.00000	0.00003	0.00066	0	0.00017	0	0	0.00012
$\#\hat{2}$	0.00000	0	0.00001	0	0	0	0	0	0
$\flat\hat{3}$	0	0.00002	0	0.00029	0	0	0	0.00001	0.00001
$\hat{3}$	0.00003	0.00001	0.00004	0.00001	0.00000	0.00088	0.00003	0	0.00000
$\hat{4}$	0.00001	0.00001	0.00000	0.00084	0	0.00004	0	0.00003	0.00006
$\#\hat{4}$	0	0	0	0.00000	0	0.00040	0.00002	0	0
$\hat{5}$	0.00001	0	0.00000	0.00037	0	0.00207	0.00006	0.00013	0.00054
$\#\hat{5}$	0	0	0	0	0	0.00001	0.00006	0	0
$\flat\hat{6}$	0	0	0	0	0	0	0	0.00003	0.00003
$\hat{6}$	0.00004	0	0.00000	0.00000	0	0.00037	0.00016	0.00001	0.00070
$\flat\hat{7}$	0	0.00000	0	0.00008	0	0	0.00000	0.00007	0.00048
$\hat{7}$	0.00003	0	0	0	0	0.00004	0.00004	0.00000	0.00001
rest	0.00003	0	0.00001	0.00023	0	0.00010	0.00003	0.00003	0.00027

the transitions for chromatic consequent tones. In table 9.2, the consequent state "rest" is used to designate tones that are followed by a notated rest, as well as tones that are explicitly notated as ending a phrase.

Table entries of "0" indicate that no instances of the transition were observed in the sampled folksong melodies. Values of "0.00000" indicate that at least one instance of the transition was observed; however, the probability of the event is less than one in fifty thousand.

The most probable melodic event in this musical sample is $\hat{3}$ followed by $\hat{2}$. With a calculated probability of 0.049, almost one in twenty pitch transitions involves moving from $\hat{3}$ to $\hat{2}$. Repetition of the dominant pitch occurs nearly as frequently, while the third most common melodic succession is from $\hat{2}$ to $\hat{1}$.

For convenience, figure 9.7 recasts some of the data in table 9.2 as a schematic diagram showing the probabilities of various scale-degree successions. Remember that these transitional probabilities are for melodies in major keys only. In this rendering, the thickness of the lines is directly proportional to the probability of occurrence. Not all transitions have been graphed. Connecting lines have been drawn only for those transitions that have a probability greater than 0.015.

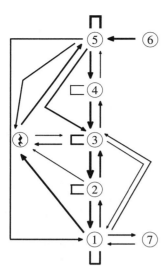

Figure 9.7
Schematic illustration of scale-degree successions for major-key melodies. The thickness of each connecting line is proportional to the probability of melodic succession. The quarter-rest symbol signifies any rest or the end of a phrase. Probabilities calculated from a large sample of Germanic folk songs. Lines have been drawn only for those transitions that have probabilities greater than 0.015.

Figure 9.7 displays many of the statistical regularities in music discussed in chapter 5. The most probable transitions involve neighboring scale tones (i.e., pitch proximity)—such as $\hat{2}$ to $\hat{3}$ or $\hat{5}$ to $\hat{4}$. In general, the most likely successive pitch is just above or below the current pitch. Notice, however, that descending steps are more common than ascending steps. Notice also that the pitches most likely to be followed by a rest (such as phrase-terminating pitches) are the tones of the tonic triad—$\hat{1}$ followed by $\hat{5}$ followed by $\hat{3}$. Scale degree $\hat{2}$ also tends to terminate phrases—as would occur, for example, with a half cadence.

In general, most pitch successions are asymmetrical. For example, the sixth scale degree is much more likely to lead to the fifth scale degree than vice versa. Similarly, the fourth scale degree is more likely to move to the third scale degree than the opposite. One of the most striking features is the sequence of descending arrows from $\hat{5}$ to $\hat{4}$ to $\hat{3}$ to $\hat{2}$ to $\hat{1}$. For Schenkerian theorists, this is strikingly reminiscent of the five-line *Urlinie*—although it should be emphasized that these transitions are note-to-note, rather than the transitions between structural tones.

Some asymmetries are counterintuitive. Notice that the arrows between $\hat{1}$ and $\hat{7}$ indicate that $\hat{1}$ to $\hat{7}$ is more probable than $\hat{7}$ to $\hat{1}$. For musicians, this seems odd.

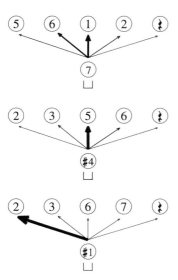

Figure 9.8
Schematic illustration of scale-degree successions for $\hat{7}$, #$\hat{4}$, and #$\hat{1}$ for major-key melodies. The thickness of each connecting line is proportional to the probability of melodic succession. The quarter-rest symbol signifies any rest or the end of a phrase. Probabilities calculated from a large sample of Germanic folk songs.

However, bear in mind that this data represents *absolute* likelihoods rather than relative likelihoods. The tonic pitch is simply more common than the leading-tone. The *relative* probabilities are more easily grasped if we isolate individual scale degrees. Figure 9.8 focuses on three tones: the leading-tone ($\hat{7}$), the raised subdominant (#$\hat{4}$), and the raised tonic (#$\hat{1}$). In each case, the five most probable continuations are plotted. Once again, the thickness of the lines is directly proportional to the probability of occurrence. In the case of the leading-tone, the affinity for $\hat{1}$ is obvious. In absolute terms, there are more instances of $\hat{1}$ going to $\hat{7}$ than $\hat{7}$ going to $\hat{1}$. But $\hat{7}$ is more likely to lead to $\hat{1}$ than $\hat{1}$ is to $\hat{7}$.

What $\hat{7}$, #$\hat{4}$, and #$\hat{1}$ share in common is that a single continuation pitch dominates all other possibilities. It is not inappropriate to call these tones "tendency tones." Recall that such tones were described in the *qualia* survey by such words as *intentional*, *motivated*, *mobile*, *unstable*, *pointing*, *restless*, and *itchy*. In contrasting the leading-tone with the tonic, it is the leading-tone we experience as having a strong tendency even though $\hat{1}$ to $\hat{7}$ is more common than $\hat{7}$ to $\hat{1}$. In other words, the phenomenal experience of *tendency* is nicely captured by the notion of a *predominant relative probability*. Said another way, individual scale degrees (such as the leading-tone) provide their own contexts. When we hear the leading-tone, it is much more likely to be accompanied by the phenomenal experience of "leading" than when we hear a pitch like the tonic.

The phenomenal experience of *tendency* arises from the brain's exquisite sensitivity to context. Consider yet another example: $\hat{1}$ is approached by $\hat{2}$ more than twice as often as $\hat{1}$ is approached by $\hat{7}$, but $\hat{7}$ evokes a stronger sense of wanting to go to $\hat{1}$ than does $\hat{2}$. First-order probabilities are relative to the context, not to the absolute probabilities of occurrence. The brain responds in a wonderfully contextual way. Instead of asking "how often does this situation arise?" the brain is asking "what is the most likely thing to happen next given the current situation?"

The strongest tendencies are associated with chromatic pitches. The importance of such tendency tones, and the tendency to hear them as linked to more stable neighbors, was vividly described by Leonard Meyer. Meyer noted, for example, that "In the music of China non-structural tones take the name of the structural tone to which they move together with the word *pièn*, meaning 'on the way to' or 'becoming.'" That is, the tendency tones are named in reference to the "resolving" tone.[25]

Measuring Tendency

Once again we can use the Shannon–Weaver equation to measure the information content for each scale degree. That is, we can measure the amount of uncertainty that attends the continuation following a given pitch. Scale tones that open outward toward many possibilities will exhibit a high information value. Conversely, scale tones that restrict the range of ensuing outcomes will exhibit a low information value. The "perfect" tendency tone would *always* be followed by the same continuation tone. Such an antecedent tone would, by definition, convey zero bits of information.

Figure 9.9 provides a summary graph showing the tendency of various scale degrees. The data for this graph were produced by Bret Aarden. Those scale tones toward the left side of the figure are "more flexible" than scale tones toward the right. Pitches like the dominant and tonic have many possible continuation tones. We might say that these tones exhibit greater "flexibility" than strong tendency tones like #$\hat{1}$ and #$\hat{4}$. If listeners acquire some knowledge of the probabilities associated with scale-degree successions, then this graph should correspond to our intuitions of *tendency*. Scale tones that are less flexible might also be characterized as evoking a greater sense of "leading" or "tending."

Accounting for Scale-Degree *Qualia*

I began this chapter by describing some of the phenomenal *qualia* experienced by musicians when imagining different scale degrees. The obvious question now is: Can

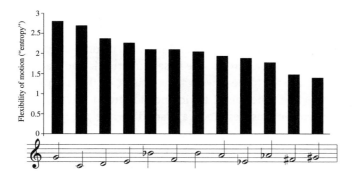

Figure 9.9

Schematic illustration of the amount of *flexibility* or (conversely) *tendency* for different scale degrees in major-key contexts. For convenience, all tones have been transposed to the key of C. The dominant pitch (G) can be followed by many different pitches. By contrast, the raised dominant (G#) tends to severely constrain possible pitch continuations. Due to small sample sizes, not all pitches are shown. Information calculated in bits. (Calculated by Bret Aarden; Aarden 2001.)

the statistical properties related to different scale degrees account for their distinctive *qualia?* Why do the different scale degrees evoke different psychological "feelings"? Why does the tonic sound pleasant in a closural position? Why does the leading-tone sound like it is "leading"?

Recall that I identified seven clusters or categories of responses in my *qualia* survey: (1) certainty/uncertainty, (2) tendency, (3) completion, (4) mobility, (5) stability, (6) power, and (7) emotion. The *certainty/uncertainty* category seems to be the most easily linked to the statistical properties of music. Two scale tones were described as "unexpected," "surprising," or "abrupt"—the lowered supertonic and the subtonic pitches. These chromatic tones occur much less frequently than other scale tones so feelings of surprise are entirely reasonable. The *tendency* category seems to correlate with the absence of statistical flexibility for pitch continuations. Scale tones described as "tending," "leading," or "pointing" included the raised dominant and the leading-tone—both tones that are statistically limited in their possible continuation tones. By contrast, the word "possibility" was applied to the most statistically flexible of pitches, the dominant. Not surprisingly, the *completion* category appears to be associated with the probability of occurrence of various tones in phrase- or work-terminating positions. Scale tones described as "restful" or "home" included the tonic and mediant pitches.

The *mobility* category is more difficult to explain. The descriptive term "movement" was applied to the supertonic pitch, while the word "drifting" was applied to the subtonic pitch. Perhaps such mobility-related terms simply designate weaker forms of "leading."

The *stable* category appears to be associated with a combination of completion and tendency. The tonic was described as "stable," while the raised supertonic and leading-tone pitches were described as "unstable." The *power* category isn't easily interpreted from a statistical learning perspective. The raised tonic and dominant pitches were described as "strong." The supertonic was described as "solid" while the mediant, submediant and subtonic pitches were described as "light."

Perhaps the most interesting *qualia* category relates to *emotion*. Here the tonic, mediant, and dominant pitches were described using such positive hedonic terms as *pleasure, warmth, contentment, beauty*, and even *love*. Negative hedonic terms like *harsh, jarring, uncomfortable*, and *anxious* were applied to tones such as the raised supertonic, the raised subdominant, and the raised dominant. Clearly, positively charged *qualia* appear linked to frequently occurring tones associated with closure. But why?

In chapter 8, we discussed the *exposure effect*—the notion that the most familiar stimulus will tend to be experienced as most pleasurable. In that chapter I suggested that the experimental data are more consistent with what I called the *prediction effect*—the notion that the most predicted stimulus will tend to be experienced as most pleasurable. For example, I noted that the so-called *repetition effect* (facilitation of mental processing for repeated visual stimuli) does not occur for pitched tones. In fact, listeners are faster when processing a *different* pitch than processing the *same* (unison) pitch. Since repeated pitches are less common in music than new pitches, this suggests that the facilitation is a consequence of statistically learned anticipations rather than repetition per se.

We can now add two more pieces of evidence in support of my claim that the *exposure effect* is better explained as a *prediction effect*. Consider the case of the tonic pitch. Is the pleasure evoked by the tonic better explained by a *prediction effect* or by an *exposure effect?* As an explanation, the exposure effect doesn't square with two musical facts. First, the dominant is the most frequently occurring pitch in both the major and minor keys. If the pleasure evoked by the tonic were due exclusively to a purported "mere exposure effect," then we would expect the dominant pitch to evoke more pleasure than the tonic. But that's not the case. Listeners report that the tonic is more pleasant than the dominant. Second, only *some* tonic pitches are perceived as pleasant. When played as a passing tone in the context of a dominant harmony, the tonic will sound unstable, transient, and not nearly as pleasant as a cadential tonic. The pleasure of the tonic is largely restricted to moments of closure.

The prediction effect provides a better account than the exposure effect for our musical observations. We have noted that (1) cadences are the *most predictable* passages in music, (2) that the tonic is the *most predictable* pitch in a cadence, and (3) the tonic can occur in less predictable circumstances (such as a passing tone in a dominant harmony) where it fails to evoke strong pleasant emotions. That is, the cases where tones evoke the greatest pleasure are precisely those circumstances where they are most predictable.

Additional support for this view can be found in the resolution of chromatic tones. While chromatic tones are highly unstable, they evoke strong expectations—that is, high first-order probabilities. When a chromatic tone is resolved, there is a sense of pleasure evoked even when the resolving pitch is also somewhat unstable. For example, when the raised dominant pitch resolves to the submediant, there is a sense of pleasure evoked despite the fact that the submediant pitch is not especially stable.

One further bit of musical evidence that supports this interpretation can be found in "out-of-the-blue" cadences. Anyone who has attended a traditional circus has heard the incidental music that a live band performs to accompany the various acts. As the circus performers accomplish certain feats, the band often stops the music in mid-phrase, and produces a "ta-da" cadence to punctuate some notable achievement. On the one hand, these ta-da cadences are pleasant enough, but they are often introduced at odd moments that make no sense in the flow of the incidental music. If the occurrence of a tonic pitch or tonic chord itself in a closural gesture were sufficient to evoke pleasure, then the circus ta-da cadence should be as satisfying as any normal cadence. However, if, as I claim, the pleasure is evoked as a reward for accurate prediction, then the circus ta-da cadence should be less satisfying than most cadences because the context for when these cadences occur is less predictable. "Out-of-the-blue" cadences would thus be less pleasurable because they are less predictable.

In light of the above discussion, we can now offer a straightforward account of the "pleasantness" *qualia* that accompany, for example, a cadential tonic pitch. In Western music the tonic pitch in a cadential context is quite simply the most predictable of pitch-related musical stimuli. The evoked pleasure originates with a limbic reward for accurate prediction that is then misattributed to the stimulus itself.

An unanswered question is why there is a correlation between the most frequently occurring pitches and the most frequently occurring closural pitches. Theoretically, there is no reason why the most predictable general pitch ought to be the most predictable phrase- or work-terminating pitch. In fact, the dominant pitch is more common than the tonic in Western music, yet the tonic is more likely in closural contexts. Still, the tonic, dominant, and mediant are more common than any other pitches, both in general and in closural contexts. However, one could imagine some music in which tones *X* and *Y* were the most likely terminating pitches, while tones *M* and *N* were the most likely overall pitches. Why are the tonic, mediant, and dominant both frequently occurring pitches *and* the most common closural pitches?

Imagine for a moment a hypothetical musical culture where different tones occur more or less frequently. Some tones are very common, others are relatively rare. Also suppose that the music of this culture consists of isochronous tones and exhibits no grouping or phrase structures. That is, the music of this hypothetical culture consists of a constant stream of tones—although some tones are more likely to occur than others. Finally, suppose that successive notes are randomly generated so there are no first-order probabilities, only zeroth-order probabilities. In this circumstance, the most predictable tone would be the most commonly occurring tone.

Now suppose that the musicians in this hypothetical culture have discovered that grouping notes together makes it easier to remember and recall melodies. These musicians have learned to demarcate such pitch groups by extending the duration of the final tone of the group. Are there some tones that would make better "cadence" tones?

The answer is "yes." Since the tones differ in their frequency of occurrence, the tones differ in their predictability, and so differ in the evoked pleasure. In general, it is better to sustain positively valenced states for a longer duration than less positively valenced states. So the overall positive emotional state can be increased by choosing the more predictable tones as the ones to receive a sustained duration.

If most segments are terminated with a particular pitch, then listeners should learn to associate that pitch with the ending of a segment, or closure. Broadly speaking, the most frequently occurring states will tend to become associated with closure. What begins as a zeroth-order favorite is likely to also become a preferred closural pitch as well.[26] All other things being equal, frequently occurring events have a tendency to be (1) the most predicted stimulus, (2) the most preferred stimulus, and (3) the stimulus that most implies closure.

Note that the pleasure of closural pitches can be enhanced by making the approach more predictable. Initially, this can be done by making the penultimate (next-to-last) note more predictable. Then the pre-penultimate note can be made more predictable . . . and so on. Increasing the predictability of the closural approach leads inexorably to highly stereotypic cadential formulas.

Interlude

By way of summary, we can now see how the probability structure of sounded events might account for at least three common *qualia* associated with scale degrees. When the first-order probabilities are high, the evoked feeling state is characterized by a sense of *tendency*. For example, the raised dominant *feels* like it wants to ascend; the subdominant *feels* like it wants to descend. The "yearning" quality of these tones appears to be a direct consequence of learned first-order probabilities.

When the first-order probabilities predict silence or pause, then the evoked feeling state is characterized by a sense of repose or *closure*. The supertonic pitch in a half-cadence *feels* like a moment of pause or rest. The final cadential tonic *feels* relaxed and complete. The incessant yearning is dispelled and a temporary or permanent sense of rest arises. Again, the closural quality of these tones appears to be a direct consequence of learned first-order probabilities.

Whenever a pitch is highly expected, a prediction effect is generated. As noted, the resulting positive emotion is typically misattributed to the sound itself. As a consequence, some scale tones sound nicer than other tones. Highly expected pitches include tones that resolve tendency tones (such as chromatic pitches). At cadence points in particular, the tonic pitch has an extraordinary power to evoke a sense of pleasure. The *qualia* of *pleasure* appears to be a direct consequence of learned high probability events.

Note that two of the three *qualia* discussed here (tendency and closure) appear to originate in the tension response. The *quale* of pleasure appears to originate in the prediction response. In either case, these *qualia* are linked to the psychology of expectation.

While "tonality" may include many other aspects not discussed here, the principal component experiences related to tonality are linked to the predictability of different sounds in various contexts. Many of the commonly reported *qualia* can be plausibly traced to statistical regularities evident in the patterns of scale degrees in Western music. While more research is needed, the subjective experiences of uncertainty, tendency, stability, mobility, closure, and emotion all appear to arise from the interplay of three psychological foundations: statistical learning, the prediction response, and the phenomenon of misattribution.

Aesthetic Caveats

At this point, it is appropriate to interject a few words about the aesthetics of tonality. As noted in the previous chapter, the idea that pleasure arises from predictability has the appearance of a defense of musical banality and an advocacy for the status quo. This is not at all my goal. As I noted in the preface, my goal in this book is to describe psychological mechanisms, not aesthetic goals. My musical aim is to provide musicians with a better understanding of the tools they use, not to tell musicians what goals they should aspire to.

In addition, I hasten to add that my account of tonality-related *qualia* must be tempered by a number of complications. One important complication is that people differ. Psychologists studying personality have established that people exhibit stable and systematic differences in their tolerance of sensation-seeking. Elsewhere I have written about the relationship between nonsocialized sensation-seeking personality attributes and limbic responses to different types of sounds.[27] In simple terms, some people are more "skittish" while others are more "thick-skinned," and these attributes are reflected in how they respond physiologically to different sound events. What some people find irritating, others find interesting, and vice versa.[28]

In addition to differences in disposition, the Israeli theorist, Zohar Eitan, has pointed out that listeners commonly have different goals at different times. Sometimes we want to relax, whereas other times we are looking for adventure. At home, we might seek a relaxed psychological state that would be best served by listening to predictable music. When attending a concert, we may be more open to novelty. Here, highly predictable music might disappoint us.

Apart from the intentions or dispositions of the listener, in many circumstances, musicians will aim to achieve a particular effect. A film composer, for example, may aim to create a sense of suspense or uneasiness for listeners. Musicians need not choose to create music that evokes pleasure. Even if a musician aims to create a wholly pleasurable effect, it bears emphasizing that there are other ways to evoke pleasure in music—including the contrastive valence mechanism discussed in chapter 2. In chapter 14 we will see how violations of expectation can lead to laughter, awe, and frisson.

Tonality and Culture

To this point, my discussion has been limited to Western music. In fact, I have focused almost exclusively on the major scale with little discussion of the minor mode. If I am correct that the pitch-related *qualia* of closure, tendency, and pleasure arise from statistical learning, then parallel phenomena should be evident in other cultures. Unfortunately, comparatively little pertinent cross-cultural work has been carried out. However, some suggestive evidence is available in three seminal probe-tone studies by Tuomas Eerola, by Ed Kessler, Christa Hansen, and Roger Shepard, and by Mary Castellano, Jamshed Bharucha, and Carol Krumhansl.

In the early 1980s, Christa Hansen and her husband Putra set out on a small motorcycle toward the remote northeastern region of the island of Bali. Whenever they met someone they asked two questions: "What is the most isolated village in this area? And does it have a gamelan?" Having reached this village, they again asked the same questions, and so continued on their quest. When they were no longer able to use their motorcycle, a footpath took them to a remote village in the shadow of the Gunung Agung volcano. There they met villagers who had never before seen a Westerner. Hansen knew that she had reached a truly isolated place when the villagers concluded that this fair-skinned stranger must be Javanese.[29] Recruiting twenty-seven participants from this village, Hansen was able to collect data from a probe-tone experiment. Her Balinese participants heard three sixteen-note melodies—one based on the Western major scale using piano tones, and two others based on the two principal Balinese scales, *pelog* and *slendro*. The pelog melodies were performed on a *gangsa* while the slendro melodies were performed on a *gender wayang*.

Participants heard the complete sixteen-note sequence followed by a probe-tone, which they rated according to its degree of fitness with the other tones. This process was repeated until all of the scale tones had been rated. For the Western melodic sequence, this meant that participants rated all twelve chromatic pitches. For the pelog and slendro melodic sequences, Hansen's participants rated all of the possible pitches available in their respective pitch sets.

With her collaborators Ed Kessler and Roger Shepard at Stanford University, these same materials were used in probe-tone experiments with twenty-one U.S. college students. Kessler, Hansen, and Shepard then subjected the data to a number of statistical analyses. Here I will focus on comparing the cross-cultural responses for just the slendro melody.

The slendro melody in mode 1 consisted of the isochronous sequence: 2, 4, 5, 4, 5, 3, 4, 5, 4, 1, 2, 3, 4, 5, 4, 3. In mode 1, the principal or gong tone is tone 2 (*dong*). While this test sequence begins with tone 2, the scale tones 3, 4, and 5 occur more frequently. Without any knowledge of a scale-related schema, an inexperienced listener might be expected to respond by choosing the most common pitches heard as the most "fitting" pitches. Thus for a Western listener hearing this slendro sequence, one might predict that they would rate most highly tone 4 (6 occurrences), followed by tone 5 (4 occurrences), followed by tone 3 (3 occurrences). On the other hand, if this sequence were heard by a listener experienced with the slendro mode 1, then a higher rating might be expected for the gong tone (tone 2), even though the gong tone appears only twice in the pitch sequence. In their analysis, Kessler, Hansen, and Shepard calculated two correlations: the correlation between the probe-tone ratings and the frequency of occurrence of the tones in the stimulus, and the correlation between the probe-tone ratings and the *a priori* hierarchy of tones as specified in Balinese musical theory. The results are plotted in figure 9.10.

As can be seen, the probe-tone ratings of Western listeners correlate most strongly with the frequency of occurrence of the various tones in the stimulus (labeled "Occurrence"). In other words, "goodness of fit" simply mirrors the amount of exposure to the different tones. By contrast, the probe-tone ratings of the Balinese listeners correlate most strongly with the tonal hierarchy for tones in the mode 1 slendro scale ("Hierarchy"). For these listeners, the gong tone (tone 2) was judged to fit well with the stimulus, even though tone 2 occurred just twice in the melodic sequence.

These results support two conclusions. First, naive listeners are sensitive to the frequency of occurrence of various tones and rate the most frequent tones as best fitting. Second, listeners who are enculturated to an appropriate pitch schema experience pitch sequences as evoking some preexisting schema and judge the various tones on

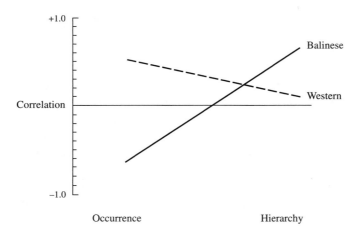

Figure 9.10
Comparison of Western and Balinese listeners exposed to a slendro melody. Western listeners judged probe-tones as most fitting when they occurred frequently in the pitch sequence ("Occurrence"). By contrast, Balinese listeners tended to ignore the frequency of occurrence of pitches within the sequence and judged probe-tones as most fitting when they fit within the general pitch hierarchy of slendro mode 1 ("Hierarchy"). Adapted from figure 14c in Kessler, Hansen, and Shepard 1984.

the basis of their frequency of occurrence in the totality of their past listening exposure rather than the frequency of occurrence in a given tone sequence.

Said another way, the behavior of the Western listeners reveals a rapid statistical learning that echoes the statistical properties of a (severely limited) musical exposure. By contrast, the behavior of the Balinese listeners reflects a statistical template assembled from a lifetime of exposure to music in slendro mode 1. The deviations of this particular pitch sequence from the normative distribution of pitches in slendro mode 1 were ignored by the Balinese listeners.

Another pertinent cross-cultural study was carried out by Mary Castellano, Jamshed Bharucha, and Carol Krumhansl. In this study, probe-tone responses were compared between north Indian and American listeners exposed to passages of north Indian music. Listeners heard passages that exemplified ten different north Indian *rags*. After these *rag*-defining contexts, listeners rated each of twelve probe tones. As in the Kessler, Hansen, and Shepard study, the probe-tone ratings of the American listeners reflected a simple statistical learning based on the presented materials. The probe-tone ratings of north Indian listeners also closely matched the statistical distribution of tones in the stimulus passages, but these ratings were also influenced by schemas representing a lifetime of exposure to the different *rags*.

Unlike the Balinese slendro and pelog scales, the Indian scale is virtually identical to the Western scale. When Westerners listen to Indian music, this similarity might be expected to cause interference from preexisting Western habits of listening. That is, we might expect that Western listeners would tend to apply the schematic expectatons of the major or minor scales to the north Indian musical contexts. However, using a multiple regression analysis, Castellano, Bharucha, and Krumhansl found no residual influence of the Western tonal hierarchy in the probe-tone ratings of the Western students listening to the north Indian music. Evidently, U.S. college students managed to avoid confusing the Indian music with Western music. They behaved like exemplary musical tourists.[30]

This study reinforces the two conclusions we saw in the Kessler, Hansen, and Shepard study. The inexperienced Western listeners were sensitive to the frequency of occurrence of various tones, and tended to rate the most frequent tones as the best fitting. The culturally experienced Indian listeners also responded according to the distribution of tones in the stimulus passages, but their responses showed the additional influence of a pitch hierarchy consistent with traditional Indian music theory.[31] To these conclusions we can add a third: although the scale tones of the Indian music were very similar to the pitches found in Western music, the Western listeners were somehow able to bracket the listening experience and avoid "contamination" from their existing Western pitch-related schemas.[32]

A more recent cross-cultural study has been carried out by Tuomas Eerola at the University of Jyväskylä in Finland.[33] Eerola's study built on earlier perceptual work with the Sami of northern Scandinavia.[34] The Sami maintain a distinctive vocal tradition in the singing of *yoiks*. Yoiks exhibit a characteristic tendency to employ certain large melodic leaps. For example, compared with Germanic folk songs, perfect fourths and fifths occur twice as often while the octave is eight times more common.

Eerola took yoik materials to Africa, and in collaboration with ethnomusicologist Edward Lebaka, Eerola collected reaction-time data from thirty-one musicians of the traditional Pedi culture in the rural northern Limpopo province of South Africa. The Pedi have had relatively little exposure to Western music and were certainly not familiar with northern Scandinavian yoik melodies. Exposed to yoik melodic sequences, the Pedi musicians provided probe-tone ratings at selected melodic points.

In analyzing the probe-tone responses, Eerola directly pitted three models against each other. One model was an auditory model proposed by Marc Leman. A second model was the two-factor simplification of Narmour's implication-realization theory as developed by Glenn Schellenberg. The third model was a simple statistical learning model that predicted responses solely on the basis of the frequency of occurrence of different pitches and intervals in the stimulus melodies. The statistical learning model proved to perform significantly better than either the auditory or Gestalt-inspired models. That is, the Pedi responses to Sami *yoiks* echoed the statistical properties of the stimulus materials themselves.

Eerola went on to compare the African Pedi responses with probe-tone responses from Scandinavian Sami listeners. Both the Pedi and Sami responses were consistent with the statistical properties of the stimulus melodies. However, the Sami responses were better predicted by long-term (schematic) statistical properties of yoiks and less influenced by the statistical features of the individual yoik stimuli. No such effect was observed in the African Pedi responses. In short, the results of Eerola's study replicate the pattern shown in figure 9.10 with two entirely different cultures.

To these studies of Sami, Balinese, and north Indian music, let me add one further anecdote. In 1997 I taught a summer course at Stanford University. One of my students was a Korean ethnomusicologist named Unjung Nam who was studying traditional Korean *p'iri* music. One day, I happened to look over her shoulder at three graphs she had produced showing the relative frequencies of occurrence for the various pitches in three different *p'iri* works. Each of the graphs had a prominent peak for a different pitch. Pointing at the peaks in each graph, I said that although I know nothing about Korean music, if I had to guess, I would predict that these tones (*hwangjong, chungryo,* and *taeju*) act as the principal or "tonic" pitches in each of their respective works. Moreover, I would predict that these same tones would tend to appear frequently at the ends of phrases. Nam looked at me like I was clairvoyant since my suggestion was entirely consistent with traditional Korean theory. A subsequent formal statistical analysis published by Nam confirmed that the target pitches were indeed much more likely to appear at breath-delineated phrase endings.[35]

By themselves, these studies are not sufficient to make the general case. In the case of the Korean *p'iri* music, it would be helpful to match the statistical analyses with psychological experiments that determine whether corresponding schemas are present for experienced Korean listeners. In these and other cultures, it would be helpful to collect qualitative descriptions of the various scale tones in order to determine whether the evoked *qualia* correlate with statistical features of the indigenous music. More empirically oriented non-Western research is needed. Nevertheless, the existing cross-cultural results are suggestive in light of what we know about statistical learning.

Reprise

In this chapter I have reiterated the theory, first advocated by Carol Krumhansl, that tonality may be viewed as a set of statistically learned pitch schemas arising from sustained exposure to the music of some culture. Where Krumhansl emphasized zeroth-order probabilities (i.e., the probabilities of individual scale tones), I have noted that higher-order probabilities (the succession of tones) are also internalized by listeners. In addition, research by Bret Aarden indicates that independent schemas arise for pitches associated with repose or conclusion.

The real magic of tonality lies in the fact that different tones are able to evoke distinctive *qualia*.[36] Tones that differ only with respect to pitch can evoke dramatically different phenomenal experiences. In a given context, a tone will sound stable, complete, and pleasant. In another context, that exact same sound will feel unstable, incomplete, and irritating. The relationships between pitches hold an amazing power to shape how we experience pitch.

I have suggested that several of the most salient *qualia* evoked by different pitches can be traced to simple statistical relationships. From a statistical-learning viewpoint, we can ask three elementary questions about each scale tone: (1) How frequently does this tone appear in music? (2) How frequently does this tone complete a phrase or terminate a work? and (3) How commonly does this tone tend to be followed by some other tone?

The predictability of a tone contributes to the hedonic experience through the prediction effect. Highly predictable tones are generally experienced more positively than unexpected tones. The probability of a tone in a closural position accounts for the phenomenal experience of *completion, arrival,* and *resolution* on the one hand, and *unfinished, hanging,* and *transitory* on the other. The subjective experience of *tending* or *leading* can be predicted on the basis of first-order probabilities evident in actual music.

Pleasantness is directly correlated with predictability. The most predictable tones and tone sequences tend to be experienced as the most pleasant—especially if listeners are not consciously aware of the high predictability. Among the most pleasurable moments are cadences, where highly predictable tones appear in highly predictable tone-successions framed by stereotypic contexts. I have suggested that when listeners describe the tonic pitch in a closural context as "sounding nice," this experience originates when a positively valenced prediction response is misattributed to the stimulus itself. Like the young men on the Capilano bridge attributing their feelings of vertigo to a woman experimenter, listeners mistakenly attribute the pleasure of accurate prediction to the sound itself. When compared with other pitches, there is nothing objectively "nice" about a cadential tonic pitch. Nor is there anything objectively "wrong" about an unresolved chromatic tone. These *qualia* are misattributions that originate in limbic responses to expectation.

Whenever a stimulus evokes a fairly consistent psychological effect, it becomes possible to use the stimulus intentionally as a means for evoking that effect. Moreover, when several different stimuli are able to evoke reliably different effects, then it becomes possible to create a palette of effects—a sort of toolkit for those wanting to intentionally evoke specific psychological outcomes. For Western musicians, this idea is captured in the concept of tonal *function*. Musicians will speak of a dominant function, or the function of the leading-tone. In conventional practice, the notion of a tonal function can be applied at several levels. For example, both the fourth scale degree and the triad based on the fourth scale degree might be deemed to serve a subdominant function. In addition, a chromatic chord such as the Neapolitan sixth chord is often regarded as serving a subdominant function. At a larger level, an entire measure or subphrase might be deemed to serve some particular function. For Western musicians, the notion of function looms large in any discussion of scale degree. The important lesson is as follows: It is the capacity of scale degrees to evoke consistent and reliable *qualia* that allows them to be musically functional. If the consistency of the evoked *qualia* originates in statistical learning, then it follows that tonal function is ultimately a product of statistical learning.

While it is possible that statistical learning is a distinctly Western phenomenon—not shared by other peoples—this view seems unlikely. Since statistical learning has been observed in many species, it is probably universal across all human cultures. Given the biological importance of accurate prediction, one might expect to see the prediction effect throughout the animal kingdom. All animals ought to tend to prefer familiar (i.e., predictable) stimuli. This suggests that any musical culture that employs recognizably distinct materials (such as scale tones) will tend to gravitate toward differentiating the probabilities of different events, and ordering successive events so that their predictability is increased. These differences also ought to lead to differences in subjective *qualia* associated with different events. If this is true, then most musical cultures should manifest psychological phenomena that are parallel or analogous to what Western musicians have called tonality. In the case of Balinese, Sami, north Indian, and Korean musics, we have seen some preliminary evidence consistent with this claim. However, further cross-cultural experimental work is needed.

In this chapter I have attempted to explain some basic phenomenological experiences associated with tonality. From a psychological perspective, tonality might be defined as a system of pitch-related expectations, where the various scale tones acquire distinctive *qualia* as artifacts of learned statistical relationships. Of course, this account is a starting point, not an ending point. Tonality is a rich phenomenon with many facets. I have provided no account of harmony, modulation, tonicization, large-scale closure, and other aspects of Western tonality. Nor does Western music provide some universal yardstick against which all musical cultures are measured: there are surely unique "tonality" phenomena to be found in other musics of the world. I have ignored rhythmic interactions, motivic organization, and phrase structure. I have not discussed the important problem of how listeners infer key, mode, or rag. I have not addressed all seven descriptive categories identified in my *qualia* survey; for example, I have not addressed the subjective impressions related to "power." Finally, my account has focused exclusively on the probabilities of individual notes and pairs of successive notes. As we will see in the next chapter, there are expectations in music that span much longer stretches of time.

So far we have been considering only pitch-related expectations. Pitch, along with tone-color or timbre, falls under the rubric of *what*-related expectations. In anticipating future events, however, listeners also form expectations about *when* events may occur.[1] Often the expected timing is very precise, as when you expect the sound of a footstep to be followed by another footstep at a particular moment. In other situations the timing may be very imprecise, as when you expect a close friend to telephone after dinner. Sometimes the timing of an expected event is delayed, as when the verb in a sentence is delayed by the appearance of a preceding adverb. In other cases, the timing is improbably early, as when a child cries "ouch" before the nurse has inserted a hypodermic needle.

Periodicity and Tactus

The most easily predicted timings are those that are periodic, such as the ticking of a clock or the clickety-clack of a passing train.[2] Periodic events are predictable for the simple reason that they establish a regular time interval that acts as a predictive template. Not all periodic events are easily anticipated, however. For example, most traffic lights are on a strictly periodic timing cycle, but the period is too long for drivers to form more than a vague impression of when the light is likely to change. For traffic engineers the uncertainty introduced by a long timing cycle may be desirable since it discourages "jack-rabbit starts" and so can increase safety on the roads.

The erosion of predictive accuracy at long periods raises a useful question: When events are perfectly periodic, at what speed are listeners most accurate in predicting the next event? Research pertaining to this question has tended to focus on a related production task: At what speed are people most accurate in maintaining a steady beat? Variations on these questions have received extensive experimental attention. Research by Herbert Woodrow, Paul Fraisse, Dirk-Jan Povel, and Peter Essens has established that the optimum period falls in the range between 0.6 and 0.75 seconds.[3] This is equivalent to metronome markings between 80 and 100 beats per minute. At this tempo the timing variation between successive taps is smallest; that is, the tapping is most accurate at this rate. This optimum period also corresponds to the average spontaneous tapping rate—the rate at which a person will typically tap when no tempo has been given. In addition, when asked to tap at a rate that is either faster or slower than this rate, performers tend to decelerate or accelerate (as appropriate) in the direction of the optimum rate.[4]

Musicians use the word *tactus* to refer to the basic beat that forms the most salient periodic pulse evident in a musical passage. The tactus often coincides with the rate at which a typical listener will spontaneously tap in time with the music, either with a hand or foot. The psychological research suggests that the tactus has a special status both for the perception of time and in accurate rhythmic production.

As we have seen, accurate expectations are biologically valuable in two ways. First, successful anticipation allows us to optimize our arousal levels and so minimize the expenditure of energy. Suppose you are sitting in a chair with a relaxed posture. From across the room, I am going to toss an apple toward you. In order to catch the apple you must raise your arms. This takes energy, and the longer you have to sustain this pose, the greater the energy expenditure. Ideally, you would not raise your arms until just prior to the arrival of the apple. If the timing of the toss is predicted accurately you will save energy.

By waiting until the last minute before raising arousal levels, you will also reduce the magnitude of the tension response. That is, successful anticipation will reduce unnecessary vigilance and arousal leading up to the anticipated event. Simply put, accurate knowledge about when events happen allows you to remain in a restful state longer.

Second, successful anticipation has a facilitating effect on attention. In the 1930s, the University of Iowa music psychologist Carl Seashore suggested that attention may be periodic.[5] Over the past quarter century, Mari Riess Jones at the Ohio State University has assembled an abundance of experimental evidence in support of Seashore's intuition. When listening to sounds, we do not pay attention equally at all moments. Instead, auditory attention is directed at particular moments in time. Specifically, attention is choreographed to coincide with the most likely moments of stimulus onsets. As Jones has shown, metric hierarchies can be understood as a structure for rhythmic attending.

In her theory of *rhythmic attending*, Jones notes that the listener's attention is most acute at strong metric positions. Consider the following experiment carried out by Mari Jones, Heather Moynihan, Noah MacKenzie, and Jennifer Puente.[6] Listeners heard an initial tone, followed by eight "distractor" tones, followed by a comparison tone. The listeners' task was to judge whether the comparison tone was higher or lower in pitch than the initial tone. In figure 10.1 the first pitch (E) is the initial tone,

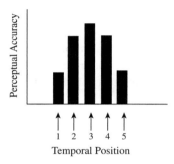

Figure 10.1
Typical stimulus used by Jones et al. (2002). Listeners heard a standard tone, followed by eight interference tones, followed by a comparison tone. Listeners were then asked to judge whether the comparison tone was higher or lower than the standard tone. The temporal position of the comparison tone was varied so that it would occur earlier or later than expected. See also figure 10.2.

Figure 10.2
Effect of temporal position on accuracy of pitch judgment. (See also figure 10.1.) Jones et al. (2002) showed that pitch judgments are most accurate when the tone judged occurs in an expected temporal position (position 3).

and the final pitch (D#) is the comparison tone. The intervening tones are random distractor tones that increase the difficulty of the task.

Jones and her collaborators manipulated the precise temporal position of the final comparison tone. In some trials, the onset of the tone coincided with the precise downbeat (position 3). Other trials were slightly earlier (position 2) or slightly later (position 4) than the downbeat. Yet other trials were considerably earlier (position 1) or considerably later (position 5) than the downbeat. It was found that the accuracy of pitch-comparison judgments depends on the precise temporal placement of the comparison tone. Listeners were most accurate in their judgments when the comparison tone coincided with the presumed downbeat. As the tone deviated from this position, perceptual judgments were degraded. This research reinforces the general principles we have already seen operating with regard to auditory expectation. Once again, accurate expectation facilitates action and perception. In the case of perception, accurate expectations about *when* a stimulus might occur helps the listener in resolving the *what* of perception.[7] Notice also that the process is entirely unconscious.

   Just as there are advantages to accurately anticipating when an event will occur, similarly, there are costs for failing to correctly anticipate the timing of some event. There are two kinds of such failures. One failure occurs when an anticipated event fails to materialize. A second type of failure occurs when an event happens whose timing was not anticipated. Such failures of temporal expectation can lead to frenzied mental activity. Suppose I dial the telephone number of a colleague. I expect my colleague to pick up the receiver and say "hello." But instead, I listen to the phone continue to ring several times. Suddenly I realize that my colleague is unlikely to answer, and that I will soon have to deal with my colleague's answering machine. Quickly, I begin to plan what message to leave. The leisurely conversation I had expected to take place will not happen. Instead I must generate an articulate, organized, coherent, and reasonably succinct monologue that doesn't leave an unprofessional impression. In this example, there is no particular event that causes me to begin making new plans. Instead, it is the absence of an expected event that precipitates all the mental activity.

Hierarchy and Hypermeter

While most music maintains a periodic pulse or beat, these beats are usually arranged into patterns that exhibit a hierarchical structure. Figure 10.3 shows a typical hierarchy for music in a simple duple meter. The figure plots the frequency of occurrence of tone onsets for a sample of children's songs from Puerto Rico.[8] The graph shows the number of tone onsets that occur at each sixteenth-note position within the measure.

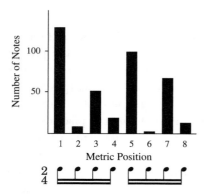

Figure 10.3
Metric organization for thirteen Puerto Rican children's songs in 2/4 meter.

Data are collapsed across all measures. Notice that there is evidence of hierarchical event patterns—what musicians refer to as *meter*. Some metric positions are more likely to coincide with note onsets than others. Specifically, the first metric position in the measure is the most likely moment of onset. The second most likely onset occurs midmeasure on the second beat (metric position 5). Metric positions 3 and 7 correspond to the second half of the first and second beats. The least frequent onsets coincide with the sixteenth-note quarter-beat positions (2, 4, 6, and 8). What musicians call the "strength" of a metric position is correlated with the likelihood of a tone onset.

If music exhibits such hierarchical event patterns, then experienced listeners should be able to take advantage of these patterns to predict the likely temporal placement of future tone onsets. Listeners probably expect tone onsets to occur at the strongest metric positions. However, I don't know of any research that directly establishes this (probably because researchers assume that this must be the case). Nevertheless, a wealth of research has established that temporal events can be coded hierarchically.[9] Other research has established that tone onsets coinciding with the most common metric positions are judged as "better fitting" with an antecedent metric context, and also that hierarchical mental coding of meter occurs.

Caroline Palmer and Carol Krumhansl carried out a set of probe-tone studies to determine how listeners rate different metric moments.[10] Palmer and Krumhansl presented stimuli that created particular metric frameworks, like 4/4 and 3/4. Following a meter-defining sequence, there was a pause, followed by a tone. Listeners were asked to judge the "goodness of fit" for each tone. Listeners assigned the highest values to those tones whose onsets coincided with the most important beats in the metric hierarchy, followed by the lesser beats, followed by the half-beat divisions, followed by tones that did not coincide with any beat.

The Palmer and Krumhansl work with temporal position was inspired by the earlier Krumhansl and Kessler approach to tonality. But the similarity between scale-degree expectation and metric expectation is not merely metaphorical or informal. Both scale degree and metric position are perceived categorically.[11] Like scale-degree pitches, metric positions provide convenient "bins" for expected stimuli. The metric hierarchy is truly homologous to a scale or scale hierarchy.

The hierarchical organization of temporal expectations does not end with the conventional musical meter. Meter signatures identify the temporal structure within musical bars or measures. However, groups of measures frequently combine in a hierarchical manner. In Western music, it is common for measures to group into eight-measure "periods" and sixteen-measure "double periods." These groupings often (though not always) coincide with the boundaries between phrases. Music theorists refer to such larger-scale temporal structures as *hypermeter*. Figure 10.4 illustrates the hypermetric organization of a string quartet by Joseph Haydn (op. 54, no. 1, 4th

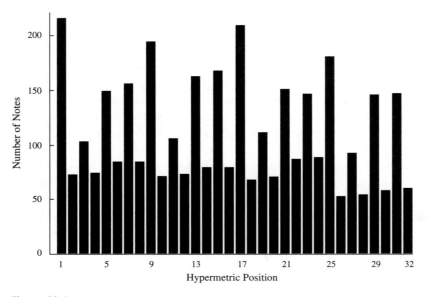

Figure 10.4

Four-measure hypermetric organization in Joseph Haydn's String Quartet, op. 54, no. 1, fourth movement. The movement is written in 2/4 meter; the graph plots the number of note onsets for all four instruments in sixteenth durations. Positions 1, 9, 17, and 25 coincide with the downbeats for the first, second, third, and fourth measures in the four-measure hypermetric unit. These positions exhibit the strong–weak–medium–weak structure commonly seen within a single measure of 4/4.

movement). Where figure 10.3 provides a histogram covering a single measure, the histogram in figure 10.4 represents a four-measure span.[12] Once again, each bar in the histogram represents a sixteenth duration. There are four measures of 2/4 meter represented. The downbeats for each of the four measures correspond to metric positions 1, 9, 17, and 25. Notice that the four downbeats exhibit a strong–weak–medium–weak pattern—a pattern usually evident for beats within a quadruple meter. Figure 10.4 collapses the onset events for groups of four measures. In other words, the normal metric hierarchy extends beyond the individual measure. In chapter 13 we will see examples of specific rhythmic patterns that help listeners become oriented to the hypermetric downbeat.

Long-Range Contingent Expectations

To this point, my discussion of temporal expectations has focused on zeroth-order patterns with a recurring cycle. That is, we have seen how event onsets are more or

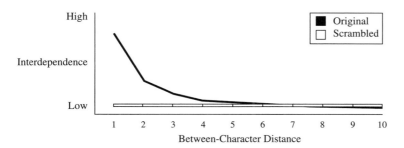

Figure 10.5
Graph showing the influence in English text of one letter on the presence of another letter displaced by *n* characters. Consecutive letters (*n* = 1) have considerable dependency. At a distance of about six letters the presence of a given letter has little measurable influence on a later letter. Interdependence is measured as entropy (in bits). From Simpson 1996.

less probable at different moments in a metric hierarchy. Rhythmic patterns also exhibit higher-order conditional probabilities. Some of these contingencies are comparatively short range, as when one event increases the likelihood of some other immediately ensuing event. However, it is often the case that an event will have a greater impact on more distant events than on neighboring events. Expectations in time appear to exhibit a range of near and far contexts.[13]

In chapter 3 we saw how information theory can be used to characterize short-range conditional probabilities. A branch of information theory known as "*m*-dependency" theory provides useful ways to characterize long-range statistical relationships between events.[14] Recall that the letter "q" tends to constrain subsequent letters—increasing the likelihood of an ensuing letter "u." But do letters influence the occurrence of letters that follow at a greater distance?

Figure 10.5 shows the interdependence of successive characters in English text. The x-axis indicates the number of characters following a given target character. The y-axis measures the dependency (in bits). As can be seen, the strongest effect is evident for a single character. This captures, for example, the strong influence that the letter "q" exerts on the immediately ensuing character. As the distance increases, the influence decreases exponentially. The lower line in figure 10.5 shows the dependencies for randomly scrambled English text. By definition, randomly rearranged characters have no influence on each other—that is, there can be no conditional dependencies. This line establishes a random baseline that is useful for comparison purposes. The figure shows that the future influence of an individual letter in English text declines to zero at a distance of about six letters.

Working at the University of Waterloo, my student Jasba Simpson applied *m*-dependency theory to analyze note-dependencies in music. Simpson examined four

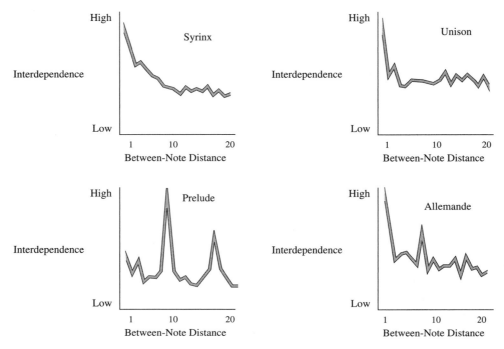

Figure 10.6
Interdependence graphs for four musical works: Claude Debussy's "Syrinx" for flute; Bela Bartók's "Unison" for piano from *Mikrokosmos*; Johann Sebastian Bach's Prelude I in C major from volume 1 of *The Well-Tempered Clavier*; and Bach's Allemande from the Partita for solo flute (BWV 1013). The graphs show long-term note dependencies. Reprinted with permission from Simpson 1996.

musical works: Debussy's *Syrinx* for solo flute, Bartók's "Unison" from *Mikrokosmos* for piano, Bach's Prelude I in C major from the first volume of *The Well-Tempered Clavier*, and Bach's *Allemande* from the Partita for solo flute. The results from Simpson's analyses are shown in figure 10.6. Once again, the graphs plot the distance over which one note influences another note.

Both the Debussy and Bartók works exhibit the exponential decay typically found when the dependencies are relatively short range. The strongest contingencies are evident when the events are temporal neighbors. As the notes grow farther apart they exhibit less of a statistical influence on one another. In the case of the two Bach works, however, there are significant peaks evident at the higher probability orders. Note especially the graph for the Bach C-major prelude. The dependencies between successive neighbors is relatively small. Instead, the greatest influence is apparent at eight-

Figure 10.7
Opening measures from Johann Sebastian Bach's Prelude I in C major from volume 1 of *The Well-Tempered Clavier*. Repetitive patterns are evident at 8 and 16 notes distance. These dependencies can be seen in the corresponding *m*-dependency graph in figure 10.6.

and sixteen-note separations. The reason for this relationship is obvious when looking at the score (see fig. 10.7).

Throughout this piece, Bach maintains a series of parallel compound melodic lines. The two voices in the bass staff are notated in a way that draws attention to their melodic independence. The monophonic series of sixteenth notes in the treble staff seems to imply a single melodic line, but this pitch sequence is perhaps better regarded as three independent voices. Each pitch has a strong relationship to pitches eight and sixteen notes distant. For example, the highest pitch (E5) in the first measure sounds like it is connected to the pitch F5 in the second measure. Such structural lines have long been described by music theorists, and research in auditory stream segregation has established that perceptions of "connectedness" are psychologically commonplace as long as the temporal separations aren't too great.[15]

These sorts of noncontiguous dependencies are not present in every musical work. But they are probably more common in music than, for example, in language. Long-range dependencies can be observed in poetry with regular rhyme schemes. However, in general, language sounds are dominated much more by short-range dependencies. The statistical methods provided by *m*-dependency theory allow us to measure and characterize such relationships.

The fact that some musical works exhibit noncontiguous statistical dependencies raises two questions. First, do listeners form the appropriate expectations when the implicative event is some distance removed from the corresponding consequence? Second, since the noncontiguous patterns differ for different works, do listeners quickly form new expectations that are tailored to the unfolding events of a given musical work?

Existing research has addressed only the first of these questions. Richard Aslin at the University of Rochester has carried out a series of studies where sounds are contingent on subsequent sounds, but the two sounds are separated by one or more statistically unrelated sounds. Aslin and his colleagues have studied successions of synthesized vowels, consonants, and pitched tones. The results of these experiments are complicated. For some kinds of stimuli, listeners form appropriate noncontiguous expectations, whereas listeners fail to form useful expectations for other kinds of stimuli. An interesting twist in this work is that Aslin and his colleagues have carried out the same experiments with cotton-top tamarins. The results for these cute little primates show that tamarins exhibit different capabilities in forming suitable expectations. It is not simply the case that tamarins are unable to form some expectations that humans readily do. For some noncontiguous stimulus patterns, tamarins succeed in forming statistically appropriate expectations where human listeners fail.[16] These interspecies differences are tantalizing, and might ultimately prove to be linked to special speech-related mechanisms for processing sound sequences.

In any event, the work of Aslin and his colleagues pertaining to medium-range temporal expectations is broadly similar to the experimental results we saw in regard to pitch-related expectations: listeners form expectations that only approximate the true underlying patterns of contingent probabilities.

The Pleasures of the Downbeat

The downbeat isn't merely that moment when events are more likely to occur in music. The downbeat *sounds nice*. One of the simple pleasures of listening to music is hearing events on the downbeat.[17] At this point, readers should be able to anticipate my proposal for why downbeats might sound pleasant. Similarly, readers should be able to anticipate why the downbeat might accrue other *qualia*, such as *closure* and *stability*.

When an event happens at an expected moment in time, the *prediction response* is positively valenced. This provides a positive reward for the heuristic used in the prediction and reinforces the use of such a heuristic in making future predictions. As noted in chapter 8, however, the positive emotion evoked by the accurate prediction is typically misattributed to the stimulus itself (the *prediction effect*). Since the downbeat represents one of the most predictable of event-moments, events that fall on the downbeat tend to evoke positive feelings. Colloquially, we say that the downbeat sounds nice.

The effect is not limited to the downbeat. Apart from downbeats, some beats and sub-beats are more probable than others, and so evoke greater or lesser pleasure via the prediction effect. Extensive metric hierarchies are evident in much of the world's music, so hypermetric downbeats (corresponding to periods or double-periods) would be experienced as especially "nice" sounding.

There is an obvious parallel between the pleasure experienced by listeners when hearing a downbeat, and the pleasure experienced by suitably enculturated listeners when hearing an expected tonic. In both cases, pleasure is evoked via predictability.

Misattribution of the prediction response to the stimulus itself leads the listener to attribute the pleasure to the downbeat and the tonic as sounded events, rather than as accurate predictions.

University of British Columbia music theorist John Roeder has described many of the formal parallels between tonality and meter.[18] I would go further and suggest that the structural similarities originate in a shared underlying psychology. Both tonality and meter are sets of enculturated mental structures—schemas that are related to a statistical hierarchy of events. Both are capable of increasing a listener's ability to anticipate and predict future sounds. They differ in that tonality relates to an aspect of the *what* of expectation, whereas meter relates to an aspect of the *when* of expectation.

I should note that the pleasure of the predictable downbeat is not the only pleasure that can be evoked through temporal organization. Syncopation, hemiola, and missing downbeats can also evoke powerful (and positive) emotions. However, I think that the mechanism for the evoked pleasure in these situations is different. Rather than manifestations of the *prediction effect*, these other rhythmic devices are forms of controlled surprise that achieve a positive affect through *contrastive valence*. We will consider the phenomenon of syncopation in detail in chapter 14.

Rhythmic Genres

As in the case of pitch perception, rhythmic expectations are related to context. Some contexts are quite general, as when we experience music in simple-duple meter, or compound-triple meter. At the other extreme, we may expect a particular temporal organization because of extensive familiarity with a particular rhythm or particular musical work. (This sort of "work-specific" expectation will be addressed more thoroughly in chapter 12.)

It is also possible that listeners form schematic expectations that are style- or genre-related. Consider, for example, the *siciliano*, a leisurely dance form popular in the seventeenth century. Ostensibly, the *siciliano* emulated a dance style characteristic of contemporary Sicily. It is generally in 6/8 meter, although occasionally it is found in 12/8. There are also stereotypic rhythms that contribute to the stylistic cliché for the siciliano. The most distinctive feature is the dotted-eighth–sixteenth–eighth figure that commonly begins the measure and may also appear in the second beat. Figure 10.8 shows the most common rhythmic patterns I found in a sample of baroque siciliani.

The Christmas carol "Silent Night" includes some of the distinctive siciliano rhythms. Figure 10.9 shows a cumulative onset histogram for a sample of bars taken from ten baroque siciliani. The graph shows the relative frequency of occurrence for various points in the 6/8 metric hierarchy. The horizontal lines marked (a), (b), and (c) correspond to the siciliano rhythms notated at the bottom of the figure.

Figure 10.8
Four rhythmic patterns commonly found in siciliano dance forms.

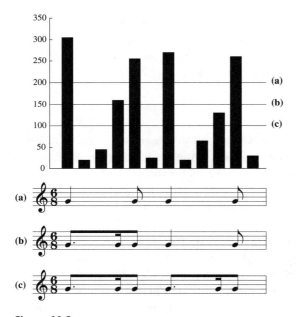

Figure 10.9
Cumulative onset histogram for a sample of measures from ten siciliano movements, showing the relative frequency of occurrence for various onset points in the 6/8 metric hierarchy.

Once such rhythms are established, listeners readily expect them. In this case, we can see that it is not simply the strict hierarchical metrical frameworks that influence a listener's temporal expectations. In addition to these *metric* expectations, listeners also form distinctly *rhythmic* expectations, which need not employ strictly periodic pulse patterns.

The siciliano rhythm is only one of hundreds of familiar rhythmic patterns. Many of these patterns are associated with various dances, such as the samba, rumba, tango, jig, reggae, limbo, pavan, beguine, polka, two-step, allemande, fox-trot, minuet, bossa nova, boureé, laendler, rock backbeat, and many others. Depending on the experience of the listener, such genres may be more or less salient and more or less distinct. Experienced listeners probably form temporal expectations that are uniquely tailored to the different rhythms that populate their acoustical environment. Like different meters, rhythmic genres are probably learned through exposure.

Nonperiodic Temporal Expectations

Although periodicity helps listeners to form temporal expectations, periodicity is not necessary for the formation of such expectations. It is important only that the listener be experienced with the temporal structure, and that some element of the temporal pattern be predictable. An illustration of this point can be found in the expectation for "bouncing" rhythms (see fig. 10.10). The sound of something bouncing is not periodic: the interbounce interval shortens as the bouncing continues. Nevertheless, listeners are able to predict, to some degree, the temporal sequence of events for a bouncing object. In music, this accelerating rhythm can be found in many musical traditions of the East, including Japanese Gagaku and Tibetan monastic music (where it is frequently played on cymbals). In Western music, there is no known instance of this accelerating rhythm prior to the twentieth century.

Further evidence for the predictability of nonperiodic rhythms has been assembled by Dirk Moelants at Ghent University, Belgium. Moelants has documented the performance stability for nonperiodic *Aksak* meters commonly found in Bulgarian dances. (These include rhythm cycles such as 3 + 2 + 2.) Moelants has also produced timing

Figure 10.10
Schematic representation of accelerating onsets characteristic of the sound produced by a bouncing object. Although the pattern is not metrically regular, it is nevertheless predictable.

measurements that confirm what musicians already know about Viennese waltzes: they are performed in a distinctly nonperiodic (though highly systematic) fashion. Viennese musicians do not simply play waltzes using a strict one-two-three, one-two-three, one-two-three. Instead the second beat is played early while the third beat is played late.[19] Nonperiodic temporal patterns can also be found in many complex west African rhythms. The nonperiodic character of certain rhythms does not prevent experienced listeners from forming accurate temporal expectations. This means that the pleasure evoked via the prediction effect is not limited to periodic beats. Even the most complex rhythms can evoke a positively valenced prediction effect if the rhythms are familiar—and thus predictable.

Speech Rhythms

Perhaps the premiere example of predictable nonperiodic rhythm is speech. People don't normally speak according to a periodic rhythm. In fact, strictly periodic syllable sequences are rare. Nevertheless, normal speech does exhibit predictable temporal patterns. Try speaking the following sentence aloud:

The quick brown fox jumped over the lazy dogs.

Most English speakers will enunciate the words "quick," "brown," and "fox" rather slowly and distinctly; by contrast, the words "over the lazy" will tend to flow in quick succession. If you were to reverse the duration pattern so that "quick brown fox" is spoken quickly and "o-" "ver" "the" "la-" "zy" is spoken slowly, the sentence would sound bizarre. Such stereotypic patterns of syllable durations are found in any spoken language. If a speaker speaks using an unorthodox temporal pattern, the speech will not simply sound unnatural; it will also be difficult for listeners to understand. Processing difficulty is one of the symptoms of inaccurate expectation. Listeners expect the temporal features of speech to conform to conventional speech patterns—even though these patterns may not be periodic in nature.

Given the importance of speech sounds in our lives, it is theoretically possible that common speech rhythms influence the experience of musical rhythm. For centuries, music scholars have speculated that music from different cultures might reflect in some way the manner in which people from that culture speak. Linguists have established that people from different cultures do speak with different rhythms. English and French, for example, provide a useful contrast. To English ears, French sounds like a smooth engine, with successive syllables all roughly the same duration, with very little stress or dynamic emphasis. French sounds like a smoothly pointillistic sewing machine. To French ears, English sounds very rugged. Some syllables are smacked hard, and these syllables tend to alternate with other syllables that nearly disappear because they are so quiet. There is some acoustical truth to the French characterization of

English as sounding like a fly buzzing near one's ears. Looking at just the duration of successive syllables, linguists have shown that French syllables tend to show relatively little variation in duration. But in English, there is a strong tendency for long and short syllables to alternate.

Working at the Neurosciences Institute near San Diego, Aniruddh Patel and Joseph Daniele carried out a study comparing instrumental melodies written by English and French composers.[20] Patel and Daniele simply measured the variability in the durations of successive notes. Assuming that a note corresponds in some sense to a syllable, one might speculate that French melodies would tend to be more isochronous, and that English melodies would tend to alternate long and short notes. That's exactly what Patel and Daniele found in a sample of three hundred melodic excerpts from instrumental music. Intrigued by this result, Joy Ollen and I carried out a replication study involving roughly ten times the number of musical passages. As in the Patel and Daniele study, we examined only instrumental works since we assumed that vocal works would surely reflect the language used in the vocal text. Our study exactly replicated Patel and Daniele's results.[21] Instrumental melodies by English composers are more likely to alternate long–short durations than are melodies by French composers. Figure 10.11 illustrates this difference.

French melodies have a slight tendency to employ successive notes of equal duration—as exemplified by "Frères Jacques." English melodies have a slight tendency to "skip" with alternating shorter and longer notes—as exemplified by "An English Country Garden." I hasten to add that the melodies in figure 10.11 are extreme examples. The average difference between French and English melodies is quite small—though statistically significant.

Apart from the controlled empirical studies, ethnomusicologists have made more informal observations linking musical patterns to speech patterns within some culture. For example, William Malm of the University of Michigan has written extensively about the relationship between Japanese speech and traditional Japanese music.[22] Once again, the rhythm patterns in the speech appear to be reflected in the music.

Figure 10.11
"Frères Jacques" and "An English Country Garden." Exemplars of a statistically significant (though weak) tendency for French melodies to employ roughly isochronous successive tones, whereas English melodies tend to "skip" with alternating shorter and longer notes. From Huron and Ollen 2003.

If the rhythms we are exposed to in speech somehow influence our music, this raises the question of how such an influence arises. At least two theories might be considered. One theory begins with the suggestion that composers of vocal music pay close attention to creating melodies that preserve the prosody of the language. This facilitates singing as well as comprehension of the vocal text. Over time, this vocal tradition establishes stylistic habits that influence the purely instrumental music as well so that all music in a given culture tends to echo the rhythmic properties of the musicians' native language. A second theory is that the common rhythmic patterns evident in some language become broadly learned as a statistical auditory pattern learned by all people within that linguistic community. These patterns then influence directly all rhythmic phenomena generated by members of that community.

Note that in either case, common speech patterns become generalized. In the first theory, the generalization is evident in the influence of vocal music on instrumental music. In the second theory, the generalization is more broadly evident.

Whatever the origin of these patterns, rhythmic influences may be much more pervasive than we think. The way we move our bodies may influence the experience of rhythm, and common rhythms may influence the way we move. For example, research has shown that paraplegics who are confined to wheelchairs have more difficulty with both rhythmic production and rhythmic perception tasks than do nonparaplegics. When movement is restricted, it seems reasonable that rhythmic production would be impeded. But why would restricted movement interfere with perception? The research seems to imply that the ability to move one's legs has an impact on rhythmic processing.

On the other hand, pervasive rhythms within a culture may affect the way people move. Percussionist John Chernoff provides a lovely description of his first trip to the west African country of Ghana. In a customs office, Chernoff had to wait while a clerk typed copies of invoices:

Using the capitalization shift key with his little fingers to pop in accents between words, [the clerk] beat out fantastic rhythms. Even when he looked at the rough copies to find his next sentence, he continued his rhythms on the shift key. He finished up each form with a splendid flourish on the date and port of entry. . . . I realized that I was in a good country to study drumming.[23]

Statistical Temporal Learning

We began this chapter by considering how periodicity might contribute to the predictability of temporal events. However, our discussion of speech rhythms suggests that periodicity may be less important than familiarity in forming rhythmic expectations. The influence of familiar speech rhythms on English and French instrumental melodies suggests a sort of generalized temporal learning through exposure. While there

Figure 10.12
Example of two perceptually distinct rhythms. In the work of Desain, Honing, and Sadakata, a series of intermediate stimuli were generated between such normative rhythms.

are other possible explanations, this phenomenon has all the earmarks of statistical learning. This suggests that we return to consider what temporal patterns real music exhibits, and whether listeners form expectations based on these statistical patterns.

Rhythms are perceived categorically. That is, a number of slightly different performed rhythms will be perceived by listeners as "the same" rhythm.[24] Consider, for example, the rhythmic figures notated in figure 10.12. The first measure contains a simple quarter–eighth–eighth pattern. With a tempo of 120 beats per minute, the nominal duration of the quarter note would be 500 milliseconds and each of the eighth notes would have a duration of 250 milliseconds. The second measure contains a quarter-note triplet. Here, the nominal duration would be 333 milliseconds for each note. However, actual musical performance exhibits a considerable range of acceptable deviation from these nominal durations. An interesting question arises when one systematically "morphs" the durations from one rhythmic pattern to another. What happens when, say, a three-note rhythmic sequence is generated where the note durations are 400 ms, 300 ms, 300 ms? What pattern do listeners hear, and why?

At the University of Nijmegen in the Netherlands, Peter Desain, Henkjan Honing, and Makiko Sadakata carried out a series of experiments that has clarified how musicians produce and perceive different three-note rhythms. The results of their research can be conveniently represented with the aid of a triangle (see figure 10.13). Successive sides of the triangle (labeled 1, 2, 3) represent the durations of the first, second, and third notes in the rhythmic pattern. Any specific three-note rhythm can be plotted as a single point within the triangle. The grid inside the triangle helps us determine the values for each of the three durations. The solid grid lines pertain to the duration of the first note, the dashed grid lines pertain to the duration of the second note, and the dotted grid lines pertain to the duration of the third note. Three sample rhythmic patterns are plotted. The point labeled "A" at the center of the graph represents a three-note rhythm in which each note has an equal duration (i.e., triplets). Point "B" at the top of the graph represents a rhythmic "pattern" in which all of the duration is assigned to the first note, while the other two-note durations are infinitely small. Point "C" represents a quarter–eighth–eighth rhythm in which the first note is 500 milliseconds while the second and third notes are 250 milliseconds each. Using this graph, it is possible to plot all possible duration ratios between three hypothetical tones.

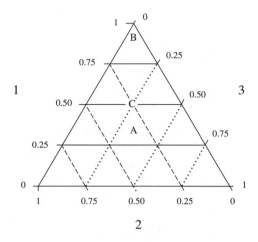

Figure 10.13
Graph representing the relative durations of three-note rhythmic patterns. Solid grid lines pertain to the duration of the first note ("1"). Dashed grid lines pertain to the duration of the second note ("2"). Dotted grid lines pertain to the duration of the third note ("3"). The point labeled "A" represents a nominal three-note "triplet" rhythm in which each note has the same duration (0.33 seconds). Point "B" represents a rhythmic "pattern" in which all of the duration (1.0 seconds) is assigned to the first note and the other two note durations are zero. Point "C" represents a quarter–eighth–eighth rhythm in which the first note is 0.50 seconds and the second and third notes are 0.25 seconds each.

Suppose we ask musicians to tap various repeated rhythms. One rhythm might consist of a quarter–eighth–eighth pattern. The upper gray area in figure 10.14 shows the range of actual performance values for musicians tapping this rhythm. If performers tapped the rhythm exactly, all values would lie near the point marked X. However, the graph shows that performers tend to lengthen the second note slightly and shorten the third note. Figure 10.14 also shows the results of tapping a repeated dotted-quarter–eighth–half rhythm. The ratios of the notes would be 3:1:4. Once again, an X marks the point corresponding to a "perfectly" tapped rhythm, while the actual performance data is indicated in the gray region that does not even include the point marked X. For this rhythm, musicians tend to significantly shorten the duration of the first note and significantly increase the duration of the second note. This raises an interesting question: why do performers produce rhythms that deviate so dramatically from the nominal or canonic timing?

To answer this question, we need to consider how listeners *perceive* these rhythms. In 2003, Peter Desain and Henkjan Honing carried out the appropriate study. In a transcription task, musician listeners heard different rhythmic patterns and were asked

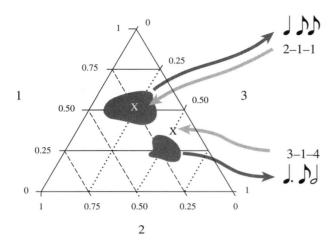

Figure 10.14

Relative durations for two 3-note rhythms tapped by musicians. The upper gray region plots performances for a 2:1:1 rhythmic ratio. The point marked X indicates the canonical or mathematically accurate ratio. The lower gray region plots performances for a 3:1:4 rhythmic ratio. The region of performance for this rhythm differs notably from the canonical or mathematically accurate ratio (marked X). From Desain and Honing 2003.

to notate them. For example, a listener might hear a repeated sequence of 240 ms, 240 ms, 520 ms—and notate this as eighth–eighth–quarter. By systematically exposing listeners to sampled points from throughout the triangular space of possible duration ratios, they were able to map the perceptual boundaries between various three-note rhythmic patterns. Some of the results are shown in figure 10.15.

Although there are some discrepancies, in general, Desain and Honing found that the perceptual categories and the performance categories match quite well. Notice that some regions, such as the 1:1:1, 1:1:2, and 2:1:1 rhythmic ratios, are quite large. By contrast, rhythmic ratios such as 2:1:3 and 1:1:4 are quite small. What accounts for the size of the rhythmic category regions, and why are the boundaries positioned where they are?

Desain and his colleagues explored one possible answer to this question. They used a large database of Western music to identify the frequency of occurrence of various three-note rhythmic patterns. They represented all of the three-note patterns using ratios, so that the patterns quarter–quarter–quarter and eighth–eighth–eighth were both coded as 1:1:1. Not surprisingly, some patterns—such as 2:1:1 (e.g., quarter–eighth–eighth)—are relatively common. Other patterns—such as 1:3:4 (e.g., six-teenth–dotted eighth–quarter)—are relatively uncommon. Many possible rhythmic patterns simply never occurred in the musical sample. For example, doubly dotted

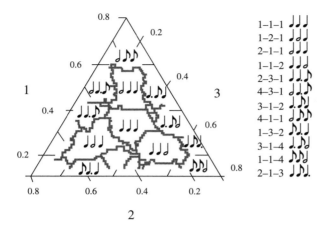

Figure 10.15
Categorical boundaries between various preceived three-note rhythms. From Desain and Honing 2003.

eighth–dotted eighth–dotted sixteenth (ratio 7:6:3). For these areas of the rhythmic map, other more common rhythms could simply encroach into these "unused" regions. The amount of encroachment is related to the frequency of occurrence: those rhythms that occur most frequently in Western music expand to include those areas associated with less common rhythms. The actual occurrences of three-note rhythmic patterns predicts very well the regions shown in figure 10.15.[25] In other words, Desain, Honing, and Sadakata found that the manner by which listeners "parcel" the (theoretically infinite number of) three-note rhythmic patterns reflects the way real music parcels this rhythmic space. In short, listeners were most likely to apprehend a rhythm in terms of their rhythmic familiarity. To put it more technically, Desain, Honing, and Sadakata found that the relationship between rhythmic perception, rhythmic production, and familiarity could be related using "Bayes' rule"—a well-known rule for statistical decision-making.

Once again, the evidence strongly suggests a form of statistical learning in which listeners perceive the world in a manner that corresponds to their past listening experience. While Desain, Honing, and Sadakata did not directly investigate the phenomenon of rhythmic expectation, their work is consistent with the patterns we have already seen for pitch perception. Listeners appear to be sensitive to the frequency of occurrence of various rhythmic patterns, and their cognitive processing of rhythmic information is disposed to interpret stimuli in terms of familiar preexisting rhythms.

Table 10.1

Metric classification	Sample meters	Percent occurrence
simple duple	2/2, 2/4, 2/8, 2/16	27.4%
simple triple	3/2, 3/4, 3/8, 3/16	32.0%
simple quadruple	4/2, 4/4, 4/8, 4/16	27.2%
compound duple	6/2, 6/4, 6/8, 6/16	9.4%
compound triple	9/2, 9/4, 9/8, 9/16	1.3%
compound quadruple	12/4, 12/8, 12/16, 12/32	1.9%
irregular	5/4, 7/8, etc.	0.8%

The Binary Default in Western Meter Perception

Just as not all rhythms are equally common in music, it is also the case that not all meters are equally common. Table 10.1 shows the results of a survey of several thousand musical works from the Western classical tradition.[26] Duple and quadruple meters occur twice as often as triple and irregular meters (66% vs. 34%). In addition, simple meters are roughly six times more common than compound meters. In other words, in Western classical music there exists a preference for binary beat groupings and a marked preference for binary beat subdivisions.

Given the predominance of binary meters, and given the evidence for statistical learning, one might suppose that listeners experienced with Western music would be biased toward binary expectations. On average, those listeners who assume an unknown rhythm to exhibit a binary structure would be more accurate in their temporal predictions than listeners who don't use this heuristic.

Evidence supporting a default "binary" metric expectation for Western listeners has been observed in neurophysiological data. Working at the University of Bourgogne in France, Renaud Brochard, Donna Abecasis, Doug Potter, Richard Ragot, and Carolyn Drake played a sequence of isochronous tones to listeners who were outfitted with electrodes to record EEG responses. Each tone in the sequence was acoustically identical, so no metrical cues existed in the stimulus itself. Brochard and his colleagues compared the evoked potentials elicited by odd-numbered versus even-numbered occurrences of the sounds. They looked only at the evoked potentials for tones beyond the tenth tone in the sequence. The odd-numbered events differed significantly from the even-numbered events—consistent with a default binary metric structure. In effect, listeners were subjectively "accenting" the odd-numbered events in the sequence.[27] Since the stimuli were identical, the observed differences in EEG must reflect a cognitive rather than a perceptual phenomenon. Since the EEG components are related to attention, the results are also consistent with Mari Jones's theory of rhythmic attention.[28] The most straightforward interpretation of this study is that greater attention is directed at alternating stimuli, and that this tendency arises from passive learning through exposure to a predominantly "binary" rhythmic environment.[29]

This study was carried out using Western listeners, so we don't know whether the results generalize to listeners from other cultures. It is conceivable that there is some innate disposition toward binary temporal grouping, but I suspect that the acoustical environment plays the preeminent role. Cross-cultural experiments could help resolve whether binary grouping is innate or learned through exposure.

The Poetry of Combining What and When

Expecting *when* something will happen is different from expecting *what* will happen. The *what* and *when* of expectation can be linked together or they can be entirely independent. In musical rhythms, for example, listeners can form a strong expectation that some sound will happen at a particular moment, even though they have little inkling of *what* sound will occur. (For example, audience members can watch the conductor's downbeat and anticipate the exact moment when the orchestra begins to play—with little idea of what sound to expect.) In other circumstances, the listener will have a good idea of *what* to expect, but will be left wondering *when* the sound will happen. More commonly, though, the *what* and *when* are interdependent and correlated. In chapter 13 we will see several musical examples where pitch and timing patterns reinforce the overall predictability.

A good place to observe the coordination of *what* and *when* is in poetry. Two features of conventional poetry are known to appeal to listeners: a *rhyme scheme* and a regular *meter* or rhythm. Consider, by way of example, the following stanza from a poem by Robert Frost:

Life's not so short
I care to keep
The unhappy days;
I choose to *sleep*.[30]

The poem maintains a duple meter: with the exception of the third line (which contains an extra syllable), each line contains two iambic (short–long) beats. Let's consider the listener's expectation at the moment just prior to the last word in the stanza (*sleep*). By establishing this regular meter, listeners expect the final syllable to coincide with the second beat. That is, the meter establishes a high expectation of *when* the final syllable will occur. At the same time, listeners will expect the final vowel to rhyme with either the "ay" of "days" or the "ee" of "keep." That is, the poem provides listeners with helpful clues of the *what* of the final syllable. The rhyme scheme directly facilitates the perception of the final vowel.

There are good reasons why people might tend to prefer poems that have a rhyme scheme and regular meter: these structures make the sounds more predictable, and so easier to perceive and process. By combining a regular rhythm and a rhyme scheme, conventional poetry makes effective use of the brain's tendency to reward itself for doing a good job of anticipating stimuli.

Apart from perception, there are also good reasons to favor rhythm and rhyme from the perspective of production. In nonliterate cultures, poetry is performed exclusively from memory. Reciting an epic poem involves enormous demands on memory. For the bard, anticipating what comes next is essential.[31]

Since increasing predictability facilitates perception, one might expect to see examples of intentional redundancy in circumstances of degraded communication. In radio communications, for example, static noise is a common problem. Organizations such as the International Civil Aviation Authority provide standard dialogue protocols that enhance intelligibility. An example is the word sequence for relaying alphabetic letters: alpha, bravo, charlie, delta, . . . x-ray, yankee, zulu.[32] This list emphasizes a two-syllable *trochee* (strong–weak) vocabulary that facilitates word recognition. An initial syllable—such as "zu"—encourages the listener to predict the consequent syllable—"lu"—which, if heard, reinforces the accuracy of the perception.

The outdoor theaters of Shakespeare's day had to contend with all kinds of noise. Whatever other function was served by Shakespeare's ubiquitous use of iambic pentameter, having the actors speak in verse increased the intelligibility of the words. In each case, a by-product of expectation-facilitated perception is a positively valenced emotion arising from the prediction response.

Representation

How are temporal expectations represented in the brain? As in the case of pitch-related representation, there are many candidates for how timed events might be mentally coded. Before addressing this question, we ought to note that the psychology of temporal organization makes a distinction between *meter* and temporal *grouping*. Grouping can be defined as the tendency for neighboring temporal events to cluster into units or chunks. Meter, by contrast, can be defined as the tendency to apply hierarchical temporal schemas for predicting recurring event onsets. The meter–grouping distinction was made forcefully in the 1950s by Herbert Woodrow and in the 1980s by Fred Lerdahl and Ray Jackendoff.[33] In research carried out in the early twentieth century, Woodrow showed that tones of long duration tend to terminate a rhythmic group, while dynamic stresses tend to initiate a rhythmic group. Lerdahl and Jackendoff refined these heuristics in a set of grouping preference rules.

As cogently argued by Bob Snyder, temporal grouping appears to be linked to short-term memory. A "group" is a sequence of events that is held together in short-term memory and processed as a unit before the brain moves on to the next group.[34] Experimental evidence in support of this interpretation is found in the work of Andrew Gregory. Working at the University of Manchester, Gregory has shown that when brief clicks are added randomly to a musical passage, well-trained listeners have trouble reporting accurately where (in time) the clicks occur. A click in the middle of a melodic sequence tends to be reported as occurring either after the sequence ends or (less commonly) before the sequence starts. That is, the clicks appear to gravitate toward group boundaries in a manner that parallels speech processing.[35] Once the auditory system begins to process a group of sounds, sounds that do not belong to the group are stored separately and dealt with later. As a result, concurrent auditory stimuli are processed sequentially rather than simultaneously. Rhythmic patterns roughly one or two seconds in length tend to be processed as mental "atoms."

Returning to the phenomenon of meter, we find that meter provides a recurring temporal template for coding and predicting event onsets. When a sequence of durations or inter-onset intervals conforms to some regular period, temporal expectations might be represented using mental oscillators of various frequencies and phases.[36] When some onset-moments are more likely than others, sound events might be coded hierarchically in terms of their *metric position* within a recurring temporal template. Mental oscillators may or may not provide the mental basis for such metric representations.

Between temporal grouping and meter there are many candidate representations that could provide a basis for mental coding. These might include onset and offset times, inter-onset intervals (IOI), duration, duration categories (such as short/medium/long), IOI "contours" (such as longer/shorter), beats, metric positions, oscillator periods, rhythmic feet (groups of two or three events linked by strong/weak relationships), rhythmic Gestalts, bars, phrases, periods, and so on. In all of these purported representations, temporal information might be coded as zeroth-order events, or as first- or higher-order relationships.

In chapter 7 I speculated that many pitch-related representations are spawned spontaneously during auditory development, and that neural competition leads to the preservation or elaboration of successful neural representations and the decay or atrophy of unsuccessful neural representations. In a similar fashion, it is possible that the brain spawns a number of competing representations for temporal expectations. Those temporal representations that survive and mature are those mental codes that prove most useful in predicting the *when* of future events.

As in the case of the various pitch-related representations, the various temporal representations will be strongly correlated with one another. In notated music, for example, I have found that *duration* and *inter-onset interval* exhibit a correlation greater than +0.98. It should be no surprise that increasing the sounded duration of a note tends to increase the inter-onset interval between successive notes. Unfortunately, such strong correlations make it more difficult to identify the precise nature of mental representations for temporal expectations. As in the case of pitch-related representations, teasing apart the many possibilities will require carefully controlled experiments.

In this chapter I have suggested that the basis for temporal perception is *not* periodicity—but *predictability*. The purpose of a good temporal representation is to predict the appearance of future stimuli, not to predict the start of a periodic cycle. It is possible that periodic stimuli are more easily coded than nonperiodic stimuli. However, it should be noted that there is no existing experimental evidence in support of this view, since none of the pertinent experiments has controlled for stimulus predictability.

In chapter 7 I suggested that brains are more favorably disposed to some forms of mental representation over others. I proposed four factors that might cause some mental representations to be favored: lower-order relationships, neighboring over distant relationships, lower derivative states, and event-related binding. The category of lower-order relationships suggests that representations will tend to involve fewer sound events or fewer relationships. In the case of rhythm, this principle would tend to favor small groups of events, such as coding of rhythmic feet, short rhythmic groups (like rhythmic motives), and bar-length patterns such as meters. The principle of neighboring over distant relationships suggests that representations will tend to favor successive events over longer-range relationships between sounded events. The category of lower derivative states suggests that representations would tend to favor events, or the simple "distance" between events, rather than the differences in the differences between events (for example, rhythmic "contour").

Music perception researchers have long emphasized the importance of inter-onset interval as a basic unit or element underlying temporal sequences. As Paul Fraisse has suggested, the stimulus is not the tick of the metronome, but rather the interval between the ticks.[37] From a biological perspective, I think this is unlikely. Once again, the biological goal of expectation is to predict future events. This goal will surely have a strong influence on the kinds of temporal representations that can exist in human brains. I have no quarrel with the notion that brains somehow keep tabs on the elapsed time between successive events, but I think these time intervals are subservient to the business of predicting the advent of a sound. Brains don't appear to predict inter-onset intervals; instead they predict sound onsets. In short, I think the ticks of the metronome truly are the stimuli. Elapsed time plays a role insofar as it is correlated with whatever representation the auditory system uses to predict when the next tick will occur. There are good reasons why brains would favor representing sound *onsets*. To the extent that stimuli provoke responses, one can see why most of the processing would be triggered by the advent of a sound. The sooner one processes a sound and formulates an appropriate response, the better.

Again my argument here is reminiscent of the discussion of pitch intervals in chapter 7. There I raised the possibility that pitch interval may not be a common mental representation; I suggested that it might be more common for brains to represent intervals as scale-degree successions. In the case of time intervals, I think the phenomenological argument is stronger. I don't know any musician who claims to hear time-spans rather than metric placement. Two rhythms are perceived to be most similar when tones are added at the most probable metric positions, and when tones are removed from the least probable metric positions. Changing a single inter-onset interval is much more disruptive—typically because the meter is affected.

Once again, notice the close psychological parallel between scale degree and metric position. Both are schematic frameworks that allow us to hear events "as" something. We hear the pitch C *as* the tonic. We hear a particular moment *as* the downbeat. In each schema, events receive mental labels that reflect their relative probability of occurrence in some commonly experienced context.

The last of my four proposed representational dispositions was *event-related binding*—the tendency for a relational attribute to be mentally assigned to a single event. In chapter 7 I suggested, for example, that a melodic interval does not exist as a percept *between* two pitches. Instead, I proposed that a melodic interval is a feeling or *quale* that adheres to the second tone of the interval: a melodic interval is a way of approaching some note. The distance between two sound events is not some disembodied property, but a property of some object—the second tone. I think the same principle of event-related binding also holds for time-related mental representations. As an illustration, consider the distinctive rhythmic *qualia* associated with syncopation.

Figure 10.16 shows two examples of an eighth note occurring immediately before a downbeat. (Both examples are assumed to occur in some metrical context that causes listeners to expect a downbeat following the barline.) In the first example, we would experience the note as syncopated. In the second example, we would experience that same note as unsyncopated. Whether the note is perceived as syncopated or not depends entirely on what happens *after* the note ends. It is the absence of an onset on the ensuing stronger metrical position that creates the syncopated experience. But the failure for an event to appear on the downbeat is ascribed retrospectively. The *quale* of syncopation is ascribed not to the silent downbeat, but to the preceding

Figure 10.16
Two passages in some established metrical context in which listeners expect a downbeat after the barline. In the first example, we hear the note as syncopated. In the second example, we hear the same note as unsyncopated.

sounded event. In general, we tend to attribute syncopation to particular sounded events rather than to particular moments. That is, we tend to hear syncopated "notes" rather than syncopated metric relationships, even though it is the relationships that cause the syncopation. As with the melodic interval, again brains are disposed to bind attributes to events, not to relationships.

This is yet another example of misattribution. Like the young men on the Capilano bridge attributing their feelings of vertigo to a woman experimenter, the feeling of syncopation is attributed to a convenient bystander. Brains may be sensitive to contexts and relationships, but these attributes tend to be coded as qualities that adhere to perceived objects or events, not to spans, intervals, or silences.

Reprise

In this chapter I have argued that meters are predictive schemas for temporal events. Traditionally, theories of meter have stressed the role of *periodicity*—a constant sequence of isochronous event onsets. I have suggested that periodicity has a special status because periodic events make it easier for inexperienced listeners to form accurate temporal expectations. However, in this chapter I have suggested that periodicity is simply a special case of the more general phenomenon—predictability. Listeners have little difficulty predicting nonperiodic event patterns, as long as the patterns are familiar. Accordingly, I have suggested that such *when*-related expectations are learned through exposure. As in the case of pitch-related schemas, temporal schemas arise through statistical learning.

In the case of pitch-related schemas we have direct evidence for statistical learning in the work of Jenny Saffran and her colleagues. In the case of temporal schemas the evidence for statistical learning is admittedly more indirect and not yet compelling. Nevertheless, the evidence is suggestive. Five forms of evidence stand out in particular. First, there is the evidence assembled by Peter Desain, Henkjan Honing, and Makiko Sadakata that the perception and reproduction of rhythmic figures by Western-enculturated listeners matches very well the actual distribution of rhythms in Western music. Listeners best process those rhythms that occur most frequently. Second, the EEG data collected by Renaud Brochard, Donna Abecasis, and their colleagues suggest that the brains of (Western-enculturated) listeners favor binary temporal grouping—a disposition that is consistent with the pervasive binary structure evident in Western music. Third, we have the existence of musics in various cultures—notably west African and Balkan—that exhibit nonperiodic metric and beat patterns. That is, there exist entire musical genres that are not based on tactus-level periodicity. Fourth, we have seen that performances of Western music exhibit stereotypic timing "deviations" that are not periodic but are nevertheless predictable for experienced listeners. An example of such systematic timing deviation is evident in the Viennese waltz, as documented by Dirk Moelants. Fifth, spoken languages are typically not periodic in their syllable timing, yet listeners form expectations based on normal speech rhythms. In this regard, we have seen that rhythms in French and English instrumental music tend to echo the prosodic features of their respective languages—although such influence may not have arisen directly from familiarity with the speech itself. Further evidence in support of the claim of rhythmic familiarity over periodicity will be given in chapter 14, where we will see that patterns of syncopation are highly stereotypic and highly predictable, despite the absence of periodicity.

Apart from the issue of statistical learning, I have suggested that the effects of temporal expectation parallel, in many ways, the effects of pitch-related expectations. First, we have seen that accurate expectations facilitate perception. The experiment carried out by Mari Jones, Heather Moynihan, Noah MacKenzie, and Jennifer Puente parallels closely the experiment by Gordon Greenberg and Willard Larkin discussed in chapter 3. There are distinct perceptual benefits for the listener who forms an accurate premonition of what pitch will occur and when it will begin. Said another way, both "aiming in time" and "aiming in pitch" confer significant mental advantages.[38] Second, we have seen that different "timing contexts" exist, such as meters and dance rhythms. These temporal templates act in a similar way to the major and minor modes in pitch-related expectation. In the Renaissance, theorists spoke of "rhythmic modes"— by analogy to pitch-related modes—instead of meters. From a psychological perspective, this analogy seems warranted. Well-known rhythms (such as dance patterns) act in a manner very similar to meters. And both meters and rhythmic schemas behave in a manner analogous to the major and minor pitch-related schemas.

Finally, I have suggested that the subjective *qualia* evoked by particular rhythmic moments can be explained statistically in a manner similar to the statistical accounting of tonality-related *qualia* discussed in chapter 9. The emotional or limbic responses are similar for both *when*-related expectations and *what*-related expectations. Positively valenced predictive rewards are evoked for highly predictable events. The downbeat is the most predictable temporal event; hence the downbeat evokes a postive prediction response. As in the case of the tonic, the positively valenced predictive reward is misattributed to the stimulus itself.

There is, however, at least one significant difference between *when*-related and *what*-related expectations. Unlike the pitch-domain, the temporal domain enables the phenomenon of "delay"—with enormous consequences for the tension response. In particular, there is a notable asymmetry between *early* and *late* onsets of events. We will explore this topic in chapter 15.

11   Genres, Schemas, and Firewalls

Every year, millions of tourists from around the world visit Britain. They visit such sites as Buckingham Palace, the cavernous interior of St. Paul's Cathedral, the lovely spires of Oxford, and the ancient monoliths of Stonehenge. But most first-time vistors also experience an unanticipated shock. Tourists from continental Europe, America, and many parts of Asia and Africa discover that the familiar act of crossing the street is far from simple. Expectations about traffic flow can be dangerously wrong. Each year, a few unfortunate visitors pay the ultimate price because entrenched mental habits are not appropriate for the British context. The British, of course, experience the same shock when they first cross the English Channel.

When forming expectations about the world, it is easy to overgeneralize from past experiences. We may not realize that our expectations have value only in a particular environment. When the context is wrong, otherwise useful intuitions may prove false, misleading, or even life-threatening. As important as it is for organisms to learn about the world, it is also important for organisms to learn to restrict inductive lessons to the appropriate domain or context in which the generalization applies. As Leda Cosmides and John Tooby have noted, there are good reasons why, in the evolution of cognitive processes, special mechanisms are needed in order to limit the scope of learned information.[1]

Consider, by way of example, harmonic progressions involving the dominant (V) and subdominant (IV) chords. In Western baroque music, the IV–V progression is much more common than the reverse (V–IV) progression. In J. S. Bach's chorale harmonizations, for example, the IV–V progression occurs more than four times as often as V–IV. By contrast, in reggae, the relationship between dominant and subdominant is reversed. In a sample of reggae music, I found that the V–IV progression occurs roughly twice as often as IV–V. This means that these chord progressions represent an eightfold asymmetrical difference in probabilities between baroque and reggae harmonies. In the baroque context, the V–IV progression is somewhat surprising, whereas in the context of reggae, the same V–IV progression is commonplace.

If the listener is to correctly anticipate the progression of acoustical events, then she must somehow bracket or segregate two different sets of expectations. If the biological goal is accurate prediction, then the listener who is able to distinguish baroque from reggae will be at a significant advantage over the listener who is unable to make such a stylistic distinction.

In the previous chapters I have made liberal use of the psychological concept of a *schema* without defining it. A schema is often described as an expectational "set." A schema provides an encapsulated behavioral or perceptual model that pertains to some situation or context.[2] Outside of music, researchers have identified all sorts of examples of psychological schemas. In music, we have already encountered evidence supporting the existence of different musical schemas. Perhaps the best documented difference is the distinction between *major* and *minor* modes.[3] Western-enculturated listeners exhibit dramatically different expectations depending on whether the music is perceived to be in a major or minor key. In addition, we've seen examples of different schemas related to time perception, such as the contrast between simple and compound meters. But the ability to form distinct schemas permeates musical experience. It is the ability of brains to form multiple schemas that provides the psychological foundation for distinguishing different styles and genres. Without this foundation, baroque and reggae would meld into a single general musical schema. Our experiences with baroque harmony would interfere with our ability to accurately predict harmonic progressions in reggae, and vice versa.

Context Cueing

How does a brain know which schema to apply to some experience? In selecting a schema it appears that brains rely on both positive and negative evidence. Positive evidence includes *environmental markers* that have a learned association with a particular schema. Negative evidence includes *inductive failures* where erroneous expectations suggest that a listener is applying the wrong schema or that the schema is faulty.

Social psychology provides innumerable illustrations of the effect of positive environmental markers on expectation. Norms of behavior are linked to particular social roles. For example, we comply with the family doctor who asks to take a look in our ears, but we would be dumbfounded if the same request were made by a taxi driver or bank teller. As sociologists have observed, cultures tend to mark different roles by characteristic cues. A common social cue is the wearing of distinctive clothing (uniforms) that are associated with various professional roles. These overt cues help us switch between different possible expectational sets or schemas.

Music provides an abundance of environmental markers—both auditory and nonauditory—that help to distinguish musical genres. One source of cues is instrumentation. Much of the world's music is characterized by the use of distinctive instruments, such as the Chinese *er-hu* fiddle, the Australian didgeridoo, or the Western electric guitar. The musical timbres themselves suggest that some continuations are more likely than others. Other environmental markers relate to location. Some forms of music occur almost exclusively in particular places, such as in a synagogue, pub, ice rink, football stadium, or elevator. Distinctive dress can also have specific musical connotations, from the ballerina's tutu to the Scottish kilt to the formal dinner jacket to the cowboy's string tie. Certain Hindu *rags* are played only at a particular time of day. For example, *Āsāvarī* is intended to be performed only in the morning.[4] Even hairstyles can have musical connotations, from the soldier's crewcut to the rocker's shaggy mane. The Rastafarian's dreadlocks might cue the harmonic heuristic "expect the progression V–IV to be more common than IV–V," whereas a powdered white wig might cue the reverse heuristic.

Environmental markers don't merely function as cues to invoke different schemas. Such markers also provide distinctive cues that help us *learn* new schemas. A particular musical style can be associated with unique instruments, performed only in specific physical locales, or played by performers dressed in a distinctive costume. My experience of American blues is indelibly associated with the *L'Hibou* ("The Owl") nightclub in 1960s Ottawa. These were my first experiences of black musicians, my first exposure to people playing harmonica and dobro, and my only exposure to music while breathing large quantities of cigarette smoke. Given the abundance of cues, it was unlikely that I would confuse this music with my activities playing flute in the Ottawa Youth Orchestra.

My experience with the blues was accompanied by highly distinctive (and memorable) cues. Such genre cueing is characteristic of encapsulated inductive learning. In their landmark book *Induction,* John Holland, Keith Holyoak, Richard Nisbett, and Paul Thagard note that inductive learning is shaped by what they call *unusualness rules.* Whenever a situation exhibits some unexpected or unusual property, there is a strong likelihood that that property will function as a conditional clause for any inductively learned rule.[5] It is not common to see a long trumpet with a flag hanging from it, so this unusual instrument evokes much narrower stylistic associations than does the common trumpet.

Sometimes, a listener is exposed to only a single token or instance of a given genre. Imagine, for example, a hypothetical listener whose only experience of Swiss yodeling consisted of a single recording. For this listener, an entire genre is represented by a single work. Should the listener encounter another instance of Swiss yodeling, the music is apt to link very directly to the more familiar work.

A nonmusical example of such "single-token genres" can be found in the story of Charles Berlitz, the well-known language educator. Charles was born into a family of linguists; he was the grandson of Maximilian Berlitz, the founder of the Berlitz language schools. When Charles first began to speak, he learned four different languages at the same time, each exclusively spoken to him by a different member of his family.[6] The young Charles had no idea that he was learning different languages. He simply learned that he needed to speak differently when interacting with his mother compared with his father, and so on. For Charles, each language had a personal identity. A language like French was not just a language; it was personified by one of his close relatives. Each language was represented by a single token—a single speaker.

Charles had cues in abundance. Here, the young Berlitz learned to form a unique communicative context for each family member. A language like Spanish was not simply an abstract form of interaction; it was the form of address that was linked to a particular face, a particular individual, a particular personality. For Charles, Spanish had a small nose, French had short hair, and English wore high heels.

Undergeneralization

Sometimes *unusualness* can interfere with a useful generalization. While the disposition to encapsulate knowledge in salient contexts can help to prevent overgeneralization, these same dispositions can sometimes prevent generalization from occurring in situations where generalization would be appropriate. A friend of mine was successfully able to train her dog to sit on voice command. Initially, the training was done while the animal was on a leash, so my friend was concerned that her dog would not obey the command once the leash was removed. Fortunately, removing the leash had no adverse effect: her dog continued to obey the "sit" command. However, she was appalled to discover later that her dog obeyed the command only when she was walking backward! Throughout the training period, my friend had been walking in front of her dog—walking backward so that she could face and address the animal. Her dog had learned to attend to the most distinctive contextual cue, namely, the rare and unusual condition of its master walking backward. If my friend failed to walk backward, the "sit" command had no effect.

It is difficult to assess whether such "undergeneralization" occurs among music listeners. Theoretically, it is possible that some listeners will fail to "transfer" expectations from a familiar context to some novel musical genre or style. (Perhaps an experienced jazz musician might fail to recognize the return of the "head" in a classical theme and variation.) However, no pertinent research has been carried out, so the phenomenon remains conjectural.

If our musical expectations change according to context, then a number of important questions arise: How many different musical schemas can a listener maintain? How fast are listeners able to identify the context and invoke the appropriate schema? When the context changes, how fast are listeners able to switch from one schema to another? What cues signal the listener to switch schemas? How do listeners learn to distinguish different contexts? How are the expectations for one schema protected from novel information that pertains to a different schema? How are schemas updated to take advantage of additional inductive lessons? How do listeners assemble a totally new schema? What happens when the events of the world straddle two different schemas?

Starting Schema

How do listeners know what schema to start with? Environmental markers can provide useful cues regarding appropriate schemas. Consider five brass players with their instruments. If the players are dressed in formal evening wear, certain associations and expectations might arise. If the players are dressed in military uniforms, our expectations would shift noticeably. If the players are dressed informally and standing on a New Orleans street corner, our expectations would again shift noticeably.

Apart from such environmental markers, listeners also rely on generalized learning to suggest how the music might unfold. We already know that an isolated tone tends to be heard by listeners as the tonic. But do listeners suppose that it is the tonic of a major or minor key? Following exposure to an isolated two-second tone, I have found that listeners are more than three times as likely to expect a tone whose pitch is a major third above as a minor third above. This implies that Western-enculturated listeners have a tendency to start by assuming a major mode.[7] The work of Brochard and Abecasis discussed in chapter 8 similarly implies that Western-enculturated listeners have a tendency to assume a binary meter. Even before the first sound is heard, listeners are prepared to invoke several musically pertinent "default" expectations. These expectations may be wrong on many occasions, but they are more likely to be right.

Once the music has begun, listeners appear to be extremely quick to detect schema-appropriate cues and to switch schemas as necessary. The split-second recognition of musical styles is apparent when listeners scan the radio dial looking for an appropriate station. Only a brief period of time is needed for most listeners to determine the style of the music and decide whether to stop or continue to the next radio station. Starting from this observation, David Perrott and Robert Gjerdingen at Northwestern University carried out an experiment to measure the speed of style identification. They exposed listeners to brief random musical segments from samples of ten different styles of music, including jazz, rock, blues, country & western, and classical, among others. They found that listeners are remarkably adept at classifying the type of music in just 250 milliseconds.[8] After one second of exposure, ordinary listeners' abilities to recognize broad stylistic categories are nearly at ceiling. That is, further exposure to the musical work does not lead to a notable improvement in style identification. If we assume that identifying a style is tantamount to activating the schema, then these observations suggest that experienced listeners can activate a schema appropriate for the genre of music they are hearing in a very short period of time.

This quick schema activation makes biological sense. A brain can't wait for a minute or two before deciding which auditory schema ought to be applied to some listening situation. If different styles or genres demand different sets of auditory expectations, then stylistic cues must be identified very rapidly. For most types of music, one second is too short to hear more than a couple of beats, so distinctive meters, rhythms, phrasings, rubatos, and repetitive patterns are not available to the listener. Listeners are often able to extract a huge amount of style-related information from a single sung tone.

These observations are at odds with many of the patterns musicologists have identified as distinguishing various musical styles. Some of the style-distinguishing patterns proposed by musicologists involve overall aspects of form. Other patterns relate to phrase construction and cadences. These patterns undoubtedly exist and undoubtedly provide useful cues for distinguishing styles. But the work of Perrott and Gjerdingen suggests that the bulk of the psychological work is done in the first 250 milliseconds. This means that *timbre* must provide more important stylistic cues than, say, large-scale *form*. Although other factors may contribute to differentiating various styles, the principal repository of stylistic information for music is timbre.

Fugal form with its distinctive monophonic opening may be one of the few "set" forms in Western classical music that can be recognized in sufficient time to evoke a unique listening schema. By contrast, the differences between sonata-allegro form and rondo form are not likely to lead to different schemas. This is not to suggest that informed listeners cannot differentiate sonata-allegro from rondo. What it suggests is that such recognition occurs at a conscious level and is not psychologically automatic. The two forms might be considered different from a formal theoretical perspective, but they almost certainly do not evoke different listening schemas such as occurs for major and minor, or for reggae and baroque. For the composer who wants to create a new genre or style that is psychologically salient, long-term structure is not a promising creative tool. New genres or styles are better established by employing distinctive timbres, textures, or moment-to-moment note transitions.

Given the rapid speed of style recognition for music, it is possible that schema recognition in music follows the same principles that have been observed in language. Linguists were surprised to discover that words are often recognized before a speaker finishes uttering the word. When a listener recognizes a word, two processes are thought to be involved—a bottom-up and a top-down process. Word recognition begins even before the advent of the first phoneme with a top-down estimate of what is likely to be said. The succession of phones then progressively trims the possibilities. For example, if a [g] sound is encountered, then words with this initial phone will be activated. With the addition of each successive phone the possibilities are reduced.

The so-called recognition point occurs when the sequence of phones uniquely determines some word. For example, in the word "glimpse" the recognition point might occur with [glimp]. The advent of the [p] would distinguish the word from similar words like "glimmer." At the same time, top-down estimates contribute to the process, so for example, syntactical and pragmatic information might cause the recognition point to occur earlier. For example, expectation of a verb might cause recognition to occur after an initial [glim] sound. This linguistic theory, known as "cohort theory," lays much emphasis on the initial sounds of an utterance. But proponents of cohort theory also argue that nonlinguistic context also contributes to word recognition. It is possible that music listeners recognize genres, styles, and keys in a manner akin to how the cohort theory claims we recognize words.[9]

The speed of style recognition in music might seem astounding, but it should not be cause for surprise. If musical expectations are shaped by statistical processes, then we ought to be able to see evidence of these processes even before any sound occurs. In most expectation-related experiments, some antecedent context is given and then the expected continuation is measured. The antecedent context "primes" the continuation. But in chapter 4, we already saw some experimental evidence of "unprimed" expectations—situations where listeners have expectations even before they hear any sound. In that experiment, I simply asked musicians to imagine tones, chords, rhythms, and other basic musical elements. Table 11.1 summarizes some of the results from that experiment.

Table 11.1
Unprimed listener expectations

	Imagined	Actual
Pitch	mean F4	mean D#4
Chord quality	major (94%); minor (3%); diminished (3%); augmented (0%)	major (72%); minor (25%); diminished (3%); augmented (0%)[1]
Chord position	root position (100%)	root position (67%); first inversion (29%); second inversion (2%)
Voice type	adult (100%), child (0%); female (56%), male (44%); vibrato (75%);	adult (99%), child (1%); female (47%), male (53%); vibrato (66%)[2]

Notes

[1] These values come from an analysis of a sample of chorale harmonizations by J. S. Bach. Ignoring the presence of 7ths, 71.8% of chords are major, 24.9% are minor, and 3.3% are diminished.

[2] These estimates come from a simple survey using 100 CD recordings from an eclectic collection of Western and world musics. The vibrato estimate was created by taking random time points in the same musical sample and judging by ear whether any corresponding vocalization included vibrato. These values should be viewed skeptically since no effort was made to assemble a representative random sample.

The leftmost column identifies the various mental tasks. The middle column summarizes the properties of the imagined sounds reported by my listeners. The rightmost column identifies comparable statistics for actual music. In the case of imagined pitch, all of my listeners imagined a tone within an octave of D4. As noted earlier, this coincides very well with the distribution of actual pitches in music.[10] Evidently, when asked to imagine a pitch, listeners tend to imagine most easily tones that lie near the center of the pitch region for real music.

In the case of chord imagination, the results are quite striking. When asked to imagine some chord, all but two of my participants imagined a major chord. Moreover, all of my participants imagined a chord in root position. Most imagined a triad, but a few imagined a four-note chord. All were in closed position. In real music, major chords are nearly three times more common than minor chords: roughly 75 percent of chords in Western music are major chords. The proportions differ by genre or style, so that minor chords are proportionally more likely in classical music than popular music; minor chords are more prevalent yet in New Age music. Yet only one of my listeners spontaneously thought to imagine a minor chord. The tendency to simply bet on the most likely outcome is characteristic of Bayesian decision making, and, as we saw in chapter 10, Bayesian-like behavior has been observed when listeners hear a rhythm.

In the final task, participants were asked to "imagine the sound of a singer singing a stable pitch." After they indicated that they had formed a vivid image I asked a series of questions: Is the voice you imagine that of an adult or child? In all cases, adult. Is the voice you imagine that of a male or female? Here the results were mixed with 56 percent reporting female and 44 percent reporting male. (I found no relationship between the sex of the imagined voice and the sex of the experimental participant.) I also asked whether the singer was singing with or without vibrato. 75 percent reported a tone with vibrato. In short, listeners tended to imagine rather prototypical sounds: an adult singing with vibrato.

In general, there is a notable similarity between the imagined sounds and the most common sounds encountered in Western culture. Even without any sound at all, listeners imagine sounds that are commonplace. If unprimed imagined sounds are at all symptomatic of unprimed expectations, then we might suggest that listeners are already disposed to hear sounds of a certain sort, even without any other cues.

Schema Switching

What about the phenomenon of *schema switching*? How rapidly can a listener switch from one schema to another? Although little research has been carried out pertaining to this question, suggestive evidence has come from the work of Carol Krumhansl and Ed Kessler working at Cornell University. Krumhansl and Kessler traced the speed with which a new key is established in modulating chord sequences.[11] According to their study, modulations to related keys are "firmly established" within three chords—a progression lasting just a few seconds. However, some residual sense of the initial key is maintained throughout the modulating passage. Since modulation is common in Western music, past experience might facilitate rapid switching between key-related schemas. It is possible that switching between more contrasting schemas might take much longer, but this seems doubtful. A switch from Calypso to Beijing opera might be wholly unexpected, but I doubt that the switch would take more than a few seconds—although the experience of surprise might last somewhat longer!

Quick schema changes are also evident in musical works that contain passages that alternate between the major and minor modes. In theme and variation forms, for example, it is often the case that one or more variations will be in the minor key—*en minore*. Listeners appear to have little difficulty making the shift between major and minor. Similarly, listeners appear to have little difficulty in switching from one meter to another: a march can morph into a waltz with only a few seconds required for listeners to adapt to the new step.

The examples of tonality and meter illustrate another useful lesson. Schemas are not simply restricted to different cultures or styles. Some schemas span multiple cultures and styles. For example, the major/minor distinction is found in nearly all Western styles—country & western, hip-hop, baroque, folk, and so on.

It is probably the case that the speed of schema switching is related to past experience. Listeners who have experienced considerable schema switching are probably more adept. The experience of bilingual speakers provides a plausible parallel. Bilingual speakers differ in their abilities to switch rapidly between different languages. Often it will take many seconds for a bilingual speaker to adapt to a change of language. But this skill appears to be related to how often speakers must change language in their daily life. Montréal taxi drivers seem remarkably adept at switching between English and French.

What cues signal the listener to switch schemas? Two plausible sources of cues for schema switching can be identified: auditory and nonauditory. One source might be obvious and persistent failures of expectation. Once again, switching between two languages is instructive. If a person has been conversing in French, then the failure of an utterance to conform to the schematic expectations for French ought to lead to a reevaluation of the language context, and so precipitate switching to a different language schema. Similarly, the failure of pitch-, rhythm-, timbre-, or other related expectations might be expected to instigate a search for a more appropriate schema.

Sometimes cues that signal a change of context are totally absent, and these situations can cause considerable anguish. Consider, for example, the difficult job of the bartender. A good bartender will engage patrons with a friendly manner. The friendliness creates a more sociable work environment and will lead to better tips. However, in most jurisdictions, bartenders hold serious statutory responsibilities. They are often held legally liable for the actions (and welfare) of drunk patrons and are legally obliged not to allow patrons to become inebriated. When faced with a patron who continues drinking, at some point, the bartender must change roles from "friendly bartender" to "stern disciplinarian." For the patron, there are no obvious external cues that signal the change of role. Since the bartender has provided drinks throughout the evening, the expectation is that the bartender will provide yet another drink. It should be no surprise that many bartenders have suffered the wrath of drunk patrons. This wrath is commonly ascribed solely to the patron's inebriated state. However, much of the anger originates in the thwarted expectation. Smart bartenders can reduce the likelihood of an angry response by providing visual cues that alert a patron to the bartender's changed role. For example, prior to cutting off a patron, the bartender might don a cap bearing the logo of a local ambulance service or fire department.

Mixed or misperceived cues can also be a source of humor. Many comedy scenarios revolve around misconceptions about what role a person is playing. The protagonist is mistakenly assumed to be a police officer, or dentist, or shop assistant. In comedy routines, part of the role of the "straight man" is to ensure that members of the audience maintain an appropriate "straight" schema, and don't simply switch to a schema that accepts absurdity as normal.

Mixed or misperceived cues can also be the source of bitter disagreement. Folk singer Bob Dylan was greeted with derision in response to his early efforts playing an electric guitar. In the early 1960s, fans regarded the sound of the electric guitar as incompatible with the folk genre. At the time, the electric guitar sound was widely associated with rock music. Pop historians have noted that the emergence of the folk-rock blend involved considerable growing pains.[12]

Sometimes such cues lead to anachronistic listening experiences. Consider, for example, the use of the saxophone in classical orchestral music. I recall my first experience as a young teenager hearing the use of the saxophone in the orchestral music of Ravel and Debussy. At the time, my only exposure to the instrument had been in the contexts of jazz, rock, and music for band. The timbre cues evoked by the saxophone did not mesh with my classical listening categories. Only later did I learn that the French penchant for orchestral saxophone predated the period when the instrument became widely associated with jazz. To an inexperienced teenager, works employing orchestral saxophone bordered on "genre mixtures"—akin to Dylan's folk-rock blend. But for Ravel and Debussy, the use of the saxophone carried no such dramatic connotations. Invented by French Belgian Adolphe Sax, the instrument seemed to be a natural expression of French musical culture.

The auditory and nonauditory cues that provoke schema switching might also provide plausible cues through which new schemas are created. The persistent failure of expectations might well raise the alarm that a novel cognitive environment has been encountered and that the listener's existing palette of schemas is inadequate. An interesting consequence of this view is that it should be difficult to form a new schema when the new context differs only slightly from an already established schema. Once again, language provides a useful illustration. Native English speakers who learn a Latinate language often experience some confusion when learning a second Latinate language. For example, a nonfluent knowledge of Spanish may generate confusion when attempting to learn Italian. Moreover, Italian vocabulary and grammar may begin to interfere retroactively with one's Spanish abilities. The difficulty appears to be the failure, from an English speaker's perspective, to sufficiently distinguish Italian from Spanish. This confusion appears to be reflected in neurological studies. It is often the case that cortical areas associated with a native language are segregated from cortical areas associated with an acquired second language. However, a third language will often share cortical regions associated with the second language. In this case, the weaker cognitive barrier between schemas is reflected in an apparently weak neurophysiological barrier.

Whatever form these barriers take, they are clearly important in order to maintain the modular structure of auditory schemas. As we noted earlier, these cognitive barriers allow a listener to be surprised by events that are common in one schema but uncommon in another. While a modern listener might be quite familiar with jazz, this same listener might well find a moment of syncopation in a renaissance motet to be somewhat shocking. Recall from chapter 9 that Mary Castellano, Jamshed Bharucha, and Carol Krumhansl found that American listeners did not carry over Western pitch expectations to the experience of listening to North Indian music. Both anecdotal and experimental evidence implies that relatively strong barriers exist between schemas. However, more research is needed to determine the extent to which one musical schema can influence another.

Cross-Over

What happens when the events of the world straddle two different schemas? The apparent modularity of auditory schemas suggests that the boundaries between schemas provide musically fruitful opportunities for playing with listeners' expectations. There are innumerable examples of musically interesting "cross-overs" and most music-lovers will be able to identify two or three favorites.

Among my favorites I would include the blend of traditional and modern elements in the Sudanese rocker Abdul Aziz el Mubarak, the comic genre-mixtures of the American musical humorist Peter Schickele (alias P. D. Q. Bach), and the King Singers' vocal renditions of Beatles tunes in a refined madrigal style. But an especially compelling example for me is found in *Bach Meets Cape Breton*—recorded by David Greenberg and the group *Puirt à Baroque*.[13] Greenberg received classical training as a baroque violin specialist, but is also an accomplished Cape Breton-style fiddler. In recording traditional baroque dance suites, Greenberg shifts easily between conventional art-music interpretations and traditional fiddling. A "gigue" by Bach will morph into a "jig." Listening to his performances, one has a palpable sense of connections being made between two formerly distinct musical schemas. A listener begins to imagine a continuum between courtly baroque dances and eighteenth-century folk dances. We will examine the phenomenon of stylistic mixtures in more detail in chapter 14.

From a musical point of view, stylistic and genre distinctions contribute to the wealth and variety of musical experience. As we have seen, experienced listeners probably form different stylistic schemas for renaissance and rock music, for bluegrass and bebop. As psychological constructs, however, genres exist as encapsulated expectation-related knowledge. The knowledge is modularized in separate schemas as the brain's way of preventing past experiences from being overgeneralized to inappropriate contexts. When creating new styles or genres, musicians take advantage of the existing evolutionary cognitive machinery for protecting an organism from misapplying local information to other environments. The fact that the brain so readily brackets novel environments suggests that musicians have considerable latitude for creating new and unprecedented musics. However, like the bartender who is forced to change roles when cutting off an inebriated patron, those composers who want to establish a new genre must provide adequate distinctive cues that will allow the listener to bracket the experience and begin the process of erecting a cognitive "firewall" around the new genre.

Schematic Taxonomies

Although differences in genre are linked to statistical patterns evident in the environment, genre is not a function of musical patterns alone. Any taxonomy for genre is a combination of the actual music and the listener's unique listening experience. Research by Robert Gjerdingen has suggested how different listeners classify different types of music. A classical music fan will distinguish many varieties of classical music (opera, chamber music, renaissance, baroque, classical, romantic, etc.). A jazz fan will distinguish many varieties of jazz (bebop, big band, ragtime, New Orleans, cool jazz, free jazz, etc.). Similarly, a rock fan will distinguish many varieties of rock (acid rock, classic rock, heavy metal, Goth, alternative, etc.). In general, people make more refined distinctions for music that is central to their taste, and then use cruder classifications for music that is peripheral to their interests. For example, while a jazz fan will distinguish a large number of varieties of jazz, other musical styles may be given broad classifications (e.g., country and western, classical, pop) with little internal differentiation. Characterizations depend on a person's listening experience.[14]

"It all sounds the same to me." This is the common verdict listeners render when they are unable to make the schematic distinctions available to the cognoscenti. The student of medieval music may be unable to distinguish Dorian from Phrygian modes—a distinction that the experienced musicologist readily hears. The teenage boy may have no difficulty distinguishing hip-hop from club music—a difference that is utterly lost on his parents. Novice ethnomusicologists engaged in field research often experience self-doubt because they cannot distinguish genres that their informants confidently make. If the schematic boundaries are absent, then it truly is the case that all of the music will "sound the same."

New schemas sometimes arise in one culture through inspiration arising from contact with another culture. Ironically, there is no guarantee that members of the appropriated culture will recognize the result. In the seventeenth century, the Ottoman Turks laid siege to the city of Vienna. Their siege was unsuccessful, but their military music-making left a lasting impression on the musically attuned Viennese who were listening on the other side of the city walls. For the next century, *alla turca* (in the Turkish or Janissary style) became a favorite musical device—a style used by Haydn, Mozart, Beethoven, and many other composers. But the Turks themselves could be forgiven if they thought *alla turca* simply sounded like typical Western classical music.

Commonly, listeners will form a broad category of "otherness" into which all deviant stimuli are, by default, indiscriminately assigned. Jonathan Bellman has documented how the *alla turca* style became synonymous with "exoticism" and subsequently became amalgamated with Hungarian and Gypsy elements in Viennese art music in the nineteenth century. In effect, Turkish, Hungarian, and Romani musical gestures fused into a single "exotic" musical language.[15] A typical Western-enculturated listener may have a handful of non-Western schematic categories available—such as Chinese music, Australian didgeridoo, and west African drumming. But for the inexperienced listener, much of the remaining world of music is clumped into a single "exotic" category. Hence, for example, Inuit, Tuvan, Papuan, and Jajouka singing would be indistinguishable to many listeners, despite the extreme cultural and geographical distances separating their Arctic, central Asian, south Pacific, and north African origins.

Alternatively, listeners may simply fail to gain sufficient exposure to bring about the creation of the new schema. Such failures are commonplace when listening to the music of an unfamiliar culture. A few years ago I was a volunteer on a project related to the Lakota. Much of the time was spent interacting with Steve (Big Bear) Emory, a traditional Lakota singer from South Dakota. Emory would regularly break into song. One evening, we were standing outside under a dark sky and he began singing. I closed my eyes and enjoyed the graceful beauty. I knew it was unlikely that he would sing a Sun Dance song or a healing song. Perhaps, I thought, he was singing a lullaby.

Instead, after he finished, he told me it was a horse-stealing song. I realized that I had completely missed the playfulness and bravado of his singing—listening for spirituality and depth when spiritedness and machismo were more appropriate. Without knowing the Lakota language, I had utterly misconstrued the musical genre. It was one of those privately embarrassing moments that highlights the discrepancy between wishes and reality.

Such failures can also occur within one's own culture. In Western music, an example can be found in the perception of atonal music. Carol Krumhansl, Gregory Sandell, and Desmond Sergeant found that listeners to atonal pitch sequences tend to divide into two groups. One group of listeners has internalized atonal conventions and judges as ill fitting those pitches that have appeared recently in the tone sequence.[16] However, a second group of listeners continued to hear the sequences according to tonal expectations. Krumhansl and her colleagues found that the two groups differ in musical background—the former group being more highly trained. This implies that greater exposure would have benefited the second group of listeners. The experience of atonal listening will be described in more detail in chapter 16.

Before leaving the subject of musical schemas, it is appropriate to draw attention to some of their shortcomings. Schemas are not merely innocent advisors that offer helpful suggestions about how to prepare and respond to the world. Schemas are also the basis for prejudice. Like racial stereotypes, schemas can bring things to the experience that are not actually present and that prevent us from recognizing elements that *are* present. Most people harbor particular musical peeves. Part of our self-conception as music-lovers is that we like certain musical styles, are lukewarm about other styles, and actively *dislike* some music. When the pop-music-lover hears the first few notes of "classical music," recognizing the style may be the cue to tune out. Similarly, the art-music-lover who hears the first few notes of a country & western tune may become dismissive or contemptuous. While schemas provide convenient ways of parcelling experience, they can also sometimes stand in the way of really listening to a musical work and attending to its unique virtues. Ears can be closed as well as opened; schemas can hinder as well as help. As we will see in the next chapter, one of the most valuable functions of consciousness is that it can permit us to revisit experiences and reappraise our responses: "I know most of you will think that you hate this kind of music, but let me just draw your attention to the following . . ."

Reprise

Building on Leonard Meyer's notion of normative archetypes, Robert Gjerdingen was the first to apply schema theory to musical genres in his *A Classic Turn of Phrase: Music and the Psychology of Convention*.[17] Different styles and genres in music appear to originate in the phenomenon of cognitive schemas. In this chapter I have suggested that the capacity to form different schemas arises from the biological need to avoid over-generalizing by limiting the scope of inductive lessons. Said another way, the ability to form multiple schemas is part of the arsenal of mechanisms developed by evolution to deal with the problem of induction.

Without musical schemas, we would hear that works resemble each other to greater or lesser degrees, but there would be no boundaries, no classes of works. Piece-specific expectations would arise for individual musical works, but listeners would experience all musics using a single overarching expectational "set." Harmonic, melodic, and rhythmic expectations would represent grand averages of all of a listener's past musical experiences.

New schemas arise in response to inductive failures. When our expectations prove wrong, the conditions are ripe for learning a new schema. Salient features in the environment (whether visual or auditory) become associated with the new inductive lessons. These same environmental markers can then serve as contextual cues that allow us to recognize future situations where invoking the new schema would be appropriate. Examples of such salient features are distinctive clothing, manners of speech, places, people, instrumentation, or anything else that proves unusual or out of the ordinary.

Listening experiences are approached with default schemas that are activated even before any sound is heard. Once the music begins, listeners are adept at switching rapidly between schemas—although some changes of schema are more common than others. The repertoire of schemas available to the individual listener is a product of that listener's unique listening history. As Gjerdingen has noted, stylistic taxonomies are listener-centered. The music heard most frequently by a listener occupies a highly differentiated central position in the listener's personal stylistic taxonomy. Less frequently heard music is less carefully differentiated, and tends to be grouped into larger more amorphous categories. Distinctive experiences may ensue when a musical experience straddles two or more existing schemas (i.e., cross over).

The brain's disposition to encapsulate knowledge into distinct domains makes it possible for musicians to differentiate styles and genres. The musical importance of such encapsulated knowledge cannot be exaggerated. For the historian and ethnomusicologist, the brain's disposition to segregate knowledge domains is surely cause for relief. If listening schemas didn't exist, a Western ethnomusicologist would never be able to experience the music of another culture without constant interference from Western listening habits. Similarly, without schemas, historians could not possibly experience the hemiolas of renaissance Latin motets without being jaded by their experience of the more audacious syncopations of modern jazz.

Although listening to the music of another culture is not unproblematic, schemas are in some ways the cognitive heroes of multiculturalism. For ethnomusicology in particular, further empirical study of musical schemas is surely warranted. Without an understanding of how schemas arise and how cognitive firewalls are erected and maintained, notions of cross-cultural listening will remain speculative.

If, as I believe, schemas are important in musical experience, then schema theory raises innumerable questions pertaining to cross-cultural musical experiences. If nonauditory environmental markers (such as ritual contexts) are important cues that provoke listeners to form new schemas, what happens when Western-enculturated listeners experience unfamiliar music in audio-only contexts? When non-Western cultures adopt Western musical instruments, are Western-enculturated listeners less likely to develop appropriate schemas? Does the use of non-Western instruments and gestures in Western cross-over music reduce the effectiveness of these timbres when forming culturally congruent listening schemas? How much exposure is required for an individual to form a style- or genre-appropriate schema? Do experienced ethnomusicologists ultimately hear a foreign music in a culturally congruent fashion, or are their schemas based on features that differ from culturally knowledgeable listeners? How do existing listening schemas interfere with or prevent the development of other listening schemas? Are all schemas acquired through statistical learning?

Over the past century, ethnomusicologists have been principally occupied with the important tasks of preserving, documenting, and interpreting the music of (often endangered) cultures. But an argument can be made that what we mean by "preserving the music" is not simply recording the sounds and maintaining the social institutions that promote ongoing creative activities. In addition to its sonic and cultural dimensions, music is a perceptual-cognitive experience, so "preserving the music" cannot happen without preservation of the culturally congruent "habits of listening." If we wish to forge effective cultural policies aimed at fostering distinctive ways of listening, we must attend to the mental mechanims that underlie the psychology of schemas.

12 Mental Representation of Expectation (II)

In chapter 7 we introduced the problem of how sounds are mentally represented. Our discussion emphasized the coded content of these representations: absolute pitch, scale degree, interval, duration, and so forth. In this chapter we return to this question of the mental representation of sounds. But here we address the structure rather than the content of these representations. In particular, I will focus on three types of memory and suggest how these different forms of memory might lead to three subtly different forms of expectation.[1] In addition, I will offer some comments on the role of conscious thought in forming expectations.

We have seen ample evidence that sound-related expectations are learned from exposure to some acoustic environment. That is, expectations derive from past experience. In the field of psychology, the mental coding of past experience is traditionally the province of memory. If expectations derive from past experience, then expectations must be linked in some way to memory.

Most of us tend to think of "memory" as a sort of library in which information is stored and sometimes retrieved. Unfortunately, this metaphor is not helpful because it fails to capture the biological origin and purpose of memory. From a biological perspective, there is nothing to be gained by simply storing information. Memory of past events is biologically useful only to the extent that these memories inform future actions. Memory exists not to allow us to relish past successes or regret past failures, but to allow us to repeat our successes and avoid future failures. The biological purpose of memory is not *recall* but *preparation*.

This suggests that memory ought to be closely linked with motor responses. In fact, neurological research suggests that memories are stored in a way that resembles the coding of motor programs—circuits that are activated when chewing, scratching an itch, or gazing to the left. Rather than thinking of memories as stored information, it is more helpful to think of them as "readiness circuits." These circuits can evoke particular motor actions or help direct attention in particular ways. At times, such circuits can also evoke particular emotional states. When these circuits activate future-oriented attention, arousal, or emotion, these neural activations are the concrete biological manifestations of expectation.

Over the past half century, experimental psychologists have produced a huge body of research related to human memory.[2] Perhaps the most important finding from this research is that there exist many types of memory. Some forms of memory appear to be differentiated according to the duration of retention. *Short-term memory* holds information for a relatively brief period. *Long-term memory* is capable of holding information for longer periods, sometimes for a lifetime. Other forms of memory are linked to specific sensory modes. For example, *echoic memory* provides a brief holding pen for sounds; *eidetic memory* is a rare long-term memory for visual images.

Memory researchers believe that long-term memory can be separated into *implicit* and *explicit* forms. *Explicit memory* is the sort of memory that can be consciously recalled and consciously memorized. Knowledge of your telephone number is an example of explicit long-term memory. Implicit memories are often difficult to describe verbally and difficult to recall through conscious effort. Knowing how a melody goes is an example of implicit memory. But failing to recall the name of the tune is a failure of explicit memory.[3]

Explicit memory can be further separated into *episodic* and *semantic* types.[4] *Episodic memory* is a sort of autobiographical memory that holds specific historical events from our past. If you recall what you ate for breakfast this morning you will be accessing episodic memory. *Semantic memory* holds much of our declarative knowledge such as names of people, places, and objects, the meanings of words, as well as the names of musical instruments and musical styles. The distinction between episodic and semantic memories is nicely demonstrated by the clinical condition of retrograde amnesia where an individual experiences the loss of episodic memories without loss of semantic memories. An amnesia patient might forget his or her own name, but still be able to speak fluently, retrieving vocabulary items and everyday facts with ease. General knowledge remains intact. Only their personal biographical history seems impaired.

Other kinds of memory include *working memory*, which provides a sort of mental "desktop" for thinking, and *motor memory*, which stores action programs or procedures such as walking, tying your shoes, or playing the violin.[5]

If expectations relate to memory, and if there are different types of memory, then an obvious question follows: Which type or types of memory are involved in expectations? What are the repercussions of these different forms of mental organization for the phenomenon of expectation? In this chapter, I will focus on just three kinds of memory: *episodic memory*, *semantic memory*, and *short-term memory*. We will see that each of these types of memory leads to a distinct form of expectation.

Episodic Memory

When I was sixteen years old, I spent the summer traveling through Europe by myself. As a security precaution, my mother had sewn a zippered pocket inside the back of my jeans. In this pocket I stored my passport and money. Arriving by boat in Calais, I and the rest of the passengers started down a long narrow hallway toward the French customs officials. Realizing that I needed to retrieve my passport, I stuck my hands into my trousers, only to discover that the zipper on the pocket was stuck. I stood there for several minutes struggling with both hands in my pants; meanwhile, the other passengers squeezed past me toward the customs agents. When I finally was able to retrieve my passport, it was already too late. I had caught the eye of a (now suspicious) customs agent. Somehow I knew this wasn't going to be easy to explain. The agent began with an outright accusation: "You have half a kilo of hashish," he declared. I was surprised, and a little offended. "No," I calmly protested. Again the agent made the accusation. "You have hashish; you have half a kilo of hashish." Again, I simply said "no." Having failed to fluster me, the agent waved me through without searching me or my knapsack.

This is a story I've recalled several times over the past thirty-five years. But it is also a story that feels oddly unreal. I have documents that establish that I really took that trip. And I have family members who recall me telling the story of my encounter with customs in Calais. But the memory seems faded, and some of the story seems far-fetched. If my zipper was stuck, I doubt that I struggled with it for as long as a minute. When we're flustered, ten or fifteen seconds can seem like an eternity. Was the hallway really so narrow that other passengers had to squeeze past me? Was a customs agent really so brazen as to accuse me of smuggling hashish?

I no longer have a vivid memory of that event. Instead, I have a bizarre story that feels more like a myth. Whenever conversations turn to odd travel adventures, it is one of many stories I can contribute. As a result, my memory is less of a past event, than the memory of a frequently retold story. As Bob Snyder has noted, there is no way to distinguish between a memory, and a memory of a memory.[6]

Research has established that episodic memories are easily distorted. In particular, episodic memories are typically transformed simply through repeated recollection and retelling. Memory researchers believe that recalling an episodic memory transforms that memory, and ultimately the recalled memory replaces the original memory.[7] The more times an episode is accessed in memory, the greater its potential transformation. This has repercussions for eye-witness testimony in legal procedings. It also has repercussions for how we experience individual musical works.

Consider, by way of example, my experience listening to Johannes Brahms' second piano concerto. Listening to any musical work starts off as an episodic memory. I first heard this work at some moment in my autobiographical past. At some point, I purchased Annerose Schmidt's recording of this work with the Dresden Philharmonic. There then followed a four- or five-year period when the CD occasionally found its way onto my stereo. If I had to guess, I expect I've heard this concerto perhaps twenty times so far in my life. The original episodic memory is gone: I can't tell you when I first heard this work. I don't even have a vague image of a place, time, companion, season, or other association. But I certainly remember the work.

Memories for well-known pieces resemble episodic memories that have been recalled many times. After a while, they can become episodic memories that are no longer tethered to a specific past moment. Unlike my story of the French customs in Calais, however, the repeated hearings of the Brahms' second piano concerto have the virtue of fidelity. Each exposure to the work is nearly identical to the previous exposure. Unlike a memorial recall, the successive renditions of the work are not being constantly reworked and distilled. The music is being experienced pretty well intact each time it is heard. This is quite unlike memorial recall, whose constant transformations resemble the proverbial game of "telephone," where a message is whispered from one person to another. In short, our memories for familiar musical works are episodic memories that have lost most of their autobiographical history, while retaining their accuracy or fidelity.

With sufficient exposure, a listener can become highly familiar with any given musical work. In some instances, an entire musical work is committed to memory. Many people, for example, have "perfect" expectations for the song "Happy Birthday." At any given point in the work, the listener knows what will happen next. (If we encounter a memory lapse with "Happy Birthday," it is apt to be a failure to remember someone's name rather than a failure to remember the melody!) Similarly, most people will have a perfect memory for their country's national anthem. Such seemingly perfect knowledge implies that no variability in expectation would be possible. At all points, the listener has complete knowledge of the ensuing events.

Of course this knowledge is not entirely perfect. To begin with, it typically requires several notes at the beginning of a work for listeners to gain confidence that the work is the one they think it is. With just one or two notes, some element of doubt will exist. Figure 12.1 shows how quickly such doubt can be dispelled. I asked listeners to try to identify several melodies using as few notes as possible. They initially heard the first note of the melody. Then they heard the first two notes, then the first three notes, and so on. After each rendition, the participants were invited to guess what the melody was, either by identifying the melody by name (explicit memory), or by singing or humming the continuation (implicit memory). Above each note is the cumulative proportion of listeners who had identified the melody by the advent of that note. The participants in my experiment were all undergraduate music students. Each was tested individually.

Figure 12.1

Recognition measurements for the openings of four melodies. The first melody (Beethoven's "Für Elise") was recognized by all listeners by the sixth note. Fifty percent recognition occurred by the second note. "The First Noël" achieved 50 percent recognition by the fourth note, but 100 percent recognition did not occur until the eighth note. The last two melodies ("Here Comes the Bride" and "O Christmas Tree") share the first four notes in common with an identical rhythm. Numbers to the right of the notation indicate the average estimated number of exposures to the melody in the past twelve months. Notice that listeners recognize "Here Comes the Bride" much sooner than "O Christmas Tree," and also estimated that they heard "Here Comes the Bride" twice as often as "O Christmas Tree."

Of twelve melodies used in the experiment, Beethoven's "Für Elise" was the most quickly recognized: 50 percent of listeners recognized it by the second note and all listeners recognized it by the sixth note. "The First Noël" shows greater variability: 50 percent recognition was achieved by the fourth note, but 100 percent recognition did not occur until the eighth note.

The third and fourth melodies shown in figure 12.1 are the Bridal Chorus from Wagner's *Lohengrin* ("Here Comes the Bride") and "O Tannenbaum" ("O Christmas Tree"). Notice that both melodies share the first four notes in common with an identical rhythm. However, the recognition points differ. With "Here Comes the Bride," 75 percent recognition occurred by the third note. By comparison, "O Christmas Tree" achieved 50 percent recognition by the fifth note with 100 percent recognition by the eleventh note (not shown).

It is possible that the differences in recognition are somehow attributable to the different meters: "Here Comes the Bride" is in quadruple meter, whereas "O Christmas Tree" is in triple meter and begins with a pickup. But a more likely explanation for the difference in recognition is frequency of exposure. At the end of my experiment I asked listeners to estimate the number of times they had heard each melody within the past twelve months. The average estimated exposure is reported to the right of each melody. My participants estimated that they had heard "Here Comes the Bride" roughly fifteen times in the past year, but estimated that they had heard "O Christmas Tree" only half as often.

Clearly, familiar musical passages can be recognized very quickly by experienced listeners. The speed with which recognition memory can be evoked appears to depend on at least two factors. First, recognition speed is correlated with exposure. This should not be surprising since we already know from the Hick–Hyman law that this is true of stimuli in general. (It is also characteristic of statistical learning.) Second, recognition speed appears to be facilitated when the melody begins in a distinctive manner. Often this involves a distinctive opening interval or rhythm. But any distinctive marker can potentially aid the listener. For example, the recognition of "Für Elise" may be facilitated by its relatively high starting pitch. When I transposed "Für Elise" down an octave, I found that recognition took slightly longer.

Apart from low familiarity and lack of distinctive markers, another source of memory uncertainty can arise from the structure of the music itself. Music typically contains repeated sections, and at particular points of repetition, the listener may be in doubt about the precise continuation. This uncertainty is most evident in performance contexts, such as the memory errors one often hears when music students play recitals or auditions. Nervous musicians will sometimes lapse into a memory "loop" where they play the same passage verbatim without taking the "second ending" or otherwise continuing as they should with the rest of the piece. The effect is a sort of slow musical "stutter." In short, even in highly familiar works, there can still exist points of uncertainty.

When listening to a familiar work, we have a pretty accurate sense of what will happen next. Psychologist Jamshed Bharucha has applied the term *veridical* to such musical expectations.[8] In order to distinguish the *memory* from the *expectation*, it is useful to preserve the difference in terminology. I will use the term *episodic* to refer to the memory and *veridical* to refer to the expectation.

Semantic Memory

If veridical expectations were the only kinds of expectations, then listening to novel musical works would leave us clueless about what to expect next—at least until we had heard the work once or twice. But clearly, listeners exhibit expectations even when they are hearing passages for the first time. We have seen plenty of evidence for such expectations, including expectations related to event timing (meter), pitch likelihood (tonality), post-skip reversal, late-phrase declination, and so on. Although these expectations are learned from exposure, they are not associated with memories for specific musical works. They are auditory generalizations.

These sorts of auditory generalizations are reminiscent of the learned categories characteristic of semantic memory. For example, the concept of an "apple" is a learned semantic category that arises, in part, from the totality of experiences we have had with individual apples.[9] Like semantic categories, schemas are generalizations formed by encountering many exemplars. Our most established schemas reflect the most commonly experienced patterns.

Schemas exist to help us deal with situations that are novel yet also broadly familiar. For example, we might recognize some object as a chair, even though we have never seen this particular type of chair before. Schemas allow the brain to process information and respond more quickly. In music, schemas represent common enculturated aspects of musical organization. The schematic expectation for pitch proximity is different in kind from the veridical expectation that the next note in "Für Elise" is D#5.

In order to distinguish the memory from the expectation, once again it is helpful to maintain different terms. I will use the terms *semantic* or *long-term* to refer to the memory and *schematic* to refer to the expectation.

Evidence supporting the distinction between veridical and schematic musical expectation is to be found in patients suffering from musical amnesia. Working at the University of Montréal, psychologist Isabelle Peretz has documented cases of neurologically damaged patients whose memories for well-known melodies have been destroyed, although their general capacity to experience (and enjoy) music shows little impairment.[10]

I should point out that there are some problems in associating veridical expectations with episodic memory, and schematic expectations with semantic memory. Familiarity with particular musical works in many ways resembles semantic memory, since the biographical episodic content is commonly missing. (Not many people remember the first time they heard "Happy Birthday.") Since all semantic memories begin as episodic information, there must be some transition between the two forms. Further research concerning the musical consequences of clinical amnesia might help illuminate such issues.[11] For now, I confess that the memory research here is simply not sufficiently advanced to make these distinctions with conviction. Nevertheless, let's see where this association takes us.

Wittgenstein's Puzzle

The difference between schematic and veridical expectations helps to resolve a long-standing paradox in musical listening. This paradox is sometimes referred to as "Wittgenstein's puzzle" after the famous Austrian philosopher, Ludwig Wittgenstein, who first posed the problem.[12] Consider the experience of listening to a *deceptive cadence*. A deceptive cadence thwarts the normal dominant-to-tonic (V–I) progression in classical music by moving to the submediant chord or (less commonly) to the subdominant chord (i.e., V–vi or V–IV). Such cadences are relatively rare. In J. S. Bach's chorale harmonizations, I have found that V–I cadences are fifty times more prevalent than V–vi.[13] The feeling of deception evoked by such cadences is quite strong for most Western-enculturated listeners, even when the listener is familiar with the work.[14] The puzzle, then, is this: how can a deceptive cadence continue to sound "deceptive" when familiarity with a work makes the progression entirely inevitable? How can we be "surprised" by an event we know will happen? Even when we are familiar with a work, how can we continue to hear moments of surprise as though we were hearing the music for the first time?

In chapters 1 and 2, we discussed a similar problem in the sound of a slamming door. A slamming door will typically evoke a startle response—a response intended to prepare us for potential danger. Now consider what happens when you catch a glimpse of the closing door just before it is about to slam. In this case, you *know* that the door is about to make a loud sound. You also know that the situation is not dangerous and that there is no need to be startled. Oddly, you still experience a startle response. To be sure, the response is often not as marked as when the door slams without any advanced warning. However, this conscious awareness is able to attenuate, but not extinguish the startle response. It is as though some part of your brain fails to get the message that there is no danger.

As we saw in chapter 2, such paradoxical experiences are possible because there exist independent neurophysiological paths related to expectation. Recall that there exists a fast "thalamo-amygdala" path and a slower "thalamo-cortico-amygdala" path. Both pathways are capable of activating stimulus-related responses. One pathway represents a "quick and dirty" reaction, while the other pathway represents a slow and careful appraisal of the same stimulus. Also recall that it is possible for the two responses to produce contradictory assessments. The ringing of a telephone, for example, might provoke a negatively valenced startle response and a positively valenced appraisal because of the expectation of receiving a call from a good friend.

Jamshed Bharucha has similarly suggested that schematic and veridical expectations can evoke independent responses.[15] In the case of the familiar deceptive cadence, the pertinent neural circuits related to veridical and schematic expectations produce different responses. In effect, the schematic brain is surprised by the "deception" while the veridical brain is not. A deceptive cadence can still evoke a physiological response characteristic of surprise, even when the listener is certain of its occurrence.

The common experience of being "surprised" by an expected deceptive cadence is consistent with the notion that veridical and schematic expectations involve different neural pathways. It should be emphasized, however, that these pathways probably differ from the fast and slow pathways discussed in chapter 2.

Of course, if a culture existed where nearly all dominant chords were followed by a submediant chord (vi), then the V–vi chord progression would no longer be perceived as deceptive. As long as the majority of dominant chords in a culture are not followed by the submediant, this progression will still retain an element of surprise.

Dynamic Expectations

Read aloud the following sequence of numbers:

5, 9, 8, 3, 5
5, 9, 8, 3, 5
5, 9, 8, 3, 5

By the time you arrived at the third repetition of this sequence, you could probably read the numbers without looking at the text. After just two repetitions, the number sequence was already resident in short-term memory. If you then heard someone speak the numbers "5, 9 . . ." you would have little difficulty anticipating the ensuing "8, 3, 5." These are expectations that arise from brief—even single—exposures. But these expectations are also volatile: it is unlikely that you will retain this number sequence beyond the end of this chapter. Since these expectations arise (and decay) dynamically, we might call them *dynamic* expectations.

Expectations of future events are not merely the product of schematic or veridical patterns that have been learned over a lifetime of exposure. Expectations can also arise from comparatively brief periods of exposure. As the events of a musical work unfold, the work itself engenders expectations that influence how the remainder of the work is experienced. The idea that listeners adapt their expectations while listening was proposed in the 1950s by Leonard Meyer.[16]

Experimental evidence in support of such adaptive expectations has been found for both controlled tone sequences and musical excerpts. In chapter 4, we discussed the work by Jenny Saffran and her colleagues where listeners formed appropriate expectations to novel stimuli given a twenty-one-minute exposure period. But twenty-one minutes of exposure is not needed to form appropriate dynamic expectations. Consider another study by Gary Marcus and his colleagues at New York University. In their study, seven-month-old infants were exposed to novel speech patterns lasting two minutes. The patterns consisted of three-syllable nonsense words, all of the form A-B-A. For example, an infant would hear words such as "bo-gu-bo," "ga-ti-ga," and "li-no-li." That is, the first and last syllables in each word were identical. After hearing these patterns for two minues, the infants were tested on either new words that had the same A-B-A pattern, or on words having an A-B-B pattern—such as "wo-fe-fe." The infants were more attentive to the novel syllable pattern. With just two minutes of exposure, the infants had readily formed expectations based on an abstract temporal pattern.[17]

In the case of more musical stimuli, evidence of rapid adaption has been demonstrated in the experiments by Tuomas Eerola and by Mary Castellano, Jamshed Bharucha, and Carol Krumhansl, discussed in chapter 9.[18] Recall that in both experiments, culturally unfamiliar melodies were played and listeners showed rapid adaptation to the frequency of occurrence of the various pitches. This was evident with Western-enculturated listeners exposed to north Indian *rags*, and with Pedi musicians from Limpopo, South Africa exposed to Sami *yoiks*. Listeners were adapting quite well to the music of another culture after hearing it for only a minute or so.

Even one minute of exposure is long compared to the rapidity in which listeners can adapt their expectations to some new stimulus sequence. The occurrence of just a single tone moves that tone into the category "likely to occur again at some point." The phenomenon of rapid adaptation was anticipated in early research in information theory. In 1958 Ted Coons and David Kraehenbuehl at Yale University proposed a dynamic probability model for experiencing music as it unfolds.[19] Kraehenbuehl and Coons imagined that a listener's statistically shaped expectations would become better adapted to a musical work as the amount of exposure increased. A listener would begin the listening experience with expectations reflecting broad or generalized probabilities arising from a lifetime of musical exposure. But as the musical piece progressed, the listener would tailor expectations that are engendered by events in the work itself. In contrast to schematic and veridical expectations, which require some coding in long-term memory, these dynamic expectations exploit short-term memory to form expectations about likely future events.

The capacity of short-term auditory memory has proved difficult to characterize. On average, it appears able to store sound sequences up to between three to five seconds in duration. However, short-term auditory memory may occasionally reach as long as ten to twelve seconds.[20] In terms of the number of events, short-term auditory memory appears able to retain roughly ten sound events. However, depending on the structure of the sound sequence, its upper limit may reach about twenty-five events.[21]

One of the keys to retaining a pattern in short-term memory is repetition. When you look up a telephone number, you can retain it by repeating it to yourself or by listening to someone else repeating it aloud. If you want to permanently memorize a telephone number so that you can recall it some time in the future, further sustained mental rehearsal is necessary. The more often one activates a pattern in short-term memory, the greater the likelihood that it will pass into so-called intermediate-term memory (ITM), and then potentially into long-term memory.

When listening to music, there is plenty of repetition to help cement patterns into memory. My collaborator Joy Ollen and I measured the amount of repetition in a cross-cultural sample of fifty musical works. Our sample included the most varied potpourri we could assemble. We studied Calypso, Inuit throat singing, Japanese New Age, Estonian bagpipe music, Punjabi pop, fifteenth-century Chinese *guqin*, Norwegian polka, a Navaho war dance, bluegrass, Macedonian singing, Ghanaian drumming, Spanish flamenco, Kalimantan ritual music, Hawaiian slack key guitar, Gypsy music, and thirty-five other works from similarly varied cultural sources. On average, we found that 94 percent of all musical passages longer than a few seconds in duration are repeated at some point in the work. Few people will be surprised to learn of this penchant for repetition in music. But consider how unique this situation is. In speech, such extreme amounts of repetition are rare. Only in political demonstrations and some religious ceremonies will one find such high amounts of repetition. Similarly, visual scenes rarely exhibit such redundancy. Music is extraordinarily repetitive compared with other stimuli in our lives.

Actually, the 94 percent figure probably underestimates the amount of repetition. Repetition need not be verbatim in order to convey useful predictive patterns. For example, the meter for many works is constant throughout the work. Even if a work were constructed using pitch sequences without any repetition, the stable meter would still help listeners predict some elements of the music. Another source of predictive patterning can be harmony. It is possible to construct a twelve-bar blues work without any verbatim melodic repetition. However, the underlying harmonic pattern will still provide an element of predictability that can be coded in memory. Similarly, stable instrumentation can become a predictable element, since most musical works exhibit comparatively few changes of instrumentation.

Repetition can serve many functions and there are several competing hypotheses about why musicians create such repetitive works.[22] Whether intended or not, repetition in music causes the repeated musical patterns to make the transition from short-term to intermediate-term memory. Musical repetition acts like an involuntary form of conscious memorization. It is perhaps no surprise that a musical *motive* is both (1) the shortest distinct unit of repetition in a work, and (2) the most memorable feature or characteristic of a work.

Bob Snyder has noted that many of the common units of repetition in music are consistent with the properties of short-term memory. Both in terms of duration and information-processing capacity, common musical units, like motives and themes, are well suited to being efficiently coded in short-term memory.[23]

Comparatively little research has been done on how one's musical expectations adapt while listening to a work. One pertinent study has been carried out by Yuet-Hon Ng at the Eastman School of Music.[24] Ng ran an experiment where listeners heard two phrases; they were then asked to judge whether the second phrase was too long, too short, or just right. Listeners showed a strong preference that the second phrase would be the same length as the first phrase. For example, if the antecedent phrase was three measures in duration, then listeners preferred a consequent phrase of three measures duration. Similarly, a four-measure antecedent resulted in a preference for a four-measure consequent phrase.

At times, the dynamic expectations evoked by a work will conflict with existing schematic expectations. Phrase length provides a good example. Although listeners will adapt to three-measure phrases, for Western-enculturated listeners, a four-measure phrase is more common. Ng likes to demonstrate this by asking people to sing the traditional Christmas carol "Joy to the World." The second phrase is notated as three measures in length, but most people sustain the final note so that the phrase is lengthened to four measures. Both long-term schemas and short-term dynamic expectations tend to converge over history. That is, the more an opus-distinctive pattern deviates from an established schema, the more repetition is required to ensure that a dynamic expectation takes precedence.

Folklorists and ethnomusicologists have long observed the tendency for traditional music and poetry to become more regularized or conventional in its structures. Just a hundred years ago, it was still common for European folk songs to exhibit irregular phrase lengths. Most folk repertoires show evidence of increasing "standardization" of phrase lengths over the decades.

Lots of examples could be cited here, but my favorite is the fiddling of the Cree Indians of northwestern Québec. In the seventeenth century, Scots from the Orkney Islands began trading with the Cree of southern Hudson's Bay. The Scots brought fiddles with them, and soon the Cree began a fiddling tradition that continued long after the Scots abandoned the fur trade. In 1980, two Cree fiddlers traveled to the Orkney Islands and met a group of modern Scottish fiddlers. The repertoire of fiddle tunes had changed little in 300 years—with one notable exception. Modern Scottish fiddling has become more regular in phrasing. In Scotland, nearly all of the seventeenth-century tunes have been shoehorned into a square four-measure phrase structure. But the Cree fiddlers have retained the more irregular phrase lengths. To the historical purist, the more "authentic" Scottish fiddlers today are probably the Cree Indians.[25]

Of course, constant repetition doesn't just cement patterns into short-term memory. This same repetition ultimately pushes the music into long-term memory. From time to time, these long-term memories will pop up to the surface. We might catch a little snatch of music from the radio of a passing car, or our footsteps might remind us of a particular musical beat. Or the pitch sequence of an elevator bell might cause us to recall the beginning of a particular melody. The well-known phenomenon of having a tune stuck in one's head has long puzzled "sufferers." Part of the mystery is that the phenomenon appears to be unique to music. Why don't verbal phrases or quilt patterns get stuck in one's head? What is it about music that causes such mental obsessions? I think an answer may lie in the extreme repetitiveness of music. We just don't hear verbal slogans often enough for them to become an unconscious preoccupation. In addition, there is another property of music that lends itself to such "ear worms." In our study of repetition in music from around the world, Joy Ollen and I found that any pattern (call it *A*) is most likely to be followed by a repetition of the same pattern *A*.[26] By comparison, a slogan like "Buy one get one free" is typically not repeated immediately. In the mental coding for music, veridical expectations tend to be linked into circular patterns where the end of the pattern points to its own beginning.

Such circular codings are evident throughout music. For listeners familiar with Philip Glass's work, what begins as a dynamic pattern is soon transferred to long-term memory:

Ko-yaa-nis-qat-si, ko-yaa-nis-qat-si, ko-yaa-nis-qat-si . . .

Intermezzo

To summarize: in the above discussion I have distinguished three forms of expectations. *Schematic expectations* represent broadly enculturated patterns of events. Different schemas may exist for different styles or genres, as well as for common patterns (like major and minor) that cross stylistic boundaries. *Veridical expectations* represent long-term patterns arising from repeated exposure to a single episode, token, or work. *Dynamic expectations* represent short-term patterns that are updated in real time, especially during exposure to a novel auditory experience such as hearing a musical work for the first time.

It is important to note that all three expectations operate concurrently and in parallel. Schematic expectations are omnipresent in all of our listening experiences. When listening to a familiar work, the dynamic system remains active even though the veridical system knows exactly what to expect. Similarly, even when listening for the first time to an unfamiliar work, the veridical system is constantly searching for a match with familiar works. The veridical system is ever vigilant, allowing us to catch the rare moments of musical quotation or allusion.

Origin of Semantic and Episodic Memory

It is helpful to ask why the brain distinguishes between semantic and episodic information. Why are some things remembered or coded as general principles, while other things are remembered or coded as specific past events?

This distinction seems especially curious since many coded bits of information begin as episodic memories that later are transformed to semantic memories. For example, if I were to ask you to name the capital of China, you would access the answer— Beijing. Most of us cannot recall when or where we learned this fact. We just know it as a general piece of information untethered to the history of its acquisition.

How and why does this transformation occur, and why aren't all memories coded semantically?

In general, it is more efficient to recall general principles rather than specific events. For example, it is simpler to remember that "Eric is untrustworthy" than to remember a series of past events that all seem to testify to Eric's untrustworthiness. When we are tempted to ask Eric to carry out an important task, it is faster and more efficient to access the general principle rather than ponder all of our past interactions. Semantic and schematic codes provide more efficient ways of interacting in the world than episodic codes. But there is a price to pay for this efficiency.

When a person concludes that "Eric is untrustworthy" based on past experience, they are making an inductive inference: forming a general proposition based on a finite set of observations. However, as we noted in chapter 4, induction is itself fallible. In chapter 5, we saw instances where observations lead to the wrong inference. Suppose, for example, that the conclusion that "Eric is untrustworthy" arises from three observations:

1. Eric failed to show up at an important meeting we had arranged, and he also failed to telephone or explain what happened.
2. I observed Eric take money from the cash box and put the money in his pocket.
3. Pat described several circumstances where Eric misbehaved.

Although these events do seem to implicate Eric, it is quite possible that we have misjudged him. When Eric failed to show up for our meeting as promised, it turned out that his mother had suffered a heart attack. He took his mother to the hospital and then spent several days arranging her affairs and visiting her. Eric was simply too busy to attend to comparatively minor obligations. When Eric took money from the cash box, it was because Karen had asked him to deposit the funds in the appropriate bank account. When Pat relayed negative gossip about Eric, it turned out that both Pat and Eric were competing for a promotion, and that Pat was unjustly attempting to tarnish Eric's reputation.

Psychologist Leda Cosmides and anthropologist John Tooby have argued that retaining episodic memory is functionally essential. In effect, episodic memory allows us to revisit "the original data" in order to evaluate alternative hypotheses. If we simply retained the generalized semantic or schematic information ("Eric is untrustworthy") and discarded the original episodic information used to form this generalization, then we would be unable to reconsider a possibly questionable inductive inference.[27]

Clearly, the brain's ability to form generalizations is important. Generalizations allow us to act more quickly, and to act without consuming a lot of mental resources. But it is also clear that the brain needs to retain some of the original observational data so that the credence of particular generalizations can be revised, questioned, or reinforced. Evolution has addressed this problem by creating two parallel memory systems: episodic and semantic. In chapter 9 we discussed the phenomenon of misattribution, the tendency to cast a wide net when emotionally charged situations lead to associative learning. In that chapter I suggested that misattribution is part of Nature's response to the difficult problem of induction. In chapter 11 we discussed the phenomenon of cognitive firewalls. There, I suggested that schemas arise from the biological need to avoid overgeneralizing by limiting the scope of inductive lessons. To those claims we can add another: the development of two memory systems is yet another part of Nature's efforts to deal with the ever-present problem of induction. Misattribution, cognitive firewalls, and the episodic/semantic distinction represent different patches in the leaky dike of inductive learning. Scale-degree *qualia*, stylistic distinctions, and deceptive cadences that remain deceptive sounding are just a few of many musical phenomena that originate from these biological mechanisms.

In the case of the auditory system, the episodic and semantic memory systems are evident in listening schemas that represent current generalizations about the world of sound, as well as a learned veridical system. In most circumstances, both of these systems agree in their expectations about future events. However, discrepancies are commonplace. Either system can be surprised. As we saw in the case of the deceptive cadence, the schematic system is surprised while the veridical system is not. Conversely, it is possible to surprise the veridical system without surprising the schematic system. Examples can be generated using "chimeric melodies." In Greek mythology, the *chimera* was a creature with the head of a lion, the body of a goat, and the tail of a serpent. Figure 12.2 shows a chimeric melody that begins with the notes of "Three Blind Mice" but elides into "Mary Had a Little Lamb." As one listens to this passage, a veridical discontinuity occurs with the last note of the second measure. The switch is surprising from a veridical perspective. But the pitch sequences themselves are commonplace, and so there is little or no schematic surprise.

Such veridical deceptions are much less common in music than schematic deceptions. It is not difficult to understand why this is the case. Schematic expectations are acquired by nearly all listeners in a culture. Acquiring these schemas does not require

Figure 12.2
Example of a chimeric melody where one melody elides into another. At the end of the second measure, a knowledgeable listener will experience a "veridical surprise" coinciding with the occurrence of the pitch D. However, the pitch sequences themselves are commonplace, and so there is no schematic surprise.

the listener to be acquainted with any specific musical work. By contrast, veridical expectations necessarily require listeners to be familiar with particular pieces. When composers make use of veridical expectations, they must explicitly take into account the musical sophistication of their audience. All listeners familiar with Western music will know that V tends to be followed by I. But fewer listeners will know that the fifth note in J. S. Bach's C minor fugue in the first volume of *The Well-Tempered Clavier* is a lowered submediant pitch. If a composer wishes to play with listeners' veridical expectations, then typically she will restrict her efforts to extremely well-known passages. Examples might include the principal motive from Beethoven's Fifth Symphony (used in Chuck Berry's "Roll Over Beethoven") or the U.S. national anthem (used in Jimi Hendrix's famous Woodstock rendition).

Less well-known veridical memories narrow the range of potential listeners who will experience the intended effect. The use of allusion, quotation, and parody is typically intended for an expert audience of cognoscenti. These are the musical equivalents of "insider jokes." In chapter 14 we will see some examples of these types of manipulations of musical expectations. As we will see, comedian–composer Peter Schickele is a master of thwarting veridical, schematic, and dynamic expectations.

The relationship between schematic and veridical expectations is always susceptible to change, depending on the listener's auditory experience. In particular, repeated listening to a single work can transform how a listener hears any veridical reference. There is a danger that the alluding or quoting work will become more familiar than the work alluded to or quoted from. This will tend to unravel the veridical expectations, so the listener's expectation for the passage is the manipulated version rather than the original version. For the classical musical listener, Chuck Berry's use of the opening motive from Beethoven's Fifth Symphony is an allusion to Beethoven. However, for a hypothetical rock-'n'-roller, an unaccustomed encounter with Beethoven's Fifth Symphony may be heard as an allusion to Chuck Berry's "Roll Over Beethoven."

Recovering from Wrong Notes in Improvisation

In the same way that schematic expectations can interact with veridical expectations, it is also possible to have interactions between schematic expectations and dynamic expectations. A good example of such an interaction is evident in the musical treatment of "wrong" notes in improvisation. Any musician who improvises must learn how to contend with unintended "accidents"—slips that would normally be considered errors. Whether one is improvising a jazz chart or realizing a figured bass accompaniment, experienced musicians have been uniform in offering novice improvisors the following advice when accidentally playing a "wrong" note. The standard advice is for the performer to return to the "wrong" note and play the passage again, including the wrong note. The goal is to convince the listener that the note was not an error, but was intentional.

First, what do we mean by an improvised note being "wrong"? From an expectational standpoint the answer is straightforward: the note has a low probability of occurrence. The note fails to conform to schematic expectations. Given its low likelihood, the initial appearance of the wrong note will inevitably sound jarring to the listener. However, repeating the passage will allow the listener to accommodate the errant note within a newly formed (dynamic) expectation.

In effect, the experienced improvisor attempts to establish the "wrong" note as a normal part of the passage. The performer can do nothing about the violation of the schematic expectation. In particular, the performer can do nothing to erase the original surprise evoked by the first appearance of the wrong note. However, by incorporating the passage as part of the work, it may be possible to persuade a listener that, in retrospect, no error was made by the performer. By repeating the passage (with the errant note), the musician establishes the note as part of the dynamic expectation— even though the wrong note continues to violate schematic expectations. In effect, the improvisor attempts to shift the "blame" to the listener: there was no error of performance—the error was the listener's presumption about how the music should go.

Unfortunately, this standard advice pertains only to improvised music, which by definition cannot evoke a detailed veridical expectation in listeners. When the performed music is part of a set repertoire, the performer will have to contend with listeners' potential veridical expectations. Violations of veridical expectations tell listeners that something is truly wrong—that the performer has messed up. For "set" compositions, like a Brahms Ballade, there is nothing a performer can do to convince a knowledgeable listener that a wrong note didn't occur. The listener will know that the performer has misplayed the work.

Conscious Expectations

To this point we have considered only those aspects of expectation that are preverbal or unconscious in origin. There is an entirely separate class of expectations that can arise from conscious reflection and conscious prediction. That is, listeners can form expectations from verbalizable knowledge. Consider first some trivial examples. You might read in a concert program that the next movement is entitled "Allegro." As a result, you might reasonably expect the ensuing music to be quick and lively. The liner notes of a recording might mention the sudden silence that follows after a massive crescendo. When attending a rock concert, your friends might have told you that a particular song always follows after a pyrotechnic display. In each case, the explicit knowledge can shape a conscious expectation or anticipation of what will happen in the future.

Such explicit knowledge is not limited to external sources of information such as concert programs, liner notes, or word-of-mouth. Explicit knowledge can also exist as part of a listener's musical expertise—often an expertise related to particular musical styles or genres. Experienced jazz enthusiasts will know that a bass solo is likely to be followed by a drum solo. Similarly, an experienced classical music listener is likely to expect the second movement in a multimovement work to have a slow tempo. People who regularly attend live concerts are likely to expect a final encore piece to be relatively short and virtuosic. A classically trained musician might have a good understanding of the sequence of events that typically occur in sonata-allegro form. An aware listener can use form-related signposts to orient herself or himself. For example, one might turn on the radio and hear a classical work already in progress. One might hear a plausible first theme followed by a plausible second theme. By noting that no modulation occurred between the two themes, the knowledgeable listener could infer that the performance is in the midst of the recapitulation section, and so the ending can be expected shortly.

Some music scholars have presumed that these kinds of large-scale form-related expectations are also present at an unconscious level. However, the existing research raises doubts about this assumption. Working in the Psychology Department at the University of California, San Diego, Vladimir Konečni and his colleagues have shown that listeners are surprisingly insensitive to reorderings of musical segments.[28] The original versions of musical works consistently fail to elicit a greater preference than altered versions for both musician and nonmusician listeners. Similar experimental results have been found by the British musicologist, Nicholas Cook.[29]

Conscious expectations sometimes arise dynamically while listening to a novel musical work. An example from my own experience is Arvo Pärt's beautiful *An den Wassern zu Babel*. The work consists of a series of well-defined sections (19 as it turns out). Each section contains a number of phrases or subphrases, and each section begins with a single note. The next phrase is longer (2 or 3 notes); the following phrase is a little longer yet (4 or 5 notes). Each successive phrase is longer than the previous phrase, until finally the section ends and a new section begins with a single note, and the cycle repeats. It doesn't take long before the listener recognizes Pärt's "lengthening" pattern. On first hearing, the listener may not decipher any more elaborate pattern, but for those listeners who are attentive to such things, Pärt's strategy is soon translated into conscious awareness and is available to inform one's expectations.

Like serial composers such as Arnold Schoenberg and Milton Babbitt, the organization of Pärt's music is infused with formal patterns. But unlike the music of Schoenberg or Babbitt, Pärt's compositional patterns can often be deciphered without having to visually analyze a score and with only a little conscious attention on the part of the listener. Pärt makes it easier for first-time listeners to predict the future.

Notice that musicians widely assume that it is better to know what is likely to happen next than to *not* know what is likely to happen next. Few things please a musician more than to be able to predict much of the sequence of events in a musical work they are hearing for the first time—especially if the work exhibits a relatively complex structure. Why would this predictive ability be valued by musicians?

The person who is quick to say "I told you so" can be irritating to the point of being obnoxious. But there is no denying the psychological gratification of being right about the future. As we have seen, there are excellent biological reasons why we might experience pleasure from accurate predictions. Such accuracy should be rewarded, not only when it is the product of unconscious mental processes, but also when it is the product of conscious rumination or verbalizable thought.

Like sensory representations, conscious thinking also requires some guidance and feedback to ensure that the thinking remains biologically adaptive. Useful thinking needs to be rewarded and encouraged, while useless thinking needs to be suppressed or discouraged. Given the biological importance of predicting the future, it seems reasonable that the prediction effect might be evoked by both conscious and unconscious predictions. In short, musicians may enjoy thinking about how the music will unfold because successful sonic prophecy is a compelling and reliable source of pleasure.

Reprise

Working at the School of the Art Institute of Chicago, composer Bob Snyder has argued that many organizational elements in music arise from various psychological properties that attend the different kinds of memory. At Northwestern University, outside Chicago, Candace Brower has argued that several aspects of musical experience can be traced to different kinds of memory. In this chapter I have offered a number of elaborations on the insights of Snyder and Brower.

I have suggested that there are at least four sources of expectations: schematic, veridical, dynamic, and conscious. Each of these four sources arises from a different type of memory. Schematic expectations arise from long-term (semantic) memory; veridical expectations derive from episodic memory; dynamic expectations originate in short-term and intermediate-term memory; and conscious expectations come from the mental desktop psychologists dub working memory. If my taxonomy is correct, then it implies that there are at least four types of surprise. A *schematic surprise* occurs when events do not conform to commonplace musical patterns such as stylistic norms. A *veridical surprise* occurs when events do not conform to a musical work (or specific musical pattern) that is familiar to the listener. A *dynamic surprise* occurs when events do not comply with expectations that have been evoked in the course of listening to the work itself. Finally, *conscious surprise* occurs when events do not conform to explicit thoughts or conjectures about what will happen.

As we've seen, distinguishing different types of expectation allows us to better understand paradoxical experiences such as how a deceptive cadence can retain an element of surprise even when we are intimately familiar with a work. Wittgenstein's paradox is resolved when we recognize that it is possible to have schematic surprises that are not veridical surprises. We have noted how experienced musicians can actively trade off different forms of surprise. For example, we have seen how experienced improvisors may be able to transform "wrong" notes into expected ("right") notes by taking advantage of dynamic expectations.

Memory remains an active area of psychological and physiological research. Although great strides have been made in memory research, many problems remain unsolved. This means that our story of musical expectation remains incomplete. As further advances are made in our understanding of memory, concomitant refinements will need to be made to the outline I have proposed in this chapter. But the principal assumption will remain: the biological purpose of memory is to prepare us for the future, and so memory forms the physiological foundation for expectation.

With this outline in place, we can now consider in more detail how musicians make use of the schematic, veridical, dynamic, and conscious expectations of listeners. In the ensuing four chapters we will look at how musicians create predictability, how they evoke surprises, how they build tension, and how they lead listeners to expect the unexpected. In chapter 14 we will see many other examples of musical surprise and how these various types of surprise can be choreographed to achieve particular effects, including awe, frisson, and laughter.

13   Creating Predictability

Music is a creative enterprise whose goals and methods are not fixed. As with all of the arts, many musicians will rightly resist any single vision of what music is, or what it ought to be. But although there is no consensus about the goals of music in general, individual composers often pursue particular goals when creating specific musical works. By analyzing music, it is occasionally possible to infer some of the techniques that the musician used to create the work. The use of certain techniques, in turn, sometimes allows us to infer one or more goals that are either implicitly or explicitly being pursued by the musician. When a technique is identified—even a technique used by a large majority of musicians—one should not presume that the technique is somehow essential to music or musicality. The role of music analysis is to identify how existing music works, not to dictate how music should be.

In the preceding chapters I've identified two psychological phenomena through which positively valenced feelings can be evoked by engaging a listener's expectations. One phenomenon is the *prediction effect*, where listeners experience positive feelings whenever a future event is successfully predicted. The second phenomenon is *contrastive valence*, where initially negative responses are supplanted by neutral or positive responses, with the limbic contrast leading to an overall positive affect. Both of these phenomena are capable of evoking pleasure when listening to sequences of sounds. The simpler phenomenon is the prediction effect, an effect that is reliably evoked when stimuli are predicted by a listener. The phenomenon of contrastive valence is more complicated. Most surprises will be dominated by a negative affect. Creating "pleasant surprises" via contrastive valence requires careful preparation.

There is no requirement that musicians create music that listeners find pleasing or pleasurable. For example, a film composer might explicitly aim to generate angst or disquiet; a contemporary composer may aim to challenge existing musical schemas; a politically motivated composer might "hold up the false to the false" in accord with Adorno's theories. Moreover, even if musicians aim to create an overtly pleasing psychological effect, there are many ways of achieving this goal without making use of expectation-related phenomena.[1] In the context of music-making, the prediction effect and contrastive valence are psychological tools, not aesthetic imperatives.[2]

Having cautioned ourselves against assuming that analysis reveals eternal artistic foundations, we can proceed to look at how the psychological phenomena of the prediction effect and contrastive valence are manifested in past and existing musical practice. In this chapter, we focus on the prediction effect. We will look in detail at many compositional and performance techniques that increase the predictability of musical events, and so increase the phenomenal pleasure experienced by many people when listening to music that uses such techniques. In the next chapter, we will turn our attention to contrastive valence. In that chapter, we will examine a number of ways musicians are able to generate the "innocuous surprises" that can result in emotions such as laughter, frisson, and awe.

By making musical events more predictable, a musician risks the possibility of listeners becoming bored, irritated, or habituated. In chapter 2, we discussed many of the relevant dangers. But for the moment, we will set aside any aesthetic misgivings, and simply focus on how a musician might exploit the prediction effect to create a pleasurable experience for listeners.

In order to evoke the prediction effect, musicians must make the musical events predictable for listeners. As we saw in the last chapter, there are four basic ways that musical events can be made predictable:

1. Schematic predictability   Here the music is constructed so that it conforms to whatever existing schemas listeners are likely to bring to the listening experience. For Western-enculturated listeners, an example of this phenomenon might be the learned expectation that a dominant seventh chord will commonly be followed by a tonic chord.

2. Dynamic predictability   Here the music is constructed so that the work itself will evoke accurate work-specific expectations. An example of this phenomenon might be an expectation that the first notes of a motivic figure will be followed by other notes that conform to previously heard instances of that motive.

3. Veridical familiarity   A simple way to make the music more predictable is to encourage listeners to hear the work many times.

4. Conscious predictability   Here the music is organized so that observant or knowledgeable listeners will be able to infer future musical events through conscious thought as the music progresses. An example of this phenomenon might be the expectation that a keyboard variation is likely to switch back to the major key after shifting to the minor.

Let's begin by first discussing veridical familiarity.

1 Veridical Familiarity

More than 99 percent of all listening experiences involve listening to musical passages that the listener has heard before. Some of the repetition is internal to the work itself. Having heard a theme once in a work, the listener can be confident that it will come around again. But even as entire works, musical experience is dominated by repetition. People sometimes reread favorite novels or watch favorite films for a second or third time, but music takes the prize for repeated exposure. A person who listens to AM radio for three hours a day will hear over 330 songs a week, of which eight or ten will be unfamiliar works. Film music nearly always introduces new music, but the music is repeated many times over the course of the film. Television shows constantly reuse music in successive episodes. Even for people with large record collections, it is estimated that just five albums in their collection will account for some 90 percent of their self-programmed listening.

Repeated listening makes the music more predictable. Veridical memories for music hold an extraordinarily refined level of detail. Listeners are highly sensitive to the slightest changes from familiar renditions. For a listener familiar with a particular recording of some musical work, recordings of the work by a different performer—or even different recordings by the same performer—often disappoint. The most minuscule changes of performance nuance leap out as deviations from a personal "norm." Contemporary composers are typically delighted to have a commercial release of a recording of one of their works. But years later, pride of achievement can sometimes turn to disappointment when their work becomes identified with a single recording—as though the recording itself defines the work.

Composer John Cage wisely suggested that repeatedly listening to an ostensibly "ugly" sound would help listeners discover its beauty. Of course there is no such thing as an objectively "ugly" sound; nor do sounds have some objective "inner beauty" waiting to be discovered. Beauty and ugliness are products of minds. To the extent that minds are changeable, it is sometimes possible to transform the ugly into the beautiful (and vice versa). The preeminent mechanism for changing minds is learning. Veridical familiarity helps listeners "learn" to enjoy musical works they may otherwise find peculiar or unsatisfying. The best advice for those who dislike modern music or non-Western musics is that they "give the music a chance" through repeated listening. There is considerable merit to Cage's recommendation that repeated listening will help banish ugliness.

Unfortunately, veridical familiarity can work against those who shape musical programming. In assembling a concert season, experienced conductors know that programming well-known "war horses" will prove more popular than programming works of comparable style that are not well known. Similarly, seasoned radio DJs know that playing familiar music draws a greater audience than playing unfamiliar music, no matter what the merit is for playing new music. Major labels know that frequent airplay is the key to successful record sales. Novelty is a surprisingly hard sell.

For aspiring composers, attempting to increase veridical familiarity is not an especially practical strategy for increasing musical familiarity. Apart from bribing DJs to play your music, or performing opportunistic encores, there is little a musician can do to influence a listener's physical exposure to his or her work.[3]

Turning briefly to *conscious predictability*, we find another largely ineffective tool for composers. Like veridical familiarity, conscious predictability is out of the composer's control, since it depends principally on the skill and sophistication of the listener. If a composer aims to increase the predictability of his or her music, this leaves the two main approaches of *schematic predictability* and *dynamic predictability*. Below we discuss these two approaches in more detail.

2   Schematic Predictability

Following the crowd has its benefits. Few musical works exist that don't follow some important musical conventions. The vast majority of works employ familiar instruments, use a familiar scale, follow a familiar meter, play familiar harmonies, and conform to a familiar style. These musical conventions obviously differ from culture to culture. Musicians typically work within the conventions of some specific culture— usually their own.

Of course, within any given culture there are numerous schematic choices available to the musician. A Western composer might choose to write in a major or minor key.[4] A Balinese musician might choose between the *slendro* or *pelog* scales. An Indian sitarist might choose from one of many *rags*.

It is important to understand that the origin of existing schemas is of little concern when creating a musical work. What matters is simply that the members of one's intended audience already hold a particular expectational schema. What makes the slendro scale important is not that it is derived from some "natural" acoustic foundation (although it might be). What makes it important is that many Balinese listeners are familiar with it. Similarly, the primary importance of the major scale is its familiarity for a large group of listeners, not that it exhibits some distinctive acoustic or formal properties.[5] As we noted in chapter 9, there are many Western musical works whose distributions of scale degrees are highly similar. This similarity is not merely a coincidence. In each case, the composer has taken advantage of existing tonality-related listening schemas.

In addition to the zeroth-order probabilities of scale tones, the predictability of music can be increased by conforming to the most likely first-order probabilities. That is, a composer will likely evoke pleasure by using the most common pitch successions associated with a particular style or genre. The most predictable pitch successions are

Table 13.1
Tallies of successive metric onsets for German folk songs in 4/4 meter. The measure is divided into 16ths. Beat onsets indicated by asterisks. Antecedent metric positions indicated in rows; consequent metric positions indicated in columns.

Consequent metric position

	→1*	→2	→3	→4	→5*	→6	→7	→8	→9*	→10	→11	→12	→13*	→14	→15	→16
1→*	36	2	600	144	2680	0	1219	0	1491	0	0	0	125	0	0	0
2→	0	0	2	0	0	0	0	0	0	0	0	0	0	0	0	0
3→	2	0	0	5	589	0	6	0	0	0	0	0	0	0	0	0
4→	0	0	0	0	147	0	2	0	0	0	0	0	0	0	0	0
5→*	4	0	0	0	0	4	760	117	2379	0	48	0	77	0	0	0
6→	0	0	0	0	0	0	4	0	0	0	0	0	0	0	0	0
7→	0	0	0	0	0	0	0	18	1969	0	3	0	0	0	0	0
8→	0	0	0	0	0	0	0	0	135	0	0	0	0	0	0	0
9→*	457	0	0	0	0	0	0	0	0	10	880	166	3720	0	367	0
10→	0	0	0	0	0	0	0	0	0	0	7	0	3	0	0	0
11→	0	0	0	0	0	0	0	0	0	0	0	13	917	0	7	0
12→	0	0	0	0	0	0	0	0	0	0	0	0	179	0	0	0
13→*	2924	0	0	0	0	0	0	0	0	0	0	0	0	26	1804	227
14→	3	0	0	0	0	0	0	0	0	0	0	0	0	0	23	0
15→	2147	0	0	0	0	0	0	0	0	0	0	0	0	0	0	50
16→	277	0	0	0	0	0	0	0	0	0	0	0	0	0	0	0

those that make use of tendency tones: those tones whose subsequent "resolutions" are most preordained.

In addition to the pitch-related *what* of expectation, the predictability of the music can also be influenced by using commonplace *when* devices. For example, pleasure arising from the prediction effect can be evoked by using a conventional meter and regular four-bar phrases. As we saw in chapter 10, certain moments can be made more predictable than others. In the first instance, composers can ensure that event onsets conform to an established metrical schema. In addition to the zeroth-order probabilities that favor particular beats, composers can also make use of first-order temporal probabilities. When a tone appears at a certain point in the metric frame, its appearance makes some ensuing moments more likely. Table 13.1 provides a useful illustration of such first-order temporal probabilities.

Table 13.1 shows the probabilities of successive metric positions based on an analysis of 544 German folk songs in 4/4 meter. Sixteen metric positions are identified, each coinciding with a sixteenth-note subdivision. Positions 1, 5, 9, and 13 correspond to the onsets of the first, second, third, and fourth beats. Antecedent metric positions are listed vertically along the left side of the table, while consequent metric positions are listed horizontally along the top of the table. For example, the table shows that

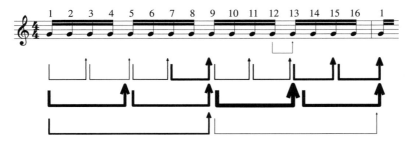

Figure 13.1
Graphical illustration of metric tendencies shown in table 13.1. The thickness of each line is proportional to the absolute probability of metric succession. Lines have been drawn only for those transitions above a minimum threshold. Notice the strong tendency for beat 3 (metric position 9) to be followed by an onset on beat 4 (metric position 13).

when an onset occurs in the first metric position (downbeat), the most likely ensuing event is an onset at metric position 5 (second beat). The table shows that 2,680 downbeat onsets are followed by a second-beat onset.

In general, the values in table 13.1 tend to cluster around a downward left-to-right diagonal. Notice, for example, that despite the predominance of zero values, metric position N always has some events that occur at metric position $N + 1$. In effect, the table shows a phenomenon analogous to pitch proximity, discussed in chapter 5. Onset moments tend to cluster together. We might refer to this tendency as *metric proximity*. Thus, we can see that two phenomena seem to dominate the *when* of music: the simple zeroth-order probability of events where some metric positions (like the downbeat) are more likely to occur, and the first-order metric proximity where an event tends to increase the likelihood of a neighboring ensuing event. Said another way, event successions are shaped by *metric hierarchy* and *metric proximity*.

The absolute probabilities evident in table 13.1 are illustrated in graphical form in figure 13.1. As before, the thickness of the connecting lines is directly proportional to the absolute probability of a given metric position being immediately followed by a tone onset at another metric position. The most common event is a note on beat 3 (position 9) being followed by a note on beat 4 (position 13). The second most common event is a note on beat 4 (position 13) being followed by a note on the downbeat of the following measure (position 1). In general, figure 13.1 shows a "beat-sequence" tendency. Beat 1 tends to be followed by beat 2, which tends to be followed by beat 3, and so on. A similar pattern is evident at the sub-beat or half-beat level. To put it another way, there is a tendency to maintain a periodic event rate: there is little evidence for syncopated rhythms in German folk songs.

Figure 13.2 illustrates the probabilities in table 13.1 from a different perspective. In this case, the graph shows only those metric-position transitions that have a probabil-

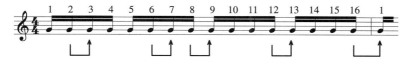

Figure 13.2
Graphical illustration of *tendency moments*—successions of metric onsets whose probabilities of co-occurrence are 1.0 in the folksong sample.

ity of 1.0. For the sampled works, the metric positions 2, 6, 8, 12, and 16 are *always* followed by the ensuing sixteenth-note position. In many ways, these metric positions are like tendency tones; there are very few possible continuations. Accordingly, we might refer to such metric positions as *tendency moments*. These are moments that virtually dictate some ensuing temporal event, at least within the genre of German folk songs.

To my knowledge, no pertinent experiments have been carried out to determine whether such tendency moments in fact evoke appropriate temporal expectations in listeners. However, given the evidence in support of statistical learning, the existence of such expectations would not be surprising. If we assume that listeners internalize the probabilities of successive onset moments, then we should predict that these metric positions will evoke a strong psychological *quale* of *tending*. At least for this repertory, tone onsets occurring at metric positions 2, 6, 8, 12, and 16 should evoke a strong sense of an event occurring at the next sixteenth position.

Of course, the sequence of temporal events in music must provide the appropriate cues that help a listener invoke the appropriate metrical schema. Various forms of stress must be coordinated. Christopher Longuet-Higgins noted the importance of duration (or *agogic*) stress in helping listeners infer the downbeat. In Western music, the prototypical meter-defining rhythm is a long-duration note followed by one or two short-duration notes. Two examples are the quarter note followed by two eighth notes, and the dotted eighth note followed by a sixteenth. These types of temporal structures make it easy for the listener to infer beat and downbeat placement. Longuet-Higgins and Lee demonstrated that an algorithm based on this principle could be used to predict the meter of common-practice Western music.[6]

The Anticipation

An increase in the predictability of ensuing events can be observed in the so-called *anticipation*. The anticipation is a kind of embellishment tone that is common in both popular and classical Western musics, and also has analogues in several non-Western cultures. An example is shown in figure 13.3. The anticipation often occurs as part of an authentic V–I cadence with the final tonic pitch anticipated. The

Figure 13.3
An example of an anticipation in a cadential V–I context.

numbers identify three moments: the (1) pre-anticipation, (2) anticipation, and (3) post-anticipation moments. It is worthwhile tracing in detail the psychological changes that accompany each of these three points in time.

In general, Western-enculturated listeners tend to expect the dominant chord to be followed by a tonic chord. When the first chord in the measure appears (moment 1), it gives no hint as to when a resolution might occur (or even whether it will occur). Uncertainty will surround both the *what* and *when* of a potential resolution. Depending on the harmonic rhythm established in the work, the most probable change of chord might be expected on the second beat, the third beat, or the first beat of the following measure. In figure 13.3, no new event happens with the second beat, so at the moment of the second beat, the most probable chord change would be either the third beat or the following downbeat.

Now consider what happens when the anticipation note appears (moment 2). Compared with the pre-anticipation sonority, the anticipation occurs on a surprisingly weak beat (the second half of the second beat). From table 13.1 we can see that this significantly raises the likelihood that an ensuing stimulus event will occur on the third beat. That is, the presence of the eighth note significantly reduces the uncertainty as to whether a significant event will appear at beat 3 or wait until the next measure. From the *when* point of view, the appearance of the anticipation greatly reduces uncertainty.

In addition, the pitch of the embellishment tone reduces some of the uncertainty concerning the ensuing *what*. We know that listeners tend to expect ensuing pitches to be close to current pitches. The presence of the C increases the likelihood that the next pitch will be a neighbor: B, D, or C itself. Since the listener is already predicting that the V chord will tend to be followed by a I chord, the appearance of the tonic pitch gives greater credibility to this prediction.

Whenever a listener encounters an anticipation, uncertainty concerning *what* is reduced somewhat, while uncertainty concerning *when* is reduced dramatically. Psychologically, the listener feels more confident or certain of what may happen next. Notice that this heightened sense of certainty sets the stage for a potentially strong prediction effect. If the ensuing events unfold as predicted, the listener will experience a positive limbic reward.

Figure 13.4
A variant anticipation in which the duration of the anticipating note is extended.

The limbic effect of the anticipation is more clearly evident if we compare the notated passage to the same passage without the anticipation. In the absence of the anticipation, the resolution to the tonic chord occurs with much less certainty. There is little to commend expecting the note on beat 3 versus waiting for the next down-beat. Nor is there any additional cue that increases the likelihood of resolving to the tonic chord. In short, although the anticipation has the negative limbic effect of introducing a sonorous dissonance, it dramatically decreases listener uncertainty about future events, and so ultimately evokes a more positively valenced prediction effect.

Before leaving the anticipation, consider the variant passage shown in figure 13.4. Here, the duration of the anticipation has been increased to a quarter note. Two important differences distinguish this case from the previous one. First, by falling on a more predictable beat, the anticipation reduces slightly the likelihood that the next event will happen on beat 3. That is, the dotted quarter/eighth of the original example makes it more certain that something will happen on beat 3. In effect, delaying the onset of the anticipation renders it more effective in helping the listener predict the *when* of the ensuing event.

The second difference is that having the anticipation occur on beat 2 rather than the second half of beat 2 makes the anticipation note itself more predictable. In effect, there is a trade-off between the predictability of the anticipation moment and the post-anticipation moment.

These are not the only psychological effects evoked by the anticipation. Later, in chapter 15, we will return to consider the anticipation (and other embellishment tones), focusing on psychological *qualia* related to feelings of tension and a sense of premonition or anticipation.

Hypermetric Anticipation

The hierarchical patterns evident in table 13.1 are not limited to the span of a measure. Longer spans are also commonly formed. In chapter 10 we saw an example of hyper-metric hierarchy in a string quartet by Haydn. Much Western music is based on four-bar periods and eight-bar double periods.

Figure 13.5

Examples of snare-drum fills (distinctive drum patterns that lead into a hypermetric downbeat). Each example represents the first entry of the snare drum in the work. The hypermetric downbeat coincides with the beginning of the next measure following the examples: (a) A single snare stroke on beat four from "Pennsylvania 6-5000" composed by Jerry Gray and Carl Sigman. (b) Fourth-beat stroke with added grace note from Duke Ellington's rendition of Vincent Youmans's "Tea for Two." (c) An entire measure of sixteenth notes from Irving Berlin's "Blue Skies" performed by Swing & Sway with Sammy Kaye.

In the same way that certain temporal patterns can help listeners infer the downbeat, there are temporal patterns that can help listeners infer hypermetric downbeats—that is, the onsets of four-bar phrases or periods. A good place to see such hypermetric cues is in drum patterns in Western popular music. When a hypermetric downbeat occurs in pop music, drummers frequently lead into that moment with so-called *fills*. A fill is a distinctive drumming sequence that precedes a major downbeat.[7] Figure 13.5 provides three examples of snare drum fills. Each example marks the first entry of the snare drum in each of their respective pieces. The simplest fill might consist of a single snare stroke on the fourth beat preceding the hypermetric downbeat. Figure 13.5a shows an example of this single-stroke fill from the big-band classic "Pennsylvania 6-5000" made famous by the Glenn Miller orchestra.[8]

Figure 13.5b shows the same fourth-beat snare stroke preceded by a grace note. An example can be found in Duke Ellington's rendition of "Tea for Two."[9] The third example shows an entire measure of sixteenths from the introduction to Irving Berlin's "Blue Skies" as performed by Swing & Sway with Sammy Kaye.[10] In each case, the final note of the fill occurs at a moment that increases the likelihood of an event on beat one. In effect, fills behave like embellished tendency tones (such as turns or trills). Like these embellishments, the presence of the fill decreases any listener uncertainty about the ensuing hypermetric downbeat.

Figures 13.6 and 13.7 show several fills from Danny & the Juniors' "At the Hop" ("Let's Go to the Hop").[11] This was a number one hit in the United States in 1958. The song is structured as a boogie-woogie style twelve-bar strophe. Figure 13.6 shows the backbeat strokes on beats 2 and 4 through the first eleven measures. Only the

Figure 13.6
Snare drum fill shown in 12-bar backbeat context from Danny & the Juniors' "At the Hop" ("Let's Go to the Hop").

Figure 13.7
Variant snare drum fills from Danny & the Juniors' "At the Hop."

snare drum is notated. At the twelfth measure, the fill begins on beat 2 and continues with a complete series of sixteenth notes.

Figure 13.7 shows other drum fills from "At the Hop." Only the last four measures are notated for each twelve-bar strophe. As can be seen, each twelve-bar strophe receives a different fill. Paradoxically, none of the fills leads to a snare drum stroke on the hypermetric downbeat of the next measure beginning a new verse or strophe. Nevertheless, the fill decreases the listener's uncertainty about the hypermeter. One can start the sound recording at a random point, but the first occurrence of a fill will dispel any confusion regarding the hypermetric structure.

In effect, the pop fill is the hypermetric equivalent of the melodic anticipation. The fill is a signal that dramatically increases listener certainty about the *when* and

Figure 13.8
"Stop-and-go" rhythm from Janis Joplin's "Buried Alive in the Blues." The hypermetric downbeat is approached by suspending the snare backbeat.

what of harmonic changes within the song. Along with the backbeat, the fill has become the principal rhythmic cliché in Western-style popular music. Whereas the backbeat varies little, the fill is the principal target for variation. The specific rhythmic pattern of the fill may vary significantly, but its position just prior to the hypermetric downbeat reflects its principal psychological role. Fills are psychologically equivalent to the precadential embellishments so characteristic of art music (cadential 6-4 chords, suspensions, etc.).

One further common variant of the fill deserves mention: the use of silence. Figure 13.8 shows an example of what might be called a "stop-and-go." The example is from "Buried Alive in the Blues" from Janis Joplin's *Pearl* album. Here the snare provides the usual quarter-note backbeats, but when the hypermetric downbeat approaches, the fill is replaced by an entire measure of rest. The snare reappears at the beginning of the hypermetric measure. Although the stop-and-go is less common than other fills, it serves the same function of rendering the hypermetric downbeat more predictable. By interrupting the flow of the rhythm, the stop-and-go acts like a melodic suspension—heightening the desire for the return of the rhythm.

Harmonic Schemata

As long as listeners are able to mentally represent some regularity, it is possible to form one or more pertinent schemas. For example, groups of pitches are able to form emergent percepts we call chords,[12] and these mental objects make possible the existence of harmonic schemas. Table 13.2 shows the frequency of various chord progressions in a sample of baroque music. Antecedent chords are identified by rows, and each column represents a different consequent chord. Rather than identifying the absolute probabilities for various chord progressions, the probabilities shown in table 13.2 have been normalized as the probability of a given chord following some antecedent chord. That is, the probabilities in each row sum to 1.0. Some progressions have a high probability of occurrence. For example, 79 percent of dominant chords are followed by the tonic. Other progressions almost never occur, like the vii°–ii progression.[13]

In contrast to table 13.2, figure 13.9 shows a schematic diagram of the absolute probability of harmonic progressions based on a sample of baroque music. Here the width of connecting arrows is proportional to the absolute probability of the

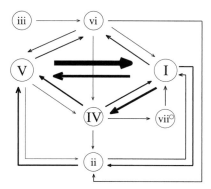

Figure 13.9
Schematic illustration of chord progressions in a sample of baroque music. The thickness of each line is proportional to the absolute probability of harmonic succession. Lines have been drawn only for those transitions above a minimum threshold. Notice the strong dominant-to-tonic (V–I) tendency.

Table 13.2

	→I	→ii	→iii	→IV	→V	→vi	→vii°
I→		0.143	0.025	0.309	0.376	0.120	0.025
ii→	0.274		0.040	0.032	0.564	0.040	0.048
iii→	0.063	0.127		0.340	0.063	0.383	0.021
IV→	0.304	0.132	0.025		0.380	0.025	0.132
V→	0.793	0.021	0.021	0.039		0.119	0.005
vi→	0.155	0.232	0.069	0.139	0.286		0.116
vii°→	0.583	0.000	0.027	0.138	0.194	0.055	

associated chord progression. Not all progressions are represented—only those above a certain threshold of probability. As can be seen, baroque harmony is dominated by the dominant–tonic progression (V–I). The second most common progression is the reverse (I–V). Some chords are highly constrained. For example, the vii° chord tends to be followed only by I.

Using the harmonic probabilities we can characterize chord progressions as more or less probable. For example, figure 13.10 shows three chord progressions. The first progression consists of chord successions that have relatively high probabilities of occurrence. The third progression consists of chord successions that have a very low probability of occurrence, while the second progression consists of chord successions with an intermediate probability. The average information (in bits) for the three progressions is 4.4, 6.9, and 10.7, respectively.[14]

$$\underset{3.05}{I} - \underset{4.08}{V} - \underset{3.05}{I} - \underset{5.08}{V} - \underset{6.61}{ii} - \underset{4.35}{IV} - I$$

$$\underset{4.08}{V} - \underset{6.99}{I} - \underset{8.99}{vi} - \underset{8.72}{ii} - \underset{8.31}{iii} - \underset{4.08}{V} - I$$

$$\underset{10.31}{v} - \underset{11.31}{IV} - \underset{8.99}{vii^{\circ}} - \underset{7.85}{vi} - \underset{11.31}{III} - \underset{4.35}{IV} - I$$

Figure 13.10
Three seven-chord progressions with transitional probabilities indicated in bits: (a) chord successions having a high probability of occurrence (average 4.4 bits); (b) chord successions having an intermediate probability of occurrence (average 6.9 bits); (c) chord successions having a low probability of occurrence (average 10.7 bits).

Style and Form

As noted in chapter 11, chord progressions sometimes differ for different styles. Western popular music, for example, exhibits a number of distinctive characteristics compared with baroque harmony. In general, individual pieces of popular music make use of a smaller variety of chords than is typical of baroque works. It is not uncommon for a pop tune to employ just two or three different chords. However, popular music in general draws from a larger and more varied palette of chords than is the case for baroque music. Roughly 30 percent of chords in pop music involve sevenths or ninths compared with only about 15 percent for baroque music. There is also a greater variety of ways of connecting chords in popular music compared with baroque music. Figure 13.11 illustrates the absolute probabilities for different chord progressions in a sample of popular music; the graph is comparable to the one shown in figure 13.9. Broadly speaking, the differences are minimal. In general, pop harmonies are less dominated by the tonic-dominant poles so evident in figure 13.9. The IV, ii, vi, and iii chords are used more frequently in popular music, while the diminished vii chord almost never appears.

Another significant difference between popular and baroque harmony is the use of chord inversions. Roughly one third of all chords in baroque music are not in root position (most often used is a first inversion chord). By contrast, only about 10 percent of chords in popular music are in inversion: the majority of chords are in root position.[15]

With the greater variety of chord transitions in pop music, one might suppose that pop harmony is less predictable than baroque harmony. This is true for both zeroth-order chord probabilities and first-order chord transitions, but not for the higher-order transitions. Pop harmony tends to be more cyclic than baroque harmony. Most pop harmonies employ a four-, six- or eight-chord progression that is repeatedly cycled in

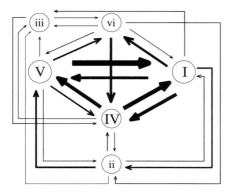

Figure 13.11

Schematic illustration of chord progressions in a sample of seventy Western popular songs, including works by John Lennon, Elton John, Bon Jovi, Marvin Gaye, Billy Joel, Vangelis, and others. The thickness of each line is proportional to the absolute probability of harmonic succession. Lines have been drawn only for those transitions above a minimum threshold. Notice the increased importance of the subdominant chord (IV) compared with baroque harmony.

accordance with the strophic structure of the song. Often two harmonic cycles are used, one for the verse and one for the chorus. In effect, the reduced schematic predictability of pop chord progressions is offset by the increased dynamic predictability of the specific progressions used in particular works.

In some cases, particular chord cycles rise to prominence and may emerge as a stylistic schema in their own right. The British musicologist, Philip Tagg, for example, has identified a class of pop works that use the cyclic progression i–♭VII–♭VI–V. Nearly all of the songs that employ this progression have lyrics suggesting "loss," "resignation," or "sadness."

Harmonic clichés may not only employ particular chord progressions. Often, a harmonic cliché is linked to a specific voice-leading arrangement. For example, in the V–I progression, Robert Gjerdingen at Northwestern University has shown how composers like Haydn and Mozart tended to rely on a specific form of the progression based on two contrapuntal lines—one falling from subdominant to mediant ($\hat{4}$–$\hat{3}$), and the other rising from leading tone to tonic ($\hat{7}$–$\hat{1}$). Gjerdingen has shown that, although this pattern received many embellishments, the basic $\hat{4}$–$\hat{3}$/$\hat{7}$–$\hat{1}$ construction became a stock-in-trade musical structure of the late eighteenth century.[16]

Apart from harmony, schematic predictability is also enhanced by using commonplace rhythms. In the case of dance music, stylistic clichés are dominated by distinctive repetitive rhythms. As we noted in chapter 10, various dances are virtually synonymous with particular rhythmic patterns, such as the cha-cha, tango, Charleston, pavan, polka, and so on.

Finally, although there is no pertinent experimental evidence, it is widely assumed that certain "set" musical forms provide useful predictive schemas for those listeners who are familiar with them. A fugue has a distinctive opening—beginning with a single musical part, which is then joined by a second part, then by a third part, and so on. For a knowledgeable listener, recognition of the fugue form may lead to particular expectations, such as the likelihood of a *stretto* passage. Other set forms, such as the *da capo* aria, rondo, and sonata-allegro form all provide useful expectations for knowledgeable listeners.

Although schemas are typically shared by a large community of listeners, it is important to remind ourselves that schemas also depend on the unique history of individual listeners. Recall that in chapter 11, we discussed research by Robert Gjerdingen showing that stylistic taxonomies are listener centered.[17] When musicians make use of existing schemas to increase predictability, they make assumptions about the general listening background of their listeners and on listeners' specific familiarity with the schemas used.

3   Dynamic Predictability

Schematic expectations are brought by the listener to the listening experience. But it is also possible to compose musical works so that the work itself will evoke work-specific expectations that increase the predictability of the music. Among the many techniques that can be used to increase the predictability of a musical work, common devices include thematic, motivic, and figurative repetition, ostinatos, and sequences. But the most straightforward technique is to repeat large segments of musical materials several times within the work itself.

Recall from the previous chapter that Joy Ollen and I found that about 94 percent of all musical passages are repeated at some point within a work. This estimate comes from a study of fifty works spanning five continents with styles ranging from bluegrass to polkas, traditional indigenous musics to orchestral works. Our sample of music explicitly excludes vocal works whose repetition structures can be strongly influenced by the narrative or poetic demands of the lyrics. In vocal music, verse and chorus structures can be expected to result in even greater amounts of repetition. If one ignores changes in lyrics, vocal music is certainly more repetitive than instrumental music. Since most of the world's music involves the voice, this means that our musical sample was probably less repetitive than the average musical work. While there are exceptions, most of the world's music exhibits a high degree of repetition.

Patterns of structural repetition are not random. In our cross-cultural study of musical form, Ollen and I found a general tendency for passages to repeat immediately. For example, if a musical work contains two main musical ideas ("A" and "B"), they are more likely to be arranged in a pattern like AAABBB or AABBBA than the pattern ABABAB. Compared with a random ordering of segments, real music exhibits a tendency to have "clumps" of repetition.[18]

In listening to any new musical work, the initial material will necessarily be novel. But after presenting the first musical segment, the musician has a choice: repeat the same segment (AA), present a modified version of the same material (AA'), or present more new material (AB). In music around the world, most musicians choose to repeat the initial segment verbatim. There are many possible reasons that might account for this clumping tendency. But notice that this strategy is consistent with the prediction effect. By repeating the first segment, the listener will already have an opportunity to benefit from predicting what will happen next.

By way of illustration, consider a hypothetical musical work that is constructed from five basic passages (A, B, C, D, E). If a composer is endeavoring to maximize the prediction effect, the worst arrangement would be to begin the work by presenting a through-composed presentation of all five passages (ABCDE). This approach would delay any prediction effect until after the appearance of the fifth passage—that is, well into the work. A better approach would be to "ration" the appearance of new material. After introducing each new passage, allow the listener to take advantage of their newly gained familiarity by repeating the same material. Although immediate repetition might lead to habituation or boredom, musicians nevertheless appear to favor this approach in structuring musical works.

Figuration

Apart from the repetition of relatively large sections of music, musical works exhibit considerable repetition at much shorter temporal spans as well. Patterns shorter than a couple of seconds in duration may consist of just a handful of notes. We might refer to these brief patterns as *figures*.

Many figures pertain to accompaniment textures. For example, an ostinato may entail a repeated arpeggio figure used for harmonic accompaniment. Or a rhythmic ostinato might be used to define a distinctive background texture. Figure 13.12 shows a typical accompaniment ostinato from Mozart's Sonata K. 545.

Sometimes ostinatos are used as foreground elements. Figure 13.13 shows examples of ostinatos from two well-known keyboard works. The triplet figure from Beethoven's *Moonlight Sonata* is ostensibly an accompaniment figure; however, for most listeners this triplet pattern is more evocative of Beethoven's piece than the actual melody line. Compared with the simple ascending triplet, the second example from Widor's most famous organ work exhibits a more complicated repeating pitch contour. It takes only a couple of ostinato figures to provide listeners with a template that makes the ensuing ostinato figures more predictable.

Figure 13.12
Typical accompaniment ostinato from W. A. Mozart, Sonata in C, K. 545, first movement. Despite the changes in chord, Mozart tends to reuse the same contour shape throughout a given musical work.

Figure 13.13
Two examples of foreground ostinatos from various keyboard works: (a) Ludwig van Beethoven, Piano Sonata op. 27, no. 2 (*"Moonlight Sonata"*); (b) Charles-Marie Widor, Finale from Organ Symphony no. 5 (1887).

All the figures shown in figures 13.12 and 13.13 consist of notes of equal durations. In some cases, figures involve both distinctive rhythms as well as distinctive pitch contours. In yet other cases, figures may be purely rhythmic in nature.

Figuration is often shared between works. For example, hundreds of keyboard works employ the same common "Alberti bass" accompaniment figures. Similarly, hundreds of popular piano works employ a "stride bass" pattern where a single bass pitch alternates with a three- or four-note chord on the offbeats. When a figuration pattern is commonplace, a listener may begin to experience it as an independent schema.

Sequence

Yet another repetition technique is the *sequence*. A sequence is a melodic figure or harmonic pattern that is repeated at different pitch heights. A sequence is much like an ostinato whose pitch level is systematically shifted. Figure 13.14 shows an example of a sequence from J. S. Bach's keyboard *Inventio* no. 8 in F major. Here, the left hand plays nine consecutive repetitions of the same figure at three different diatonic pitch heights while the right hand plays the same sequence at two different pitch heights.

Figure 13.14

Sequence from J. S. Bach's *Inventio* no. 8 (BWV 779).

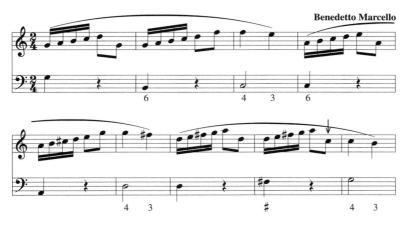

Figure 13.15

Excerpt from Marcello's Sonata in A minor for flute, measures 46 to 54. Three instances of a sequence are shown. In the third instance, the pitches C5 and B4 are an octave lower than would be expected. However, the harmonic sequence is preserved.

A slightly longer sequence is shown in figure 13.15. In this flute sonata by Benedetto Marcello, each statement of the sequence is three measures in length. In the first and second statements, the 4–3 suspensions correspond to the high point in the phrase. However, in the third instance of the sequence, the suspension drops down an octave (arrow) from where it might have been expected. This example demonstrates an interesting issue related to similarity and mental representation. Expectations rely on some underlying mental representation. Listeners expect something concrete—like a particular pitch, or a particular harmony, or tone color. In the third statement of the sequence, the pitches C5 and B4 are an octave lower than would be expected—given the preceding statements.

The octave displacement at the arrow would be surprising if the passage is mentally represented using pitch contours or intervals. However, this passage would not be surprising if the music is mentally represented using pitch-classes, scale degree,

"pitch-class contour," and so on. Moreover, these changed notes still preserve the underlying harmonic sequence. The *continuo* part harmonizes each sequence as a V-of harmony
ending in a 4–3 suspension. By way of summary, the final three notes evoke "surprise"
for pitch, contour, and interval representations, whereas the notes are entirely expected
for pitch-class, pitch-class contour, scale degree, and harmonic representations.

The sequence in figure 13.15 suggests that a passage might be both potentially
surprising and expected at the same time. The degree of surprise will depend on the
nature of the listener's mental representation for music. It is theoretically possible that
different listeners will find the passage exhibits different amounts of expectedness,
depending on the listener's predominant mental representation for music. A passage
deemed surprising from the perspective of one representation might be entirely
expected from the perspective of another representation. When we speak of musical
similarity, these are the sorts of factors that might significantly influence how listeners
judge musical "nearness."

The above examples provide merely anecdotal illustrations. To my knowledge, no
pertinent experimental research has established that musical figures and sequences
facilitate coding in short-term or intermediate-term memory. Nor has research shown
that these patterns facilitate dynamic expectations. But such musical structures suggest
potentially fruitful areas for future research.

Themes and Motives

Whereas certain figures are often shared between hundreds of works, other figures may
be unique to individual musical works. Intuitively, we sense that some aspects of a
musical work are more characteristic of the work than other aspects. Most works
contain passages that are commonly found in other works. For example, roughly one
third of Western musical themes contain the pitch sequence $\hat{3}$–$\hat{2}$–$\hat{1}$. The sequence $\hat{5}$–
$\hat{4}$–$\hat{3}$ is also quite common.[19] Most musical works exhibit scale-like passages, and many
works exhibit arpeggios of different sorts. Figure 13.16 shows three examples of commonplace musical segments or figures. There is little about these passages that uniquely
brings to mind particular musical works.

Other figures are characteristic of particular works. For example, figure 13.17 provides two well-known rhythms that are work-specific. These rhythms are the dynamic
equivalents to rhythmic schemas (like the cha-cha). I should note that these well-
known examples also benefit from veridical memory. That is, they are works that have
benefited from frequent exposure for most Western-enculturated listeners.

In themselves, these rhythms are no more distinctive than the patterns that characterize various dances—like the tango or samba. Ravel's *Bolero* is an instructive
example since Ravel borrowed both the rhythm and the title from an already existing
dance form in Spain. For most modern listeners, the rhythm denotes Ravel's *Bolero*.

Figure 13.16
Three common Western musical patterns.

Figure 13.17
Two work-specific rhythms: (a) Gustav Holst's "Mars, the Bringer of War" from *The Planets*; (b) Maurice Ravel's *Bolero*.

But for listeners familiar with Spanish dance music it denotes boleros in general. A similar point might be made about the limbo and the macarena. For most people who have any familiarity with these, the dance forms are associated with specific popular musical works rather than a group of works or genre.

In short, what makes a figure a *theme* or a *motive* is that it is associated uniquely with a particular work. The same figure could function as a way of distinguishing a genre or style. Themes or motives are figures that occur frequently within some work, but rarely occur in other works.

Until around the mid-twentieth century, the identification of themes and motives was regarded as a central task in music analysis. By midcentury, thematic and motivic analysis was considered old-fashioned and somewhat naive. Today it is possible to rely less on intuition and provide a more formal understanding of themes and motives. In characterizing themes and motives, the main task is describing a succinct feature that is truly distinctive of the work in question.

In attempting to identify a distinctive musical pattern for a given work, it is easy to mistakenly describe a musical commonality instead. A striking illustration of this problem can be found in a well-known analysis by Allen Forte of Johannes Brahms' op. 51, no. 1 string quartet.[20] The opening of the first movement is shown in figure

Figure 13.18
Johannes Brahms, String Quartet op. 51, no. 1, first movement, measures 1 to 4.

13.18. Forte proposed that the principal motive for this work can be described in set-theoretic terms by the interval-class set (2,1). This refers to four formally related three-note sequences: (1) three ascending pitches—rising by first two semitones and then one semitone; (2) three descending pitches—falling by first two semitones and then one semitone; (3) three descending pitches—falling by first one semitone and then two semitones; and (4) three ascending pitches—rising by first one semitone and then two semitones. The prime, inversion, retrograde, and retrograde-inversion forms of the motive are illustrated in figure 13.19.

When I first encountered Forte's analysis, it seemed to me that there was nothing to be gained by using a set-theoretic formulation. Although Forte's allegiance to analytic rigor is laudable, his figure definition seems unduly impoverished. Rising and falling sequences of tones and semitones are commonplace in music, so it seemed unlikely that this interval-class set would provide a useful description of a distinctive feature of this work. Forte's analysis inspired me to carry out a statistically based

Figure 13.19
Some sample sets from Forte's motivic analysis of Brahms op. 51, no. 1, first movement.

Figure 13.20
Schematic representation of the principal motive in Brahms op. 51, no. 1, first movement, as developed using a comparative analysis method.

analysis of what feature distinguishes this string quartet.[21] I used a computer to help calculate the most succinct musical figure that is common in this work, but not common in other (similar) works. In order to pursue this approach, one must select a "control" sample of music against which the specific work can be contrasted. I chose movements from Brahms' two other string quartets. As it turned out, the motive identified by Forte occurs more frequently in both of Brahms' other quartets than in the opus 51, no. 1.

Nevertheless, Forte's intuition seems warranted, even if the description is problematic. Using a statistical approach, I was able to progressively refine Forte's motive until it became genuinely distinctive of the quartet movement in question. The statistical analysis is too tedious to describe here—interested readers should refer to the published analysis.[22] But the final result of my analysis is shown in figure 13.20. In order to render the three-note motive distinctive, it must be linked to a long–short–long rhythm. In addition, the feature tends to start a phrase or slur, follow a rest, occur in an outer voice, and begin on a strong metric position. Finally, my statistical approach eliminated the inversion, retrograde, and retrograde inversions of Forte's motive: only the prime form proved distinctive of opus 51, no. 1. All of these attributes contribute to the distinctiveness of the feature—compared with other string quartets by Brahms.

My proposed alternative to Forte's interval-class set bears more than a superficial resemblance to the opening statement in the first violin. In traditional tonal analysis, this feature would have been informally labeled "the principal motive." My lengthy analysis of this work merely formalized the evidence in support of this informal intuition.

Like sectional repetitions and figures, themes and motives help listeners to form dynamic expectations about what is likely to happen next. Some traditional musical forms invite phrase- or period-length repetition—such as the Chaconne, where some bass line is repeated over and over again. But much of the facilitation of listener expectation can be traced to shorter segments of figures, themes, and motives. Repetition can occur at many temporal levels, from long-term repetition of entire sections of music to brief motivic repetition.

Themes and motives are not merely statistically distinctive. They are also the parts of the music that are most likely to be spontaneously recalled, and they are the passages most likely to help us remember the rest of a musical work. If asked to recall something from a musical work, we are not likely to recall the sorts of banal passages illustrated in figure 13.16.

Using information theory, we might say that what distinguishes one work from another are those elements that have a higher entropy than other works, but a low entropy in the context of the work itself. Said another way, we would look for passages or features that are (1) not commonly found in other works, but (2) occur frequently in the work under consideration. Formally, we can define a "distinctive feature" to be those passages or figures that exhibit a high ratio of external-to-internal entropy. Such measures of "distinctiveness" have long been used in quantitative stylistics, such as research used to determine the authorship of some text.

Perhaps surprisingly, such measures were proposed for music analysis as long ago as the 1950s.[23] However, despite some initial enthusiasm, the use of information theory in music analysis waned in the 1960s. The original enthusiasts suffered from a lack of computational resources—including suitably large databases of music. By the time the technology had caught up with the theoretical ideas, information theory had lost much of its appeal among music theorists.

It is not surprising that a statistical approach to music analysis would fail to ignite the imaginations of music scholars. Quantitative approaches can seem antithetical to the spirit of the arts. But given what we now know about statistical learning, we should not be surprised by the utility of a statistical approach in identifying distinctive musical features that conform well with our musical intuitions.

What Is a Musical Work?

The above discussion of thematic and stylistic features has repercussions for the thorny aesthetic issue of defining a musical work. For most of us, the question of whether two performances represent the same or different musical works seems like an arcane and uninteresting philosophical question. We think it is obvious what a musical work is, and find such questions pedantic and academic. However, there is much to learn by considering such questions.

Most English-speaking readers will regard "Baa, Baa, Black Sheep," the "Alphabet Song" and "Twinkle, Twinkle, Little Star" as different children's songs. But non-English speakers will recognize that the melodies are the same and wonder why they aren't considered different verses of the same song.

Consider the problem posed to me by a musician I met in Iceland: There is a well-known song that you have heard hundreds of times. This song has thousands of verses, only a few of which are sung for any given performance. It is written for solo voice and guitar. Sometimes other instruments are added, or the guitar figuration is changed. Sometimes the tempo is changed. This work has no official title, but an appropriate name might be "Twelve-Bar Blues." In other words, why are Bessie Smith's "Young Woman's Blues," B. B. King's "Three O'Clock Blues," and John Lee Hooker's "Hobo Blues" considered to be different works? Why aren't these all considered "arrangements" of the same song?

In the real world there exists a continuum. At one end of the continuum we can play a single sound recording twice and most listeners will say that the performances are identical—it is the same work. At the opposite extreme, we can juxtapose works from different cultures that are as different as one can imagine. But in between these two extremes we can create an almost perfect continuum. We can have two different flutists play Debussy's *Syrinx*. We can arrange Bach's 'cello suites for viola, or Vivaldi's violin concertos for organ. Charles Gounod can add a vocal melody to Bach's Prelude no. 1 from *The Well-Tempered Clavier* and call it "Ave Maria." Percy Faith creates an "easy listening" version of J. S. Bach's Minuet in G and calls it "Lover's Concerto." Albert Ahlen makes a jazz arrangement of Beethoven's "Für Elise" and calls it "Elise-a-Go-Go." Leroy Carr can take the twelve-bar blues form and create "Alabama Woman Blues." Anton von Webern can use Schoenberg's method of composing with twelve tones and create the opus 30 Variations.

I would like to suggest that the distinction people make between a "work" and a "genre" has no objective basis. There is nothing in the external world that delineates these two classes of auditory experience. They are not "natural kinds." Rather, the distinction between "work" and "genre" is entirely a subjective phenomenon; it is probably an artifact of the way human memory is structured. Specifically, I propose that what distinguishes a work from a genre or style is the type of memory coding. What we call a "work" is a veridical coding of an auditory memory. If two different musical stimuli activate the same veridical coding we call them "renditions" (of the same "work"). What we call a "style" or "genre" is a schematical coding of an auditory memory.

The value of this way of understanding the definition of a work is that it accounts for the different experiences of musical novices and experts. I recall the first time I heard recordings of Inuit throat singing. The singing was strikingly different from any human vocalization I had heard before. In Inuit throat singing, two women stand face-to-face, hang on to each other's clothing, and virtually sing into each other's mouths. I listened to the first "song" with a sense of astonishment. But when the recording moved on to the second track, the music was virtually indistinguishable from track one. The liner notes identified the title of each selection and gave some background about the meaning and use of each song. For example, some throat songs were identified as lullabies. But to my ears, all of the selections were cut from the same cloth. Each had the characteristic antiphonal back-and-forth pattern. Each had the same gruff vocalization. Each selection ended with the two singers breaking into laughter—a state probably induced by hyperventilation. To my naive ears, all of the tracks amounted to different performances of the same work.

Consider an often-observed phenomenon in children's listening. With four-year-olds, play two different melodies (A and B) on a trumpet. Then repeat one of the melodies (A) on a flute. Then ask each child which melodies were the same. Young children are much more likely to say that the two different melodies played by the trumpet are the same. In other words "same" and "different" are defined primarily by instrumental timbre rather than by pitch or time.

Whether you hear twelve-bar blues as a "work" or a "genre" depends on your experience. No experienced blues listener could identify with my Icelandic acquaintence for whom it all sounded like one piece. Nor would a traditional Inuit singer sympathize with my experience of hearing Inuit throat songs as slightly different renditions of the same piece. A central New Guinea highlander inexperienced with Western music might hear piano pieces by Skriabin, Jelly Roll Morton, and Mozart as "that piano work."

From a psychological perspective, the question is "how is the experience coded in memory?" If "Baa, Baa, Black Sheep" and "Twinkle, Twinkle, Little Star" are coded as separate veridical memories, then they are, by my reckoning, different works. If different Inuit throat songs fail to be encoded as distinct veridical memories, then I will hear them as renditions of a single token. It is only through long exposure that renditions will be mentally segregated and achieve an independent veridical identity. With exposure, the audiophile will hear recordings of the same piece by Gould and Horowitz as different works. By linking the notion of work with veridical memory and genre with schematic memory, we provide a better way of understanding why such distinctions arise. There is no philosophically necessary reason why we should distinguish works (and their various renditions) from genres. The distinction emerges, I believe, from the way brains work, not from some objective physical difference and not from some disembodied aesthetic concept.

Of course it is easier to distinguish individual tokens when the perceptual differences are large. Within cultures and genres, however, there are many commonalities. With so much music employing the same melodic, rhythmic, harmonic, stylistic, and other schemas, what is there to distinguish one work from another? If a composer wants to create a work that is more easily distinguished as a unique token within a genre, how does one create a distinctive character?

There is a sort of catch-22 for any musical feature that is intended to distinguish one work from another. On the one hand, such features must be sufficiently novel that they are truly unique to a particular musical work. But novelty alone can raise problems. Suppose, for example, that a composer created an otherwise stereotypic and nondescript work, except that the performers *cough* midway through the work. This single feature is logically sufficient to distinguish the work from all other musical works. If necessary, one might create two or three such highly unique "markers." No one could doubt that the work differs from all others.

But such a strategy for creating distinctiveness raises at least two problems. The first problem is that until the first "identity marker" appears, the work would sound banal, boilerplate, stereotypic. There would be no sense of the work's identity until the advent of the first marker. The second problem is that the markers, by definition, would be completely unpredictable. If a sense of uniqueness can be conveyed only by departing from the well-worn schematic paths, then such single-event markers will necessarily sound out of place.

We already have evidence that such isolated identity markers don't work. When we sing "Happy Birthday," there is little sense that it is a different musical work depending on whether we sing it to Mary or Bert. The differences in lyrics fail to confer a distinct identity on the piece. We don't end up with two pieces: "Happy Birthday, Mary" and "Happy Birthday, Bert." The reason why is easy to see: both versions tap into the same veridical expectations. Adding a cough to the middle of Bach's *Goldberg Variations* doesn't make it "my" piece. Experienced listeners will be hearing the work according to already established veridical expectations.

Since uniqueness *must* involve some departure from schematic norms, the only way to ensure that the "markers" sound "in-place" is to place them in the context of dynamic expectations. This means that some sort of repetition is needed. Instead of creating an identity for a work by introducing distinctive one-time events, a better approach is to repeat the markers frequently. That is, "markers" ideally should consist of distinctive musical patterns that are repeated frequently. Also, to prevent listeners from invoking an inappropriate veridical expectation, these frequently repeated markers should be introduced soon after the piece begins.

In summary, if we are seeking to create a unique mental identity for a sound experience, we might seek auditory "markers" that: (1) appear frequently throughout the experience, (2) exhibit distinct or unique features compared with other experiences, and (3) tend to be presented soon after the experience begins. In the language of Western music, examples of such patterns include *themes* and *motives*. Such distinctive figures provide the sorts of memory hooks that make it possible to form independent veridical memories. They help to differentiate the work from other, possibly similar or indistinguishable works.

The distinctive pitch and rhythm properties of themes and motives are not the only ways to establish a piece's identity. One can also create a distinctive identity through the use of texture, treatment, or timbre. For example, one could achieve a unique identity for a work by performing otherwise banal material using a distinctive instrumental combination—say, handbells and electric guitar. Alternatively, one might play works using a distinctive tremolo treatment. But the range of possible treatments is small compared with the combinatorial explosion of possibilities offered by pitch and rhythm. In most cultures, the number of distinct instrumental combinations is quite small. Perhaps this explains why manipulations of pitch, rhythm, and lyrics provide the most common identity markers for musical works.

Memory's Progress

At this point it is important to remind ourselves that memory is dynamic rather than static. When we experience an auditory stimulus for the first time, the experience is initially coded in short-term memory. This short-term memory provides the basis for dynamic expectations as the auditory experience continues to unfold. If our experience is sufficiently salient it will be retained in episodic memory—meaning that we will be able to recall the experience as an event in our autobiographical past. We can use this episodic memory to form veridical expectations that inform future listening experiences. If we hear many nearly identical performances, the original autobiographical memory may become obscured and the veridical expectation will no longer be linked to the memory of a specific exposure. If broadly similar auditory stimuli are experienced many times over a long period of time, then the memory will be transformed into a mental schema that provides the basis for schematic expectations.

These dynamic changes in memory interacting with the totality of past auditory experience are what allow us to hear something as a *motive* rather than a commonplace *figure*, as a *work* rather than a *rendition*, and as elements that define a *genre* or *style* rather than a particular work or performance. These distinctions, I believe, arise from a combination of the specific history of a listener's musical exposure interacting with the physiological structures of human memory.

Reprise

This chapter has explored some of the ways that listening experiences can be made more predictable. I have distinguished four broad approaches to shaping predictability: veridical, schematic, dynamic, and conscious. In the previous chapter I suggested that each of these forms of expectation is associated with a different type of auditory memory: episodic, semantic, short-term, and working. I also suggested that these different types of memory owe their origins to different biological functions.

In the case of schematic predictability, the vast majority of musical works employ familiar instruments, use a familiar scale, follow a familiar meter, play familiar harmonies, and conform to a familiar style. Most musical works make use of a host of culturally defined schematic norms. In Western music, for example, we've identified several of the many melodic, rhythmic, harmonic, and other norms. Melodies typically exhibit central pitch tendency, pitch proximity, and step declination. Rhythms tend to exhibit metric hierarchy and metric proximity. Phrases lean toward arch-shaped trajectories and four- and eight-bar hypermeters. Harmonies tend to rely on common chord progressions, stable harmonic rhythms, and cadential clichés. These represent only a handful of the commonly used musical schemas.

Apart from schematic norms, musical works avail themselves of a variety of dynamic structures. For example, nearly all musical works make use of internal repetition. Entire musical passages are commonly repeated in music—and this observation holds for music throughout the world. In addition to these broad repetitive strokes, nearly all musical works also employ smaller-scale figurative repetitions, and many works make use of ostinatos and sequences. Individual musical works also tend to exhibit unique repetitive figures that distinguish the work from other works. Examples of such work-specific figures include themes and motives.

Along with schematic and dynamic forms of repetition, veridical repetition is common in music. A striking fact about music is our tolerance—indeed our desire—to listen to the same music again and again. As noted earlier, although people occasionally do reread favorite novels or view favorite films more than once, music takes the prize for repeated exposure. With the possible exception of dance and meditation, there is nothing else in common human experience that is comparable to music in its repetitiveness. Narrative artifacts like movies, novels, cartoon strips, stories, and speeches have much less internal repetition. Even poetry is less repetitive than music. Occasionally, architecture can approach music in repeating some element, but only sometimes. I know of no visual analogue to the sort of trance-inducing music that can engage listeners for hours. Although dance and meditation may be more repetitive than music, dance is rarely performed in the absence of music, and meditation tellingly relies on imagining a repeated sound or *mantra*.

On rare occasions, a musician will set out to build his or her own unique musical language—seemingly from scratch. Perhaps the best example of this can be found in the music of the twentieth-century American composer, Harry Partch. Partch created his own forty-three-note scale and invented his own distinctive musical instruments. He trained his own performers and composed exclusively for such instruments as *chromelodeon*, *bloboy*, and *zymo-xyl*. The result is a strikingly novel music.[24]

In many ways, Partch created not just his own musical style, but his own musical culture. For most listeners, the experience of listening to Partch's music is best described as colorful and exotic. Yet despite its foreign-sounding character, Partch's music is accessible and, for most listeners, pleasant. Given the fact that first-time listeners to Partch have no appropriate schema for his forty-three-note scale and no familiarity with his unique instruments, how does Partch manage to create a pleasing effect? I think the answer lies in two features of his music. First, Partch's rhythmic language is conventional. The meters and rhythmic patterns are recognizably Western, and many fast-paced passages are very predictable rhythmically. Partch does not abandon the well-worn paths of Western rhythmic schemas. Second, Partch's music follows conventional Western practice in its motivic organization. That is, he makes effective use of dynamic expectations.

In this chapter I have interpreted the various schematic, dynamic, and veridical devices as supporting the hypothesis that musicians often seek to evoke listener pleasure through the prediction effect. This is admittedly speculative. Since we can't climb inside the heads of musicians to determine their conscious or unconscious motives, we can't say that musicians *intend* to make the auditory experience more predictable for listeners. Indeed, some musicians would claim that their goal is to make their music unpredictable. (In chapters 14 and 17 we will look more carefully at the musically unexpected.) However, for most music, claims of great novelty are not easily reconciled with the actual musical organization.

It is not simply the case that music is repetitive. Three converging pieces of evidence support the view that musicians may be unconsciously attracted to make use of the prediction effect. In addition to sheer repetitiveness, the reliance on existing schemas increases predictability without necessarily increasing repetitiveness. Moreover, many common musical devices, such as the anticipation and the "fill," have the effect of reducing listener uncertainty—apart from whether they increase repetitiveness or whether they conform to preexisting schemas. That is, while repetitiveness alone can increase predictability, there are also plenty of other nonrepetition devices musicians use that are consistent with efforts to reduce listener uncertainty.

Music commentators and scholars like to focus on novelty. We are often eager to identify "firsts": the first use of some device, an unprecedented technique, a novel arrangement, or a new venue. Focusing on innovation is understandable: both cleverness and deviance will be found in the unusual. But observers of music have generally failed to draw attention to the single most characteristic feature of music around the world—its extraordinary repetitiveness.[25] In this chapter I have suggested that a plausible explanation for such rampant repetition can be found in the main psychological correlate of repetition—namely, predictability.

With this background, we are now ready to turn our attention to compositional novelty. In the next chapter we consider how (and perhaps why) musicians generate musical surprises.

14 Creating Surprise

Suppose some mischievous gremlin were let loose on a musical score. The gremlin begins making random changes—adding an accidental to a note, deleting a beat, changing a diminished triad to an augmented triad, or reordering two phrases. Almost all of the changes our gremlin could make would cause the music to be less predictable in some way. That is, the majority of possible changes would result in some element of surprise. For most listeners, most of the changes would be irksome or annoying.

In the previous chapter, we looked at a number of techniques that increase the predictability of musical events and so tend to increase the phenomenal pleasure of listeners via the prediction effect. In this chapter, we will turn our attention to musical surprises. When composers or performers make a passage less predictable, they may have mischief in mind (like the gremlin). One of their goals may be to make listeners feel some element of discomfort or uneasiness. But although all surprises begin with an initial negative affect, surprises can sometimes be crafted to evoke a distinctly positive psychological effect through the mechanism of *contrastive valence*. In this chapter we will look at both kinds of surprise: those that are intentionally irksome, and those that are crafted to delight.

There are four basic ways by which musical events can be experienced as surprising:

1. Schematic surprise   Here the music is constructed so that it violates some existing schema that listeners have brought to the listening experience.
2. Dynamic surprise   Here the music is constructed so that the work itself will set up some work-specific expectation that is then violated.
3. Veridical surprise   Surprises can also be evoked by violating a listener's existing knowledge of a given musical work. Such violations may arise, for example, through performance error, misquotation, or intentional parody.

All three of these forms of surprise act at an *unconscious* level. Listeners do not need to think consciously about the music in order to experience these sorts of surprise.

However, it is also possible to reflect about the music and form explicit conscious thoughts about what might happen next. This allows us to distinguish our fourth type of surprise:

4. Conscious surprise   Here the music leads a knowledgeable listener to consciously form an expectation about a future event that is then thwarted.

A consideration in all surprises is that repeated listening to a work will render the surprises expected. However, as we have seen, a distinction must be made between veridical expectations and schematic expectations. Familiarity with a particular work will erode and eventually extinguish the veridical surprise. But it remains possible that a work will retain a schematic surprise. We will see that the phenomenon of surprise holds some surprises.

Schematic Surprises

All of the familiar elements of music within some culture provide opportunities for creating surprises. These include surprising changes of dynamics, instrumentation, scales, meters, harmonies, intervals, styles, and so on. Surprises can be created by sudden changes of loudness, switching instrumentation, violating the current key, transgressing the meter, using a rare chord progression, prematurely terminating a phrase, adding an improbable melodic leap, delaying a resolution, jumping to a different style, and many other manipulations.[1]

Some surprises start right from the moment a work begins. When Igor Stravinsky began his *Rite of Spring* with a solo bassoon, he violated several well-worn conventions in classical music. The vast majority of Western orchestral works do not begin with a solo. Moreover, the bassoon is one of the least likely orchestral instruments to perform by itself. Finally, Stravinsky placed the instrument at the very top of its range. In other words, Stravinsky began the *Rite of Spring* in a highly unorthodox (that is, improbable) way.

Surprises are most reliably evoked when the musician establishes a context in which the surprise is framed. That is, surprises are best ensured when they are "set up." Such setups might be achieved via nonauditory cues, such as manner of dress or performance venue. A violinist wearing a tuxedo might surprise us by launching into a bluegrass fiddle tune. Stepping into an elevator, we might be surprised to hear Gregorian chant. The biggest surprises occur when the context has especially strong associations. In a cathedral sanctuary, most listeners would be surprised if a brass ensemble began to play mariachi. Conversely, if the context lies outside of our experience it will fail to evoke any strong sense of expectation. For example, Murray Schafer's *Music for a Wilderness Lake* places the musicians in canoes on a lake. In this context, listeners standing on the shore have little relevant experience to inform their expectations.

Although social or physical environment may be important in establishing the context of a surprise, more commonly the context is established through the music itself. For example, after a duple meter is established, switching to a triple meter will be more surprising than if the work simply began in triple meter. After establishing a "gallant" musical style, switching to boogie-woogie will be highly unexpected. Each of these surprises arises through the violation of some experience-based schema.

In Western music, perhaps the quintessential example of a schematic violation is the deceptive cadence. In chapter 12 we discussed how the deceptive cadence thwarts the expectation for the more probable dominant-to-tonic progression. We saw, for example, that in the chorale harmonizations by J. S. Bach, V–I cadences are fifty times more prevalent than V–vi. There does not appear to be any natural affinity between V and I apart from learned exposure. That is, there doesn't seem to be any obvious reason why V–I should sound better than some other progression (although such a reason might exist). The deceptive *quale* evoked by the V–vi progression seems to reside solely in the fact that it is much less common than V–I.[2]

More surprising than the deceptive cadence are *chromatic mediant* progressions. Chromatic mediant chords are major and minor chords based on the third and sixth scale degrees; they are chords that do not conform to the key (hence the designation "chromatic"). In any given key, there are six chromatic mediant chords. In the key of C major, for example, the chromatic mediant chords include the triads E major, E-flat major, E-flat minor, A major, A-flat major, and A-flat minor. In the key of C minor, the chromatic mediant chords include the triads E major, E minor, E-flat minor, A major, A minor, and A-flat minor.

Chromatic mediant progressions are rare, and consequently surprising. These sorts of progressions are commonly used in film music where they are associated with moments of high emotion. They are chords that appear to evoke quite specific *qualia* in the listener. In order to characterize these *qualia* I played a series of progressions involving chromatic mediant chords to musician and nonmusician listeners and asked them to provide adjectives that describe their feelings. For both the major and minor keys, I played a key-defining scale, followed by a progression (I–IV–V–I or i–iv–V–i), followed by one of the six chromatic mediant chords. The adjectives provided by the listeners are reported in tables 14.1 and 14.2. Major and minor chords are designated by upper- and lowercase Roman numerals respectively. Preceding sharps or flats indicate roots that are raised or lowered from the diatonic pitches (regardless of the actual accidental). I have distributed the descriptive adjectives into four categories: (1) adjectives related to feelings of surprise, (2) adjectives related to feelings of tendency, (3) adjectives related to positive or negative feelings, and (4) adjectives that don't fit into the other three categories.

Compared with diatonic chord progressions, chromatic mediant chords are clearly unexpected. The most common characterization of these chords is "surprising." With

Table 14.1
Reported qualia for chromatic mediant chords in a major key context

Chord	Expectedness	Tendency	Valence	Other
VI	surprising, bold	leading, unresolved, forward-leaning, strong tendency, heralding change, anticipatory, tense, suggestive, dangled	bright, joyful	quizzical
♭VI	sudden, abrupt, surprising, shocking, daring, bold	suggestive	hopeful, open, bright, airy, powerful, solid, heroic, majestic	confident, sure, strident, enigmatic
♭vi	unexpected, surprising		dark, mysterious, serious, sad, gloomy, negative, wrenching, anguished, sorrowful, angst, troubled	stately, impassioned
III	different	leading, directed, unresolved, stable, final	warm, homely, mellow, simple, light, airy, solemn, firm, duller	questioning
♭III	sudden, jolting, shifty	strong, solid	positive, bright, sunny, joyful, buoyant, luminous	resolute
♭iii	surprised, unusual, weird	retiring, tentative	somber, desolate, dramatic, empty, despairing, tragic, gloomy, sad, resigned, hopeless, stark, serious, reflective, hollow, pensive	

regard to tendency, there is no obvious pattern. The minor chords appear to be more stable or restful, whereas the major chords seem more likely to evoke a leading or forward tendency. This is probably an artifact of the use of major chords as secondary dominants. For example, in a major key, the VI chord is nearly always used in a V-of-ii function. Major chromatic mediant chords are probably more constrained by what happens next than is the case for minor chromatic mediants.

With regard to valence, there is a marked division between major and minor chords. In general, major chromatic mediant chords tend to elicit descriptive terms such as "bright," "warm," "positive," and sometimes "upbeat" or "hopeful." In the case of minor chromatic mediant chords, the most common descriptive terms include "mysterious," "dark," and "serious." What is striking about these descriptions is how much

Table 14.2
Reported qualia for chromatic mediant chords in a minor key context

Chord	Expectedness	Tendency	Valence	Other
#VI	novel, futuristic, bold, conventional	stable, settled, complete, final, leading, urging, pushy	upbeat, energetic, bright	whole, heightened, strong, simple, uncomplicated, plain
#vi	surprising, challenging	confident, resolute, enticing, incomplete, stable, established, shifty, open-ended	weighty, airy, serious, majestic	melodious, strident, expansive, solid
vi	unexpected, different, newness, abrupt, eccentric		mysterious, cheerless, somber, dark, tragic, despairing, death, depressed	
#III	surprising, edgy, sudden	transitional, falling, promising, temporary, committed, directed, suggestive, drawing in, settled, resolved	satisfying, positive,	simple, plain, hollow, crisp
#iii	surprise	restful, resigned	somber, sad, mysterious, serious, solemn, stately, solid, melancholic	whimsical, light
iii	surprising, unprepared	compelling, foreboding, insistent, leading, tentative	dark, ominous, murky, solemn, mysterious, ethereal, disturbed, anxious	rich, fuzzy, cozy, sensitive, detached

more valenced they are than descriptions of comparable major and minor chords *within* the key.

These exaggerated psychological *qualia* appear to be related to an interesting psychological phenomenon found in harmony perception. A simple experimental task is to ask musicians to identify as quickly as possible whether a given chord is major or minor. For isolated chords, experienced musicians can do this task quite quickly. However, in a key context, the speed of chord quality recognition is typically reduced (contrary to intuition). For example, in the context of C major, musicians are slower to identify a D-minor triad as "minor." By contrast, in the context of C major, an A-flat minor triad sounds more obviously minor, and this is reflected in a faster reaction time. It is as though the key context tends to cause the chord qualities of "major" and "minor" to become muted. Or said another way, chords better retain the psychological qualities associated with major and minor triads when they are isolated than when played in a common progression.

In chapter 9, I suggested that the *qualia* evoked by different scale degrees arise from learned statistical properties. Zeroth-order probabilities appear to determine the sense of *stability,* whereas first-order statistical probabilities appear to account for the feelings of *tendency.* Here I would like to suggest that the distinctive *qualia* associated with chromatic mediant chords can also be attributed to statistical properties. (1) The chords themselves have a low probability of occurrence and so tend to evoke a sense of surprise, novelty, or unusualness. (2) With the exception of some major chromatic mediant chords (which can be heard as secondary dominants), chromatic mediant chords fail to evoke a strong sense of tendency and so typically convey a feeling of repose or pause, though not closure. (3) In light of their poor statistical linkage to the preceding and following chords, the qualities of "major" and "minor" come to the fore. Major chromatic chords tend to sound more distinctly "major," and so are somehow "brighter" or more "positive" than major chords within the key. Similarly, minor chromatic chords tend to sound more obviously "minor"—with the consequence that these chords will sound more "serious," "sad," or "tragic" than their diatonic counterparts.[3]

Music theorists commonly refer to chromatic mediant chords as *nonfunctional color chords.* The adjective "nonfunctional," I would suggest, acknowledges that these chords do not usually evoke strong first-order probabilities either in their approach or departure. The adjective "color" suggests an awareness of the fact that they are highly evocative, even as isolated chords.

If we join together the "unusualness," "weirdness," or "strangeness" (arising from their low probability of occurrence) with the *qualia* evoked by major and minor chords in isolation, we can better understand why chromatic mediant chords evoke such specific feelings. Minor chromatic mediant chords tend to evoke feelings of "surprising darkness," often expressed as "mystery," "seriousness," "sadness," or "gloom." Similarly, major chromatic mediant chords tend to evoke feelings of "surprising brightness," often expressed as "hopeful," "majestic," "luminous," or "joyful."

A simple example of a chord progression involving a chromatic mediant chord is the opening to Franz Liszt's *Il Pensieroso* shown in figure 14.1. The work's title echoes the title of Auguste Rodin's famous sculpture *The Thinker.* For Western-enculturated listeners, Liszt's opening exudes "profundity." On the basis of past statistical exposure, listeners are apt to assume that the initial octave E's represent either the tonic or dominant pitches. At least initially, the most probable inferred key is either E or A major or (less likely) minor. Listeners will therefore tend to hear the first (C# minor) chord as a mediant chord evoking both surprise and seriousness. Repeating the pattern into the second measure, the ensuing (A minor) chord holds a chromatic mediant relation to the first chord and so will reinforce the *qualia* of surprise and seriousness.

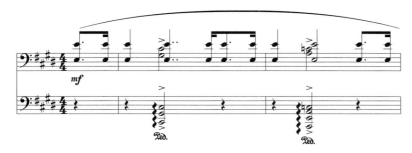

Figure 14.1
An example of a chord progression involving a chromatic mediant chord: Franz Liszt's "Il Pensieroso" ("The Thinker") from *Années de Pèlerinage* (volume 1).

Figure 14.2
Chromatic mediant progression from Giuseppe Verdi's *Requiem* (final cadence of the *Dies Irae*).

Within the the first two measures, Liszt's "thinker" manifests both "strange" and "serious" qualities. The effect is heightened by the slow ("ponderous") tempo.

In contrast to minor chromatic mediant chords, major chromatic mediants evoke a much more positive valence. Figure 14.2 provides an example from Verdi's *Requiem*. The passage is from the end of the *Dies Irae*, which is some forty minutes in length. As befits a requiem mass, the atmosphere is somber. But it is also essential that a requiem provide gestures of spiritual hope. The *Lacrymosa* is set in B-flat minor, but the movement ends with a raised or Picardy third on B-flat major. In addition to this surprising tonic chord, Verdi has the choir sing "Amen" on a ♭VI chord. In the context of B-flat minor, both the B-flat major and G major chords are "positive surprises." They are both evocative of a distinctively "hopeful" *quale*.[4]

Veridical Surprises

Apart from violating general (schematic) expectations about music, musicians can also arrange to violate a listener's specific knowledge of a particular musical work or

Figure 14.3
Ludwig van Beethoven, Symphony no. 5 in C minor, op. 67, second movement, first theme.

Figure 14.4
Peter Schickele, "Adagio" from *Quodlibet for Small Orchestra*. Compare with figure 14.3.

passage. Such veridical surprises are the stock in trade of musical humor. By way of example, consider the following passage from Peter Schickele's *Quodlibet for Small Orchestra* (1959). The work is assembled entirely from musical quotations from other works. In the live Vanguard recording of this work, the biggest laugh in the "Adagio" movement is reserved for a remarkably delicate and lyrical moment. After preparing a quiet transition, Schickele moves into a direct quotation of the famous 'cello theme from the second movement of Beethoven's fifth symphony. The well-known theme is shown in figure 14.3.

Schickele's modified version of this theme is shown in figure 14.4. Staring at the notation will give you no sense of how funny this is: I recommend that readers pause and sing the two examples, or better yet, listen to the Schickele recording. The two passages are identical until the beginning of the fourth measure. Where Beethoven follows the B flat with an E natural, Schickele follows the B flat with an A flat (see marked intervals). In the original, Beethoven's theme branches into a new key area, but Schickele simply brings the phrase to a stereotypic close. Here the listener's surprise is veridical rather than schematic. Schickele's version is much more consistent with the norms of Western classical music. Most of Schickele's gags involve doing something absurdly unexpected. But in this situation, Schickele rejects the adventurousness of Beethoven's original theme, and replaces it with a conventional four-bar phrase ending on the tonic. The effect is heightened by the performance nuances in which the final cadence is approached by a delicate but clearly final ritard. In fact, this single four-bar phrase forms the ending for the Adagio movement, but it takes the audience several seconds to realize this. The laughter is sustained and then shifts to applause as the ending gesture is fully comprehended. In Beethoven's original, the theme signals the start of something new. In Schickele's hands, the theme is simply the end.

To get a sense of the surprise here, I calculated the probabilities of the two melodic transitions. In the original Beethoven melody, the second scale degree (B flat) is followed by the raised fifth scale degree (E natural)—the interval of a descending tritone. Of all the possible successions from $\hat{2}$, the movement to #$\hat{5}$ is the rarest, with a probability of less than 0.0007. By contrast, the succession from $\hat{2}$ to $\hat{1}$ is the most common, with a probability of 0.33.[5] This means that the probability of going from B flat to A flat is some 400 times more likely than going from B flat to E natural.

This passage represents precisely the sort of "veridical deception" I posited as a theoretical possibility in chapter 12. In that chapter I concocted a chimeric melody that begins with "Three Blind Mice" and then elides into "Mary Had a Little Lamb." A veridical expectation is subverted even though the continuation conforms to schematic norms.

In my opinion, what Schickele does here amounts to one of the cleverest moments in the history of musical humor. Schickele takes a beautiful and well-known melody, changes a single note, and produces a terrifically funny result. Moreover, the change he makes is not one of introducing some wacky improbable note. Instead, he changes an improbable note in the original melody to a highly probable one. Notice that this passage is psychologically the polar opposite of the deceptive cadence. For listeners familiar with a work, the deceptive cadence involves a violation of a schematic expectation while fulfilling a veridical expectation. In Schickele's modified quote from Beethoven, a veridical expectation is violated while the schematic expectation is fulfilled.[6]

The most common forms of veridical surprises are to be found not in the activities of composers, but in the activities of performers. In the simplest case, a veridical surprise can arise simply as a result of performance error. For listeners familiar with the work, the error will evoke an immediate sense of surprise—a surprise typically with no redeeming qualities. The slower appraisal response will usually judge the surprise to be symptomatic of a lack of skill or some other lapse. Unless the listener is *hoping* that the performer will make an error (as in a music competition), no positively valenced limbic response can be expected.

More often, veridical surprises arise from differences in performance nuance. Since the advent of sound recording, it has become commonplace for listeners to acquire an intimate familiarity with particular recordings of a work. We may be surprised when another rendition fails to duplicate the familiar interpretive gestures. Compared with what we are used to, a performance can generate veridical surprises by failing to ritard, using different dynamic levels, different articulation, different tempos, or different phrasing.

Dynamic Surprises

In a dynamic surprise, the music is constructed so that the work itself sets up some work-specific expectation that is then violated. There are many ways to generate such surprises. Perhaps the most familiar example of a dynamic surprise in Western classical music occurs in Joseph Haydn's Surprise Symphony (no. 94). The "surprise" from which the symphony gets its nickname occurs in the slow second movement. The well-known theme is shown in figure 14.5.

Haydn assigns a dynamic level of *piano* to the movement, and nearly the entire movement is played with the quiet ambience typical of a second (slow) symphonic movement. The movement begins by stating the main theme in full once. The surprise version is rendered during the second statement. The "surprise" consists of a dominant chord played *fortissimo* on the second beat.

Most of the elements of the surprise can be traced to schematic rather than purely dynamic violations of expectation. An isolated fortissimo chord does not commonly occur in slow, quiet music. Some element of metric surprise is also evoked by placing the strongly accented chord on the second (weaker) beat of the measure. But clearly an important factor contributing to the surprise is the fact that Haydn has already presented this theme without the presence of the fortissimo chord. When Haydn reiterates the main theme a second time, first-time listeners can be forgiven for assuming that the passage is likely to unfold in a similar manner to the first rendition.

Another example of a dynamic surprise can be observed in Beethoven's familiar setting of Schiller's "Ode to Joy" from the fourth movement of Symphony no. 9. The principal theme consists of four phrases with nearly identical second and fourth phrases (see figure 14.6). The surprise amounts to a single syncopated moment when the fourth phrase begins a quarter-note prior to the downbeat. As in Haydn's "surprise," this unexpected onset occurs after Beethoven has already presented the phrase in its unsurprising form. In fact, each of the first three phrases begins on a downbeat.

Figure 14.5
Main theme from Joseph Haydn's Symphony no. 94 ("Surprise"), second movement (Andante).

Figure 14.6
Early onset from the "Ode to Joy" in Ludwig van Beethoven's Symphony no. 9, op. 125, fourth movement.

For the first-time listener, the expectation here is for the fourth phrase to begin on the downbeat of the next measure.

Whereas the "surprise" in Haydn's Surprise Symphony involves a *what*-related violation of dynamic expectation, the "premature" note in Beethoven's "Ode to Joy" entails a *when*-related violation. In addition, the two passages tend to produce somewhat contrasting experiences for listeners. Haydn's surprise tends to evoke amusement—or, for those who are sleepier, bewilderment. By contrast, the premature onset in Beethoven's "Ode to Joy" typically leads to neither amusement nor bewilderment. Among the people I have informally polled about this passage, the most common characterization of this moment is "thrilling."

Neither the Haydn nor the Beethoven works are the best examples of dynamic violations of expectation. Both involve some element of schematic violation as well. In the Beethoven, there is a violation of the metric schema, and in the Haydn there is a violation of the dynamic norm for lyrical quiet passages. Unequivocal examples of dynamic violations are difficult to find in music. Most involve some element of schematic violation as well. Lest readers think that "pure" examples of dynamic violation do not exist, let me at least propose what such a passage might look like. Imagine, for example, a musical work whose main theme involves a single syncopated event. Over the course of the work this theme might be repeated several times, each time with the syncopation present. Finally, the theme is reiterated without the syncopation. In this case, the absence of the syncopation would violate only the dynamic expectation—not the schematic expectation for meter to which the rhythm now conforms.

Garden Path Surprises

In our discussion of surprises, one further type of surprise needs to be mentioned: the "garden path" phenomenon. The "garden path" phenomenon is well known in linguistics. It describes the situation in which earlier parts of a sentence, thought to be understood, must be reanalyzed in light of a later part. The following grammatically correct sentence provides a good example:

Figure 14.7
Ludwig van Beethoven, Piano Sonata, op. 14, no. 2, beginning of the third movement.

The old man the boats.

The words "old man" would normally be parsed as an adjective ("old") followed by a noun ("man").[7] However, the sentence makes sense only if the word "old" is parsed as a noun and the word "man" is parsed as a verb. Notice that the word "old" is used more commonly as an adjective than a noun, and that the word "man" is used more commonly as a noun than a verb. Viewed probabilistically, the words "old man" are much more likely to be an adjective-noun sequence than a noun-verb sequence.

The distinctive subjective experience is dubbed the "garden path" phenomenon because most listeners will be led down the garden path by the more common interpretation—a presumption that will ultimately render the sentence as a whole unparseable. A moment of confusion will ensue, and if the sentence is available in written form (as above), most people will reread the sentence until it parses successfully.

The pertinence of the garden path phenomenon to music was first proposed by David Temperley of the Eastman School of Music. Figure 14.7 reproduces an example of a musical garden path experience described by Temperley. The example is from Beethoven's Piano Sonata op. 14, no. 2.[8]

Ostensibly, the movement is written in 3/8 meter. However, the opening rhythm leads unsuspecting listeners down a different metrical path. The repeated short–short–long rhythmic pattern implies a duple meter with the eighth note receiving the metric stress. The agogic stress associated with the third, sixth, and ninth notes is more consistent with a 2/8 meter—where the first two notes form a pickup. If listeners hear the passage in this way, then the third bar will lead to a moment of confusion. The quarter-note D at the beginning of the third measure will be assumed to span an entire measure. The end of the phrase at the beginning of the fourth measure will sound like a strong-to-weak ending rather than a weak-to-strong ending. Most listeners are apt to hear the passage as beginning with a 2/8 meter and switching to 3/8 at the third measure. A metric "glitch" is thus introduced.

Notice that the garden path phenomenon defies straightforward classification as either schematic or dynamic surprise. On the one hand, we might argue that it is a form of schematic surprise, because the passage disrupts the expectations arising from an active listening schema. On the other hand, we might argue that it is a form of dynamic surprise, because it is the music itself that leads listeners to adopt the "wrong" initial schema. The surprise itself is schematic, but the setup is clearly passage-specific. As long as we understand the sequence of mental events, it doesn't really matter whether we classify the experience as a "schematic surprise" or a "dynamic surprise." The passage remains surprising.

Psychological Effects of Surprise

In chapter 2 I noted that the phenomenon of surprise indicates a biological failure. If the purpose of expectation is to enhance readiness, then failing to correctly anticipate ensuing events represents a genuine mental failure. Although musical surprises do not hold the dire consequences of other possible surprises, music nevertheless is able to activate the biological machinery that reacts to such surprises.

In chapter 2 I suggested that the "fast" neurological circuit evoked by surprise can lead to one of three fear-related behavioral responses: *fight*, *flight*, or *freeze*. I further suggested that each of these responses tends to be associated with a particular emotional response: *frisson*, *laughter*, and *awe*. Recall that I linked frisson with the fight response: bristling hair is characteristic of both aggressive display and frisson. I also linked awe with the freeze response: breath-holding is characteristic of both fear-induced freezing and the "breathtaking" experience of awe. Finally, I linked laughter with the flight response: panting is characteristic of flight, while punctuated exhaling is characteristic of laughter. It is now time to consider in detail some musical examples that evoke these various responses.

Frisson

In 1991, John Sloboda from Keele University carried out a seminal study of musically evoked frisson. Sloboda distributed a questionnaire soliciting information from music-lovers concerning passages that evoked strong emotions, including "shivers" or "chills."[9] Some eighty-three responses were received. Many included accompanying letters describing in exquisite detail various aspects of the individual's experience. Sloboda assembled notated scores for the identified passages and carried out a series of analyses in an attempt to determine some of the musical properties that correlate

Figure 14.8
Piano reduction of bars 225 to 230 from Arnold Schoenberg's *Verklärte Nacht*. A passage identified by one of John Sloboda's respondents as reliably evoking a frisson ("chills") response.

with listener's reports of frisson. Sloboda found that tears (or a lump in one's throat) are correlated with melodic appoggiaturas and sometimes with harmonic sequences. He found that shivers or chills (frisson) are correlated with sudden changes of harmony and with abrupt changes in dynamic level.

A sample passage identified by one of Sloboda's respondents is shown in figure 14.8. This passage, from Arnold Schoenberg's *Verklärte Nacht* ("Transfigured Night"), includes three elements of surprise that all coincide with the onset of the D-major chord at the beginning of measure 229. In the key of G minor, the D-major chord is the dominant: a progression from E-flat major (VI) to V would be a relatively common progression. However, in approaching this passage, there is no hint of G minor, and the E-flat chord is minor rather than major. In short, the D-major chord would be highly unexpected given the preceding harmonic context. In addition to the harmonic surprise, there is also an abrupt change of dynamic level—from the preceding *pianissimo* to the *forte* accompanying the D-major chord at measure 229. Finally, a third element of surprise is evident in the timing of the event. Prior to measure 229, the chord onsets have been systematically avoiding the downbeat. In approaching measure 229, the sense of meter has been significantly eroded for listeners, so although the D-major chord occurs on the downbeat, this moment is no longer expected for most listeners. In short, the onset of this loud D-major chord is a pretty surprising event. For at least one listener, we know that this passage evokes marked shivers running up and down the spine.

Another example of musically induced frisson is reported in a study by neurophysiologist Jaak Panksepp, working at Bowling Green University. Panksepp found a passage in Pink Floyd's *The Final Cut* that displayed a high probability of evoking frisson experiences in his undergraduate listeners. The vocal melody for the most important passage is shown in figure 14.9. The passage occurs roughly 2:50 into the recording. Unlike the Schoenberg example, which involves several concurrent elements of surprise, this example seems to exhibit only a single element of surprise: a dramatic shift

Would you send me packin'?   Or would you send me home?

Figure 14.9
Vocal melody from Pink Floyd's *The Final Cut*. One of the frisson-inducing passages studied in Panksepp 1995.

from a *pianissimo* dynamic level to *fortissimo*. The frisson effect is nevertheless robust. Several of my students reported frisson responses on hearing this passage, and although I am not a Pink Floyd fan, I too experienced a distinct frisson response on my first hearing.

While other examples of frisson-inducing passages might be cited from the research literature, these examples illustrate the main finding of frisson-related studies of music. Frisson is strongly correlated with marked violations of expectation—in particular, with dynamic, metric, and harmonic violations. In general, when a change of dynamic level evokes frisson, it is usually an increase in dynamic level that causes the surprise. However, frisson experiences are also reported when a high dynamic level is unexpectedly followed by a dramatic reduction in loudness (i.e., *subito piano*).

One further observation about frisson relates to its reliability. In Sloboda's study, respondents reported that even after listening to a passage fifty times, the passage continued to be able to evoke a frisson response. As Sloboda points out, "listening to a piece of music very many times does not always entail a diminishing of strong emotional response to it."[10] This finding has been replicated by Panksepp, who has suggested that works may be *more* likely to evoke frisson when they are familiar.[11] In my own listening experience, I've noticed that frisson appears to be more easily evoked when the ambient temperature is low. Although the Pink Floyd example normally evokes frisson for at least some of my students, the passage typically fails to evoke any frisson when the classroom is unusually warm. (There may be good aesthetic reasons for maintaining an air-conditioned concert hall.)

Laughter

Musical comedy can be observed in many of the world's cultures. In Western music, *opera buffa* and Gilbert-and-Sullivan-like operetta have been popular forms of entertainment. Since the plots and libretti texts account for much of the humor, these genres are less ideal repertoires for studying music-evoked laughter. From time to time, composers have engaged in overt humor within a purely instrumental idiom. Famous examples include Haydn's "Joke Quartet" (op. 33, no. 2 in E-flat) and Mozart's *Ein musikalischer Spass* (A musical joke), K. 522.[12] There are plenty of more modern examples, such as *The Jingle Cats* (popular Christmas songs arranged with sampled cat meows).

Earlier in this chapter we saw an example from the music of Peter Schickele. Schickele is one of the most prolific musical humorists. He has written nearly a hundred works of musical humor, from "The O.K. Chorale" to the "Erotica" Variations. I have found that Schickele's music provides a rich resource for the study of musical expectation.[13]

Some of the humor devices used by Schickele involve visual gags. For example, Schickele's "Pervertimento" involves a stationary bicycle outfitted with a pitch generator. The pitch is increased or decreased by pedaling faster or slower. Part of the humor arises from the melodic requirement that the performer pedal very fast. Other aspects of Schickele's music depends on plays on vocal text. For example, in Schickele's "Ground Rounds," the words sung by the baritone and by the tenor are innocuous madrigal clichés. However, when the two texts are interleaved so that the tenor sings one word, and the baritone sings the next, the result is lewd and ribald.

But beyond the visual gags and language-based humor, most of Schickele's humor devices are to be found in the core musical domains of pitch, time, and timbre. Most of Schickele's music has been recorded, and the majority of these recordings include a live audience. A four-CD compilation of Schickele's music includes over 600 moments of audible audience laughter. Conveniently, these laughter moments provide a useful opportunity for testing theories of musical humor. In a detailed study of Schickele's music, I have identified nine kinds of devices that form the basis for his musical humor:[14]

1. Incongruous sounds   In his works, Schickele often makes use of unusual sound sources such as duck whistles, kazoos, and slide whistles. His *Sinfonia Concertante*, for example, is composed for string orchestra and six solo instruments: lute, balalaika, ocarina, sewer pipe, double-reed slide music stand, and bagpipe.

Very few of Schickele's works are written exclusively for bizarre instrumentation. Typically, Schickele will mix some bizarre instrument with conventional instruments of the classical orchestra. This is no coincidence. In order for something to sound out of place, one must first establish a "place." The sound of the classical orchestra provides the foil against which the unconventional sounds appear especially incongruous. That is, the sounds of the orchestra evoke conventional symphonic schemas in listeners, which makes the unconventional sounds sound much more out of place, much more disruptive. In short, the role of the normal orchestral timbres is analogous to the "straight man" in a comedy duo. Absurdity is more successful as a humor device when it is placed in the context of normalcy.

2. Mixed genres   Schickele will switch abruptly between different styles. For example, in the Andante-Allegro from Schickele's "*Unbegun*" Symphony, the movement begins

with a slow lyrical andante. After about a minute, there is a slow transition that moves abruptly to an unexpected allegro with the trumpet playing "De Campdown Races" and other "fast" tunes. In the commercial live recording of this work, the audience laughs at the moment where there is an unexpected change in musical mood and style.

In creating such passages, Schickele's most common tactic is to juxtapose "high art" and "low art" styles. Typically, the "high art" style is established first, followed by interjections of "low art" materials. Critical to the success of such incongruous juxtapositions is that the audience recognize the tunes used. In his selection of both "high art" and "low art" melodies, Schickele restricts himself to using tunes that are well known—at least to American audiences.

3. Drifting tonality   After the Renaissance, modulations to different keys became commonplace in Western music. Nevertheless, changes of key can be highly disruptive if not prepared in a predictable manner. One of Schickele's techniques is to abruptly shift to a different key. Many of these changes move to keys that are at the interval of a tritone. Such tritone key shifts are both the least predictable (most surprising) and also the most disruptive in maintaining a tonal center.

In popular music, a common form of key shifting is the so-called *pump up*. A pump up occurs when the key rises by a diatonic or chromatic step. Often a pump up is introduced near the end of the work when a chorus is being repeated. In Schickele's music, an occasional key-shift device is what might be dubbed the "pump down." Here the music abruptly shifts down a semitone or more. Shifts of key downward by a step are rare in Western music. While there are hundreds of examples of pump ups in Western pop music, I know of no examples of pump downs. In this regard, Schickele's pump downs are truly improbable occurrences.

When shifts of key occur frequently, the sense of tonality itself is lost or ambiguous. Perhaps the paradigmatic example of key ambiguity as a source or humor is Mozart's *Ein musikalischer Spass* (A musical joke), K. 522. The work was written in 1787 and is scored for a small chamber group consisting of two violins, viola, bass, and two horns. Of the many comic devices used in Mozart's *Ein musikalischer Spass*, the most memorable is the bizarre final cadence: six instrumentalists finish in five different keys.

4. Metric disruptions   In the same way that tonality may be disrupted, it is also possible to disrupt meter. A simple technique is to eliminate or add extra beats to a measure. A waltz in 3/4 might lose a beat, or a march might gain half of a beat. Schickele often resorts to what might be called "peg-leg" rhythms. Where changes of key thwart the listener's *what*-related expectations, changes of meter thwart the listener's *when*-related expectations.

5. Implausible delays   Another humor device used by Schickele is to delay highly expected resolutions. Good examples of humor include appoggiaturas that fail to resolve at the expected moment. Figure 14.10 shows a passage from Schickele's *Concerto*

Figure 14.10
P. D. Q. Bach (Peter Schickele), *Concerto for Horn and Hardart*, second movement ("Tema con variazione").

for Horn and Hardart. The passage shown is played by the violins in the stylistic context of a minuet performed by a chamber orchestra.

The breach of expectation occurs in the delay of the D# chromatic appoggiatura resolving to the E. In the classical style, the appoggiatura would normally resolve on the second beat of the second measure. A less likely possibility is that the appoggiatura would be held until the beginning of the ensuing bar—that is, the resolution would be delayed until the downbeat of the third measure. In the Vanguard recording of this work, a live audience breaks into laughter within one second of the downbeat of the third measure. This is consistent with a broad recognition of the failure of the D# appoggiatura to resolve at the beginning of the measure. Further sporadic laughter erupts as the D# is sustained for a full four measures. This is a clear violation of the learned schema for classical appoggiaturas.

6. Excessive repetition   In chapter 13, we saw that repetition is commonplace in music. However, Schickele occasionally will repeat a passage many more times than is the musical norm. Once again, an example can be found in the first movement of Schickele's *Concerto for Horn and Hardart* where one eight-note passage is repeated twelve times in a row. The result is a sort of "broken record" effect. In the Vanguard recording, the audience laughs in the midst of the fourth repetition—consistent with a norm of three repetitions before changing the musical pattern.[15]

7. Incompetence cues   Another device used by Schickele is to have musical passages performed in a crude or unrefined manner. This includes bad pitch intonation, implausibly loud sounds, and obnoxious or crude instrumental or vocal timbres.

8. Incongruous quotation   Musical quotations provide opportunities to juxtapose veridical expectations against an improbable schematic context. Schickele will often mix a quoted melody with an incongruous style. For example, in one of Schickele's works he combines the opening of Bach's first suite for unaccompanied cello with the opening strains of the Latin pop song "Brazil."

9. Misquotation   Earlier in this chapter we discussed Schickele's misquotation of Beethoven's famous 'cello theme from the second movement of the fifth symphony. In the Vanguard compilation of Schickele's works, this misquotation represents one of the most successful laughter-inducing moments in the entire collection.

Recall that where Beethoven's theme branches into a new key area, Schickele simply brings the phrase to a stereotypic close. As noted earlier, the humor here is linked to the violation of a common veridical expectation while rendering the passage schematically more normative. Once again, this effect is psychologically the opposite of the deceptive cadence.

What is striking about these nine devices is that they all involve violations of expectation. Incongruous sounds violate expectations related to norms of musical timbres. Drifting tonality and metric disruptions violate *what*-related pitch schemas and *when*-related temporal schemas. Mixed genres violate the maintenance of schematic-stylistic norms, while incongruous quotations violate veridical-stylistic norms. Implausible delay thwarts the norms of temporal succession, while excessive repetition confounds expectations of form-related structure. Incompetence cues violate a number of performance-related schematic norms. Misquotation violates veridical expectations.

I have spent considerable time on musically evoked laughter in order to drive home an important point. All of the musical passages that succeed in evoking laughter do so by violating listener expectations. Most of these violations involve schematic expectations. Some involve violations of veridical expectations, and a few involve violations of dynamic expectations. But all of the laughter-evoking moments can be traced to a violation of listener expectation. In my study of laughter episodes in recordings of Schickele's music, all of the interpretable bouts of the laughter could be attributed to one of the nine categories described above.[16]

Although musically engendered bouts of laughter might be attributed to violations of expectation, not all violations of expectation lead to laughter. For example, there is an asymmetry with respect to "high" and "low" culture. The interruption of a "high-brow" minuet by a "low-brow" popular tune is more likely to generate laughter than vice versa. The interruption of a string quartet by a bagpipe is funnier than interrupting pipers with a string quartet.

Like the experience of frisson, laughter is not a common response to music. But, also like frisson, laughter is linked to specific auditory violations. This raises the question of what it is about some thwarted expectations that leads to *laughter* rather than *frisson*. I think there are at least three pivotal factors.

One factor is the magnitude of the violated expectation. Laughter-inducing passages are much more surprising than frisson-inducing or awe-inducing passages. In the case of Schickele's misquotation of Beethoven, it was possible to compare the probability of the actual music with the probability of the expected continuation. Here we found a 400-fold difference between the expected and actual transitional probabilities. Normally, these probabilities cannot be calculated for laughter-inducing musical passages because the events themselves are so rare. But it is clear that laughter-inducing events have very low probabilities of occurrence.

A second difference is linked to the appraisal of intent. In the case of musical humor, the context appears to be overtly one of playfulness and parody. The interjection of "low art" gestures into ostensibly "high art" contexts provides an important social signal of playfulness. (Audiences are effectively given permission to laugh.) Similarly, the use of absurd sounds in an ostensibly normal musical context also conveys the message that the intent is one of light-heartedness or a lack of seriousness. By contrast, the musical passages leading to frisson all occur in contexts that are typically appraised as serious or solemn. Laughter is facilitated if the musician signals that laughter is expected or allowed.

Apart from the compositional intent and the magnitude of the violation, the immediate social environment of the listener also plays a role in exactly how the listener reacts. Recall from chapter 2 that Robert Provine has estimated that people are thirty times more likely to laugh in the presence of another person than when they are alone.[17] A sociable group dynamic can render even somber stimuli funny. Laughter is facilitated if one's social peers signal that laughter is expected or permitted. Conversely, when listening by oneself, ostensibly humorous music may fall flat.

Awe

The feeling of "awe" is a distinctive emotion in which fear and wonder are intermingled. A sense of awe might be evoked by a fearful reverence inspired by something sacred or mysterious. Awe can also represent a submissive fear in the presence of some great authority or power. In short, awe might be defined as a sort of "sublime fear." "Awe" combines mystery, wonder, and reverence with a touch of dread.

In chapter 2 I identified several situations in which one is likely to experience awe: standing on the edge of a cliff, encountering a snake, observing a thunder storm, viewing a ferocious animal at close quarters. An important qualification to add is that these situations must be encountered in relative safety. To experience awe, we must view the ferocious animal from behind glass or bars. If not, we will simply experience acute fear or terror. That is, while fear forms an important part of awe, it is tempered by feelings of intense curiosity, compelling interest, or even admiration.

Five physiological indicators are associated with the experience of awe: (1) gasping, (2) breath-holding, (3) lowered chin with the mouth slightly opened, (4) immobility or stillness, and (5) reduced blinking. Gasping and breath-holding are especially telltale indicators. While the idea that music can "take one's breath away" has been frequently expressed, in practice, breath-holding in response to music appears to be rare.

Working at Uppsala University in Sweden, Alf Gabrielsson and Siv Lindstrom carried out a large survey involving over 800 individuals. Using the media to solicit participants, they asked respondents to describe their strongest or most intense experiences involving music. They received about a thousand written reports. Gabrielsson and his colleagues then embarked on a series of content analyses. Among the most commonly reported physiological symptoms were feelings of bodily tension, shivers, goose flesh, bristling of hair, actual or incipient weeping, relaxation, dizziness, and difficulty speaking. In addition, listener reports identified periods of stillness or immobility, and changes of breathing, including difficulty breathing.[18]

Compared with laughter and frisson, awe appears to be an even less common experience. Nevertheless, for centuries, artists have worked hard to evoke this highly prized emotional state. Consider an example from visual art. Frederic Church was a nineteenth-century American landscape painter who is justly remembered for his especially large canvases. For example, his painting *Under Niagara* (1858) is roughly six square meters in area. Although not as big as a modern cinema screen, in his day, these paintings impressed audiences throughout North America and Europe. In the 1860s, Church exhibited his painting *Heart of the Andes* in a special-purpose room where viewers paid twenty-five cents to attend. In the darkened room the curtains were opened and the painting then dramatically illuminated with gas lamps. According to period reports, the effect was astonishing. Visitors gasped at the experience. A modern equivalent today might be attending an IMAX movie.[19]

Evoking awe is often a goal of filmmakers. Consider, for example, the popular science-fiction film *The Matrix*, written by Larry and Andy Wachowski. A pivotal plot moment occurs roughly thirty-three minutes into the film (scene 10). Here, the main protagonist (played by Keanu Reeves) "awakens" to discover that his whole life has been lived in an artificial dream world. He finds himself in a transparent pod that is attached to a gigantic dark tower. Reeves sits up and looks out to discover that he is just one of millions of people attached to dozens of enormous towers. As far above and below him as he can see, there are human beings attached to the matrix. Leading up to this moment, Don Davis's music makes use of tone clusters, creating a dark foreboding atmosphere. But at the moment when the audience finally sees the enormous vista of the matrix, a massed choir sings a sustained D-minor chord, which then shifts to a B-flat major chord joined by orchestral brass. The sound is loud, sustained, expansive, and voluminous, as the chorus moves from an "oh" to an "ah." Combined with the visual spectacle of the enormous space and the precarious cliff-face location of Reeve's character, the effect is one of terrifying awe mixed with amazement. Throughout the scene, Reeve's mouth remains slightly open and he doesn't blink. While this scene doesn't cause me to gasp or hold my breath, that the cinematic goal is to evoke awe seems clear.

A less whiz-bang example might be found in the final movement ("Neptune, the Mystic") of Gustav Holst's *The Planets*. The musical texture here is much lighter than Davis's score for *The Matrix*—but more mysterious. Forty-six measures before the end of his suite, Holst introduces a choir of women's voices. The principal surprise here is the distinctive change of tone color. The potpourri of orchestral timbres is displaced by a chorus of female voices singing the vowel "ah." The emotion here seems to be a combination of mystery and awe. Once again, this is not a passage that causes me to gasp or hold my breath. Yet Holst's efforts to create a mysterious sense of cosmic wonder do largely succeed.

Unfortunately, there are not many documented instances of musically evoked awe, so identifying its musical characteristics is notably speculative. Some possible characteristics might include: high dynamic level, frequent use of choral textures, large numbers of instruments or voices, sustained major or minor chords, and reverberant or spacious auditory image.

Weirdness

Not all surprises evoke frisson, laughter, or awe. All three of these responses to surprise rely on contrastive valence to generate a positive affect. This contrastive valence entails either an appraisal response or another reaction response that ultimately judges the surprising transgression positively. Moreover, unless the surprise is sufficiently large, the amygdala will not initiate the respiratory or topical (skin-related) physiological changes that are needed to produce frisson, laughter, or awe. Of course, it is possible for unexpected events to evoke only negatively valenced prediction, reaction, or appraisal responses with no tempering positive element.

Musical examples of such trangressions are relatively uncommon. If we assume that musicians usually seek to evoke positive listener responses, the rarity of these transgressions seems to make sense. But musicians do produce such surprises. In the music of Sergey Prokofiev, such transgressions amount to a stylistic signature. Consider, for example, the well-known theme from Prokofiev's *Peter and the Wolf* (figure 14.11). The work begins with "Peter's theme"—a bouncy, "happy" tune in C major. At the third measure, Prokofiev abruptly shifts to a lowered submediant harmony. But the real surprise occurs in the melody line, which alternates between E flat

Figure 14.11
Opening measures from Sergey Prokofiev's *Peter and the Wolf*, op. 67. Numbers indicate the information conveyed by selected scale-degree transitions (in bits).

and B natural. The B natural clashes with the C of the accompanying harmony. More disruptive yet is the low probability of the melodic sequence. Figure 14.11 shows some of the transitional probabilities for successive scale degrees expressed in bits. Based on a large database of melodic intervals in major keys, typical scale degree dyads lie in the range between three and five bits. However, the E flat/B natural alternation jumps out. The probability of $\hat{7}$ being followed by $\flat\hat{3}$ is just 0.00004. Compared with the melodic intervals in the first two measures, the intervals of the third measure are strikingly improbable. The pitches sound "wrong"—as though Prokofiev had mistakenly written B4 rather than C5. In fact, it has become commonplace for theorists to refer to such transgressions as "wrong-note" harmonies or "wrong-note" melodies.[20]

Theorist Deborah Rifkin has chronicled a number of such "wrong-note" passages in Prokofiev's music.[21] Notable examples can be found in Prokofiev's piano sonatas, violin concertos, and in works such as the *Cinderella Suite* and the *Classical Symphony*. These "wrong notes" display a number of characteristic properties. The notes typically involve semitone displacements from tonally appropriate notes. Often the pitches are flat by a half step. The "wrong notes" are typically neither prepared nor resolved: they are often approached and left by melodic leaps—violating the expectation for pitch proximity. They commonly appear in mid- or late phrase without warning.[22] As in the above example, Prokofiev tends to immediately repeat the wrong-note sequence—as if to say "yes, I really intended that pitch." In doing this, Prokofiev is following the standard advice regarding improvisational errors discussed in chapter 12. Repeating "wrong notes" allows Prokofiev to tap into dynamic prediction.

Prokofiev's "wrong notes" are probably not unrelated to his penchant for neoclassical writing. In choosing to write music with conventional tonal and phrase structures, Prokofiev's "wrong notes" are more obvious to listeners accustomed to the musical language of the classical period.[23] Like Peter Schickele's reliance on "highbrow" music as the foil or "straight man" for his musical humor, Prokofiev's conventional classical style provides the background schema that adds emphasis to his "wrong notes." In some ways, Prokofiev's "wrong notes" are the pitch-related equivalents of syncopation: the classical style serves the role of the metric schema, against which disruptions are introduced.[24]

The *qualia* evoked by Prokofiev's "wrong-note" music have been variously described as "quirky," "unexpected," "weird," "impertinent," and "impudent."[25] It is largely Prokofiev's wrong-note passages that established his reputation as a compositional "bad boy." These *qualia* can be directly attributed to the low schematic probability of such notes. By placing these notes within a conventional tonal context, they truly evoke a sense of being "wrong." At the same time, repetition assures listeners that the notes are clearly intentional. It is not inappropriate for listeners to interpret "intended wrongness" as a symptom of "impertinence."

Prokofiev's use of "wrong notes" is episodic or occasional. Most of his music unfolds in a fairly predictable way with the wrong-note events adding musical "spice." Not all composers are so reserved. In some works, the thwarting of expectation may be sustained throughout the music. If the music is constructed in an appropriate fashion, listeners can experience a nearly total predictive failure. That is, the events cannot be attributable to a delayed fulfillment, incorrect genre, garden path phenomenon, or a misapprehended context. In these circumstances the listener will be unable to reconcile the actual events with any existing perceptual schema. The psychological consequence is that the listener will experience a relatively high degree of stress and discomfort.

The best example of such failure can be found in a Western-enculturated listener who has had little or no experience with atonal music. For this listener, sequences of notes may systematically fail to conform with any preexisting schema. The music is likely to be experienced as weird, stressful, and uncomfortable. With repeated exposure, the listener may develop the kinds of expectations shown by experienced atonal listeners; and with this new schema in place, subsequent listening experiences will likely prove significantly less stressful. In chapter 16 we will consider the psychological effects of atonal music in more detail.

Effects of Repeated Listening

In carrying out my analyses of musical humor I spent a lot of time listening to recordings of Peter Schickele's music. Repeated listening does reduce the effectiveness of the humor. When I first heard Schickele's works, I frequently laughed out loud. With increasing familiarity, however, I rarely laughed. The social nature of humor is evident when I play excerpts for other listeners. I can anticipate the moments when someone else is likely to laugh, and although I still may not laugh, I will smile and enjoy the fact that someone else laughs.

The effect of repeated listenings for humor in music is in marked contrast with the effect of repeated listenings for frisson. Recall that Sloboda found that repeated listenings had little effect on the incidence of frisson, whereas Panksepp has suggested that frisson may be more common when works are familiar. Listeners continue to experience frisson, even for passages they have heard dozens of times. In my own listening to Schickele, I have found that the musical devices he uses shift relatively quickly into the "oddball" category. Over repeated listenings, what is initially experienced as humorous becomes simply "weird." Veridical familiarity is not kind to humor: the joke is too familiar to be funny. Rather than evoking humor, one simply hears the music as peculiar. With familiarity, I find that I am most likely to laugh only when I imagine someone else listening to the passage for the first time.

Why is musically induced frisson so different from musically induced laughter? And why, incidentally, is musically induced "awe" so rare?[26] I would like to suggest that these differences can be traced to their origins in the fight, flight, and freeze responses. Recall that the fight, flight, and freeze responses can be ordered according to the manageability of the induced fear. The freeze response is most indicative of helplessness: "there is nothing I can do except hope the danger passes." By contrast, the fight response is the most pro-active: "I can prevail over this danger." The flight response is somewhere in the middle: "I can't prevail here, but I might successfully escape." Since we "survive" repeated listenings, I propose that veridical expectations have a tendency to attentuate any reactive threat. Like the lion trainer entering the lion's cage, the first time was much more unnerving than the hundredth time. But like the lion trainer, the element of fear is never truly extinguished.

I propose that it is the magnitude of the evoked fear that accounts for our different observations. I would like to suggest that there are two main reasons why experiences of "awe" are relatively rare in music. First, music has a limited capacity to generate the most extreme forms of fear—as exemplified by the freeze response. Musical sounds don't bring us face-to-face with a cliff's edge or a rattlesnake. Second, with repeated listenings, the "breathtaking" experience of "awe" tends to be replaced by the more controlled frisson experience. That is, the tendency to experience a freeze response is replaced by the milder fight response.

In the case of laughter, the problem is that most of the final (appraisal) states are not positive. Laughter-evoking passages typically hit listeners with the expectational equivalent of a brick bat. Unlike, say, the deceptive cadence, the deceptions of humor-related devices are simply too wacky. There is no contrastive valence: the initial schematic surprise is not followed by a positive appraisal of the outcome. It is as though the children of my sixth-grade class had painted their faces in a ghoulish manner at Ms. Bradley's surprise party. Although the initial surprise would be enhanced, the subsequent appraisal might have been less positive: the whole event might have seemed too weird to enjoy. Nor is veridical expectation kind. If you knew that there was a group of people permanently stationed in your basement always ready to shout "surprise" each time you entered, how often would you visit the basement?

The effect of repeated listenings on these major emotions testifies to the fact that expectations change as we become more familiar with musical works.[27] Repeated listenings provide the listener with more accurate veridical expectations. On the one hand, these veridical expectations allow one to imagine (and anticipate) the surprise and laughter of novice listeners and to render a positive conscious appraisal of the passages. On the other hand, the same veridical expectations draw attention to the oddball character of the passages. One cannot listen to musical comedy in the same way as regular music.

It is this transformation that I think accounts for the fact that frisson is far more common than either awe or laughter when listening to music. Both awe and laughter are more fragile. Veridical familiarity with a musical work tends to transform awe to the less "fearful" response of frisson. In the case of laughter, veridical familiarity tends to transform comedy to oddity.

Expecting the Unexpected

As we've seen, surprises can be made to be predictable. Normally, familiarity reduces veridical surprise while leaving schematic surprises intact. However, with enough exposure, it is possible to create new schemas that help us anticipate commonplace forms of surprise in unfamiliar works. "Expecting the unexpected" is commonplace in jokes. Many jokes, for example, follow well-worn rhetorical patterns that both alert the listener of the light-hearted or ironic intention and simultaneously prepare the listener for surprise:

"Have you heard the one about . . ."

"There once was a man from . . ."

Common rhetorical patterns (such as the limerick form above) are established through repeated exposure. In effect, there are recognizable "surprise devices"—we can learn to expect the unexpected.

In chapter 16 we will see some direct empirical evidence of such surprise-based schemas in music. But for the present discussion, let's focus on one of the most ubiquitous surprise-based schemas in popular music—*syncopation*. Syncopation probably began as isolated effects that served particular surprise-related functions. However, syncopation evolved to become a commonplace pattern, and so, like the limeric structure, became a schema in its own right.

Syncopation

Waiting for a local bus on the Pacific island of Tutuilla, I heard a woman quietly singing a Samoan pop song. The pitches would be straightforward to notate, but the gentle syncopated performance was a masterpiece of temporal complexity. Most people would consider the melody to be simple. But many literate musicians would be intimidated by the corresponding rhythmic notation.

Syncopated passages can be found throughout the history of Western music. Until the mid-nineteenth century, most syncopated passages were isolated effects (although the Scottish "snap" syncopation has existed for hundreds of years). Syncopation emerged as a prominent musical element in the West around 1880 or so. Almost certainly an African transplant to the Americas, syncopation has taken the musical world

Figure 14.12
Syncopated and unsyncopated passages. The first passage is deemed more syncopated because of the absence of an event coinciding with the onset of the second beat ("onset syncopation").

by storm over the past century. It has become a standard part of popular musical vocabulary from Tutuilla to Taiwan, and is one of life's little delights. The phenomenon of syncopation provides important lessons related to expectation. Let's begin with some very simple examples. Figure 14.12 shows two passages that differ by a single note. The first example is syncopated whereas the second is not.

What makes the first example syncopated is the absence of an event coinciding with the onset of the second beat. In many ways, this syncopation is the antithesis of the anticipation. In the anticipation, the note onset in a weak metric position increases the probability that an ensuing note will occur at the next stronger metric position. Syncopation, by contrast, occurs when this heuristic is broken. Syncopation occurs whenever a note onset fails to occur at the next higher metric position.

Both the anticipation and the syncopation depend on the fact that, while events may happen in weak metric positions, they are (nearly always) followed by events that occur on the next strongest metric position. In the case of the anticipation, uncertainty of the "when" of the ensuing event is reduced. In the case of the syncopation shown above, the failure of the ensuing note to appear as expected has the effect of a delayed note: we are still waiting for the note to happen. The result is an increase in tension. The listener is like the man with outstretched arms waiting for a bag of clothing to drop out of the sky.

Another simple example of syncopation is shown in figure 14.13. Here the second beat receives a dynamic accent—that is, its salience is increased due to an increased loudness. The transgression here relates to the learned norm that strong beats are (nearly always) followed by weaker beats of lesser dynamic intensity. A similar example can be created using harmonic patterns. In figure 14.14, the syncopation is harmonic. Here the syncopation is only indirectly caused by the change of harmony on the second beat. The real cause of the syncopation is the failure of the harmony to also change on the third beat. Harmonic changes on weak beats are (nearly always) followed by strong beats that also change harmony. The syncopation arises from breaking this learned norm.

Figure 14.13
"Dynamic syncopation" arising from an unexpected dynamic accent coinciding with a relatively weak beat.

Figure 14.14
"Harmonic syncopation" arising from an unexpected failure to change harmony on the third beat.

Figure 14.15
"Agogic syncopation" arising from an unexpected durational contrast where longer durations coincide with weaker beats.

Duration can also be used to create syncopation. Figure 14.15 shows a passage where short duration notes occur on strong beats with longer notes occurring on the weak beats. The syncopation arises from breaking the learned norm that agogic stresses on weak beats are (nearly always) followed by equally large or larger agogic stresses on the next stronger beat.

The above examples have been concocted to represent four simple forms of syncopation: onset, dynamic, harmonic, and agogic. In real music, syncopation often combines several forms of syncopation simultaneously—what might be called *mixed syncopation*. For example, figure 14.16 shows an agogic-harmonic-onset syncopation in which duration, harmony, and onset all fail to conform to metrical norms. What

Figure 14.16
"Mixed syncopation" that combines unexpected harmonic, agogic, and onset properties.

is interesting about this example is the phenomenal experience of *where* the syncopation occurs. The violation of expectation occurs at the third beat. But it is not the (uneventful) third beat that is perceived as syncopated; instead, it is the second-beat chord. Recall that in chapter 10, I suggested that this phenomenon arises from the brain's disposition to bind properties to events rather than to non-events. Mental attributes or *qualia* are not allowed to float freely. Having experienced a violation of expectation, the evoked feeling of surprise is tagged to the most proximate stimulus. The sense of "unusualness" that characterizes syncopation is misattributed to the proximate precipitating event rather than to the non-event. Objectively, it is the absence of a chord on the third beat that causes the syncopation. But subjectively, the blame is assigned to the second-beat chord.

What musicians call "syncopation" can be defined as a certain class of violations of temporal expectation, where these violations occur against the background of some established temporal schema, and where the violations fail to dislodge the schema itself. A notable caveat to add is that simply slowing down or speeding up the tempo does not constitute syncopation.

Tonal Syncopation

If this view of syncopation is correct, then we ought to be able to observe syncopated events in otherwise unnoticed (or poorly noticed) situations. A good example is provided by a fifth basic form of syncopation—*tonal syncopation*. Consider, for example, the ascending sequence of melodic thirds and fourths illustrated in figure 14.17. In the case of ascending thirds, Western-enculturated listeners tend to hear the *lower* note as accented. By contrast, in the case of ascending fourths, listeners tend to hear the *higher* note as accented. What accounts for this difference in perception?

Given the importance of statistical learning, we should first consider that the difference in perceptual dispositions might be attributable to different treatments in typical Western music. Perhaps it is the case that the metrical context for ascending thirds more typically places the lower pitch on the more stressed beat than the higher pitch. Conversely, perhaps ascending fourths tend to place the higher pitch on the

Figure 14.17
Ascending melodic thirds and fourths. In the case of the thirds, listeners tend to hear the lower note in each third as accented. In the case of the fourths, listeners tend to hear the higher note in each fourth as accented. Why?

Table 14.3a
Metrical context for ascending melodic intervals

Interval	Strong–Weak	Weak–Strong	Same	Total
P1	53.8%*	40.7%	5.5%	59,825
+m2	32.3%	62.6%*	5.1%	18,046
+M2	39.5%	54.3%*	6.2%	37,725
+m3	48.0%	46.0%	6.0%	13,948
+M3	62.0%*	32.6%	5.4%	8,783
+P4	30.4%	64.5%*	5.1%	12,695
+A4	50.0%	43.8%	6.3%	96
+P5	32.0%	61.2%*	6.8%	3,253
+m6	50.9%*	41.2%	7.9%	860
+M6	33.3%	62.0%*	4.7%	2,092
+m7	41.0%	56.1%	2.9%	615
+M7	40%	40%	20%	15
+P8	42.8%	50.9%	6.4%	582

more stressed beat. Tables 14.3a and 14.3b tabulate the frequency of occurrence of various melodic intervals in three different accentual contexts. For any given melodic interval, we can determine whether the two tones forming the interval occur in a strong-to-weak or weak-to-strong context. For example, in 2/4 meter, an interval between notes on the first and second beats will form a strong-to-weak metrical context. Moving from the second beat to the first beat in the next measure will form a weak-to-strong metrical context. In addition, there is a third possibility: both tones forming the interval may occur on equally important beats in the metric hierarchy—as where both tones occur at the beginning of successive measures.

Tables 14.3a and 14.3b were generated by examining intervals in a large sample of folk songs.[28] The number of occurrences of each interval size were tabulated, and classified according to the metrical levels of the two participating tones. Consider first the

Table 14.3b
Metrical context for descending melodic intervals

Interval	Strong–Weak	Weak–Strong	Same	Total
−m2	45.0%	50.1%	4.9%	24,074
−M2	47.2%	47.4%	5.5%	59,328
−m3	56.1%*	37.2%	6.7%	16,961
−M3	59.3%*	34.7%	6.0%	7,781
−P4	58.1%*	35.4%	6.5%	5,311
−A4	72%	20%	8%	79
−P5	47.0%	45.5%	7.5%	2,644
−m6	65.7%*	26.6%	7.7%	930
−M6	63.3%*	29.5%	7.2%	569
−m7	63.2%*	32.7%	4.1%	220
−M7	15%	69%	15%	13
−P8	67.2%*	23.2%	9.6%	384

case of ascending thirds. Ascending minor thirds show no significant difference between strong-to-weak and weak-to-strong instances. However, ascending major thirds are somewhat more likely to occur in a strong-to-weak accentual context. By contrast, ascending perfect fourths are more than twice as likely to occur in a weak-to-strong accentual context. In short, the disposition of listeners to hear the ascending thirds and fourths differently is consistent with statistical learning.

There are other interesting relationships evident in table 14.3a. For example, unisons are more likely to occur in a strong-to-weak accentual context. This is consistent with the use of unisons as simply extending the effective duration of a primary tone. In contrast with unisons, ascending major and minor seconds are more likely to occur in a weak-to-strong context.

The pertinence of these patterns to the phenomenon of syncopation can be illustrated by using the information in tables 14.3a and 14.3b as a template for generating random or stochastic pitch sequences. Figure 14.18 shows two randomly generated pitch sequences based on tables 14.3a and 14.3b. The first and last pitches were set as C. Random intervals were selected from the above tables, but if the generated pitch failed to conform to the pitches of the C-major scale, it was discarded and another interval generated instead.

The first pitch sequence (labeled "a") was generated so that the first interval was selected from one of the intervals bearing an asterisk in the strong-to-weak column. The second interval was then selected from one of the intervals bearing an asterisk in the weak-to-strong column. This procedure was repeated for intervals three and four, and so on. The consequence of this procedure is that the randomly generated melody

Figure 14.18
Two random pitch sequences generated using the information in tables 14.3a and 14.3b. Sequence 1: generated to be most consistent with a strong–weak–strong–weak accentual pattern. Sequence 2: generated to begin with a strong–weak pattern which then switches to a weak–strong pattern at the point indicated.

should tend to evoke a persistent "strong–weak–strong–weak . . ." accentual pattern throughout the melody. The second pitch sequence (labeled "b") was constructed so that the first five pitches conform to the strong–weak pattern. But beginning with the fifth pitch (marked with an arrow), the generating algorithm switched to a weak–strong–weak–strong pattern. The goal here was to create a disruption in metric expectation. This example shows that it is possible to generate "syncopation" using isochronous pitches without any dynamic or other forms of accent. A weak sense of meter can be created merely through interval patterns, as long as these patterns are consistent with statistical norms in the music to which we are exposed. Syncopated *qualia* arise whenever there are temporal violations of expected norms.

As we've seen in earlier chapters, the presence of a statistical pattern in music doesn't always mean that listeners become precisely sensitive to the pattern. The above illustrations notwithstanding, it would be nice to have direct experimental evidence that listeners are attuned to the statistical patterns shown in table 14.3. Working in my laboratory, postdoctoral fellow Simon Durrant carried out an experiment in which listeners heard a repeatedly alternating pair of pitches. For example, listeners might hear the alternating pitches C4 and E4. Each tone sequence was slowly faded in and faded out so that there was no sense of which pitch "began" the sequence. For hundreds of intervals, listeners were asked to judge which of the two pitches—the higher or lower—seemed more accented. In the case of the major third, for example, listeners tended to hear the *lower* of the two pitches as more accented. By contrast, listeners tended to hear the *higher* pitch as more accented for the interval of a perfect fourth. Durrant's experiment formally establishes that there is a close, though not precise, relationship between the perceptual disposition of listeners and the statistical accentual tendencies for different intervals.

In earlier chapters, we also noted that just because listeners are sensitive to certain patterns doesn't mean that their mental representation of the pattern conforms to the representation one might assume. The tone sequences shown in figure 14.18 might be better viewed as scale-degree successions rather than successions of melodic inter-

Figure 14.19
Measures 17 to 20 from Scott Joplin's "Maple Leaf Rag."

vals. If one assumes that closural pitches (like the tonic, dominant, and mediant) tend to occur on stronger metric positions, then many of the strong–weak interval relationships associated with particular intervals are reminiscent of how one might approach a closural pitch. For example, the association of the ascending minor second with a weak-to-strong metric relationship might be attributable to the tendency for the leading tone to precede the (metrically stressed) tonic. Similarly, the ascending perfect fourth with a weak-to-strong association might be an artifact of the tendency for the dominant to move to the tonic. Whether the metric associations are mentally coded as intervals or scale degree dyads is moot, but in either case, statistical learning is implicated.

Some forms of syncopation are more common than others. Onset syncopation (omitting strong-beat onsets) and mixed onset-agogic syncopation are the most common forms of syncopation. Harmonic, agogic, and tonal syncopation are comparatively rare. Dynamic syncopation is rarely notated in scores, but it appears to be fairly common in actual performance. Syncopation is often combined with other forms of melodic embellishments, such as appoggiaturas. Figure 14.19 shows a typical musical example from a piano rag by Scott Joplin.

More generally, figure 14.20 shows a distribution of note onsets from a broad sample of Joplin's piano rags. The data were gathered from sixty randomly selected measures from works in 2/4 meter. The eight columns represent successive sixteenth-note positions in the meter for 2/4. The tallies indicate the number of tone onsets in the corresponding metric position. Tallies represent only the presence of an onset, and ignore the number of notes that might appear in a chord. Separate onset tallies were made for the left and right hands (bass and treble staves), and both tallies are combined in figure 14.20.

Like the ordinary metric hierarchy shown in chapter 10, the most likely events have onsets falling on the downbeat at the beginning of the measure. However, the second beat (occurring in the middle of the measure) is not the next most common onset point in these works. Instead, the second half of beats 1 and 2 are more probable onset points. There is one further deviation from the common duple meter hierarchy.

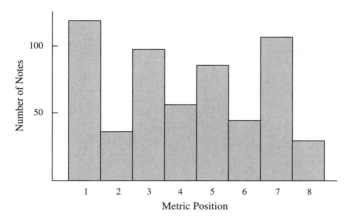

Figure 14.20
Distribution of note onsets in a sample of bars from Scott Joplin rags. Sample was taken from rags in 2/4 meter.

Typically, long–short–short patterns are evident at all levels of a (nonsyncopated) metric hierarchy. In the Joplin rags, this pattern is present when comparing metric positions 2 and 4, but it is reversed in positions 6 and 8. That is, in unsyncopated music, one would normally expect metric position 8 to attract more onsets than metric position 6.

Joplin's syncopation is quite constrained and highly stereotypic. On average, there is only one syncopated event per measure, sometimes two, and rarely three. The "Maple Leaf Rag" notwithstanding, syncopations are not especially common on the downbeat at the beginning of the measure, and the left-hand accompaniment tends to maintain a conservative unsyncopated "stride bass" of alternating bass pitches and chords.

Notice that Joplin's emphasis on the second half of beats 1 and 2 seems to be a forerunner of the *backbeat* that later becomes the hallmark of rock and roll. Viewed as a quadruple rather than duple meter, we can see the emphasis on beats 2 and 4 that defines the backbeat. With the advent of rock in the 1950s, the energy of the downbeat is further eroded. Over the ensuing decades there continues to be a de-emphasis on beats 1 and 3, leading to the emergence of reggae in which the great majority of the energy is reserved for beats 2 and 4 alone.

Expecting Syncopation

All of the above remarks concerning syncopation assume nonsyncopated music as the background norm for forming expectations. Of course, repeated exposure to syncopated music results in new expectations. As we saw in chapter 9, when new norms are established, it is possible for experienced listeners to form new mental schemas, and so a new genre appears. Arguably, syncopated music forms such a distinctive genre, of which ragtime, rock and roll, and reggae are instances. In a large sample of recorded popular music spanning the period 1890 to 1940, historical musicologist Ann Ommen and I found little change over time in the specific syncopation patterns used by musicians. What changed was the amount of syncopation: over the fifty-year survey period we found an approximate doubling of the number of syncopations per unit of time.[29]

Syncopation only *challenges* metric perceptions; it never annihilates meter. In order for syncopation to exist, it is essential to maintain normal (unsyncopated) metric expectations. Syncopated schemas piggyback on unsyncopated ones. The meter provides the schema against which *when*-expectations are formed. Meter and pulse are preserved. Later, in chapter 16, we will see examples where rhythmic events truly destroy the perception of an underlying meter.

Reprise

At the beginning of this chapter I suggested that most of the changes one can make to a score will tend to render the music less predictable in some way. Setting a gremlin loose on a musical score is apt simply to produce surprises that listeners find irksome or annoying. In some cases, composers—like our hypothetical gremlin—may be motivated by the goal of psychological mischief. However, musicians can also choreograph surprises in ways that have a distinctly positive psychological effect. In Beethoven's "Ode to Joy," a single early note may generate a memorable thrill for many listeners.

In this chapter I have suggested that there are four basic forms of surprise: *schematic*, *dynamic*, *veridical*, and *conscious*. A *schematic surprise* arises when a commonplace (schematic) event is displaced by an event of lower probability. Musical examples of such surprises include deceptive cadences and chromatic mediant chords. A *dynamic surprise* arises in response to events that have a low probability given the listener's encounter with previous passages in that same work thus far. Musical examples include rhythmic hemiola, and the "surprise" chord in Haydn's Surprise Symphony. A *veridical surprise* arises in response to events that have a low probability of occurrence given past experiences with the work. Musical examples of such surprises include performance errors, intentional misquotations (such as Schickele's thematic joking), and unfamiliar interpretive nuances applied to works that are otherwise highly familiar to a listener. A *conscious surprise* is a rare form of surprise that we have not discussed in this chapter. It arises when a knowledgeable listener consciously infers some future event, which then does not take place.

The key to understanding the emotional consequences of surprise is the recognition that surprise represents a biological failure. Any failure of an organism to anticipate future events constitutes a potentially grave danger. Understandably, surprises tend to generate a negatively valenced limbic response, even if only briefly. In chapter 2, I suggested that these negative responses activate classic fear-related physiological changes. The most important of these mechanisms is the fight–flight–freeze constellation of responses that can be observed in nearly all multicellular organisms. The most extreme of these three responses is the freeze response, where an organism ceases all motor movement and holds its breath. The least extreme of these responses is the fight response where the organism prepares to attack and prevail over the offending stimulus. This often entails elements of a display of aggression, including bristling hair.

In our examination of musical passages that evoke laughter, awe, or frisson, the underlying commonality is that they all involve a significant element of surprise. It appears that musicians cannot generate laughter, awe, or frisson without violating the listener's expectations. The negatively valenced initial responses evoked by these surprises are often usurped or truncated by a slower appraisal or another reactive response that is neutral or positive. The resulting contrastive valence leads to a generally positive aura or feeling. Without the contrastive valence, surprising events are experienced as merely oddball or weird.

Repeated listening seems to have different consequences for the various responses. Familiarity with laughter-evoking passages tends to attenuate the humor and transform the passage into something "odd" or "peculiar." Familiarity with frisson-evoking passages tends to either enhance the frisson experience or leave the experience unchanged. Awe-evoking passages tend to be difficult to replicate. Familiarity with awe-evoking passages tends to lead to frisson rather than awe.

If the thwarting of an expectation becomes commonplace, then listeners can learn to expect the unexpected. For example, in the context of joke-telling, we expect the joke to entail some unexpected twist or turn. In music, perhaps the foremost example of such "institutionalized surprise" is syncopation. On the local level, syncopated moments entail significant disruption of a listener's temporal expectations. However, patterns of syncopation can themselves become highly predictable. We are simultaneously surprised and yet not surprised.

In the following chapter we will turn our attention to the *tension response*. We will see that this response plays a large role in one of the quintessential contrastive valence devices used by musicians—the musical climax.

15 Creating Tension

In the preceding chapters we have considered how listeners respond *after* events have happened: chapter 13 dealt with expected events, whereas chapter 14 dealt with surprising events. In the psychology of expectation, however, the quintessential phenomena are to be found in the experiences leading up to some event.

The ITPRA theory distinguishes two classes of pre-outcome responses: the imagination response and the tension response. Recall that the *imagination response* entails those feelings that are evoked from thinking or day dreaming about possible future outcomes. Thoughts about the future are accompanied by feelings that make the various outcomes emotionally palpable. These vicarious emotions in turn shape our subsequent actions. For example, you might choose to clean up your kitchen before the arrival of guests because you can imagine the embarrassment you would feel if your guests were to see such a mess. In the experience of music, imagination responses are not common, but we will see some examples later in this chapter.

In the ITPRA theory, the *tension response* refers to a pre-outcome limbic reaction that arises from changes in arousal and attention, in preparation for some expected event. These arousal and attention preparations lead to a phenomenal sensation akin to stress. In chapter 1, I offered two illustrations of the tension response in action. In the case of the baseball outfielder, I suggested that tension peaks with the throwing of each pitch. Between pitches, the fielder can relax, both physically and mentally. But as the pitcher prepares to throw the ball, the fielder's arousal and attention will increase. The anticipatory tension is evoked whether or not the fielder must take action. There is no uncertainty regarding the *when* of the event, only about the *what* (i.e., whether one must play the ball).

The second example I gave was that of the man awaiting bundles of clothing dropped from a poorly visible second-floor balcony by his wife. Here, there was no uncertainty regarding the *what:* bundles would surely be hurled over the railing. The only question was *when* the bundles would appear. In this case, the man stood with his outstretched arms, in a continuous state of mental vigilance and heightened arousal.

In both examples, there is an increased attentiveness or vigilance as well as an increased arousal or action-readiness. Changes in attention and arousal cause mental and corporal changes that affect how we feel. In chapter 1, I claimed that such tension responses are, properly speaking, *artifacts*. The feelings simply accompany the physiological changes, such as increased heart rate, epinephrine release, muscle tension, decreased blinking, and so on. In short, what I have dubbed the *tension response* is a pre-outcome limbic activation that accompanies heightened arousal and/or heightened attention in anticipation of particular outcomes.

The Feeling of Anticipation

As we saw in chapter 13, some events have a very strong tendency to be followed by other events. The feelings that precede highly expected events are quite distinctive. The *qualia* might be characterized as tending, urging, cleaving, leaning, driving, propelling, pushing, or craving. In labeling this feeling, psychologist Jamshed Bharucha has suggested the term "yearning." Music theorist Eugene Narmour uses the term "implicative"; while theorist Elizabeth Margulis has coined the technical term "tension-S."[1] I prefer the more straightforward term "anticipation." Unfortunately, the word "anticipation" has the disadvantage that Western-trained musicians already use it to refer to the particular embellishment tone first discussed in chapter 13. To avoid confusion, I will use the phrase "feeling of anticipation" to refer to the sense of expectancy. When a listener is certain of some future event, we may say that the listener is experiencing a strong feeling of anticipation.

In light of the brain's disposition toward statistical learning, it is likely that the feeling of anticipation is greatest when the probability of an event approaches certainty. For zeroth-order probabilities, it is not common for events to be certain. Without some context, there are usually many possible events. However, many first-order probabilities really do approach statistical certainty. For Western-enculturated listeners, examples of strong feelings of anticipation include the feeling that a chromatic tone should resolve to a diatonic neighbor, and the feeling that a drum fill should lead to a hypermetric downbeat.

Consider, once again, the anticipation tone. In chapter 13 we traced how the prediction response changes during the course of an anticipation in a dominant-to-tonic harmonic context. Let's return to this passage to consider what happens with the tension response. Even if we are certain that a dominant chord will be followed by a tonic chord, recall from chapter 13 that it may not be clear *when* this resolution will take place. Figure 15.1 shows the three most likely moments of resolution for a dominant chord whose onset begins on the first beat in a 4/4 metric context. The most probable points of tonic resolution include the second beat (uppermost), the third beat (middle), or the downbeat of the next measure (lowermost). The expectation of

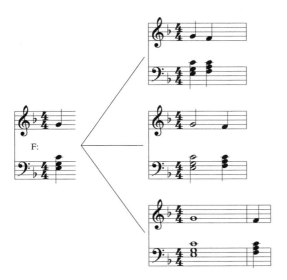

Figure 15.1
A dominant chord in F major, showing three typical moments of resolution to the tonic chord.

resolution will lead to a degree of tension. That is, a slight amount of psychological stress will arise as each moment of possible resolution approaches.

This stress will ebb and flow according to the unfolding metric probability. For example, if we expect a tonic chord to appear on the third beat of the measure, then tension will rise as the third beat approaches. If the chord fails to appear on the third beat then the tension will subside slightly—since the chord is less likely to appear on the fourth beat (or any of the intervening partial beats). As the downbeat of the next measure approaches, the tension will again rise, since this is the next moment when the tonic chord is likely to occur. Notice that "tension" is almost the exact opposite of "surprise." Tension builds as we approach expected event onsets. Tension drops as the listener passes through moments in which events are unexpected. If an event occurs sooner than expected the tension response fails to reach its potential peak. However, the surprise of an unexpectedly early event will likely evoke a negatively valenced *prediction response*. Surprise happens *after* events; tension happens *before* events. Nevertheless, both tension and surprise are able to evoke physiological stress.

Now consider what happens if we add the tone shown in figure 15.2. Several continuations are possible. The pitch F4 might be a passing tone leading to the pitch E4, or F4 might be a lower neighbor tone leading back to G4. Both of these possibilities would involve the dominant harmony being sustained. In the context where a listener

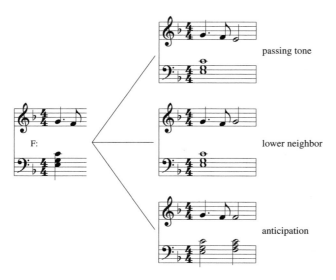

Figure 15.2
Dominant chord in F major with tonic embellishment, showing three possible continuations.

expects a dominant–tonic resolution, however, the F4 is most likely to suggest an anticipation. The *anticipation* is the quintessential expectation-related embellishment. In chapter 13 we saw that the introduction of the anticipation reduces uncertainty about both the *what* and *when* of the ensuing resolution. This increased certainty leads to a more positive (post-outcome) prediction response.

But what happens before the anticipation is resolved? What *qualia* are evoked by the anticipation tone itself? The first thing to note is that the sonority is now more dissonant.[2] That is, apart from expectation, the sonorous moment is likely to evoke a comparatively negative valence. Said another way, the *reaction response* to the introduction of the pitch F4 is negative.

At the same time, the advent of F4 dramatically increases the expectation of resolution. Experienced listeners will have a fairly good idea of what will happen next. This increased certainty concerning the future increases the yearning, craving, or the feeling of anticipation. Paradoxically, reducing the uncertainty has the effect of increasing the tension.

In chapter 13 I noted how decreasing uncertainty had the effect of increasing the limbic reward for the (post-outcome) prediction response. In addition to this effect, we can now add the high (pre-outcome) tension response. When the resolution occurs, the tension dissolves—that is, the sense of yearning or expectancy abates. I would suggest that the contrast between the high pre-outcome tension and the positive post-outcome prediction response provides another limbic contrast—another contrastive valence that contributes to the experience of pleasantness that accompanies the reso-lution. All other things being equal, a cadence that includes an anticipation tone should be more pleasant than one without it.

The Suspension

A similar phenomenal experience accompanies the so-called *suspension*. Figure 15.3 shows a typical 4–3 suspension. The suspension shown occurs as part of a tonic–dominant progression in which the movement of the tonic pitch (F) to the leading tone (E) is delayed. The numbers identify the (1) pre-suspension, (2) suspension, and (3) post-suspension moments.

Consider first the pre-suspension moment (moment 1). As a I chord, it is quite stable and so may evoke no strong sense of continuation. Consequently, there is little feeling of anticipation and little tension. Consider next the moment when the suspended sonority appears (moment 2). The sonority is now more dissonant, so the reaction response has a comparatively negative valence. For a listener experienced with Western music, the suspended pitch creates a very high expectation that it will move to the E. In other words, the *what* of the next moment is almost perfectly predicted. In fact, the post-suspension event is more predictable than the comparable moment for the anticipation. As we saw, the anticipation shown in figure 15.2 might be a passing tone or a lower neighbor tone. But the characteristic dissonant sonority associated with the suspension is much less ambiguous. The probability of the F falling to the E is near certainty.

The *when* of the post-suspension moment is a little more uncertain. The resolution might occur on the next beat, or it might be delayed until the next major downbeat at the beginning of the next measure. Despite this, however, the uncertainty accom-panying the *when* is relatively mild. Only a couple of choices are likely. Since the overall uncertainty is low, there is a strong feeling of anticipation attending the sus-pended moment.

Figure 15.3
Prototypical suspension. A tonic chord is followed by a dominant chord with the tonic pitch suspended. The suspended pitch resolves downward by step.

Finally, the anticipated moment of resolution occurs (moment 3). In the first instance, there is a large positive prediction response. The listener's confident prediction of this moment is realized, accompanied by a high positively valenced predictive reward. At the same time, the formerly dissonant sonority has been replaced by a chord with comparatively low sensory dissonance. Consequently, the reaction response will exhibit a relatively high positive valence.

Resolving the suspended tone is not the end of the matter. In a sample of baroque music, I found that 87 percent of 4–3 suspensions involving a dominant chord are followed by a tonic chord. The dominant chord itself then evokes a sense that it will return back to the tonic chord. That is, the resolution of the suspension will simultaneously evoke a strong anticipation of an ensuing tonic resolution. The entire cadential cliché will evoke a series of positively valenced prediction responses while simultaneously evoking a series of "yearnings" or anticipatory feelings. Notice that the anticipatory feelings pertain to the immediately following event. The experienced listener will expect each sonority to follow the previous one according to the norms of Western harmony. We cannot, for example, skip directly from the suspended sonority to the final I chord without first resolving the suspension to the V chord. It is not simply that listeners yearn for the cadential tonic chord; listeners yearn for each successive moment as the cadence unfolds.

In many listening situations, a listener may direct no explicit attention to the music, and may show no awareness of the listening act. For convenience, we might call this listening mode "stream-of-consciousness" listening. In stream-of-consciousness listening, the *imagination* and *appraisal* components of ITPRA are rare or attenuated. That is, the listener is not engaged in consciously imagining various possible future scenarios. Nor is the listener engaged in consciously appraising each event after it happens. This listening mode reduces ITPRA to TPR—*tension, prediction,* and *reaction.* Even for musician listeners, these three component responses probably account for most of the expectation-related feelings experienced. Since *imagination* and *appraisal* may be idiosyncratic to different listeners, the TPR components also probably account for the majority of shared expectation-related experiences within a community of listeners. Reducing our analyses to stream-of-consciousness elements may provide a useful simplification.

Table 15.1 summarizes the sequence of *qualia* associated with each successive moment in the classic 4–3 suspension, reporting only those elements found in stream-of-consciousness listening: tension, prediction, and reaction responses. The table distills the reaction response to the simple categories of "consonant" and "dissonant." There is more to the reaction response, but consonance/dissonance is an important component. At this point it is appropriate to pause and consider the meaning of these words. Fifty years ago, music theorists began to use the term "dissonant" to refer to the subjective feeling that accompanies the sense of a need for resolution. For example,

Table 15.1
Summary expectation analysis of a suspension

	Reaction	Prediction	Tension
pre-suspension	consonant	—	low tension
suspension	dissonant	moderate predictive success due to pitch proximity	very high tension; strong expectation of ensuing resolving pitch
post-suspension	consonant	extremely high predictive success	continued high tension; strong expectation of returning to tonic chord
cadence end	consonant	very high predictive success	closure; weak expectation of ensuing events, so low tension

any dominant function would be referred to as "dissonant" insofar as it needs resolution. Formerly, the term "dissonant" was used mostly to refer to the unpleasant clangorousness of certain chords or intervals with no regard for the context of these sonorities. After the 1960s, some theorists suggested that isolated sonorities had no innate dissonance and that dissonance arises exclusively from (learned) context. Pivotal evidence in support of this view was the harmonic interval of the perfect fourth. In medieval times, the perfect fourth was considered highly consonant and stable. But for modern Western-enculturated listeners, the isolated interval of the fourth tends to sound like a suspension yearning to be resolved to a third.

Calling a tonic triad "consonant" and a dominant triad "dissonant" has the important advantage of drawing attention to the difference in subjective tension associated with each moment. Yet perceptual research does not support the notion that context *alone* determines the subjective sense of annoyance or satisfaction associated with isolated sonorities. At the same time that music theorists were abandoning the notion that sonorities had any innate consonance or dissonance, hearing scientists like Donald Greenwood, Reinier Plomp, and Willem Levelt were identifying the physiological basis for classic dissonance. We now face a terminological conundrum: how should we use the word "dissonant"? One possibility is that we might return to the classic usage and reserve it for the subjective sense of clangorousness or irritation evoked by a static vertical sonority. We might then use terms like "yearning" or "tension" to refer to the dynamic feelings evoked at various moments. Alternatively, we might use a broader notion of dissonance to refer to both static and dynamic feelings of uneasiness. We might then use "sensory dissonance" to refer to the static experience of clangorousness, and "tension dissonance" to refer to the dynamic aspects. Unfortunately, neither of these suggestions is consistent with the current way that music scholars use the word "dissonant." We can muddle through this terminological conundrum, as long as we are clear in defining our terms as they arise. In table 15.1,

I am using the terms dissonance and consonance to refer to the sensory irritation evoked by a vertical sonority.

Notice, incidentally, that statistical learning provides a plausible explanation for why the perfect fourth is experienced differently by modern listeners compared with medieval listeners. Western music over the past four centuries has tended to follow isolated harmonic fourths by thirds. Listeners have learned to expect this first-order probability, and so modern listeners hear a perfect fourth as evoking the *quale* of anticipating an ensuing third. Listeners who are highly familiar with medieval music appear to form a separate schema that allows the perfect fourth to be heard as stable.

The Oddball Note

Given the preceding analyses of the anticipation and suspension, a skeptical reader might conjecture that the introduction of any note would have a similar effect of reducing uncertainty—and so produce a positively valenced prediction response. As a control case, consider the concocted passage shown in figure 15.4. This example shows a dominant–tonic progression with an "oddball" note interposed. A brief analysis follows.

With an already established key context, the dominant chord would have a high probability of being followed by a tonic chord, and the supertonic pitch would have a good chance of being followed by the tonic. Accordingly, there would be a fairly strong anticipation of the *what* component. The predicted *when* for this outcome would be less certain. Plausible event onsets might occur on beats 2 or 3, or the downbeat of the next measure.

With the advent of the oddball note (D flat), the resulting sonority is now more dissonant, so the reactive response would have a comparatively negative valence for this moment. Both the pitch (D flat) and the onset timing are poorly predicted, so the prediction response would also be highly negatively valenced. The D flat does not

Figure 15.4
Oddball event. The pitch D flat has a low probability of occurrence. The tone occurs at an unexpected moment and is approached in a disjunct manner. The ensuing tonic "resolution" similarly occurs at an unexpected moment and the D flat is followed by an unexpected leap.

belong to the key and so has a low probability of occurrence. In addition, the D flat is remote in pitch from the preceding G, and is approached by the unlikely interval of a diminished fifth. The D flat might be considered part of a dominant ninth chord—a chord borrowed from the minor key. However, in a major key without any previous instance of a D flat, this event would still have a low probability of occurrence. A prediction effect is unlikely, so the advent of this tone will not be positively valenced.

Turning to the tension response, the appearance of the D flat would tend to evoke a fairly clear expectation of a subsequent note. The lowered sixth scale degree is typically anchored to the dominant pitch, so if a listener heard the D flat as a lowered sixth degree, then there would be a strong prediction that it would be followed by C. On the other hand, if the D flat is experienced as a raised dominant degree (i.e., C#), then there would be a strong prediction that it would be followed by D. With regard to temporal expectations, the appearance of the D flat leads to a fairly clear expectation of the timing of the subsequent note. Like the anticipation, the timing of the D flat strongly implies that the next event should occur on beat 3. Most experienced listeners would therefore confidently predict the occurrence of either C5 or D5 on beat 3. Both the *what* and *when* are highly predictable. Although the oddball note evokes negatively valenced outcome and prediction responses, it evokes a comparatively strong tension response.

In figure 15.4 the third beat passes without a new event. The consequence is that the *when*-related expectation is completely thwarted. This prediction failure leads to a negatively valenced prediction response beginning at beat 3. At the same time, the high sense of anticipation remains. For the listener, the expectation that D flat/C sharp will be resolved to either C or D remains, so the feeling of anticipation does not go away.

Finally, the next event appears on the second half of the third beat. At this point, the listeners' confident predictions of the resolution pitches are proved wrong. Both the *when* and the *what* fail to conform to expectations. Only the fact that the chord is a tonic function was predicted. As a result, the prediction response is predominantly negative. Nevertheless, the final chord has a low sensory dissonance so the reactive response is somewhat positive. With regard to closure, the capacity for the tonic to evoke closure following the dominant function is weakened by the timing. By appearing on the second half of the third beat (rather than, say, the downbeat of the next measure), the tonic here evokes little sense of closure—with the consequence that it also evokes little sense of repose or relaxation.

With only slight modifications, our oddball example might be transformed into an appoggiatura (see figure 15.5). An appoggiatura would have the D flat resolving downward to the C on beat 3. A more likely appoggiatura might employ a D natural instead of the D flat. But consider how this appoggiatura would evoke different

Figure 15.5
Oddball example from figure 15.4 is transformed into an appoggiatura. Compared with figure 15.4, both the onset of the D flat and the onset of the resolution are made more predictable. In addition, the pitch resolution entails a more predictable conjunct motion, plus a post-skip reversal of contour.

Table 15.2
Summary expectation analysis of an oddball note

	Reaction	Prediction	Tension
pre-oddball	consonant	—	moderate to low tension; relatively strong expectation of the ensuing resolving pitch
oddball note	dissonant	poor predictive success; surprising	high tension; strong expectation of ensuing resolving pitch
post-oddball	consonant	poor predictive success; surprising	partial closure; weak expectation of ensuing events, so relatively low tension

expectation-related responses compared with the oddball passage. Both the oddball passage and the appoggiatura produce a dissonant moment, accompanied by a high expectation of the ensuing event. In the case of the appoggiatura, the subsequent resolution conforms to the expectation—creating a positive prediction response in addition to the positive reaction response. However, in the oddball passage, the subsequent "resolution" fails to conform to expectations, hence evoking a negatively valenced prediction response.

Emotional Effect of Delay

A potent factor influencing the tension response is delay. We noted earlier that the tension response increases as the moment of the predicted outcome approaches. The goal is to be optimally prepared just before the anticipated event. If the outcome occurs earlier than expected, then the tension response will fail to reach its potential peak. On the other hand, if the outcome is late, then the tension response will reach a peak and may be sustained as we wait for the presumed outcome to materialize. This delay, as a result, creates a longer and more intense period of tension.

Table 15.3
Summary expectation analysis of an appoggiatura

	Reaction	Prediction	Tension
pre-appoggiatura	consonant	—	moderate to low tension; relatively strong expectation of the ensuing resolving pitch
appoggiatura	dissonant	poor predictive success; surprising	high tension; strong expectation of ensuing resolving pitch
post-appoggiatura	consonant	extremely high predictive success	closure; weak expectation of ensuing events, so low tension

The mental consequences of anticipating an event that is delayed is quaintly captured in the following *Reader's Digest* anecdote:

An amateur golfer challenged his club pro to a match. "But," said the amateur, "you've got to give me a handicap of two 'gotchas.'" Although the pro had no idea what a "gotcha" was, he was confident and agreed to the terms. Just as the pro was about to tee off, the amateur crept up, grabbed him around the waist and shouted, "Gotcha!" They finished the game without incident, but the pro played terribly and was beaten. Asked why he had lost, he mumbled, "Have you ever played 18 holes of golf waiting for a second 'gotcha'?"[3]

Here, uncertainty regarding *when* results in considerable stress. In effect, the golf pro in the story experiences a heightened tension response throughout the eighteen-hole round. This anecdote describes a largely *conscious* mental tension, but most tensions related to uncertainty are unconscious.

As we saw in chapter 2, the effect of delay is most marked when expectations are most certain. (We have the most to lose when we are virtually certain of a good outcome, and the most to gain when we are virtually certain of a bad outcome.) This means that the effect of delay in music will be greatest when applied to the most predictable, stereotypic, or clichéd of events or passages. For listeners experienced with Western music, the most predictable chord progression is V–I; the most predictable tone successions are tendency tones (such as chromatic tones); the most predictable metric moment is the downbeat; the most predictable passages are cadences. These are also the points where performers are most likely to slow down. By increasing tension through delay, performers are increasing the limbic contrast that will ensue when the expected outcome generates a positive prediction response. In the context of highly predictable stimuli, delay amplifies the contrastive valence and so evokes greater pleasure at the moment of resolution.

Over the past eighty years, numerous studies concerning performance nuance have been carried out. Many of these studies have focused on the intentional speeding-up and slowing-down that characterize performers' *rubato*. Perhaps the most important discovery has been the characteristic *ritardando/accelerando* to be found at phrase boundaries. Performers typically slow down when approaching the ends of phrases and just before hypermetric downbeats. They then accelerate as the new phrase, period, or section begins. The amount of tempo change is correlated with the structural importance of the phrase boundary. Subphrase boundaries are typically approached with a modest ritard, whereas major transitions between large musical sections tend to provoke more dramatic slowing.[4] The final ending is commonly marked by the greatest reduction in tempo. It might appear that the biggest ritard is reserved for the points of greatest closure. Traditionally, music theorists have interpreted the ritard as a gesture that clarifies the musical structure.

Notice that there is another possible interpretation for such ritardandos. Typically, the final cadence involves approaching the most predictable pitch, the most predictable chord, and the most predictable metric moment. *High predictability* provides an opportunity to heighten the tension response and thereby to increase the pleasure evoked by contrastive valence. In performed music, highly marked ritards may occur just prior to the resolution of a tendency tone—but this resolution may not necessarily coincide with an important structure division. The resolution of a 4–3 suspension, for example, is often accompanied by slowing down, even though the moment is not closural and does not delineate a structural boundary.

At the risk of offending many fellow theorists, I would like to suggest that the principal motivation for such ritards is to enhance contrastive valence, rather than enhancing closure or delineating structure. Performers are attracted to these moments of high predictability because they provide the greatest opportunities to leverage tension. Approaching closure is correlated with the use of the ritard because closural approach is associated with high predictability. It is therefore understandable why the musical function of the ritard might be misconstrued as exclusively closural.

Of course the frequent use of the ritard in cadential passages will inevitably become a learned association. When we hear the music slow down, we might reasonably regard this as a signal of impending closure. But I would like to suggest that the original motivation for slowing was to heighten an emotional effect, not to delineate the musical syntax. The best evidence in support of this view is the ubiquitous tendency for performers to slow down at moments of high predictability, even when these moments are not closural or structural.

The ritard itself is progressive: the longest delay precedes the final note of the cadence or section. Interestingly, Ulf Kronman and Johan Sundberg have shown that the shapes of tempo curves in real performances resemble Newtonian mechanics: what musicians mean by "slowing down" is the same as Isaac Newton's conception of a body coming to rest.[5] Performers execute ritardandos using the same trajectory as a rolling ball coming to rest.

If the performer fails to slow down at cadences, the emotional impact of the music tends to be flattened. A computer performance of a score without any rubato sounds mechanical and devoid of emotion or feeling. Tellingly, listeners report that such mechanical performances fail to evoke as much pleasure as listening to a performance that involves interpretive rubato.

A simple dominant–tonic cadence embellished using an anticipation and performed with a touch of ritard evokes a veritable bouquet of psychological effects. The highly probable sequence of events produces strong feelings of anticipation accompanied by the stresses of heightened attention and arousal. As the predicted cadential passage unfolds, pleasure is evoked by each event through the prediction effect. At the same time, the high tension in each pre-outcome epoch provides the contrastive "foil" against which the prediction rewards become amplified. The ritard adds to the tension so that the contrastive valence is rendered even more contrastive. Yet the ritard itself proceeds according to a predictable trajectory, so the tension is maximized without disrupting the predictability of individual notes. The final arrival of the tonic evokes additional *qualia* of stability and closure. Without the ritard, the tension is reduced and so the contrastive valence is more muted. Without the anticipation embellishment, predictive certainty is reduced and so the prediction effect is less strong. If the final chord is omitted, then only the sense of tension remains—no predictive reward, no contrastive valence, no stability, and no closure.

The use of delay to amplify emotion is not limited to music. Its effects can be observed, for example, in the use of slow motion in film. Slow motion is most useful when the plot is highly predictable. Consider a cliché Hollywood script where the ending involves some sort of conflict between the good guys and the bad guys. The conflict might be a fight, chase, or a sporting competition, for example. For audience members, the outcome is preordained—the good guys will prevail (at least in Hollywood). But this very predictability of the outcome makes it difficult for the filmmaker to ensure an appropriate emotional response for viewers. How can the filmmaker maximize the positive valence evoked for viewers? What can the filmmaker do to enhance the contrastive valence? Like the musician's precadential ritard, a common device is delay. One way to do this is to render the decisive moment in the conflict in slow motion. Another device is to interrupt or suspend the decisive moment by moving to another scene. Yet another delaying device is to have the protagonist fail in what seems like the decisive moment, only to subsequently prevail in what will later prove to be the decisive moment. All of these delaying tactics will sow the seeds of doubt in an otherwise jaded audience that knows very well what the final outcome will be. Each of the devices used in film was used first in music.

Slowing the tempo is not the only means for delaying the resolution of a cadence. The history of Western music is replete with cadential delaying tactics. In fact, many

Figure 15.6
An early example of a fade-out ending. "Neptune, the Mystic" from Gustav Holst's *The Planets* (1914). The passage is for female chorus. The performance instruction reads: "The chorus is to be placed in an adjoining room, the door of which is to be left open until the last bar of the piece, when it is to be slowly and silently closed. This bar to be repeated until the sound is lost in the distance."

of the most seminal harmonic techniques originated as cadential interlopers. This includes the addition of the subdominant pitch in the creation of the dominant seventh chord, the suspension, the cadential 6–4, augmented sixth chords, the Neapolitan sixth, the pedal tone, the augmented triad, the dominant ninth and thirteenth chords, the preterminal false modulation, the interminable terminating I chord, and the deceptive cadence. The number of ways to delay the musical end is legion.

In the late romantic period, composers such as Richard Wagner established the elided phrase in which cadence moments were avoided: the anticipated cadence would instead begin the ensuing phrase. In some ways, this delaying tactic reached its apex in the twentieth century with the advent of the *fade-out*. In Gustav Holst's *The Planets*, the final fade-out is achieved mechanically (by closing a door), but with electronic sound recording fade-outs became routine. With the fade-out, music manages to delay closure indefinitely. The "end" is predictable, even though the music doesn't "stop." The "stop" gesture is replaced by a gesture toward the "infinite."

Ritards are most commonly associated with the highest-probability events, but research has shown that slowing also accompanies low-probability events. Working at the Royal Institute of Technology in Stockholm, Johan Sundberg has observed that performers will often slow down when approaching a (low-probability) chromatic melody tone or chromatic chord. Sundberg has suggested that the reason for this slowing is to reduce the likelihood that listeners will experience the event as an unintended error. In effect, these ritards are used to signal deliberateness: the ritard says to the listener "I intend precisely this."

Premonition

Normally, when we anticipate events, tension doesn't tend to rise until very near the moment when the event is expected. However, tension can sometimes rise well in advance of an event. These "early warning" expectations can lead to a vague sense that something may be about to happen. We might call these "premonitions."

I experience this effect in the first movement of Beethoven's "Emperor" Concerto (Piano Concerto no. 5). The pertinent passage is notated in figure 15.7. To my ears this is the most beautiful passage in the entire concerto. The orchestra gives way to an emerging piano solo. At first the piano continues with some of the high energy of the preceding passage. But the energy gradually dissipates (measures 406–407) and two variations of the second theme appear. The first variation consists of a two-against-three treatment that begins at measure 408. The second variation begins at measure 415 and is a lovely, delicate passage: a single flowing line played in the uppermost register of the piano accompanied by a light bass harmony. The sound is gentle, relaxing, and beautiful.

Around measure 419 or 420 I find that the sense of relaxation wanes and I become acutely tense.[6] Four measures later, the passage will end abruptly with a full orchestra *tutti* playing a strident sequence of block chords (beginning just before measure 424). Oddly, the tension I feel arises at least a dozen beats before the anticipated *tutti*. Although I am still hearing that delicate lyrical line, my body already starts to prepare for the inevitable boisterous interruption. My muscles feel tense and my ears feel like they are squinting—as though I am preparing for an explosion. All the loveliness between measures 419 and 422 is poisoned: my body simply won't let me experience the delicate lyrical music in a relaxed fashion.

Why does the tension arise so far in advance of the actual *tutti* passage? For first-time listeners, the loud *tutti* comes as a complete surprise. A strongly negative reactive response is generated, and this limbic response ensures that the event (and its musical antecedent) will be indelibly imprinted on memory: next time the listener will know better. Still, why does the tension need to rise so far in advance of the *tutti*?

One possibility is that larger changes in physiological arousal require more preparation time. (One cannot simply climb out of bed and begin running a marathon; nor can a marathon runner simply hop into bed and fall asleep after completing a race.) If the goal is to reach an arousal level that is congruent with the anticipated event, then large changes in arousal should require more time to achieve the needed physiological transformation. Another possibility is that big surprises simply cause memory to be efficient: more of the antecedent context may be retained in long-term memory.

In composing this passage, Beethoven, I suspect, was probably designing an effect for first-time listeners. The naive listener would simply enjoy the delicacy of the

Figure 15.7
Measures 406 to 424 from Ludwig van Beethoven, op. 72, Piano Concerto no. 5 ("Emperor"),
first movement.

Figure 15.8
From Jacques Offenbach's "Barcarolle" from *Tales of Hoffmann*. Example (a) shows the main melody (strings). Example (b) shows the main accompaniment figure (flute)—a figure also used in the lengthy introduction prior to the appearance of the melody.

passage for its full duration, and then be surprised by the *tutti*. For the seasoned listener, however, reduced surprise is purchased at the price of experiencing the lyrical passage with a certain element of foreboding. I doubt that the experience of seasoned listeners figured as strongly in Beethoven's thoughts.

Of course premonitions can also lead to more positive musical experiences. One can build tension leading toward a long-expected pleasant moment or passage. The best example I know of this phenomenon is to be found in Jacques Offenbach's Barcarolle from the *Tales of Hoffmann*. The melody for the Barcarolle is well known and much loved. Figure 15.8 shows the melody (a) along with an important accompaniment figure (b). The melody is played by the strings while the accompaniment figure is predominantly carried by the flute. The main melody does not appear until nearly a minute of tantalizing introduction. The introduction is so evocative of the (absent) melody that the introduction continues for what seems like an eternity. For listeners familiar with the Barcarolle, the anticipation of the melody is wonderfully palpable. When listening to this introduction I sometimes feel like one of Pavlov's dogs awaiting the delivery of food after having heard the ringing of the bell.

How does Offenbach create such a strong sense of anticipation? The key, I think, is the accompaniment figure played by the flute (figure 15.8b). Apart from a few measures at the beginning and end of the work, the accompaniment figure occurs throughout the entire span of the Barcarolle. If you are at all familiar with Offenbach's melody, you will be familiar with the accompaniment figure as well.

The accompaniment figure doesn't simply evoke strong associations with the melody; it also bears a strong resemblance to the melody. The figure uses the same quarter–eighth rhythmic alternation that characterizes the melody. It also preserves much of the same up-and-down pitch contour. Offenbach's accompaniment figure sits precariously on the fence, rocking back and forth between $\hat{5}$ and $\hat{6}$. Both the close resemblance and strong association combine to build an expectation for the melody— at least for those listeners who are familiar with the work. I expect that few musical introductions so reliably cue the ensuing main melody. Anyone familiar with

Offenbach's Barcarolle will feel a sense of acute anticipation waiting for the introduction to finally give way to the melody.

For the experienced listener, the veridical knowledge of this piece will include both the melody as well as the rocking $\hat{5}$ to $\hat{6}$ accompaniment figure. In fact, the $\hat{5}$ to $\hat{6}$ figure is the most commonly heard element in the Barcarolle. This implies that the accompaniment figure will prove very effective in cuing the veridical expectation for the melody itself. It is the use of this veridical knowledge of the accompaniment that makes it possible for Offenbach to build the premonition tension as listeners anticipate the start of the melody.

Notice that Offenbach makes ubiquitous use of anticipations. The pitches on each beat and downbeat are anticipated. Moreover, given the dominant harmony in the second and third measures of the melody, the F# actually forms a suspension, which is resolved to the E and G of the dominant seventh chord. This means that the anticipations of the F# in the second and third measures are actually anticipations of tones that turn out to be suspensions. Only the F# anticipation to the fourth measure of the phrase anticipates a true chordal tone in the tonic triad.

The first thirty notes of Offenbach's melody make use of just three neighboring pitches: E, F#, and G. There are no abrupt leaps, no chromatic tones, and no unusual rhythms. Nevertheless, Offenbach piles on the tension. He delays the advent of the melody for nearly a minute. When the melody appears, nearly half of all the melody tones are either anticipations or suspensions. The tensions arise solely from expectation. Offenbach's Barcarolle is a textbook illustration of how to use expectation to add drama and tension to an otherwise graceful and serene work.

Climax

The premonition tension evoked by Offenbach's introduction to the Barcarolle resembles, in many respects, the most famous of dramatic devices—the *climax*. In theater and film, a climax is a point of heightened tension or conflict. It often coincides with a moment of physical or mental struggle, and its outcome typically establishes an important element in the plot or story line. Climaxes are also part of dance, theatrical magic, fireworks, carnival shows, and sexual intercourse. The temporal placement of climaxes differs for different activities. The theatrical magician will leave the most astounding trick until the end of the program. Similarly, the high-wire acrobat will place the most difficult maneuver last; and the fireworks artist will save the most impressive display for the finale. Since laughter facilitates more laughter, comedians, by contrast, will often place their best jokes near the beginning of a routine. In figure skating, the most difficult jumps are typically spread over the course of the program in order to minimize the effects of fatigue and nervousness. Of course there may be more than one climax; late romantic orchestral music in particular will often exhibit several climactic moments. The climactic intensity may be more or less muted, and much music exists where there are no discernible climactic passages.

The psychological tension generated in musical climaxes is not limited to the phenomenon of expectation. There are numerous other methods musicians use to evoke tension. Among the features characteristic of climaxes, three have long been identified by music theorists: high pitch, loud dynamic level, and relatively dissonant sonorities.[7] In addition, several other elements appear to contribute to the sense of climax. These include timbre changes associated with physical intensity, the use of vibrato, accelerating event sequences, increased "volume," upward pitch trajectory, decreased predictability, and tactical delays. Let's look at some of these in turn, beginning with volume.

Working at Harvard University in the 1930s, the famous experimental psychologist, Smith (S. S.) Stevens, proposed that *volume* is a basic attribute of sound—like pitch, loudness, and timbre.[8] By "volume," Stevens meant the subjective sense of auditory size, mass, or spaciousness. When the volume is increased, the sound isn't simply louder, it is also "bigger" in some sense. The legacy of Stevens's term can be observed today on audio equipment where the big knob is still labeled the "volume" control. The label is wholly deceptive. Equipment manufacturers thought that "volume" would appeal to customers more than either "loudness" or "amplitude." In fact, when we adjust the "volume" we are simply increasing or decreasing the amplitude (which is strongly correlated with loudness). However, Stevens's notion of volume was much more nuanced and interesting than what happens when we adjust a volume control on a stereo. Volume is increased when the sound appears more massive or monumental. One way to increase the volume is by augmenting the number of sound sources—as when more orchestral instruments are employed. Volume is also increased when switching from monophonic to stereophonic or surround-sound reproduction. For Stevens, increasing the number of singers in a chorus would increase the subjective sense of volume, not just the loudness. Many musical climaxes are accompanied by such an increase in volume; often the instrumental or vocal resources are augmented. The sound appears "bigger."

Also in the 1930s, University of Iowa psychologist Carl Seashore carried out a number of studies on vibrato.[9] When we are angry or fearful, the body releases large amounts of the hormone epinephrine (also known as adrenaline). Epinephrine has a facilitating effect on muscle movement. When released in large quantities, epinephrine causes muscle tremors—that is, spontaneous intermittent muscle flexing. When we are angry or fearful, the trembling is a consequence of the epinephrine release. The presence of epinephrine affects every muscle in the body, including the muscles of the vocal cords. As a result, when we are angry or fearful, the vocal cords tremble and so the pitch of the voice wavers. The musical vibrato is a more controlled form of pitch trembling.[10] For listeners, the presence of pitch trembling is a reliable signal of both a high state of arousal as well as a high state of emotionality. Although not all musical climaxes involve the use of vibrato, a marked increase in vibrato can often be observed at points of musical climax. Conversely, *secco* (dry) or *senza vibrato* passages typically convey a low level of affect, calmness, control, innocence, or project a feeling of emotional desolation.

Throughout the twentieth century, numerous ethological studies were carried out to determine the purpose or meaning of various animal calls and signals. Loud sounds are generally associated with high arousal in a vast array of animals. Low-pitched loud sounds are associated with aggression, whereas high-pitched loud sounds are associated with alarm. High-pitched quiet sounds are often associated with deferrence or submissiveness, while low-pitched quiet sounds are associated with both contentment and threat.[11]

The basic connotations of various sounds for human listeners has been explored extensively by Klaus Scherer at the University of Geneva. In one study, Scherer and his colleague James Oshinsky synthesized tone sequences whose basic acoustic properties were systematically manipulated. Listeners then described the emotions suggested by the different sound sequences. Scherer and Oshinsky found that anger and fear are associated with high pitch level, ascending pitch contours, and fast event sequences. In vocal production, all of these acoustical characteristics are associated with high metabolic arousal. When we are excited we speak faster, we speak at a higher pitch level, and we are more likely to glide upward than downward in pitch.[12] These same features are often evident in musical climaxes.

Another common feature of musical climaxes is the use of timbres that employ rich spectra containing many harmonics—especially higher harmonics. The presence of high energy in upper harmonics is associated with high physical tension in an acoustic vibrator accompanied by a relatively high activating energy. The presence of intense, rich spectra is one of the acoustical properties that Scherer and Oshinsky found are associated with *anger* and *fear*. When we are relaxed, both the tension in our vocal cords and the activating pneumatic energy are relatively low, and so the resulting spectrum contains relatively little energy in the upper partials. Conversely, when we are aroused or anxious, increased tension in the vocal cords and increased pneumatic energy tend to evoke a subjectively "harsher," less mellow timbre. The timbres associated with musical climaxes are more likely to be characterized as intense or harsh rather than mellow or warm.

The concept of dissonance is one of the most complicated and contentious in music scholarship. Once again, we will sidestep the myriad of issues by focusing on just one aspect of dissonance—the phenomenon of sensory dissonance. The subject of extensive experimental research,[13] sensory dissonance is known to be linked to physiological interference along the basilar membrane of the cochlea. In effect, the presence of one (pure) tone component tends to interact with other (pure) tone components in a way that renders the hearing organ less able to discern the various spectral components present in the environment. The phenomenon can be likened to visual *glare* where a bright light source or reflection interferes with our ability to see. That is, a visual stimulus degrades the performance of the visual system so that we are less able to gather information from the environment. The accompanying phenomenal experience is one of annoyance or irritation. Similarly, some sonorities result in stimulus-engendered degradation of the auditory system. In simple terms, some sounds make it more difficult to "hear" than other sounds. These "glaring" sounds include the sorts of sonorities that music theorists have conventionally characterized as "dissonant" such as tritone and semitone intervals, and dense loud sonorities containing many close pitches. Once again, such sounds have a tendency to appear at moments of musical climax.

As we have already seen, delay tends to magnify the tension response. In particular, delay has the greatest limbic effect when the outcome is most predictable. At first, the use of delay to increase stress appears to be in conflict with the use of accelerating events to increase arousal. How can a composer both increase the tempo and also delay the onset of events? Notice, however, that delay is most effective when an event is most predictable. This means that increasing tempo can be mixed with the occasional use of delay for those events that are most expected.

Notice that tension arises when a future event is highly predictable. But for the prediction response, the greatest stress arises when an event is unexpected or surprising. Once again, at first there seems to be a contradiction: stress is heightened when a future event is predictable; stress is heightened when an actual event is unpredictable. But notice that it is possible to evoke both forms of stress when a strongly held expectation is thwarted. Climaxes often involve such "bait-and-switch" constructions. Thwarted expectations can be achieved by introducing nonscale tones, unprepared changes of key, unusual harmonies, uncommon melodic intervals, odd sonorities, unconventional rhythms, abrupt changes of meter, or other musical devices that introduce an element of surprise. These events will generate stress through a negatively valenced prediction response.

Notice that all of the above climactic devices are associated with the evocation of fear. Loud sounds are more likely to evoke fear than quiet sounds. "Large" or "massive" sounds are potentially more fear-evoking than sounds with less "volume." Harsh sounds (generated by tight vibrators) are more likely to be indicative of high arousal or high emotion than are the mellow sounds produced by more relaxed vibrators. Faster sound sequences are more likely to indicate high arousal or high energy states, which again hold the potential for evoking greater concern. Vibrato is indicative of "trembling"—suggesting that the agent producing the sound is in a high state of arousal or is emotionally distraught. Sensory dissonance is associated with high levels of auditory masking. Masking, in turn, is a form of sensory degradation—a condition that is potentially dangerous, and sufficient cause to feel irritation or annoyance. Throughout the animal kingdom, loud high-pitched sounds are associated with alarm. Descending pitch glides are associated with calm, whereas upward pitch glides are associated with high arousal. In addition, stress is evoked when unpredictable events occur, and tension is evoked when predicted events are delayed. In short, musical climaxes tend to assemble a range of acoustical devices that are linked to the evocation of fear, alarm, or annoyance.

Apart from what composers write, it is revealing to look at the typical interpretive techniques used by performers when approaching a climax. In Western culture, performers are given relatively little latitude in modifying what the composer's score dictates. However, when approaching climactic moments, performers frequently accelerate, play more loudly, use more intense timbres, add vibrato, accentuate dissonant elements, introduce large delays prior to the most expected moments, and sometimes even fill out chords with additional notes. All of these manipulations are consistent with the goal of amplifying negatively valenced physiological responses.

Aside from climaxes, in most circumstances where listeners experience contrastive valence, the transition from negative to positive is accomplished quickly—typically in less than half a second. It is this rapid transition that makes it difficult for listeners to become aware of the initial negative limbic response. In the musical climax, by contrast, the negative condition typically lasts much longer—often several seconds. This means that listeners can better recognize the clangorous, disorienting, and stressful character of the climactic build-up. In this context, the resolution or denouement is also more apparent to listeners.

The climax may represent the epitome of contrastive valence in music making. The high sensory dissonance, high physiological arousal, high physiological stress, and vivid feelings of anticipation combine to set the stage for a dramatic limbic reversal. The psychological result sometimes borders on the euphoric. Several music scholars have noted a striking parallel to sexual orgasm. Listeners find musical climaxes memorable, and familiarity with a musical climax can lead experienced listeners to form premonitions of approaching climactic moments. Even as the climax reaches its most clangorous peak, experienced listeners are already anticipating the release in tension and the sense of pleasure that will follow. The music lover rides through the most dissonant build-ups with hopeful excitement.

Sweet Anticipation—The Role of Consciousness

To this point, all of our pre-outcome discussion has focused on the unconscious tension response. However, as I noted at the beginning of this chapter, the ITPRA theory also proposes an imaginative pre-outcome response, a response that entails those feelings that are evoked from thinking or daydreaming about possible future outcomes. Thoughts about future outcomes are accompanied by feelings, which in turn shape our actions. Recall that the *imagination response* can be evoked long before an anticipated event.

Listening to music can be a highly enjoyable experience. The very act of going to a concert or turning on the stereo is shaped by the expectation that we will enjoy ourselves. That is, the decision to expose ourselves to music often arises from an imaginative assessment. The positing of future pleasure provides the motivational amplifier. Even if all musical experiences were pleasant, there would be much less music listening if people couldn't recall and predict that they are likely to enjoy listening.

In some ways, the sweet anticipation of knowing in advance that we are likely to find a listening experience enjoyable is the most important of musical expectations. It is this expectation that ultimately makes us return again and again to the act of listening. People who are in the business of marketing music know that a history of enjoyable experiences is the key to getting people out of their homes to attend a concert. Many times I have come out of a concert feeling glad that I had overcome my initial reluctance to go. Music marketers know that the principal challenge is reaching the potential audience who don't yet have a past history of musical enjoyment that could provide the engine for seeking musical experiences. At the same time, those who organize concerts that fail to engage listeners are in the business of destroying not just their own audiences, but potentially the audiences for other musicians as well.

Imagination responses are not limited to our own experiences. They can also arise by entertaining empathetic thoughts—as when we imagine how someone else might feel. These empathetic experiences are not uncommon. Every music lover has had the experience of introducing a fellow music-lover to a new listening experience. We get a vicarious thrill out of the thought that someone else will also find this music thrilling. One of the joys of teaching music is the pleasure of introducing students to some wonderful musical moments.

Such empathetic imagination responses can sometimes revitalize an otherwise jaded palette. For example, in working with the music of Peter Schickele, I have listened to some humorous passages dozens of times. In the previous chapter I noted that extreme familiarity with various passages tends to reduce if not eliminate the humor. However, when I play these highly familiar examples to others, I find myself anticipating the moments when they might laugh, and the passages regain their humor for me. Anticipating how others might respond to a passage can have the effect of rekindling our own responses.

This empathetic experience is not limited to the community of listeners. Imagining how others might respond is one of the creative engines available to performers and composers. When composing, a composer will sometimes imagine how people are likely to respond to a particular passage or device. Similarly, performers will sometimes imagine the experience of listeners, or even the responses of friends or critics. The ability to imagine how others might experience something is arguably the cornerstone for all artists and entertainers. The theatrical magician Doug Henning once said that only magicians get to see the real magic. For the magician there is no mystery in the trick: the trick involves straightforward manipulations of physical objects in a peculiar way. The true magic is seeing how these manipulations evoke a sense of utter astonishment in those who watch the trick. The true magic is the evoking of astonishment, not the peculiar movement of objects.

Although imagining the responses of others can become excessive or pathological, some sensitivity to the experiences of others is healthy. The good artist may ignore the critics, but the good artist will not completely discount the experiences of others.

Reprise

In this chapter we have addressed some of the *qualia* listeners experience before an anticipated event. When a future event is highly probable, listeners experience a strong sense of the inevitability of that outcome—an experience we can call the "feeling of anticipation." Anticipating events leads to changes of attention and arousal whose physiological concomitants are akin to stress. The amount of tension experienced is proportional to the predictability of the ensuing event. The most predictable events evoke the strongest feelings of tension.

If the actual outcome conforms to the listener's prediction, there ensues a stong positively valenced prediction response. When musicians speak of "tension and release" or "tension and resolution," much (though not all) of what they are speaking of can be understood as anticipation followed by a positively valenced prediction response. Such tension-and-release experiences are most likely to occur when musical events are highly predictable. In Western music, examples of such highly predictable event sequences include the movement of chromatic tones to neighboring diatonic pitches, commonplace embellishments like anticipations and suspensions, and highly stereotypic cadences.

A common way to increase the feeling of anticipation (and the accompanying tension) is through *delay*. By delaying the advent of the expected event, the state of anticipation can be sustained and so made more salient for a listener. Performers often hesitate or slow at points of high certainty, such as phrase endings, downbeats, hypermetric downbeats, tendency tones, and final cadences. The same use of delay can be observed in other performing arts such as film, mime, and dance.

Perhaps the epitome of contrastive valence in music is the climax. In addition to using "delay-of-the-expected" to increase tension, climaxes often make use of a vast array of devices to evoke a negatively valenced limbic state prior to the release. As noted, all of these devices can be plausibly linked to stimuli that tend to induce some element of fear.

Not all feelings of anticipation pertain to the immediately ensuing events. In "premonition tension," a listener may experience some apprehension or tension related to an event that may be many seconds away.

Finally, another form of anticipatory *quale* arises through imagination. By imagining the enjoyment of others, we may be motivated to introduce our friends to favorite musical works. By imagining critical acclaim, a performer or composer might shape a particular passage for maximum musical effect. By imagining the enjoyment we might experience from listening to music, we might decide to attend a concert or turn on the radio. The sweet anticipation of future pleasure is one of the main motivators for engaging with music.

Two months after the terrorist attacks of September 11, 2001, Swiss police carried out a dawn raid at a hotel in Basel. There they arrested a suspected French terrorist who had publicly advocated the bombing of the Paris Opera. The suspected terrorist was seventy-six-year-old composer and conductor Pierre Boulez. In a 1967 interview, Boulez had infamously suggested that "the most elegant solution to the problem of opera is to blow up the opera houses."[1] Not known for their sense of humor, the Swiss police were having trouble distinguishing between intemperate avant-garde rhetoric and incitement to commit terrorism. An aging artist like Boulez must have felt truly honored.[2]

By any yardstick, the twentieth century was a remarkable period in music history. The century witnessed an explosive growth in popular music. Major genres, such as jazz, Broadway, blues, and rock, emerged. As the century advanced there was an increasing awareness of and appreciation for the musical riches of non-Western cultures. Unprecedented numbers of Westerners were exposed to the musics of India, China, Japan, Indonesia, Africa, and other regions. At the same time, technological developments transformed the experience of music listening. Prior to the introduction of sound recording and broadcasting, music had been experienced as a fleeting pleasure to be savored in relatively infrequent concerts or domestic soirées. By the end of the twentieth century, music had become a soundtrack to daily life.

In addition to these changes, Western art music experienced a dramatic and profound transformation. Sometime between 1910 and 1920, Western art music took a distinctly modernist turn. Nearly every established element of music was probed, explored, and extended—from tuning systems and scales to performance venues and playing techniques; from instruments and timbres to political and social agendas. Melody, harmony, rhythm, timbre, and form were stretched in a multitude of directions. The advent of *modernism* raises special challenges for understanding the role of expectation in musical experience.[3]

Although modernism is typically associated with the early decades of the twentieth century, its roots extend back to the late nineteenth century. Many historians regard

Richard Wagner as the principal precursor of musical modernism. Not content with writing the music of his time, Wagner proposed that his job as a composer was to write *Zukunftsmusik*—the music of the future. By shifting the musical emphasis from the present to the future, Wagner endorsed the growing idea of an advanced guard or *avant-garde*. With the turn of the century, the main figures of musical modernism emerged: Debussy, Satie, Stravinsky, Bartók, Schoenberg, Webern, Prokofiev, Varèse, Messiaen, Cage, and many others. Of the many composers of the first half of the century, perhaps the preeminent figures of musical modernism were Arnold Schoenberg and Igor Stravinsky—composers whose innovations had a widespread effect on the language of art music.

An enormous body of arts scholarship has addressed the phenomenon of "modernism."[4] In characterizing modernism, many themes have emerged. One strain of modernism focuses on themes such as progress, novelty, technology, and invention. This is essentially a future-oriented, often overtly optimistic strain. A second strain of modernism is somewhat darker, emphasizing alienation, isolation, parody, irony, absurdity, and fragmentation. The common element to be found in both the optimistic and pessimistic strains of modernism is the effort by artists to "go against the grain"—to snub orthodoxy and replace it with the unorthodox.

The French painter Georges Braque was only one of many artists who said that art should disturb. It was an idea that reverberated throughout avant-garde musical circles. There was a widespread feeling that the arts were too tame. On the one hand, the arts needed to better divorce themselves from the banality of popular entertainment. On the other hand, the arts needed to be freed from the polite refinements of bourgeois respectability. Pierre Boulez was not the only artist to propose radical solutions.

If one's goal is to disturb listeners, there are many ways to achieve this. Music scholars have drawn attention to the increased use of dissonance in modern music. Certainly, one way to go against the grain is by adding more of the auditory spice we call dissonance. A more radical approach might reverse the musical roles of consonance and dissonance—using consonance where one would normally use dissonance, and using dissonance where one would normally use consonance. In the language of egalitarian politics, dissonance could be "emancipated." Dissonance could be set free from its formerly courteous constraints.

To be sure, the twentieth century saw a significant increase in the proportion and variety of dissonant sonorities. However, I think the emphasis on dissonance as a defining character of musical modernism detracts from a more fundamental characteristic. The essence of unorthodoxy is to be found in the psychology of expectation. To be unorthodox is to fail to conform to what is expected. Norms are challenged by confronting and reversing established expectations.

In this chapter, I propose to examine briefly three composers who made major contributions to the language of musical modernism: Richard Wagner, Arnold

Schoenberg, and Igor Stravinsky. As we will see, each composer introduced compositional innovations whose implicit or explicit goal was to go against established musical
expectations. Long before Wagner, composers had endeavored to thwart listeners'
expectations in various ways, such as through the deceptive cadence. However,
prior to the modern period, these compositional efforts to thwart expectations
were momentary, episodic, and fleeting. With Wagner, we see what appears to be the
first *sustained* effort to systematically thwart expectations—to consistently *not* give
listeners what they expect. These same efforts can also be observed in the musics of
Schoenberg and Stravinsky and other modernist composers. I will refer to this disposition as the *contrarian aesthetic*. One might call it a "negative" or "anti" aesthetic, but
I prefer the word "contrarian" for two reasons. First, "contrarian" has more positive
connotations than these other designations. Second, "contrarian" better evokes
the resolute, persistent, and often stubborn character of these musical mavericks.
Going against the grain is sure to provoke criticism—even anger or revulsion. No
one can sustain such a revolution without a tenacious, iconoclastic, or contrarian
personality.

In the case of Wagner, this contrarian aesthetic is most evident in the simple
cadence. Especially in his later works, Wagner did everything in his power to
avoid, disguise, elide, suspend, or delay cadential closure. One might say that
Wagner wrote "contra-cadential" music. In the case of Schoenberg, this contrarian
aesthetic is most evident in his avowed avoidance of tonality. As we will see shortly,
tonality plays a significant role in the organization of Schoenberg's music. But its
role is that of a "reverse psychology" in which Schoenberg explicitly sets out to unravel
any latent tonal implications. I will suggest that his music is not "atonal;" rather,
it is "contratonal" in structure. Finally, in the case of Stravinsky, the contrarian aesthetic is most evident in his periodic unraveling of meter. As with Schoenberg's view
of tonality, Stravinsky wasn't simply "agnostic" when it came to meter. Instead, segments of his music exhibit a systematic organization whose purpose is to actively
subvert the perception of meter. Although his music remains highly rhythmic, some
of Stravinsky's most distinctive passages are methodically "contrametric" in
structure.

All three composers were controversial during their lifetimes. The music of
Schoenberg and Stravinsky in particular was greeted by howls of protest from unsuspecting audiences. By looking in detail at the musical organization we will be able to
see how the psychology of expectation accounts for the betrayal felt by many listeners
of the time, and why the music continues to confound many present-day listeners.
At the same time, the psychology of expectation will help us understand how some
listeners have adapted to the contrarian aesthetic, and have internalized the same
contrarian principle as a basis for auditory expectation. Experienced listeners can come
to expect the unexpected.

Wagner's Contracadential Music

Richard Wagner (1813–1883) wrote philosophy, literature, chamber music, and poetry, but primarily, he composed operas. In Wagner's lifetime, his music was both loved and reviled. He attracted both a fervent audience of devotees and a choleric army of critics. Even today, his music tends to polarize listeners for both musical and political reasons. Scholars have found Wagner to be an especially compelling subject for study: few musicians can claim to have received a comparable amount of scholarly attention.[5]

Music scholars have pointed to a number of characteristic aspects of Wagner's music. These include an expressive chromatic language, rich orchestration, a preference for continuous melody, dramatic dynamic shading, and a unique system of denotative motives. But commentators seem to have been most happy when describing their emotional responses to Wagner. Wagner's music is variously described as expressive, passionate, or intense. My favorite description, however, is John Freeman's character-ization of Wagner's musical language as "the language of longing."[6] There are at least two ways to interpret this phrase. One interpretation views "longing" as a quintes-sentially "romantic" emotion. For some, Wagner represents the apex of romanticism. His libretti are often luridly passionate stories where love, betrayal, and power are intermingled. Wagner takes personal emotions and raises them to cosmic significance.

There is also a second, more literal interpretation of Freeman's phrase. The "language of longing" also draws attention to the yearning *qualia* that are so often evoked by Wagner's music. This yearning sensation is evident even when listeners are clueless about the programmatic stories. The longing or yearning character can be traced in large part to Wagner's chromatic harmony, and in particular, to his manipulation of classical cadential gestures.

Some of Wagner's works employ fairly conventional cadences. Examples include *Tannhäuser* and *Lohengrin*. But much of Wagner's music displays consistently uncon-ventional cadential treatments. Where other composers were content to rely on exist-ing cadential clichés, Wagner used cadential clichés as the raw material for something far more radical.

As we saw in chapter 15, psychological tension can be magnified by delaying expected outcomes. The effect of delay is greatest when the expectations are strongest. Since cadences are among the most predictable musical structures, cadences provide fruitful opportunities for delay-induced tension. Wagner did not originate the delayed cadence, but he certainly made extensive use of it. Figure 16.1 shows a simple example from the overture to Wagner's *The Flying Dutchman*. The theme leads to a fortissimo diminished seventh chord, which is followed by silence. When the music resumes following the grand pause, the diminished chord continues as an arpeg-

Figure 16.1
Measures 316 to 320 from the overture to Wagner's *The Flying Dutchman*.

Figure 16.2
Measures 217 to 221 from the overture to Wagner's *Tannhaüser*.

giated figure in the strings, and continues for another six measures before it is finally resolved.

The importance of the delayed cadence in Wagner is most easily observed by looking at his use of rests. In most music (both popular and classical), rests are most likely to appear immediately after a cadence. Rests often mark the boundary between the end of one phrase and the beginning of the next. Yet in Wagner, notated rests commonly occur, not as post-cadential moments of repose, but in the middle of the cadence itself—typically at the moment when anticipation of some resolution is greatest. In other cases, Wagner dispenses with the resolution. He simply stops mid-cadence, pauses, and then goes on to a new musical idea as though a final resolving chord were unnecessary. In effect, he abandons the cadence.

Sometimes, an "abandoned cadence" involves an elided phrase where the end of one idea marks the beginning of a new idea. Figure 16.2 shows a typical example from Wagner's *Tannhäuser.* Here, the end of a solo clarinet passage coincides with a new motivic idea featured in the violas. The underlying harmony reinforces the failure to bring clear closure before proceeding with the next idea. A German sixth leads to a second-inversion tonic chord, followed by a dominant seventh chord. All expectations point to a tonic F-sharp major chord. But Wagner adds the minor seventh to the expected chord, causing the tonic to act as a secondary dominant that launches the new musical motive.

One could regard the cadence here as a "deceptive" cadence. A more generic designation might be a "thwarted cadence"—meaning simply a cadence whose final

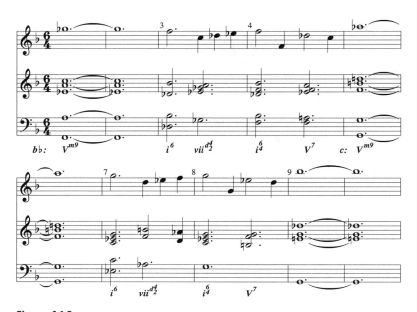

Figure 16.3
Excerpt from Richard Wagner's overture to *The Flying Dutchman*. The excerpt begins ten measures before rehearsal letter "H."

outcome is contrary to expectation. The expectation here originates in a predictable cadential formula. Particularly noticeable is the use of the pre-cadential 6–4. In the classical style, the tonic 6–4 chord tends to be followed by a dominant chord, followed by a resolution to the tonic in root position. Many theorists prefer to regard the tonic 6–4 chord as a dominant chord with a double suspension. This view draws attention to the great psychological instability or strong sense of tendency that this chord evokes for listeners familiar with the Western classical style.

Figure 16.3 shows another example of how Wagner uses the pre-cadential 6–4 formula to set up a strong expectation that is then thwarted at the moment of antici- pated resolution. The first 6–4 chord appears in the fourth measure. Here we see a minor tonic 6–4 followed by a dominant seventh chord. The B-flat minor key-area here has been solidly established: in the preceding measures Wagner resolves an extended dominant minor ninth to the tonic, followed by a diminished-seventh-to- tonic progression. For good measure, Wagner adds a minor thirteenth (D flat) to the dominant harmony in the fourth measure and begins the cliché of following the thirteenth with a passing tone (C) that would normally lead to the tonic pitch (B flat). The passing tone eliminates uncertainty of when the resolution will occur: a tonic chord will surely follow at the beginning of the fifth measure.

But instead of the highly expected resolution to a tonic B-flat minor chord, Wagner surprises us with a chord that shares only one pitch with the expected chord—the pitch F. This pitch should be a stable component of the tonic triad, but instead appears as the seventh of a new secondary dominant chord that tonicizes the unrelated key of C minor. Instead of the anticipated B-flat minor chord, Wagner gives us a dominant minor ninth chord in the key of C. He then reinforces the surprise value by sustaining the unexpected chord for two complete measures.

Wagner then repeats the entire scenario. Using the dominant minor ninth, he tonicizes the key of C minor by going ahead with a dominant–tonic progression, followed by a diminished-seventh-to-tonic progression. By the eighth measure, we once again hear the formulaic pre-cadential 6–4 followed by a dominant seventh with the added minor thirteenth. Once again the cliché resolution of the thirteenth involves a passing tone leading to the presumed tonic. Just as we are certain to hear a C minor resolution in the next measure, Wagner gives us a diminished seventh chord from an extraneous key.

This example is also instructive regarding Wagner's treatment of tonic chords. Figure 16.3 contains four points where a tonicizing dominant or diminished chord leads to an expected tonic. But Wagner has a strong reluctance to place the tonic in root position. The most common root position chord in Wagner is the dominant. The least common root position chord in Wagner is the tonic. Wagner needs the tonic in order to ensure that an appropriate tonicized key schema is evoked for listeners. But by avoiding root position tonics, he maintains a psychological experience of instability. Wagner needs the dominant to evoke the strongest sense of anticipation or tendency. This sense of expectancy is better ensured when the dominant is in root position.

Apart from delayed, elided, abandoned, and thwarted cadences, Wagner sometimes avoids cadences altogether. Consider, for example, the Prelude to act 3 of *Parsifal*. The Prelude has a duration of roughly five and a half minutes, yet there is not a single cadence or cadence-like moment anywhere. The Prelude does not even end with a cadence: it simply "morphs" into the first scene of the final act. Despite the absence of points of repose, Wagner makes use of cadential clichés as the basis for his harmonic writing. Figure 16.4 shows how Wagner uses harmonic progressions with strong cadential implications in a noncadential context.

Wagner approaches the dominant seventh chord in the fourth measure with the diminished seventh and subdominant chords. There is a strong sense of the key of B-flat minor, and the progression evokes a vivid expectation that a tonic resolution will occur on the third beat of the fourth measure. Instead, Wagner interjects a diminished seventh chord, which tonicizes the unrelated key of C minor. Replacing a tonic chord by a diminished seventh from an unrelated key is Wagner's most common form of "deceptive" cadence. But unlike the previous example, this progression is not even a

Figure 16.4
Measures 3 and 4 from the Prelude to act 3 of Wagner's *Parsifal*.

"cadence." There is no pause or catching of breath—no effort to close an idea or delineate a group of notes. It is just one moment in an endless progression of seething harmonies.[7]

One might be tempted to call Wagner's music "noncadential" or even "acadential." But the cadence is not simply an object of cavalier disregard. On the contrary, Wagner displays a consummate mastery of the cadential language inherited from the composers of the classical style. His pre-cadential harmonies follow the most stereotypic patterns to be found in Haydn, Mozart, and Beethoven. Wagner seems to love every aspect of the classical cadence except three: the resolution, the persistent reinforcing of a single key area, and the tendency to interrupt the musical flow. In short, Wagner is attracted to the strong "tending" quality of cadential patterns, but repulsed by the evoking of closure or repose. He makes constant use of cadential elements while pointedly avoiding the actual cadence—the resolution. It would not be inappropriate to characterize this compositional practice as *contracadential*.

In the classical style, cadences provide the principal means for delineating formal segments or sections. However, the McGill University theorist William Caplin has pointed out that not all cadential passages serve such a syntactic function. In many ways, Wagner provides an extreme example: the cadential content is almost entirely divorced from perceptual or formal segmentation.[8]

The passages described above are isolated examples rather than a representative statistical sample of Wagner's music. There are numerous works and passages that employ a more conventional cadential language. Nevertheless, the above examples reflect much of Wagner's mature harmonic style. The examples are highly suggestive in light of what we know about the importance of statistical learning in auditory expectation. Wagner's harmonic practice relies on those elements of Western music that are the most clichéd and so the most evocative. In the classical style, chords like the dominant seventh, the dominant minor ninth, the diminished seventh, and even the tonic 6–4 chord exhibit the most constrained first-order probabilities. From a statistical standpoint, we could call them *tendency chords*. Wagner's music is dominated by such chords. Nor is Wagner's harmony limited to first-order tendencies. In using cadential formulas like the German sixth followed by the tonic 6–4 followed by the dominant, Wagner regularly taps into second- and higher-order probabilities that would have been highly familiar to his nineteenth-century European audience. The phenomenal experiences evoked by Wagner's music are closely linked to his use of statistical patterns of tendency, while avoiding the statistical patterns related to repose or closure.

The psychological effects of this way of composing are noteworthy. For over a century, listeners have been remarkably consistent in describing how Wagner's music makes them feel. The feeling of "endless longing" and "unsettled yearning"[9] can be directly related to statistical learning. Wagner sought out those musical patterns that most evoked strong expectancies. Using delay and misdirection, he sought to heighten the tension that accompanies strong feelings of anticipation. At the same time, he added to the intensity of the experience by avoiding points of closure or repose. Wagner's music "yearns." It is the music of hunger, rather than of fulfillment. It is music that leans and points, portends and implies, urges and compels. To the extent that Wagner avoids cadential resolutions, it is also music that is unrequited. It is music that tempts and titillates, denies and frustrates, deceives and thwarts. Not everyone is comfortable sitting on the edge of their seats. But no Western-enculturated listener can deny the intensity of the Wagnerian experience.

Schoenberg's Contratonal Music

In an often-quoted passage published in 1948, Arnold Schoenberg laid out the logic that led him to his most influential musical invention:

I have stated in my *Harmonielehre* that the emphasis given to a tone by a premature repetition is capable of heightening it to the rank of a tonic. But the regular application of a set of twelve tones emphasises all the other tones in the same manner, thus depriving one single tone of the privilege of supremacy. It seemed in the first stages immensely important to avoid a similarity with tonality. (1948, p. 246)

In the development of the twelve-tone method, Schoenberg (1874–1951) explicitly set out to devise a system that would help circumvent tonal implications in his music. Schoenberg's famous solution to this problem was the precompositional "tone row." The only formal criterion espoused by Schoenberg in creating the tone row was the necessity of circulating through all twelve pitch-classes without omission or later repetition. That is, Schoenberg's method for circumventing tonality consisted of a remarkably simple system that ensured that all pitch-classes would appear with the same frequency.

Figure 16.5
A twelve-tone row that begins with a strong C-major implication and ends with a strong pentatonic sense. From Huron and von Hippel 2000.

Notice that Schoenberg made an explicit perceptual claim in the above quoted
passage. He claimed that the frequent occurrence of a given pitch-class will tend to
confer on it the status of tonic. Some seventy years after Schoenberg composed his
first twelve-tone work, Cornell University psychologist Carol Krumhansl advocated
this same theory based on her experimental evidence. Yet many musicians regarded
her theory as naive, apparently overlooking the fact that Schoenberg's invention of
the twelve-tone row assumed the same theory of tonality.[10]

In chapter 9 we saw that much of our experience of tonality can indeed be traced
to exposure-based statistical learning—in particular, the zeroth-order pitch-class probabilities. But a flat distribution of pitch-classes alone does not guarantee the erasure
of tonality. Even if one cycles through all twelve pitch-classes, it is possible to create
short pitch sequences that evoke "local" key implications. Figure 16.5 shows a hypothetical tone row that has strong tonal connotations—implying first a major scale and
then a pentatonic scale. Although all tone rows exhibit the same uniform distribution
of pitch-classes, it is clear from figure 16.5 that portions of some rows might strongly
evoke or suggest a tonal center. That is, although the row as a whole is tonally ambiguous, portions of the row might well be less ambiguous.

In actual practice, there is more to Schoenberg's approach than merely treating each
pitch roughly equally. Both theoretical works and subsequent perceptual experimentation suggests that tonal implications are also related to pitch successions—apart from
the simple distribution of pitch-classes.[11] Working at Ohio State University, David
Butler and Helen Brown carried out a series of experiments establishing that first-order
pitch relationships influence the perception of tonality when the zeroth-order pitch-
class distributions are held constant.[12] As we saw in chapter 9, pitch-related schemas
are shaped by both first-order pitch relationships as well as zeroth-order pitch-class
frequencies.

If Schoenberg's aim was to avoid evoking a sense of key, then we might expect to
see evidence of this goal at both the global and local level. One might expect to see
efforts on his part to avoid moment-to-moment key-evoking patterns. Recall that the
tonal implications of a group of pitches can be estimated using the Krumhansl–
Schmuckler key-estimation method. Although far from perfect, this method provides
a convenient tool for examining the moment-to-moment tonal implications in twelve-
tone rows.

Table 16.1

Pitch sequence	Key correlation
c g e♭	.89
c g e	.83
c g f	.79
c g d	.79
c g a	.72
c g b♭	.69
c g b	.67
c g a♭	.66
c g f#	.55
c g c#	.51

Consider the pitch sequence C followed by G. These pitches will tend to evoke a C major (or C minor) key for typical Western-enculturated listeners. If a composer were endeavoring to avoid evoking a strong key, what tone would be appropriate for a third ensuing note? We might think that the worst possible continuation would be the pitches E or E flat, as these tones would complete a C major or C minor tonic triad. The pitch F might suggest do–so–fa in C major, or so–re–do in F major. Similarly, the pitches D and A would have fairly strong tonal implications. The pitch B flat would imply a dominant seventh chord in F major or F minor. The pitch F sharp would imply a G-major tonality. The pitch A flat might suggest the key of C minor. The pitch B is consistent with both C major and (perhaps) G major. Of all the possible continuations following C and G, most musicians would consider C sharp to be the best candidate for suppressing any latent tonal implication.

These musical intuitions are echoed by the results of the Krumhansl–Schmuckler key-estimation algorithm—shown in table 16.1. The table shows the maximum key correlation following the addition of the third note indicated. Table items are ordered from the most tonally evocative to the least tonally evocative. The pitch C# is rated lowest. Notice that we can then apply this same technique to determine which pitch would best follow the C#. That is, we could continue to use the Krumhansl–Schmuckler key-estimation algorithm to select each successive pitch in the tone row so as to minimize the local key implications. If we start with a single pitch, we can use this approach to create a "minimally tonal" twelve-tone row.[13] Owing to a series of numerical ties, this procedure in fact leads to several dozen "minimally tonal" tone rows.[14]

The more interesting question is to examine actual compositional practice. In real twelve-tone rows, do ensuing pitches tend to reinforce or efface the implied tonality of the antecedent pitch sequence? Do the actual tone rows used by Schoenberg tend to show evidence of such moment-to-moment minimization of tonal implications?

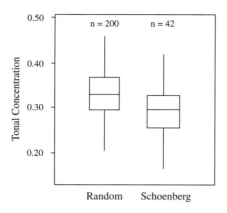

Figure 16.6

Box plots comparing random twelve-tone rows with actual twelve-tone rows composed by Arnold Schoenberg. Random twelve-tone rows exhibit significantly greater tonal concentration than the composed tone rows. This result suggests that Schoenberg explicitly organized his tone rows so as to minimize possible local tonal implications. The actual tone rows are consistent with a "contratonal" compositional goal.

Paul von Hippel and I tested this hypothesis. We used a collection of forty-two twelve-tone rows—all of the tone rows used in Schoenberg's dodecaphonic compositions.[15] We also generated 200 random tone rows as "controls." The research question was formulated as follows: on the basis of tonal implications alone, can we distinguish the random tone rows from the tone rows actually used by Schoenberg?

We calculated the "tonal concentration" for each twelve-tone row by averaging the maximum key correlation for all successive pitch-class subsets. The results are displayed in the boxplots of figure 16.6. Each boxplot presents five pieces of information. The horizontal line through the middle of the box represents the mean or average value. The box itself outlines values spanning one standard deviation above and below the mean. Roughly 70 percent of the measurements fall within the box. The vertical line above and below the box extend to the highest and lowest values measured.

The results show that Schoenberg's tone rows have significantly lower tonal concentrations than random tone rows. This result suggests that Schoenberg actively sought to minimize possible tonal implications within his tone rows. Most twelve-tone rows contain short segments that tend to imply or evoke a sense of tonal area or key. But in composing his twelve-tone music, Schoenberg avoided such tone rows. A typical example is shown in figure 16.7. This tone row, from Schoenberg's opus 24 *Serenade*, has a characteristically low tonal concentration. Unlike the tone row shown in figure 16.5, there is little sense of key evoked by the moment-to-moment succession of pitches.[16] In some ways, this result shouldn't be surprising. After all,

Figure 16.7
Tone row from Arnold Schoenberg's *Serenade*, op. 24 (fourth movement, "Sonett"). The row exhibits very little local aggregate key correlations with the Krumhansl–Kessler key profiles.

Schoenberg explicitly claimed that his goal was to write music that avoided tonal implications.

A common criticism levied at Schoenberg was that his musical organization was driven by formalist conceptions entirely devoid of perceptual considerations. Our study of Schoenberg's twelve-tone rows suggests that it is a mistake to regard his music as unrelated to perception. In fact, Schoenberg's twelve-tone rows show a strong link to perceptual research on tonality: the shadow of learned major and minor key schemata is evident in the detailed construction of these precompositional rows. Tonality is present—albeit as part of a sort of reverse psychology.[17]

Schoenberg knew what he was doing. He articulated a perceptual–aesthetic goal of writing music that avoided tonal implications. In the first instance, his "method of composing with twelve tones" is a remarkably effective, simple, yet perceptually grounded technique that contributes to the achievement of this goal. By cycling through all twelve pitch-classes, Schoenberg ensured a "flat" pitch-class distribution that confounds the evoking of a major or minor key schema.[18] But Schoenberg went further. In creating his twelve-tone rows, he purposely avoided those rows that contained segments that might evoke momentary key implications. Both the concept of the twelve-tone row and the pitch-to-pitch construction of his rows are in accord with his espoused goal of avoiding tonality.

Schoenberg himself disapproved of the term "atonal" as a description for his music. As we have seen, there are good reasons for agreeing with Schoenberg's objection: tonality is not irrelevant to his music. A more accurate description of the pitch-related aspects of his twelve-tone music is *contratonal*.[19]

Of course the avoidance of tonality was not the only aesthetic goal Schoenberg pursued in his twelve-tone compositions. There are other factors influencing the organization of Schoenberg's twelve-tone rows—not all of which pertain to avoiding tonal implications. Throughout the history of serial music, composers have been attracted to various formal properties of tone rows, including various symmetries and other phenomena. Schoenberg's music exhibits evidence of both formalist concepts as well as perceptual and psychological considerations.

There is no mystery about the psychological consequences of this way of composing. If any listener applies a key-related schema to the listening experience, then their pitch predictions will fail miserably. Using a major or minor schema to predict Schoenberg's pitches will not just prove unreliable: the predictive accuracy will be worse than chance. Without accurate expectations, there will be no successful prediction effect. As a result, tonally oriented listening will evoke the *qualia* of confusion and discomfort. These feelings will then be misattributed to the sounds themselves, so the phenomenal impression will be that the music itself is chaotic and ugly.

Nor is the schematic failure limited to key schemas. The average interval size in Schoenberg's twelve-tone works is more than double the average for music from around the world. Only Swiss yodeling regularly contains wider melodic intervals than twelve-tone music. For the listener, this means that even the expectation of pitch proximity is likely to be thwarted. This will contribute further to the impression that the music is chaotic and ugly—at least for the procrustean listener who tries to it hear using conventional schemas.

There is at least one more important violation of expectation that is engendered by twelve-tone music. Recall that people are motivated to attend concerts because of the sweet anticipation of enjoyment. Most listeners have learned to *expect* music to evoke a state of pleasure. Apart from the failure to predict musical events, unsuspecting listeners who attend a concert of twelve-tone music may also feel betrayed by the fact that the music fails to evoke much pleasure. Their imaginative anticipation of musical enjoyment will lead to disappointment. No wonder audiences were so disturbed by Schoenberg's music.

In chapter 7 I suggested that predictive failure is the foremost signal to the brain that a new schema is needed. In the operation of the brain, false prophecies are the hallmarks of false prophets. An important empirical question is whether experience with twelve-tone music leads to the abandonment of scale-related schemes as a way of predicting pitch successions. By circumventing a sense of key, did Schoenberg successfully prevent listeners from using tonal schemas? Do experienced listeners form new pitch-related schemas that are better able to predict pitch sucessions in twelve-tone music? We will return to these questions later in this chapter.

Stravinsky's Contrametric Music

Schoenberg was a fastidious composer: he worried constantly about many organizational details and was haunted by larger questions of his responsibilities as an artist. Igor Stravinsky (1882–1971), by contrast, was much more eclectic and less tormented by compositional decisions. He used innumerable compositional devices and readily adopted (and discarded) ideas from many sources—including twelve-tone organization. His inspiration could come from the simple expedient of playing different chords with his left and right hands on the piano.

Among the most striking aspects of Stravinksy's music are the unusual rhythmic elements. In many passages, Stravinsky maintains a steady beat—sometimes inces-

Figure 16.8
Excerpt from the "Augurs of Spring" from Stravinsky's *Rite of Spring*. The accents notated above the staff identify Stravinsky's actual accent pattern. Accents in parentheses below the staff were generated randomly using a probability distribution for 2/4 metric hierarchy.

santly so. In other passages, the metric and rhythmic elements seem to be tangled messes. Stravinsky's rhythms are often difficult to conduct and play. Stravinsky sometimes struggled with how best to notate them.

By way of illustration, consider a well-known passage from Stravinsky's *Rite of Spring*. In the "Augurs of Spring," the notated meter remains constant, but an unusual accent pattern is superimposed (see figure 16.8). The passage features a single repeated eighth-note chord within a 2/4 meter. Stravinsky stresses a number of the chords as indicated by the accent marks above the staff. Accents in parentheses below the staff were generated randomly using a probability distribution for a 2/4 metric hierarchy similar to the distribution shown in figure 10.3 in chapter 10. In Stravinsky's work, two of the six accents coincide with metric downbeats, while four of the accents coincide with weak metric positions. By contrast, four of the randomly generated accents coincide with downbeats, while the remaining two accents coincide with secondary beat positions.

Using a zeroth-order metrical distribution we can calculate the information content for both the actual accent pattern composed by Stravinsky and the random (control) pattern. For Stravinsky's pattern, the zeroth-order information is 2.31 bits. For the random pattern, the zeroth-order information is 1.73 bits. Could it be that Stravinsky's accents are less predictable than randomly generated accent patterns? A better approach to this question would look at the relationship between successive accents rather than focusing on zeroth-order probabilities. In chapter 13 I presented some transitional probabilities for first-order onset distributions. Recall, for example, that an onset on the third beat of a quadruple meter tends to be followed by an event on the fourth beat. Moreover, an onset on the final sixteenth of a measure virtually ensures that an event will occur on the downbeat of the next measure (see figure 13.2). Using comparable statistics we can calculate the first-order probabilities for the accent patterns shown above.

Consider first the first-order probabilities for the random accent pattern shown under the staff in figure 16.8. For the random accent pattern, the average transitional probability is 0.40 (1.32 bits). For Stravinsky's accent pattern, the average first-order transitional probability is 0.01 (6.64 bits). In other words, this randomly generated accent pattern is forty times more probable than Stravinsky's actual accent pattern.

This relationship is not limited to the sample random pattern shown below the staff in figure 16.8. Generating 100 random accent patterns, I calculated the average transitional probability to be 0.41 (1.29 bits). I found that 98 of the 100 random accent patterns exhibited a higher average transitional probability than the actual accent pattern used in this six-bar excerpt from Stravinsky's "Augurs of Spring." Stravinsky's accent pattern is not just improbable, it is less predictable than a random pattern of accents.

Perhaps the most notable characteristic of Stravinsky's music is its irregular metric organization. It is not that Stravinsky avoids pulse: on the contrary, his music typically maintains a constant pulse-stream or tactus. As we saw in chapter 10, meter should be viewed as a system of temporal expectations—a schema for expected event onsets. That is, meter establishes a hierarchy of expectations concerning when events might be likely to occur.

Passages such as the above excerpt from the "Augurs of Spring" are not simply metrically odd. They appear to be *contrametric* in organization. Stravinsky's rhythms make it extremely difficult for first-time listeners to predict the next accented moment. How difficult? Stravinsky's accents are forty times more difficult to predict than a purely random sequence of accented moments generated using a normative metrical distribution. For listeners inexperienced with the modernist aesthetic, the psychological *qualia* evoked by such passages will be dominated by feelings of confusion and chaos.

It bears emphasizing that passages with these features occur only sometimes. Unlike Schoenberg's twelve-tone organization, Stravinsky's contrametric passages do not permeate his music. Contrametric organization is episodic and occasional rather than ubiquitous.

Modernism

Richard Wagner, Arnold Schoenberg, and Igor Stravinsky have long been regarded as among the seminal figures in the development of musical modernism. The above analyses are not intended to be comprehensive studies of their compositional practices. Instead, I have focused on quite narrow aspects: cadential harmony in Wagner, tonal organization in Schoenberg's twelve-tone rows, and rhythmic stress in a distinctive passage by Stravinsky. In each case, we have seen that the compositional practices are consistent with a shared psychological goal. It appears that each of these "modernist" composers was actively endeavoring to create sound patterns that would contradict established expectations.

Of course, earlier composers also engaged in writing passages that thwarted the expectations of experienced listeners—as, for example, in the deceptive cadence. But such breaches of expectation were occasional and fleeting. Composers used them to achieve a momentary effect—often to create the sorts of surprising effects we discussed in chapter 14. With the music of Wagner, however, we see sustained efforts to persistently thwart expected norms. Extraordinary effects become the vernacular language.

I don't think it is a coincidence that Wagner targeted the cadence. As we have seen, the cadence is the most stereotypic and cliché gesture in music. If one's aim is to thwart expectations, then the greatest opportunities are provided by those structures that are the most predictable. In his later works, Wagner's enthusiasm for chromatic harmony ultimately led him to write music in which the sense of key is rendered obscure. Picked up by Gustav Mahler, Anton Bruckner, and the young Richard Strauss, it was this obscuring of tonality that proved to be so compelling for the impressionable Arnold Schoenberg. However, Schoenberg was not content with composing music that merely rendered the key area sometimes vague. With his twelve-tone method, he created a music that was systematically contrary to tonal expectations. This contratonal goal is evident both in the zeroth-order probabilities of the twelve pitch-classes as well as in his first-order choices of successive notes within his tone rows.

While Schoenberg was subverting schemas related to *what* (pitch), Stravinsky was subverting schemas related to *when* (meter). It bears emphasizing that Schoenberg and Stravinsky differed in their zeal for the contrarian aesthetic. Stravinsky wrote contrametric passages only occasionally in his music. By contrast, once Schoenberg had chosen the twelve-tone path, he remained true—rarely deviating from his contratonal mission.

There is a long history of efforts to portray Stravinsky and Schoenberg as contrasting composers. Like many rhetorical polarities, these juxtapositions are usually overstated and oversimplistic. I don't want to give the impression that Schoenberg was exclusively obsessed with the *what* of expectation whereas Stravinsky was exclusively obsessed with the *when* of expectation. Both composers exhibited many, sometimes conflicting, motivations. Schoenberg, for example, introduced several rhythmic novelties, and Stravinsky famously took up twelve-tone composition following Schoenberg's death. However, as a first approximation, this what/when characterization of the two composers seems to have some merit.

Modernism's Reception

The reception of modern music by audiences is illuminating. While Wagner, Schoenberg, and Stravinsky all attracted devoted followers, many other contemporary listeners found their music unpleasant or even loathsome. Even today, despite decades of periodic exposure and the expansion of the modernist language by other composers, many listeners still find the music unpleasant. As we have seen, listeners tend to describe Wagner's music using terms such as "longing" or "yearning." Other evoked *qualia* including unsettling, incessant, or frustrating. Listeners commonly describe Schoenberg's music as angular, confusing, dissonant, or ugly. And Stravinsky's music is commonly described as crude, disorganized, cumbersome, or barbaric. The music created under the contrarian aesthetic is experienced by most listeners as annoying or irritating. This should not be a surprise when the musical organization persistently transgresses the expectations of listeners who are enculturated to Western musical norms—especially the norms of the classical style.

However, another experience is also possible. The very persistence of the contrarian organization provides a novel pattern that some listeners have been able to internalize. Inexperienced listeners find these transgressions unsettling, but at least some experienced listeners adapt to this strategy and learn to expect the unexpected. In chapter 11 we discussed the experimental work of Carol Krumhansl, Gregory Sandell, and Desmond Sergeant.[20] Recall that their listeners divided into two groups when listening to atonal pitch sequences. Some of their listeners continued to hear the sequences according to tonal expectations. However, a second group of listeners had internalized atonal conventions and judged as ill-fitting those pitches that appeared recently in a tone sequence. Krumhansl and her colleagues found that the latter group were musically more highly trained than the former group.

Those who spend a lot of time listening to modern music don't simply form contrarian expectations based on the emergence of a "contrarian schema." Extensive listening experience will also make a listener familiar with individual musical works from the modernist repertoire. As with Max Meyer's oriental-like melodies, repeated exposure will lead to increased liking. Musical literati have typically heard excerpts from the *Rite of Spring* hundreds of times. A teacher of twelve-tone music will probably be highly familiar with specific dodecaphonic works, such as Anton Webern's Concerto opus 24. For these listeners, accurate veridical expectations will temper the violations of common tonal and metric schemas.

Another difference between experienced and inexperienced listeners relates to the sweet anticipation of enjoyment. Experienced listeners know what they are getting into, and so are less prone to a sense of disappointment or betrayal when attending a concert of modern music. A cynic might say their expectations are lowered. Minus the cynicism, I think this is true—but only of the sensory and unconscious cognitive processes involved. The disappointment of an inexperienced listener encountering modern music is, in part, the disappointment of someone receiving *Coquilles Saint-Jacques* when expecting ice cream.

For the musical cognoscenti, the combination of a contrarian schema plus veridical expectations plus lower expectations of being entertained will render modernist works considerably less disturbing. The "sharp edges" that dominate the phenomenal experiences of less experienced listeners will be much duller. This is not to say that experienced listeners to modern music will not retain some of the experiential "sharpness." Like the deceptive cadence, veridical awareness of what is going to happen cannot fully extinguish the normative schematic responses. Similarly, experienced listeners to modern music may continue to feel some of its "edge" without experiencing the trauma that greeted many of the premiere audiences for works like the *Rite of Spring*. More experimental research is needed to determine whether contrarian auditory schemas indeed exist and how widespread they are among listeners.

The reception of modernist music forms a marked contrast with the reception of that other major twentieth-century musical enthusiasm: syncopation. Where musical modernism failed to capture much of an audience beyond the halls of academia, the reception for syncopated music could hardly have been warmer. The language of musical syncopation has been exported around the world and has been wildly successful. Like the contracadential and contratonal efforts of Wagner and Schoenberg, syncopation involves a systematic violation of schematic expectations. Like Wagner's chromatic harmony, syncopated music tends to be syncopated from beginning to end. So why do audiences find syncopation more acceptable than the methods of Wagner or Schoenberg?

The pervasive use of syncopation in some Western music was already at least forty years old at the time Stravinsky was writing his early ballets. Even more so than Stravinsky's contrametric passages, syncopation is an effect that is typically sustained throughout a composition. But syncopation is not contrarian in the sense of turning expectations upside down. Three notable features of syncopation make it more accessible and enjoyable for listeners. The first is that syncopation never eliminates metric schemas. The *when*-related predictive framework we call "meter" remains intact despite the occasional slings and arrows of shifted temporal events. In Stravinsky's contrametric passages, it is often the meter itself that is thwarted, not just particular beat-onsets. A second feature is that the patterns of syncopation are stereotypic and so highly predictable.[21] As we saw in chapter 14, just one or two syncopated rhythms will dominate a given syncopated work. In effect, just a handful of syncopated patterns will provide templates that aid dynamic prediction. Finally, syncopated rhythms are brief:

as temporal patterns they are much more easily coded in short-term memory than, say, a sequence of twelve pitches forming a tone row. Like the deceptive cadence, the effect of syncopation relies on some element of surprise. But unlike the contrarian efforts of composers like Arnold Schoenberg and Igor Stravinsky, the surprises of syncopation remain highly predictable and don't undercut other existing expectational schemas.

As a psychological phenomenon, syncopation is not likely to be unique. There are probably other aspects of musical organization that are ripe for similar treatments. Perhaps timbre, articulation, melodic contour, or the predictability of spatial location might have analogs of syncopation that could prove popular with future audiences.

Reprise

Like most artistic movements, the revolution of "modern art" is extraordinarily rich and multifaceted. It has many dimensions, including historical, political, social, cultural, technological, and institutional aspects. Scholars have offered innumerable interpretations of modernism. "Modernism" was certainly not limited to music; nor was it restricted to the arts.[22] In attempting to build an explanatory account of modern art, it is dangerous to offer glib generalizations. Nevertheless, I think there are some broad patterns that can be identified.

In this chapter I've suggested that, at least in the case of music, there is an important psychological dimension to modernism. There are characteristic features of modern music whose most straightforward interpretation is the goal of *psychological irritation* or *unease*. Many of the musical devices used by Wagner, Schoenberg, Stravinsky, and others make sense only when viewed as serving the goal of psychological disruption through thwarted expectation.

As we saw in earlier chapters, cadences, tonality, and meter are among the most stereotypic and predictable elements to be found in music. If one wants listeners to experience a sense of discomfort or unease, cadences, tonality, and meter are among the best targets a composer might find. For musical humorists, they offer some of the most attractive points of manipulation. It is surely more than a coincidence that three of the foremost figures in the development of musical modernism—Wagner, Schoenberg, and Stravinsky—placed so much emphasis on cadence, tonality, and meter, respectively. In attempting to evoke the subjective experience of "uneasiness," modernist composers were drawn to the "big buttons" provided by the psychology of expectation.

In making my case for a contrarian psychological basis underlying modernism, I have relied on just three composers. Of course this is too small a sample from which to form a reliable generalization about musical modernism. One could imagine making similar contrarian cases for other twentieth-century composers. For example, the music of Edgar Varèse challenged expectations related to musical timbres. Terry Riley violated Western norms of repetition. Miles Davis violated harmonic expectations. John Adams violated genre distinctions between popular and classical music. Filippo Marinetti and John Cage persistently violated audience schemas for what constitutes a musical work. Clearly, further analytic research is needed in order to test this psychological interpretation of modernism.

In discussing twelve-tone music I have largely ignored the wealth of formal properties and relationships that have captured the imaginations of many theorists. The various properties of tone rows and associated pitch-class sets are a proper subject for theoretical and analytic investigation—whatever the origin or purpose of these structures. Nor is it wrong for theorists to offer speculative theories or ideas about how such structures might influence the listening experience. In fact, it is *good* that theorists offer such speculations, since theorizing is essential to furthering our understanding of music. Of course most theories are ultimately shown to be incompatible with empirical observations. The implicit and explicit claims about how certain set-theoretic properties might influence listening attracted the empirical attention of both skeptics and admirers. As we saw in chapter 7, experiments by Francès, Thrall, Largent, Lannoy, Millar, Bruner, Gibson, Samplaski, and others have shown that many of the formal properties of music that have excited theorists are not in fact perceptually salient for the listener. These theoretical failures should not deter theorists from forming or offering new (testable) theories. But empirical failures usually suggest that we cast the net more widely in trying to figure out what is going on.

The evidence suggests that the most important organizational patterns to be found in twelve-tone rows are their contratonal properties. These properties are not just formal abstractions. They are structures that reach directly into the messy world of auditory experience. The actual twelve-tone rows used by Arnold Schoenberg are very much the products of perception: they have "tonality" written all over them. Even the very concept of a twelve-tone row is imbued with the perceptual principles that underlie tonality. Schoenberg's definition of the twelve-tone row was a direct challenge to the zeroth-order pitch-class distributions that we know contribute to the sense of tonality. Moreover, the actual note-to-note transitions used by serial composers again directly challenge the learned first-order pitch successions that also contribute to the perception of tonality.

For decades, music scholars have known that twelve-tone rows make the perception of tonality difficult. But we have failed to investigate in any depth how twelve-tone rows manage to circumvent tonality. It is cognitively inspired theory that has helped to solve the riddle. The pitch sequences are less tonal than random tone rows, which is consistent with a compositional *intent* to create contratonal organizations. The pitch sequences are intentionally difficult to predict—except insofar as sophisticated listeners can learn to expect the unexpected.

In many ways, both Schoenberg's critics and his devotees missed the mark. Schoenberg's critics typically felt that he had violated some natural laws. He was widely thought to have created a "formalist" approach to music making that paid no attention to human perceptual capacities, and that creating a "system" of composition was antithetical to the humanistic spirit. What his critics interpreted as a breach of natural law was simply the fact that they found the music to be psychologically disturbing—an experience, incidentally, that was shared by at least one of Schoenberg's ardent proponents, Theodor Adorno. Schoenberg's defenders either argued that perception was incidental (and perhaps irrelevant) to the artifice of music, or they offered torturous (and often implausible) views of how serial music might be perceived. Schoenberg was not unconcerned with the psychology of the listener. He was wrong about some things, but on other things his intuitions were largely correct. For example, in his *Fundamentals of Musical Composition*, he explicitly raised the issue of what listeners could and could not comprehend, and argued (rightly) that appropriate subdivision facilitates understanding.[23] In his creation of the twelve-tone row, Schoenberg exhibited remarkable sensitivity and intuition regarding human perception. If his aesthetic goal was to create psychological unease, he was masterful in his use of the tools of psychology. On the other hand, Schoenberg's intuitions about human memory were deficient—as, for example, when he believed that future music lovers would be whistling tunes from his works on city streets.

Twelve-tone music is perhaps the clearest example of a psychological structure arising from the contrarian aesthetic. However, a similar pattern is also apparent in the cadential machinations of Wagner, the metric disruptions of Stravinsky, and even the "wrong-note" treatments used by composers like Prokofiev.

In proposing the notion of the contrarian aesthetic, I don't mean to suggest that what motivated modernism was some sort "orneriness" (although I wouldn't discount ornery personalities as a contributing factor). I doubt that modernist composers were more ornery than the composers of previous centuries. I confess that I don't have any intuitions why the contrarian aesthetic found favor among many composers and artists of the early twentieth century. Some well-known theorists have linked modernism with various political interpretations. With Theodor Adorno, for example, one could interpret the contrarian aesthetic as an artistic expression of the alienation thought to necessarily accompany advanced capitalism. Or Italian futurists might have interpreted the contrarian aesthetic as an artistic expression of *machismo*. However, I suspect that these purported motivations are convenient post hoc accounts. I doubt that they played much of a role in composers' thinking. Schoenberg was a monarchist who probably didn't understand Adorno's negative dialectic of "holding up the false to the false."

Perhaps the contrarian aesthetic arose as an unintended by-product of the pursuit of artistic novelty. A spirit of artistic inventiveness might have initially encouraged a certain insensitivity to the psychological experiences evoked by various devices. In the real world, transgressing expectations causes an organism to sit up and take notice. The experiences are memorable, even if they aren't initially all that pleasant. Having inadvertently generated such experiences, these same experiences might then have become the target of further exploration and embellishment. But this suggestion is entirely speculative.

My main point is that a detailed examination of the devices of modern music reveals the hallmarks of psychological intent. If, as several artists argued, the goal was to disturb audiences, then some of the techniques used by composers like Schoenberg and Stravinsky are psychologically consistent with this goal. Even if modernist composers intended to pursue different musical goals from their predecessors, they still resorted to using the same psychological tools in order to evoke particular experiences for their listeners. Schoenberg wielded the same psychological tools of expectation that Mozart did, even if he sculpted very different works. The fact that some listeners are able to internalize the contrarian organization and form repertoire-appropriate expectations is a hopeful sign for the future development of music. If we want music to be all that it can be, then such "advance guards" provide essential explorations.

Scholarship on musical modernism has tended to focus almost exclusively on one of two approaches. One approach emphasizes formalist theoretical analysis. The second approach emphasizes social and political interpretations. In this chapter I have suggested that psychological studies can provide a fruitful third path to understanding musical modernism.

17 A Sense of Future

School children are commonly taught that there are five senses—taste, touch, smell, sight, and hearing. Over the past century, physiologists have established that in fact there exist many more than five. For example, we have a sense of balance (equilibrium) and a sense of body position (proprioception). Even our sense of touch turns out to entail four distinct sensory systems for heat, cold, pressure, and pain.

In many ways, *expectation* can be regarded as yet another sense: a *sense of future*. In the same way that the sense of vision provides the mind with information about the world of light energy, the sense of future provides the mind with information about upcoming events. Compared with the other senses, the sense of future is the closest biology comes to magic. It tells us not about how the world is, but how the world will be. It arose through natural selection's myriad efforts over millions of years to produce organisms capable of clairvoyance and prophecy. A stockbroker might value the ability to predict the future as a way to becoming rich. But for Nature, the value of predicting the future is the more precious gift of living longer.

Our senses are not transparent windows onto the world. Instead, our senses are adaptations that select, distill, augment, and (sometimes) deceive. We tend to accept our sensations as truthful reflections of reality. But in fact, our senses evolved not to decipher the truth, but to enhance our chances of survival and procreation. We perceive "ugliness" even though there is nothing in the world that is objectively ugly. When night falls we perceive the world in shades of gray, but nighttime objects remain just as colorful. We experience the temperature of ocean water as cold, where a whale finds the same water to be warm. We find the smell of roses more attractive than the smell of a dead carcass, and are disgusted to discover that our pet dog has the opposite experience.

Some deceptions are artifacts of the way sensory organs or brains work. For example, the visual system engages in a little creative fiction when it fills in the empty canvas left by the blind spot of the retina. This sort of deception is really an attempt to compensate for a biological design flaw. Similarly, the sense of future deceives us when the onset of an expected stimulus evokes positive feelings toward that stimulus. The positive feelings evoked by the tonic pitch and by the downbeat are artifacts of accurate prediction, not objective properties of the stimuli themselves.

Other deceptions appear to be integral to Nature's blueprint. They are deceptions that enhance the propagation of our genes. When a woman becomes pregnant, for example, she will often exhibit a hypersensitivity to food, especially during the first trimester. Formerly favorite foods may provoke feelings of nausea or disgust. Although these foods would be healthy for her to eat, they sometimes contain small quantities of teratogens that may endanger the health of the developing fetus. Nature follows a conservative path by promoting picky eating and frequent purgings. The woman's aesthetic experience of food is deliberately warped to conform to Nature's goals.[1]

Similarly, the sense of future regularly deceives us when we are surprised or startled. The vast majority of startling stimuli are utterly innocuous, but the sense of future amplifies and exaggerates the feelings of danger. Evolution has determined that it is better to be conservative rather than realistic: it is better to be wrongly startled a thousand times than to miss the one situation where being startled preserves life. Visiting a city park with a handful of peanuts, we can marvel at the extraordinary caution of a hungry squirrel in accepting the food. The squirrel will bolt at the slightest provocation. But when it comes to the experience of surprise, humans are just as tightly wound as any skittish squirrel.

In this book I have suggested that the psychology of expectation shapes many aspects of our lives. In drawing information from the world, our attention waxes and wanes according to what the world has to say and when the world might speak to us. In preparing to act in the world our arousal rises and falls according to what we anticipate will be appropriate responses. We imagine various future scenarios and in so doing experience muted feelings that help us choose between different courses of action. We feel the mental and corporal tensions that sometimes precede anticipated moments—moments that may or may not arrive. Many feelings are a direct consequence of expectation, including surprise, anticipation, suspense, boredom, comfort, and sleepiness. Expectation also plays a leading role in many other emotional experiences, such as awe, chills, and laughter.

In the first chapter I suggested that it is no coincidence that the performing arts have figured prominently in attempts to shape human emotional experiences. Since expectations can lead to different emotions, the manipulation of expectation provides one of the most potent resources available for playwrights, novelists, poets, film directors, choreographers, comedians, theatrical magicians, and others. Compared with the other arts, music has perhaps faced the most onerous challenges since music relies predominantly on abstract nonrepresentational sounds. But, as argued by Leonard Meyer half a century ago, the psychology of expectation provides an ample starter-kit with which musicians can work their wonders.

As we have seen, expectation appears to shape many aspects of musical organization. I have suggested that tension and resolution, tendency, syncopation, garden paths, deception, closure, stylistic cross-over, and other phenomena relate directly to expectation. Many common musical devices, such as anticipations, suspensions, and cadential formulae, appear to owe their origins to schematic expectation, as do large-scale structures such as genres and styles. Tonality is a manifestation of *what*-related schemas, whereas meter is a manifestation of *when*-related schemas. I have also suggested that patterns of repetition and form, motivic structure, and ostinatos are all linked to dynamic expectancy.

Two general lessons might be highlighted from among the arguments presented in this book. The first is that many musical devices can be plausibly traced to the "deep structure" of evolutionary psychology. The mental mechanisms involved in musical expectation are biological adaptations that arose through natural selection. At the same time, musical expectations are intimately linked to culture. The expectations listeners form echo the structures of the acoustical worlds they inhabit. In the case of music, those acoustical worlds are defined largely by culture. Both culture and biology shape the phenomenal experience of musical expectation.

Summary of the ITPRA Theory

At the core of this account of musical expectation lies my ITPRA theory of general expectation. The ITPRA theory is admittedly somewhat complicated; but by itself, complexity doesn't make the theory less plausible. In fact, in linking the worlds of biology and culture, one shouldn't be surprised that a proposed theory has a lot of parts.

Unfortunately, the greater the number of parts, the greater the likelihood for making mistakes. Having identified and discussed many aspects of the ITPRA theory of expectation, it is useful to gather together all of the main points. The following numbered summary is intended to clarify the logic of my theory. This summary should also help to expose weaknesses, inconsistencies, gaps in logic, and other problems. I also hope that this summary can provide a guide for which parts of the theory are most in need of empirical testing. After the summary, I will provide some further discussion regarding the musical repercussions of the theory.

Prediction

1. The ability to anticipate future events enhances survival in three main ways. First, accurate expectations improve perception by anticipating the *what, when*, and *where* of likely stimuli. Second, accurate expectations speed up appropriate motor responses. Third, expectations help us select more favorable futures by allowing us to anticipate

the consequences of various actions. The mental systems involved in anticipating the future probably arose through evolution by natural selection.[2]

2. Accurate prediction is biologically valuable even when the predicted outcome is unpleasant.

3. It is possible to form relatively accurate expectations only because real-world events exhibit structure. The capacity to form expectations relies on the brain's ability to create mental structures that emulate environmental structures. Ideally, the principles underlying expectations would precisely reflect the actual principles that structure the environment in a particular way.[3] For example, if gravity operates according to an inverse-square law, then mental intuitions about gravity would ideally be based on the same inverse-square principle.

4. Expectations are automatic, ubiquitous, and (mostly) unconscious. We cannot turn off the mind's tendency to anticipate events and we are usually unaware of the mind's disposition to make predictions. Except when we are surprised, or when the outcomes are important, we may not be cognizant of the specific predictions our minds make. Minds are disposed to anticipate all types of stimuli—even those stimuli (like music) that appear to be unimportant for survival.

ITPRA

5. The psychological responses to expectation can be classified into five categories, grouped into *pre-outcome* and *post-outcome* phases. In the *pre-outcome* phase, an individual might consciously imagine different possible outcomes and vicariously experience some of the feelings that would be expected for each outcome. This *imagination response* provides an important mechanism for motivating an individual to take courses of action that increase the likelihood of a positive outcome.

6. Also in the *pre-outcome* phase, appropriate states of arousal and attention need to be evoked in preparing for an imminent event. These preparations can include corporeal changes (such as changes in muscle tone or respiration) or changes in mental engagement (such as increased vigilance). These changes are accompanied by distinctive feelings. This *tension response* tailors the arousal and attention to match the degree of uncertainty and the importance of the possible outcomes. The response becomes more marked as the anticipated moment of the outcome approaches. The tension response is commonly manifested as stress.

7. In the *post-outcome* phase, the accuracy of an individual's predictions is assessed in the *prediction response*. A positive response occurs when the outcome matches the individual's expectation. A negative response arises when the outcome is unexpected.

8. When a stimulus appears, a "quick and dirty" response is evoked. This *reaction response* is defensive in function. At the same time, a slower process of cognitive evalu-

ation is initiated that takes into account complex social and situational factors. This *appraisal response* is able to inhibit or facilitate the initial reaction response, or evoke a wholly different response. The purpose of these emotions is to act as behavioral motivators, reinforcing the achievement of positive states, and punishing the achievement of negative states.

9. For a fast reaction response to remain effective in dealing with danger, it must be protected from habituation or unlearning. Reaction responses must be evoked reliably, even when there is an overwhelming history of false alarms. The vast majority of these responses are ultimately inhibited or suppressed by the slower, more accurate, appraisal process. As a result, fast reaction responses are typically short lived and rarely reach conscious awareness. Our brains and bodies engage in frequent skirmishes with ghostly dangers while we remain blissfully unaware.

10. The distinction between fast and slow responses reflects the neurological embodiment of two usually contradictory goals: (1) the need to respond as *quickly* as possible to dangerous circumstances, and (2) the need to judge as *accurately* as possible the value of some event or situation.

11. The overall feeling state evoked by events arises from a combination of the imagination, tension, prediction, reaction, and appraisal responses. These responses may all be positively valenced, or they may all be negatively valenced. But most experiences involve a complex mix of positively and negatively valenced responses.

Learning

12. Theoretically, expectations might have exclusively innate or learned origins. When an environment remains stable over millions of years, it is possible for efficient innate expectations to evolve. However, when an environment is highly variable, the capacity to form expectations through *learning* provides a better biological strategy.[4]

13. In human hearing, innate processes are evident in such auditory functions as the *orienting response* and in the *azimuth* component of *localization*. However, the existing research implicates learning as the preeminent source for auditory expectations. This suggests that the auditory environments in which humans evolved were highly variable. Sounds that in one context might indicate danger might, in another context, indicate opportunity.

14. Whether innate or learned, expectations are typically formed through exposure to an environment. Expectations arise through a process of *induction,* in which generalizations are formed from a finite number of specific experiences. Since inductive inference is known to be fallible, the generalizations formed through listener experience are also fallible. That is, the principles underlying expectations are likely to be imperfect approximations of the actual principles that shape the world.[5]

15. From a broad sample of melodies, several simple principles have been identified that appear to underlie the objective organization of certain types of music. One principle is the tendency for successive pitches to be relatively close. This tendency is probably a consequence of physical constraints on changes of frequency for vibrating objects. Experienced listeners appear to form an appropriate expectation for *pitch proximity*. A second principle is that pitches exhibit a *central tendency*. Again, this tendency is probably a consequence of physical constraints on vibrating objects. A mathematical consequence of central tendency is *regression to the mean*: extreme values (far from the mean) tend to be followed by less extreme values (closer to the mean). However, experienced listeners do not form the precisely appropriate expectation for melodic regression. Instead, experienced listeners expect *post-skip reversal*—an approximation of melodic regression. A third principle is that large intervals tend to ascend while small intervals tend to descend. Again, experienced listeners do not form the precisely appropriate expectations. Instead, experienced listeners expect *step-inertia*—which appears to arise from a combination of the tendency for pitch proximity and the tendency for intervals to descend. A fourth principle is that melodic phrases in Western music tend to exhibit an *arch-shaped contour*. Experienced listeners expect pitches to descend in the latter half of phrases, but they do not expect the pitches in the first half of phrases to ascend. That is, experienced listeners appear to expect *late phrase declination*.[6]

Statistical Learning

16. In a stable environment, the most frequently occurring events of the past are the most likely events to occur in the future. Thus, a simple yet optimum inductive strategy is to *expect the most frequent past event*. Acquiring such knowledge through exposure is referred to as *statistical learning*. The simple frequency of isolated events ("zeroth-order probability") appears to provide the foundation for unconsciously learned expectations.

17. An example of frequency-dependent learning in music can be seen in the phenomenon of *absolute pitch*. Those individuals who acquire this remarkable ability to identify pitches out of context are faster when identifying pitches that occur frequently (like G), and are slower when identifying less common pitches (like G#).[7] Another example of frequency-dependent learning in music is the sensitivity of listeners to the distribution of scale degrees—as documented by Carol Krumhansl and elaborated by Bret Aarden.

18. Zeroth-order or noncontexual statistical learning is most clearly evident in the assumptions listeners make about how a musical work is likely to begin. For example, Western-enculturated listeners tend to assume that music will begin with pitches in the central pitch region, that the music is more likely to be in a duple rather than a triple meter, and that the music will be in a major rather than a minor key.

19. In addition to zeroth-order probabilities, listeners also learn the contextual or contingent probabilities of neighboring or co-occurring events. The distance separating contingent events can range from immediate neighbors to long-range relationships. In addition, contingent probabilities can be influenced by the number of prior events that combine to influence a particular ensuing event. These probability orders can range from a single preceding event (first-order probability) to many preceding events (higher-order probabilities).

20. Direct experimental evidence for contingent-frequency learning in tone sequences can be seen in the work of Jenny Saffran, Richard Aslin, and their collaborators. Contingent-frequency learning in music is evident in the probability of various scale-degree successions, such as the tendency for chromatic tones to lead to specific diatonic neighbors.[8]

Emotion

21. Expectations provoke emotional responses. The evolutionary purpose of emotions is to act as motivational amplifiers that encourage behaviors presumed to be adaptive while discouraging behaviors presumed to be maladaptive. There are no neutral emotions: emotions are either positive or negative (although both positive and negative emotions can be evoked concurrently).

22. Expectations that prove to be correct represent successful mental functioning. Successful predictions are rewarded by the brain.[9]

23. Successful expectations can be measured: when a person's expectations are correct, information related to the expectation will be processed faster and more accurately.

24. Successful predictions evoke positive feelings, which we may then mistakenly attribute to the outcome itself, a phenomenon known as *misattribution*. As a result, we tend to prefer a predicted outcome. In addition, if we repeatedly make successful predictions for a given outcome, then the predicted outcome can itself evoke positive feelings through classical conditioning.

25. Because commonplace events tend to be more predictable, there is a tendency to prefer frequently occurring stimuli (formerly, the *exposure effect*). However, the preference for such stimuli arises from *predictability* rather than frequency (*prediction effect*).

26. An example of the *prediction effect* in music can be found in the phenomenon of tonality. Once a tonal context is established, listeners tend to experience some pitches as more pleasant or preferable than others. Another example of the prediction effect is found in the phenomenon of meter. Once a metrical context is established, listeners tend to experience events that occur at the most expected moments to be more pleasant or preferable to other states.

27. Although expected events are generally preferred, highly predictable environments can lead to reduced attention and lowered arousal—often leading to sleepiness.

This tendency can be counteracted to some extent by using energetic sounds, or other sounds that have an innate tendency to increase arousal.

28. Expectations that prove to be incorrect represent failures of mental functioning. Unsuccessful expectations evoke a form of mental "punishment," typically in the form of stress. Failures of expectation provide important information that helps brains select between competing mental representations for events. Mental representations that prove to be poor future predictors atrophy.

Surprise

29. A classic response to expectational failure is *surprise*. The open mouth and wide eyes characteristic of surprise originate in increased arousal (an open mouth facilitates oxygen uptake) and increased attention (open eyes facilitate gathering information).

30. Although it is possible to have "good surprises," the surprise itself always indicates a biological failure to anticipate the future. Thus, surprises activate a fast neural pathway that initiates one of three conservative responses: *fight, flight,* or *freeze*. These responses can be subsequently suspended, inhibited, or amplified by another reaction response or by a slower appraisal process. In the case of music, appraisal responses typically conclude that the situation is safe, and so the fast responses are rapidly extinguished.

31. The *fight* response initiates an aggressive display characterized by piloerection (hair standing on end). The *flight* response causes increased arousal, including panting. The *freeze* response initiates rapid inspiration and/or breath-holding. For surprises that are subsequently appraised as nonthreatening, these three responses are typically manifested as *frisson, laughter,* or *awe,* respectively.

32. It is extremely difficult to "unlearn" fast reaction responses, but it is beneficial to learn to recognize new circumstances where a reaction response should be evoked ("quick to learn, slow to unlearn"). One of these circumstances is when worldly events fail to conform to expectations. Learned *schemas* provide the basis for recognizing such failures, and so learned schemas provide the basis for evoking some of the fast reaction responses. Other reaction responses may be innate (such as reacting to loud sounds).

Qualia

33. Apart from positive or negative emotions, musical events commonly evoke distinctive feelings or *qualia*. Many of these feelings can be plausibly attributed to statistical properties of the stimulus in a particular context. The most important statistical properties include the zeroth-order probability of a stimulus, first-order tendencies between successive stimuli, and the likelihood that no further stimuli will occur. Some of the *qualia* that can be linked to these statistical properties include feelings of uncer-

tainty, inevitability, tendency, stability, mobility, yearning, anticipation, premonition, surprise, abruptness, weirdness, climax, incompletion, and closure.

Memory

34. In biological systems, the sole purpose of memory is to help future behaviors to be more adaptive.

35. There are different types of memory, such as episodic memory, semantic memory, short-term memory, and working memory. Semantic memory is the basis for schematic expectations. Episodic memory is the basis for veridical expectations. Short-term memory is the basis for dynamic expectations. Working memory is the basis for conscious or ruminative expectations. Schematic expectations represent generalizations learned from a lifetime of exposure. Veridical expectations represent invariant sequences learned from frequent exposure to a particular stimulus. Dynamic expectations arise from the immediately preceding experience. Conscious expectations arise from conscious reflection or thought.

36. Different types of expectation may predict different outcomes. In some cases an event can be both simultaneously surprising and unsurprising. For example, a deceptive cadence doesn't entirely lose its "deceptive" character, even when a listener's familiarity with a work indicates that a deceptive cadence is imminent. As a result, the same event may evoke a schematic surprise without evoking a veridical surprise (and vice versa).

37. There is no objective distinction between a *work* and a *style*. These distinctions depend on an individual's listening experience interacting with the structure of memory. A sound experience is deemed a work when it is coded veridically; the sound experience is deemed a style or genre when it is coded schematically. Similarly, the difference between a *motive* and a *figure* is that motives are veridically coded whereas figures are coded schematically or dynamically.

38. Often, certain patterns of organization are evident only in a particular context or environment. It is important for an organism to learn to distinguish these environments and to prevent inferential lessons from influencing expectations that pertain to other environments.[10] Neural mechanisms exist that help segregate different contexts (*cognitive firewalls*). Such barriers allow listeners to distinguish various kinds of musical experiences, including styles and genres. Each listener develops a unique stylistic taxonomy that reflects his or her particular history of musical exposure.

39. At least three aspects of memory can be plausibly viewed as biological responses to the problem of induction. When emotionally charged situations lead to associative learning, *misattribution* arises when the brain casts a wide net in order to increase the likelihood of catching a true correlate. *Cognitive firewalls* endeavor to avoid overgeneral learning by limiting the scope of inductive lessons. Finally, the preservation of *episodic*

memories allows potentially erroneous inductive generalizations to be revisited in light of a reinterpreted behavioral history.

Mental Representation

40. Expectations rely on underlying mental representations. In the case of pitch, for example, hypothetical representations include absolute pitch, pitch-class, scale degree, interval, interval class, scale-degree dyad, interval dyad, contour, and so on. Several representations may operate concurrently in the forming of expectations. It appears that not every listener has access to the same representations. For example, most people do not have access to an absolute pitch representation. Moreover, musicians with absolute pitch often exhibit inferior interval abilities compared with non-AP musicians. Such differences may originate in the individual listener's history of auditory exposure. A major difference between AP possessors and nonpossessors is that AP possessors tend to have been exposed to musical works early in life that were always in the same key. It is possible, as argued by Otto Abraham, that the practice of singing songs in different keys reduces the value of coding absolute pitch. If absolute pitch has little predictive value for a listener then it would make sense for the listener's auditory system to ignore such pitch height information.

41. Different mental representations can lead to different expectations. For example, one element (such as pitch-class) may be highly expected, whereas another element (such as contour) may be highly unexpected. That is, apart from the different types of memory, divergent predictions might also arise from different representations.

42. Different listeners may have different expectations. Individual differences may be attributable to four possible sources. (1) Listeners may differ in their underlying representation codes. For example, one listener may favor an absolute pitch representation whereas another listener favors a scale degree representation. (2) Listeners differ in their exposure to music, so some listeners will have had less opportunity to develop appropriate schemas. (3) A listener may fail to distinguish expectational sets that may be appropriate for different genres of music. For example, as Krumhansl has shown, some listeners may continue to apply a tonal schema to an atonal listening experience. (4) Listeners may differ in the accuracy of their predictive heuristics. For example, it is theoretically possible that a listener experiences melodic contours in accordance with a regression-to-the-mean heuristic rather than a post-skip-reversal heuristic.

Aesthetic Opportunities

43. The overall feeling state evoked by some event appears to be strongly influenced by *contrast*. If we initially feel bad and then feel good, the good feeling tends to be stronger than it would be had the good experience occurred without the preceding

bad feeling. Conversely, if we initially feel good and then feel bad, the bad feeling tends to feel worse. The five components of the ITPRA theory provide many possible interactions that might lead to such *contrastive valence*.

44. The delaying of an expected outcome has the effect of extending the period of tension. When the outcome finally appears, the resulting contrastive valence often increases the sense of pleasure evoked by the resolution. Many performance and compositional techniques can be regarded as efforts to delay expected outcomes. Such delaying techniques tend to produce their greatest effect when the passage is highly stereotypic or cliché.

45. Not all repetitions lead to the prediction effect, and not all violations of expectation lead to contrastive valence. Repetition can lead to (unconscious) habituation and to (conscious) boredom. Violations of expectation can lead to irritation and annoyance.

46. When the circumstances are appropriate, listeners may come to expect the unexpected. That is, a sort of "reverse psychology" may arise. The twelve-tone rows of Arnold Schoenberg are organized in a manner consistent with such a reverse psychology.

47. The fact that learning plays a preeminent role in forming expectations, in addition to the fact that expectations can adapt dynamically to ongoing stimuli, suggests that there exist considerable opportunities to craft a range of musics for which listeners may form appropriate expectations.

Some Musical Repercussions

It is important to understand that this book has focused on those aspects of musical emotion that relate only to expectation. Music can also evoke emotions through many other means—apart from whether sounds are expected or not. Sounds often have distinctive timbral qualities that we experience as harsh, cute, urgent, sexy, mellow, disgusting, edgy, and so on.[11] Sounds can be uncomfortably loud or annoyingly quiet. Emotional reactions can arise to sonorous dissonance or consonance.[12] Clear localization cues are experienced as pleasant (hence listeners prefer stereo over mono reproduction). Elsewhere I have described how clear part-writing can evoke pleasure for listeners.[13] Listeners can become habituated, bored, or irritated by sounds. Emotions can arise from empathetic performance nuance, dynamic shape, tempo, and other factors. Most of all, emotions can arise from a vast range of learned associations.[14]

If the theory I have proposed in this book were true, it would hold a number of repercussions for composers, performers, music theorists, historians, ethnomusicologists, and aesthetic philosophers. Like all theories, there will be problems—including, perhaps, problems that could render the entire approach wrong-headed. Many of my fellow music theorists are apt to find my "psychological" approach worrying, whereas many psychologists will be uncomfortable with my efforts to link the cognitive aspects of expectation to evolutionary origins. Given that my theory (like any theory) might completely miss the mark, it is nevertheless worthwhile to explore some of its repercussions, as the repercussions themselves might help clarify how the theory is problematic or how it might be improved. The following discussion assumes the theory to be correct and offers appropriate lessons for composers and performers, music theorists, historians, ethnomusicologists, and aesthetic philosophers.

Repercussions for Composers and Performers: Choreographing Expectations

My theory does assume that music often evokes pleasure in listeners. But there is no requirement whatsoever that artists create works of art that evoke pleasure. Art has no predefined function, which means that it can be harnessed to serve any number of purposes—including no purpose at all. Sometimes art is successful because it educates us, inspires us, challenges us, disturbs us, or even insults us. But if art never offered any element of pleasure, it would cease to play much role in human affairs. Of course there are different ways to evoke pleasure.

In the case of music, not all pleasure arises from the experience of listening. One can delight in a concept, such as the philosophical perspective underlying John Cage's *4'33"* ("Silence"). As a music scholar, I regularly take pleasure in ideas about how works are constructed. Ideas about music are sometimes more compelling than the associated sounds. Sometimes I enjoy the social atmosphere of a concert more than the music. Sometimes I prefer reading a score to listening to it. Sometimes I crave a radically different musical experience. Like most music teachers, my collection of sound recordings is filled with oddities that provide compelling class demonstrations, but these are typically not recordings that I listen to for the simple pleasure of listening. If music is to remain compelling as a sonic experience, then at least some of its pleasure must arise through ordinary stream-of-consciousness listening.

With regard to expectation, I have proposed two phenomena that tend to evoke pleasure. First, I have suggested that accurate predictions are rewarded through the prediction effect. The most predictable events are the events that occur most often. Commonly experienced sounds or sound patterns are more likely to evoke a positively valenced affect. In pointing this out, I don't mean to suggest that listeners don't also experience habituation and boredom. But the extraordinary repetitiveness found throughout the world's music is more apt to please listeners than bore them.

Second, I have suggested that negatively valenced feelings can form a backdrop against which positively valenced feelings seem even more positive. This phenomenon of contrastive valence occurs in two general circumstances. When events are surprising, the surprise evokes an initially negative limbic response which in some circumstances can be displaced by subsequent reactive or appraisal responses that are more positive. When events are fully expected, the feeling of anticipation evokes a somewhat negative preparatory tension, which is often displaced by subsequent positive feelings arising from the prediction effect.

If a musician wishes to evoke a predictive reward, then musical events must be made predictable. The most straightforward way of creating predictable events is to follow existing musical conventions such as relying on traditional scales, meters, timbres, harmonies, genres, and styles. That is, events are more predictable when a musician taps into already existing listening schemas. The maxim "Know your audience" provides a useful reminder that it is the schemas of listeners, not the musician's own schemas, that are pertinent. Predictable events include both zeroth-order probabilities (such as the prominence of the dominant pitch and the downbeat) and higher-order conditional probabilities (such as tendency tones, anticipations, fills, periods, and forms). Sometimes it is possible to borrow nonmusical schemas to help increase musical predictability. For example, one might use the characteristic speech rhythms within some linguistic population to increase the predictability of musical rhythms.

A second way to make events predictable is to use repetition within musical works. Repetition facilitates the development of dynamic expectations. The work itself then provides background experiences that increase the predictability of subsequent events as the work unfolds. In poetry, such predictability can be achieved through repeated metric feet and the use of rhyme schemes. In music, using repeated figures, ostinatos, motives, themes, and rhythmic patterns will increase the likelihood of predictive success for listeners.

In addition to repetition, events can be made more predictable within works by creating passages that are *similar*. Where continued repetition ultimately leads to boredom or habituation, similarity allows elements of novelty to be introduced that help forestall these potentially negative experiences while simultaneously allowing some predictive accuracy. Variation techniques such as the ground bass, the sequence, modal and tonal transposition, various forms of embellishment, reharmonization, dynamic contrast, and other techniques can preserve dynamic predictability while circumventing boredom.

For composers who aim to evoke pleasure, the more a musical work departs from schematic conventions, the greater the importance of repetition and self-similarity. This principle also applies to listeners: when experiencing the music of another culture for the first time, the most accessible works will be those that tend to be the most repetitive and self-similar. Of course, the capacity for a work to evoke pleasure will also increase with repeated listenings.

Tension-related contrastive valence can be evoked by delaying the onset of highly expected events. This can be achieved through simple pauses, using slower tempos, or using a progressive slowing or *ritardando*. Other delaying tactics include interposing embellishments, Neapolitan chords, and other interjections. In light of the predictability of cadences, cadences are especially suitable sites for introducing delays. The most predictable aspect of the cadence is the final chord or note. So the greatest potential for tension occurs immediately prior to this event. The characteristic slowing of natural bodies (such as rolling objects) provides a familiar temporal schema: emulating the natural trajectory of a slowing object allows for increasing delay while simultaneously making the delay process itself predictable. If the delay is excessively long, then the listener may lose the feeling of tendency, and so the effect will be lost.

Another way to evoke contrastive valence is through specially crafted surprises. By itself, surprise induces a form of fear. But "pleasant" surprises can be produced by ensuring that the initially negative response is superceded by an innocuous or positive response. Surprises might involve unexpected pitches (such as appoggiaturas), unexpected chords (such as chromatic mediant chords), unexpected chord progressions (such as deceptive cadences), unexpected event timings (such as syncopations), unexpected sonorities (such as suspensions), unexpected dynamics (such as *subito piano*), or various other techniques. Depending on the strength or magnitude of the violated expectation, the music can evoke frisson, laughter, or awe. If the violation is especially large, listeners are apt to experience the event as "weird."

Musicians have exploited many of the psychological phenomena related to expectation, but there remain many unexplored opportunities. Since auditory expectation is preeminently a matter of learning, there is plenty of scope for musicians to create new listener expectations. Where this process is most evident is in the perpetual creation of new musical styles. Each new style builds a distinctive schematic context that provides new opportunities for both thwarting expectations and confirming expectations. Musicians have the freedom to create new styles, but the listener's penchant for predictability restrains the speed with which new styles can be spawned. Musicians create musical culture, but not just as they please.

In addition to the repercussions for practicing musicians, the psychology of expectation has repercussions for how we study music. There are pertinent lessons for music theorists, historians, aesthetic philosophers, and ethnomusicologists.

Repercussions for Music Theory: Form and Function

Over the centuries, music theorists have identified hundreds of structures and structural devices in music. These structures range in scale from the minuscule to the monumental. Musical structures include various ornaments and embellishments, motivic and thematic structures, chords and chord progressions, phrases, periods, forms, genres, styles, networks of intertextual quotation, allusion, Schenker's *Urlinie*, and many more.

Having identified this cornucopia of structures, the obvious next question relates to purpose. What purpose (if any) do these structures serve? Why do these structures exist? Few topics in arts scholarship are more thorny than the relationship between *form* and *function*. Identifying form is not the same as identifying function. This issue is not limited to the arts, so in seeking some wisdom on this matter we can cast a wide net. In biology, for example, the difference between form and function is formalized in the division between *anatomy* and *physiology*. Anatomy is a descriptive discipline whose purpose is to identify and characterize the component parts of organisms and their interconnections. Physiology is a discipline whose purpose is to decipher how things work. An anatomist will describe some organ such as the kidney, whereas the physiologist will endeavor to explain the purpose and operation of the kidney.

Historically, anatomy has nearly always been more advanced than physiology. That is, in most cases, detailed descriptions of organs existed before anyone had a good idea of what their function was. For this reason, anatomists were held in higher esteem than physiologists throughout much of medical history. Describing biological function is inherently more speculative than describing anatomical form. Nevertheless, the principal motivating interests have been physiological rather than anatomical. Biologists are more interested in understanding how organisms work than in descriptions of their form.

As in biology, the big questions in music pertain to function rather than form. Most music scholars would love to understand how music works. Unfortunately, as in the case of biology, deciphering musical function has proved much more difficult than describing musical form.

A common mistake in thinking about function is to assume that all structures contribute to the same overarching purpose. We will surely be wrong if we assume that all structures serve an aesthetic purpose, or that all structures serve some psychological function. A particular chord arrangement might exist because of a composer's small hands. A particular repeat sign might exist for purely financial reasons. Structures might reflect systems of beliefs, idiomatic aspects of an instrument, economic imperatives, social aspirations, or simply traditional ways of doing things. And, like the human appendix, some common musical structures may serve no purpose at all.

Most music theorists understand that identifying structure is not the same as identifying function. Throughout the latter half of the twentieth century, many music theorists endeavored to avoid making functional claims for the musical structures they described. The functional claims made by Heinrich Schenker at the beginning of the twentieth century have been largely ignored by his followers. Young theorists are taught to avoid "psychologizing" musical structures precisely because this involves making functional claims that are difficult to support. Other theorists retain the word "function" but apply it to the formal relationship between elements without positing any concrete purpose. In other words, over the past half century, music theorists have largely worked on problems of musical "anatomy" (describing the structures of music) rather than problems of musical "physiology" (describing the purpose of these structures). In light of the difficulty of identifying function, many music theorists have accepted that describing structure is the intellectually more defensible occupation.[15]

Despite the sense that music theory ought to focus on structure, it is difficult to avoid wanting to talk about function, origin, or purpose. In the same way that anatomists lapse into physiological speculation, music theorists are frequently tempted to speculate about musical function. The challenge of inferring function from form is not unique to music scholarship. The same problems can be found in fields as diverse as archeology, ethology, jurisprudence, architecture, and neurology. I am persuaded, however, that the most informative lessons about form and function are to be found in the field of physiology. A particularly useful insight can be traced to the esteemed nineteenth-century French physiologist Claude Bernard—and his debate with contemporary anatomists. It is worthwhile spending a few moments to recount an important cautionary tale.

Unfortunately, anatomists often felt that the purpose of an organ was obvious. In the early nineteenth century, for example, biologists were convinced that they understood the function of the lungs. For over a century, they had been aware that oxygen is essential to combustion. They also knew that sugars could be converted to heat and energy in the presence of oxygen. Thus, they argued, obviously, food energy was converted to metabolic energy in the lungs. Moreover, since the exhaled air was warmer than the inhaled air, and the exhaled air contained less oxygen, it seemed clear that metabolic energy was created in the lungs. This view is now known to be false. Metabolic energy is created throughout the tissues of the body. The lungs simply collect and transport one of the essential ingredients—oxygen—but do so only indirectly, through the conveyance of hemoglobin in the bloodstream.

It took Claude Bernard the better part of his life to convince anatomists that they were wrong about the functioning of the lungs. Bernard is celebrated in the history of biology, not just for his physiological discoveries. The principal lesson from Bernard's work was that it is impossible to infer the functioning of some structure without careful experimentation in which conditions are methodically manipulated and the results systematically observed. Bernard vividly exposed the gap between form and function in biology, and he responded to this problem by establishing a set of famous experimental principles that to this day are used by biologists.

Though it is not as dramatic as Claude Bernard's story, music theorists experienced their own epiphany regarding the gap between form and function. We recognized that there isn't a one-to-one relationship between musical structure and function, and we also recognized that not all of the structures evident in music can be related to some purpose, such as social or perceptual goals. As I've noted, the main response to this awareness has been to retreat to the anatomical realm of describing musical structure and structural relationships.

However, as I've said, even for the most careful descriptive theorist it is often difficult to avoid lapsing into the assumption that a particular structure serves some function. For example, a scholar might presume that a particular structure leads to a greater sense of unity or coherence. A more careful scholar would remove the words "sense of" so that it sounds less psychological. Other scholars will avoid making any claim about the structure or structural relationship they describe. But there is still the implication that a particular structure is "good"—or at least "interesting," maybe even "cool." (Not surprisingly, it is difficult to get published if readers don't find a described structure interesting.) But notice that these evaluative terms are extrastructural; they all imply some sort of function.

Times change. My own experience has convinced me that it may be possible to understand the function of some musical structures, such as the anticipation or the deceptive cadence. I think that the tools of empirical research have advanced sufficiently that music theory can once again rekindle the dream of earlier generations of theorists—the goal of understanding how music works its magic. Claude Bernard's experimental methodology provides a useful model and inspiration. Of course the quest to understand musical function using experimental methods will not be without difficulty. But I think that empirical approaches will help music theory reinvigorate our quest to understand musical function.

Note that even if we were to agree that the purpose of music theory ought to be restricted to the task of describing musical structure, there are plenty of obstacles that stand in the way of even this modest path. As long as the task of identifying structures is carried out by human beings, there is the possibility that the structures we identify are subjective appearances rather than objective realities. Many purported patterns of organization are not borne out by careful examination of musical scores or sounds. And several of the patterns purportedly observed about musical organization actually describe the listener's experience instead. In chapter 6 we noted that a person who believes that subjective perception is the same as objective reality is called a *naive realist*. In music theory, naive realism is evident in two assumptions: that the structures we see in the notated music are the ones we experience, and that the structures we experience can be seen in the notation. Those who aim to describe the music as it is can do so only by abandoning the path of naive realism. Sophisticated realism begins by acknowledging the separation between the subjective and objective worlds.

Sophisticated realism is possible only by making use of empirical methods of observation.

Sadly, this is not a new insight. Music psychologists have made these arguments for a long time. In 1938, for example, the music psychologist Carl Seashore concluded his final book by noting that listeners both fail to recognize patterns evident in the music and simultaneously bring things to the experience that are not present in the physical sound. He warned against any assumption that there is a one-to-one relationship between the physical sound and the mental experience of music. The objective and subjective worlds are related but not equivalent.[16]

I think that music theory will benefit greatly by embracing two important lessons that have been hard won in the natural and social sciences. From psychology, music theory will benefit by making a systematic distinction between the world of notational artifacts (or sound recordings) and the world of subjective phenomenal experience. Controlled observation is essential if we want to determine whether a structure exists in sounds, in scores, or in minds.[17] From physiology, music theory will benefit by recognizing that one cannot decipher function through descriptive analysis alone. (Careful description of the human appendix cannot establish that it serves no function.) Experimental manipulation is essential if we want to understand the possible functions of some structure. As Hal Hellman has written regarding Bernard's work, the reason the biomedical world got into trouble was the "belief that structure and function in the human body [are] perfect correlates."[18] Unfortunately, this same misconception has haunted analytic scholarship throughout the arts.

I think that music theorists should continue the task of describing musical structures. But I think we should be frank about our interest in understanding musical function. The task of identifying function will always be difficult and full of opportunities to make mistakes. But the impetus to talk about function is healthy. Until recently, we just didn't have good ways to investigate the matter. In my opinion, if we want to identify musical function we have to heed Claude Bernard's lessons: as music theorists, we need to roll up our sleeves and engage in some experimental work.

Of course, music theorists are free to reject this call and decide to remain "musical anatomists." But if we want to continue talking about form and avoid function, then we need to recognize two facts. First, it will be a constant battle to avoid slipping into functional presumptions. We will have to maintain a perpetual vigil to avoid implying that a particular structure might have one or another function. We will have to avoid any implication that a particular structure makes a piece interesting, good, unified, coherent, pleasant, memorable, well formed, or easy to perform. More important, we will need to accept the fact that most people will find our work irrelevant since most folks (including composers and performers) are more interested in how music functions than in abstract descriptions of musical structure.

Repercussions for Musical Aesthetics: Pleasure Reconsidered

For the better part of three centuries, aesthetic philosophers in the West have resisted the idea that the arts have anything to do with "mere pleasure." The famed music philosopher Eduard Hanslick regarded physiological or psychological responses to music as "pathological."[19] In Western culture, most aesthetic philosophers use the word "pleasure" to imply a sort of crude bodily sensation. The "pleasure principle" is regarded as some unrefined and perhaps demeaning motive, unworthy of sophisticated people.

Few ideas have been more harmful in impeding our efforts to understand the arts. In departing from the traditional view, let me begin by pointing out that all pleasure is biological. Without a brain there is no pleasure. There is no separate realm of aesthetic pleasure that is experienced independent of biology. Second, pleasure guides most human and animal behaviors. Even deferred gratification is motivated by imaginative appraisals of future pleasure. The function of pleasure is evident in the myriad of possible activities humans could pursue, but don't. A person could spend hours scrubbing a horse's tail against the bark of trees, but nobody does this. Instead, people spend hours drawing horse hair over violin strings. A person could turn off her computer and spend hours enthralled by the sounds emitted by the clicking made by typing on the keys. Instead, people spend hours enthralled by the sounds that are emitted by pressing the keys of pianos. A person could spend hours in the bathroom enthralled by the act of gargling with mouthwash. Instead, people join community choirs and spend hours enthralled by the act of blowing air through their vocal cords. The idea that music making and listening are not motivated primarily by pleasure is biologically implausible.

The brain is the most complicated object we have encountered in the universe. All of the indications suggest that there are many pleasure-evoking mechanisms in the brain. Pleasure is not limited simply to putting candy in one's mouth. The phenomenon of contrastive valence suggests that even negative limbic responses can provide a prelude to pleasure. As we have seen, slapstick comedy, spine-tingling chills, and the expansive sensation of "awe" begin by engaging the physiological machinery for fear. The masochist's propensity for self-inflicted pain does not tell us that pleasure and pain are relative or interchangeable. Rather, the lesson from masochism is that the biology of pain and pleasure is more complicated than we might have supposed. The main path to understanding masochism lies not in understanding deviance, alienation, or modernism, but in understanding biology.

Of course, one of my readers might now go out and spend a couple of hours scrubbing a horse's tail against the bark of trees. But wouldn't the motivation for this act be the psychological satisfaction of proving me wrong? Pleasure cannot easily be dismissed as the ultimate motivator. In arts scholarship, rather than pooh-poohing "mere" pleasure, we need to recognize that the biological phenomenon of pleasure is a proper starting point for understanding the psychology of artistic experience.

This is not to say that the only reason anyone does anything is to maximize pleasure. As I have already noted, there is no requirement whatsoever that artists create works of art that make people feel good. But art will not exist for long without some attention to the evoking of pleasure. I simply want to claim that pleasure is more complicated than aesthetic philosophers have assumed, and that pleasure is more pervasive and fundamental to the arts than many arts scholars would care to admit. If aesthetic philosophers are genuinely interested in understanding the phenomenon of beauty, they cannot achieve this goal without taking into account the operation of the human brain and its predilection for pleasure.

Repercussions for Musicology: Psychological History

In telling the story of music, music historians, like all historians, attempt to place an episode or incident in its broader context. Historians try to identify the contributing factors or causes that lead to particular historical events. Typically, historians appeal to larger political movements, or social, cultural, religious, technological, economic, and other factors. At the same time, historians might identify "local" factors, such as the personalities of the major players, or the personal circumstances or motivations that might have disposed people to take certain actions.

When it comes to music history, I think musicologists can benefit from the experiences of historical linguists. Historical linguistics is typically preoccupied with tracing how languages change, or reconstructing historically dead languages. There are important historical transformations that have shaped languages. A good example is the so-called Great Vowel Shift that dramatically transformed English pronunciation between the fifteenth and eighteenth centuries. For example, words involving the vowel "eh" were changed to "ee," and "oh" was gradually transformed to "oo."[20]

Languages change for many reasons. Sometimes they change because of major migrations of peoples, famines, wars, or diseases. Sometimes technological innovations have an impact on language—such as the advent of writing systems, or the advent of national broadcasting. Often changes originate in efforts to distinguish social classes or because of language "fashions." But there are many other aspects of language change that arise for simple psychological and physiological reasons. For example, some phonemes are more difficult to pronounce than others. Some phonemes become difficult to distinguish perceptually and so fuse. In other cases phonetic contrasts become exaggerated in order to aid perception.

When historical linguists attempt to explain the historical changes in some language, they make use of a broad range of explanatory phenomena. This includes the usual political, social, cultural, religious, technological, and economic factors that form the stock-in-trade of all historians. But it also includes the cognitive, perceptual, physiological, and other biological phenomena that are known to shape language production and language perception. Since music is also shaped by a wealth of psychological factors, one would expect that the writing of music history can only benefit by the addition of psychological phenomena to the toolkit of historical explanation. In chapter 16 I provided an example of such an approach in the contrarian psychological motivations apparent in musical modernism. The emergence of musical modernism is linked, at least in part, to a compelling interest in a particular psychological effect.

Another example of a psychological approach to music history can be found in my work with historical musicologist Joshua Veltman.[21] Veltman and I carried out statistical analyses of medieval chants. We found that the Phrygian and Hypomixolydian modes are statistically indistinguishable, and that the "mode profiles" cluster in a manner consistent with a theory of mode offered by the eleventh-century theorist Johannes Cotto. More important, the statistical clustering of mode profiles suggests the beginnings of a major–minor polarization that may have paved the way for the subsequent (17th-century) emergence of the modern major–minor system. This pattern is reminiscent of the phenomenon of "merger" in historical linguistics, where acoustically similar phonemes collapse into a single perceptual category.

Schemas are not fixed. Over time, some schemas merge together, old schemas disappear, and new schemas are spawned. For example, there is a cognitive history to be traced in the gradual transformation of stride-bass accompaniment into the "backbeat" metric schema that is the hallmark of rock and roll. As Robert Gjerdingen has noted, the history of schematic change in music awaits detailed description.

These particular cognitive/historical accounts may not stand up to further scrutiny. Nevertheless, I remain convinced that historical musicologists have much to gain by emulating the experiences of historical linguists. At least some of the changes in musical language might be expected to arise from cognitive dispositions.

In drawing attention to such cognitive processes, I don't want to leave the impression that social, cultural, and political currents haven't had a major impact on the events of music history. Nor do I want to suggest that the personal dispositions and motivations exhibited by individual musicians haven't been important. I'd simply like to propose that, in addition to these factors, there are basic perceptual and cognitive phenomena that shape human auditory experiences, and that these phenomena have contributed directly both to the organization of musics and to the dynamics of musical change. As cognitive research in music advances, I expect that music historians will be able to draw on a wider conceptual toolkit in attempting to form accounts of the musical past.

Repercussions for Ethnomusicology: Opening Minds

Compared with spoken language, music certainly seems more universally accessible. Westerners might not understand a word of Tibetan, but when we listen to Tibetan music, many of us will feel that we somehow get the gist of it. Have we truly grasped some essential kernel of the music? Or are we simply deceiving ourselves?

What does it mean to understand the music of another culture? Over the past century, ethnomusicologists have documented some of the many forms of music-related knowledge possessed by people in different cultures. Musical "understanding" can involve many aspects. A musically knowledgeable person can have specialized knowledge of language, mythology, cosmology, history, poetry, dance, ritual practices, social, political and religious significance, allusion, quotation, and parody, as well as specialized performance skills, knowledge of repertory, instrument-making skills, methods of instruction, and distinctive listening habits.

The music of some non-Western cultures does indeed seem to be organized differently from Western music. But as we saw in chapters 5 and 6, musical structure is not the same as musical experience. We don't really know how differently people experience music. With a few exceptions, researchers typically have not engaged in the sort of experimental work that would allow us to peer inside people's heads and determine how different folk hear music differently.

The theory I have presented in this book holds a number of repercussions for ethnomusicology. In the first instance, the ITPRA theory assumes that all the world's peoples share a common biological heritage, even though the specific forms of expectation may differ radically between cultures and over time. That is, the theory presumes that everyone exhibits the same types of memory, the same inductive learning processes, the same tendency to form multiple mental representations, the same physiological responses to surprise and habituation, and the same imagination, tension, prediction, reaction, and appraisal components. Ethnomusicologists are naturally skeptical of purported universals, and such skepticism is surely warranted. The theory should be tested as opportunities and funding permit.

However, suppose, for the sake of argument, that the basic outline of the ITPRA theory is correct. What would it mean for our understanding of cultural difference in music? The theory offers both good news and bad news for ethnomusicology. The good news is that people learn from simply being exposed to some acoustical environment. The evidence in support of statistical learning affirms ethnomusicologists' claims regarding the importance of cultural milieu. This suggests, for example, that a person unfamiliar with the music of another culture might be able to develop a culturally appropriate way of listening, simply by immersing him- or herself in the music of that culture.

Further good news is that it may be possible to hear music from past ages in a historically appropriate manner. That is, those who immerse themselves in, say, medieval music are likely to develop new schemas that are appropriate to the music of that age. Moreover, these schemas should be relatively impervious to interference from modern listening habits.

For the seasoned ethnomusicologist, perhaps the most worrisome thought is that even after decades of studying the music of some culture, they have mistaken familiarity for understanding, and have failed to experience the music in a culturally congruent way. In part, the extant cognitive research goes some way toward allaying these fears.

Now for the bad news. Although new auditory schemas may be relatively easy to learn, the underlying mental representations are probably much less flexible. As we have seen, mental representations for music probably develop through exposure during early childhood. After that, they probably are resistant to change. In the same way that the stability of a pitch environment may influence whether or not a listener acquires absolute pitch, different musical cultures may lead listeners toward one or another constellation of mental representations for music. If our first exposure to the music of a particular culture is delayed until adolescence or adulthood, then the way in which our minds represent sounds may diverge (perhaps considerably) from a culturally normative listener. We may be hearing *intervals* whereas culturally experienced listeners may be hearing *scale tones* (or vice versa).

This is not merely of concern for those of us who wish to become conversant with the music of another culture. It also has repercussions for people who might regard themselves as belonging to that culture. Suppose, for example, that an adolescent in South Korea listens almost exclusively to modern Korean pop music. While the lyrics are in Korean, the musical language is thoroughly Western. Now suppose that later in life, this same individual takes an interest in the traditional music of Korea. In "rediscovering" one's cultural roots, it is possible to develop a great deal of expertise without developing a parallel auditory expertise.

Notice that having facility with the language, knowledge of the traditional mythology, poetry, and history, awareness of the social, political and religious contexts, expertise in performing the music on authentic instruments, familiarity with traditional repertoire, and knowledge of the history and significance of individual works will not, in themselves, necessarily allow a person to experience the succession of sounded events according to a psychological pattern that resembles a traditional culturally knowledgeable listener. Although a culturally inexperienced listener may be able to develop a new auditory schema that is shaped by exposure, the underlying mental representation may fail to provide a culturally congruent foundation. In addition, the auditory schema may be insufficiently broad. These problems are not overcome by familiarity with individual musical works. The experimental research suggests that familiarity with individual works is not the same as familiarity with cultural schemas. A listener could be familiar with a couple dozen musical works from some culture, and so exhibit knowledgeable veridical expectations. But veridical expectations alone are not sufficient for a culturally congruent listening experience. Said another way, a person can be intimately familiar with a given repertory while failing to experience the music in a manner consistent with the culture.

In the case of linguistic knowledge, the acid test for whether we have truly mastered some language is our ability to understand what is being said. However, in the case of music, there may be no comparable test. Both familiarity and enjoyment can be our enemies. Veridical familiarity gives us the sense that we know what will happen next, and this feeling is easily mistaken for schematic musical expertise. When we enjoy music, this experience of enjoyment is something we will share with culturally expert listeners—an experience that may give us a false sense of belonging. Thus, compared with language, the sense of musical expertise is wide open to self-deception.

Perhaps the closest to an acid test for musical cultural understanding is that of musical humor. As we saw in chapter 14, musically induced laughter arises from gross violations of learned expectations. If a listener does not have the appropriate schematic or veridical expectations, then a major discrepancy between actual events and normative events is not likely to evoke laughter. Getting musical jokes may be the ethnomusicologist's best test of cultural understanding.

Having said all of this, it is important not to treat authenticity as some supreme transcultural value. Having a culturally congruent experience is not the only worthy musical goal. One's experience of music need not embrace all of the elements that historians, ethnomusicologists, music theorists, or cognitive psychologists say are important. In any event, it is unlikely that we can preserve or protect all the world's musical cultures. Western music, especially Western popular music, has been making inroads in virtually every corner of the world. For many non-Western listeners, Western music has become their first or natal environment for musical exposure. This means that both the mental coding for music, and their schemas, are being shaped by, and adapted to, the languages of Western music.

Clearly, we must be responsive to the goals and aspirations of different peoples. Many non-Westerners are understandably uninterested in becoming living museum pieces. As Mr. Tutii Chilton told me on the Micronesian island of Koror: "Protection is a word used by outsiders. What we want is respect, not protection."

No one wants the arts to become fossilized. Arts are creative, dynamic enterprises. We want and expect the arts to change and grow, to variegate, to explore, and to challenge. We want music to be all that it can be.[22] In this creative venture, the musics of other cultures are important because other cultures bear testimony to other ways of being—other ways in which music can be effectively organized.

Our passion for novelty can occasionally take us far away from human needs. Adventurous artists can sometimes produce ineffective constructions that fail to push listeners' buttons. By contrast, the musics of other cultures have withstood the test of time: although we may not fully grasp or appreciate the music of some culture, we know that this music is compelling to some minds.

Perhaps the best we can hope for is to learn. Learning how other minds work has the potential to greatly expand our own horizons. Of course it is possible that the lessons to be learned from other musical cultures will ultimately prove to be trivial or inconsequential. It may be that all of the important lessons regarding music can be found in Western music. But who would be so presumptuous as to assume this to be the case before we investigate the matter thoroughly? We should be concerned about the loss of cultural diversity for the same reason that biologists worry about the loss of biodiversity: we don't yet know what the loss will mean, but we do know that the loss will be irreversible. As I have argued elsewhere, the danger in current ethnomusicology is that we will assemble wonderful archives of cultural recordings and descriptive interpretations, but we will have lost the minds to experience them and even the knowledge of how they were once experienced.[23]

My points here are the same as those I made regarding music theory. Research with Western listeners provides some sobering lessons. First, describing the musical organization is not the same as describing the phenomenal experience. Just because we observe a distinctive pattern in some music or ritual does not mean that the pattern is salient to culturally knowledgeable individuals. More important, significant patterns of perception and cognition may be nowhere to be found in the sounds, transcriptions, or videos. Second, if we want to understand what is going on we must supplement descriptive scholarship with careful experimentation. If we don't do this, we will have failed to truly open our minds to the minds of others.

If the arts are to achieve all that can be achieved, we must be vigilant in recognizing and identifying how and why minds differ. We need to focus not merely on the structure of artifacts, but on the structures of individual minds—especially minds that experience the world in ways that seem alien to us. At this point in history, we have only a few tools to help us in this venture. "Thick description" alone is not sufficient to understand how minds differ.

Coda

In this final chapter I have tried to highlight how psychological knowledge might have an effect on practical music making, music theory, historical musicology, ethnomusicology, and philosophical aesthetics. I have suggested that cognitively inspired research can help enrich and propel each of these fields of study. More brazenly, I have argued that the best way to expand artistic horizons and foster creativity is by better understanding how minds work.

In this book I've attempted to describe some of the psychological mechanisms involved in music making. My musical aim has been to provide musicians with a better understanding of some of the tools they use, not to tell musicians what goals they should follow. Where I've offered advice, I have tried to bracket the advice by indicating that it assumes the musician is seeking to evoke pleasure for listeners. It's not easy to keep to an explanatory agenda, so I expect that my text contains some lapses.

Beyond the musical aims, this work has attempted to describe how expectation in general works. In particular, I have attempted to explain some of the ways that expectation can account for different feelings, emotions, and *qualia*. I have offered a model that I hope proves useful beyond music—to drama, literature, film, dance, comedy, theatrical magic, industrial design, and other fields of activity. I am all too aware of the many outstanding questions regarding expectation that remain to be addressed. If any expectation about the future is warranted, it is the expectation that more research awaits. If the past is any guide, future insights concerning expectation are themselves worthy of some sweet anticipation.

Notes

Preface

1. A search for "sweet anticipation—musical examples" should point you to the right location.

2. See Fred Lerdahl's "Cognitive constraints on compositional systems" (1988), and further discussions in Lerdahl's (2001) book, *Tonal Pitch Space*. More generally, see Melvin Konner's revised edition of *The Tangled Wing: Biological Constraints on the Human Spirit* (2003).

Chapter 1

1. I believe that Leonard Meyer was right to emphasize the importance of expectation in musical experience. However, I believe that Meyer was wrong to downplay the importance of representational elements in music listening. Elsewhere I have argued that auditory denotation and connotation contribute significantly to the evocation of emotion while listening to music. I hope to expand on these arguments on another occasion. But in the current volume, I will restrict my discussion to expectation. In focusing on expectation, readers should not assume that I agree with Meyer's position that representational aspects of music are of little consequence.

2. The pertinent research tends to fall into three broad approaches: perceptual and cognitive experimentation, studies in music theory and analysis, and empirical analyses of scores inspired by information theory.
   Experimental investigations of musical expectation include studies by Aarden (2002, 2003); Abe and Oshino (1990); Bharucha (1994, 1996); Bigand and Pineau (1997); Carlsen (1981); Cuddy and Lunney (1995); Dowling and Harwood (1986); Federman (1996); Francès (1958); von Hippel (1998, 2000a,b, 2002); Jones (1990); Jones and Boltz (1989); Krumhansl (1995a,b, 1997); Krumhansl et al. (1999); Margulis and Levine (2004); Oram and Cuddy (1995); Rosner and Meyer (1982); Schellenberg (1996, 1997); Schmuckler (1988, 1989, 1990, 1997); Sloboda (1992); Thompson, Balkwill, and Vernescu (2000); Unyk (1990); and Werbik (1969). Cognitively inspired theorizing about music and expectation includes work by Gaver and Mandler (1987); Kubovy (1999); and Rozin (1999).

Investigations inspired by music theory and analysis include works by Berger (1990); Gjerdingen (1988); Knopoff and Hutchinson (1983); Kramer (1982); Larson (1997, 2002); Lerdahl and Jackendoff (1983); Margulis (2003, 2005); Meyer (1956); and Narmour (1990, 1991, 1992, 1999, 2000). Many other music theorists discuss expectation in the context of other musical phenomena, e.g., Aldwell and Schachter (1989); Hindemith (1943); Piston (1978); Rameau (1722); Riemann (1903); and Schenker (1906).

Information-theoretic and score-based empirical studies include works by Cohen (1962); Coons and Kraehenbuehl (1958); Goldstone (1979); von Hippel and Huron (2000); Huron (1996, 2001a); Huron and von Hippel (2000); Kraehenbuehl and Coons (1959); Moles (1958/1966); Pinkerton (1956); Reimer (1964); and Youngblood (1958).

3. See Tomkins 1980.

4. See Richmond, Liu, and Shidara 2003; Matsumoto, Suzuki, and Tanaka 2003; Damasio 1994.

5. For a discussion of the importance of daydreaming, see Klinger 1990. A significant body of research has examined how people predict future emotions. Most of this research emphasizes conscious prediction and some of the errors in prediction that commonly arise. See March 1978 and Loewenstein and Schkade 1999.

6. See Bechara et al. 1994, described in Damasio 1994, pp. 212–217.

7. See Lange and James 1922. William James was a philosopher and psychologist, and brother of the famous American writer Henry James. Carl Lange was a Danish physiologist (whose name is pronounced "Long").

8. See James 1884, p. 190.

9. See Hohmann 1966; James 1894; Lange and James 1922; Marañon 1924; Schachter and Singer 1962; Tomkins 1975.

10. See Strack, Stepper, and Martin 1988.

11. A further study by Stepper and Strack 1993 has established a similar effect of posture on emotion.

12. See Cornelius 1996 for a pertinent review.

13. I owe this insight to my colleague, Simon Durrant.

14. See Mandler 1975.

15. See Olson, Roese, and Zanna 1996.

16. For a good description of the wide range of feeling states, see *The Subtlety of Emotions* by Aaron Ben-Ze'ev (2000).

Chapter 2

1. LeDoux has been the principal advocate of the dual-path theory of fear. See LeDoux 1996.

2. See Li, Stutzmann, and LeDoux 1996.

3. For a general discusssion of the neural pathways involved in fear, see LeDoux and Phelps 2000.

4. See Simons 1996.

5. McGraw 1999.

6. The effect of suprise on emotion remains an active area of psychological research. The amplifying influence of surprise is predicted both by norm theory (Kahneman and Miller 1986) and by decision-affect theory (see Mellers et al. 1997; Mellers, Schwartz, and Ritov 1999).

7. See Bandura et al. 1988. See also Bolles and Fanselow 1980; Malow 1981.

8. An extensive literature addresses issues related to limbic contrast. The most influential psychological model has been Richard Solomon's "opponent process" theory (Solomon 1980). Inspired by his research on eating chili peppers, Rozin (1999) has proposed a "benign maso-chism" theory which he has used in discussing music. Limbic contrast also forms the basis for a theory of music proposed by Gaver and Mandler (1987). Limbic contrast has often figured in writings on aesthetics. For example, Edmund Burke (1757) characterized the sublime as "When we have an idea of pain and danger, without being actually in such circumstances." Similarly, in his *Critique of Judgment* (1790) Immanuel Kant wrote: "There accompanies the reception of an object as sublime a pleasure, which is only possible through the medium of pain." A useful dis-cussion of negative hedonic states in the psychology of art can be found in the work of Aiken (1998).

9. See Gabrielsson and Lindstrom 1993.

10. The basic elements of the expression are captured admirably in Edvard Munch's famous painting *The Scream*.

11. The best single source for research on laughter is Provine 2000.

12. Provine 2000, p. 45.

13. But different languages describe laughter differently. Provine (2000, p. 62) notes, for example, that the English "ha-ha-ha" is rendered as "ah ah ah" in French and Italian.

14. Provine 2000, p. 57.

15. Provine 2000, p. 79.

16. Provine 2000, p. 86.

17. See Wheelock 1992 (p. 172) and Provine 2000 (p. 13).

18. Singer et al. 2004. Singer and her colleagues recorded fMRI activity while administering alternate electrical shocks to one of two volunteers who were romantic partners. Participants received signals indicating that their loved one—present in the same room—was receiving a similar pain stimulus. They found common brain activity in both the "self" and "other" conditions. While brain activity related to the sensory components of pain were absent in the "other" condition, brain areas related to the affective components of pain were activated in both the "self" and "other" conditions.

19. Marion 1990, p. 59.

20. Sustaining the peek-a-boo surprise for three hours entails a certain amount of inventiveness in trying to increase uncertainty about *when* the face will appear. Also, peek-a-boo doesn't simply involve the element of visual surprise. In observing this game, I've noticed that low-pitched threatening sounds often accompany the build-up to the moment of surprise.

21. Although see Dick Higgens' "Danger Music" for an exception (Hansen 1965).

22. My thanks to Paul von Hippel for drawing my attention to social panting in dogs. After writing this chapter, I discovered a research report by Patricia Simonet and her colleagues at Sierra Nevada College concerning dogs and social panting. Simonet has identified a special form of panting whose acoustic structure includes a broader range of spectral frequencies and is therefore easier to detect than ordinary panting. Simonet has explicitly speculated that this form of panting resembles laughter. (See Simonet, Murphy, and Lance 2001; also Milius 2001.)

23. Later I will argue that the creation of music is one of the ways human culture has expanded on the agreeable feelings evoked by the contrast between negative reaction feelings and neutral/positive appraisal feelings.

24. There is yet another, more subtle version of the gasp, where one simply stops breathing momentarily (without the rapid inhaling characteristic of the gasp).

25. See Panksepp 1995, p. 203.

26. Studies of musically induced frisson include Gray 1955; Goldstein 1980; Sloboda 1991, 1992; Panksepp 1995; Blood, Zatorre, and Evans 1999; and Blood et al. 1999.

27. Further support for the idea that laughter is linked to the flight response (rather than the fight response) is evident in the rough-and-tumble play that is often associated with laughter in humans and other primates. Recall that in these play situations, it is the socially submissive animal that is more likely to laugh. Often the more dominant animal is chasing, holding, or mock-threatening the more submissive animal. The submissive animal responds not by fighting back, but instead by attempting to flee. The paradigmatic situation is a submissive animal being chased by a more dominant playmate, with the submissive animal laughing.

28. Studies of personality indicate that susceptibility to fear is a stable factor that distinguishes people. More fearful individuals are less likely to take risks. In susceptibility to fear and risk taking, there are reliable differences between men and women. In general, women are more risk aversive and more likely to experience fear. Note that studies of musically evoked emotions

reliably show differences between men and women: women are significantly more likely to experience strong emotions evoked by music compared with men. (See, e.g., Sloboda 1991.) It is possible that these differences are an artifact of reporting—women appear to be more open in reporting emotional experiences. Another possibility is that the differences between men and women reflect a unique characteristic arising from Western enculturation. However, a third possibility is that the greater reported tendency for women to experience strong emotions while listening to music is a consequence of their relative ease in experiencing fear.

29. See Rozin 1999 for an insightful comparison between eating chili peppers and music.

30. In addition to Meyer 1956, see also Meyer 1989, notably chapter 1. Also, Gretchen Wheelock has quite rightly drawn attention to the views of Hans Teuber: "[Jokes] point simultaneously at the value and at the limitations of all schemata. They force us to realize that the communication process . . . cannot do without the schemata." See Wheelock 1992, p. 14.

31. In John Sloboda's survey of emotional responses to music, of 12 physical responses, "shivers down the spine" and "laughter" were the first and second most commonly reported responses (Sloboda 1991, p. 112).

Chapter 3

1. See Olson, Roese, and Zanna 1996.

2. Greenberg and Larkin 1968.

3. Howard et al. 1984.

4. There is a large volume of research that supports the principle that accurate expectation facilitates perception. This discovery can be traced at least as far back as 1949 when Bruner and Postman published research showing that violations of expectancy interfered with accurate perception.

5. Carlsen, Divenyi, and Taylor 1970.

6. Carlsen 1981.

7. Incidentally, Carlsen found that his Hungarian participants were much less inhibited about singing or improvising a melodic continuation than his German and American participants.

8. Lake 1987.

9. Schmuckler 1988, 1989, and Povel 1995.

10. Larson 1997, 2002.

11. Schmuckler 1990.

12. Krumhansl and Shepard 1979.

13. Shepard 1964.

14. See Krumhansl 1990.

15. See Eerola, Toiviainen, and Krumhansl 2002.

16. Von Hippel, Huron, and Harnish 1998 (manuscript only).

17. A related problem with the betting paradigm is that the method can be confounded by the prior betting experience of the participants. In the case of our Balinese experiment, we originally chose the betting paradigm because we were aware that gambling is pervasive in Indonesian culture. We thought that asking our participants to wager would make the experiment less alien and more familiar. However, this led to an unanticipated problem. The results of our experiment showed that the Balinese participants were much more successful in placing their bets than the American participants. What if this greater success was merely an artifact of the Indonesian's greater gambling experience? How could one claim that the greater success was attributed to their more accurate musical expectations? Fortunately, in the post-experiment interviews, we discovered that all four Balinese musicians had been raised in religious homes where gambling was forbidden. It is therefore unlikely that the differences we found between the American and Balinese participants can be ascribed to greater gambling experience for the Balinese participants.

18. For a discussion of these variants see Kagan 2002, p. 121.

19. See Weiss, Zelazo, and Swain 1988, as cited in Kagan 2002, p. 117.

20. See Aarden 2003. An early use of reaction time measures to musical expectation is found in Janata and Reisberg 1988.

21. To motivate participants to respond as quickly and accurately as possible, Aarden sometimes presents the experiment in terms of a competition in which participants try to achieve the highest score. Response errors and reactions times are echoed in a continuously updated "score," which participants can see throughout the experiment. High scores are given for fast responses. Lower scores are given for inaccurate or slower responses. Participants are encouraged to produce better scores than the others.

22. It is possible that reducing the tempo might tend to reduce the influence of musical context on listener responses. That is, a slower tempo might emphasize local note-to-note expectations over more holistic or integrated perceptions of musical melodies. To encourage his listeners to experience the tone sequences as intact musical melodies, Aarden (2003) added a follow-up task after each stimulus sequence. Aarden replayed the entire stimulus sequence at the correct tempo with a 50% probability that one of the notes would deviate from the original sequence. Listeners were then required to indicate whether the slower and faster versions of the sequence were the same or different. Bonus scores were given for correct responses. The purpose of this auxiliary task was to encourage participants to hear the tone sequence more holistically.

23. It might be thought that another problem with the reaction-time method is that the reaction-time data pertain not to the expectedness of specific tones, but to the expectedness of specific contours. For example, if a participant responds quickly to a descending pitch contour, one might suppose that we cannot claim that the participant regards this lower pitch as highly

expected. Instead, it may be that a *different* lower pitch was expected and this expectation facilitated the responses to all lower pitches. However, the experimental evidence does not support this view. When an unexpected stimulus occurs, this causes momentary confusion and tends to reduce reaction time—even if the response is identical to the response that would have ensued if the stimulus had corresponded to the most expected result. In short, testing for contour is a sufficient means of testing for expectedness.

24. See, e.g., Ritter et al. 1999.

25. See Kagan 2002, p. 100, for discussion.

26. See Shannon 1948; Shannon and Weaver 1949; and Moles 1958/1966.

Chapter 4

1. See Bayes 1763; Popper 1934/1959; Hattiangadi 1983; Neyman and Pearson 1928, 1967.

2. See Johnston 1999, p. 136.

3. Baldwin 1896, 1909.

4. See, e.g., Hasher and Zacks 1984; Gallistel 1990; Kelly and Martin 1994; Reber 1993.

5. Hick 1952; Hyman 1953.

6. The research literature on the subject of absolute pitch is extensive. Some pertinent references include Abraham 1901; Cohen and Baird 1990; Crozier 1997; Cuddy 1968; Halpern 1989; Levitin 1994; Marvin and Brinkman 2000; Meyer 1899; Miyazaki 1988, 1990, 1993; Simpson and Huron 1994; Stumpf 1883; Takeuchi and Hulse 1991, 1993; Ward 1999. Research on possible genetic correlates with absolute pitch includes Baharloo et al. 1998; Gregersen 1998.

7. Miyazaki 1990. See also Takeuchi and Hulse 1991.

8. Simpson and Huron 1994. This is the first of many statistical measures about music that I will report throughout the remainder of this book. The measures are derived from several musical databases, including the Essen Folksong Collection assembled by Helmut Schaffrath (1995), and the MuseData materials produced at the Center for Computer Assisted Research in the Humanities. The database of pop chord progressions was encoded by Tom Recchia. The non-Western musical corpora I encoded myself. All analyses were carried out using the Humdrum Toolkit software (Huron 1995a). Methodological and measurement issues, including error rates, are discussed elsewhere (e.g., Huron 1988a).

9. This study was reported in my 1999 Ernest Bloch Lectures, University of California, Berkeley.

10. For 4,310 American and European folk melodies in major keys, my tallies were: 1431 (do), 21 (re), 394 (mi), 6 (fa), 2,433 (so), 17 (la), 8 (ti). The frequency of occurrence of initial pitches alone does not account for the reaction time results.

11. I purposely asked participants not to sing or hum the pitch of the tone they were imagining. The purpose was to avoid their imagined pitch being transposed up or down in order to fit within their vocal range. Instead, I used probe tones until we matched the pitch of the imagined tone.

12. See Huron 2001b.

13. The estimate that root position chords are more common than chords in other inversions is based on the frequency of occurrence of chords in chorale harmonizations by J. S. Bach.

14. There is further evidence that listeners are sensitive to the statistical properties of opening gestures. The distinguished British musicologist, Donald Francis Tovey, once observed that "if a composer begins by hammering out the note C, you grow more and more certain that it will prove to be, not the tonic of C, but the dominant of F" (quoted in Cook 1959, p. 45).

Statistically, we've already noted that "so" is the most likely initial pitch in a work. This would suggest that it is already prudent to predict that the first pitch of a work is the dominant. But what about Tovey's intuition about repeating a tone? In general, the pitch "so" occurs about 15% more often than "do." However, when we look at successive repetitions of the same pitch, the difference in probability increases. "So-so" occurs about 42% more often than "do-do." In general, it doesn't matter how many times a note is repeated. There are more repetitions of "so" than of "do," and this difference is greater than would be expected given the overall do–so proportion. In other words, the statistics are consistent with Tovey's observation. Repetitions of a single pitch increase the likelihood that the pitch is "so" rather than "do."

15. Saffran et al. 1999.

16. Saffran, Newport, and Aslin 1996.

Chapter 5

1. In fact, it has been shown (Huron 2001a) that comparative probabilistic analysis can be used to identify the motivic features that distinguish one musical work from another. This work will be discussed in chapter 13.

2. See Moles 1958/1966; Cope 2001.

3. See Ortmann 1926; Merriam, Whinery, and Fred 1956; and Dowling 1967.

4. From Huron 2001b.

5. See Boomsliter and Creel 1979.

6. Aarden 2003.

7. Vos and Troost 1989.

8. The musical sample used was assembled by Eric Berg. Since the Indian sample was small, this result should not necessarily be interpreted as a stylistic feature of north Indian classical music.

9. For Russian laments see Mazo 1994; for Australian aboriginal music see Ellis 1969; for Lakota (Sioux) music see Densmore 1918.

10. See Pike 1945; Lieberman 1967; 't Hart, Collier, and Cohen 1990.

11. Narmour (1990) uses the term "process"; I prefer von Hippel's term "step inertia."

12. See von Hippel 2002 and Aarden 2003.

13. See von Hippel 1998.

14. See von Hippel and Huron 2000.

15. Von Hippel and Huron 2000.

16. See von Hippel manuscript in preparation.

17. See Huron 1996 for details.

Chapter 6

1. In unpublished work, Paul von Hippel has determined that the distribution of pitches in most melodies meets statistical tests of normality.

2. Voss and Clarke 1978; Gardner 1978.

3. Though highly speculative, one possible origin might be found in early exposure to lullabies. Unyk et al. (1992) studied lullabies from a number of different cultures and noted that, compared with culturally matched non-lullabies, lullabies exhibit a greater tendency to employ descending pitch contours. That is, lullabies are even more prone to descending intervals than other forms of music. Since lullabies are intended to soothe infants and encourage sleep, the preponderance of descending pitch contours might have an innate tendency to reduce physiological arousal. If infants are frequently exposed to lullabies or lullaby-like stimuli, then they might develop a general expectation for descending intervals that continues to shape their listening as adults.

4. See Narmour 1990, 1992.

5. See Schellenberg 1996 for a summary description.

6. See Cuddy and Lunney 1995.

7. Schellenberg 1996, 1997.

8. Schellenberg 1997.

9. Von Hippel 2002.

10. Rosner and Meyer 1982; Schmuckler 1989.

11. See von Hippel 2000b. As part of that publication, with the cooperation of Rosner and Meyer, von Hippel was able to reanalyze their original experimental data and showed that their results were more consistent with a regression-to-the-mean model than a gap-fill model.

12.   Pearce and Wiggins 2004.

13.   One example of such discontinuous frequency jumps in music is Swiss yodeling.

14.   Where the biological premise is adaptive accuracy, the musical premise is one of psychological conformity. However, note that I am not *advocating* psychological conformity. I am simply observing that psychological conformity is a prerequisite if a composer wishes individual listeners to hear a musical work in broadly similar ways. As we learn more about individual psychological differences, in the future it might be possible for composers to tailor works for particular subgroups or even individual listeners.

15.   *Naive realism* can be contrasted with *qualified realism*. Both philosophical positions hold that there are objects and events in the world whose existence does not depend on being perceived or thought about. However, qualified realism regards perceptions as partial and fallible, whereas naive realism regards perceptions as direct and accurate.

16.   There are many examples of this process: consider the perception of visual edges. When I look at my desk, I see clear edges that delineate different surfaces and that form boundaries that distinguish one object from another. Unfortunately, these impressions are deceptive – as computer scientists have discovered. Researchers in machine vision have attempted to program computers to identify objects from photographs. When they began this work several decades ago they were amazed to discover that the sharp edges that we see around objects simply do not exist in photographic images. It turns out that these edges are created by the visual system, which amplifies contrasts, interprets, interpolates, and otherwise manufactures the distinct edges we experience.

Chapter 7

1. I am using the term "mental code" loosely here. My only assumption is that auditory expectations are manifested in distinctive brain states. For example, expected sounds might be represented by distributed action potentials that are only implicitly coded.

2. One caveat needs to be noted, however: since the size of a person's head grows larger until adulthood, we can infer that even in the case of sound localization, some adaptive learning must be involved.

3. See Hofman and Van Opstal 1998.

4. See Hofman et al. 2002.

5. The difference between the actual spectral shape and the normative spectral shape for the class of sound is also important. In addition to the spectral effects of the pinna, the spectrum is also influenced by so-called head-related transforms (HRTs).

6. I think this hypothesis is more plausible than the others, for reasons given later in this chapter.

7. In fact, spacialization has been integral to a number of works by contemporary musicians, including such composers as Louis Andriessen, Pierre Boulez, Gavin Bryars, Elliot Carter, Ambrose Field, Pauline Oliveros, R. Murray Schafer, Karlheinz Stockhausen, Iannis Xenakis, and others. For discussions of the musical significance of sound location see Bernard 1983 and Trochimczyk 2001.

8. See Edelman 1987 and Calvin 1996.

9. My use of the word "atrophy" here pertains to the neural function, not necessarily to the physiological structures themselves.

10. As Daniel Levitin has pointed out, absolute pitch really entails two skills—the ability to recognize or generate a particular pitch and the ability to label or name that pitch. Musicians with "perfect pitch" have both the ability to recognize and name the pitch. But Levitin has identified nonmusicians who have "absolute pitch" only in the sense that they recognize specific pitches—even though they don't know the conventional musical names. Such a person will sing a song in the correct key without knowing it. A repair technician, for example, may recognize that a refrigerator is faulty because the pitch of its hum is a semitone flat.

11. See Gergersen 1998; Baharloo et al. 1998.

12. See Cohen and Baird 1990; Crozier 1997.

13. A number of testimonials have been circulated by adults attesting to their success in acquiring absolute pitch. Naturally, reports of failure tend not to circulate. Peter Sellmer's failure occurred after a year of methodical effort. He wore a tuning fork around his neck and frequently referred to it over the course of his daily activities. Each week he tested himself using a computer program with randomized stimuli. Despite concerted effort to acquire AP he failed. Advocates of adult-acquired AP will argue that such failures are due to inadequate technique. To my knowledge, none of the commercial systems has been properly evaluated—especially controlling for childhood involvement with music.

14. See, e.g., Crozier 1997. Crozier affirms the evidence in support of a critical period in early development. But Crozier also argues that more research is needed concerning the "elimination" of AP rather than its "acquisition."

15. Miyazaki 1990; Takeuchi and Hulse 1991; Simpson and Huron 1994.

16. Miyazaki 1993.

17. Research by Jay Dowling (1978), for example, implies that for melodies, the most important pitch-related representations are scale degree and contour.

18. See, e.g., Cozby 1989, pp. 36ff.

19. See Butler and Ward 1988 for an evaluation of the effectiveness of this "tonal eraser" procedure.

20. We may even consider expanding the number of mnemonic tunes used in ear-training classes to include other key contexts where a given interval commonly occurs (such as "re–ti" and "fa–re" for major sixths).

21. There are other representations that are known not to be accessible to introspection. For example, Daniel Levitin at McGill University has shown that there are people who have absolute pitch but don't know it. For these individuals, their absolute-pitch coding is not available to consciousness.

22. See, e.g., Forte 1973; Rahn 1980; Morris 1988.

23. See Davy Temperley's important article on the purposes of music theory (Temperley 1999).

24. See Huron 1995b and Huron 2001b, pp. 56, 58.

25. This research has had little discernible influence in music theory. To my knowledge, no set theorist has ever cited any of these studies. However, see the work of Elizabeth West Marvin for a nuanced interpretation and further pertinent research (Marvin 1997).

26. See Gergersen 1998; Baharloo et al. 1998.

27. See Barkow, Cosmides, Tooby 1992.

28. See Shepard 1982 for a description of the tonal torus structure.

29. Janata et al. 2002.

Chapter 8

1. Meyer 1903.

2. See, e.g., Meyer 1903; Gordon 1917; Moore and Galliland 1924; Washburn, Child, and Able 1927; Henkin 1957; Mull 1957; Getz 1966; Heingartner and Hall 1974; Leman et al. 2003; Szpunar, Schellenberg, and Pliner 2004.

3. In the 20-year period following Zajonc's 1968 study, Robert Bornstein (1989) was able to identify 134 published studies reporting on 208 individual experiments related to the exposure effect.

4. See Mita, Dermer, and Knight 1977.

5. See the review by Bornstein 1989.

6. This line of investigation started with a series of experiments begun by Moreland and Zajonc 1977.

7. See Bornstein 1989, p. 275.

8. See Kihlstrom 1987; Bornstein 1990.

9. Burgess and Sales 1971.

10. See Bornstein 1989, p. 279.

11. In his meta-analysis of the exposure effect, Bornstein (1989) identified 22 studies that used auditory stimuli.

12. See Wilson 1975, 1979.

13. See Bornstein 1989, pp. 270–271.

14. See Berkowitz 2000.

15. Bornstein and D'Agostino 1994.

16. In retrospect, it is possible to recognize a number of early precursors in the discovery of misattribution. See, e.g., Marañon 1924.

17. Aarden 2003.

18. See Bertelson 1961; Hyman 1953.

19. Aarden 2003.

Chapter 9

1. For the Western major scale, the most well-known names are the solfège syllables *do, re, mi, fa, so, la,* and *ti*. Music theorists prefer the names *tonic, supertonic, mediant, subdominant, dominant, submediant,* and *leading tone*. Actually, these technical names prove more convenient since they apply both to the major and minor scale steps, whereas the solfège syllables cause confusion in the minor key. Fortunately, it is also common to refer to the technical scale degrees by numbers: $\hat{1}, \hat{2}, \hat{3}, \hat{4}, \hat{5}, \hat{6},$ and $\hat{7}$.

The following table identifies the scale degree terminology for Western tonal theory. These same names are used for both the major and minor scales, despite the fact that some of the pitches differ. Chromatic (nonscale) tones are identified as either "raised" or "lowered" modifications of a neighboring scale tone.

Scale step	Name	Sample Pitch (Major Key)	Sample Pitch (Minor Key)
$\hat{1}$	Tonic	C	C
$\hat{2}$	Supertonic	D	D
$\hat{3}$	Mediant	E	E flat
$\hat{4}$	Subdominant	F	F
$\hat{5}$	Dominant	G	G
$\hat{6}$	Submediant	A	A flat
$\hat{7}$	Leading tone	B	B
	Subtonic	B flat	B flat

2. No list of references could do justice to the breadth and volume of writings on the subject of tonality. A partial list might include Cohen 1991; Cook 1987; Cuddy 1997; Dahlhaus 1968/1990; Deliège 1984; Forte 1973; Krumhansl 1990; Lerdahl 2001; Norton 1984; Proctor 1978; Schenker 1906, 1935; Salzer 1952; Thomson 1999; Yasser 1932.

3. See Francès 1958; Krumhansl and Shepard 1979; Krumhansl 1979; Krumhansl and Kessler 1982; Deliège 1984; Brown 1985; Cook 1987; Janata and Reisberg 1988; Butler and Ward 1988; Krumhansl 1990; Cohen 1991; Huron and Parncutt 1993; Brown, Butler, and Jones 1994; Butler and Brown 1994; Povel 1995; Cuddy 1997; Butler 1998; Van Egmond and Butler 1997; Huron and von Hippel 2000; Janata et al. 2002.

4. *Qualia* remains an active and contested topic in the philosophy of mind. An early exposition can be found in Clarence Irving Lewis's *Mind and the World Order: Outline of a Theory of Knowledge* (1929). A contemporary critique of the notion of *quale* can be found in Daniel Dennett's *Consciousness Explained* (1991).

5. Cook 1959, especially pp. 45–47.

6. The music sampled for these distributions included European folksong melodies. More complex keyboard and orchestral works tend to contain passages that modulate to another key, and so were excluded from the sampled music.

7. Each work in volumes 1 and 2 of *The Well-Tempered Clavier* is written in a different key.

8. Using the Krumhansl and Kessler distributions (discussed later in this chapter) produces slightly less impressive results: the estimated keys for *The Well-Tempered Clavier* results in 3 wrong classifications and an average correlation of +0.84.

9. See Huron 1992 for an assessment of the effectiveness of the Krumhansl–Schmuckler algorithm. See Huron and Veltman (2006) for a discussion of the use of Euclidean distance rather than correlation as a superior method of calculating similarity.

10. Aarden 2003.

11. "Listeners appear to be very sensitive to the frequency with which the various elements [pitch chromas] and their successive combinations are employed in music. It seems probable, then, that abstract tonal and harmonic relations are learned through internalizing distribution properties characteristic of the style" (Krumhansl 1990, p. 286).

12. Krumhansl and Kessler 1982.

13. Aarden 2003.

14. For these calculations I used a sample of 300 German folksongs from the Essen Folksong collection; see Schaffrath 1995. The standard deviations for the two measures are 1.42 and 1.29, respectively.

15. For these calculations I used a sample of 50 chorale harmonizations by J. S. Bach. Chords in different inversions were treated as distinct information states, as were chords with sevenths. Chord successions across phrase boundaries were excluded.

16. More technically, the cadence is referred to as a *bókazó* cadence. See Bellman 1993, pp. 118–119.

17. See, e.g., Kramer 1982.

18. See also Manzara, Witten, and James 1992.

19. The Chinese *bawoo* melody is transcribed from *Huan Le Ge* performed by Li He (1992). The Jajouka melody is transcribed from "The Middle of the Night" on Island Record's *The Master Musicians of Jajouka* (1992). The Pawnee cadence is from a transcription of "Song Concerning Mother Moon" as sung by Tsastawinahiigat (Effie Blain) circa 1919. See Densmore 1926.

20. See 't Hart, Collier, and Cohen 1990.

21. All reported values here are based on a musical sample of roughly 4,600 songs containing roughly 200,000 intervals.

22. Margulis 2003, p. 263.

23. As Margulis (2003) has noted, closure segments the melody into implicative chunks. See Margulis 2003, p. 39.

24. See Eberlein and Fricke 1992. In addition to the experiments reported, their book contains a useful history of the cadence in Western music.

25. Meyer 1956, p. 56.

26. The logic might be summarized by the following causal sequence:

· frequently occurring events provide the best predictions for future states;
· since successful predictions are rewarded, frequently occurring events tend to become associated with positive emotions (nominally "neutral" stimuli may thus acquire a positive valence);
· it is preferrable for long-duration states to have a positive valence;
· by definition, the terminating event in a sequence is a long-duration state; in creating a sequence of states, pleasure is increased if frequently occurring events tend to be placed at the ends of segments; and
· through repeated exposure, terminating events become associated with closure and repose or stability; hence frequently occurring events tend to become associated with closure and repose/stability.

27. See my "Foundations of Cognitive Musicology," Ernest Bloch Lectures, University of California, Berkeley, 1999.

28. See Dimberg 1989.

29. Kessler, Hansen, and Shepard 1984.

30. We will consider this issue further in the next chapter.

31. See Jairazbhoy 1971 for a description of a pertinent theoretical analysis of traditional north Indian *rags*.

32. Castellano, Bharucha, and Krumhansl 1984.

33. See Eerola 2004.

34. See Krumhansl et al. 2000.

35. Nam 1998.

36. Another theory of music that emphasizes the evoked subjective *qualia* can be found in the work of Steve Larson (2002). Larson's theory appeals to metaphorical "forces" in accounting for basic melodic tendencies. For example, Larson refers to as "magnetism" the tendency of an unstable note to move to the nearest stable pitch. "Inertia" is the tendency of a pattern of musical motion to continue in the same fashion, whereas "gravity" is the tendency of a high pitch to descend.

Chapter 10

1. The phenomenon of musical rhythm has attracted voluminous attention by both music theorists and psychologists. No single note could do justice to the wealth of pertinent research. Music scholars who have approached rhythm from a psychological perspective include Cooper and Leonard Meyer (1960); Gabrielsson (1974); Berry (1976); Benjamin (1984); Clarke (1985, 1987, 1999); Lester (1986); Kramer (1988); Rothstein (1989); Brower (1993); Hasty (1998); and Snyder (2000). Psychologists who have studied musical rhythm include Povel (1981, 1995); Povel and Essens (1985); Michon (1985); Fraisse (1978, 1982, 1987); Handel (1991); Jones (1981, 1982, 1990, 1992); and Deutsch (1999).

2. For a pertinent discussion, see Hasty 1998.

3. See Woodrow 1951; Fraisse 1978, 1982; Povel and Essens 1985.

4. The neurological origins of the spontaneous tactus are not currently known.

5. See Seashore 1938, p. 140.

6. See Jones et al. 2002.

7. In this sense, temporal expectation is akin to the *orienting response*—a behavior whose purpose is to improve perception.

8. This analysis is based on a set of Puerto Rican infant songs collected by Maria Cadilla de Martinez 1940. My analysis included only songs in 2/4 meter.

9. See Povel 1981; Handel and Todd 1981; Jones, Kidd, and Robin Wetzel 1981; J. Smith 1983.

10. See Palmer and Krumhansl 1990.

11. See Burns and Ward 1978; Clarke 1987.

12. In assembling this histogram, I synchronized four-measure spans with the main thematic statements. Haydn sometimes adds an additional measure or two to the period. These extensions were omitted in tabulating the onset moments.

13. See Jones 1992.

14. See Wong and Ghahraman 1975.

15. See Bregman 1990; Schenker 1906.

16. See Hauser, Newport, and Aslin 2001.

17. To be sure, syncopation and missing downbeats can also evoke pleasure, but for other reasons. Read on.

18. Roeder 2003 refers to the downbeat as a "beat-class tonic."

19. See Moelants 1999.

20. See Patel and Daniele 2003.

21. See Ollen and Huron 2003.

22. See Malm 1980. Of particular interest is the *ma* concept, the tension and release in rhythmic changes, and the "sliding door" phenomenon related to simultaneous rhythms.

23. Quoted from Chernoff's delightful book (1979), p. 94.

24. See Clarke 1987.

25. Desain, Honing and Sadakata (2003).

26. For this survey I used the Barlow and Morgenstern *Dictionary of Musical Themes* (1948). The meters for some 8,356 themes were included. Most works contain more than one theme, and hence the number of works is significantly smaller than the number of themes.

27. Brochard et al. 2003.

28. See, e.g., Jones and Boltz 1989.

29. Early speculation concerning a binary rhythmic "default" can be found in work by Robert Lundin (1953/1967, p. 107), who also mentions similar speculations by Kurt Koffka (1909) and Carl Seashore (1947). My thanks to David Butler for drawing my attention to this literature.

30. From Frost's "The Birds Do Thus."

31. See Lord 1960; Parry 1971; Rubin 1995.

32. A number of these sorts of alphabets exist.

33. Woodrow 1951; Lerdahl and Jackendoff 1983.

34. Snyder 2000.

35. Gregory 1978.

36. See Large and Jones 1999.

37. Fraisse 1982.

38. Greenberg and Larkin 1968. See also Deutsch 1978; Boomsliter and Creel 1979.

Chapter 11

1. Cosmides and Tooby 2000.

2. The application of schema theory to music has been discussed by a number of writers, including Leonard Meyer (1956, 1989), Jay Dowling and Dane Harwood (1986), and Robert Gjerdingen (1988).

3. Krumhansl 1990.

4. Wade 1979, p. 76.

5. Holland et al. 1986.

6. Berlitz 1982, p. ix.

7. A survey of European folk songs indicates that melodies in major keys are roughly twice as common as melodies in minor keys. This suggests that even the choice of initial schema may be sensitive to the frequency of occurrence of various contexts.

8. Perrott and Gjerdingen 1999.

9. See Marslen-Wilson and Tyler 1980.

10. In 1992 I calculated the average notated pitch in a large sample of notes drawn from various musical works, including a large diverse sample of Western instrumental music, as well as non-Western works including multipart Korean and Sino-Japanese instrumental works. The average pitch in this sample was found to lie near D#4. See Huron 2001b, p. 9, for details.

11. Krumhansl and Kessler 1982; Krumhansl 1990, p. 221.

12. See, e.g., Spitz 1991.

13. Greenberg and MacMillan 1996.

14. See Gjerdingen 2003.

15. Bellman 1993.

16. Krumhansl, Sandell, and Sergeant 1987.

17. Gjerdingen 1988.

Chapter 12

1. An informative discussion of the relationship between musical experience and different types of memory is found in the work of Candace Brower (1993).

2. The breadth and depth of research pertaining to memory is voluminous and impressive. A partial list of citations would include Tulving 1972; Tulving and Craik 2000; Dowling 1978; Dowling and Bartlett 1981; Butler and Ward 1988; Halpern 1989; Huron and Parncutt 1993; Levitin 1994; Schachter and Tulving 1994; Snyder 2000; Schachter 2001; Squire and Schachter 2002.

3. See Squire 1994, p. 204; cited in Snyder 2000, p. 73.

4. The distinction between episodic and semantic memory was first proposed by the University of Toronto psychologist Endel Tulving in 1972.

5. See Snyder 2000 for a fine introduction to memory as it relates to sound and music.

6. Snyder 2000, p. 75.

7. See Schachter 2001.

8. Bharucha 1994.

9. Eugene Narmour has speculated that common musical figures behave as psychological prototypes. Although no empirical research has addressed this matter, it is an interesting view.

10. See Peretz 1996.

11. Significant work in this area has been carried out by Isabelle Peretz and her colleagues at the University of Montréal. See in particular Peretz 1996; Belleville, Peretz, and Arguin 1992; and Belleville, Peretz, and Malenfant 1996. Also see Hebert and Peretz 1997; Gaudreau and Peretz 1999; and Belleville, Caza, and Peretz 2003.

12. See Dowling and Harwood 1986, p. 220; Wittgenstein 1966.

13. This result is based on an analysis of 50 randomly selected chorale harmonizations.

14. Audio examples of deceptive cadences can be found at the Web site supplement to this book.

15. See Bharucha et al. 1999; Bharucha and Stoeckig 1986.

16. Meyer 1956.

17. Marcus et al. 1999.

18. Eerola 2004; Castellano, Bharucha, and Krumhansl 1984.

19. See Coons and Kraehenbuehl 1958; Kraehenbuehl and Coons 1959.

20. See the review in Snyder 2000, p. 50.

21. See Fraisse 1982, p. 157; cited in Snyder 2000, p. 50.

22. See Ollen and Huron 2003, 2004, for a summary of the various ideas.

23. Snyder 2000, p. 50.

24. Ng 2003.

25. The differences between modern Scottish and Cree fiddling are chronicled in the film *The Fiddlers of James Bay*, National Film Board of Canada 1980.

26. Ollen and Huron 2003.

27. See Cosmides and Tooby 2000.

28. See Gotlieb and Konečni 1985; Karno and Konečni 1992.

29. Cook 1987.

Chapter 13

1. E.g., voice-leading: see Huron 2001b.

2. The presumption that "what is" is "what ought to be" is referred to by philosophers as the naturalistic fallacy. Artists have long believed that the goals and methods of art do not need to agree with past artistic goals and methods. Art perpetually holds to the possibility of reinvention. Nowhere is the naturalistic fallacy less welcome than in the arts.

3. Some other possibilities include (1) creating a compelling work that people want to hear, and (2) creating memorable "hooks" that get stuck in people's heads. With a good hook, the repetition is done by the listener, rather than the musician.

4. For Western-enculturated listeners, the blues scale might also be included here. See Huron 1994 for an examination of the appeal of different scales.

5. In saying this, I don't mean to imply that there are no "natural" foundations or origins for certain musical schemas. In fact, I think there are some pertinent foundational phenomenon that dispose listeners to favor certain structures over others. But these foundations are best viewed as "bootstraps" that bias the learned schemas in particular directions, not as essential or immutable necessities that trump all other possibilities.

6. Longuet-Higgins and Lee 1982.

7. For a discussion of the psychological importance of fills see also Snyder 2000, p. 174.

8. Jerry Gray and Carl Sigman, "Pennsylvania 6-5000" as recorded by the Glenn Miller orchestra. From *The Glenn Miller Story* (1985), MCA Records, Universal City Studios, MCABD-1624. The passage in question occurs at 0:27.

9. Duke Ellington's rendition of Vincent Youmans's "Tea for Two." From *Best of Big Band* (2003), Madacy Entertainment Group, THF2 3948. The passage occurs at 1:20.

10. From Irving Berlin's "Blue Skies" performed by Swing and Sway with Sammy Kaye. From *Jazz Classics* (2001), BMG Special Products, 75517 459492. The passage occurs at 0:16.

11. Words and music by Arthur Singer, John Medora, and David White.

12. A theory of the emergent perceptual properties of chords was proposed by psychoacoustician Ernst Terhardt and elaborated by Richard Parncutt (1989).

13. An important early survey of chord frequencies was published by Helen Budge in 1943.

14. The information values for these calculations were based on a sample of chorale harmonizations by J. S. Bach. Chord inversions, sevenths, and ninth chords were treats as root position triads. Calculations were made using the Humdrum Toolkit.

15. The sample of works used in these calculations included 70 popular songs from Joel Whitburn's *The Ultimate Pop Rock Fake Book* (1996). My thanks to Tom Recchia for encoding the chords used in these calculations.

16. Gjerdingen 1988.

17. Gjerdingen 2003.

18. Ollen and Huron 2003.

19. The pitch sequence $\hat{3}$–$\hat{2}$–$\hat{1}$ is found in 3,349 of 9,324 classical themes in Barlow and Morgenstern, while 2,902 of 7,787 folksong incipits include the sequence (Essen Folksong Collection). The pitch sequence $\hat{5}$–$\hat{4}$–$\hat{3}$ occurs in 3,017 of 9,324 classical themes and 2,166 of 7,787 folksong incipits.

20. Forte 1983, reprinted as Forte 1987.

21. Huron 2001a.

22. Huron 2001a.

23. E.g., Coons and Kraehenbuehl 1958; Kraehenbuehl and Coons 1959.

24. See Partch 1949/1979.

25. An exception to this generalization can be found in the writings of ethnomusicologist Curt Sachs (1962) who described the often extreme repetitiveness found in several non-Western musics. Sachs thought that high levels of repetition were symptomatic of "primitive" musics and represented a less advanced stage of musical development (pp. 123–124). Sachs's view was broadly resonant with the attitudes of early twentieth-century musicians. Arnold Schoenberg thought that repetition was an "insult" to intelligent listeners. With the advent of modernism in the West, the repetitiveness of common music seemed to have become a source of embarrassment for professional art musicians. In chapter 16, our discussion of modernism in music will address this issue more directly.

Chapter 14

1. The majority of composed surprises in music probably originate with schematic surprises of some sort. I say "probably" because the pertinent analytic studies have not been carried out.

2. The deceptive cadence does preserve the presence of the tonic pitch. Whether the deception arises through V–Vi or V–IV, the presence of the tonic pitch is the one commonality that these progressions share with the more usual V–I.

3. Of course this points up the question of why major and minor chords tend to evoke the *qualia* of "happy" and "sad" for listeners experienced with Western music. One possible explanation is that these chords have prior associations. In the same way that Pavlov's dogs could associate the arbitrary sound of a bell with food, listeners might simply learn to associate the minor chord with sadness. This account sidesteps the "bootstrap" question of how such an association got started. Interested readers might refer to lecture 4 of my Ernest Bloch Lectures.

4. My thanks to Elizabeth Sayres for suggesting this example.

5. The statistics here were calculated using the combined corpus of the Barlow and Morgenstern *Dictionary of Music Themes* and the Essen Folksong Collection. Of 57,829 melodic continuations from the supertonic, 43 were found to be followed by either the raised dominant or the lowered submediant for major keys ($p = 0.0007$). Given the rarity of occurrence, many of these tritones are apt to be database errors.

6. As we will see later in this chapter, not all veridical surprises lead to humor, nor is humor limited to veridical surprises. Incidentally, since most musical works do not quote from other works, the very act of quoting some passage can evoke surprise.

7. This example comes from David Temperley (2001, p. 210). Linguist Steven Pinker gives other examples of garden path sentences: "The man who hunts ducks out on weekends"; "The cotton clothing is usually made of grows in Mississippi." Pinker 1994, p. 212.

To my knowledge, Leonard Meyer was the first music theorist to propose that listeners could mis-hear a passage by applying the wrong schema. In *Emotion and Meaning in Music* Meyer wrote: "the same physical stimulus may call forth different tendencies in different stylistic contexts. . . . For example, a modal cadential progression will arouse one set of expectations in the musical style of the sixteenth century and quite another in the style of the nineteenth century" (Meyer 1956, p. 30).

8. See Temperley 2001.

9. Sloboda's survey also collected responses concerning musically evoked tears and laughter, as well as frisson.

10. Sloboda 1991, p. 113. See also Sloboda 1992.

11. Panksepp 1995.

12. Scholarly studies of musical humor include Gretchen Wheelock's (1992) study of humor in Haydn, and Helen Mull's (1949) study of Rameau's *La Poule*.

13. See Huron 2004a.

14. Huron 2004a.

15. In fact, after the eighth repetition, Schickele begins to "deconstruct" the texture by progressively removing notes out of the passage. The passage ends by the conductor interjecting and

counting out loud—as though the orchestral musicians had got stuck or lost. From *The Dreaded P. D. Q. Bach Collection*, volume 1, track 3, beginning at 0:39 seconds.

16. Huron 2004a.

17. See Provine 2000, p. 45.

18. See Gabrielsson and Lindstrom 1993; Gabrielsson 2001.

19. My thanks to Ray Montemayor for drawing Church's paintings to my attention.

20. Deborah Rifkin (2000) provides a list of writers who have used the term "wrong note" in connection with Prokofiev's music. Among other theorists, the term has been used by Jonathan Kramer, William Austin, Richard Bass, Patricia Ashley, Rebecca Kaufman, and Neil Minturn.

21. See Rifkin 2000.

22. See Bass 1988.

23. See Rifkin 2000, p. 5.

24. Syncopation will be discussed later in this chapter. Notice that wrong-note harmonies may, in the future, emulate the history of syncopation. The disruptions of syncopation ultimately developed into a normative schema in which stereotypic displacements from a prevailing meter came to be expected. In the future, wrong-note harmonies might similarly develop into a normative schema for predicting stereotypic displacements from commonly expected harmonies. That is, syncopation might provide a *when*-related prototype for the *what*-related disruptions of wrong-note harmonies.

25. Rifkin 2000, p. 1.

26. A survey of emotional responses by John Sloboda (1991) found that frisson and laughter were reported as the first and second most common physiological responses to music (of 12 reponse categories provided in the survey). Ninety percent of respondents reported experiencing "shivers down the spine" within the previous five years. Eighty-eight percent reported musically evoked laughter within the previous five years. Breath-holding was not included among the survey categories.

27. See also Cone 1977/1989.

28. The sample included nearly 6,000 melodies from the Essen Folksong Collection (Schaffrath 1995). Intervals spanning rests were ignored. Tied notes were treated as a single pitch. In characterizing the metrical level of a note, possible differences in hypermetric level were ignored. For example, all downbeats were treated as identical levels, even though music often exhibits metric hierarchies that span several measures.

29. Huron and Ommen in press.

Chapter 15

1. My view of tension is the same as that offered by Elizabeth Margulis (see Margulis 2003, pp. 150 ff). If there is a single highly probable event, then the tension-S is high. If the most likely

ensuing event has a relatively low absolute probability, then the tension-S is low. Of tension-S, Margulis says it "pertains not to the degree to which an event satisfies or denies expectations created by preceding events, but to the strength of expectation generated by an event about future ones. . . . Tension-S creates an impression of urgency or precariousness" (p. 150). According to Margulis, tension-S is similar or equivalent to Bharucha's notion of "yearning" (p. 152). It is a tension generated by a strong implication.

2. The term "dissonance" is used in a wide variety of senses. In this context, the word is intended to refer to the perceived clangorousness of the vertical moment, sometimes called "sensory dissonance" (or tonal consonance). Psychoacousticians have established that this type of dissonance originates in tonotopic interactions of the basilar membrane. See Greenwood 1961; Plomp and Levelt 1965; Kameoka and Kuriyagawa 1969a,b; Huron and Sellmer 1992.

3. *Reader's Digest*, September 1977, p. 665, as quoted in Simons 1996, p. 88.

4. See especially Shaffer and Todd 1994. Early research on musical performance was carried out by the University of Iowa psychologist Carl Seashore. More recently, important performance-related research has been carried out by Henry Schaffer, Neil Todd, and Eric Clarke in Britain, Johan Sundberg and his colleagues in Sweden, Henkjan Honing and Peter Desain in the Netherlands, and Bruno Repp and Caroline Palmer in North America.

5. See Kronman and Sundberg 1987; Huron 1988b.

6. This passage occurs twice in the movement: first near measure 163 and later near measure 424.

7. Pertinent research includes the work on melodic "peaks" by Zohar Eitan 1997.

8. See Stevens and Davis 1938.

9. Seashore 1932. See also Dejonckere, Hirano, and Sundberg 1995.

10. See Sundberg 1987.

11. See Ohala 1984; Morton 1994.

12. See Scherer and Oshinsky 1977.

13. See Greenwood 1961; Plomp and Levelt 1965; Kameoka and Kuriyagawa 1969a,b; Huron and Sellmer 1992.

14. Recall that the imagination response relates to the activity of contemplating various future states. There is a case to be made that the vast majority of listening is done *teleologically*. That is, music listening is dominated by a sense of inevitability, where the listener is unable to entertain alternative ways in which the music might unfold. When I became active as a composer, I was amazed that it was possible to listen to well-known compositions with a composer's sense of "choices." That is, one could listen to a composer like Beethoven with a sense that certain passages could have been different: Beethoven might have added another variation of the current theme, or brought back a theme used earlier, or shortened a section of the development. In other

words, the experience of composing made it possible to listen without the sense that the music is inevitably the way it is, and not some other way.

In ordinary music listening, it is likely that the imagination response is largely absent or muted. This is obviously a convenient point of view, since attempting to analyze the nonteleological or imaginative component to listening would be extremely daunting.

Chapter 16

1. Boulez 1967/1968.

2. See Henley 2001 and Ben Parsons's inspiring review article (Parsons 2004).

3. In this chapter I use the word "modernism" as a synonymn for "modern art" and its affiliated social, political, and other manifestations. Over the past decade, the meaning of the word "modernism" has shifted, largely owing to the growing influence of postmodern scholarship. For postmodernists, the term "modernism" refers to the broad Enlightenment enterprise that assumes social, scientific, and technological progress. That is, "modernism" refers to the principal intellectual beliefs that have shaped Western culture for the past 300 years.

4. No list of citations would do justice to the breadth and volume of published research pertaining to modernism. A sample of pertinent scholarship would include Rosenberg 1959; Poggioli 1962; Bürger 1974; Calinescu 1977; Berman 1982; Marcus 1989; Berman 1994; Levenson 1999; Danius 2002; and Cunningham 2003.

5. See, e.g., Glasenapp 1977; Mack and Voss 1978; Breig, Dürner, and Mielke 1998.

6. Freeman 1992.

7. My discussion here of Wagner's avoidance of closure is necessarily partial. Other factors contributing to the minimizing of closure include rhythmic elements (such as the use of feminine endings), and phrase structures (such as the Wagner's violations of the classical "bar form" described by Alfred Lorenz). See also Meyer 1989, pp. 46–48, for additional discussion of closure in Wagner's music.

8. A fine discussion of the classical cadence can be found in Caplin 2004.

9. See Freeman 1992.

10. See Huron 1992, where I first suggested that Schoenberg's method of composing with twelve tones assumes a theory of tonality that is in close accord with Krumhansl's experimental presentation.

11. See Browne 1981.

12. Butler and Brown 1994.

13. An example of such a minimally tonal tone row is: C, F#, G#, D, A#, E, F, B, C#, G, D#, A. (This row is just one of an extensive class of equivalent minimally tonal tone rows.)

14. The Krumhansl–Schmuckler key-estimation agorithm is based on the Krumhansl–Kessler key-profiles (1982). In chapter 9 we saw that Bret Aarden's experiments suggest that the Krumhansl–Kessler key-profiles relate predominantly to the psychological experience of closure. When the Krumhansl–Kessler profiles are replaced by the major and minor distributions calculated by Aarden, I have found that the key estimation accuracy improves significantly. Nevertheless, the research reported here made use of the original Krumhansl–Schmuckler algorithm rather than using the revised algorithm.

15. The rows were taken from an unpublished catalog of twelve-tone rows compiled by Paul Metz of the University of Cincinnati.

16. Von Hippel and I also applied this same method to the tone rows of Anton Webern and Alban Berg. Like Schoenberg, Webern's tone rows were consistently more contratonal than the matched random tone rows. In fact, Webern's tone rows tend to be slightly more contratonal than Schoenberg's. However, Berg's tone rows are equivocal. Note first that with only 8 tone rows, little can be concluded about Berg's overall compositional goal. Several of Berg's tone rows are more contratonal than the random controls. But in general Berg's tone rows appear to be more tonal than the random controls. That is, Berg was as likely to have pursued tonal implications as to have avoided them. Anyone familiar with Berg's music will not be surprised by this result.

17. On the one hand, it would appear that this research seems to give short shrift to the Browne–Butler–Brown approach to tonality. However, as we have demonstrated, order matters in the organization of tone rows, which was precisely the main point of contention between Krumhansl and Butler.

18. Leonard Meyer has also described how the principles of tone-row construction tend to circumvent the perception of tonality. See Meyer 1967, pp. 240–242.

19. The term "contratonal" was first proposed in Huron and von Hippel 2000.

20. Krumhansl, Sandell, and Sergeant 1987.

21. See Huron and Ommen in press for an analysis and inventory of common syncopation patterns.

22. Refer to the third note in this chapter for a clarification regarding the use of the word "modernism."

23. My thanks to Joy Ollen for pointing this out.

Chapter 17

1. See Profet 1992.

2. Daniel Dennett has suggested that "All brains are, in essence, anticipation machines" (1991, p. 177).

3. The reknowned Stanford University psychologist, Roger Shepard, referred to this agreement between the psychological structures and environmental structures as *complementarity* (Shepard 1981).

4. See Baldwin 1896.

5. This argument is made forcefully in von Hippel 2002.

6. See Aarden 2003.

7. Recall that this difference is not related to a difference between white and black keys. More common black keys (like F sharp and B flat) are more quickly identified than less common black keys (like D sharp and A flat). See Takeuchi and Hulse 1991. See also Miyazaki 1990; Simpson and Huron 1994.

8. See Saffran, et al. 1999; Bharucha 1984.

9. See Olson, Roese, and Zanna 1996.

10. See Cosmides and Tooby 2000.

11. See, e.g., the research by Scherer and Oshinsky 1977.

12. See Greenwood 1961; Plomp and Levelt 1965; Huron and Sellmer 1992.

13. See Huron 2001b, pp. 56ff.

14. A discussion of music-related associations can be found in Balch, Myers, and Papotto 1999. For a broad survey of music and emotion see Juslin and Sloboda 2001. An attempt to formulate a comprehensive theory of music and emotion can be found in the fourth of my Ernest Bloch lectures (1999). See also Huron 2002.

15. There are several notable exceptions to this generalization. For example, feminist theorist Susan McClary (2002) has offered strong claims about the relationship between musical structure and misogynist social structures.

16. Seashore wrote as follows:

let us not delude ourselves into thinking that the situation is simple or solved. If there were a one-to-one relationship between the physical sound and the mental experience or response which it elicits, our problem would be simplified. However, such relationships scarcely if ever exist. The mental process never corresponds exactly to the physical event, and it is in this situation that the real problem of the psychologist begins in the task of discovering law and order in the deviations of the mental event from the physical event. This leads us first to the staggering realization that in musical art, "All is illusion." Without the blessing of normal illusions, musical art would be hopelessly stunted. Our profoundest appreciations of nature and of art are detachments from the physically exact and constitute a synthesis through the medium of normal illusions. But the composer, the performer, and the listener all deal with the physical medium and all the theories of form and interpretation of message and response must in the long run be grounded upon a true cognizance of the nature of this medium and its possible roles. (1938, p. 378)

when a message is transmitted from the sender to the listener, a great deal of the message is lost. . . . Hearing music is subject to vast limitations. . . . On the other hand, the listener may put a great deal more into the music than was originally intended or is actually present. . . . Fundamental to this issue is the fact that there is not a one-to-one relationship between music as performed and music as experienced. (1938, p. 382)

17. See also Temperley 1999.

18. Hellman 2001, chapter 4, p. 55.

19. Hanslick 1854/1885.

20. See, e.g., Dobson 1968; Baugh and Cable 1993.

21. See Huron and Veltman in press.

22. Of course, the idea of wanting music to be "all that it can be" may be a Western value that is not shared by other cultures.

23. See Huron 2004b.

Glossary

absolute pitch (AP) The ability found in a minority of listeners, where the pitch of a tone can be accurately identified without relying on an external reference pitch. Also called perfect pitch.

aggression display See *threat display*.

agogic Pertaining to duration.

agogic syncopation Syncopation that arises when metrically unstressed notes are longer in duration than metrically stressed notes. Compare *onset syncopation*. See also *syncopation; dynamic syncopation; harmonic syncopation; tonal syncopation; meter*.

Aksak meter Any of a class of irregular meters commonly found in Bulgarian dances. For example, a repeated rhythmic cycle of 3 + 2 + 2.

amygdala An almond-shaped brain structure located in both right and left temporal lobes that is involved in emotional responses, especially fear.

antecedent state An event that precedes some other event—as in the first note in a melodic interval. Compare *consequent state*.

anticipation 1. The subjective experience accompanying a strong expectation that a particular event will occur; also referred to as the *feeling of anticipation*. 2. In Western music theory, a type of melodic *embellishment* in which an expected note is immediately preceded by the same pitch. E.g. The "ta" in the "ta-dah" cadence. See also *premonition*.

AP *Absolute pitch.*

appoggiatura 1. In Western music theory, a type of melodic *embellishment* in which an important melody pitch is preceded by two tones that form a large pitch interval (*leap*) followed by a *step* in the opposite direction. 2. The second tone in the three-tone pattern just described.

appraisal response The fifth and final component of the *ITPRA* theory of expectation. Any of one or more feelings that can arise after an outcome is fully assessed. Feelings might include jealousy, anger, suspicion, boredom, relief, pride, embarrassment, irritation, disgust, sadness, confusion, and joy, to name just a few. See also *ITPRA; imagination response; tension response; prediction response; reaction response*.

arousal   The body's readiness for action. A low state of arousal is accompanied by feelings of lethargy or sleepiness, whereas a high state of arousal is accompanied by feelings of energy and excitement. Physiological features of low arousal include slow heart rate, low blood pressure, slow respiration, low cellular glucose uptake. Compare *attention*.

association   A learned link or correlation between a stimulus and a response, or between two stimuli.

attention   A network of mental processes that selects which sensations or thoughts become the subject of contemplation. Also, the extent or magnitude of interest or disinterest.

authentic cadence   The most common cadence in Western music. A closing gesture that is defined by two successive harmonies: a *dominant* chord followed by a *tonic* chord. E.g. In the key of C major, a G major chord followed by a C major chord. See *cadence*. See also *deceptive cadence*.

awe   An emotion in which wonder and fear are combined. Often associated with gasping or breath-holding and general motor immobility ("freeze").

azimuth   The left–right horizontal component of sound *localization*. Azimuth cues are known to be related to interaural time and amplitude differences. An aspect of audition that is resistent to learning. See also *elevation*.

backbeat   The tendency in a recurring four-beat sequence to emphasize the second and fourth beats rather than the first and third beats. The most characteristic feature of rock and roll, typically played on a snare drum.

Baldwin effect   Variously interpreted. The idea, proposed by James Baldwin, that evolution favors the development of learning (in preference to innate responses) whenever the environment changes relatively rapidly.

Baroque   A stylistic period in Western music spanning roughly 1600 to 1750. Associated with the music of such composers as J. S. Bach and G. F. Handel.

basilar membrane   A long, thin tissue in the cochlea that contains the sensory neurons responsible for hearing. Through a complicated biomechanical arrangement, the basilar membrane achieves a form of spectral analysis where high and low frequencies cause maximum activation toward opposite ends of the membrane.

beat   A recurring moment when tone-onsets are more expected. In contrast to *tactus*, beats are differentiated from strong to weak and occur within a repeating pattern of beats, called a *meter*.

betting paradigm   An experimental method used to infer the subjective probability of different outcomes by having participants place monetary bets on possible future events.

binary meter bias   The tendency for (Western-enculturated) listeners to assume that *beats* and subbeats will form strong–weak (or weak–strong) pairs. Listeners tend not to expect *triple meters* or *compound meters*. See Brochard et al. 2003. See also *statistical learning*.

binding problem   The problem of how the mind integrates the various properties of a stimulus (e.g., *pitch* and *timbre*) into a single perceptual experience. A classic problem in cognitive science.

bit   Binary digit. A logarithmic representation useful for characterizing the amount of information or uncertainty. Two states can be represented by a single bit. Four states can be represented by two bits. Eight states can be represented by three bits, etc.

bradycardia   The momentary slowing of the heart rate in response to a stimulus. Typically, bradycardic responses occur when the individual pays *attention*. Bradycardic responses are symptomatic of *interest* (as opposed to boredom or fear).

cadence   A stereotypic musical pattern that evokes a sense of full or partial completion or *closure*. Cadences are evident in virtually all musical cultures. In Western music, different types of cadences are often associated with different harmonic progressions. See *authentic cadence; deceptive cadence.*

central pitch tendency   The tendency for pitches in a melody to cluster around a middle region. By contrast, few pitches in a melody will be especially high or especially low. Central pitch tendency is likely an artifact of the mechanics of pitch production: pitches in a particular region or tessitura are usually easier to generate than outlying pitches. See also *regression to the mean.*

chills   See *frisson.*

chimeric melody   A pitch sequence constructed by linking together two different melodies. A tune that begins with one melody, but then shifts to another melody. See also *elision; quodlibet.*

chroma   In psychology, the subjective phenomenon by which tones in different octaves sound similar. The tones C#4, C#5, C#6, etc. differ in *pitch* but evoke the same *chroma*. Compare *pitch class.*

chromatic   An adjective applied to any pitch or chord that does not belong to the perceived *key*. Compare *diatonic.*

closure   The subjective sense of ending or completion—as when experiencing the end of a sentence. In music, ending gestures are called *cadences*. Narmour has defined closure as the absence of psychological expectations. See also *cadence.*

compound meter   Any *meter* in which the beats are subdivided into three. E.g. **1**-2-3-**4**-5-6 (compound duple), **1**-2-3-**4**-5-6-**7**-8-9 (compound triple). Compare *simple meter.* See also *binary meter bias.*

consequent state   An event that follows after some preceding event—as in the second note in a melodic interval. Compare *antecedent state.*

consonance   The idea that some sounds or sound-combinations are more beautiful or euphonious than others. An ancient but disputed idea that has received numerous treatments. Psychoacoustic research suggests that consonance may be regarded as the absence of sensory dissonance. See *dissonance.*

context cue   An unusual or distinctive feature that provides information about which of several *schemas* to invoke in some situation. Context cues might include distinctive forms of dress, manners of speech, environment or locale, etc. See also *schema.*

contingent frequency   The likelihood of some event given the occurrence of some other event. For example, the likelihood of a *downbeat* given an event on the preceding upbeat.

contour   The up-and-down of pattern pitch changes in a melody.

contracadential   As used here, the compositional strategy, evident especially in the music of Richard Wagner, where *cadence*-like passages do not lead to the experience of *closure*.

contrametric   As used here, the compositional strategy, evident especially in some passages by Igor Stravinsky, where the music is designed to thwart the listener's ability to infer a regular *meter*.

contratonal   As used here, the compositional strategy, evident especially in the 12-tone compositions of Arnold Schoenberg, where the 12-tone row is organized to thwart the listener's ability to infer a tonal center or *key*.

contrarian aesthetic   The artistic goal, associated with certain modernist artists and musicians, where works of art are created to provoke psychological discomfort or unease. See also *contracadential; contrametric; contratonal*.

contrastive valence   A conjecture that the *hedonic* value of an experience is amplified when preceded by a contrasting hedonic state. See also *valence*.

cortical   Pertaining to the cerebral cortex. That is, pertaining to the outer surface of the brain commonly associated with conscious thought. Contrasts with subcortical.

critical learning period   The idea that learning is facilitated during a particular period of animal development. Critical learning periods are typically proposed during childhood.

cross-over   In music or art, the mixing of two or more styles, such as the blending of "folk" and "rock" to create "folk rock."

deceptive cadence   A type of *cadence* where a *dominant* chord is not followed by the (normal) *tonic* chord. Commonly, a deceptive cadence involves a dominant chord that is followed by either a *submediant* chord or a *subdominant* chord. See also *cadence; authentic cadence; progression*.

declination   The general tendency for successive pitches to decline. Commonly observed in speech where the pitch of the voice tends to fall until the speaker inhales. See also *step declination; tumbling strain*.

deduction   The process of deriving statements (called propositions) from a set of assumptions (called axioms). If *all humans are mortal* and *Socrates is human*, then it may be deduced that *Socrates is mortal*. Compare *induction*.

degree   See *scale degree*.

diatonic   An adjective applied to any pitch or chord that belongs to the perceived *key*. Compare *chromatic*.

diatonic interval   An *interval* between two pitches, both of which belong to a single major *key*. See also *diatonic; chromatic*.

dishabituation   After habituating to a repeated stimulus, the phenomenon whereby an organism regains its sensitivity to the same stimulus. See also *habituation*.

dissonance   The idea that some sounds or sound-combinations are less euphonious than others. An ancient but disputed idea that has received numerous treatments. Psychoacoustic research supports a low-level auditory irritation dubbed "sensory dissonance" that is related to the timbre, register, and interval content for sonorous moments. See also *consonance.*

dominant   1. The fifth *scale degree* in the Western major or minor scales. 2. The major chord built on the fifth scale degree (dominant chord). 3. The harmonic function associated with the dominant chord.

downbeat   The first beat in a measure. The moment in a metric schema that is most likely to coincide with an event onset. See also *meter.*

duple meter   Any *meter* that exhibits two main beats per measure. Duple meters may be either *simple* (beats are subdivided into 2) or *compound* (beats are subdivded into 3). See also *triple meter; meter.*

duplex theory of pitch   A theory proposed in the 1950s by Licklider that pitch is neurologically represented by two factors: the *place* of maximum excitation on the *basilar membrane*, and the *rate* of neural firing.

dyad   Pair. Two items, such as two notes, or two intervals.

dynamic syncopation   Syncopation that arises when events are louder at metrically weaker moments. See also *agogic syncopation; harmonic syncopation; onset syncopation; tonal syncopation; meter.*

dynamic expectation   An expectation that arises "on the fly." These expectations are shaped by immediate experience, as when exposure to a novel work causes a listener to expect similar passages as the work continues. Dynamic expectations are linked to short-term memory. See also *schematic expectation; veridical expectation.*

echoic memory   A brief sensory memory that retains a sound impression for roughly a second.

elevation   The component of sound *localization* that pertains to the vertical height of a sound source. Elevation cues are related to the shape of the outer ear (pinna). Elevation appears to be learned. See also *azimuth.*

elision   Overlapping—as when the last note of one musical phrase is also the first note of the ensuing phrase. See also *chimeric melody.*

embellishment   A class of tones found in melodies that are commonly regarded as subservient to neighboring "structural" tones. The most important embellishment tones include *anticipations, appoggiaturas,* passing tones, neighbor tones, and suspensions. Also called "nonharmonic," "nonchordal," or "unessential" tones.

epinephrine   A hormone associated with increased *arousal* that causes elevated respiratory, circulatory, and other changes appropriate for increased movement. See *arousal; norepinephrine.*

episodic memory   Autobiographical memory; a memory for particular past events.

event-related binding   The conjecture that properties of sounds (including the relationships between successive sounds) are mentally assigned to sound onsets. For example, the idea that the *qualia* evoked by melodic intervals are experienced as the way in which a tone is approached.

exposure effect   Also called "mere exposure effect." The tendency, evident in all animals, to prefer stimuli to which they have been most frequently exposed. It is argued in this book that the exposure effect is better viewed as a *prediction effect*.

fast track   Any neural pathway that takes less than about 150 milliseconds to respond to some stimulus. Typically, such fast responses do not involve the neocortex. In general, "fast track" processes are concerned with protection or defense. Compare *slow track*.

fight response   The tendency for an organism to attack in response to fear-inducing stimuli. One of three classic physiological responses to fear. See also *flight response; freeze response; surprise; threat display; frisson*.

firewall   Also *cognitive firewall*. The hypothetical physiological mechanism through which brains are able to segregate inductive lessons into distinctive contexts. The capacity for brains to protect *schemas* from overgeneralized learning.

first-order   The probability of an event occurring given the prior occurrence of a single other event. Compare *zeroth-order*.

flight response   The tendency for an organism to flee in response to fear. One of three classic physiological responses to fear. See also *fight response; freeze response; surprise; laughter*.

folk psychology   The name given by professional psychologists to describe common intuitive theories about human behavior. Folk psychologies are often captured in sayings or aphorisms such as "Never cry wolf." Psychologists have noted that many folk psychologies are inconsistent or contradictory. For example, people may concurrently hold to be true "Absence makes the heart grow fonder" and "Out of sight, out of mind."

freeze response   The tendency for an organism to become immobile in response to fear. One of three classic physiological responses to fear. See also *fight response; flight response; surprise; gasp; awe*.

frisson   The sensation of chills, thrills, or shivers running up and down one's spine. Also associated with goose flesh and piloerection (one's hair standing on end). Commonly evoked by cold temperatures and acute fear. The word "frisson" is borrowed from French. See also *piloerection; skin orgasm*.

gap fill   A general psychological principle, proposed by Leonard Meyer, that listeners expect a stimulus sequence to return to any states that have been omitted in some sequence. For example, if a melody ascends along some scale and skips one of the scale tones, Meyer suggested that there would arise a psychological craving to return at some point and "fill" the gap that had been created. Meyer proposed that gap fill constituted a formerly overlooked Gestalt principle. See *post-skip reversal*.

gasp   A reflex motor response characterized by (1) open mouth, (2) rapid inhale, followed by (3) breath-holding. Gasping may be audible or inaudible. Sometimes breath-holding (and immobility) may occur without the rapid inhaling. See also *awe; freeze response; surprise*.

genre   In music, a broad class or type of music. Genres are defined in various ways, such as by instrument (music for accordion, didgeridoo), by instrumental group (chamber orchestra, music for gamelan), by style (country & western, Gregorian chant), by culture (gagaku, bossa nova, flamenco), by spectacle (opera, puppet theater, jig), by texture (monody, polyphony, heterophony), by technical musical features (minor key, slendro, compound meter), etc. See also *schema*.

goose flesh   See *piloerection*.

habituation   The process of decreasing responsiveness to a recurring stimulus. The simplest form of learning. See also *dishabituation*.

harmonic syncopation   Syncopation that arises when chord changes coincide with metrically weaker (rather than metrically stronger) moments. See also *agogic syncopation; dynamic syncopation; onset syncopation; tonal syncopation; meter*.

hedonic   Pertaining to pleasure.

hemiola   A syncopation-like effect created when a musical passage changes meter for one or two measures. See also *syncopation*.

heuristic   Rule of thumb. A rule that proves helpful in most (though not all) cases.

Hick–Hyman law   The speed of processing a stimulus is inversely proportional to the familiarity of the stimulus.

hypermeter   A recurring pattern of *beats* whose period of repetition is longer than a single bar or measure. In Western music, hypermeter commonly involves two- or four-measure patterns. See *meter; downbeat*.

hippocampus   A structure found in the right and left temporal lobes known to be involved in short-term memory and spatial representation.

imagination response   The first component of the *ITPRA* theory of expectation. The feelings that are evoked by imagining some future outcome, such as imagining being embarrassed by not completing a project, or feeling pride at the thought of graduating from college. See also *ITPRA; tension response; prediction response; reaction response; appraisal response*.

implication-realization theory   A theory of musical expectation developed by Eugene Narmour. The theory distinguishes circumstances where listeners form strong expectations (implicative contexts) from circumstances where listeners form weak expectations. For implicative contexts, the theory proposes a number of Gestalt-like principles that shape the listener's expectations.

induction   The process by which general lessons are drawn from a finite set of experiences or observations. Compare *deduction*.

interval   In music, the distance between two successive pitches (melodic interval) or two concurrent pitches (harmonic interval). In Western music, intervals are characterized by either their distance in semitones, or by their diatonic/chromatic relationship.

irregular meter   As used by Western musicians, any *meter* that does not employ a recurring cycle of 2, 3, or 4 beats, or where beats are not subdivided in the same way. See *Aksak meter*.

isochronous   Equivalent in duration.

ITPRA   A mnemonic for the sequence of five expectation-related responses: *Imagination response, Tension response, Prediction response, Reaction response, Appraisal response.*

James–Lange theory   The theory proposed by William James and Carl Lange that feeling states arise from sensing physiological changes (e.g., we are sad *because* we cry).

key   1. The name or designation given to an absolute pitch scale, or a musical passage conforming to such a scale. Key designations include the *tonic* (first scale tone) and the mode (major or minor)—as in the key of "F major." 2. The scale schema evoked by some musical passage or sequence of tones.

key closure   See *long-term closure.*

laughter   An innate respiratory reflex involving a characteristic punctuated exhaling. Commonly evoked by initially fearful stimuli that are subsequently appraised as innocuous. May be evoked by nervousness, surprise, sadism, slapstick, social politeness, or humor. See also *flight response.*

leading tone   The seventh scale degree in either the Western major or minor scales. A pitch that often evokes the *qualia* of "yearning" to resolve to the *tonic.*

late phrase declination   The tendency exhibited by Western-enculturated listeners to expect pitches to descend in the latter half of phrases. An expectational *heuristic* that may originate in the *melodic arch.* See also *declination; tumbling strain; Urlinie.*

leap   A large melodic pitch interval. Traditionally, a leap is defined as an interval larger than two or three semitones. Contrasts with *step.*

localization   The sense of spatial position of a sound source, including left–right *azimuth*, high–low *elevation*, and near–far proximity.

long-term closure   Also called "key closure." 1. The practice of ending a musical work in the same key in which it begins. 2. The theory that ending a musical work in the same key in which it begins evokes a stronger psychological sense of *closure.*

long-term memory   Memories that may be retrieved days, months, or years later.

lower-order   The probability of an event occurring in light of little knowledge of other prior events. Examples of lower-order probabilities include *zeroth-order* and *first-order* relationships. Contrasts with higher-order.

macroemotions   See *microemotions.*

McDonald's effect   The tendency for long melodic arches to display a midphrase dip. The average pitch height graph for long phrases exhibits an M-shape akin to the golden arch logo used by McDonald's restaurants. See also *melodic arch.*

major key bias   The tendency for (Western-enculturated) listeners to assume that musical passages will be in a major (as opposed to minor) key. See also *statistical learning.*

mediant   The third *scale degree* in the Western major or minor scales.

melodic arch   The tendency in Western (and some other) musical cultures, for melodic phrases to exhibit a rising then falling pitch contour. Also the tendency for an ascending phrase to be followed by a descending phrase. See *late phrase declination.*

mental representation   The way that brains code the external world.

meter   1. A recurring pattern of *beats* that, in Western music, coincides with the duration of a bar or measure. 2. A beat *schema* that typically involves a cycle of between 2 and 5 beats with a distinctive way of subdividing beats. See *compound meter; simple meter; duple meter; triple meter; irregular meter; Aksak meter; hypermeter; contrametric; binary meter bias; beat; downbeat.*

microemotions   Slight feelings of pleasantness or discomfort that occur throughout a normal day, and which are rarely accessible to conscious awareness. Examples include the irritation that causes a person to shift posture, or the enjoyment of stroking fur. Contrasts with macroemotions—major emotional experiences, such as feeling fear at the sight of a snake, or the joy of being reunited with a loved one.

misattribution   The psychological tendency to attribute or associate feelings or emotions with any distinctive or noticeable stimulus or environment.

naive realism   The belief that the world exists as it appears and that our senses do not deceive us. See also *sophisticated realism.*

neural Darwinism   The neurological theory that mental functions compete for the use of cortical tissues.

norepinephrine   A hormone associated with increased brain activity. See *arousal; attention; epinephrine.*

oddball note   A single tone that is experienced as "out of place."

onset syncopation   Syncopation that arises when note onsets coincide with metrically weaker (rather than metrically stronger) moments. Compare *agogic syncopation.* See also *syncopation; dynamic syncopation; harmonic syncopation; tonal syncopation; meter.*

panting-laughter   A form of laughter, found in nonhuman primates, that involves both inhaling and exhaling.

paradoxical expectation   An event that is simultaneously expected and not expected. A phenomenon that can be traced to diverging *schematic, veridical,* or *dynamic* expectations. See also *Wittgenstein's puzzle; deceptive cadence.*

pianissimo   Italian for *very quiet* or *soft.* Contrasts with *fortissimo.*

piloerection   The physiological reflex that causes hair follicles to constrict so that one's hair stands on end. See *threat display; frisson.*

pitch class   In music theory, the property by which tones in different octaves are deemed to be the same—as in the set of all Cs, or the set of all C#s, etc. Compare *chroma.*

pitch proximity   1. The tendency, found in most of the world's music, for successive tones to be near in pitch. 2. The tendency for listeners to expect successive tones to be near in pitch.

post-event epoch   The period of time immediately following the advent of some expected or unexpected event. In the *ITPRA* theory, this epoch includes the *prediction response*, the *reaction response*, and the *appraisal response*. Compare with *pre-event epoch*.

post-skip reversal   1. The tendency for melodic *leaps* or large pitch intervals to be followed by a change in pitch direction. 2. The psychological expectation that a melodic leap will be followed by a change of direction. See *gap fill; regression to the mean*.

pre-event epoch   The period of time preceding the advent of some expected or unexpected event. In the *ITPRA* theory, this epoch includes the *imagination response* and the *tension response*. Compare *post-event epoch*.

prediction effect   The tendency to *misattribute* positive or negative feelings generated by the *prediction response* to the stimulus. That is, the tendency to experience predicted stimuli as positive, and unpredicted stimuli as negative. Compare *exposure effect*.

prediction response   The third component of the *ITPRA* theory of expectation. The positive or negative feelings that are evoked in response to the relative success or failure in predicting some outcome. Also referred to as the *primary affect* in some theories of expectation. See also *ITPRA; imagination response; tension response; reaction response; appraisal response*.

premonition   A long-range feeling of *anticipation*.

primary affect   See *prediction response*.

problem of induction   The philosophical problem, identified by David Hume, that no amount of observation can ever establish the truth of some general proposition. For example, no matter how many white swans one observes, one can never prove that *all* swans are white. All *learning* is constrained by the problem of induction.

progression   Also "harmonic progression." The succession of chords in a musical work or passage.

pump-up   An abrupt modulation, common in some popular musics, where the *key* shifts upward by one or two semitones. Typically appears toward the end of a work.

qualia   The distinctive subjective or phenomenological "feel" of some experience.

quodlibet   A musical work constructed primarily of quotations from other works. See also *chimeric melody*.

reaction response   The fourth component of the *ITPRA* theory of expectation. Any one of several fast responses that might be immediately evoked after an outcome. Reaction responses are automatic (unconscious) and are typically defensive in nature. Reaction responses might include innate reflexes such as the startle response or the orienting response, or learned quick responses. See also *ITPRA; imagination response; tension response; prediction response; appraisal response*.

realism   The belief that there exists an objective, physical world. See also *naive realism; sophisticated realism*.

recognition point   The moment in time when a stimulus is recognized. It will take several tones before an individual can recognize a familiar melody.

regression to the mean   The tendency for an extreme value to be followed by a more moderate value.

relative pitch   The mental coding of pitches by their successive relationships rather than according to their fixed pitch level. Examples of relative pitch include *pitch interval* and *scale degree succession*. Relative pitch is evident when the same song can be sung at several different pitch levels without changing the essential character of the song. Compare *absolute pitch.*

rhythmic attending   The theory, proposed by Mari Riess Jones, that *attention* waxes and wanes according to periodic pulses ("attentional pulses"). Listeners are more attentive at particular moments in time.

ritard   The slowing down of a musical passage, commonly done at the ends of musical phrases. Especially marked at the ends of musical works.

rubato   The intentional speeding-up and slowing-down when performing music.

scale degree   A relative system for naming pitches according to their position in some scale. For Western music, seven scale degrees are commonly identified. For the major scale, the most well-known names are the "solfa" syllables: do, re, mi, fa, so, la, ti. For both the major and minor scales, theorists use the names: *tonic, supertonic, mediant, subdominant, dominant, submediant, leading tone*, or more simply, the numbers $\hat{1}$, $\hat{2}$, $\hat{3}$, $\hat{4}$, $\hat{5}$, $\hat{6}$, $\hat{7}$.

Schadenfreude   The pleasure evoked by others' misfortunes. A word borrowed from the German.

schema   A mental preconception of the habitual course of events.

schematic expectation   Expectations that arise from general knowledge of how events typically unfold—such as familiarity with the "language" of jazz. Expectations linked to *long-term memory.* Compare *dynamic expectation; veridical expectation.*

Schenkerian analysis   A method of music analysis devised by Heinrich Schenker in the early 20th century. Schenker conceived of tonal works as an elaboration of one of three background templates or scaffolds. One scaffold consists of three descending pitches—mi, re, do. A second scaffold consists of five descending pitches—so, fa, mi, re, do. A third (more rare) scaffold consists of an eight-pitch descending line—do, ti, la, so, fa, mi, re, do. Using a sophisticated series of "rewrite" rules, Schenkerian analysts progressively distill a musical foreground to a successively reduced set of structural tones until finally, an entire work or movement is reduced to a 3-, 5-, or 8-line scaffold called an *Urlinie*. See also *declination; Urlinie.*

simple meter   Any *meter* in which the beats are subdivided into two. E.g., **1**-2-**3**-4 (simple duple), **1**-2-3-**4**-5-6 (simple triple). Compare *compound meter.* See also *binary meter bias.*

skin orgasm   Term coined by Jaak Panksepp; synonymous with *frisson.*

slow track   Any neural pathway that takes more than about 150 milliseconds to respond to some stimulus. Typically, such slow responses arise because of the involvement of the neocortex. In general, "slow track" processes are concerned with accurate appraisal. Compare *fast track.*

sophisticated realism   The belief that there exists an objective, physical world apart from human experience. A belief that this reality is interpreted and filtered by our sensory systems and that sensations are only indirect apprehensions of the presumed external world. See also *naive realism.*

Strack effect   Flexing the zygomatic muscles makes people feel happier. For example, holding a pencil with your teeth causes you to feel happier than holding it with your lips. (You can feel happy *because* you smile.) See also *James–Lange theory; tension response.*

statistical learning   Learning based on how frequently a particular event occurs, or how tightly two or more events are correlated.

step   The pitch distance between two successive tones in some scale. The precise size of a step may vary from one to three semitones. See *pitch proximity; step declination; step inertia.*

step declination   A disposition evident in Western musical notation for a descending melodic *step* to be followed by a subsequent lower pitch. Compare *step inertia.*

step inertia   A psychological disposition exhibited by (Western-enculturated) listeners to expect that a melodic *step* will be followed by a subsequent pitch that continues in the same direction. Originally proposed by theorist Eugene Narmour, the idea received experimental support in work by Paul von Hippel. N.B. Notated Western music does *not* exhibit step inertia. Compare *step declination.*

stop-and-go   A musical device in which the music stops completely for a moment, and then resumes.

stream-of-consciousness listening   A common form of music listening where the listener is unaware or pays no conscious attention to the listening experience. In this form of listening, the *imagination* and *appraisal* responses are muted or attenuated, and so a simplified analysis (reducing *ITPRA* to *TPR*) may be appropriate.

strong beat   A recurring moment when tone-onsets are especially expected. See *beat; downbeat; meter.*

subito   Italian word meaning "sudden," as in *subito piano* (suddenly quiet).

subdominant   1. The fourth *scale degree* in the Western major or minor scales. 2. The major or minor chord built on the fourth scale degree ("subdominant chord"). 3. The harmonic function associated with the subdominant chord.

subjective probability   The perceived or apparently likelihood (rather than the actual likelihood).

submediant   1. The sixth *scale degree* in the Western major or minor scales. 2. The major or minor chord built on the sixth scale degree ("submediant chord"). 3. The harmonic function associated with the submediant chord. See also *deceptive cadence.*

supertonic   The second *scale degree* in the Western major or minor scales.

surprise   A common response to unexpected stimuli. A characteristic facial expression may be evoked where the mouth remains open (facilitating breathing) and the eyelids remain retracted (facilitating perception). See also *fight response; flight response;* and *freeze response.*

surprise laughter   Laughter evoked by some unexpected event or stimulus, such as the bursting of a balloon.

sweet anticipation   As used in this book, the positive feelings that arise from conscious thought about some future event (such as the thought of attending a concert).

syncopation   A distinctive rhythmic effect produced by a class of violations of temporal expectation. Specifically, where an event coinciding with a relatively weak metrical moment fails to be followed by an event on an ensuing stronger metrical moment. See also *agogic syncopation; dynamic syncopation; harmonic syncopation; onset syncopation;* and *tonal syncopation.*

tactus   A basic pulse that typically falls in the range between 0.6 and 0.75 seconds (80 to 100 events per minute). The rate at which a listener will spontaneously tap while listening to music. The tactus commonly coincides with the beat rate. However, where *beats* are perceived as stronger or weaker events within a recurring *meter*, the tactus remains an undifferentiated pulse.

tendency moment   Moment within a *meter* that evokes a strong expectation of an event onset coinciding with some ensuing metrical moment. An example of a tendency moment is the pickup, upbeat, or anacrusis. See also *tendency tone; meter.*

tendency tone   In music theory, a tone that evokes a strong expectation of some ensuing tone. Common examples of tendency tones include chromatic (nonscale) tones, the *leading tone,* and the seventh in a dominant seventh chord.

tension   As used in this book, a term reserved to describe those feelings that arise immediately prior to an expected event. See *tension response.*

tension response   The second component of the *ITPRA* theory of expectation. Feelings that arise due to preparations for an expected event—often feelings evoked by an increase in arousal or vigilance. See also *James–Lange theory; ITPRA; appraisal response; imagination response; prediction response; reaction response.*

theme   A relatively brief musical passage that is (1) characteristic of the work in question, and (2) has a tendency to be memorable. The "main musical idea" of a work.

threat display   A characteristic component of the *fight response,* where an animal endeavors to appear fierce. Typically involves the showing of teeth, making eye contact, leaning forward, *piloerection* (hair standing on end), and vocalization.

thrills   See *frisson.*

timbre   (TAM-bur) A catch-all term denoting those properties of a sound (other than pitch or loudness) that contribute to the sound's distinctive character or identity. Also called "tone color" or "tone quality."

tonal syncopation   Syncopation that arises when pitch patterns fail to coincide with the prevailing meter. See also *agogic syncopation; dynamic syncopation; harmonic syncopation; onset syncopation; meter.*

tonality   1. A system for interpreting pitches or chords through their relationship to a reference pitch, dubbed the *tonic.* The relationships are designated using scale-degree names or numbers. 2. Any musical system in any culture that relates scale tones to a final or reference pitch. 3. The major/minor system of pitch organization that has dominated Western music since the 16th century (contrasts with *modality* and *atonality*). 4. A broad-ranging interrelated system of musical organization that includes *cadences*, modulations, thematic key areas, and *long-term key closure*. See also *scale degree*.

tonic   The first *scale degree* in the Western major and minor scales. The pitch in a scale that sounds most stable or closed.

triple meter   Any *meter* that exhibits three main beats per measure. Triple meters may be either *simple* (beats are subdivided into 2) or *compound* (beats are subdivded into 3). See also *duple meter; meter*.

tumbling strain   Name given by ethnomusicologist Curt Sachs to denote music that exhibits a distinctive tendency to fall in pitch with each musical phrase. Compare *melodic arch*. See also *declination; step declination; Urlinie*.

Urlinie   Concept proposed by theorist Heinrich Schenker to denote a fundamental line or deep structure that is presumed to underlie all aesthetically constructed tonal music. See also *Schenkerian analysis; declination; step declination; late phrase declination; tumbling strain*.

valence   The positive or negative quality of emotions. (There are no neutral emotions.) See also *contrastive valence*.

veridical expectation   Expectations that arise from past knowledge of a familiar sequence of events—such as familiarity with a particular musical work. Expectations linked to *episodic memory*. See also *dynamic expectation; schematic expectation*.

Wittgenstein's puzzle   The paradox, posed by the Austrian philosopher Ludwig Wittgenstein, of how it is possible to be surprised by musical events that one knows will happen. How, for example, can a *deceptive cadence* continue to sound deceptive, even when a listener is familiar with the music? See also *paradoxical expectation*.

zeroth-order   The raw probability of an event occurring without any consideration of the possible influence of surrounding or neighboring events. Compare *first-order*.

References

Aarden, B. (2001). An empirical study of chord-tone doubling in common era music. Masters' thesis. School of Music, Ohio State University.

Aarden, B. (2002). Expectancy vs. retrospective perception: Reconsidering the effects of schema and continuation judgments on measures of melodic expectancy. In C. Stevens, D. Burnham, G. McPherson, E. Schubert, and J. Renwick (eds.), *Proceedings of the 7th International Conference on Music Perception and Cognition*, pp. 469–472. Adelaide: Causal Productions.

Aarden, B. (2003). Dynamic melodic expectancy. Ph.D. dissertation. School of Music, Ohio State University.

Abe, J., and E. Oshino (1990). Schema driven properties in melody cognition: Experiments on final tone extrapolation by music experts. *Psychomusicology* 9: 161–172.

Abraham, O. (1901). Das absolute Tonbewusstein. *Sammelbände der Internationalen Musikgesellschaft* 3: 1–86.

Aiken, N. E. (1998). *The Biological Origins of Art.* Westport, Conn.: Praeger.

Aldwell, E., and C. Schachter (1989). *Harmony and Voice Leading.* Orlando, Florida: Harcourt Brace Jovanovich.

Aristotle (1927). *The Poetics.* Trans. by Hamilton Fyfe. London: Heinemann.

Baharloo, S., P. A. Johnston, S. K. Service, J. Gitschier, and N. B. Freimer (1998). Absolute pitch: An approach for identifying genetic and non-genetic components. *American Journal of Human Genetics* 62: 224–231.

Balch, W. R., D. M. Myers, and C. Papotto (1999). Dimensions of mood in mood-dependent memory. *Journal of Experimental Psychology: Learning, Memory, and Cognition* 25 (1): 70–83.

Baldwin, J. M. (1896). A new factor in evolution. *American Naturalist* 30: 441–451, 536–553.

Baldwin, J. M. (1909). *Darwin and the Humanities.* Baltimore: Review Publishing.

Bandura, A., D. Cioffi, C. B. Taylor, and M. E. Brouillard (1988). Perceived self-efficacy in coping with cognitive stressors and opioid activation. *Journal of Personality and Social Psychology* 55 (3): 479–488.

Barkow, J. H., L. Cosmides, and J. Tooby (1992). *The Adapted Mind: Evolutionary Psychology and the Generation of Culture.* Oxford: Oxford University Press.

Barlow, H., and S. Morgenstern (1948). *A Dictionary of Musical Themes.* New York: Crown Publishers.

Bass, R. (1988). Prokofiev's technique of chromatic displacement. *Music Analysis* 7: 197–214.

Baugh, A. C., and T. Cable (1993). *A History of the English Language,* 4th edition. Englewwod Cliffs, NJ: Prentice-Hall.

Bayes, T. (1763). An essay toward solving a problem in the doctrine of chances. *Philosophical Transactions* 53: 370–418.

Bechara, A., A. R. Damasio, H. Damasio, and S. Anderson (1994). Insensitivity to future consequences following damage to human prefrontal cortex. *Cognition* 50: 7–12.

Bellman, J. (1993). *The Style Hongrois in the Music of Western Europe.* Boston: Northeastern University Press.

Belleville, S., N. Caza, and I. Peretz (2003). A neuropsychological argument for a processing view of memory. *Journal of Memory and Language* 48 (4): 686–703.

Belleville, S., and I. Peretz (1996). Examination of the working memory components in normal aging and in dementia of the Alzheimer type. *Neuropsychologia* 34 (3): 195–207.

Belleville, S., I. Peretz, and M. Arguin (1992). Contribution of articulatory rehearsal to short-term memory: Evidence from a case of selective disruption. *Brain and Language* 43 (4): 713–746.

Ben-Ze'ev, A. (2000). *The Subtlety of Emotions.* Cambridge, Mass.: MIT Press.

Benjamin, W. (1984). A theory of musical meter. *Music Perception* 1 (4): 355–413.

Berger, J. (1990). A theory of musical ambiguity. *Computers in Music Research* 2: 91–119.

Berkowitz, L. (2000). *Causes and Consequences of Feelings.* Cambridge: Cambridge University Press.

Berlitz, C. (1982). *Native Tongues.* New York: Grosset and Dunlap.

Berman, A. (1994). *Preface to Modernism.* Urbana: University of Illinois Press.

Berman, M. (1982). *All That Is Solid Melts into Air: The Experience of Modernity.* New York: Simon and Schuster.

Bernard, J. W. (1983). Spatial sets in recent music of Elliot Carter. *Music Analysis* 2: 5–34.

Berry, W. (1976). *Structural Functions in Music.* Englewood Cliffs: Prentice-Hall.

Bertelson, P. (1961). Sequential redundancy and speed in a serial two-choice responding task. *Quarterly Journal of Experimental Psychology* 13: 90–102.

Bharucha, J. (1984). Anchoring effects in music: The resolution of dissonance. *Cognitive Psychology* 16: 485–518.

Bharucha, J. (1994). Tonality and expectation. In R. Aiello (ed.), *Musical Perceptions*, pp. 213–239. Oxford: Oxford University Press.

Bharucha, J. (1996). Melodic anchoring. *Music Perception* 13 (3): 383–400.

Bharucha, J. J., and K. Stoeckig (1986). Reaction time and musical expectancy: Priming of chords. *Journal of Experimental Psychology: Human Perception and Performance* 12 (4): 403–410.

Bharucha, J. J., and K. Stoeckig (1987). Priming of chords: Spreading activation or overlapping frequency spectra? *Perception & Psychophysics* 41 (6): 519–524.

Bigand, E., and M. Pineau (1997). Global context effects on musical expectancy. *Perception & Psychophysics* 59 (7): 1098–1107.

Blood, A. J., R. J. Zatorre, P. Bermudez, and A. C. Evans (1999). Emotional responses to pleasant and unpleasant music correlate with activity in paralimbic brain regions. *Nature Neuroscience* 2 (4): 382–387.

Blood, A. J., R. J. Zatorre, and A. C. Evans (1999). Intensely pleasant emotional responses to music correlate with CBF modulation in paralimbic and other subcortical brain regions. *Society of Neuroscience Abstracts* 25: 2146.

Bolles, R. C., and M. S. Fanselow (1980). A perceptual-defensive-recuperative model of fear and pain. *Behavioral and Brain Science* 3: 291–323.

Boomsliter, P. C., and W. Creel (1979). Prestimulus perceptual activity in perception of tone in musical sequences. *Journal of the Acoustical Society of America* 65 (1): S123.

Bornstein, R. F. (1989). Exposure and affect: Overview and meta-analysis of research, 1968–1987. *Psychological Bulletin* 106 (2): 265–289.

Bornstein, R. F. (1990). Critical importance of stimulus unawareness for the production of subliminal psychodynamic activation effects—A meta-analytic review. *Journal of Clinical Psychology* 46 (2): 201–210.

Bornstein, R., and P. D'Agostino (1994). The attribution and discounting of perceptual fluency: Preliminary tests of a perceptual fluency/attributional model of the mere exposure effect. *Social Cognition* 12 (2): 103–128.

Boulez, P. (1967/1968). Jan Buzga: Interview mit Pierre Boulez in Prag. *Melos* 34: 162–164. English translation provided in *Opera* vol. 19 (1968), pp. 440–450.

Bregman, A. S. (1990). *Auditory Scene Analysis: The Perceptual Organization of Sound*. Cambridge, Mass.: MIT Press.

Breig, W., M. Dürner, and A. Mielke (1998). *Chronologiches Verzeichnis der Briefe von Richard Wagner. Wagner-Briefe-Verzeichnis (WBV)*. Wiesbaden: Breitkopf und Härtel.

Brochard, R., D. Abecasis, D. Potter, R. Ragot, and C. Drake (2003). The "ticktock" of our internal clock: Direct brain evidence of subjective accents in isochronous sequences. *Psychological Science* 14 (4): 362–366.

Brower, C. (1993). Memory and the perception of rhythm. *Music Theory Spectrum* 15 (1): 19–35.

Brown, H. (1985). The effects of set content and temporal context of pitches on musicians' aural perception of tonality. Ph.D. dissertation, School of Music, Ohio State University.

Brown, H., D. Butler, and M. R. Jones (1994). Musical and temporal influences on key discovery. *Music Perception* 11 (4): 371–407.

Browne, R. (1981). Tonal implications of the diatonic set. *In Theory Only* 5 (6–7): 3–21.

Bruner, C. L. (1984). The perception of contemporary pitch structures. *Music Perception* 2 (1): 25–39.

Bruner, J., and L. Postman (1949). On the perception of incongruity: A paradigm. *Journal of Personality* 18: 206–223.

Budge, H. (1943). *A Study of Chord Frequencies Based on the Music of Representative Composers of the Eighteenth and Nineteeth Centuries.* Contributions to Education, No. 882. New York: Teachers College, Columbia University.

Bürger, P. (1974). *Theorie der Avantgarde.* Frankfurt: Suhrkamp Verlag. Trans. by M. Shaw as *Theory of the Avant-Garde.* Minneapolis: University of Minnesota Press (1984).

Burgess, T. D., and S. M. Sales (1971). Attitudinal effects of mere exposure: A reevaluation. *Journal of Experimental Social Psychology* 7: 461–472.

Burke, E. A. (1757/1759). *A Philosophical Inquiry into the Origin of Our Ideas of the Sublime and Beautiful.* London: Dodsley.

Burns, E. M., and W. D. Ward (1978). Categorical perception—phenomenon or epiphenomenon: Evidence from experiences in the perception of melodic musical intervals. *Journal of the Acoustical Society of America* 63 (2): 456–468.

Butler, D. (1998). Tonal bootstrapping: Re-thinking the intervallic rivalry model. In Suk Won Yi (ed.), *Music, Mind, and Science*, pp. 7–12. Seoul: Seoul National University Press.

Butler, D., and H. Brown (1994). Describing the mental representation of tonality in music. In R. Aiello and J. Sloboda (eds.), *Musical Perceptions,* pp. 191–212. Oxford: Oxford University Press.

Butler, D., and W. D. Ward (1988). Effacing the memory of musical pitch. *Music Perception* 5 (3): 251–259.

Calinescu, M. (1977). *Faces of Modernity: Avant-Garde, Decadence, Kitsch.* Bloomington: Indiana University Press.

Calvin, W. H. (1996). *The Cerebral Code: Thinking a Thought in the Mosaics of the Mind.* Cambridge, Mass.: MIT Press.

Caplin, W. E. (2004). The classical cadence: Conceptions and misconceptions. *Journal of the American Musicological Society* 57 (1): 51–117.

Carlsen, J. C. (1981). Some factors which influence melodic expectancy. *Psychomusicology* 1: 12–29.

Carlsen, J. C., P. L. Divenyi, and J. A. Taylor (1970). A preliminary study of perceptual expectancy in melodic configurations. *Council for Research in Music Education Bulletin* 22: 4–12.

Castellano, M. A., J. J. Bharucha, and C. L. Krumhansl (1984). Tonal hierarchies in the music of North India. *Journal of Experimental Psychology: General* 113 (3): 394–412.

Chernoff, J. M. (1979). *African Rhythm and African Sensibility: Aesthetics and Social Action in African Musical Idioms.* Chicago: University of Chicago Press.

Churchland, P. S. (2002). *Brain-Wise: Studies in Neurophilosophy.* Cambridge, Mass.: MIT Press.

Clarke, E. F. (1985). Some aspects of rhythm and expression in performances of Erik Satie's "Gnossienne no. 5." *Music Perception* 2 (3): 299–328.

Clarke, E. F. (1987). Categorical rhythm perception: An ecological perspective. In A. Gabrielsson (ed.), *Action and Perception in Rhythm and Music*, pp. 19–33. Stockholm: Royal Swedish Academy of Music.

Clarke, E. F. (1999). Rhythm and timing in music. In D. Deutsch (ed.), *The Psychology of Music*, (revised edition), pp. 473–500. San Diego: Academic Press.

Cohen, A. J. (1991). Tonality and perception: Musical scales primed by excerpts from *The Well-Tempered Clavier* of J. S. Bach. *Psychological Research/Psychologische Forschung* 53 (4): 305–314.

Cohen, A. J., and K. Baird (1990). Acquisition of absolute pitch: The question of critical periods. *Psychomusicology* 9 (1): 31–37.

Cohen, J. E. (1962). Information theory and music. *Behavioral Science* 7 (2): 137–163.

Cone, E. T. (1977). Three ways of reading a detective story—Or a Brahms Intermezzo. *Georgia Review* 31: 554–574. Reprinted in R. Morgan (ed.), *Music: A View from Delft. Selected Essays.* Chicago: Chicago University Press (1989).

Cook, D. (1959). *The Language of Music.* Oxford: Oxford University Press.

Cook, N. (1987). The perception of large-scale tonal closure. *Music Perception* 5 (2): 197–206.

Coons, E., and D. Kraehenbuehl (1958). Information as a measure of structure in music. *Journal of Music Theory* 2: 127–161.

Cooper, G., and L. B. Meyer (1960). *The Rhythmic Structure of Music.* Chicago: University of Chicago Press.

Cope, D. (2001). *Virtual Music: Computer Synthesis of Musical Style.* Cambridge, Mass.: MIT Press.

Cornelius, R. R. (1996). *The Science of Emotion: Research and Tradition in the Psychology of Emotions.* Upper Saddle River, N.J.: Prentice-Hall.

Cosmides, L., and J. Tooby (2000). Consider the source: The evolution of adaptations for decoupling and metarepresentations. In D. Sperber (ed.), *Metarepresentations: A Multidisciplinary Perspective*, pp. 53–115. Oxford: Oxford University Press.

Cozby, P. C. (1989). *Methods in Behavioral Research* (4th edition). Mountain View, Calif.: Field.

Crozier, J. B. (1997). Absolute pitch: Practice makes perfect, the earlier the better. *Psychology of Music* 25: 110–119.

Cuddy, L. L. (1968). Practice effects in the absolute judgment of pitch. *Journal of the Acoustical Society of America* 43: 1069–1076.

Cuddy, L. L. (1997). Tonal relations. In I. Deliège and J. Sloboda (eds.), *Perception and Cognition of Music*, pp. 329–352. London: Psychology Press.

Cuddy, L. L., and C. A. Lunney (1995). Expectancies generated by melodic intervals: Perceptual judgments of melodic continuity. *Perception & Psychophysics* 57 (4): 451–462.

Cunningham, D. (2003). A time for dissonance and noise. *Angelaki: Journal of the Theoretical Humanities* 8 (1): 61–74.

Dahlhaus, C. (1968/1990). *Untersuchungen über die Entstehung der harmonischen Tonalität*. Trans. by R. Gjerdingen as *Studies on the Origin of Harmonic Tonality*. Princeton: Princeton University Press.

Damasio, A. (1994). *Descartes' Error: Emotion, Reason, and the Human Brain*. New York: G. P. Putnam's Sons.

Danius, S. (2002). *The Senses of Modernism: Technology, Perception, and Aesthetics*. Ithaca, N.Y.: Cornell University Press.

Dejonckere, P., M. Hirano, and J. Sundberg (1995). *Vibrato*. San Diego: Singular.

Deliège, C. (1984). *Les fondements de la musique tonale: une perspective analytique post-schenkerienne*. Paris: J.C. Lattès.

Dennett, D. C. (1991). *Consciousness Explained*. Boston: Little, Brown.

Densmore, F. (1918). *Teton Sioux Music*. Washington: Government Printing Office. Bulletin no. 61 of the Smithsonian Institution, Bureau of American Ethnology.

Densmore, F. (1926). *Pawnee Music*. Washington: Government Printing Office. Bulletin no. 93 of the Smithsonian Institution, Bureau of American Ethnology.

Desain, P., and H. Honing (2003). The formation of rhythmic categories and metric priming. *Perception* 32 (3): 341–365.

Desain, P., H. Honing, and M. Sadakata (2003). Predicting rhythm perception from rhythm production and score counts: The Bayesian approach. Paper presented at the Society for Music Perception and Cognition 2003 Conference, Las Vegas, Nevada, June 18.

Deutsch, D. (1978). Delayed pitch comparisons and the principle of proximity. *Perception & Psychophysics* 23: 227–230.

Deutsch, D. (1999). Grouping mechanisms in music. In D. Deutsch (ed.), *The Psychology of Music* (revised edition), pp. 299–348. San Diego: Academic Press.

Dimberg, U. (1989). Perceived unpleasantness and facial reactions to auditory stimuli. Uppsala, Sweden: Uppsala Psychological Reports, no. 414.

Dobson, E. J. (1968). *English Pronunciation 1500–1700*, 2 vols. (2nd edition). Oxford: Clarendon Press.

Dowling, W. J. (1967). Rhythmic fission and the perceptual organization of tone sequences. Ph.D. dissertation, Harvard University, Cambridge, Mass.

Dowling, W. J. (1978). Scale and contour: Two components of a theory of memory for melodies. *Psychological Review* 85: 341–354.

Dowling, W. J., and J. C. Bartlett (1981). The importance of interval information in long-term memory for melodies. *Psychomusicology* 1 (1): 30–49.

Dowling, W. J., and D. L. Harwood (1986). *Music Cognition.* San Diego: Academic Press.

Dutton, D. G., and A. P. Aron (1974). Some evidence for heightened sexual attraction under conditions of high anxiety. *Journal of Personality and Social Psychology* 30 (4): 510–517.

Eberlein, R., and J. P. Fricke (1992). *Kadenzwahrnehmung und Kadenzgeschichte: ein Beitrag zu einer Grammatik der Musik.* (Cadence perception and the history of the cadence: A contribution to a grammar of music.) Frankfurt am Main: Verlag Peter Lang.

Edelman, G. (1987). *Neural Darwinism: The Theory of Neuronal Group Selection.* New York: Basic Books.

Eerola, T. (2004). Data-driven influences on melodic expectancy: Continuation in north Sami Yoiks rated by South African traditional healers. In S. D. Lipscomb, R. Ashley, R. O. Gjerdingen, and P. Webster (eds.), *Proceedings of the 8th International Conference on Music Perception and Cognition*, pp. 83–87. Evanston, Ill.: Casual Productions.

Eerola, T., P. Toiviainen, and C. L. Krumhansl (2002). Real-time prediction of melodies: Continuous predictability judgments and dynamic models. In C. Stevens, D. Burnham, G. McPherson, E. Schubert, and J. Renwick (eds.), *Proceedings of the 7th International Conference on Music Perception and Cognition.* Adelaide: Causal Productions.

Eitan, Z. (1997). *Highpoints: A Study of Melodic Peaks.* Philadelphia: University of Pennsylvania Press.

Ellis, C. J. (1969). Structure and significance in aboriginal song. *Mankind, Australia* 7 (5): 3–14.

Federman, F. (1996). A study of various representations using NEXTPITCH: A learning classifier system. Ph.D. dissertation, City University of New York.

Forte, A. (1973). *The Structure of Atonal Music*. New Haven: Yale University Press.

Forte, A. (1983/1987). Motivic design and structural level in the first movement of Brahms's string quartet in C minor. *Musical Quarterly* 69: 471–502. Reprinted 1987 in M. Musgrave (ed.), *Brahms 2: Biographical, Documentary, and Analytic Studies,* pp. 165–196. Cambridge: Cambridge University Press.

Fraisse, P. (1978). Time and rhythm perception. In E. C. Carterette and M. P. Friedmans (eds.), *Handbook of Perception*, vol. 8, pp. 203–254. New York: Academic Press.

Fraisse, P. (1982). Rhythm and tempo. In D. Deutsch (ed.), *The Psychology of Music*, pp. 149–180. New York: Academic Press.

Fraisse, P. (1987). A historical approach to rhythm as perception. In A. Gabrielsson (ed.), *Action and Perception in Rhythm and Music*, pp. 7–18. Stockholm: Kungliga Musikaliska Akademien.

Francès, R. (1958/1988). *La perception de la musique*. Translated 1988 by W. J. Dowling as *The Perception of Music*. Hillsdale, N.J.: Lawrence Erlbaum.

Freeman, J. W. (1992). The language of longing: Only at the final cadence does "Parsifal" resolve its musical question. *Opera News* 56 (March 28): 26–29.

Frost, R. (1969). *The Poetry of Robert Frost: The Collected Poems, Complete and Unabridged*. New York: Henry Holt.

Gabrielsson, A. (1974). Performance of rhythm patterns. *Scandinavian Journal of Psychology* 15: 63–72.

Gabrielsson, A. (2001). Emotions in strong experiences with music. In P. N. Juslin and J. A. Sloboda (eds.), *Music and Emotion: Theory and Research*, pp. 431–449. New York: Oxford University Press.

Gabrielsson, A., and S. Lindstrom, (1993). On strong experiences of music. *Musikpsychologie: Jahrbuch der Deutschen Gesellschaft für Musikpsychologie* 10: 118–139.

Gallistel, C. R. (1990). *The Organization of Learning*. Cambridge, Mass.: MIT Press.

Gardner, M. (1978). Mathematical games—white and brown music, fractal curves, and one-over-f fluctuations. *Scientific American* 238 (4): 16–32.

Gaudreau, D., and I. Peretz (1999). Implicit and explicit memory for music in old and young adults. *Brain and Cognition* 40 (1): 126–129.

Gaver, W. W., and G. Mandler (1987). Play it again, Sam: On liking music. *Cognition and Emotion* 1: 259–282.

Gergersen, P. K. (1998). Instant recognition: The genetics of pitch perception. *American Journal of Human Genetics* 62: 221–223.

Getz, R. P. (1966). The effects of repetition on listening response. *Journal of Research in Music Education* 14 (3): 178–192.

Gibson, D. B. Jr. (1986). The aural perception of nontraditional chords in selected theoretical relationships: A computer-generated experiment. *Journal of Research in Music Education* 34 (1): 5–23.

Gibson, D. B. Jr. (1988). The aural perception of similarity in nontraditional chords related by octave equivalence. *Journal of Research in Music Education* 36 (1): 5–17.

Gibson, D. B. Jr. (1993). The effects of pitch and pitch-class content on the aural perception of dissimilarity in complementary hexachords. *Psychomusicology* 12 (1): 58–72.

Gjerdingen, R. O. (1988). *A Classic Turn of Phrase: Music and the Psychology of Convention.* Philadelphia: University of Pennsylvania Press.

Gjerdingen, R. O. (2003). Social factors in the categorization of genre. Paper presented at the Society for Music Perception and Cognition Conference. Las Vegas, Nevada.

Glasenapp, C. F. (1900–1908). *Das Leben Richard Wagners.* Translated (1900–1908) by W. A. Ellis as *Life of Richard Wagner*, 6 volumes, London: Kegan Paul, Trench, Trübner. Reprinted 1977, New York: Da Capo Press.

Goldstein, A. (1980). Thrills in response to music and other stimuli. *Physiological Psychology* 3: 126–129.

Goldstone, J. A. (1979). A general mathematical theory of expectation models of music. Ph.D. dissertation, University of Southern California.

Gordon, K. (1917). Some tests on the memorizing of musical themes. *Journal of Experimental Psychology* 2 (2): 93–99.

Gotlief, H., and V. J. Konečni (1985). The effects of instrumentation, playing style, and structure in the Goldberg Variations by Johann Sebastian Bach. *Music Perception* 3 (1): 87–102.

Gray, R. M. (1955). The pilomotor reflex in response to music. Masters' thesis, University of Kansas.

Greenberg, D., and S. MacMillan (1996). *Bach Meets Cape Breton.* Audio CD. Canada: Marquis Records no. 181. ASIN: B000003WHK.

Greenberg, G. Z., and W. D. Larkin (1968). Frequency-response characteristic of auditory observers detecting signals of a single frequency in noise: The probe-signal method. *Journal of the Acoustical Society of America* 44 (6): 1513–1523.

Greenwood, D. D. (1961). Critical bandwidth and the frequency coordinates of the basilar membrane. *Journal of the Acoustical Society of America* 33 (4): 1344–1356.

Gregersen, P. K. (1998). Instant recognition: The genetics of pitch perception. *American Journal of Human Genetics* 62 (2): 221–223.

Gregory, A. H. (1978). Perception of clicks in music. *Perception & Psychophysics* 24 (2): 171–174.

Halpern, A. R. (1989). Memory for the absolute pitch of familiar songs. *Memory and Cognition* 17: 572–581.

Handel, S. (1991). *Listening: An Introduction to the Perception of Auditory Events*. Cambridge, Mass.: MIT Press.

Handel, S., and P. Todd (1981). The segmentation of sequential patterns. *Journal of Experimental Psychology: Human Perception and Performance* 7 (1): 41–55.

Hansen, A. (1965). *A Primer of Happenings and Time/Space Art*. New York: Something Else Press.

Hanslick, E. (1854/1885). *Vom Musikalisch-Schönen*. Translated in 1891 by Gustav Cohen as *The Beautiful in Music*, Indianapolis: Bobbs-Merrill.

Hasher, L., and R. T. Zacks (1984). Automatic processing of fundamental information. *American Psychologist* 39: 1372–1388.

Hasty, C. (1998). *Meter as Rhythm*. Oxford: Oxford University Press.

Hattiangadi, J. N. (1983). A methodology without methodological rules. In R. Cohen and M. Wartofsky (eds.), *Language, Logic and Method*, pp. 103–151. Dordrecht, Holland: D. Reidel.

Hauser, M. D., E. L. Newport, and R. N. Aslin, (2001). Segmentation of the speech stream in a nonhuman primate: Statistical learning in cotton top tamarins. *Cognition* 78: B53–B64.

Hebert, S., and I. Peretz (1997). Recognition of music in long-term memory: Are melodic and temporal patterns equal partners? *Memory and Cognition* 25 (4): 518–533.

Heingartner, A., and J. V. Hall (1974). Affective consequences in adults and children of repeated exposure to auditory stimuli. *Journal of Personality and Social Psychology* 29 (6): 719–723.

Hellman, H. (2001). *Great Feuds in Medicine: Ten of the Liveliest Disputes Ever*. New York: John Wiley.

Henkin, R. I. (1957). The prediction of behavior response patterns to music. *Journal of Psychology* 44: 111–127.

Henley, J. (2001). Swiss terror swoop discomposes Boulez. *Guardian*, December 5, 2001.

Hick, W. E. (1952). On the rate of gain of information. *Quarterly Journal of Experimental Psychology* 4: 11–26

Hindemith, P. (1943). *A Concentrated Course in Traditional Harmony*. New York: Associated Music Publishers.

Hofman, P. M., and A. J. Van Opstal (1998). Relearning sound localization with new ears. *Nature Neuroscience* 1: 417–421.

Hofman, P. M., M. S. M. G. Vlaming, P. J. J. Termeer, and A. J. Van Opstal (2002). A method to induce swapped binaural hearing. *Journal of Neuroscience Methods* 113: 167–179.

Hohmann, G. W. (1966). Some effects of spinal cord leisons on experienced emotional feelings. *Psychophysiology* 3: 143–156.

Holland, J. H., K. J. Holyoak, R. E. Nisbett, and P. R. Thagard (1986). *Induction: Processes of Inference, Learning, and Discovery.* Cambridge, Mass.: MIT Press.

Howard, J. H., A. J. O'Toole, R. Parasuraman, and K. B. Bennett (1984). Pattern-directed attention in uncertain-frequency detection. *Perception & Psychophysics* 35 (3): 256–264.

Huron, D. (1988a). Error categories, detection, and reduction in a musical database. *Computers and the Humanities* 22 (4): 253–264.

Huron, D. (1988b). Alf Gabrielsson (ed.): Action and perception in rhythm and music. *Psychology of Music* 16 (2): 156–162.

Huron, D. (1992). Carol Krumhansl: The cognitive foundations of musical pitch. *Psychology of Music* 20 (1): 180–185.

Huron, D. (1994). Interval-class content in equally-tempered pitch-class sets: Common scales exhibit optimum tonal consonance. *Music Perception* 11 (3): 289–305.

Huron, D. (1995a). *The Humdrum Toolkit: Reference Manual.* Stanford, Calif.: Center for Computer Assisted Research in the Humanities.

Huron, D. (1995b). Nicholas Cook: Music, imagination, and culture. *Music Perception* 12 (4): 473–481.

Huron, D. (1996). The melodic arch in Western folksongs. *Computing in Musicology* 10: 3–23.

Huron, D. (2001a). What is a musical feature? Forte's analysis of Brahms's opus 51, no. 1, Revisited. *Music Theory Online* 7 (4). Available at http://www.societymusictheory.org/mto/issues/mto.01.07.4/mto.01.7.4.huron.html.

Huron, D. (2001b). Tone and voice: A derivation of the rules of voice-leading from perceptual principles. *Music Perception* 19 (1): 1–64.

Huron, D. (2002). A six-component theory of auditory-evoked emotion. In C. Stevens, D. Burnham, G. McPherson, E. Schubert, and J. Renwick (eds.), *Proceedings of the 7th International Conference on Music Perception and Cognition*, pp. 673–676. Adelaide: Casual Productions.

Huron, D. (2004a). Music-engendered laughter: An analysis of humor devices in PDQ Bach. In S. D. Lipscomb, R. Ashley, R. O. Gjerdingen, and P. Webster (eds.), *Proceedings of the 8th International Conference on Music Perception and Cognition*, pp. 700–704. Evanston, Ill.: Casual Productions.

Huron, D. (2004b). Issues and prospects in studying cognitive cultural diversity. In S. D. Lipscomb, R. Ashley, R. O. Gjerdingen, and P. Webster (eds.), *Proceedings of the 8th International Conference on Music Perception and Cognition*, pp. 93–96. Evanston, Ill.: Casual Productions.

Huron, D., and P. von Hippel (2000). Tonal and contra-tonal structure of Viennese twelve-tone rows. Paper presented at the Society for Music Theory Conference, Toronto, Canada.

Huron, D., and J. Ollen (2003). Agogic constrast in French and English themes: Further support for Patel and Daniele (2003). *Music Perception* 21 (2): 267–271.

Huron, D., and A. Ommen (in press). An empirical study of syncopation in American popular music, 1890–1939. *Music Theory Spectrum.*

Huron, D., and R. Parncutt (1993). An improved model of tonality perception incorporating pitch salience and echoic memory. *Psychomusicology* 12 (2): 154–171.

Huron, D., and P. Sellmer (1992). Critical bands and the spelling of vertical sonorities. *Music Perception* 10 (2): 129–149.

Huron, D., and J. Veltman (2006). A cognitive approach to medieval mode: Evidence for an historical antecedent to the major/minor system. *Empirical Musicology Review* 1 (1): 33–55.

Hyman, R. (1953). Stimulus information as a determinant of reaction time. *Journal of Experimental Psychology* 45: 423–432.

Jairazbhoy, N. (1971). *The Rags of North Indian Music: Their Structure and Evolution.* London: Faber and Faber.

James, W. (1884). What is an emotion? *Mind* 19: 188–205.

James, W. (1894). The physical basis of emotion. *Psychological Review* 1: 516–529.

Janata, P., J. L. Birk, J. D. Van Horn, M. Leman, B. Tillmann, and J. J. Bharucha (2002). The cortical topography of tonal structures underlying Western music. *Science* 298 (5601): 2167–2170.

Janata, P., and D. Reisberg (1988). Response-time measures as a means of exploring tonal hierarchies. *Music Perception* 6 (2): 161–172.

Johnston, V. S. (1999). *Why We Feel: The Science of Human Emotions.* Reading, Mass.: Perseus Books.

Jones, M. R. (1981). Music as a stimulus for psychological motion: Part 1. Some determinants of expectancies. *Psychomusicology* 1: 34–51.

Jones, M. R. (1982). Music as a stimulus for psychological motion: Part 2. An expectancy model. *Psychomusicology* 2: 1–13.

Jones, M. R. (1990). Learning and the development of expectancies: An interactionist approach. *Psychomusicology* 9 (2): 193–228.

Jones, M. R. (1992). Attending to musical events. In M. R. Jones and S. Holleran (eds.), *Cognitive Bases of Musical Communication*, pp. 91–110. Washington, D.C.: American Psychological Association.

Jones, M. R., and M. Boltz (1989). Dynamic attending and responses to time. *Psychological Review* 96: 459–491.

Jones, M. R., M. Boltz, and G. Kidd (1982). Controlled attending as a function of melodic and temporal context. *Perception & Psychophysics* 32: 211–218.

Jones, M. R., G. Kidd, and R. Wetzel (1981). Evidence for rhythmic attention. *Journal of Experimental Psychology: Human Perception and Performance* 7: 1059–1073.

Jones, M. R., H. Moynihan, N. MacKenzie, and J. Puente (2002). Temporal aspects of stimulus-driven attending in dynamic arrays. *Psychological Science* 13 (4): 313–319.

Juslin, P. N., and J. A. Sloboda (eds.) (2001). *Music and Emotion: Theory and Research*. Oxford: Oxford University Press.

Kagan, J. (2002). *Surprise, Uncertainty, and Mental Structures*. Cambridge, Mass.: Harvard University Press.

Kameoka, A., and M. Kuriyagawa (1969a). Consonance theory. Part I: Consonance of dyads. *Journal of the Acoustical Society of America* 45: 1451–1449.

Kameoka, A., and M. Kuriyagawa (1969b). Consonance theory. Part II: Consonance of complex tones and its calculation method. *Journal of the Acoustical Society of America* 45: 1460–1469.

Kant, I. (1790). *Kritik der Urteilskraft*. Trans. (1914) by F. M. Miller as *Critique of Judgment*. London: Macmillan.

Karno, M., and V. J. Konečni (1992). The effects of structural interventions in the first movement of Mozart's symphony in G minor K.550 on aesthetic preference. *Music Perception* 10 (1): 63–72.

Kelly, M. H., and S. Martin (1994). Domain-general abilities applied to domain-specific tasks: Sensitivity to probabilities in perception, cognition, and language. *Lingua* 92: 105–140.

Kessler, E. J., C. Hansen, and R. N. Shepard (1984). Tonal schemata in the perception of music in Bali and in the West. *Music Perception* 2 (2): 131–165.

Kihlstrom, J. (1987). The cognitive unconscious. *Science* 237 (4821): 1445–1452.

Klinger, E. (1990). *Daydreaming*. Los Angeles: Tarcher.

Knopoff, L., and W. Hutchinson (1983). Entropy as a measure of style: The influence of sample length. *Journal of Music Theory* 27 (1): 75–97.

Koffka, K. (1909). Untersuchungen zur Lehre von Rhythmus. *Zeitschrift für Psychologie* 52: 1–109.

Konner, M. (2003). *The Tangled Wing: Biological Constraints on the Human Spirit* (2nd edition). New York: Owl Books.

Kraehenbuehl, D., and E. Coons (1959). Information as a measure of the experience of music. *Journal of Aesthetics and Art Criticism* 17: 510–522.

Kramer, J. D. (1982). Beginnings and endings in Western art music. *Canadian University Music Review/Revue de musique des universites canadiennes* 3: 1–14.

Kramer, J. D. (1988). *The Time of Music*. New York: Schirmer Books.

Kronman, U., and J. Sundberg (1987). Is the musical ritard an allusion to physical motion? In A. Gabrielsson (ed.), *Action and Perception in Rhythm and Music*, pp. 57–68. Stockholm: Royal Swedish Academy of Music.

Krumhansl, C. L. (1979). The psychological representation of musical pitch in a tonal context. *Cognitive Psychology* 11: 346–374.

Krumhansl, C. L. (1990). *Cognitive Foundations of Musical Pitch.* Oxford: Oxford University Press.

Krumhansl, C. L. (1995a). Effects of musical context on similarity and expectancy. *Systematische Musikwissenschaft/Systematic Musicology/Musicologie systematique* 3 (2): 211–250.

Krumhansl, C. L. (1995b). Music psychology and music theory: Problems and prospects. *Music Theory Spectrum* 17 (1): 53–80.

Krumhansl, C. L. (1997). Effects of perceptual organization and musical form on melodic expectancies. In M. Leman (ed.), *Music, Gestalt, and Computing: Studies in Cognitive and Systematic Musicology*, pp. 294–320. Berlin: Springer Verlag.

Krumhansl, C., and E. J. Kessler (1982). Tracing the dynamic changes in perceived tonal organization in a spatial representation of musical keys. *Psychological Review* 89: 334–368.

Krumhansl, C. L., J. Louhivuori, P. Toiviainen, T. Järvinen, and T. Eerola (1999). Melodic expectancy in Finnish folk hymns: Convergence of statistical, behavioral, and computational approaches. *Music Perception* 17 (2): 151–195.

Krumhansl, C., G. J. Sandell, and D. C. Sergeant (1987). The perception of tone hierarchies and mirror forms in twelve-tone serial music. *Music Perception* 5: 153–184.

Krumhansl, C., and R. N. Shepard (1979). Quantification of the hierarchy of tonal functions within a diatonic context. *Journal of Experimental Psychology: Human Perception and Performance* 5 (4): 579–594.

Krumhansl, C. L., P. Toivanen, T. Eerola, P. Toiviainen, T. Järvinen, and J. Louhivuori (2000). Cross-cultural music cognition: Cognitive methodology applied to North Sami yoiks. *Cognition* 76 (1): 13–58.

Kubovy, M. (1999). On the pleasures of the mind. In D. Kahneman, E. Diener, and N. Schwarz (eds.), *Well-Being: The Foundations of Hedonic Psychology*, pp. 134–154. New York: Russell Sage Foundation.

Lake, W. (1987). Melodic perception and cognition: The influence of tonality. Ph.D. dissertation, University of Michigan.

Lange, C. G., and W. James (1922). *The Emotions.* Baltimore: Williams and Wilkins.

Lannoy, C. (1972). Detection and discrimination of dodecaphonic series. *Interface* 1: 13–27.

Large, E. W., and M. R. Jones (1999). The dynamics of attending: How people track time-varying events. *Psychological Review* 106: 119–159.

Largent, E. J. (1972). An investigation into the perceptibility of twelve-tone rows. Ph.D. dissertation, Ohio State University.

Larson, S. (1997). Continuations as completions: Studying melodic expectation in the creative microdomain Seek Well. In M. Leman (ed.), *Music, Gestalt, and Computing: Studies in Cognitive and Systematic Musicology*, pp. 321–334. Berlin: Springer Verlag.

Larson, S. (2002). Musical forces, melodic expectation, and jazz melody. *Music Perception* 19 (3): 351–385.

LeDoux, J. (1996). *The Emotional Brain*. New York: Simon and Schuster.

LeDoux, J., and E. Phelps (2000). Emotional networks in the brain. In M. Lewis and J. Haviland-Jones (eds.), *Handbook of Emotions* (2nd edition), pp. 157–172. New York: Guilford Press.

Lerdahl, F. (1988). Cognitive constraints on compositional systems. In J. Sloboda (ed.), *Generative Processes in Music: The Psychology of Performance, Improvisation, and Composition*, pp. 231–259. Oxford: Oxford University Press. Reprinted in *Contemporary Music Review* 6: 97–121.

Lerdahl, F. (2001). *Tonal Pitch Space*. New York: Oxford University Press.

Lerdahl, F., and R. Jackendoff (1983). *A Generative Theory of Tonal Music*. Cambridge, Mass.: MIT Press.

Lester, J. (1986). *The Rhythms of Tonal Music*. Carbondale, Ill.: Southern Illinois University Press.

Levenson, M. (ed.) (1999). *Cambridge Companion to Modernism*. Cambridge: Cambridge University Press.

Levitin, D. (1994). Absolute memory for musical pitch: Evidence from the production of learned melodies. *Perception & Psychophysics* 56: 414–423.

Lewis, C. I. (1929/1991). *Mind and the World Order: Outline of a Theory of Knowledge*. New York: Dover.

Li, X. F., G. E. Stutzmann, and J. L. LeDoux (1996). Convergent but temporally separated inputs to lateral amygdala neurons from the auditory thalamus and auditory cortex use different post-synaptic receptors: *in vivo* intracellular and extracellular recordings in fear conditioning pathways. *Learning and Memory* 3: 229–242.

Lieberman, P. (1967). *Intonation, Perception, and Language*. Cambridge, Mass.: MIT Press.

Locke, J. (1689). *An Essay Concerning Human Understanding*. London.

Loewenstein, G., and D. Schkade (1999). Wouldn't it be nice? Predicting future feelings. In D. Kahneman, E. Diener, and N. Schwarz (eds.), *Well-Being: The Foundations of Hedonic Psychology*, pp. 85–105. New York: Russel Sage Foundation.

Longuet-Higgins, H. C., and C. S. Lee (1982). Perception of musical rhythms. *Perception* 11: 115–128.

Lord, A. (1960). *The Singer of Tales*. Cambridge, Mass.: Harvard University Press.

Lundin, R. F. (1953/1967). *An Objective Psychology of Music*. New York: Ronald Press.

Mack, D., and E. Voss (1978). *Richard Wagner. Leben und Werk in Daten und Bildern.* Frankfurt am Main: Insel.

Malm, W. P. (1980). Some of Japan's musics and musical principles. In E. May (ed.), *Musics of Many Cultures: An Introduction*, pp. 48–62. Berkeley: University of California Press.

Malow, R. M. (1981). Effects of induced anxiety on pain perception. *Pain* 11: 397–405.

Mandler, G. (1975). *Mind and Emotion.* New York: J. Wiley.

Manzara, L. C., I. H. Witten, and M. James (1992). On the entropy of music: An experiment with Bach chorale melodies. *Leonard Music Journal* 2 (1): 81–88.

Marañon, G. (1924). Contribution à l'étude de l'action émotive de l'adrénaline. *Revue Française d'Endorinologie* 2: 301–325.

March, J. (1978). Bounded rationality, ambiguity, and the engineering of choice. *Bell Journal of Economics* 9: 587–608.

Marcus, G. (1989). *Lipstick Traces: A Secret History of the 20th Century.* Cambridge, Mass.: Harvard University Press.

Marcus, G. F., S. Vijayan, S. Rao, L. Bandi, and P. M. Vishton (1999). Rule learning by seven month old infants. *Science* 283: 77–80.

Margulis, E. H. (2003). Melodic expectation: A discussion and model. Ph.D. dissertation, Columbia University.

Margulis, E. H. (2005). A model of melodic expectation. *Music Perception* 21 (4): 663–714.

Margulis, E. H., and W. H. Levine (2004). Melodic expectation: A priming study. In S. D. Lipscomb, R. Ashley, R. O. Gjerdingen, and P. Webster (eds.), *Proceedings of the 8th International Conference on Music Perception and Cognition*, pp. 364–366. Evanston, Ill.: Casual Productions.

Marion, R. (1990). *The Boy Who Felt No Pain.* Reading, Mass.: Addison-Wesley.

Martinez, M. C. de (1940). *Juegos Y Canciones Infantiles de Puerto Rico.* San Juan, P.R.: Talleres Graficos Cas Baldrich.

Marvin, E. W. (1997). Tonal/atonal: Cognitive strategies for recognizing transposed melodies. In *Music Theory in Concept and Practice*, pp. 217–236. Rochester: University of Rochester.

Marvin, E. W., and A. R. Brinkman (2000). The effect of key color and timbre on absolute pitch recognition in musical contexts. *Music Perception* 18 (2): 111–137.

Marslen-Wilson, W., and L. K. Tyler (1980). The temporal structure of spoken language understanding. *Cognition* 8 (1): 1–71.

Matsumoto, K., W. Suzuki, and K. Tanaka (2003). Nueronal correlates of goal-based motor selection in the prefrontal cortex. *Science* 301: 229–232.

Mazo, M. (1994). Lament made visible: A study of paramusical elements in Russian lament. In *Themes and Variations: Writings on Music in Honor of Rulan Chao Pian*, pp. 161–211. Hong Kong: Chinese University Press.

McClary, S. (2002). *Feminine Endings: Music, Gender, and Sexuality.* Minneapolis: University of Minnesota Press.

McGraw, A. P. (1999). Expectations and emotions in sports. Master's thesis. Psychology Department, Ohio State University.

Mellers, B. A., A. Schwartz, K. Ho, and I. Ritov (1997). Decision affect theory: Emotional reactions to the outcomes of risky options. *Psychological Science* 8 (6): 423–429.

Mellers, B. A., A. Schwartz, and I. Ritov (1999). Emotion-based choice. *Journal of Experimental Psychology: General* 128 (3): 332–345.

Merriam, A. P., S. Whinery, and B. G. Fred (1956). Songs of a Rada community in Trinidad. *Anthropos* 51: 157–174.

Meyer, L. B. (1956). *Emotion and Meaning in Music.* Chicago: University of Chicago Press.

Meyer, L. B. (1967). *Music, the Arts, and Ideas.* Chicago: University of Chicago Press.

Meyer, L. B. (1989). *Style and Music: Theory, History, and Ideology* Philadelphia: University of Pennsylvania Press.

Meyer, M. (1899). Is the memory of absolute pitch capable of development by training? *Psychological Review* 6: 514–516.

Meyer, M. (1903). Experimental studies in the psychology of music. *American Journal of Psychology* 14: 456–475.

Michon, J. A. (1985). The compleat time experience! In J. A. Michon and J. L. Jackson (eds.), *Time, Mind, and Behavior*, pp. 21–52. Berlin: Springer Verlag.

Milius, S. (2001). Don't look now, but is that dog laughing? *Science News* 160 (4): 55.

Millar, J. K. (1984). The aural perception of pitch-class set-relations: A computer-assisted investigation. Ph.D. dissertation, North Texas State University.

Mita, T. H., M. Dermer, and J. Knight (1977). Reversed facial images and the mere-exposure hypothesis. *Journal of Personality and Social Psychology* 35 (8): 597–601.

Miyazaki, K. (1988). Musical pitch identification by absolute pitch possessors. *Perception and Psychophysics* 44: 501–512.

Miyazaki, K. (1990). The speed of musical pitch identification by absolute-pitch possessors. *Music Perception* 8 (2): 177–188.

Miyazaki, K. (1993). Absolute pitch as an inability: Identification of musical intervals in a tonal context. *Music Perception* 11 (1): 55–72.

Moelants, D. (1999). Perceptual analysis of "aksak" meters. In M. Leman (ed.), *New Techniques in Ethnomusicology: Proceedings of the 11th Meeting of the FWO Research Society on Foundations of Music Research*, pp. 3–26. Ghent: IPEM, University of Ghent.

Moles, A. (1958/1966). *Théorie de l'information et perception esthétique.* Paris. Trans. (1966) as *Information Theory and Aesthetic Perception.* Urbana, Ill.: University of Illinois Press.

Monahan, J. L., S. T. Murphy, and R. B. Zajonc (1997). Subliminal exposure effects: Specific, general, or diffuse? Unpublished study. Reported in Berkowitz 2000, p. 30.

Moore, H. T., and A. R. Galliland (1924). The immediate and long-term effects of classical and popular phonograph selections. *Journal of Applied Psychology* 8: 309–232.

Moreland, R. L., and R. B. Zajonc (1977). Is stimulus recognition a necessary condition for the occurrence of exposure effects? *Journal of Personality and Social Psychology* 35: 191–199.

Moreland, R. L., and R. B. Zajonc (1979). Exposure effects may not depend on stimulus recognition. *Journal of Personality and Social Psychology* 37: 1085–1089.

Morris, R. (1988). *Composition with Pitch-Classes: A Theory of Compositional Design.* New Haven: Yale University Press.

Morton, E. (1994). Sound symbolism and its role in non-human vertebrate communication. In L. Hinton, J. Nichols, and J. Ohala (eds.), *Sound Symbolism*, pp. 348–365. Cambridge: Cambridge University Press.

Mull, H. K. (1949). A study of humor in music. *American Journal of Psychology* 62: 560–566.

Mull, H. K. (1957). The effect of repetition upon the enjoyment of modern music. *Journal of Psychology* 43: 155–162.

Nam, U. (1998). Pitch distribution in Korean court music: Evidence consistent with tonal hierarchies. *Music Perception* 16 (2): 243–247.

Narmour, E. (1990). *The Analysis and Cognition of Basic Melodic Structures: The Implication-Realization Model.* Chicago: University of Chicago Press.

Narmour, E. (1991). The influence of embodied registral motion on the perception of higher-level melodic implication. In M. R. Jones and S. Holleran (eds.), *Cognitive Bases of Musical Communication*, pp. 69–90. Washington, D.C.: American Psychological Association.

Narmour, E. (1990). *The Analysis and Cognition of Basic Melodic Structures: The Implication-Realization Model.* Chicago: University of Chicago Press.

Narmour, E. (1992). *The Analysis and Cognition of Melodic Complexity: The Implication-Realization Model.* Chicago: University of Chicago Press.

Narmour, E. (1999). Hierarchical expectation and musical style. In D. Deutsch (ed.), *The Psychology of Music* (2nd edition), pp. 441–472. San Diego: Academic Press.

Narmour, E. (2000). Music expectation by cognitive rule-mapping. *Music Perception* 17 (3): 329–398.

National Film Board of Canada (1980). *The Fiddlers of James Bay.* Directed by Bob Rodgers, 29 minutes.

Neyman, J., and E. S. Pearson (1928). On the use and interpretation of certain test criteria for purposes of statistical inference. *Biometrika* 20: 175–240, 263–294.

Neyman, J., and E. S. Pearson (1967). *Joint Statistical Papers.* Cambridge: Cambridge University Press.

Ng, Yuet-Hon (2003). Temporal expectancy at the level of musical phrases: A study of expectancy length. Paper presented at the Society for Music Perception and Cognition, 2003 Conference, Las Vegas, Nevada.

Norton, R. (1984). *Tonality in Western Culture: A Critical and Historical Perspective.* University Park: Pennsylvania State University Press.

Ohala, J. (1984). An ethological perspective on common cross-language utilization of F0 in voice. *Phonetica* 41: 1–16.

Ollen, J., and D. Huron (2003). Musical form and habituation theory. Poster presented at the Society for Music Perception and Cognition, 2003 Conference, Las Vegas, Nevada.

Ollen, J., and D. Huron (2004). Listener preferences and early repetition in musical form. In S. D. Lipscomb, R. Ashley, R. O. Gjerdingen, and P. Webster (eds.), *Proceedings of the 8th International Conference on Music Perception and Cognition*, pp. 405–407. Evanston, Ill.: Casual Productions.

Olson, J. M., N. J. Roese, and M. P. Zanna (1996). Expectancies. In E. T. Higgens and W. Kruglanski (eds.), *Social Psychology: Handbook of Basic Principles*, pp. 211–238. New York: Guilford Press.

Oram, N., and L. L. Cuddy (1995). Responsiveness of Western adults to pitch-distributional information in melodic sequences. *Psychological Research* 57 (2): 103–118.

Ortmann, O. R. (1926). *On the Melodic Relativity of Tones.* Princeton, N.J.: Psychological Review Company. (Vol. 35, no. 1 of *Psychological Monographs.*)

Palmer, C., and C. Krumhansl (1990). Mental representations for musical meter. *Journal of Experimental Psychology: Human Perception and Performance* 16 (4): 728–741.

Panksepp, J. (1995). The emotional sources of "chills" induced by music. *Music Perception* 13 (2): 171–207.

Parncutt, R. (1989). *Harmony: A Psychoacoustical Approach.* Berlin: Springer-Verlag.

Parry, M. (1971). *The Making of Homeric Verse: The Collected Papers of Milman Parry.* Oxford: Clarendon Press.

Parsons, B. (2004). Arresting Boulez: Post-war modernism in context. *Journal of the Royal Musical Association* 129 (pt. 1): 161–176.

Partch, H. (1949/1979). *Genesis of a Music* (2nd edition). New York: Da Capo Press.

Patel, A. D., and J. R. Daniele (2003). An empirical comparison of rhythm in language and music. *Cognition* 87: B35–B45.

Pearce, M. T., and G. A. Wiggins (2004). Rethinking Gestalt influences on melodic expectancy. In S. D. Lipscomb, R. Ashley, R. O. Gjerdingen, and P. Webster (eds.), *Proceedings of the 8th International Conference on Music Perception and Cognition*, pp. 367–371. Evanston, Ill.: Casual Productions.

Peretz, I. (1996). Can we lose memory for music? A case of music agnosia in a nonmusician. *Journal of Cognitive Neuroscience* 8 (6): 481–496.

Perrott, D., and R. O. Gjerdingen (1999). Scanning the dial: An exploration of factors in the identification of musical style. Paper presented at the Society for Music Perception and Cognition Conference, Evanston, Ill.

Pike, K. L. (1945). *The Intonation of American English.* Ann Arbor: University of Michigan Press.

Pinker, S. (1994). *The Language Instinct.* New York: William Morrow.

Pinkerton, R. C. (1956). Information theory and melody. *Scientific American* 194 (2): 77–86.

Piston, W. (1978). *Harmony.* 4th ed. New York: Norton.

Plomp, R., and W. J. M. Levelt (1965). Tonal consonance and critical bandwidth. *Journal of the Acoustical Society of America* 37: 548–560.

Poggioli, R. (1962). *Teoria dell'arte d'avanguardia.* Società editrice il Mulino. Trans. (1968) by G. Fitzgerald as *The Theory of the Avant-Garde.* Cambridge, Mass.: Harvard University Press.

Popper, K. (1934/1959). *Logik der Forschung.* Vienna, 1934. Trans. as *The Logic of Scientific Discovery.* New York: Basic Books, 1959.

Povel, D.-J. (1981). Internal representation of simple temporal patterns. *Journal of Experimental Psychology: Human Perception and Performance* 7: 3–18.

Povel, D.-J. (1995). Exploring the elementary harmonic forces in the tonal system. *Psychological Research* 58 (4): 274–283.

Povel, D.-J., and P. Essens (1985). Perception of temporal patterns. *Music Perception* 2 (4): 411–440.

Proctor, G. M. (1978). Technical bases of nineteenth-century chromatic tonality: A study in chromaticism. Ph.D. dissertation, Princeton University.

Profet, M. (1992). Pregnancy sickness as adaptation: A deterrent to maternal ingestion of teratogens. In J. Barkow, L. Cosmides, and J. Tooby (eds.), *The Adapted Mind: Evolutionary Psychology and the Generation of Culture*, pp. 325–365. Oxford: Oxford University Press.

Provine, R. (2000). *Laughter: A Scientific Investigation.* New York: Penguin.

Rahn, J. (1980). *Basic Atonal Theory.* New York: Longman.

Rameau, J.-P. (1722). *Traité de l'harmonie reduite à ses principes naturels*. Paris.

Reber, A. S. (1993). *Implicit Learning and Tacit Knowledge: An Essay on the Cognitive Unconscious*. Oxford: Oxford University Press.

Reimer, B. (1964). Information theory and the analysis of musical meaning. *Council for Research in Music Education Bulletin* 2: 14–22.

Richmond, B. J., Z. Liu, and M. Shidara (2003). Predicting future rewards. *Science* 301: 179–180.

Riemann, H. (1903). *System der musikalischen Rhythmik und Metrik*. Leipzig.

Rifkin, D. (2000). Tonal coherence in Prokofiev's music: A study of the interrelationships of structure, motives, and design. Ph.D. dissertation, Eastman School of Music, University of Rochester.

Ritter, W., E. Sussman, D. Deacon, N. Cowan, and H. G. Vaughan (1999). Two cognitive systems simultaneously paired for opposite events. *Psychophysiology* 36 (6): 835–838.

Roeder, J. (2003). Beat-class modulation in Steve Reich's music. *Music Theory Spectrum* 25 (2): 275–304.

Rosenberg, H. (1959). *The Tradition of the New*. Chicago: University of Chicago Press.

Rosner, B. S., and L. B. Meyer (1982). Melodic processes and the perception of music. In D. Deutsch (ed.), *The Psychology of Music*, pp. 317–341. New York: Academic Press.

Rothstein, W. (1989). *Phrase Rhythm in Tonal Music*. New York: Schirmer Books.

Rozin, P. (1999). Preadaptation and the puzzles and properties of pleasure. In D. Kahneman, E. Diener, and N. Schwarz (eds.), *Well-Being: The Foundations of Hedonic Psychology*, pp. 109–133. New York: Russell Sage Foundation.

Rubin, D. C. (1995). *Memory in Oral Traditions: The Cognitive Psychology of Epic, Ballads, and Counting-Out Rhymes*. Oxford: Oxford University Press.

Sachs, C. (1962). *The Wellsprings of Music*. The Hague: Martinus Nijhoff.

Saffran, J. R., R. N. Aslin, and E. L. Newport (1996). Statistical learning by 8-month-old infants. *Science* 274 (5294): 1926–1928.

Saffran, J. R., E. K. Johnson, R. N. Aslin, and E. L. Newport (1999). Statistical learning of tone sequences by human infants and adults. *Cognition* 70: 27–52.

Salzer, F. (1952). *Structural Hearing: Tonal Coherence in Music*. New York: C. Boni.

Samplaski, A. G. (2000). A comparison of perceived chord similarity and predictions of selected twentieth-century chord-classification schemes, using multidimensional scaling and clustering techniques. Ph.D. dissertation, School of Music, Indiana University.

Samplaski, A. G. (2004). The relative perceptual salience of Tn and TnI. *Music Perception* 21 (4): 545–559.

Schachter, D. L. (2001). *The Seven Sins of Memory: How the Mind Forgets and Remembers.* Boston: Houghton Mifflin.

Schachter, D. L., and E. Tulving (eds.) (1994). *Memory Systems 1994.* Cambidge, Mass.: MIT Press.

Schachter, S., and J. E. Singer (1962). Cognitive, social, and physiological determinanats of emotional state. *Psychological Review* 69: 379–399.

Schaffrath, H. (1995). *The Essen Folksong Collection.* Ed. D. Huron. Stanford, Calif.: Center for Computer Assisted Research in the Humanities.

Schellenberg, E. G. (1996). Expectancy in melody: Tests of the implication-realization model. *Cognition* 58: 75–125.

Schellenberg, E. G. (1997). Simplifying the implication-realization model. *Music Perception* 14 (3): 295–318.

Schenker, H. (1906). *Harmonielehre: Neue musikalische Phantasien und Theorien, Heft 1.* Stuttgart: Cotta. Abridged trans. by E. Mann Borgese, edited by O. Jonas (1954) as *Harmony.* Chicago: University of Chicago Press.

Schenker, H. (1935). *Der freie Satz.* Vienna: Universal. Trans. by E. Oster, edited by O. Jonas (1956) as *Free Composition; Volume III of New Musical Theories and Fantasies.* New York: Longman.

Scherer, K. L., and J. S. Oshinsky (1977). Cue utilization in emotion attribution from auditory stimuli. *Motivation and Emotion* 1 (4): 331–346.

Schmuckler, M. A. (1988). Expectation in music: Additivity of melodic and harmonic processes. Ph.D. dissertation, Cornell University.

Schmuckler, M. A. (1989). Expectation in music: Investigation of melodic and harmonic processes. *Music Perception* 7 (2): 109–150.

Schmuckler, M. A. (1990). The performance of global expectation. *Psychomusicology* 9: 122–147.

Schmuckler, M. A. (1997). Expectancy effects in memory for melodies. *Canadian Journal of Experimental Psychology* 51 (4): 292–305.

Schoenberg, A. (1948). Composition with twelve tones (Part 2). Reprinted 1975 in L. Stein (ed.), *Style and Idea*, London: Faber and Faber.

Schoenberg, A. (1967). *Fundamentals of Musical Composition.* Ed. G. Strang and L. Stein. New York: St. Martin's Press.

Seashore, C. E. (1932). *The Vibrato.* Iowa City: University of Iowa Press.

Seashore, C. E. (1938). *The Psychology of Music.* New York: McGraw-Hill.

Seashore, C. E. (1947). *In Search of Beauty in Music.* New York: Ronald Press.

Shaffer, L. H., and N. P. M. Todd (1994). The interpretive component in musical performance. In R. Aiello and J. A. Sloboda (eds.), *Musical Perceptions.* London: Oxford University Press.

Shannon, C. E. (1948). A mathematical theory of communication. *Bell System Technical Journal* 27: 379–423, 623–656.

Shannon, C. E., and W. Weaver (1949). *The Mathematical Theory of Communication.* Urbana, Ill.: University of Illinois Press.

Shepard, R. N. (1964). Circularity in judgments of relative pitch. *Journal of the Acoustical Society of America* 36: 2346–2353.

Shepard, R. N. (1981). Psychophysical complementarity. In M. Kubovy and J. R. Pomerantz (eds.), *Perceptual Organization*, pp. 279–341. Hillsdale, N.J.: Erlbaum.

Shepard, R. N. (1982). Geometrical approximations to the structure of musical pitch. *Psychological Review* 89 (4): 305–333.

Simonet, P., O. M. Murphy, and A. Lance (2001). Laughing dog: Vocalizations of domestic dogs during play encounters. Paper given at Animal Behavior Society Conference, July 14–18, Corvallis, Oregon.

Simons, R. C. (1996). *Boo! Culture, Experience, and the Startle Reflex.* Oxford: Oxford University Press.

Simpson, J. (1996). A formal analysis of note-interdependence in selected works. Unpublished manuscript. Available at http://www.geocities.com/jasba_simpson/research/inter/inter.htm.

Simpson, J., and D. Huron (1994). Absolute pitch as a learned phenomenon: Evidence consistent with the Hick-Hyman law. *Music Perception* 12 (2): 267–270.

Singer, T., B. Seymour, J. O'Doherty, H. Kaube, R. J. Dolan, and C. D. Frith (2004). Empathy for pain involves the affect but not sensory components of pain. *Science* 303 (5661): 1157–1162.

Sloboda, J. A. (1991). Music structure and emotional response: Some empirical findings. *Psychology of Music* 19 (2): 110–120.

Sloboda, J. A. (1992). Empirical studies of emotional response to music. In M. R. Jones and S. Holleran (eds.), *Cognitive Bases of Musical Communication*, pp. 33–50. Washington, D.C.: American Psychological Association.

Smith, J. (1983). Reproduction and representation of musical rhythms: The effects of musical skill. In D. Rogers and J. A. Sloboda (eds.), *Acquisition of Symbolic Skills.* New York: Plenum.

Snyder, B. (2000). *Music and Memory: An Introduction.* Cambridge, Mass.: MIT Press.

Solomon, R. L. (1980). The opponent process theory of acquired motivation. *American Psychologist* 35: 691–712.

Spitz, B. (1991). *Dylan: A Biography.* New York: Norton.

Squire, L. R. (1994). Declarative and nondeclarative memory: Multiple brain systems supporting learning and memory. In D. Schacter and E. Tulving (eds.), *Memory Systems, 1994.* Cambridge, Mass.: MIT Press.

Squire, L. R., and D. L. Schachter (eds.). (2002). *Neuropsychology of Memory* (3rd edition). New York: Guilford Press.

Stepper, S., and F. Strack (1993). Proprioceptive determinants of emotional and non-emotional feelings. *Journal of Personality and Social Psychology* 64: 211–220.

Stevens, S. S., and H. Davis (1938). *Hearing: Its Psychology and Physiology.* New York: Wiley.

Strack, F., S. Stepper, and L. L. Martin (1988). Inhibiting and facilitating conditions of the human smile: A nonobtrusive test of the facial feedback hypothesis. *Journal of Personality and Social Psychology* 43: 768–777.

Stumpf, C. (1883). *Tonpsychologie I.* Liepzig: Hirzel Verlag.

Sundberg, J. (1987). *The Science of the Singing Voice.* DeKalb: Northern Illinois University Press.

Szpunar, K. K., E. G. Schellenberg, and P. Pliner (2004). Liking and memory for musical stimuli as a function of exposure. *Journal of Experimental Psychology: Learning, Memory, and Cognition* 30 (2): 370–381.

Takeuchi, A. H., and S. H. Hulse (1991). Absolute pitch judgments of black- and white-key pitches. *Music Perception* 9: 27–46.

Takeuchi, A. H., and S. H. Hulse (1993). Absolute pitch. *Psychological Bulletin* 113 (2): 345–361.

Temperley, D. (1999). The question of purpose in music theory: Description, suggestion, and explanation. *Current Musicology* 66: 66–85.

Temperley, D. (2001). *The Cognition of Basic Musical Structures.* Cambridge, Mass.: MIT Press.

't Hart, J., R. Collier, and A. Cohen (1990). *A Perceptual Study of Intonation: An Experimental-Phonetic Approach to Speech Melody.* Cambridge: Cambridge University Press.

Thompson, W. F., L. L. Balkwill, and R. Vernescu (2000). Expectancies generated by recent exposure to music. *Memory and Cognition* 28 (4): 547–555.

Thomson, W. (1999). *Tonality in Music: A General Theory.* San Marino, Calif.: Everett Books.

Thrall, B. (1962). The audibility of twelve-tone serial structure. Ph.D. dissertation, Ohio State University.

Tomkins, S. S. (1975). The phantasy behind the face. *Journal of Personality Assessment* 39: 551–562.

Tomkins, S. S. (1980). Affect as amplification: Some modifications in theory. In R. Plutchik and H. Kellerman (eds.), *Emotion: Theory, Research, and Experience*, pp. 141–164. New York: Academic Press.

Trochimczyk, M. (2001). From circles to nets: On the signification of spatial sound imagery in new music. *Computer Music Journal* 25 (4): 39–56.

Tulving, E. (1972). Episodic and semantic memory. In E. Tulving and W. Donaldson (eds.), *Organization of Memory*, pp. 381–403. New York: Academic Press.

Tulving, E., and F. I. M. Craik (eds.) (2000). *The Oxford Handbook of Memory*. Oxford: Oxford University Press.

Unyk, A. M. (1990). An information-processing analysis of expectancy in music cognition. *Psychomusicology* 9 (2): 229–240.

Unyk, A. M., and J. C. Carlsen (1987). The influence of expectancy on melodic perception. *Psychomusicology* 7: 3–23.

Unyk, A. M., S. E. Trehub, L. J. Trainor, and E. G. Schellenberg (1992). Lullabies and simplicity: A cross-cultural perspective. *Psychology of Music* 20: 15–28.

Van Egmond, R., and D. Butler (1997). Diatonic connotations of pitch-class sets. *Music Perception* 15 (1): 1–29.

von Hippel, P. (1998). Post-skip reversals reconsidered: Melodic practice and melodic psychology. Ph.D. dissertation, Stanford University.

von Hippel, P. (2000a). Redefining pitch proximity: Tessitura and mobility as constraints on melodic intervals. *Music Perception* 17 (3): 315–327.

von Hippel, P. (2000b). Questioning a melodic archetype: Do listeners use gap-fill to classify melodies? *Music Perception* 18 (2): 139–153.

von Hippel, P. (2002). Melodic-expectation rules as learned heuristics. In C. Stevens, D. Burnham, G. McPherson, E. Schubert, and J. Renwick (eds.), *Proceedings of the 7th International Conference on Music Perception and Cognition*. Adelaide: Causal Productions.

von Hippel, P., and D. Huron (2000). Why do skips precede reversals? The effect of tessitura on melodic structure. *Music Perception* 18 (1): 59–85.

von Hippel, P., D. Huron, and D. Harnish (1998). Melodic expectation for a Balinese melody: A comparison of Balinese and American musicians. Unpublished manuscript.

Vos, P. G., and J. M. Troost (1989). Ascending and descending melodic intervals: Statistical findings and their perceptual relevance. *Music Perception* 6 (4): 383–396.

Voss, R. F., and J. Clarke (1975). 1/f noise in music and speech. *Nature* 258: 317–318.

Voss, R. F., and J. Clarke (1978). 1/f noise in music: Music from 1/f noise. *Journal of the Acoustical Society of America* 63 (1): 258–263.

Wade, B. C. (1979). *Music in India: The Classical Traditions*. Englewood Cliffs, N.J.: Prentice-Hall.

Ward, W. D. (1999). Absolute pitch. In D. Deutsch (ed.), *The Psychology of Music* (2nd edition), pp. 265–298. New York: Academic Press.

Washburn, M. F., M. S. Child, and T. M. Abel (1927). The effects of immediate repetition on the pleasantness or unpleasantness of music. In M. Schoen (ed.), *The Effects of Music*. New York: Harcourt, Brace.

Watt, H. J. (1924). Functions of the size of interval in the songs of Schubert and of the Chippewa and Teton Sioux Indians. *British Journal of Psychology* 14: 370–386.

Weiss, M. J., P. R. Zelazo, and I. U. Swain (1988). Newborn response to auditory stimulus discrepancy. *Child Development* 59: 530–541.

Werbik, H. (1969). L'indétermination et les qualités impressives des modèles stimulants mélodiques. *Sciences de l'Art* 1–2: 25–37.

Wheelock, G. (1992). *Haydn's Ingenious Jesting with Art: Contexts of Musical Wit and Humor*. New York: Schirmer Books.

Whitburn, J. (ed.) (1996). *The Ultimate Pop Rock Fake Book* (3rd edition). Winona, Minn.: Hal Leonard.

Wilson, W. R. (1975). Unobtrusive induction of positive attitudes. Ph.D. dissertation, University of Michigan.

Wilson, W. R. (1979). Feeling more than we can know: Exposure effects without learning. *Journal of Personality and Social Psychology* 37: 811–821.

Wittgenstein, L. (1966). *Lectures and Conversations on Aesthetics, Psychology, and Religious Belief*. Compiled from notes taken by Yorick Symthies, Rush Rhees, and James Taylor. Ed. Cyril Barret. Oxford: Blackwell.

Woodrow, H. (1951). Time perception. In S. S. Stevens (ed.), *Handbook of Experimental Psychology*, pp. 1224–1236. New York: Wiley.

Wong, A. K. C., and D. Ghahraman (1975). A statistical analysis of interdependence in character sequences. *Information Sciences* 8: 173–188.

Yasser, J. (1932). *A Theory of Evolving Tonality*. New York: American Library of Musicology.

Youngblood, J. E. (1958). Style as information. *Journal of Music Theory* 2: 24–35.

Index